THE CAMBRIDGE HISTORY OF
THE GOTHIC

This first volume of *The Cambridge History of the Gothic* provides a rigorous account of the Gothic in Western civilisation, from the Goths' sacking of Rome in 410 AD through to the mode's various manifestations in British and European culture of the long eighteenth century. Written by an international cast of leading scholars, the chapters explore the interdisciplinary nature of the Gothic in the fields of history, literature, architecture and fine art. As much a cultural history of the Gothic as an account of the ways in which the Gothic has participated within a number of formative historical events across time, the volume offers fresh perspectives on familiar themes while also drawing new critical attention to a range of hitherto overlooked concerns. From writers such as Horace Walpole and Ann Radcliffe to eighteenth-century politics and theatre, the volume provides a thorough and engaging overview of early Gothic culture in Britain and beyond.

ANGELA WRIGHT is Professor of Romantic Literature at the University of Sheffield, and a former co-president of the International Gothic Association (IGA). Her books include *Britain, France and the Gothic: The Import of Terror, 1764–1820* (Cambridge University Press, 2013), *Mary Shelley* (University of Wales Press, 2018), and the co-edited volumes *Ann Radcliffe, Romanticism and the Gothic* (with Dale Townshend, Cambridge University Press, 2014) and *Romantic Gothic: An Edinburgh Companion* (with Dale Townshend, Edinburgh University Press, 2016).

DALE TOWNSHEND is Professor of Gothic Literature in the Manchester Centre for Gothic Studies, Manchester Metropolitan University. He has published widely on Gothic writing of the eighteenth and nineteenth centuries. His most recent monograph is *Gothic Antiquity: History, Romance, and the Architectural Imagination, 1760–1840* (Oxford University Press, 2019).

THE CAMBRIDGE HISTORY OF
THE GOTHIC

How to write the history of a cultural mode that, for all its abiding fascination with the past, has challenged and complicated received notions of history from the very start? *The Cambridge History of the Gothic* rises to this challenge, charting the history of the Gothic even as it reflects continuously upon the mode's tendency to question, subvert and render incomplete all linear historical narratives. Taken together, the three chronologically sequenced volumes in the series provide a rigorous account of the origins, efflorescence and proliferation of the Gothic imagination, from its earliest manifestations in European history through to the present day. The chapters in Volume I span antiquity and the long eighteenth century (*c.* 1680–1800), covering such topics as the Gothic Sack of Rome in AD 410, the construction and reception of the Gothic past in eighteenth-century Britain, the revival of Gothic architecture, art and literature in British and European culture and their imbrication during the revolutionary decades, 1770–1800. Elaborating upon several of the themes introduced in the first volume, the chapters in Volume II address the Gothic cultures of Britain, America and Europe during the nineteenth century (1800–1900), thus covering while moving well beyond those areas that have traditionally been demarcated as the 'Romantic' and the 'Victorian'. Engaging with the themes of the earlier volumes, the chapters in Volume III also explore some of the myriad forms that the Gothic has assumed in the twentieth and twenty-first centuries (*c.* 1896–present), beginning with an account of the appropriation of the mode in early cinema and concluding with the apocalyptic Gothic turns of much recent cultural production. Resolutely interdisciplinary in focus, *The Cambridge History of the Gothic* extends the critical focus well beyond literature and film to include discussions of Gothic historiography, politics, art, architecture and counterculture. All three volumes in the series are attentive to the ways in which history has been refracted through a Gothic lens, and are as keen to chart the inscription of Gothic in some of the formative events of Western history as they are to provide a history of the Gothic mode itself. Written by an international cast of contributors, the chapters bring fresh scholarly attention to bear upon established Gothic themes while also highlighting a number of new critical concerns. As such, they are of relevance to the general reader, the student and the established scholar alike.

THE CAMBRIDGE HISTORY OF THE GOTHIC

*

VOLUME 1
Gothic in the Long Eighteenth Century

*

Edited by
ANGELA WRIGHT
University of Sheffield

DALE TOWNSHEND
Manchester Metropolitan University

Shaftesbury Road, Cambridge CB2 8EA, United Kingdom

One Liberty Plaza, 20th Floor, New York, NY 10006, USA

477 Williamstown Road, Port Melbourne, VIC 3207, Australia

314–321, 3rd Floor, Plot 3, Splendor Forum, Jasola District Centre, New Delhi – 110025, India

103 Penang Road, #05–06/07, Visioncrest Commercial, Singapore 238467

Cambridge University Press is part of Cambridge University Press & Assessment, a department of the University of Cambridge.

We share the University's mission to contribute to society through the pursuit of education, learning and research at the highest international levels of excellence.

www.cambridge.org
Information on this title: www.cambridge.org/9781108460170

DOI: 10.1017/9781108561044

© Cambridge University Press & Assessment 2020

This publication is in copyright. Subject to statutory exception and to the provisions of relevant collective licensing agreements, no reproduction of any part may take place without the written permission of Cambridge University Press & Assessment.

First published 2020
First paperback edition 2025

A catalogue record for this publication is available from the British Library

Library of Congress Cataloging-in-Publication data
NAMES: Wright, Angela, 1969 May 14– editor. | Townshend, Dale, editor.
TITLE: The Cambridge history of the Gothic / edited by Angela Wright, University of Sheffield ; Dale Townshend, Manchester Metropolitan University.
DESCRIPTION: Cambridge, UK ; New York : Cambridge University Press, 2020–. | Includes bibliographical references and indexes. | Contents: v. 1. Gothic in the long eighteenth century – v. 2. Gothic in the nineteenth century –
IDENTIFIERS: LCCN 2019058624 (print) | LCCN 2019058625 (ebook) | ISBN 9781108662017 (three-volume set) | ISBN 9781108472708 (v. 1 ; hardback) | ISBN 9781108472715 v. 2 ; hardback) | ISBN 9781108561044 (v. 1 ; ebook) | ISBN 9781108561082 (v. 2 ; ebook))
SUBJECTS: LCSH: Gothic fiction (Literary genre) – History and criticism. | Gothic revival (Literature) – History and criticism. | Fantastic fiction – History and criticism. | Architecture, Gothic. | Art, Gothic.
CLASSIFICATION: LCC PN3435 .C285 2020 (print) | LCC PN3435 (ebook) | DDC 809.3/8729–dc23
LC record available at https://lccn.loc.gov/2019058624
LC ebook record available at https://lccn.loc.gov/2019058625

ISBN – 3 Volume Set 978 1 108 66201 7
ISBN – Volume I 978 1 108 47270 8
ISBN – Volume II 978 1 108 47271 5
ISBN – Volume III 978 1 108 47272 2
ISBN 978-1-108-46017-0 Paperback

Cambridge University Press & Assessment has no responsibility for the persistence or accuracy of URLs for external or third-party internet websites referred to in this publication and does not guarantee that any content on such websites is, or will remain, accurate or appropriate.

Contents

List of Figures page x
Notes on Contributors xii
Acknowledgements xvi

Introduction: The Gothic in/and History 1
DALE TOWNSHEND, ANGELA WRIGHT AND CATHERINE SPOONER

1.1. The Goths in Ancient History 22
DAVID M. GWYNN

1.2. The Term 'Gothic' in the Long Eighteenth Century, 1680–1800 44
NICK GROOM

1.3. The Literary Gothic Before Horace Walpole's *The Castle of Otranto* 67
DALE TOWNSHEND

1.4. Gothic Revival Architecture Before Horace Walpole's Strawberry Hill 96
PETER N. LINDFIELD

1.5. Horace Walpole and the Gothic 120
STEPHEN CLARKE

1.6. Shakespeare's Gothic Transmigrations 141
ANNE WILLIAMS

1.7. Reassessing the Gothic/Classical Relationship 161
JAMES UDEN

Contents

1.8. 'A World of Bad Spirits': The Terrors of Eighteenth-Century Empire 180
RUTH SCOBIE

1.9. In Their Blood: The Eighteenth-Century Gothic Stage 198
PAULA R. BACKSCHEIDER

1.10. Domestic Gothic Writing after Horace Walpole and before Ann Radcliffe 222
DEBORAH RUSSELL

1.11. Early British Gothic and the American Revolution 243
JAMES WATT

1.12. Gothic and the French Revolution, 1789–1804 262
FANNY LACÔTE

1.13. The Aesthetics of Terror and Horror: A Genealogy 284
ERIC PARISOT

1.14. Ann Radcliffe and Matthew Lewis 304
ANGELA WRIGHT

1.15. The Gothic Novel Beyond Radcliffe and Lewis 323
YAEL SHAPIRA

1.16. Oriental Gothic: Imperial-Commercial Nightmares from the Eighteenth Century to the Romantic Period 345
DIEGO SAGLIA

1.17. The German 'School' of Horrors: A Pharmacology of the Gothic 364
BARRY MURNANE

1.18. Gothic and the History of Sexuality 382
JOLENE ZIGAROVICH

1.19. Gothic Art and Gothic Culture in the Romantic Era 406
MARTIN MYRONE

Contents

1.20. Time in the Gothic 426
ROBERT MILES

Select Bibliography 450
Index 484

Illustrations and Captions for Volume I

Fig.4.1:	Nicholas Hawksmoor, *North Quadrangle towers and east range, All Souls College, Oxford*. Author's photograph. *page*	105
Fig.4.2:	Sir John Vanbrugh, *Sketch plan and elevation of Inveraray Castle, Argyll*. c.1720. E.2124:79–1992. © Victoria and Albert Museum, London.	108
Fig.4.3:	William Kent, *Cartoon of The Redcross Knight Introduced by Duessa to the House of Pride*. c.1729–40. E.876–1928. © Victoria and Albert Museum, London.	111
Fig.4.4:	After Luke Sullivan, *Detail of A View of Esher in Surrey, the Seat of the Rt. Hon. Henry Pelham Esq*. 1759. B1978.43.1075. Yale Center for British Art, Paul Mellon Collection.	113
Fig.4.5:	William Kent, *A Screen Erected before the Choir in the Cathedral Church of Gloucester*, 1741. Plate 49 from John Vardy, *Some Designs of Mr. Inigo Jones and Mr. Wm. Kent* (1744). Folio A N 63. Yale Center for British Art, Paul Mellon Collection.	114
Fig.5.1:	John Carter, *The Entry of Prince Frederick [sic] into the Castle of Otranto* (1790). Courtesy of the Lewis Walpole Library, Yale University, lwlpr15827.	135
Fig.5.2:	John Carter, Unpublished illustration of 'The Death of Matilda' from Horace Walpole's *The Castle of Otranto* (1791). RIBA Collections.	136
Fig.9.1:	Susanna Highmore Duncombe, *Manfred Pursuing Isabella in Front of the Portrait. A Scene from The Castle of Otranto*. Courtesy of the Lewis Walpole Library, Yale University, 24 17 765 Copy 4.	205
Fig.10.1:	Anatomy of the heroine's heart from Nicholson's *The Solitary Castle* (1789). The British Library Board. © British Library Board. All Rights Reserved/Bridgeman Images 12611.a.23, vol.1, p. 52.	226
Fig.12.1:	Graph of the number of French translations of the English Gothic novel and the number of French *romans noirs* published per year (1789–1822).	263
Fig.19.1:	John Constable, *Hadleigh Castle, The Mouth of the Thames – Morning after a Stormy Night* (1829). Yale Center for British Art, Paul Mellon Collection.	411
Fig.19.2:	Print made by Luigi Schiavonnetti after William Blake. Title page to Robert Blair's *The Grave, a Poem* (1808, published 1813). Yale Center for British Art, Paul Mellon Collection.	412
Fig.19.3:	Theodor von Holst, Frontispiece to Mary Shelley's *Frankenstein* (1818), revised edition published by Colburn and Bentley, London 1831. Steel engraving in book 93 x 71 mm. Wikimedia Commons.	413

List of Illustrations and Captions for Volume I

Fig.19.4: Robert Thew after Henry Fuseli, *Hamlet, Prince of Denmark: Act I, Scene iv, Platform before the Palace of Elsineur [sic] – Hamlet, Horatio, Marcellus and the Ghost* (1803). Yale Center for British Art, Yale Art Gallery Collection, Gift of John Gerli, B.A. 1932.   416

Fig.19.5: Engraving after Henry Fuseli's *The Nightmare*. Wellcome Collection. CC BY.   419

Fig.19.6: John Raphael Smith after Henry Fuseli, *Belisane and Parcival under the Enchantment of Urma* (1782). Paul Mellon Fund. Courtesy of the National Gallery of Art, Washington.   421

Notes on Contributors

PAULA R. BACKSCHEIDER is Philpott-Stevens Eminent Scholar at Auburn University and a former president of the American Society for Eighteenth-Century Studies. She is the author of many articles and several books, including *Spectacular Politics: Theatrical Power and Mass Culture in Early Modern England* (1993); *Daniel Defoe: His Life* (1989), which received the British Council Prize; and *Eighteenth-Century Women Poets and Their Poetry: Inventing Agency, Inventing Drama* (2005), which received the MLA Lowell Prize. She is currently completing a book on theatrical representations of wartime women, 1660–1810.

STEPHEN CLARKE is a Fellow of the Society of Antiquaries and an Honorary Research Fellow of the University of Liverpool. He is Chairman of Dr Johnson's House Trust and of the Beckford Society, a member of the Board of Managers of the Lewis Walpole Library at Yale University, and was from 2005 to 2018 a trustee of Strawberry Hill House. His research interests centre on Horace Walpole, William Beckford, Samuel Johnson, antiquarianism and book history. His most recent book is *The Selected Letters of Horace Walpole* (2017), which he edited for Everyman's Library.

NICK GROOM is Professor of Literature in English at the University of Macau. He has written extensively on the Gothic, and among his books are *The Gothic: A Very Short Introduction* (2012) and *The Vampire: A New History* (2018), as well as editions of *The Castle of Otranto*, *The Monk*, *The Italian*, and *Frankenstein*, all for Oxford World's Classics.

DAVID M. GWYNN is Reader in Ancient and Late Antique History at Royal Holloway, University of London. He is the author of a number of recent books, including *The Roman Republic: A Very Short Introduction* (2012), *Christianity in the Later Roman Empire: A Sourcebook* (2014) and *The Goths: Lost Civilizations* (2017).

FANNY LACÔTE holds a PhD in French and English Literature from the Université de Lorraine, France, and the University of Stirling, Scotland. Having worked as a Teaching Assistant in French and English Studies at the University of Stirling, she is now a Post-doctoral Research Fellow in French at the University of Oxford, associated with the 'CAT19' project and the creation of a bibliography of novels published in French between 1800 and 1830. Her personal research focuses on the Gothic novel and the French Revolution, and in particular the process of translation from English into French at the turn of the nineteenth century.

Notes on Contributors

PETER N. LINDFIELD FSA is a Senior Research Associate at Manchester Metropolitan University working on forged antiquarian material culture in Georgian Britain. He has published widely on the Gothic Revival, and his second monograph, *Unbuilt Strawberry Hill* (2020), explores the unrealised designs for Horace Walpole's important villa, Strawberry Hill, Twickenham.

ROBERT MILES is Professor of English at the University of Victoria. He is the author of *Gothic Writing 1750–1820: A Genealogy* (1993), *Ann Radcliffe: The Great Enchantress* (1995) and *Romantic Misfits* (2008). His most recent book is *The Gothic and Theory: An Edinburgh Companion* (2019), edited with Jerrold E. Hogle.

BARRY MURNANE is Associate Professor of German at the University of Oxford. His main areas of research are the literature and culture of the 'threshold period' between 1780 and 1830, modernism and contemporary drama. He has published widely on the Gothic, Anglo-German relations and medical humanities, including a monograph on Franz Kafka (2008), edited volumes on the German *Schauerroman* in 2011 and 2012 (with Andrew Cusack), on Hanns-Heinz Ewers in 2014 (with Rainer Godel), and Gothic Revival architecture in Germany in 2015 (with Heinrich Dilly).

MARTIN MYRONE is Senior Curator, British Art to 1800, at Tate Britain, London, and has been Visiting Tutor in the History of Art at the University of York and at the Courtauld Institute of Art. As a specialist in eighteenth- and nineteenth-century British art, he has delivered a range of exhibition and display projects at Tate Britain, including 'Gothic Nightmares: Fuseli, Blake and the Romantic Imagination' (2006). His latest book is *Making the Modern Artist: Culture, Class and Art-Educational Opportunity in Romantic Britain* (2020).

ERIC PARISOT is a Senior Lecturer in English at Flinders University (Adelaide, Australia), and a Research Investigator with the Australian Research Council's Centre of Excellence for the History of Emotions. His primary interests lie within the literature and culture of the British long eighteenth century, including Graveyard poetry and funereal writings, the representation and aesthetics of death and suicide, the history of emotions and the Gothic. He is also the author of *Graveyard Poetry: Religion, Aesthetics and the Mid-Eighteenth-Century Poetic Condition* (2013).

DEBORAH RUSSELL is Lecturer in the Centre for Eighteenth-Century Studies and the Department of English and Related Literature at the University of York. Her research interests focus on the Gothic, with a particular emphasis on women's writing and discourses of national identity. Her publications include essays on Charlotte Smith and on Gothic romance, and her forthcoming monograph on eighteenth-century women's Gothic fiction is entitled *Domestic Gothic*. She has also begun research for a book project on Romantic-era theatre, focusing on adaptation and the politics of silence.

DIEGO SAGLIA is Professor of English Literature at the University of Parma, Italy. His research centres on Romantic-period literature and culture, and in the field of Gothic studies he has worked and published on Ann Radcliffe, William Beckford, drama and melodrama and narrative verse. He has produced the first critical edition of Robert Southey's *Roderick, the Last of the Goths* (2012) and has contributed to *Ann Radcliffe,*

Romanticism and the Gothic (ed. Dale Townshend and Angela Wright, 2014), *The Gothic World* (ed. Glennis Byron and Dale Townshend, 2014) and *Romantic Gothic: An Edinburgh Companion* (ed. Angela Wright and Dale Townshend, 2016). His latest publication is the monograph, *European Literatures in Britain, 1815–1832: Romantic Translations* (2019).

RUTH SCOBIE is Stipendiary Lecturer in English Literature at Mansfield College, University of Oxford. She is the author of *Celebrity Culture and the Myth of Oceania in Britain, 1770–1823* (2018), and has published articles about ideas of the global in the works of authors including Mary Shelley, Frances Burney and Samuel Foote.

YAEL SHAPIRA is Senior Lecturer in English literature at Bar-Ilan University in Israel and the author of *Inventing the Gothic Corpse: The Thrill of Human Remains in the Eighteenth-Century Novel* (2018). Her work has appeared in journals such as *Narrative, Women's Writing, Eighteenth-Century Fiction, Eighteenth-Century Life, Romantic Textualities* and in the collection *Shakespearean Gothic* (2009). Her current research focuses on the forgotten 'trade Gothic' novels of the Romantic period and the challenge they present to established narratives of Gothic literary history.

CATHERINE SPOONER is Professor of Literature and Culture at Lancaster University. Her six books include *Fashioning Gothic Bodies* (2004), *Contemporary Gothic* (2006) and, with Emma McEvoy, *The Routledge Companion to Gothic* (2007). Her most recent book, *Post-Millennial Gothic: Comedy, Romance and the Rise of Happy Gothic* (2017), was awarded the Allan Lloyd Smith Memorial Prize for advancing the field of Gothic Studies 2019. She was co-president of the International Gothic Association, 2013–2017.

DALE TOWNSHEND FSA is Professor of Gothic Literature in the Manchester Centre for Gothic Studies, Manchester Metropolitan University. His most recent publications include *Writing Britain's Ruins* (with Peter N. Lindfield and Michael Carter, 2017) and *Gothic Antiquity: History, Romance, and the Architectural Imagination, 1760–1840* (2019).

JAMES UDEN is Associate Professor of Classical Studies at Boston University. His research focuses on Latin poetry, the cultural history of the Roman Empire, and Classics in English literature (especially in the eighteenth century). He is the author of *The Invisible Satirist: Juvenal and Second-Century Rome* (2015) and of the forthcoming *Spectres of Antiquity: Classical Literature and the Gothic*.

JAMES WATT is Senior Lecturer in the Department of English and Related Literature and the Centre for Eighteenth Century Studies at the University of York. He is the author of *Contesting the Gothic: Fiction, Genre, and Cultural Conflict 1764–1832* (1999) and *British Orientalisms, 1759–1835* (2019), and he has produced an edition of Clara Reeve's *The Old English Baron* for Oxford World's Classics.

ANNE WILLIAMS is Emeritus Professor of English at the University of Georgia. She has published numerous essays on British Romantic topics, the Gothic and the intersections of opera and Gothic literature. Her books include *Prophetic Strain: The Greater Lyric in the Eighteenth Century* (1984) and *Art of Darkness: A Poetics of Gothic* (1995). She has edited *Three Vampire Tales* (2002) and co-edited (with Christy Desmet) *Shakespearean Gothic* (2009). She is currently completing a psychobiography of Horace Walpole.

ANGELA WRIGHT is Professor of Romantic Literature in the School of English at the University of Sheffield. A former co-president of the International Gothic Association (IGA), she is completing a Leverhulme-funded project entitled *Fostering Romanticism*, and working upon the author Ann Radcliffe. Her books include *Britain, France and the Gothic: The Import of Terror* (2013) and *Mary Shelley* (2018). With Dale Townshend, she has also edited *Ann Radcliffe, Romanticism and the Gothic* (2014) and *Romantic Gothic: An Edinburgh Companion* (2016).

JOLENE ZIGAROVICH is Associate Professor of English in the Department of Languages and Literatures at the University of Northern Iowa. Her book publications include *Writing Death and Absence in the Victorian Novel: Engraved Narratives* (2012), and she is editor of *Sex and Death in Eighteenth-Century Literature* (2013) as well as *TransGothic in Literature and Culture* (2017). Her current project considers death, the body and materialism in eighteenth-century fiction and culture.

Acknowledgements

The *Cambridge History of the Gothic* was conceived in 2015, when Linda Bree, then Editorial Director at Cambridge University Press, first suggested the idea to us. After much discussion and writing, what began life as a modest single-volume project became a larger and far more ambitious three-volume work. Our thanks are due to Linda Bree for her early encouragement and for taking this project at proposal stage through peer review, syndicate and contracting. Shalini Bisa and Tim Mason efficiently oversaw much of the initial paperwork. Since then, Bethany Thomas has become our patient, encouraging and responsive editor who has supported the project indefatigably. We are enormously grateful to both Linda and Bethany, and to the extraordinary team who has worked alongside them at Cambridge University Press, including Natasha Burton, content manager Sarah Starkey, copy-editor Denise Bannerman and indexer Eric Anderson of Arc Indexing Inc. Jayavel Radhakrishnan at Integra Software Services has been the most helpful and efficient of project managers.

Of course, there would be no *Cambridge History of the Gothic* were it not for the exciting scholarship on the Gothic that has been produced by researchers across the globe. Our heartfelt thanks are also thus due to the scholars who, with such enthusiasm and diligence, signed up to write chapters for these volumes and who patiently endured the sometimes arduous processes of review, editing and revision. They have been extremely generous with their time and scholarship, and we remain forever in their debt. Our respective institutions have been encouraging of, and patient with, us as we have wrestled with the enormity of this project. Angela Wright wishes to thank the School of English at the University of Sheffield, and especially those colleagues who have listened and, in several cases, contributed work to these volumes. Particular thanks are due to Andy Smith, Maddy Callaghan, Joe Bray, Hamish Mathison, Anna Barton, Amber Regis and Frances Babbage. Dale Townshend wishes to thank his friends and colleagues in the

Manchester Centre for Gothic Studies at Manchester Metropolitan University, as well as Jess Edwards and Antony Rowland. In a more personal capacity, the editors also wish to thank their families. For Angela, Hamish, Jess and Antonia have provided fun, amusement and understanding, and for Dale, Howard, Shannon and Stephen and Dickens the cat have, as ever, been long-suffering sources of laughter, comfort and support.

Introduction: The Gothic in/and History

DALE TOWNSHEND, ANGELA WRIGHT AND CATHERINE SPOONER

> History is a Romance that is believed; romance a history that is not believed
>
> (Horace Walpole)[1]

History in the Gothic

In the first Preface to *The Castle of Otranto* (published late 1764; dated 1765), Horace Walpole's literary avatar, the editor and translator William Marshal, tethers the story to follow to a precise year: 'It was printed at Naples, in the black letter, in the year 1529.' In the very next sentence, however, Marshal tempers this precision with the following cautious disclaimer: 'How much sooner it was written does not appear.'[2] The transition from the precise dating of the printed volume to the vagueness and ambiguity surrounding the original work is immediately arresting: 1529, after all, was an important year in the history of England, one in which Henry VIII's infamous Legatine Court, established to annul his marriage to Catherine of Aragon, finally took place after extended delays by papal emissaries. It was a year in which a royal marriage, and most particularly the virginity and fecundity of a Queen, was opened up to intense scrutiny for the reading public, a year that saw the rupture of the English throne from the Catholic Church. The break between Henry VIII and Catherine of Aragon is rehearsed on a literal level in *The Castle of Otranto* when Manfred, Prince of Otranto, seeking to secure his family line, makes an appeal to the Catholic Church in an attempt at abandoning his long-

---

[1] Horace Walpole, *The Works of Horatio Walpole, Earl of Orford*, 5 vols (London: Printed for G. G. and J. Robinson and J. Edwards, 1798), vol. 4, p. 368.
[2] Horace Walpole, *The Castle of Otranto*, edited by Nick Groom (Oxford: Oxford University Press, 2014), p. 5.

time devoted spouse Hippolita in the hopes of coercing the younger Isabella, his would-be daughter-in-law, into marriage.

More figuratively, the opening page of *The Castle of Otranto's* first Preface alludes to the Protestant Reformation and subsequent counter-Reformation that took place in England in the wake of the annulment of Henry and Catherine's marriage. The manuscript, we are told, was 'found in the library of an ancient catholic family in the north of England', an established, presumably landed family which cannot be named, since to do so would be to risk displaying too great an intimacy and familiarity with the reviled Catholic faith. For similar reasons, the manuscript's temporal and locational origins, moreover, must not and cannot be uncovered, since to do so would be to reveal too much knowledge on the part of William Marshal. This first Preface to one of the most foundational texts of the Gothic thus boldly yokes historical precision to obscurity, hesitation and uncertainty. There is an irresolution here between the historiographical impulses of the Enlightenment, and the darkness of earlier ages, a fascination with historical process, but a caution in exercising it. Thus, *The Castle of Otranto* reveals the blandishments and risks of history. While the risks are absorbed through the work's imbrication of history and romance, the blandishments are foregrounded in the antiquarian paratextual materials that frame the 'discovered' document. 'Within the Gothic', argues David Punter, 'we can find a very intense, if displaced, engagement with political and social problems, the difficulty of negotiating those problems being precisely reflected in the Gothic's central stylistic conventions.'[3] The Gothic's 'stylistic conventions', one could further argue, also teach us much about the ways in which we apprehend, consume and narrativise history itself. For while the Gothic may critique the present moment through the figurations of the past, so too does it interrogate the modes through which we have learned about that past, the distancing historiographical devices that have given us access to, yet also alienated us from, the painful realities of Catherine of Aragon's marriage to King Henry, and from the attendant brutalities of the Protestant Reformation.

As these opening comments suggest, it would be remiss to introduce a three-volume history of the Gothic from antiquity to the present day without at least reflecting on the complex relationship that the Gothic mode has always had with the theory and practice of history itself. On the one hand,

---

3 David Punter, *The Literature of Terror: A History of Gothic Fictions from 1765 to the present day*, 2nd edition, 2 vols (Harlow: Longman, 1996), vol. 1, p. 54.

Introduction: The Gothic in/and History

there is little doubt that the 'rise' in the latter part of the eighteenth century of what has subsequently come to be known as 'Gothic literature' was part of a broader epistemic and discursive shift, one in which notions of history, historicity and a sense of the historical past came to assume ever-increasing explanatory, conceptual and intellectual prominence. As Michel Foucault, the so-called 'father' of New Historicism, argued in *The Order of Things* (1966; translated 1970), the transition from the 'classical' to the 'modern' episteme that occurred across Western culture from the end of the eighteenth century onwards brought with it the dawning of a profound historical awareness, to the extent that it is to this period that we might look for the origins of modern notions of history itself.[4] The philosopher, historian and economist David Hume registered something of this burgeoning historical interest when, in a well-known letter to the publisher William Strahan in August 1770, he declared that 'I believe this is the historical Age and this the historical Nation', the observation as much a reflection on his own contribution to the field of historical enquiry in his influential *The History of England* (1754–62) as an acknowledgment of the work of William Robertson, Robert Henry, Adam Ferguson, Gilbert Stuart and other 'philosophical historians' of the Scottish Enlightenment.[5]

Hume's enthusiastic tribute in 1770 to the 'historical Age' of the present in the 'historical Nation' that was contemporary Scotland was occasioned by his reading of draft sections of, and a detailed plan for, what would eventually become *The History of Great Britain, from the First Invasion of It by the Romans Under Julius Cæsar* (1771–93). In its published form, this was a six-volume tome of an anticipated ten-volume series on British history, from Roman times up to the present day, written by the Church of Scotland minister and historian Robert Henry. 'I have perus'd all his Work', Hume's letter to Strahan continues, 'and have a very good Opinion of it. It conveys a great deal of Good Sense and Learning, convey'd in a perspicacious, natural, and correct Expression.'[6] Hume's sole reservation with Henry's study was its sheer capaciousness, the very concern that, in the end, would prevent Strahan from purchasing the copyright to it and necessitate the author financing its publication himself: 'his Specimen contains two Quartos', Hume writes, 'and yet gives us only the History of Great Britain from the Invasion of Julius

---

4 See Michel Foucault, *The Order of Things: An Archaeology of the Human Sciences* (Abingdon and New York: Routledge, 2002).
5 David Hume, 'Letter XLII', in *Letters of David Hume to William Strahan*, edited by G. Birkbeck Hill (Oxford: Clarendon Press, 1888), pp. 155–7 (p. 155).
6 Hume, 'Letter XLII', p. 155.

Cæsar to that of the Saxons: One is apt to think that the whole, spun out to the same Length, must contain at least a hundred Volumes'.[7] For the rest, Hume was unstinting in his praise, not only recommending the work to Strahan as a performance of 'very considerable merit', but deeming its author, too, to be 'a very good Character in the World, which renders it so far safe to have dealings with him'.[8]

While its length made publication by Strahan financially unfeasible, it is clear that Henry's *The History of Great Britain* volubly articulated the intellectual priorities and methodological principles of the late Enlightenment. Though based on Antoine-Yves Goguet's *De l'origine des loix, des arts, et des sciences et leurs progrès chez les anciens peuples* (1758), this was a study that was self-consciously 'written on a new plan', and in its proposed aims to provide exhaustive coverage of seven different topics, from civil and military history to the history of manners and customs, in each of the historical periods that it surveyed, it participated in the same impulses expressed in that other ambitious project of the European Enlightenment, the *Encyclopédie, ou dictionnaire raisonné des sciences, des arts et des métiers* (1751–72) of Denis Diderot and Jean le Rond d'Alembert. 'This is all that falls within the province of general history', Henry would write in the General Preface to the first published volume of the *History*, and 'all that can be universally useful and agreeable, or reasonably desired and expected in a work of this kind'.[9] In the late eighteenth century, the category of 'historiography' was comprehensive to the point of being all-encompassing.

The legitimacy of Henry's entire historiographic endeavour, however, required that the disruptive, overly imaginative forces of romance be strenuously kept at bay, and so to vouch for the integrity of his study, the author, writing in the third person, duly records in the opening volume the authentic documentary and monumental sources that he has consulted in his searching account of the nation's past, explaining that 'If he does not write romance instead of history, he must have received his information from tradition—from authentic monuments—original records—or the memoirs of more ancient writers; and therefore it is but just to acquaint his readers from whence he actually received it.'[10] Henry was not alone in his cautious exclusion of romance from the annals of true history: Hume had maintained a similar distinction between history and romance throughout *The History of*

---

7 Hume, 'Letter XLII', p. 156.   8 Hume, 'Letter XLII', p. 156.
9 Robert Henry, *The History of Great Britain, from the First Invasion of It by the Romans under Julius Cæsar*, 6 vols (London, 1771–93), vol. 1, p. xi.
10 Henry, *The History of Great Britain*, vol. 1, p. xi.

England, as did most other historiographers of the period. Contemporary essayists, aestheticians and cultural commentators, for their part, continuously enumerated the differences between history and romance, while writers of fiction often pondered the relations between the two in Prefaces and other paratextual materials. As Hugh Blair explained in *Lectures on Rhetoric and Belles Lettres* (1783), the 'primary end' of history was 'to record Truth, Impartiality, Fidelity, and Accuracy', all of these, in turn, said to be the 'fundamental qualities' of the historian himself.[11] In relation to such priorities, however, the fanciful and idealising tendencies of the romance mode could only ever be perceived as counter-historical. Substituting the excesses and vagaries of fiction for empirically verifiable historical fact, *The History of Great Britain* thus presented itself as an exercise in legitimate historical writing, participating, in this way, in what scholars such as Karen O'Brien, Mark Salber Phillips and others have shown to be the climate of extraordinary historiographic interest, variety and innovation in British culture of the eighteenth century.[12]

Even a cursory perusal of a selection of titles and subtitles alone is sufficient to indicate that, in its earliest forms, Gothic fiction was driven by similar historicist impulses, from the 'Gothic Story' added to the second edition of Walpole's *The Castle of Otranto* in 1765, through the 'Gothic Story' that was Clara Reeve's *The Champion of Virtue* (1777) and the 'Tale of Other Times' of Sophia Lee's *The Recess* (1783–5), and into the 'Gothic Tale', 'Gothic Story' and 'Gothic Times' variously invoked in the subtitles of many other fictions. As Clara Reeve put it in the Preface to what she in 1778 now titled *The Old English Baron*, this story, like *The Champion of Virtue* before it, was 'distinguished by the appellation of a Gothic Story' primarily insofar as it purported to offer 'a picture of Gothic times and manners'.[13] For the late eighteenth-century writer of fiction, the term 'Gothic' signified, first and foremost, a sense of the distant, somewhat barbaric historical past, but also included the imaginative literary tradition – ghosts, goblins, fairies, wonders and enchantments – with which that past was most closely associated. In one sense, then, Gothic literature appears to have been the child of its cultural moment, for in its jettisoning of the contemporary and near-contemporary

---

11 Hugh Blair, *Lectures on Rhetoric and Belles Lettres*, 2 vols (London, 1783), vol. 2, p. 260.
12 See, for example, Karen O'Brien, *Narratives of Enlightenment: Cosmopolitan History from Voltaire to Gibbon* (Cambridge: Cambridge University Press, 1997) and Mark Salber Phillips, *Society and Sentiment: Genres of Historical Writing in Britain, 1740–1820* (Princeton, NJ: Princeton University Press, 2000).
13 Clara Reeve, *The Old English Baron*, edited by James Trainer, intro. by James Watt (Oxford: Oxford University Press, 2003), p. 1.

settings of the eighteenth-century realist novel, and through its self-conscious revival of the 'Gothic' forms and times of medieval and Renaissance romance, Gothic fiction, drama and poetry, as Markman Ellis has put it, itself constituted 'a theory of history' and a popular form through which history could be apprehended and consumed.[14]

On the other hand, however, it is clear that, as our opening comments suggest, the Gothic adopted a sceptical and at times critical stance in relation to history and antiquarianism, the very historiographic modes of enquiry with which its genesis and cultural consolidation towards the end of the eighteenth century was contemporary. It is instructive in this regard to consider Horace Walpole's responses to Henry's *The History of Great Britain*, the same study that had provoked such enthusiastic responses from Hume in his letter to Strahan in 1770. As Walpole, having read a volume of Henry's published work, wrote to the author in March 1783, 'In one word, Sir, I have often said that *History in general is a Romance that is believed, and that Romance is a History that is not believed;* and that I do not see much other difference between them.'[15] Whereas Hume had celebrated Henry and his work as the epitome of the 'historical Age', Walpole insouciantly dismisses the historian's entire enterprise as little more than an exercise in imaginative fiction. The audaciousness of Walpole's comment here cannot be overstated: relegating the soaring, overarching stadial narratives of the conjectural historian to the realm of literary fiction in the same gesture that he elevates the imaginative musings of a romancer to the level of authentic history, Walpole strikes at the heart of the Enlightenment historiographer's attempts to separate out truth from falsehood. History and romance, he irreverently argues, derive their differences not from any absolute or inherent qualities so much as from the levels of credibility that their readers invest in each. That these were sentiments that Walpole 'often' expressed is easily corroborated, for variations on the claim worked their way into several of Walpole's letters and throughout his published and unpublished works, to the extent that they became a Walpolean refrain of sorts.[16] But what is particularly striking about its iteration in the letter to Robert Henry in 1783 is the observation that follows the assertion, one that complicates and undoes the very equivalences

---

14 Markman Ellis, *The History of Gothic Fiction* (Edinburgh: Edinburgh University Press, 2003), p. 11.
15 Horace Walpole to Robert Henry, 15 March 1783, in W. S. Lewis (ed.), *The Yale Edition of Horace Walpole's Correspondence*, 48 vols (New Haven: Yale University Press, 1937–83), vol. 15, p. 173.
16 See Dale Townshend, *Gothic Antiquity: History, Romance, and the Architectural Imagination, 1760–1840* (Oxford: Oxford University Press, 2019), pp. 29–30.

between history and romance that Walpole has only just set in place: 'nay, I am persuaded that if the dead of any age were to revive and read their own histories, they would not believe that they were reading the history of their own time'.[17] Ghosts or the reanimated spirits of the dead, in other words, can only ever prove the conclusions of the historian wrong. Though romance and history, for Walpole, might, in essence, be indistinguishable, spectres, the stuff of Gothic romance from *Otranto* onwards, always exceed the historian's scrupulous gaze. Situated in a realm well beyond historiography's reach and remit, the ghosts conjured up by the Gothic romancer look down in contempt and disbelief at any attempt at rational, historical reasoning.

Of course, the fractious relationship between history and romance that Walpole would articulate here was already in place in *The Castle of Otranto* from nearly two decades before. The Preface to the first edition, as we have already observed, framed it as an exciting antiquarian discovery: a translated and edited text that, though printed in 1529, was, in all likelihood, written in Italian between 1095 and 1243, and, as such, a relic of 'the darkest ages of christianity'.[18] If this framing technique courted the stultifying 'dryness' of the antiquarian method that Walpole bemoaned elsewhere, he was determined to thwart these expectations in the narrative that followed with a tale of magic, wonder and enchantment. Indeed, during the eighteenth century, the distinction between romance and history often superimposed itself upon the distinction between romance and the realist novel, to the extent that Walpole's self-professed aim, as the second Preface to *Otranto* put it, to rejuvenate contemporary prose fiction with the fanciful resources of romance was thus as much a statement of literary intent as it was a riposte to what he took to be an unimaginative and moribund historical and antiquarian tradition.

Subsequent Gothic fictions articulated as powerful a challenge to the work of the eighteenth-century antiquary and historiographer through the pointed modifications that they made to the Walpolean trope of the recently discovered document. Although Walpole's 'Gothic Story', for all its professed antiquity, had remained remarkably intact, these historical documents were reduced in the hands of subsequent writers to a pile of incomplete and inconclusive fragments, to manuscripts that frustratingly disintegrate into illegible traces at precisely that crucial moment in the narrative in which they are expected to yield their burning secrets. In the 'Advertisement' to *The Recess*, for instance, Lee observed that 'The depredations of time have left

17 Walpole, *Correspondence*, vol. 15, p. 173.   18 Walpole, *The Castle of Otranto*, p. 4.

chasms in the story, which sometimes only heightens the pathetic.'[19] Though Lee's editorial persona subsequently claims that what she calls an 'inviolable respect for truth' would not would not permit her to 'connect' these disparate fragments in the story 'even where they appeared faulty', it is quite clear that *The Recess* depends wholly upon the powers of romance to synthesise and make sense of otherwise unfathomable historical material, as if the latter, without such interventions, were fundamentally lacking in significance, meaning and narrative potential.[20] Though taking her historical bearings from William Robertson's *The History of Scotland During the Reigns of Queen Mary and James VI* (1759) and Hume's *The History of England*, Lee in *The Recess* supplements formal historiography with a Gothic tale of anxiety, suffering and female incarceration, boldly inventing twin daughters for Mary, Queen of Scots, as a means of amplifying her text's feminist politics. Faced with such a feminised, romantic assault upon the largely (but by no means exclusively) masculine historiographic tradition, it is perhaps unsurprising that a critic in *The Gentleman's Magazine* in 1786 complained that 'we cannot entirely approve the custom of interweaving fictitious incident with historic truth; and, as the events related approach nearer the aera we live in, the impropriety increases; for the mind, preoccupied with real facts, rejects, not without disgust, the embellishments of fable'.[21]

Adeline, the heroine of Ann Radcliffe's *The Romance of the Forest* (1791), similarly bears witness to the limits of historical sense-making and interpretation when she discovers a manuscript that purportedly relates the truthful history of her late father: 'She attempted to read it, but the part of the manuscript she looked at was so much obliterated, that she found this difficult, though what few words were legible impressed her with curiosity and terror, and induced her to return with it immediately to her chamber.'[22] Perusing the document later, Adeline encounters in it no clear, concise and linear narrative but a near-illegible historical record that is plagued by impenetrability, decay and the elision of crucial information. The typography of the text in volume II represents these gaps in historical evidence and documentation through a preponderance of asterisks – * * * * – the same lacunae that facilitate in the

---

19 Sophia Lee, *The Recess; or, A Tale of Other Times*, edited by April Allison (Lexington: The University Press of Kentucky, 2000), p. 5.
20 Lee, *The Recess*, p. 5.
21 Review of *The Recess* from *The Gentleman's Magazine* in 1786, quoted in E. J. Clery and Robert Miles (eds), *Gothic Documents: A Sourcebook 1700–1820* (Manchester and New York: Manchester University Press, 2000), p. 181.
22 Ann Radcliffe, *The Romance of the Forest*, edited by Chloe Chard (Oxford: Oxford University Press, 1986), p. 116.

heroine the florid imaginings of Gothic romance, what Radcliffe refers to as 'the mystic and turbulent promptings of imagination'.[23] Intense and often incapacitating romantic conjecture steps in to fill those gaps in the narrative for which historical records alone cannot account. As Jonathan Dent has shown, the relationship between eighteenth-century Gothic and contemporary historical writing remained throughout the period one of antagonism and conflict, subversion and critique, with fictional narratives from Walpole, through Reeve and Lee and into Radcliffe, often exposing and foregrounding that about which formal historiography in the period had little or nothing to say.[24] Consequently, to read historical documents in the Gothic is always to open oneself up to the possibility of egregious misinterpretation, most embarrassingly so in the case of Catherine Morland's misreading of the laundry list in Jane Austen's *Northanger Abbey* (written 1798–9; published late 1817; dated 1818). When Charles Robert Maturin utilised the well-worn convention of the discovered document in his meta-textual commentary on the then somewhat belated Gothic tradition in *Melmoth the Wanderer* (1820), he returned to Radcliffe's earlier treatment of the trope, signifying the 'blotted and illegible' pages of the 'discoloured, obliterated, and mutilated' manuscript that John Melmoth reads early on in the story through a characteristic preponderance of asterisks * * * * *.[25] Like the mental reveries of Radcliffe's heroines, the numerous fictional narratives and narratives-within-narratives in Maturin's text arise as if as a means of compensating for these gaps and silences within the official records of historiography. Stories gives rise to more stories in an interminable process that, while attempting to fix the ever-shifting historical ground, only generates further textuality.

Early Gothic writing, in this respect, is the writing of Jacques Derrida's 'archive fever', the mode that anxiously sets about the recording, arrangement and narrativisation of history even as it tirelessly confronts the deathly *pulsion* towards archival incompletion, obliteration and lack.[26] The simultaneity of historical retrieval *and* erasure, recovery *and* loss is central to the form, a doubleness to which the Gothic responds with the further engendering of romance. Political theorist, philosopher and Gothic novelist William Godwin articulated the grounds for what we might describe as a distinctly 'Gothic'

---

23 Radcliffe, *The Romance of the Forest*, pp. 132–44.
24 Jonathan Dent, *Sinister Histories: Gothic Novels and Representations of the Past, From Horace Walpole to Mary Wollstonecraft* (Manchester: Manchester University Press, 2016).
25 Charles Robert Maturin, *Melmoth the Wanderer*, edited by Douglas Grant, intro. by Chris Baldick (Oxford: Oxford University Press, 1989), pp. 39, 28.
26 See Jacques Derrida, *Archive Fever: A Freudian Impression*, trans. by Eric Prenowitz (Chicago: University of Chicago Press, 1996).

conceptualisation of historiography in his essay 'Of History and Romance' in 1797, in which he countered the 'general' histories of such eighteenth-century conjectural or philosophical historians as Hume, Robertson, Edmund Burke and Edward Gibbon with the 'particular' histories told by the modern 'historical romancer'. While the former traded in abstraction, and subordinated an interest in the particular to the greater aims of narrating the teleological progress of the nation from civilisation to barbarism, the historical romancer dealt always with the individual, with the human subject as located tightly within history and with the historical narratives that recounted his or her experiences accordingly demonstrating a penchant for the conditional, the detailed and the particular. As Godwin sees it, formal Enlightenment history, the historiography of the contrasting variety, is as plagued by difficulties remarkably similar to those explored in contemporary Gothic fictions:

> He who would study the history of nations abstracted from individuals whose passions and peculiarities are interesting to our minds, will find it a dry and frigid science. It will supply him with no clear ideas. The mass, as fast as he endeavours to cement and unite it, crumbles from his grasp, like a lump of sand. Those who study revenue or almost any other of the complex subjects above enumerated are ordinarily found, with immense pains to have compiled a species of knowledge which is no sooner accumulated than it perishes, and rather to have confounded themselves with a labyrinth of particulars, than to have risen to the dignity of principles.[27]

Historical evidence turns to fragments in the historian's hands, and, like a character in Gothic fiction, he is left to flounder in a labyrinth of unsynthesised conjectures. A history of the particular is thus Godwin's favoured historical mode, but if this is an approach to narrating the past that is best wielded by what he terms the 'historical romancer', it is because Godwin, like Walpole before him, remained convinced of the formal, thematic and methodological equivalences between romance and history. 'It must be admitted indeed that all history bears too near a resemblance to fable', he writes, for 'Nothing is more uncertain, more contradictory, more unsatisfactory than the evidence of facts'; 'If then history be little better than romance under a graver name', he boldly continues, 'it may not be foreign to the subject here treated, to enquire into the credit due to that species of literature, which bears the express stamp of invention, and calls itself romance or novel.'[28] Like the

---

27 William Godwin, 'Of History and Romance' <www.english.upenn.edu/~mgamer/Etexts/godwin.history.html> (last accessed 17 June 2019).
28 Godwin, 'Of History and Romance'.

Gothic reader of an incomplete and partially illegible manuscript, the historical romancer must take what evidence they can from the traces which remain, including 'the broken fragments, and the scattered ruins of evidence'. 'From these considerations', Godwin reasons, 'it follows that the noblest and most excellent species of history, may be decided to be a composition in which, with a scanty substratum of facts and dates, the writer interweaves a number of happy, ingenious and instructive inventions, blending them into one continuous and indiscernible mass.'[29] A Gothic romance such as *The Recess* comes to mind here, as does the work of Antoine François Prévost, whom Godwin in the essay approvingly cites. Historical romance for Godwin is the mode that remains infinitely superior to the Enlightenment's noble and sanctioned historiographic tradition. As Robert Miles has argued, Godwin's 'Gothic' conceptualisation of history in this essay would be worked out in similar terms in his own political Gothic fiction *Caleb Williams* (1794), as well as in Herman Melville's *Pierre; or, The Ambiguities* (1852).[30] Taken together, Gothic writers in this vein, for Miles, preempt the genealogical turn of Michel Foucault and New Historicism, since both fictions turn out to be remarkably modern histories of the 'present' and the play of power in which that present is inscribed. Even though Walter Scott, too, would theorise the mutual imbrication of history and romance in 'An Essay on Romance' (1824), his own historical novels adopt a far more confident and considerably less self-conscious approach to the task of narrating the past than that found in the Gothic. Instead, Scott's historical fictions seem to take their cue from the teleological narratives of Enlightenment historiography, often resolving or repressing their Gothic elements in the interests of forging national and historical unity, coherence and closure. To write a history of the Gothic is thus to engage with a literary mode that resists the tidy, linear and teleological compulsions of history itself, compulsions all too often associated with the Gothic through the numerous 'Whiggish' critical accounts of its 'rise' and 'development' across time.

This early Gothic's deep distrust of traditional historiography would continue throughout later periods. Through its mutating forms, nineteenth-century Gothic continues to interrogate the ethics of representing history, the modes of assimilating the past. The very form of Mary Shelley's *Frankenstein* (1818), hailed simultaneously as Gothic, Romantic and as a

---

29 Godwin, 'Of History and Romance'.
30 Robert Miles, 'History/Genealogy/Gothic: Godwin, Scott and Their Progeny', in Jerrold E. Hogle and Robert Miles (eds), *The Gothic and Theory: An Edinburgh Companion* (Edinburgh: Edinburgh University Press, 2019), pp. 33–52.

work of science fiction, dissects our urges to represent the past as it occurs to us in the present. Its epistolary form seems at once immediate, but, upon closer inspection, it points us to letters apparently composed during the 1790s. This, combined with the novel's repeated invocations of reported dialogue, retrospective narrative and editorial alterations, finds its embodiment in the fractured and hastily assembled parts of the creature's monstrous form. The novel's vexed and distanced relationship with history is there, too, in the ways in which the creature interrogates his own readings of history and fiction, the two modes or genres existing side by side as though they were entirely interchangeable with one another: self-educated, his reading of John Milton's *Paradise Lost* (1667; 1674) as a 'true history' sits uncomfortably alongside his anatomisation of good and bad historical figures.

Mary Shelley's fascination with the limitations of history persisted throughout her later writing. It is no coincidence that as she completed *Frankenstein*, she had already begun research for a major historical novel subsequently entitled *Valperga: or, The Life and Adventures of Castruccio, Prince of Lucca* (1823). Here, in examining the life of the Italian warlord Castruccio del Antelminelli of Lucca, Shelley problematises our modes of assimilating and knowing the past through the mouthpiece of her second heroine Euthanasia. When faced with the loss of her beloved castle Valperga at the hands of Castruccio, Euthanasia utters the following remarkable words:

> We look back to times past, and we mass them together, and say in such a year such and such events took place, such wars occupied that year, and during the next there was peace. Yet each year was then divided into weeks, days, minutes, and slow-moving seconds, during which there were human minds to note and distinguish them, as now. We think of a small motion of the dial as of an eternity; yet ages have past, and they are but hours; the present moment will soon be only a memory, an unseen atom in the night of by-gone time.[31]

Shelley's heroine here ventriloquises one of the Gothic mode's key problematisations of historical representation; that is, how 'we mass together' 'times past' rather than separate out the 'unseen atoms' that comprise it. Euthanasia's observations also serve as Shelley's self-conscious reflection on the process of her own writing. As she suggests, the miniscule moments that make up a sense of linear time – the time of the historiographer and historical novelist – might only be synthesised through an act of narrative violence, a

---

31 Mary Shelley, *Valperga: or, The Life and Adventures of Castruccio, Prince of Lucca*, edited by Tilottama Rajan (Peterborough, Ont.: Broadview Press, 1998), p. 305.

forcing together of the individual moments that comprise 'history' and 'historical fiction' that is as unethical as it is unreliable. Despite these reservations, Shelley forges in *Valperga* precisely those 'connections' between disparate events and temporal fragments that Sophia Lee had been reluctant to make. Artificial though the end-product might be, such a recourse to the power of fiction is both necessary and inevitable, the only possible approach to a historical field that is forever collapsing into weeks, days, minutes and slow-moving seconds.

Shelley would confront the same problems of historical interpretation and representation in *The Last Man* (1826), framing her post-apocalyptic vision of the extermination of human life in the twenty-first century with an Introduction that self-consciously alluded to the paratextual devices of earlier Gothic fictions. It was during a visit to Naples in 1818, she writes, that she and her unnamed companion discovered in the cave of the Cumaean Sibyl 'piles of leaves, fragments of bark, and a white filmy substance, resembling the inner part of the green hood which shelters the grain of the unripe Indian corn'.[32] Though these are subsequently identified by Mary's companion as Sibylline Leaves, those prophesies of the future that the Cumaean Sibyl writes on leaves of oak in Virgil's *Aeneid*, they fulfil the same functions as the crumbling, partially illegible manuscripts of earlier Gothic writing. Seemingly unconnected with each other, and written in scripts and languages that neither Mary nor her companion can fully decipher, these 'thin scant pages' pose somewhat of a hermeneutic challenge.[33] Having returned to the cave on several subsequent visits so as to amass more of these inscrutable fragments, Shelley later sets about the task of decipherment. Though we are told that their 'meaning, wondrous and eloquent, has often repaid [her] toil, soothing [her] in sorrow, and exciting [her] imagination to daring flights', it is clear that, as this very invocation of the imagination suggests, the aggregation of seemingly unrelated historical materials cannot be achieved without the synthesising functions of romance: 'I present the public with my latest discoveries in the slight Sibylline pages. Scattered and unconnected as they were, I have been obliged to add links, and model the work into a consistent form.'[34] William Godwin had argued much the same point in 'Of History and Romance', and Shelley had interrogated both the ethics and efficacy of such acts of historigraphic 'connection' in *Valperga*. What distinguishes her endeavour in *The Last Man*, however, is the way in which it turns the problematics

---

32 Mary Shelley, *The Last Man*, edited by Morton D. Paley (Oxford: Oxford University Press, 1994), p. 5.
33 Shelley, *The Last Man*, p. 5.   34 Shelley, *The Last Man*, p. 6.

of history in the Gothic into a careful meditation on thinking and conceiving, writing and representing the future.

Between June and November 1826, the same year in which *The Last Man* was published, the periodical press in France and Britain was preoccupied with the strange case of Roger Dodsworth, apparently the son of the seventeenth-century Yorkshire antiquarian of the same name who, having fallen into a coma in the Swiss Alps in the late seventeenth century, had been miraculously revived and reanimated in the modern present. The most famous version of this hoax came from the pen of Mary Shelley, who in her short story 'The History of Roger Dodsworth: The Reanimated Englishman' (published posthumously in 1863), voiced a playful yet pointed critique of antiquarians, poets and historians, including her own father Godwin, for their overweening preoccupations with this curious 'relic' from the distant past:

> The antiquarian society had eaten their way to several votes for medals, and had already begun, in idea, to consider what prices it could afford to offer for Mr Dodsworth's old clothes, and to conjecture what treasures in the way of pamphlet, old song, or autographic letter his pockets might contain. Poems from all quarters, of all kinds, elegiac, congratulatory, burlesque and allegoric, were half written. Mr Godwin had suspended for the sake of such authentic information the history of the Commonwealth he had just begun. It is hard not only that the world should be baulked of these destined gifts from the talents of the country, but also that it should be promised and then deprived of a new subject of romantic wonder and scientific interest.[35]

The 'reanimated Englishman', in Shelley's witty retelling of events, becomes an object for antiquarian, biographical and historiographical scavengers, scholars who are interested less in the stupendous fact of his reanimation than in his value as an historical artefact. Shelley's rendition of the often-rehearsed hoax in 1826 uncannily echoes the observations of Horace Walpole of so many years before: 'nay, I am persuaded that if the dead of any age were to revive and read their own histories, they would not believe that they were reading the history of their own time'.[36] When, at last, we hear from the character himself, Roger Dodsworth finds it hard to believe that England once more has a king, just as his interlocutor finds it impossible to understand Dodsworth's royalist sensibilities from the age of the Commonwealth. As

---

35 Mary Shelley, 'Roger Dodsworth: The Reanimated Englishman', in Betty T. Bennett and Charles E. Robinson (eds), *The Mary Shelley Reader* (New York and Oxford: Oxford University Press, 1990), pp. 274–82 (p. 274).
36 Walpole, *Correspondence*, vol. 15, p. 173.

Shelley's fiction repeatedly tells us, the past has always disappeared and evaporated into the atoms of miniscule moments that constitute it, leaving the returning ghosts of the dead somewhat bewildered as to how the official narratives of history have been forged.

Those authorised versions of the past increasingly come under interrogation in modern and contemporary Gothic, as new ideas generated by Marxism, psychoanalysis, postmodernism and post-structuralism begin to shape historical thinking. At the turn of the twentieth century, Jonathan Harker in Bram Stoker's *Dracula* (1897) records of the vampire Count that 'I asked him a few questions on Transylvanian history, and he warmed up to the subject wonderfully. In his speaking of things and people, and especially of battles, he spoke as if he had been present at them all.'[37] Anticipating the imminent ascendancy of Sigmund Freud, history in *Dracula* is personal history; it is history experienced and recounted in the first person. Freud's influence on Gothic would be far-reaching precisely because it conceived of personal history in terms of narrative, a story told on the analyst's couch, in which crucial information would necessarily be obscured, forgotten or misunderstood but could be revealed and become malleable through the process of retelling and interpretation. If Dracula's personal history does not quite have this resonance (in the way that other characters' histories in the novel do), it is because Dracula's voice is filtered through Harker; Dracula's self-authored account of his own history, we might say, is the figurative line of asterisks in Stoker's multi-voiced novel.

Dracula's exclusion from the assemblage of narratives that make up the novel points to another crucial twentieth-century development, one that is expressed most forcibly in Hayden White's *Metahistory* (1973). This is the shift towards understanding history as, precisely, *historiography*, as a form of writing, subject to literary devices and therefore, like fiction, unreliable in its claim to truth. A statement at the beginning of *Dracula*, attributed to the figure of the author himself, outlines the methodology undertaken in communicating his story:

> All needless matters have been eliminated, so that a history almost at variance with the possibilities of latter-day belief may stand forth as simple fact. There is throughout no statement of past things wherein memory may err, for all the records chosen are exactly contemporary, given from the standpoints and within the range of knowledge of those who made them.[38]

37 Bram Stoker, *Dracula*, edited by Glennis Byron (Peterborough, ON: Broadview, 1998), p. 59.
38 Stoker, *Dracula*, p. 29.

What is striking about this comment is that it explicitly acknowledges the novel's textuality even as it frames it as history. Its truth claim, however, is thrown into relief by Jonathan Harker's discovery at the end of the novel that among the papers recording its events 'there is hardly one authentic document; nothing but a mass of typewriting'.[39] This is a moment of radical textual instability that suggests the fundamental unreliability of historical narrative and its status as *writing*. As such, *Dracula* anticipates a wide array of twentieth-century Gothic texts that increasingly foreground their own inauthenticity and explicitly question the ways in which history is constructed, positioning themselves as what Linda Hutcheon calls 'historiographic metafiction', or self-conscious fiction about history.[40] 'It is a black art, the writing of a history, is it not?' enquires the opening line of Patrick McGrath's novel of the American Revolution, *Martha Peake* (2000), casting into doubt the narrator's veracity and asking the reader to contemplate the infernal processes by which he conjures up historical figures for their amusement.[41]

In the twentieth century, those gaps and silences foregrounded by the Gothic text become increasingly politicised, drawing attention to *who* writes history and speaking back to the often-quoted line (attributed to numerous historical figures), 'History is written by the victors.' Thus modern writers have read Dracula's comparative silence as an open invitation to provide the vampire's own diverging account of events, as in Fred Saberhagen's *The Dracula Tape* (1975), or to attempt to reconcile Stoker's narrative with broader histories of Eastern Europe, as in Francis Ford Coppola's *Bram Stoker's Dracula* (1992) and Gary Shore's *Dracula Untold* (2014), or to locate Dracula's power in his own skill as an archivist who controls the flows of knowledge around him, as in Elizabeth Kostova's *The Historian* (2005). Further afield, feminist and postcolonial writers have drawn on Gothic techniques to question whose stories are told and the moral responsibility of the author in channelling the voices of the dead. 'Is history to be considered the property of the participants solely?' asks the narrator of Salman Rushdie's most overtly Gothic novel, *Shame* (1984), a reimagining of the events following the founding of Pakistan: 'Can only the dead speak?'[42]

---

39 Stoker, *Dracula*, p. 419.
40 Linda Hutcheon, *A Poetics of Postmodernism: History, Theory, Fiction* (London: Routledge, 1988).
41 Patrick McGrath, *Martha Peake: A Novel of the Revolution* (London: Penguin, 2001).
42 Salman Rushdie, *Shame* (London: Picador 1984), p. 28.

The inauthenticity of the typewritten manuscript at the end of *Dracula* anticipates one of the most fundamental ways in which twentieth- and twenty-first-century Gothic has problematised history. Drawing on Fredric Jameson's description of the past within postmodernity as a depthless repository of images, Allan Lloyd Smith compares the Gothic's 'ransacking of an imaginary museum of pastness' to 'the postmodern cannibalisation of images from the detritus of global history'.[43] For Lloyd Smith, this results in a sort of vagueness or imprecision about meaning within many late twentieth-century texts: '*Something* is evidently at stake, but it is difficult to say what that something is.'[44] That bold yoking of historical precision to obscurity, hesitation and uncertainty that we identified in Walpole, however, still remains at play in contemporary texts, and apparently 'empty' Gothic aesthetics may in themselves produce historical meaning. On screen, the self-conscious, gleeful embrace of inauthenticity, anachronism, stylistic excess and horror imagery in films like Tim Burton's *Sleepy Hollow* (1999) and Guillermo del Toro's *Crimson Peak* (2015), or television shows like *Penny Dreadful* (Showtime, 2014–16), troubles the verisimilitude, cosy nostalgia and covert nation-building of what Andrew Higson designates the 'heritage film'.[45] Similarly, in visual arts and fashion, the juxtaposition of historically dissonant images may allow new meanings to emerge. A sumptuous, blood-red ball gown by John Galliano for Dior's Spring 2006 collection, for example, brings together ostentatious eighteenth-century panniers with an exaggerated high collar strategically drawing attention to the neck, provocatively equating couture with the *ancien régime* while also revelling in the imagery of its destruction. On its skirts, a sumptuously embroidered image of the Marquis de Sade, accompanied by the words, 'Is it not by murder that France is free today?', invites reflection on the horrors that underlie nation- building and specifically France's history as the leader of international fashion.[46] Across numerous media, then, contemporary Gothic draws attention to the telling of the story, and encourages its consumers to ask questions of history, to refuse to accept acknowledged truths and to beware unwanted returns.

---

43 Allan Lloyd Smith, *American Gothic Fiction: An Introduction* (New York and London: Continuum 2004), p. 126.
44 Allan Lloyd-Smith, *American Gothic Fiction*, p. 126.
45 Andrew Higson, *English Heritage, English Cinema: Costume Drama Since 1980* (Oxford: Oxford University Press, 2003).
46 Quoted in 'Gothic: Dark Glamour', *The Museum at FIT*, <http://sites.fitnyc.edu/depts/museum/Gothic/Dior.html> (last accessed 26 July 2019).

A History of the Gothic / The Gothic in History

Of course, the discussion above is not to detract from what remains our primary editorial objective in *The Cambridge History of the Gothic* – the compilation of a comprehensive cultural history of the Gothic that runs from antiquity to the present day, and which spans across three chronologically ordered and thematically arranged volumes: the long eighteenth century, 1680–1800 (with an important opening chapter on the Goths in ancient history); the nineteenth century, 1800–1900; and the twentieth and twenty-first centuries, 1896–present. Both within and across all three volumes, *The Cambridge History of the Gothic* charts key moments of change, development, innovation and transition in and of the Gothic mode, for the most part jettisoning the more familiar 'generic' or 'formal' approaches to the field to be found in a host of available 'Companions' to the Gothic.[47] Moreover, while such volumes have been largely (though not exclusively) focused on the Gothic in its manifold literary, filmic and televisual forms, the chapters assembled here collectively demonstrate that the history of the Gothic, the account of its manifestation and persistence through historical time, is necessarily interdisciplinary by nature, encompassing as it does considerations of the Gothic tribes of antiquity, the appropriation of 'Gothic' politics in seventeenth- and eighteenth-century British thought, Gothic architecture (both 'survivalist' and 'revivalist') and the Gothic in art history as well as the more familiar Gothic literature and film. In its interdisciplinary dimensions, *The Cambridge History of the Gothic* seeks to recover the particular ways in which 'Gothic', as a complex cultural signifier of literary, political, architectural, subjective, subcultural and filmic import, was, and continues to be, read and appropriated. Combining sustained textual analysis with an attention to key historical moments, the chapters across all three volumes chart

---

47 See, for example, Jerrold E. Hogle (ed.), *The Cambridge Companion to Gothic Fiction* (Cambridge: Cambridge University Press, 2002); Catherine Spooner and Emma McEvoy (eds), *The Routledge Companion to Gothic* (Abingdon and New York: Routledge, 2007); Andrew Smith and William Hughes (eds), *The Victorian Gothic: An Edinburgh Companion* (Edinburgh: Edinburgh University Press, 2012); David Punter (ed.), *A New Companion to the Gothic* (Chichester: Blackwell, 2011); Glennis Byron and Dale Townshend (eds), *The Gothic World* (London and New York, 2014); Jerrold E. Hogle (ed.), *The Cambridge Companion to the Modern Gothic* (Cambridge: Cambridge University Press, 2014); Angela Wright and Dale Townshend (eds), *Romantic Gothic: An Edinburgh Companion* (Edinburgh: Edinburgh University Press, 2016); Jason Haslam and Joel Faflak (eds), *American Gothic Culture: An Edinburgh Companion* (Edinburgh: Edinburgh University Press, 2016); and Xavier Aldana Reyes and Maisha Wester (eds), *Twenty-First-Century Gothic: An Edinburgh Companion* (Edinburgh: Edinburgh University Press, 2019).

the 'rise' of the Gothic in Anglo-American, European and, eventually, global culture in relation to time, place, discipline and event, providing a novel and engaging historical account of the Gothic mode and its mutations across time and cultural space.

In this and other respects, our editorial decisions have been guided by a strongly revisionist impulse. In the first volume, for instance, the opening chapters sketch out a 'pre-history' of the Gothic in literature, politics and architectural aesthetics that counters the inveterate tendency to trace the literary Gothic back to a spontaneous and somewhat unprecedented 'event': the publication of Horace Walpole's *The Castle of Otranto* in London in late 1764. In the second volume, a reading of key historical moments in Gothic cultural production of nineteenth-century Britain, Europe and America, the chapters collectively challenge the once-prevalent critical argument that held that, following Maturin's *Melmoth the Wanderer* of 1820, the Gothic went 'underground' for much of the period, prior to enjoying a concerted 'renaissance' in popular fiction of the Victorian *fin de siècle*. Instead, the chapters in this volume focus upon significant moments and cultural events that drove the generation of Gothic textuality across the nineteenth century, while also exploring how the mode in America, Britain and Europe interacted with other cultural forms. The same could be said for the twentieth century, the chapters on which in the third volume reject the commonplace idea that Gothic faded out after the Edwardian period only to be revived by postmodernism, emphasising instead that the mode continued to play a dynamic role within Modernism, and tracing forms of Gothic cultural production in diverse media throughout the century. In those places where the volumes return to consider some relatively familiar critical territory – such as the Gothic on the eighteenth-century stage or the German influences on early Gothic in the first volume; the Victorian ghost story or Gothic sensation fiction in the second; or the relationship between the Gothic and feminism or psychoanalysis in the third – our aim has been to commission chapters by both established and emerging scholars that provide fresh and original accounts, invariably situating these among essays on topics that have remained, to date, critically unexplored. While each of the three volumes is intended as a discrete, stand-alone entity, they have nonetheless been conceived with certain echoes, parallels and continuities between them in mind: themes of war and revolution, for instance, feature across all three, as do notions of gender, sexuality, empire and the national Gothic traditions of Britain, Europe and America. If the Gothic has taught us one thing, however, it is that no history, however comprehensive, may ever presume to be complete; as our discussion above has shown, the Gothic continuously interrogates the reliability and legitimacy of sanctioned versions of the past, if not of the very practice of historiography itself. Comprehensive though they are, the volumes inevitably contain certain elisions, gaps and silences – those *** of early Gothic romance. And if the histories of the national Gothic traditions assembled here exclude direct or sustained considerations of, say, Australian, African, Central and South American Gothic, this is because our focus is more historical than geographical.[48] While this has inevitably amounted to certain geographical oversights – exclusions no doubt determined by our own partial perspectives as editors working within the Western, Anglophone academy – we nonetheless warmly invite scholars of other Gothic traditions worldwide to engage with the various perspectives that we have brought together here.

There remains one final sense in which this project comprises a 'history' of the Gothic, and that is in the ways in which several of the chapters in all three volumes explore the inscription or implication of the Gothic within some of the most significant events in Western history, from the Goths' sacking of Rome, through the seventeenth, eighteenth and nineteenth centuries, and into the modern and contemporary period. Each volume, that is, includes essays that situate the Gothic in relation to key historical moments and processes, such as the French and American Revolutions in the first; the Summer of 1816, the coming of the railways and the publication of evolutionary theory in the second; and the Great War, the rise of feminism and the global environmental crisis in the third. As critics have long acknowledged, and as many of the chapters here further attest, the Gothic is, and has always been, extraordinarily sensitive to historical events, sometimes simply reflecting them, at other times registering their magnitude, but always providing some manner of response to them through the mode's characteristic tendency to shape-shift, mutate and change. To read Gothic is to look through a glass darkly at the events, crises and traumas that constitute a sense of history. Alternatively, to write a history of the Gothic is also to produce a particularly Gothic version of history. But the Gothic also frequently has to exceed and move beyond history in order to maintain its distinctive purchase upon wonder, horror and terror. When, in the wake of the cataclysmic events in

---

48 For recent critical accounts of some of these national traditions, see Justin D. Edwards and Sandra Guardini Vasconcelos, *Tropical Gothic in Literature and Culture: The Americas* (New York and Abingdon: Routledge, 2016) and Rebecca Duncan, *South African Gothic: Anxiety and Creative Dissent in the Post-Apartheid Imagination and Beyond* (Cardiff: University of Wales Press, 2018).

France from 1789 onwards, the Marquis de Sade in 1800 described the Gothic as 'the necessary fruit of the revolutionary tremors felt by the whole of Europe', he went on to say that, in order to confer some interest on their productions, writers of this school were forced to 'appeal to hell for aid and to find chimeras in the landscape: a thing which one perceived at the time by a mere glance through the history of mankind in this age of iron'.[49] History had become Gothic, and the Gothic was forced to make further recourse to supernatural, infernal aid so as to define, constitute and sustain itself.

49 Quoted in Victor Sage (ed.), *The Gothick Novel: A Casebook* (Basingstoke: Macmillan, 1990), p. 49.

1.1
The Goths in Ancient History

DAVID M. GWYNN

The 'Gothic' has come to hold many different meanings over the last millennium. From medieval cathedrals through novels and films to contemporary music and fashion, the sheer breadth of modern Gothic interpretations seems to defy a single all-encompassing definition. Yet certain fundamental principles always remain consistent. The Gothic stands at the forefront of constantly evolving dialogues between 'civilisation and 'barbarism', social values and personal freedoms. And the Gothic is rooted in history, for whenever we speak of the Gothic the past interacts with the present. This historical vision can be both positive and negative, with images of barbaric destruction offset by appeals to human liberty and the need for new energy to challenge outmoded assumptions. It is a vision that finds its genesis in the original Goths, the Germanic people who played a crucial role in the fall of the Roman Empire and the rise of medieval Europe.

Inevitably, the relationship between what we now refer to as Gothic and these original Goths can become exceedingly weak. The Goths did not build the medieval cathedrals, let alone write Gothic novels or enjoy Gothic films. They were a Germanic tribal people who migrated from their semi-mythical homeland of Scandza to spread across Europe. In August AD 410, a Gothic army led by Alaric sacked the imperial city of Rome, and, at the end of the fifth century, kingdoms ruled by Visigoths and Ostrogoths dominated much of the post-Roman West. The last of those kingdoms was destroyed in 711, when Visigothic Spain fell to the Muslim Arabs, yet the Gothic legacy endured. The Renaissance depiction of the Goths as destructive barbarians

> All references to ancient and late antique sources follow a traditional notation system similar to that used for the Bible, with references given by book and/or paragraph number rather than by page number in a specific edition. This universal system ensures that references are consistent across all editions and translations of a given work, including those accessible online.

was balanced by the Reformation's respect for Gothic vigour and freedom, which gathered momentum in Germany and particularly England and, in turn, inspired the cultural revival from which the modern Gothic emerged. To understand in full the attraction of the Gothic from the seventeenth century onwards, we must therefore look back even if only briefly to the Goths of history, for the weight of that history is an essential element of what makes the Gothic so significant today.[1]

Sources

The Goths did not develop a written culture until they came into close contact with the Roman Empire and Christianity. Our knowledge of early Gothic history thus depends on oral traditions preserved in later collections, combined with the material remains identified by archaeologists. Even after the Goths entered the Roman world, the vast majority of surviving texts were written by Greek and Latin authors who were strongly influenced by the Classical opposition of civilisation and barbarism. Many of those writers lived during the fourth and fifth centuries AD, and so witnessed first-hand the Gothic migrations into the Roman Balkans and subsequently across Italy, Gaul and Spain. In addition, a number of works were composed by Romans living under Gothic rule, reflecting the process of cultural interaction and shifting identities that took place within those Germanic kingdoms. We therefore see the Goths primarily through the eyes of outsiders, with the one notable exception being the Gothic historian, Jordanes.[2]

Our essential guide to the arrival of the Goths into the Empire and their victory over the eastern emperor Valens at the Battle of Adrianople in 378 is Ammianus Marcellinus's *Res Gestae* (c. 390). Although an unusually even-handed author, Ammianus naturally regarded the Goths as a threat and knew

---

[1] For a general introduction to the Goths and their history see Peter Heather, *The Goths* (Oxford: Blackwell Publishing, 1996). The wider background of the Germanic migrations and the transformation of early medieval Europe receives sweeping treatment from differing perspectives in Walter Goffart, *Barbarian Tides: The Migration Age and the Later Roman Empire* (Philadelphia: University of Pennsylvania Press, 2006); Guy Halsall, *Barbarian Migrations and the Roman West, 376–568* (Cambridge: Cambridge University Press, 2007); and Peter Heather, *Empires and Barbarians: Migration, Development and the Birth of Europe* (London: Macmillan, 2009). The complex relationship between the historical Goths and the later Gothic is explored in David M. Gwynn, *The Goths: Lost Civilizations* (London: Reaktion Books, 2017).

[2] There is a detailed discussion of the problems raised by our early Gothic evidence in Peter Heather, *Goths and Romans, AD 332–489* (Oxford: Clarendon Press, 1991); see also Walter Goffart, *The Narrators of Barbarian History (A.D. 550–800): Jordanes, Gregory of Tours, Bede, and Paul the Deacon* (Princeton, NJ: Princeton University Press, 1988).

little of Gothic history before the fourth century. His narrative ends in 378, and no source of equal quality illuminates the following decades, which witnessed the rise of Alaric, the Sack of Rome, and the creation of the first Visigothic kingdom in southern Gaul. Alaric's rivalry with the Roman general Stilicho is described in vivid, if partisan, detail by Stilicho's court poet Claudian (early 400s), while some useful detail can be gleaned from the contrasting narratives of the Christian Orosius's *Seven Books of History against the Pagans* (c. 416) and the pagan Zosimus's *New History* (late fifth century). The fragments from the lost history of Olympiodorus of Thebes (c. 440) offer brief glimpses of Alaric's successors, notably his brother-in-law Athaulf, while the early Visigothic kingdom of southern Gaul is revealed particularly through the letters and poems of the Gallo-Roman nobleman and later bishop, Sidonius Apollinaris (writing c. 455–89).

The sources surviving from Ostrogothic Italy and Visigothic Spain are somewhat more extensive. The Italian aristocrat Cassiodorus served at the Ostrogothic court in the early sixth century, and his *Variae* (c. 538) preserved a collection of official letters composed for Theoderic, the founder of the kingdom, and his heirs. Cassiodorus also wrote a history of the Goths, now sadly lost, which was used by Jordanes. Other contemporary authors were less positive towards Theoderic than Cassiodorus, including Boethius, who wrote *The Consolation of Philosophy* (c. 524) while awaiting execution on Theoderic's orders, and the source known as The Anonymous Valesianus (mid-sixth century) which offers a bitterly hostile account of Theoderic's last years. The subsequent destruction of the Ostrogothic state by the eastern emperor Justinian is narrated in detail from the eastern perspective in Procopius's *Wars* (c. 551–4). Our literary evidence for Visigothic Spain ranges from the official records of the royal councils of Toledo to Christian theological treatises and hagiographies, and reaches a peak during the kingdom's cultural golden age in the seventh century. Isidore of Seville, the most renowned scholar of that golden age, contributed among many other works a short *History of the Kings of the Goths* (c. 621–5) and his masterpiece the *Etymologies* (c. 621–36), a compendium of knowledge that was hugely admired in the Middle Ages. For the dramatic train of events culminating with the Arab conquest that overran Visigothic Spain in 711, we depend upon the hindsight of later chronicles. To these textual witnesses to the life and death of the Gothic kingdoms, we must further add the material evidence of archaeology, from settlement patterns and pottery to the great Ostrogothic churches of Ravenna and the golden crosses and votive crowns of the Visigothic Treasure of Guarrazar.

There then remains our only significant historical work written by an actual Goth: the *De origine actibusque Getarum* ('The Origin and Deeds of the Getae/Goths') or *Getica* of Jordanes (c. 551). Classically educated, Jordanes was certainly not a stereotypical 'barbarian', and he wrote the *Getica* in Latin while residing in imperial Constantinople. Nevertheless, he was fiercely proud of his Gothic heritage, and he drew upon both Gothic oral tradition and Roman literary sources in constructing his narrative. Jordanes traced the history of the Goths all the way from their legendary origins to his own time in the mid-sixth century. The desire to glorify his people is clear throughout the *Getica*, but Jordanes above all preserved how the Goths themselves remembered their past, and no other single work has exerted a greater influence on later interpretations of the Goths and their legacy.

The Problem of Names

One immediate challenge that confronts any student of Gothic history flows directly from the limitations of our sources. When we speak of 'the Goths', to whom does that name actually apply? Do we think of the historical Goths as a single tribal people, or do we use the word 'Gothic' in a collective sense rather than expressing a specific political or ethnic identity? How did the original Goths become divided into 'Visigoths' and 'Ostrogoths', and when did those divisions first appear? These questions have troubled later scholars, from medieval times down to the present day, and their roots go all the way back to Jordanes's *Getica* and his construction of Gothic origins.

When Jordanes prepared his account of the Goths' migrations before they entered the Roman Empire, he combined Gothic oral traditions with stories told by Greek and Latin writers of other tribal peoples, like the Scythians, from the same geographic regions. A number of independent Germanic tribes similarly became incorporated into Jordanes's Gothic narrative, notably the Gepids who later defeated the Huns. This accumulation of different elements encouraged the use of 'Gothic' to refer to all Germanic peoples, an interpretation that became increasingly popular from the Renaissance onwards as Classical and biblical visions of history intertwined. Both Jordanes's *Getica* and Tacitus's earlier *Germania* (c. 98) were rediscovered in the fifteenth century and were claimed in support of a single Gothic–Germanic identity. The Bible attributed the origins of all peoples to Shem, Ham and Japhet (Genesis 10–11), the sons of Noah who repopulated the world after the Flood. Japhet and his children were believed to have entered Europe, with the Goths becoming the archetypal Germans descended from

Japhet's second son, Magog.[3] Against this Classical–biblical background every European culture, from Sweden and Spain to Germany and England, could make some appeal to the shared heritage represented by 'the Goths'. Almost anything Germanic or medieval could therefore be described as 'Gothic', and it was this universal meaning that shaped the modern definitions of Gothic architecture, literature and contemporary culture.

From the historical perspective taken in the present chapter, the name 'the Goths' has a more precise significance. The Goths were a Germanic tribal people who, by the mid-third century, had settled north of the Black Sea. Jordanes wrongly dated the division into Ostrogoths and Visigoths back to this early time: 'Part of them who held the eastern region and whose king was Ostrogotha, were called Ostrogoths, that is, eastern Goths, either from his name or from the place. But the rest were called Visigoths, that is, the Goths of the western country.'[4] In reality, that separation did not yet exist. When the lands north of the Black Sea were overrun by the Huns, some of the Goths fell under Hun rule, while two Gothic tribes, the Tervingi and Greuthungi, fled to the Danube River in 376 and entered the Roman Empire. Over the next 40 years, the remnants of the Tervingi and Greuthungi migrated westward and eventually settled in southern Gaul in 418. Their migration saw them incorporate a number of other tribal groupings and by 418 they had forged a new identity as the Visigoths, who ruled first in Gaul and later in Spain. The Goths who had been absorbed under Hun rule only broke free when the Hunnic confederation collapsed in the 450s. They became the Ostrogoths, who settled first in the Balkans and then Italy. When Jordanes completed his *Getica* in *c*. 551, it was natural for him to assume that the divisions of his own time had existed in the distant past, an assumption that misled scholars well into the twentieth century. The appearance of the Visigoths and Ostrogoths as independent peoples was a direct consequence of the impact of the Huns and the subsequent Gothic movements into the Roman Empire.

---

3 According to Isidore of Seville, the eldest sons of Japhet were Gomer and Magog: 'Gomer, from whom sprang the Galatians, that is, the Gauls; Magog, from whom people think the Scythians and the Goths took their origin'. See Stephen A. Barney, W. J. Lewis, J. A. Beach and Oliver Berghof (eds), *The Etymologies of Isidore of Seville*, trans. by Stephen A. Barney, W. J. Lewis, J. A. Beach and Oliver Berghof (Cambridge: Cambridge University Press, 2006), 9.2.26–7. The Goths were thus the oldest Germanic people, although the Celtic Gauls were even older.

4 Jordanes, *Getica*, 14, translated in Charles C. Mierow, *Jordanes: The Origin and Deeds of the Goths* (Cambridge: Speculum Historiale; New York: Barnes & Noble, 1960).

Migration from Scandza

Gothic origins are shrouded in mystery. According to the oral traditions known by Jordanes, the birthplace not only of the Goths but many other tribes was the great island of Scandza.[5] This island, which Jordanes described as 'a hive of races (*officina gentium*) or a womb of nations (*vagina nationum*)', was located in the northern Ocean opposite the mouth of the River Vistula, which flows through modern Poland into the Baltic Sea.[6] Scandza therefore equates at least approximately to Scandinavia, and it was from this legendary homeland that the Goths began their long migrations.[7] Led by King Berig, they crossed the sea and landed in Europe. Several generations later, as their population expanded, the Goths then travelled on southward under King Filimer and settled in the fertile country of Scythia (roughly modern Ukraine), near to the Black Sea.

These early Goths are depicted as fierce warriors and hard-working farmers, who nevertheless were not deficient in learning. They lived in villages under tribal leaders and worshipped a god of war (identified by the Romans as Mars), with spoils taken from defeated enemies and hung from trees in the god's honour.[8] The savage rituals ascribed to the pagan Goths resemble elements from the later Scandinavian sagas, yet Jordanes also celebrates Gothic wisdom. Taught by learned men, the Goths studied ethics and logic, astronomy and botany. Thus, reasoned Jordanes, 'the Goths have ever been wiser than other barbarians and were nearly like the Greeks'.[9]

Jordanes's narrative undoubtedly combines mythical embellishments with exaggerated praise of his Gothic ancestors. Still, his outline of early Gothic history may be broadly accepted. A Scandinavian origin cannot be proven but fits with our limited knowledge of Gothic customs, while the southward migration towards Scythia probably began during the late second century AD. In the regions north of the Danube River and the Black Sea, archaeology has confirmed the presence of a largely uniform culture that began to flourish around the mid-third century. Two cemeteries were excavated independently in the early 1900s, at Sîntana de Mureş in central Transylvania and

---

5 Jordanes, *Getica*, 1.   6 Jordanes, *Getica*, 4.
7 On the myth of Scandza, see Robert W. Rix, *The Barbarian North in Medieval Imagination: Ethnicity, Legend, and Literature* (New York and London: Routledge, 2015). The Scandinavian origins claimed for the Goths would later fuel Swedish imperialist ambitions. See Kurt Johannesson, *The Renaissance of the Goths in Sixteenth-Century Sweden*, trans. by James Larson (Berkeley and Los Angeles: University of California Press, 1991).
8 The Scythian god Zamolxis is depicted together with the Norse god Odin on the northern (Gothic) wall in Alexander Pope's *The Temple of Fame* (1715), lines 123–4.
9 Jordanes, *Getica*, 5.

Černjachov near Kiev. More than 3,000 sites from this Sîntana de Mureş-Černjachov culture have now been excavated from eastern Romania to the southern Ukraine, all dated to the period of Gothic settlement beyond the frontiers of the Roman Empire.[10]

The archaeological evidence for the Sîntana de Mureş-Černjachov culture reveals an agricultural population living in organised farming villages. Houses were built in wood and earth more often than in stone, with cereal crops (wheat, barley, millet) cultivated alongside a variety of domesticated animals (cattle, sheep, goats, pigs). Most villages had both a pottery kiln and a smithy, and styles of pottery and of iron and bronze metalwork were fairly consistent across the culture. Finds of Roman amphorae and glassware attest to ongoing trade, possibly in exchange for slaves, and Roman coins circulated in increasing numbers north of the Danube frontier across the fourth century. Despite the overall uniformity of the Sîntana de Mureş-Černjachov culture, however, we should not assume that a united ethnic or political power bloc controlled the entire expanse from the Danube River to the northern Black Sea steppe. Local variations in housing, craftwork and burial customs strongly hint at distinct tribal groups, with the Goths probably the single most dominant force.

Goths, Huns and Romans

The Sîntana de Mureş-Černjachov culture flourished from the mid-third to the later fourth century AD. These were the same years, our literary sources attest, in which Goths and Romans first came regularly into contact.[11] The third century was a period of turmoil for the Roman Empire, and from the 230s onwards we hear of Gothic raids into the Balkans and even across the Black Sea into Bithynia and Cappadocia. At the battle of Abrittus in 251, the Gothic chieftain Cniva defeated and killed the emperor Decius (otherwise remembered chiefly for his persecution of Christianity) and only gradually were the Goths driven back, with Claudius II (emperor, 268–70) taking the title *Gothicus* to celebrate his victories. The Roman frontier was secured along the line of the River Danube, and over the next hundred years relations

---

10 The archaeological evidence is conveniently summarised in Peter Heather and John Matthews, *The Goths in the Fourth Century* (Liverpool: Liverpool University Press, 1991), pp. 47–95.

11 Michael Kulikowski, *Rome's Gothic Wars: From the Third Century to Alaric* (Cambridge: Cambridge University Press, 2007).

between Romans and Goths were generally peaceful, with isolated outbreaks of violence followed by treaties to restore the status quo.

Close proximity increased the influence of Roman culture on Gothic society. Most significant of all was the arrival of Christianity. Ulfila, the 'apostle to the Goths' (and their first bishop (c. 340)), was descended from Christian captives taken during the Gothic raids into Cappadocia. It was Ulfila who devised the Gothic alphabet in order to translate the Bible, and it was his teachings that the Goths brought with them when they founded their later kingdoms in Gaul, Italy and Spain.[12] Crucially, the 'Homoian' doctrine of the Christian Trinity preached by Ulfila proclaimed that the Son was 'like' (Greek: *homoios*) to the Father but did not share the Father's essence (*ousia*). This teaching was imperial orthodoxy for much of Ulfila's lifetime, but was condemned by the Roman Church in the late fourth century as 'Arian' (the heresy named after the Egyptian presbyter Arius, who was condemned at the first ecumenical council of Nicaea in 325). Tensions between 'heretical' Goths and 'orthodox' Romans would continue throughout the subsequent centuries until Visigothic Spain officially adopted Catholic Christianity in 589.

By the middle years of the fourth century, relative harmony seems to have descended upon the regions from the Danube River and north around the Black Sea coast. Then everything changed. In summer 376, two Gothic tribes advanced upon the Roman frontier. Men, women and children camped near the riverbank in tens of thousands, for the Tervingi and Greuthungi came not as raiders but as refugees seeking permission to settle within the Empire. The Goths of the Sîntana de Mureş-Černjachov culture were sedentary farmers, and, among the refugees, non-combatants outnumbered warriors by 4:1 or 5:1. What had driven such a people on this dangerous migration? Our contemporary sources, particularly the historian Ammianus Marcellinus, leave little room for doubt. The Tervingi and Greuthungi had fled from their homes to escape a terrible new enemy: the Huns.

Little evidence survives from the Huns themselves.[13] They left no written culture and the only descriptions come from their Roman and Gothic foes.

---

12 Ulfila is said to have translated the entire Scriptures except the books of Kings, as the Goths required no further encouragement to go to war (Philostorgius, *Ecclesiastical History* [c. 440], 2.5). Extensive fragments of the Gothic Bible survive, most notably the magnificent *Codex Argenteus* from Ostrogothic Italy, but no passages from Kings. On Ulfila's teachings and Gothic 'Arianism', see the chapters collected in Guido M. Berndt and Roland Steinacher (eds), *Arianism: Roman Heresy and Barbarian Creed* (Farnham: Ashgate, 2014).

13 For the evolution of modern scholarly approaches to the Huns, compare the treatments of Otto J. Maenchen-Helfen, *The World of the Huns: Studies in Their History and Culture* (Berkeley and London: University of California Press, 1973); E. A. Thompson,

Yet the Huns were one of the greatest nomadic peoples ever to sweep across the Russian steppe, their impact only exceeded centuries later by the Mongols. To Romans and Goths alike, the Huns seemed alien and somehow inhuman. Ammianus spoke of them as two-legged animals, while Jordanes traced Hun ancestry to witches driven out by the Goths, who then mated with the unclean spirits of the Scythian wilderness.[14] Whatever their true origins, the Huns struck the tribes living north of the Black Sea like a thunderbolt. Mounted on swift-moving horses and equipped with powerful composite bows the nomads overran the Greuthungi, who either fled or were absorbed under Hun rule. Those who were absorbed would re-emerge in the 450s – after Hun power dissolved – as the Ostrogoths. The Greuthungi who fled joined the Tervingi in the long march towards the Danube.

The arrival on the frontier of perhaps 100,000 Gothic men, women and children placed the eastern Roman emperor Valens (364–78) in a difficult position. The Goths offered a potentially valuable source of manpower, but their numbers were too great for the Romans to control easily. An attempt to separate the Tervingi from the Greuthungi failed, and by early 377 both tribes had successfully crossed the river into Roman territory. Ammianus records a grim story of mismanagement and Roman corruption, which ended in the Battle of Adrianople on 9 August 378.[15] Valens was killed, together with between 10,000 and 20,000 Roman soldiers. With the benefit of hindsight, the disaster at Adrianople set both Goths and Romans on the path that led to the Sack of Rome and the eventual collapse of the western Roman Empire. In the short term, the eastern Roman Empire had been weakened, and the Tervingi and Greuthungi Goths had secured their first foothold on Roman soil.

The Age of Alaric

Following their victory at Adrianople, the Tervingi and Greuthungi tribes sought land on which to farm. In October 382, a treaty was signed between

---

revised by Peter Heather, *The Huns* (Oxford: Blackwell Publishing, 1996); and the chapters in Michael Maas (ed.), *The Cambridge Companion to the Age of Attila* (Cambridge: Cambridge University Press, 2015).

14 Ammianus, *Res Gestae*, 31.2, translated in Walter Hamilton, *Ammianus Marcellinus: The Later Roman Empire (A.D. 354–378)*, intro. and notes by Andrew Wallace-Hadrill (London: Penguin Books, 1986); Jordanes, *Getica*, 24. In Bram Stoker's *Dracula* (chapter 3), the vampire count himself alludes scornfully to Jordanes's legend when proclaiming his descent from the ancient Scandinavians and Huns.

15 Ammianus, *Res Gestae*, 31.1–13. See further Noel Lenski, *Failure of Empire: Valens and the Roman State* (Berkeley and London: University of California Press, 2002).

the Goths and the new eastern emperor Theodosius I (379–95), allowing the tribes to settle in the Balkans south of the Danube River. That agreement came at a price. The Goths were required to provide military support to Theodosius, and their position in the Balkans made them vulnerable to the Huns further north and to tensions between the eastern and western halves of the Roman Empire. Theodosius twice fought civil wars against usurpers in the west and his barbarian allies suffered heavy losses – notably at the battle of the River Frigidus in 394, where 10,000 Goths are said to have died.[16] The confused nature of Gothic society heightened their vulnerability to Roman exploitation. The tribes that had crossed the Danube may have shared a common culture, but they lacked a strong identity or political hierarchy. In the chaos of their flight the ruling structures of the Tervingi and Greuthungi had been destroyed, while the later groupings known as the Visigoths and Ostrogoths did not yet exist. It was within this vacuum of authority that Alaric, the Goths' greatest early chieftain, rose to power.

According to Jordanes, Alaric 'came from the family of the Balthi, who because of their daring valour had long ago received among their race the name *Baltha*, that is, The Bold'.[17] In reality, Alaric's rise to power rested not on a legendary 'Balthi dynasty' but on personal charisma and ability. He witnessed first-hand the Gothic losses in the Frigidus campaign and, after Theodosius died in January 395, Alaric inspired the combined Tervingi and Greuthungi to revolt. Exploiting the tensions between Theodosius's sons, Arcadius (395–408) in the east and Honorius (395–423) in the west, Alaric raided Greece in the late 390s and then, in 401–2, turned his Goths towards Italy. There he encountered his most formidable rival, the half-Vandal Roman general Stilicho who commanded Honorius's army. Two hard-fought battles followed at Pollentia and Verona, forcing Alaric to withdraw back to the Balkans.[18]

Stilicho had saved Italy, yet the Gothic threat still loomed and wider events now shook the western Roman Empire. In 405–6, the continuing advance of the Huns into the Great Hungarian Plain triggered a further wave of

---

16 Andrew T. Fear, *Orosius: Seven Books of History against the Pagans*, trans. by Andrew T. Fear (Liverpool: Liverpool University Press, 2010), 7.35.19. Speaking for many Romans, Orosius happily declared that 'to lose them was a gain and their defeat was a victory'.
17 Jordanes, *Getica*, 29.
18 Claudian's *The Gothic War* (402) gives a greatly exaggerated account of his patron Stilicho's success. On Claudian, see Alan Cameron, *Claudian: Poetry and Propaganda at the Court of Honorius* (Oxford: Oxford University Press, 1970); Ian Hughes, *Stilicho: The Vandal Who Saved Rome* (Barnsley: Pen & Sword Military, 2010) provides an accessible introduction to Stilicho and his rivalry with Alaric.

Germanic migrations towards the Roman frontiers.[19] Stilicho crushed the first threat to emerge: the independent Gothic chieftain Radagaisus who led his people across the Alps into northern Italy. The defeat of this new enemy while also holding off Alaric, however, forced Stilicho to summon additional troops to Italy. On 31 December 406, the weakened Rhine River frontier broke and tribes of Vandals, Alans and Sueves rampaged across Gaul and into Spain. Alaric seized his chance, sweeping into Italy once more in the spring of 408. Stilicho was executed by emperor Honorius and many of Stilicho's Germanic soldiers deserted to join Alaric, including the survivors from Radagaisus's Goths. The path was now open for Alaric to march on Rome.

Alaric's intention was not to destroy the ancient imperial city. He wanted to force concessions from Honorius, and the fifth-century historian Zosimus – in his *New History* – preserved the demands that Alaric made.[20] Those demands are highly revealing. Alaric wanted an annual payment of gold and grain, land for his followers around the Adriatic coast and a Roman military title. For the Gothic tribes, the essential desire remained a stable food supply and secure land to farm. For Alaric, gold to reward loyalty and official Roman recognition strengthened his leadership, founded as it was on the unstable platform of personal charisma. If Honorius had yielded, later interpretations of the Goths and their legacy might have been very different. Safe in Ravenna, Honorius refused to compromise, and in late August 410 Alaric and the Goths sacked Rome. In the words of Jerome: 'When the brightest light of the world was extinguished, when the very head of the Roman Empire was severed, the entire world perished in a single city.'[21]

Rome's fate sent shockwaves echoing across the Empire. Jerome wrote his lamentation in distant Bethlehem, while in North Africa Augustine of Hippo began to compose his *City of God* (412–26), partly to reassure Christians struggling to understand why God had permitted such a catastrophe. Later centuries looked back on the Sack of Rome as proof of Gothic barbarism, symbolising the Goths' role in the decline and fall of the western Roman Empire. In reality, for contemporaries no less than for future generations, the psychological impact of the Gothic Sack far outweighed the practical consequences. Alaric's forces roamed the city for three days, but the death toll

---

19 Peter Heather, *The Fall of the Roman Empire: A New History* (London: Macmillan, 2005), pp. 191–211.
20 Zosimus, *New History*, 5.48–9
21 Jerome, *Commentary on Ezekiel* (410–14), prologue. Translated in Philip Schaff (ed.), *The Principal Works of St. Jerome*, trans. by W. H. Freemantle (Grand Rapids: Wm. B. Eerdmans Publishing, 1892).

was low and relatively few buildings were damaged, not least because the Christian Goths spared Rome's churches and those who took sanctuary inside.[22] Rome itself had not been a regular imperial residence for more than a century, and the attack on the city had little political or military significance for the Empire as a whole. The Gothic Sack of 410 was just one episode in the gradual collapse of Roman power in the west, which culminated with the deposition of the last western emperor, Romulus Augustulus, in 476.

The Sack of Rome turned Alaric into a legend, but his triumph was bittersweet. By marching into Rome, he abandoned any hope of agreement with Honorius and his quest to secure a lasting settlement for his people ended in failure. Travelling south through a hostile Italy, Alaric died early in 411. The site of his burial was hidden by diverting a river, thus concealing his body and the treasures taken from Rome.[23] Nevertheless, in the history of the Goths, Alaric was more than a great warrior chieftain. Under his leadership a new Gothic identity took shape. The surviving Tervingi and Greuthungi tribes merged with other Germanic peoples – who had joined Alaric during his campaigns – to become the Visigoths, the eventual founders of the first independent Gothic kingdom in western Europe.

The First Visigothic Kingdom

On Alaric's death, leadership passed to his brother-in-law Athaulf, who inherited the challenge of securing settlement for the Goths and recognition of his status as chieftain. Leaving Italy behind, Athaulf and his followers entered the fertile lands around Narbonne and Bordeaux. With them travelled Galla Placidia, the sister of emperor Honorius, who had been captured in the Sack of Rome. Early in 414, Athaulf married Galla Placidia in a Roman ceremony in Narbonne.[24] It was an impressive statement of ambition, particularly as Honorius remained childless while Galla Placidia immediately bore a son who received the imperial name Theodosius. Sadly, the new

---

22 This is attested by both Jerome in letter 127.13 in 412, in Philip Schaff (ed.), *The Principal Works of St. Jerome* and Augustine in Henry Bettenson, *St Augustine: City of God*, intro. by John O'Meara (London: Penguin Books, 1984), 2.2, although neither explicitly acknowledges the religious motives of the 'heretical' Goths.
23 Jordanes, *Getica*, 30.
24 Olympiodorus of Thebes, fragment 24, in R. C. Blockley, *The Fragmentary Classicising Historians of the Later Roman Empire*, 2 vols (Liverpool: Francis Cairns, 1981–3). On the remarkable life of Galla Placidia, see Hagith Sivan, *Galla Placidia: The Last Roman Empress* (Oxford: Oxford University Press, 2011).

Theodosius died in infancy, and Athaulf's ambitions alarmed not only Honorius but also some Goths who feared that their chieftain was becoming too Roman. Driven into Spain, Athaulf was murdered in Barcelona in 415, while Galla Placidia was traded back to Honorius in exchange for wheat. The next few years saw a confused sequence of short-lived Gothic leaders fighting for and against the western Empire, until finally the Goths allied with the Romans to subdue the rival tribes that had crossed the Rhine frontier back in 406. As reward for that service, the Goths in 418 were at last permitted to settle in their own kingdom in south-west Gaul.

The original Visigothic kingdom of Aquitaine extended from Toulouse and along the Garonne valley to Bordeaux.[25] In effect, the Goths now controlled an independent state, although they still provided military aid to the embattled western Empire. The local Roman population had little choice but to accept their new rulers, and indeed the Goths offered welcome stability amid the ongoing turmoil. Theoderic I (418–51), the first Visigothic king, held power for a remarkable 33 years and consolidated his authority over much of southern Gaul. For the western Roman emperors, by contrast, the outlook was bleak. Piece by piece, the territories once controlled by the Empire fell into 'barbarian' hands. Visigothic Aquitaine was an early marker in this downward spiral. Britain was abandoned, Spain plunged into chaos and North Africa fell to the Vandals, who had entered the Empire during the great Rhine crossing. Each lost territory reduced imperial resources of taxation and manpower and so made the remaining regions more difficult to defend, until no imperial power remained.[26]

In the midst of this period of confusion, an old enemy reared its head once more. For two generations, the Huns had been moving further westward. Now led by Attila, the greatest Hun of all, they crossed the Rhine River in 451 and rampaged through Gaul.[27] The Visigothic reaction, on hearing that the terror that drove them from their Black Sea homeland had followed them halfway across the Roman world, can only be imagined. King Theoderic and his warriors joined a coalition army led by the western Roman general

---

25 The precise terms of the settlement of 418 are not extant. For discussion, see the chapters collected in John Drinkwater and Hugh Elton (eds), *Fifth-Century Gaul: A Crisis of Identity?* (Cambridge: Cambridge University Press, 1992) and Ralph W. Mathisen and Danuta Shanzer (eds), *Society and Culture in Late Antique Gaul: Revisiting the Sources* (Aldershot: Ashgate, 2001).

26 See Heather, *Fall of the Roman Empire*; Bryan Ward-Perkins, *The Fall of Rome and the End of Civilization* (Oxford: Oxford University Press, 2005).

27 Christopher Kelly, *Attila the Hun: Barbarian Terror and the Fall of the Roman Empire* (London: Vintage Books, 2008).

Flavius Aetius, and together they confronted Attila at the Battle of the 'Catalaunian Fields'.[28] After hours of fierce fighting, in which Theoderic was killed, Attila was forced to retreat. The coalition victory was not complete, however, and the Hun threat was only finally removed by Attila's death in 453 and the disintegration of Hun power that followed. Aetius was then murdered in 454, as the western Roman Empire spiralled deeper into decline. In 455 the Vandals sacked Rome, an attack far more devastating than the more famous Gothic sack 45 years earlier, and a succession of ephemeral emperors were unable to preserve their few remaining territories. When Romulus Augustulus was deposed in 476, the western Empire as a political entity ceased to exist.

As imperial prestige weakened, Visigothic Aquitaine grew in strength and independence. The Goths were the military elite within their new state, but for administration and social harmony they needed the cooperation of the local aristocracy and Christian clergy. One such individual was Sidonius Apollinaris, a Gallo-Roman nobleman who became bishop of Clermont-Ferrand. His writings reveal the interaction of Roman and Germanic elements which occurred in all the Gothic kingdoms, from law and taxation to art and literature, and Sidonius offered a glowing portrait of Visigothic king Theoderic II (453–66), praising the king's nobility and playing down his heretical 'Arian' Christianity.[29] The peak of early Visigothic power came under Theoderic's brother and successor Euric (466–84), who was suspected of murdering his elder sibling for the throne. Euric was the first Gothic king known to have ordered a Latin legal code, the *Codex Euricianus*, combining Roman written law with Germanic customary law. It was also under Euric that the Visigoths expanded their dominion to include almost the entire Spanish peninsula, which for the next two centuries became the heartland of the most enduring Gothic realm in western Europe.

By the late fifth century, the Visigoths ruled over the largest Germanic kingdom in the post-Roman west. Yet, in the history of France, the Gothic presence was only fleeting, superseded by the people from whom the modern country takes its name. The Franks emerged from the northern banks of the Rhine to challenge Visigothic authority in Gaul, and at the Battle

---

28 'That portion of the earth became the threshing-floor of countless races' (Jordanes, *Getica*, 36).

29 Sidonius, *Letter* 1.2 (early 460s), in W. B. Anderson, *Sidonius Apollinaris: Poems and Letters*, trans. by W. B. Anderson, 2 vols (Cambridge, MA and London: Harvard University Press, 1936). On Sidonius and his times, see further Jill Harries, *Sidonius Apollinaris and the Fall of Rome, A.D. 407–485* (Oxford: Oxford University Press, 1994).

of Vouille in 507 the Frankish king, Clovis (*c.* 481–*c.* 511), defeated and killed the Visigothic king, Alaric II. Victory ensured Frankish pre-eminence, while the conversion of Clovis and his followers to Catholic Christianity unified Franks and Romans to a degree that the 'Arian' Goths were unable to achieve.[30] The Visigoths were thus eclipsed, supplanted by the triumphal vision of 'Francia' led first by the Merovingian dynasty of Clovis and then by the Carolingians of Charles Martel and Charlemagne. It was in Spain that the Visigothic legacy survived, until their last bastion was overrun by the Arab conquest of 711.

The Rise and Fall of the Ostrogoths

At the Battle of the 'Catalaunian Fields' in 451, the Visigoths of Aquitaine had found themselves fighting against other Gothic warriors serving in the army of Attila. These were descendants of those Goths who had not fled to the Danube in 376, but were absorbed under Hun rule. When Attila died in 453, the Huns' subject peoples rose in revolt. Led by the Gepids, they defeated the Huns on the banks of the Nedao River, and Hun power simply evaporated.[31] Much like the different tribal blocs that eventually combined to form the Visigoths, however, the varied Gothic groups that broke free as the Hunnic confederation collapsed originally lacked a coherent focus of identity. Only gradually did that identity take shape, under the inspired leadership of Theoderic the Amal. By the early 480s, Theoderic had brought almost all the remaining Balkan Goths together into a single union: the Ostrogoths. Then in 489, with the agreement of the eastern Roman emperor Zeno (474–91), Theoderic led his new people westward into Italy, retracing the route taken by their distant kinsmen almost a century earlier. The Germanic chieftain Odovacer, who had ruled Italy since Romulus Augustulus's deposition in 476, was besieged in Ravenna and in 493 he died. For the next thirty years, Theoderic reigned over Ostrogothic Italy, his fame placing him alongside Alaric at the head of the Goths' heroic pantheon.[32]

---

30 This union is reflected in the writings of the Catholic bishop Gregory of Tours, who depicted Clovis with some exaggeration as an orthodox crusader who refused to accept 'Arians' occupying part of Gaul. See Lewis Thorpe, *Gregory of Tours: The History of the Franks* (Harmondsworth, Penguin Books, 1974), 2.37.

31 Jordanes acknowledged that the Gepids led the revolt, but in the *Getica* the Gepids were themselves of Gothic descent and derived their name from *gepanta* (slow) after falling behind in the original migration from Scandza.

32 For an introduction to Theoderic see John Moorhead, *Theoderic in Italy* (Oxford: Oxford University Press, 1992), and on Ostrogothic Italy see also Patrick Amory, *People and Identity in Ostrogothic Italy, 489–554* (Cambridge: Cambridge University

When the eastern historian Procopius began to narrate the Justinianic reconquest of Italy, he offered up a virtual panegyric praising the founder of the Ostrogothic kingdom: 'Although in name Theoderic was a usurper, in fact he was as truly an emperor as any who have distinguished themselves in this office from the beginning; and love for him among both Goths and Italians grew to be great.'[33] Theoderic had faced the challenge of unifying his followers, perhaps 150,000 Goths and other Germanic peoples, with the existing Italian population. Crucial to his success was the respect that he displayed for Roman culture. Like the Visigothic kings in Gaul and, later, Spain, Theoderic relied upon the local aristocracy, particularly in the fields of administration, taxation and law. Cassiodorus was the most prominent of the Italian aristocrats who held high office at Theoderic's court, and Cassiodorus's *Variae* preserves the letters and edicts that he wrote on behalf of Theoderic and his successors. Through those letters, Theoderic addressed the Roman Senate, the eastern imperial court, and other western Germanic kings. The image that he constructed, with Cassiodorus's assistance, was of a king worthy of inheriting from the Roman emperors of old. The Senate and the eastern emperor were treated with deference, while Theoderic claimed moral superiority over his Germanic rivals as the mediator between them and the Empire. Theoderic reinforced his diplomacy with marriage alliances, uniting himself with the Visigoth Alaric II, the Vandal king Thrasamund in North Africa, and Clovis of the Franks. Such diplomacy was not always successful, however, and Theoderic failed in his efforts to prevent the war between Clovis and Alaric II which led to the latter's death.[34] Nevertheless, Theoderic did secure thirty years of peace for Italy, a feat that would not be achieved again for centuries.

Theoderic's accomplishment was all the more remarkable in light of the tensions that constantly simmered just below the surface of his kingdom. The Ostrogoths chiefly settled in northern Italy around Ravenna and Verona, and Theoderic's Gothic and Roman subjects rarely intermixed. Two languages remained in use, Gothic and Latin, and two legal systems when Roman written law and Gothic customary law could not be reconciled. Most significantly of all, the Ostrogoths, like the Visigoths, followed the 'Homoian'

Press, 1997) and the chapters collected in Jonathan J. Arnold, M. Shane Bjornlie and Kristina Sessa (eds), *A Companion to Ostrogothic Italy* (Leiden: Brill, 2016).

33 Procopius, *Wars*, 5.1, in H. B. Dewing (ed.), *Procopius: History of the Wars*, 5 vols (Cambridge, MA and London: Harvard University Press, 1914–28).

34 Cassiodorus, *Variae*, 3.1–4, in S. J. B. Barnish, *Cassiodorus: Selected Variae* (Liverpool: Liverpool University Press, 1992).

Christian teachings of the apostle Ulfila, which made them 'Arian' heretics in the eyes of the Catholic Italians. Theoderic avoided open violence for most of his reign, but the ongoing separation was symbolised in his own city of Ravenna by the presence of two richly decorated baptisteries, 'Catholic' and 'Arian', very similar in artistry, yet serving different communities.[35]

The consequences of the divisions were laid bare in Theoderic's final years. In the east, the accession of the militantly orthodox Justin (518–27) offered the Italian aristocracy an emperor to whom they might look as an alternative to their heretical barbarian king. Two leading Roman nobles, Symmachus and his son-in-law Boethius, were executed in c. 524 on charges of conspiring with the eastern Empire against Theoderic. Boethius defended his innocence in *The Consolation of Philosophy*, written during his incarceration, while also meditating on the fickleness of fortune and the abuses committed by the Goths. Shortly afterwards, in 526, Bishop John of Rome went on embassy to Constantinople and received such a welcome from emperor Justin that when John returned to Ravenna, he was imprisoned and left to die. These events cast a dark shadow over Theoderic's legacy, and when the king himself died later in 526 his fate was hailed by the Catholic author of The Anonymous Valesianus as the judgement of God:

> [On Wednesday, 26 August 526, Theoderic ordered] that on the following Sabbath the Arians would take possession of the Catholic basilicas. But He who does not allow His faithful worshippers to be oppressed by unbelievers soon brought upon Theoderic the same punishment that Arius, the founder of his religion, had suffered. For the king was seized with diarrhoea, and after three days of open bowels lost both his throne and his life on the very same day on which he rejoiced to attack the churches.[36]

The Ostrogothic kingdom declined rapidly after Theoderic's death. In an attempt to strengthen his charismatic hold on authority, Theoderic had exalted his family, the Amals, as the chosen rulers of the Gothic people.[37] Unfortunately, in a patriarchal world Theoderic's only legitimate child was a

---

35 The religious symbolism of the churches of Ostrogothic Ravenna, including the twin baptisteries, receives careful analysis in Bryan Ward-Perkins, 'Where Is the Archaeology and Iconography of Germanic Arianism?', in David M. Gwynn and Susanne Bangert (eds), *Late Antique Archaeology 6: Religious Diversity in Late Antiquity* (Leiden: Brill, 2010), pp. 265–89.

36 Anonymous Valesianus, in J. C. Rolfe, *Ammianus Marcellinus, Vol. III: Latter Part: The History of King Theoderic* (Cambridge, MA and London, Harvard University Press, 1939), 16.94–5.

37 The Amal genealogy claiming descent from heroes of the Gothic migratory period was probably constructed by Cassiodorus and was repeated in Jordanes, *Getica*, 14.

daughter, Amalasuintha, whose husband Eutharic died in *c.* 522. The resulting succession crisis added to the tensions of the 520s, and Theoderic's grandson Athalaric was just ten when he ascended to the throne. Many Goths feared that the young king would grow up more Roman than Gothic under the influence of his mother and Cassiodorus, and on Athalaric's early death in 534, a coup broke out. Amalasuintha was killed, and amidst the resulting chaos the eastern army of Justin's nephew Justinian (527–65) invaded Italy.[38] Justinian's general, Belisarius, had already crushed the North African Vandals in 533 and after landing in Sicily in 535, he advanced northward to take Ravenna in 540. The Ostrogoths, however, were not easily overcome. Aided by Belisarius's recall to Constantinople and the outbreak of bubonic plague in the east, the Goths rallied under their new king, Totila (541–52). Another decade of warfare laid waste to Italy, and Totila was particularly remembered in the Renaissance for twice sacking Rome until he was finally defeated and killed in 552 by a reinforced imperial army led by the eunuch Narses at the Battle of Busta Gallorum.[39] Sporadic fighting continued for several years to come, but as an independent people the Ostrogoths disappeared from history.

Ostrogothic rule over Italy lasted little more than two generations. The devastation caused by 20 years of warfare was followed by the invasion of the Lombards in 568, and a united Italian state would only emerge again in the nineteenth century. The decades of peace under Theoderic were largely forgotten, and even the churches of Ostrogothic Ravenna were redecorated by Justinian's craftsmen.[40] Seen through the eyes of the Italian Renaissance, the Goths were the barbaric destroyers of the Classical tradition and inspired the excesses of 'Gothic' medieval architecture. And yet Theoderic in particular remained a figure of veneration as well as condemnation in later centuries. His reputation as a heretical persecutor was recalled by Pope Gregory the Great (590–604), who depicted the king being cast into a south Italian volcano by his victims Symmachus and Pope John.[41] But Theoderic was also a warrior hero, the greatest Germanic chieftain of his generation.

---

38 The chapters in Michael Maas (ed.), *The Cambridge Companion to the Age of Justinian* (Cambridge: Cambridge University Press, 2005) provide a convenient overview of the complex world of Justinian and the imperial reconquest.
39 These were the years in which Jordanes composed the *Getica* in Constantinople, honouring Justinian and Belisarius as worthy conquerors of the Goths.
40 Most famously, the Ostrogothic royal chapel, known today as Sant' Apollinare Nuovo, where the mosaic of Theoderic's palace was reworked to replace the original figures (possibly including an image of Theoderic himself) with plain tesserae and curtains.
41 Gregory the Great, *Dialogues* (593–4) <www.tertullian.org/fathers/index.htm#Gregory_Dialogues> (last accessed 8 August 2019), 4.30.

Charlemagne honoured his memory, and the High German epic poem *Das Nibelungenlied (The Song of the Nibelungs, c.* 1200) reimagined Theoderic as the noble knight, Dietrich von Bern. Theoderic's mausoleum still stands today just outside of Ravenna, its design modelled on the tomb of the first Roman emperor, Augustus, as a monument to the union of Goths and Romans that Theoderic had desired.[42]

Visigothic Spain and the End of Gothic History

In AD 500, Gothic kingdoms dominated the territories once ruled by the western Roman emperors. The imperial heartland of Italy was held by the Ostrogoths, while Visigothic power extended from southern Gaul across the Iberian peninsula. Sadly, 'Gothia' was not destined to replace 'Romania'. The Franks rose to seize control over Gaul and with the collapse of Ostrogothic Italy, only one independent Gothic state remained. Visigothic Spain was once regarded as little more than a barbaric backwater of the early medieval Dark Ages. More recent assessments, however, have shown greater appreciation for the cultural achievements of this Spanish kingdom, the longest surviving of all the Gothic realms in post-Roman Europe, which endured for two centuries and eventually fell not to western enemies but to the new and unexpected threat of Islamic invaders from North Africa.[43]

After the Frankish victory at Vouillé in 507, which drove the Visigoths almost entirely out of Gaul, the centre of Visigothic authority was focused first around Barcelona and then more centrally around Toledo. The Iberian peninsula is split by mountains and river valleys, a geographical layout which has always hindered effective government, while the Goths were once again a small minority ruling over a predominantly Roman population. Visigothic control over Spain was thus initially weak and not aided by a sequence of coups and royal murders. The key figure in reviving the Visigothic monarchy was King Leovigild (568–86), who brought almost the entire peninsula, including what is now Portugal, under his sway. Leovigild consolidated political and religious power in his capital, Toledo, and sought to unify his subjects by issuing a new law code, binding to Goths and Romans alike and

---

42 For a brief survey of the contrasting Renaissance and Reformation images of Theoderic and the Ostrogoths, see Gwynn, *The Goths*, pp. 83–98.
43 The standard introduction to Visigothic Spain is Roger Collins, *Visigothic Spain 409–711* (Oxford: Blackwell Publishing, 2004); see also the chapters and scholarly debates recorded in Peter Heather (ed.), *The Visigoths from the Migration Period to the Seventh Century: An Ethnographic Perspective* (Woodbridge: The Boydell Press, 1999).

encouraging intermarriage. In one crucial sphere, however, this programme of unification failed. Like Theoderic in Italy, the Visigothic king was unable to reconcile 'Arian' Goths and Catholic Romans. In his efforts to uphold the Gothic Christianity originally preached by Ulfila, Leovigild clashed repeatedly with Catholic bishops such as Masona of Merida and had to defeat his own rebellious son Hermenegild, who had converted to Catholicism.[44] As recorded by Isidore of Seville, the resolution of the tensions had to wait for Leovigild's death and the succession of his second son, Reccared (586–601):

> [Reccared] was a devout man, very different from his father in his way of life. For while the one was irreligious and had a very warlike disposition, the other was pious and outstanding in peace; while the one was increasing the dominion of the Gothic people through the arts of war, the other was gloriously elevating the same people by the victory of the faith. For in the very beginning of his reign, Reccared adopted the catholic faith, recalling all the peoples of the entire Gothic nation to the observance of the correct faith and removing the ingrained stain of their error.[45]

Visigothic Spain was the only Gothic state officially to embrace Catholic Christianity. Reccared condemned the 'Arian heresy' at a council of Toledo in 589. These councils were a distinctive feature of the kingdom, with regular gatherings of bishops debating both ecclesiastical and secular affairs in the royal presence.[46] Reccared's decision provoked some minor rebellions but no concerted resistance, and a shared religious identity in turn promoted social unity. The stage was thus set for the Spanish cultural renaissance of the seventh century, headed by Isidore, bishop of Seville (c. 600–36).[47] An active theological and ecclesiastical writer, Isidore also compiled the short *History of the Kings of the Goths*, echoing Cassiodorus in depicting the Gothic people as worthy inheritors of the Roman Empire. Far more influential on subsequent generations was Isidore's greatest work, the vast encyclopaedia of Classical

---

44 Bishop Masona's heroic resistance to Leovigild is celebrated in the anonymous *Lives of the Fathers of Merida* (mid-seventh century), 5.4–9. Hermenegild was remembered by Isidore of Seville as a rebel who was justly put down, but over time the rebel son became a martyr hero whose veneration was approved by the papacy in 1586 at the urging of Philip II of Spain.
45 Isidore of Seville, *History of the Kings of the Goths*, 52, in Kenneth Baxter Wolf, *Conquerors and Chroniclers of Early Medieval Spain*, 2nd edition (Liverpool: Liverpool University Press, 1999).
46 Rachel L. Stocking, *Bishops, Councils, and Consensus in the Visigothic Kingdom, 589–633* (Ann Arbor: University of Michigan Press, 2000).
47 On Isidore's vision of historical and religious identity in Visigothic Spain, see Jamie P. Wood, *The Politics of Identity in Visigothic Spain: Religion and Power in the Histories of Isidore of Seville* (Leiden: Brill, 2012).

and Christian learning known as the *Etymologies*. This work was a monument to Isidore's breadth of scholarship and was, for the next millennium, one of the most widely studied books in western Europe after the Bible.[48] Isidore did not stand alone. He dedicated the *Etymologies* to King Sisebut (612–21), a patron of literature and a poet in his own right, while Isidore's disciple, Braulio of Zaragoza (bishop 631–51), continued the promotion of Classical learning. Alongside the outstanding literary production, high-quality metalwork was also still being crafted, most famously the gold crosses and votive crowns preserved in the Treasure of Guarrazar (discovered in *c*. 1858 not far from Toledo), including a golden crown set with sapphires and pearls dedicated by King Reccesuinth (649–72). Seen in this light, the seventh-century Visigothic kingdom scaled heights of cultural expression unrivalled in the west until the Frankish revival under Charlemagne.

Unfortunately, the cultural attainments of the Visigothic kingdom were no guarantee of royal stability. The reigns of strong kings like Reccesuinth were interspersed with repeated outbreaks of civil war, which increased the kingdom's vulnerability should an external threat arise. Even so, the Visigoths can be forgiven for failing to grasp the full extent of the danger from an enemy that first emerged in distant Arabia. The Islamic conquests that followed the death of Prophet Muhammad in 632 swept east into Iran and Iraq and west across Egypt and North Africa. By the early eighth century the Muslims were poised opposite Spain, ready to exploit any opportunity. On the death of Wittiza (694–710), the last strong Visigothic king, yet another crisis broke out and Wittiza's sons are alleged to have requested Muslim aid against their rival, Roderic (710–11). Whatever the exact circumstances, an Arab–Berber army crossed the straits in summer 711 led by Tariq ibn Ziyad, who gave his name to *Jabal Ṭāriq* ('mountain of Tariq' or Gibraltar). A decisive battle was fought at Guadalete in southern Spain, where Roderic was killed, and Visigothic rule came to an abrupt end.[49] For

---

48 'The knowledge of a word's etymology often has an indispensable usefulness for interpreting the word, for when you have seen whence a word has originated, you understand its force more quickly. Indeed, one's insight into anything is clearer when its etymology is known', Isidore, *Etymologies*, 1.29.2.

49 'Weighed down by the quantity of their sins and exposed by the treachery of the sons of Wittiza, the Goths were put to flight. The army, fleeing to its destruction, was almost annihilated. Because they forsook the Lord and did not serve Him in justice and truth, they were forsaken by the Lord so that they could no longer inhabit the land that they desired' (*Chronicle of Alfonso III* (late ninth century), 7, in Baxter Wolf, *Conquerors and Chroniclers of Early Medieval Spain*).

the next five hundred years, it was the power of Islam that dominated the Iberian peninsula.[50]

The fall of Visigothic Spain brought a dramatic end to the history of the Goths as an independent people. Populations with Gothic ancestry still remained, from the Black Sea to Portugal, and Gothic culture did not vanish overnight. But no subsequent Gothic kingdom arose, and no medieval state looked back to the Goths as their forefathers. Alaric and Theoderic were superseded in the medieval consciousness by Charlemagne, while the Italian Renaissance remembered the barbaric destroyers of Classical civilisation. Across all the territories where Goths had once ruled, only the Spaniards later recalled their Gothic descent with pride, through the Christian *Reconquista* and the sixteenth-century Spanish Empire.

Paradoxically, it was further north, where the original Goths had never set foot, that belief in the Gothic inheritance exerted the most powerful influence. Reformation appeals to the Goths as symbols of freedom against Roman oppression helped to inspire the movement for German unification, since German nationalists saw the Gothic tradition as a means to develop a shared national identity. And in England the principle of representative government was attributed to the 'Gothic constitution' that came to Britain through the Anglo-Saxons. During the tumultuous years of the English Civil War, the Parliamentarian Nathaniel Bacon traced English political liberty to the 'ancient Gothique Law' (*An Historicall Discourse of the Uniformity of the Government of England*, 1647). A generation later, after the Glorious Revolution of 1688 and the Bill of Rights in 1689, Sir William Temple represented the Saxons as one of many Gothic nations swarming from the 'Northern Hive' of Scandza, bringing not only the foundations of English government but trial by juries and the institutions of feudal society (*An Introduction to the History of England*, 1695). Such arguments promoted claims to the 'Gothic' heritage, and fuelled the Gothic cultural revival. By the seventeenth century, the Goths of history were increasingly fading into the past. The Gothic legacy, however, was still continuing to unfold.

---

50 The afterlife of the Visigoths, both historical and legendary, is explored in detail in J. N. Hillgarth, *The Visigoths in History and Legend* (Toronto: Pontifical Institute of Mediaeval Studies, 2009).

I.2

The Term 'Gothic' in the Long Eighteenth Century, 1680–1800

NICK GROOM

In a withering review of August Wilhelm Iffland's play *Die Mündel* (1785), translated from the German into English by Hannibal Evans Lloyd in 1799 as *The Nephews*, the *Monthly Review* for 1800 remarked that,

> Our resistance to the irruption of northern barbarians has hitherto been tolerably successful. We have asserted the independance [sic] of the British theatre, and have endeavoured to persuade our readers that, whatever reform might be necessary, we ought to begin it at home, instead of submitting to the yoke of foreign invaders: – but what can be now done, when HANNIBAL is at the gates? Harassed as we are, we must '*crush our old limbs in ungentle steel,*' and repel the swarthy champions of the black-letter from the citadel of taste.[1]

The Goths of antiquity (the 'northern barbarians') are of the same stock – on the same page – as the romantic poets of the Middle Ages ('champions of the black-letter'). Moreover, here they are seen as 'foreign invaders' – the 'yoke' suggesting the Normans – against which the British stage must assert its 'independance' in Shakespearean terms.[2] Yet all this is strange: the *Monthly* was politically a Whig publication – that late seventeenth- and eighteenth-century political faction and party that, as the following chapter will argue, more usually embraced and promoted the Gothic in the face of neoclassical aesthetics. But, on this particular occasion, it was too tempting not to attack the Tory lapdog Hannibal Evans Lloyd through his Carthaginian namesake, and so, even for the fiercest Whiggish advocates of the Goths and the Gothic – be they Norman, medieval, Anglo-Saxon, Norse, Celtic or Germanic – the terms never lost their derogatory associations.[3]

---

1 Anon., 'Art. 42', *Monthly Review* 2nd series 32 (1800): 323–5 (p. 323).
2 William Shakespeare, *1. Henry IV*, edited by A. R. Humphreys (London: Arden Shakespeare, 2000), V.i.13.
3 Lloyd was later appointed to the Foreign Office by Lord Bathurst, High Tory and Foreign Secretary.

There was no such thing in the eighteenth century as a 'Gothic novel', and the term barely had meaning in the nineteenth century either.[4] Certainly, Horace Walpole subtitled the second edition (1765) of *The Castle of Otranto* 'A Gothic Story', and later writers occasionally adopted the adjective – John Stagg, the 'Blind Bard' of Cumberland, for example, subtitled his *The Minstrel of the North* a 'Poetical Miscellany of Legendary, *Gothic*, and Romantic Tales' (1816, my emphasis). But these were not fleeting references to an emergent sense of the Gothic as an eerie cultural movement; rather, they were deliberate allusions to what the Gothic had already meant from the seventeenth century onwards. And it meant a great deal: rebellion and ruin, ferocity and freedom, chivalry and anti-classicism, pointed arches and Protestantism, couplets and quirkiness, barbarousness and bad weather, and the constitutional monarchy and destiny of the nation.[5]

In this context, the eighteenth-century understanding of the Gothic is broadly made up of various recognisable, if braided, threads. First, the reception of the history and reputation of the ancient Goths themselves as the barbarians of antiquity. Second, the reputed social organisation of ancient Gothic society: their characteristic system of government, and its influence on the British constitution and contemporary politics. And third, the developing taste for the culture of the Middle Ages, particularly in architecture, design and literature – often tied to a growing sense of nationalistic pride in industry and empire. But very quickly – and at the same time – this Gothicism also became supernatural and mysterious.

Antiquity to 1680

The Goths, considered as a Germanic tribe from the depths of central and Eastern Europe, only occasionally emerge from under the vast wings of the Roman Empire. Julius Caesar referred to the *Germani* in his history of the *Gallic Wars* (58–49 BC), and 150 years later, Tacitus scrutinised the Germanic peoples in his ethnographical survey *Germania* (AD 98). In AD 376, however, the Goths took centre stage when, led by Alaric, they crossed the Danube and sacked Rome. This was the primal trespass on the Roman Empire and Classical culture, and its reverberations would resonate through history; it was also only the first incursion. Over the next century, and by now

---

4 The *Oxford English Dictionary (OED)* first records the term in 1889.
5 See, for example, Nick Groom, 'Eighteenth-Century Gothic before *The Castle of Otranto*', in Joanne Parker (ed.), *The Harp and the Constitution: Myths of Celtic and Gothic Origin in Modern Europe* (Leiden and Boston: Brill, 2016), pp. 26–46.

established in the imperial capital, Goths spread across much of Europe. But what is central to the meaning of Gothic in the seventeenth and eighteenth centuries (and indeed to a large extent in the nineteenth century) is how this momentous historical event – or series of events – figured in the later historical analysis of the genesis of Europe, particularly in forging a distinctive English, and then a British, national identity.[6]

The Goths were persistently represented as the ransackers of Rome, the defilers of Classical learning. The word was a synonym for rank ignorance, brutish vulgarity and mindless violence – and continued as such throughout the eighteenth century. The anonymous 'Cynick Philosopher', for example, could only express his extraordinary encounter with one of the rude savages of Yorkshire by coining new verbs: 'beyond *Northallerton*, meeting with a Herdsman, I was almost frighted out of my Wits, for this Fellow was a strange Creature, wonderfully *Goth'd*, and be *Vandall'd*, even to Barbarity itself. He was really a Clown in grain, an uncultivated Boor, a Beast of the Herd in Humane Shape.'[7]

Nevertheless, these barbarians were treated seriously by antiquaries such as William Camden in his pivotal work *Britannia* (Latin edition 1586, English edition 1607). Camden proposed that the Goths originally 'liv'd beyond the Ister, near the Euxine Sea, and were formerly called *Getes*'.[8] Ister, another name for Scythia, covers the region east of the Black (i.e. the Euxine) Sea and extending to the Aral Sea (today being southern Russia, Kazakhstan, eastern Ukraine, Azerbaijan, Georgia, Belarus and parts of the Baltic States). The Scythians – proto-Goths – were 'a most ancient people . . . invincible themselves, and free from any foreign yoke'.[9] The seventeenth-century diplomat and cultural historian Sir William Temple likewise saw the Baltic region as a Gothic heartland, suggesting that 'The *Saxons* were one Branch of those *Gothick* Nations, which swarming from the Northern Hive, had under the Conduct of *Odin*, possessed themselves anciently of all those mighty Tracts of Land that surround the Baltick Sea.'[10]

---

6 Johann Jakob Mascov, *The History of the Ancient Germans; Including that of the Cimbri, Celtæ, Teutones, Alemanni, Saxons, and Other Ancient Northern Nations*, 2 vols (London and Westminster, 1737 [1738]), vol. 1, Book VII, pp. 385–463.

7 [J. Hinton?], *The Comical Pilgrim; or, Travels of a Cynick Philosopher, thro' the most Wicked Parts of the World, namely, England, Wales, Scotland, Ireland, and Holland* (London, 1722), pp. 27–8; republished in Anon., *A Collection of Welsh Travels, and Memoirs of Wales* (London [1748]), p. 26.

8 William Camden, *Britannia; or, A Chorographical Description of Great Britain and Ireland, together with the Adjacent Islands*, 2 vols (London, 1722), vol. 1, p. xlviii.

9 Camden, *Britannia*, vol. 1, xlvii.

10 William Temple, *An Introduction to the History of England* (London, 1695), p. 44.

As implied by this remark, the Goths were a restless people. Having resisted threats of foreign invasion and subjugation, they overran northern Europe in waves that were both inexorable and chaotic. As the Catholic ethnographer Richard Verstegan had declared in *A Restitution of Decayed Intelligence* (1605):

> And whereas some do call us a mixed nation by reason of these Danes and Normannes coming in among us, I answer ... that the Danes and the Normannes were once one same people with the Germans, as were also the Saxons; & wee not to be accompted mixed by having only some such joined unto us againe, as somtyme had one same language and one same originall with us.[11]

The barbarousness of the Goths meant that, in contrast to the twin pillars of Classical civilisation – the Roman and the Hellenic – and also in keeping with the tendency of Classical historians who had compounded all the northern barbarian tribes, Gothic became a catch-all term. Antiquaries consequently spilt much ink in first disentangling and then interlacing these races together through their supposed movements and settlements, making all the non-Roman migrations that had settled in England – the Angles, Saxons, Jutes, Danes and Normans – effectively Gothic. Moreover, in the revised and abridged version of Camden's *Britannia* that appeared at the beginning of the eighteenth century, so too were some of the Scots: those Scots 'who inhabit the East part of the Country, are not really Scots, but of the same German Original with us English'.[12] Ultimately, such Gothic ancestry ran through the major dynasties of Europe:

> It cannot be disgraceful to the Scots, to own themselves the Progeny of the Goths: since the most Potent Kings of Spain value themselves upon that Extraction; and the Noblest Italian Families either derive their Pedigree from the Goths, or, at least, pretend to do it And the Emperor *Charles* V. was wont to say, in good earnest, That all the Nobility of *Europe* were deriv'd from *Scandia* and the Goths.[13]

The consequences of the Gothic usurpation of Classical history were therefore immense and far-reaching: they were seen as the primeval non-Classical race, the founders of medieval Europe.

---

11 Richard Verstegan, *A Restitution of Decayed Intelligence: In Antiquities Concerning the Most Noble and Renowned English Nation* (Antwerp, 1605), p. 187.
12 Camden, *Britannia*, vol. 1, pp. xlviii–xlix; Camden, *Camden's Britannia Abridg'd; with Improvements, and Continuations, to this Present Time*, 2 vols (London, 1701), vol. 1, p. 42.
13 Camden, *Britannia Abridg'd*, vol. 1, p. 45.

Such antiquarian theories were of paramount importance in the politics of the period. By, for example, promulgating an aboriginal unity between the English and the Scots, the myth of Gothic origins was, unsurprisingly, promoted in the debates surrounding the 1707 Acts of Union, suggesting that Great Britain, the consequence of the union, was a recovery and a restitution of natural order. In one reductive version:

> If the *Goths*, of whom, as it's [sic] said, the *English* are partly come, be *Scythians*, and that the *Scythians* are *Scots*, then in common consequence the *Scots* and *English* must have the same Original, and been at first one People; and if so, it is no wonder, that after they were severed they should be so desirous now to unite.[14]

Comparable arguments were made to integrate Wales more closely with England and Scotland. In 1716, the Presbyterian Jeremy Owen preached on St David's Day that in the Hanoverian monarch (and native German speaker) George I, 'we find flowing in his Veins the Blood of the *Tudors*, derived from our own *Ancient Stock*, that we may justly triumph in him as one from among ourselves, by far the most worthy of any that could be found *to bear rule over us*'.[15] This Hanoverian Gothic compact effectually eradicated any lingering doubt over the retrospective unionist legislation of the Tudor king Henry VIII in 1536: 'we were compleatly [sic] incorporated into the *English* Nation, and enjoy'd thenceforth the same Laws and Privileges with themselves'.[16] Hanoverian loyalists also milked the Gothic bloodline of the German dynasty – in 1723, for example, the physician and poetaster Sir Richard Blackmore – who had already received a knighthood from William III for his epic *Prince Arthur* (1695) – dedicated his twelve-book poem *Alfred* (1723) to Prince Frederick of Hanover with the toadying encomium that Alfred the Great was 'a Prince sprung from the ancient *Saxon* Race of your own native Land'.[17]

This eagerness to read contemporary politics as Gothic reveals a very different interpretation of the Gothic legacy than one of barbarism and wilful destruction: there was another, much more positive perception of the Goths in Britain during the long eighteenth century. The historians Cassiodorus and

---

14 *A Perswasive to the Union Now On Foot, by Arguments from Nature, Reason, and Mutual Advantage* (London, 1706), p. 26.

15 Jeremy Owen, *The Goodness and Severity of God, in his Dispensations, with respect unto the Ancient Britains* (London, 1717), p. [2] [italics reversed]; see Bethan M. Jenkins, *Between Wales and England: Anglophone Welsh Writing of the Eighteenth Century* (Cardiff: University of Wales Press, 2017), chapter 1.

16 Owen, *Goodness and Severity*, p. 15.

17 Sir Richard Blackmore, *Alfred. An Epick Poem* (London, 1723), sig. a4r.

Jordanes (both Goths themselves) claimed that their race had originated in Scandza, a northern Scandinavian island and the 'hive of nations', before sweeping down to Scythia. Scandza (which does not exist) was compared by Jordanes to Britain (which of course does): it was a land of mist and moors and mountains, of dark forests and perilous wilderlands. In line with Aristotelian theories of racial environmentalism in which climate and topography engendered temperament, this unforgiving landscape bred a race that was not only hardy but also vigorous and martial and fertile – and with such characteristics went values of courage and loyalty, and an instinctive love of freedom and resistance to tyranny. From the seventeenth century onwards, this spirit of liberty increasingly came to characterise attitudes to the Goths. In this context, the Sack of Rome could be viewed as a heroic resistance against imperial tyranny and decadent corruption. The Goths could, moreover, be seen as an instrument of divine justice, enacting holy revenge upon pagan Rome. William Temple reasoned that the 'infinite Swarm of that vast Northern-Hive' which had 'shook the World like a great tempest, and overflow'd it like a Torrent; changing Names, and Customs, and Government, and Language, and the very face of Nature, where-ever they seated themselves' had abated with their conversion to Christianity.[18] Thereafter, 'of all the Northern Nations, the *Goths* were esteemed the most civil, orderly, and vertuous'.[19]

This view of the Goths as champions of liberty underscored their political significance, positioning the Gothic as an alternative northern historical dynamic to the conventional Classical Mediterranean hub. It was insistently argued that north European forms of government had their roots in 'Gothick polity' and an antipathy to tyranny in all its forms, manifested in the Middle Ages as rule by a constitutional monarch and by feudal land management. The sovereign, an assembly of barons and an assembly of commoners formed a 'Government of Free-men', which, according to Temple, was not only common to all the northern nations, but also seen in Poland, Hungary and parts of Spain and Portugal: 'this Constitution has been celebrated, as framed with great Wisdom and Equity, and as the truest and justest Temper that has been ever found out between Dominion and Liberty'.[20] Furthermore, one corollary of this representative form of rule was trial by a jury of one's

---

18 William Temple, 'Observations on the United Provinces of the Netherlands', in *The Works of Sir William Temple, Bart.*, 2 vols (London, 1720), vol. 1, pp. 10–11.
19 William Temple, 'Of Heroick Virtue', in *Miscellanea: The Second Part* (London, 1690), pp. 218–19 [separately paginated].
20 Temple, 'Of Heroick Virtue', *Miscellanea II*, p. 103.

peers – considered to be a cornerstone of both the Saxon and the Norman legal codes, and central to English and Scottish law.[21] Gothic feudalism, meanwhile, entailed land tenure being conferred and held 'in feu' by vassals, who in turn made a reciprocal payment or served the landowner in some way, further cementing social bonds and safeguarding future stability.[22]

Gothic governance may have been decidedly medieval in its operation, but it evidently had a strong contemporary appeal, protecting civil and political liberties by explicitly opposing absolutism and the exercise of arbitrary and unchallenged power. In the wake of the Civil Wars and the execution of Charles I – a monarch who had entertained precisely such despotic desires – the idea of the '*Gothick* Constitution' was not only deeply appealing but also provided a powerful historical legitimation of Whig parliamentary politics, particularly after the so-called 'Glorious Revolution' of 1688.[23] In *Jure Divino* (1706), for example, Daniel Defoe presents the '*Gothick* rules of Government' as the steadfast custodians of natural order and human rights through 'Native Liberty', and as the scourge of tyranny – a word that resounds through the political verse of the period.[24] Likewise the Scottish writer James Thomson, responsible for the anthem 'Rule, Britannia' and the writer of *The Seasons* (1729–30), the best-selling poem of the age, also celebrated English Gothicism and the British constitution in his political poem, *Liberty* (1735–6):

> Of *Gothic* Nations This the final Burst;
> And, mix'd the Genius of these People all,
> Their Virtues mix'd in one exalted Stream,
> Here the rich Tide of *English* blood grew full.[25]

In England, this fascination with Gothic descent contributed to a belief in English exceptionalism: an ancient form of government that allegedly had its roots in Saxon *witenagemots*, and was emphatically Protestant and uniquely progressive. As such, the Saxons, according to both Camden and the Protestant martyrologist John Foxe, were not only the ancestors of the English – thus distancing the genesis of the nation from Galfridian claims of

21 Temple, *Introduction to History of England*, p. 160.
22 See Temple, 'Of Heroick Virtue'; on feudal society, see Robert Hepburn, *A Discourse concerning Fews and Superiorities, Shewing That the Rigid Observance of Them Is Inconsistent with the Nature of the British Constitution* (Edinburgh, 1716), pp. 3–4.
23 Gilbert Burnet, *A Collection of Several Tracts and Discourses Written in the Years 1677, to 1704*, 3 vols (London, 1704), vol. 3, p. 8.
24 Daniel Defoe, *Jure Divino: A Satyr. In Twelve Books* (London, 1706), Bk VIII: p. 28 [separately paginated].
25 James Thomson, 'Liberty', in *The Works of Mr. Thomson*, 2 vols (London, 1736), vol. 2, p. 41 (part IV, ll. 742–5).

Trojan settlement as well as from possible biblical origins – but also practiced a nascent form of Protestantism.[26]

The celebrated and oft-invoked '*Gothick* Constitution', then – understood to be a form of government based on progressive freedoms and on parliamentary checks and balances of the power of the monarch – was rapidly extended across Britain. Indeed, by the middle of the century Scottish Enlightenment thinkers were unequivocally identifying their own values with Gothicism. As Andrew McDouall, the Scottish judge and author of *An Institute of the Laws of Scotland* (1751-3) whiggishly confirmed in his 1747 account of land management and feudal holdings, 'It is to the *Gothick* Constitution that we owe our Parliaments, which are the Guardians of our Rights and Liberties.'[27]

In addition to the representative government and law of the '*Gothick* Constitution', the Gothic spirit was also intuitively cooperative. Even Tories, such as the political economist Charles Davenant, made the link between the Goths and commercial enterprise, maintaining that they 'did not make their hazardous Migrations and blindly follow Cheifs [*sic*] and Leaders without any Conditions', but rather that their territorial conquests were pointedly similar to the profit-driven colonial ventures of eighteenth-century Britain:

> 'tis evident from History, that they who accompany'd the Princes that made those Expeditions from the North assisted with Men and Mony in the Enterprize and were to participate both as to Property in the Land, and as to Authority in Governing the Territories and Dominions which with their joint Forces they purposed to Invade. There was, what we now call, an Original Compact among 'em.[28]

Yet at the same time, the '*Gothick* Constitution' was a barbed legacy. For all the love of liberty and freedom that constitutional historians increasingly celebrated, the Goths and Gothic rebellion had been a bloody affair throughout history – not only in the Sack of Rome but in the Baronial Wars of the Middle Ages, in the Reformation and especially its historically unfathomable (to the Whig mind) backlash in the counter-Reformation, and in the recent Civil Wars and their aftermath. Political

---

26 See Graham Parry, *The Trophies of Time: English Antiquarians of the Seventeenth Century* (Oxford and New York: Oxford University Press, 1995), pp. 37-8.
27 Andrew McDouall [MacDowall], Lord Bankton, *An Essay upon Feudal Holdings, Superiorities, and Hereditary Jurisdictions, in Scotland* (London, 1747), p. 28.
28 Charles Davenant, *Essays upon I. The Balance of Power. II. The Right of Making War, Peace, and Alliances. III. Universal Monarchy* (London, 1701), p. 236.

progress and the state of the nation were haunted by guilt over the history of bloodshed that had secured these advances.

Cultural Politics

Although political debate was shot through with Gothic motifs, the remains of the Gothic heritage were most noticeable in the built environment. If little survived of the earliest pre-Roman architecture of Britain, what did remain certainly fired the imagination: enigmatic barrows, menhirs and stone circles. Such monuments were gigantic memorials to mortality, either burial tombs or, in the popular imagination, the sites of human sacrifice. They were also sublime. In his influential *A Philosophical Enquiry into the Origin of Our Ideas of the Sublime and Beautiful* (1757), Edmund Burke dedicated a chapter to the sublime effect of the most renowned of these megaliths: 'Stonehenge, neither for disposition nor ornament, has any thing admirable; but those huge rude masses of stone, set on end, and piled on each other, turn the mind on the immense force necessary for such a work. Nay, the rudeness of the work increases this cause of grandeur, as it excludes the idea of art, and contrivance.'[29]

In contrast to the dearth of early structures, however, the Middle Ages had produced 500 years of non-Classical architecture and decorative arts, the buildings typified by pointed-arch windows, vaultings and flying buttresses, the ornamentation epitomised by stained glass, heraldic carvings, gargoyles and macabre *memento mori* – features that characterised both ecclesiastical buildings and crenellated castles, as well as manors and merchant houses. For the Tory, Roman Catholic neoclassical poet Alexander Pope, these 'Dark Ages' (as this period was dubbed as early as 1730) were one long Gothic night, the Middle Ages a sorry echo of the indelicacy of the Gothic hordes:

> A second Deluge Learning thus o'er-run,
> And the *Monks* finish'd what the *Goths* begun.[30]

For others, however, this architectural succession confirmed that the country – a country whose very landscape was riven with history – did indeed enjoy a direct Gothic lineage. Architectural historians thus distinguished between ancient Gothic and modern Gothic. The former was 'massive, heavy, and

---

29 Edmund Burke, *A Philosophical Enquiry into the Origin of Our Ideas of the Sublime and Beautiful*, edited by Adam Phillips (Oxford: Oxford University Press, 1990), p. 71 (part II, section 12).
30 Alexander Pope, *An Essay on Criticism* (London, 1713 [1712]), p. 34.

coarse', encompassing the triliths of Stonehenge, Norman churches and castles, and the Tower of London. In contrast, modern Gothic (primarily decorated and perpendicular Gothic, notable examples being Westminster Abbey and Lichfield Cathedral) was highly decorative – 'light, delicate, and rich to Excess' – and was exemplified by an 'Abundance of little, whimsical, wild, and chimerical Ornaments' in which 'Every Thing is cramm'd with Windows, Roses, Crosses, Figures, &c.'[31]

The exuberance of Gothic embellishment clearly set modern Gothic apart not only from the austere might of Stonehenge and the doughty simplicity of Norman buildings, but also distinguished it from the severity of Classical styles. The Gothic and the Classical were repeatedly presented as binary opposites, and – despite much blurring at the edges – this dichotomy was fundamental in establishing the meanings and associations of these terms. Gilbert Burnet, for example, identified Gothic style with the Goths and Vandals, then with the Normans, and finally with the majesty of medieval cathedrals – it was both non-Classical and northern.[32] Predictably, such Gothic architecture was heavily favoured by the Whigs. In *The History of Tom Jones* (1748), the Whig novelist Henry Fielding underlines the Old English credentials of Squire Allworthy by installing him in an appropriate ancestral home: 'THE Gothick Stile of Building could produce nothing nobler than Mr. *Allworthy*'s House. There was an Air of Grandeur in it, that struck you with Awe, and rival'd the Beauties of the best *Grecian* Architecture.'[33] There was also a Gothic vogue for interior décor: designers such as Batty Langley and Thomas Chippendale, for example, produced both patterns and examples of Gothic furniture, fixtures and fittings, from chairs to fireplaces.[34] Others, however, were unconvinced. The poet Charles Leslie (probably 'Mussel-Mou'd Charlie', Jacobite ballad singer and old-school Tory) was sceptical of the aesthetic qualities of medieval architecture. While admitting that these vast works are unrivalled in their structural magnitude and the fine detail of the masons, they are nevertheless a 'wild disorder' of devices and decorations:

---

31 Anon., *The Builder's Dictionary: or, Gentleman and Architect's Companion*, 2 vols (London, 1734), vol. 1, [fol. 439], p. v.
32 Gilbert Burnet, *Some Letters, containing An Account of What Seem'd Most Remarkable in Travelling Through Switzerland, Italy, Some Parts of Germany, &c.*, 3rd edition ([London?] 1708), pp. 213, 202, 277, 280, 290.
33 Henry Fielding, *The History of Tom Jones, A Foundling*, 6 vols (London, 1749), vol. 1, 16.
34 Thomas Chippendale, *The Gentleman and Cabinet-Maker's Director: Being a Large Collection of the Most Elegant and Useful Designs of Household Furniture, in the most Fashionable Taste*, 3rd edition (London, 1762), plates 44 and 48.

> Grov'ling conceits with noble figures plac'd,
> A motley mixture, speak the *Gothic* taste.[35]

Yet if this instantly recognisable and nationally prevalent architecture provided a strong reminder of the native history of the nation, it was primarily because so much of it lay in ruins – the victim of the Reformation and the Dissolution of the Monasteries. These towering edifices may have been inspired by the Roman Catholic faith, but in their collapsed and decaying condition they were evidence of the triumph and iconoclastic zeal of Protestantism. Catholicism remained a ubiquitous threat in the eighteenth century – the perception being that Roman Catholic individuals and institutions owed their allegiance not to the monarch nor to Parliament, but beyond the nation's borders to the jurisdiction of the Pope – and so Great Britain was to a large degree defined by a fiercely anti-Catholic Protestantism. In the early sixteenth century, the Reformation had overturned Papal authority and when the threat of a Catholic monarch rose again at the end of the seventeenth century, Protestant succession to the throne was secured through Act of Parliament. Consequently, the Reformation could be figured as a rebellion against Roman Catholic authoritarianism via the historical narrative of the *translatio imperii ad Teutonicos*, a neat historical echo of Gothic resistance to Classical Roman oppression.

The cataclysmic devastation attending the Dissolution of the Monasteries and the overthrow of a millennium of ecclesiastical culture and social order further paralleled the havoc wrought by the Goths in antiquity. Progress was literally ruinous. These are the terms on which the Royalist poet Sir John Denham evaluated the devastating might of Henry VIII in his widely quoted and influential topographical poem, *Coopers-Hill* (1642):

> Who sees these dismal Heaps, but would demand.
> What barbarous Invader sack'd the Land?
> But when he hears, no Goth, no Turk did bring
> . . .
> This desolation, but a Christian King;
> What does he think our Sacrilege would spare,
> When such th' effects of our Devotion are.[36]

In Scotland, the Roman Catholic cleric Thomas Innes likewise saw the fall of Roman civilisation echoed in the Scottish Reformation. Attacking the prominent reformer John Knox, he railed that 'It is *Knox* himself who

---

35 Charles Leslie, *Masonry: A Poem* (Edinburgh, 1739), p. 10.
36 John Denham, *Coopers-Hill. A Poem* (London, 1709), p. 10.

hounded out, or led on the furious mobb in this wretched expedition, ...
more becoming the *Goths* or *Vandals*, than an apostolical man, as he
pretended to be.'[37]

For Leslie, meanwhile, the architectural vision of the Middle Ages, 'The best, the noblest of the *Gothic* kind', carried in it the seeds of its own destruction:

> Illustrious monuments of former Art,
> Domes, Pillars, Arches, Figures, every part
> Now mangl'd, with their last remains, upbraid
> The spite and fury of hot zeal run mad.[38]

These shattered monuments are evidence of Protestant extremism (known at the time as 'enthusiasm') – salutary reminders of the self-destructive contradictions at the heart of the Gothic ideology. Nevertheless, the Gothic splendour of country piles, such as that of Fielding's Squire Allworthy, ran parallel with a vogue for ruins: it was as fashionable to have medieval remains on one's estate as it was to inhabit a Gothic (or Gothicised) country house, as such architectural wrecks were reminders of the Baronial Wars and the Reformation: these decaying and overgrown castles and abbeys stood as reminders of the progress of the nation through the Gothic spirit of liberty.

The imaginative and emotional impact of the Dissolution was, then, persistently expressed through analogy with Gothic history. One consequence was that these ruins, deliberately left to bear witness to iconoclasm, became sites of poetic reflection on national history that both celebrated the Reformation as the advent of Protestantism, yet at the same time lamented its violence. They inspired meditative and melancholy contemplation in the poetry of the Graveyard School led by Robert Blair (1743), and such works as Mark Akenside's *Pleasures of Imagination* (1744) and Edward Young's *Night Thoughts* (1742–6). The past and its myriad thwarted futures held a sublime power – profoundly felt by Thomas Gray, for example, whose *Elegy Wrote in a Country Church-Yard* (1751) pondered human mortality, the caprices of historical chance and the chilling possibilities of what might have been – as well as the savagery of recent history that had nevertheless helped to bring the country to its current prosperous state. Moreover, Gray's imagination reached far beyond the bloodbath of the Civil War to Edward II's campaign to fortify English nationhood through Welsh genocide in 'The Bard' (1757),

---

37 Thomas Innes, *A Critical Essay on the Ancient Inhabitants of the Northern Parts of Britain, or Scotland*, 2 vols [continuously paginated] (London, 1729), vol. 2, p. 569, also p. 573.
38 Leslie, *Masonry*, pp. 9–10.

and the grisly battlefield atrocities of Norse culture that linked directly both to Gothic martial lore and even to primitive megalithic ruins ('The Fatal Sisters'; written 1761, published 1768). Although the chronology of English constitutional history appeared to be driven by defying absolutism and extremism, and sharing increasing rights and liberties, this process had, in little more than a century, condoned regicide, fomented civil war, colluded in the country's invasion by a foreign power (William of Orange), instigated the self-styled 'Bloodless Revolution' (anything but bloodless in Ireland) and triggered the Jacobite insurgency that culminated in the brutal Battle of Culloden (1746), which had in its aftermath of systematic slaughter, mass executions and the Highland Clearances. Writers were literally haunted by such guilt.

'The Visionary Tribe'

Yet the Gothic shaped literature in more ways than simply acquiescing to the nation's shameful hidden history. The most sustained early analysis of Gothic literature is William Temple's influential essay 'Of Poetry' (1690). In this, Temple, part of the inner circle of Whigs who supported the accession of William of Orange, explained how the Gothic instinct of freedom was expressed through the 'runic' poetry of the Goths, in which the imagination was not only ignited, but transformed into conjuration. Gothic verses were literally spellbinding. Although the 'true Flame of Poetry' was rare among the Goths, the '*Gothick Runers*' – *Runæ*, runers, or runic bards – nonetheless had powers of enchantment that substituted for the 'Sublime and Marvellous'. They turned their rhymes into 'Incantation and Charms' by which they endeavoured 'to raise Storms, to Calm the Seas, to cause Terror in their Enemies, to Transport themselves in the Air, to Conjure Spirits, to Cure Diseases and Stanch Bleeding Wounds, to make Women kind or easy, and Men hard or invulnerable'. Thus, their poets became '*Wizards* or *Witches*', and the sorceries of '*Gothick* Wit' underpinned later superstitions, folklore and medieval romance: 'all the visionary Tribe of *Fairies*, *Elves*, and *Goblins*, of *Sprites* and of *Bul-baggers*'.[39]

In literature, then, the Gothic manifested itself as supernatural. For the Whig leader of taste Joseph Addison,

---

39 Temple, 'Of Poetry', in *Miscellanea II*, pp. 41–2 [separately paginated]; see Thomas Warton, *Observations on The Fairy Queen of Spenser*, 2nd edition, 2 vols (London, 1762), vol. 1, p. 1.

THERE is a kind of Writing, wherein the Poet quite loses sight of Nature, and entertains his Reader's Imagination with the Characters and Actions of such Persons as have many of them no Existence, but what he bestows on them. Such are Fairies, Witches, Magicians, Demons, and departed Spirits.

Shakespeare was the master of such imaginative writing due to his 'Extravagance of Fancy', which allowed him 'to touch the weak superstitious Part of his Reader's Imagination' – as he wrote himself in *A Midsummer Night's Dream* (c. 1594–5):

> as imagination bodies forth
> The forms of things unknown, the poet's pen
> Turns them to shapes, and gives to airy nothing
> A local habitation and a name.[40]

Such poetry blossoms from 'an Imagination naturally fruitful and superstitious' – it 'depends on the Poet's Fancy ... and must work altogether out of his own Invention', making it 'more difficult than any other'.[41]

Although the imagination had been seen as a perilous realm by many writers – indeed, for Shakespeare himself, 'The lunatic, the lover, and the poet / Are of imagination all compact' – it nevertheless offered abundant riches when the supernatural was given free rein.[42] For the Whig poet and literary critic Edward Young, the supernatural was a catalyst for originality, the imagination was an 'empire of Chimeras' that fed upon ancient monuments and medieval ruins.[43] Young's own poetic statement on the powers of the individual imagination was *Night Thoughts*, which pulsated with elusive and intangible forces ('Night the Fifth', 1743):

> I widen my Horizon, gain new Powers,
> See Things invisible, feel Things remote,
> Am present with Futurities.[44]

William Duff, the Scottish minister and primitivist theorist, meanwhile celebrated 'the vigorous effort of a creative Imagination' that enabled the poet to call 'shadowy substances and unreal objects into existence. They are present to his view, and glide, like spectres, in silent, sullen majesty, before

---

40 William Shakespeare, *A Midsummer Night's Dream*, edited by Harold Brooks (London: Arden Shakespeare, 2004), V.i.14–17.
41 *The Spectator*, 8 vols (London, [1712–13] [1713]), vol. 6, p. 127 (No. 419).
42 Shakespeare, *Midsummer Night's Dream*, V. i. 7–8.
43 Edward Young, *Conjectures on Original Composition* (London, 1759), p. 37.
44 Edward Young, *The Complaint* (London, 1743), p. 24 (Book V. ll. 339–41).

his astonished and intranced [sic] sight.'⁴⁵ Even Samuel Johnson's remarks on Shakespeare, published a decade later in 1765, attended to the Gothicism of the playwright. Just as Temple had characterised 'all the visionary Tribe' as Gothic, so too Johnson perceived in *A Midsummer Night's Dream* the same 'Gothick mythology of fairies'.⁴⁶

Alongside Shakespeare, Edmund Spenser also exemplified the Gothic turn in literature in his medievalist epic, *The Faerie Queene* (1590–6), with its evocation of the chivalry and intrigue of the Middle Ages. Despite some grudging admiration, Addison had in the early years of the century unfavourably compared Spenser with Classical writers, at one point dismissing the 'Gothick Manner in Writing' (meaning medievalist romance) as a 'wrong artificial Taste upon little fanciful Authors and Writers of Epigram', in direct contrast to elegant (i.e. neoclassical) 'Simplicity of Thought'.⁴⁷ Nevertheless, Spenserian imitation was in vogue throughout the century.⁴⁸ 'Strange lays, whose power had charmed a Spenser's ear' are invoked in William Collins's 'Ode on the Popular Superstitions of the Highlands of Scotland' (written 1749, published 1788), a poem of the supernatural undead that uncannily anticipates James Macpherson's later Ossianic works, themselves brimming with megalithic remains and teeming with attendant ghosts who 'on their twilight tombs aerial council hold' – meaning that in one sense, Ossianic Scotland and Scottish Gothic is a reworking of English Spenserianism.⁴⁹ Thomas Gray, too, summons the dead of Wales in his necromantic poem 'The Bard' (1757):

> 'They do not sleep.
> 'On yonder cliffs, a grisly band,
> 'I see them sit, they linger yet,
> 'Avengers of their native land.'⁵⁰

Spenser's appeal was not, however, confined to poets. In his 1715 edition of *The Faerie Queene*, John Hughes countered Addison by suggesting that

---

45 William Duff, *An Essay on Original Genius; and Its Various Modes of Exertion in Philosophy and the Fine Arts, particularly in Poetry* (London, 1767), p. 177; the allusion is to Shakespeare's Owen Glendower, 1. *Henry IV*.
46 William Shakespeare, *The Plays of William Shakespeare*, edited by Samuel Johnson, 8 vols (London, 1765), vol. 1, p. xxi.
47 *The Spectator*, vol. 1, pp. 397–8 (No. 70).
48 For example, Alexander Pope, 'The Alley'; James Thomson, 'The Castle of Indolence'; William Shenstone, 'The School-Mistress'; and William Collins, 'Ode on the Poetical Character' in Roger Lonsdale (ed.), *The New Oxford Book of Eighteenth-Century Verse* (Oxford: Oxford University Press, 1984), pp. 87–8, 193–6, 305–7, 379–81.
49 *The Poems of Thomas Gray, William Collins, Oliver Goldsmith*, edited by Roger Lonsdale (London and New York: Longman, 1969), p. 504 (l. 39).
50 Lonsdale (ed.), *Poems of Gray, Collins, Goldsmith*, p. 188 (ll. 43–6).

judging Spenser's epic by the standards of *The Odyssey* or *The Aeneid*, 'wou'd be like drawing a Parallel between the *Roman* and the *Gothick* Architecture. In the first there is doubtless a more natural Grandeur and Simplicity: in the latter, we find great Mixtures of Beauty and Barbarism, yet assisted by the Invention of a Variety of inferior Ornaments.'[51] The historian and later poet laureate Thomas Warton elaborated this argument in the 1750s and 1760s. For Warton, *The Faerie Queene* provides a starting point for a taxonomy of English architecture from the Saxons to the Reformation, divided into four different orders: Saxon Gothic, Absolute Gothic, Ornamental Gothic and Florid Gothic.[52] For Warton, too, Gothic architecture and Gothic literature were united by a mutual endeavour: he praised the original 'Gothic state' of St Paul's as 'one of the noblest patterns of that kind of architecture' and reasoned that it had influenced John Milton's 'Il Penseroso' (1645).[53] Poetry, to adapt a later axiom, was frozen architecture.[54]

Both Richard Hurd and Horace Walpole made the same point. For Hurd, 'When an architect examines a Gothic structure by Grecian rules, he finds nothing but deformity. But the Gothic architecture has it's [sic] own rules, by which when it comes to be examined, it is seen to have it's merit, as well as the Grecian.'[55] He then went on to evaluate Spenser's poetry and fashions in gardening on these terms. In like manner, Walpole argued that the term '*Gothic Architecture*' was originally 'inflicted as a reproach on our ancient buildings in general by our ancestors who revived the Grecian taste, is now considered but as a species of modern elegance, by those who wish to distinguish the Saxon style from it', before memorably declaring:

> It is difficult for the noblest Grecian temple to convey half so many impressions to the mind, as a cathedral does of the best Gothic taste – a proof of skill in the architects and of address in the priests who erected them. The latter exhausted [expended] their knowledge of the passions in composing edifices whose pomp, mechanism, vaults, tombs, painted windows, gloom and perspectives infused such sensations of romantic devotion; and they were happy in finding artists capable of executing such machinery. One must have

---

51 Edmund Spenser, *Works*, edited by John Hughes, 6 vols (London, 1715), vol. 1, p. lx.
52 See Thomas Warton, *Observations on The Fairy Queen of Spenser*, vol. 2, pp. 185–98.
53 Thomas Warton, *Observations on the Faerie Queene of Spenser* (London, 1754), p. 246 [1762 edition, vol. 2, p. 135].
54 Though often attributed to Goethe, Madame de Staël popularised the description of music as 'frozen architecture': see Paul Johnson, *The Birth of the Modern: World Society, 1815–1830* (London: Phoenix Giant, 1996), p. 119.
55 Richard Hurd, *Letters on Chivalry and Romance* (London, 1762), p. 61.

taste to be sensible of the beauties of Grecian architecture; one only wants passions to feel Gothic.[56]

This recurrent kinship between Gothic architecture and medievalist literature, a touchstone of eighteenth-century Gothic thinking, is one reason for the architectonic features of later Gothic novels.

Despite so often being pitted against Classical taste, it is worth emphasising that Gothicism was not unambiguously Whiggish any more than neoclassicism was a uniquely Tory style. 'Jacobite Gothick' was a recognised medievalist architectural movement, linking to medieval Catholicism as well as to absolutist monarchy, and Alexander Pope, for example, wrote Chaucerian and Spenserian verse as well as editing Shakespeare, the darling of the Gothic critics. Indeed, despite his Toryism, Pope was broadminded enough in judging Shakespeare's plays to use the same argument as Hughes had with Spenser: 'one may look upon his works, in comparison of those that are more finish'd and regular, as upon an ancient majestick piece of *Gothick* Architecture, compar'd with a neat Modern building: The latter is more elegant and glaring [dazzling], but the former is more strong and more solemn.'[57] Similarly, Gilbert West's poem *The Institution of the Order of the Garter* (1742) was an ancient British pageant filled with Gothic bards and druids that reflected the progressive Toryism of Henry St John, Viscount Bolingbroke, author of *The Idea of a Patriot King* (circulating in manuscript from 1738).

Yet while the supernatural had had a place in poetry and drama since time immemorial, prose narratives – at least in Britain, and especially in the eighteenth century – tended to be far more grounded. That is not to say that magical tales were completely absent from the early English novel. The Christian allegory of John Bunyan's *Pilgrim's Progress* (1678), based on the more moderate divine interventions in his spiritual autobiography *Grace Abounding to the Chief of Sinners* (1666), was a key influence on later dissenting narratives such as Daniel Defoe's *Robinson Crusoe* (1719) and *Moll Flanders* (1722), both of which, for all their materialism, have metaphysical events woven into their plots (the footprint and dreams in *Crusoe*; the call to Jemy to 'come back' in *Flanders*). Similarly, following the first publication of *The Arabian Nights' Entertainments* in France in 1704 there had been a vogue for

---

56 Horace Walpole, *Anecdotes of Painting in England; with Some Account of the Principal Artists; and Incidental Notes on Other Arts*, 4 vols (Strawberry Hill: Printed by Thomas Farmer, 1762–71 [i.e. 1780]), vol. 1, pp. 107–8.
57 Alexander Pope (ed.), 'The Preface', *The Works of Shakespear*, 6 vols (London, 1725), vol. 1, p. xxiii.

fantastical Eastern tales popularised by writers as diverse as Addison and Johnson (*Rasselas*, 1759), as well as popular chapbook accounts of ghostly occurrences. In spite of these, however, Horace Walpole's *Castle of Otranto*, first published on Christmas Eve in 1764, is highly significant for its prodigal use of the supernatural. For all its heady mix of extreme sentimentalism, sumptuous medievalism, fervent Shakespearean imitation and Whig power politics, it was the supernaturalism of *Otranto* that initiated a new form of fiction – precisely the passions, superstition and witchery that is lacking from other medievalist novels of the time such as Thomas Leland's thirteenth-century saga *Longsword, Earl of Salisbury* (1762).

Further to its literary influence, Gothic also had textual and linguistic dimensions. The Goths were celebrated for their written runic language, considered comparable to the ancient Egyptian achievement of hieroglyphs. Consequently, it was argued that the Gothic Runers had formed an elite cultural caste. They 'studied Nature, Astronomy and Magick, and without their Advice nothing of publick Importance was transacted', and they summoned with demons who led them in 'impious Rites and Ceremonies', taught them to read the future in the entrails of their enemies, led them in building their 'barbarous Monument[s]', and accompanied them into battle.[58] And in addition to consorting with their supernatural familiars, the Runers were also the custodians of written laws and the guardians of the constitution: literature and liberty were part of their sorcery.[59]

Rhyme, meanwhile, had long been associated with the barbarian nations, and so William Temple also contended that the prevalence of rhyming verse in Italian, Spanish, French and English poetry had its origin in the monosyllabic 'Gingle' of the Gothic language, again in contrast to the metre and measure of Classical poetry.[60] As the Tory poet and dramatist John Dryden contemptuously put it, the pure current of Virgilian Latin 'bears along with it the filth and ordures of the *Goths* and *Vandals*'.[61] Likewise, the Whig philosopher Anthony Ashley Cooper, third Earl of Shaftesbury, complained of 'the GOTHICK *Model* of Poetry' being 'the horrid Discord of jingling Rhyme'.[62]

---

58 John Webb, *A Vindication of Stone-Heng Restored: in which the Orders and Rules of Architecture Observed by the Ancient Romans, are Discussed*, 2nd edition (London, 1725), p. 86.
59 Henry Spelman, *Reliquiæ Spelmannianæ*, 2 vols (London, 1723), vol. 2, p. 102.
60 Temple, 'Of Poetry', *Miscellanea II*, p. 38.
61 John Dryden (trans.), *The Works of Virgil: Containing His Pastorals, Georgics and Æneis*, 3 vols, 3rd edition (London, 1709), vol. 1, p. 8 [italics reversed].
62 Anthony Ashley Cooper, Earl of Shaftesbury, 'Advice to an Author' [first published 1710], in *Characteristicks of Men, Manners, Opinions, Times*, 5th edition, 3 vols (London, 1732), vol. 1, p. 217.

Moreover, Gothic had introduced into the English language not only rhymes but also harsh sounds and 'stubborn Consonants': a *'Goth-like'* sound, characteristic of indigenous names such as 'Bubb' and 'Hop'.[63] One unexpected consequence of this attention to textual Gothics is that, if it meant anything, eighteenth-century 'Gothic literature' originally implied whimsical and eccentric writing: 'the little *Gothick* Ornaments of Epigrammatical Conceits, Turns, Points, and Quibbles, which are so frequent in the most admired of our *English Poets*'.[64] If the emergence of neo-Gothic building styles and fashions for interior décor revelled in profuse and extravagant adornment, neo-Gothic literature was densely compacted, compressed to the point of opacity. In 1710 *The Tatler* printed a skit by the Tory Jonathan Swift that parodied the Gothic vogue as 'directly contrary to the Example of the *Greeks* and *Romans*, altogether the *Gothick* Strain, and a natural Tendency towards relapsing into Barbarity':

> SIR,
> I *Cou'd n't* get the Things you sent for all *about Town* —— I *thôt* to *ha'* come down my self and then *I'd h' brôt 'um*; but I *ha'n't don't*, and I believe I *can't do't*, that's *Pozz* —— ... *Will Hazard* has got the *Hipps* ... He has promis't me upon *Rep*, to leave off Play; but you know 'tis a Weakness *he's* too apt to *give into*, *thô* he has as much Wit as any Man, *no body more*. He has lain *incog* ever since —[65]

This is a sardonic blueprint for 'sentimentalism', and on such terms Laurence Sterne's *Tristram Shandy* (1759–67) is modish English *'Gothick'*. Besides, Johnson described the 'Teutonick' ancestry of the English language in the 'Grammar' prefaced to the first volume of his *A Dictionary of the English Language* of 1755.[66]

Taking its cue from the embodiment of *'Gothick* Wit' in its variety of cultural forms, Gothic values began to define eighteenth-century English society and its heritage. The Goths were not only a martial society but revered as the most courageous of the ancient races: hence they had surely developed the chivalric code of the Middle Ages that persisted in pockets of

---

63 'Miranda', 'To Lady Harvey, on a Conversation concerning Names', in *Miscellaneous Poems and Translations. By Several Hands*, edited by Richard Savage (London, 1726), p. 247.

64 'Ned Softly', in Richard Steele, *The Lucubrations of Isaac Bickerstaff Esq; in Five Volumes*, 5 vols (London, 1720), vol. 3, p. 199 (*The Tatler*, No. 163).

65 [Jonathan Swift], in Steele, *Lucubrations of Bickerstaff*, vol. 4, pp. 145, 144 (*The Tatler*, No. 230).

66 Samuel Johnson, 'A Grammar of the English Tongue', *A Dictionary of the English Language*, 2 vols (London, 1755–6), vol. 1, p. x.

good manners, loyalty and respect for women. In the pictorial arts, they were acclaimed as the innovators of 'Hereditary Marks of Honour', or heraldry – that colourful blaze of fantastic beasts and visual puns which remained a cornerstone of eighteenth-century pageantry and aristocratic legitimacy, connecting the ruling classes with the country's warlike past.[67] Jousts and tournaments, meanwhile, had morphed and modernised into the leisured class's taste for hunting, while honour was defended through duels.[68] Even chess was seen as a war game of strategy and tactics: a *'Gothick* Game'.[69] Indeed, almost anything that connected with medieval culture could be seen as Gothic: in printing, the black-letter fount (𝔱𝔥𝔲𝔰) used in legal documents and primers was a direct descendant of the earliest typefaces, and so stood as a reminder of the nation's medieval birth right communicated through the literacy of the Gothic Runers and the Middle Ages.

Conclusion: The Gothic

The 1760s is the crucible of English Gothic literature. It was the decade of Walpole's *The Castle of Otranto*, Hurd's *Letters on Chivalry and Romance*, and Johnson's edition of Shakespeare (and also his entanglement with the Cock-Lane Ghost); it was the decade of Sterne's textual *tour de force Tristram Shandy*, the decade of 'Wilkes and Liberty' – a radical spin on the political Gothic myth – and of the unforgiving political satires of Charles Churchill, including the allegorical farrago *The Ghost* (1762–3). The 1760s was also the decade of three writers whose work was in different ways haunted by questions of forgery, authenticity and legitimacy – areas that would become characteristic tropes of later Gothic literature.

James Macpherson's 'Ossianics' comprised the works of the third-century blind Celtic bard Ossian, last of his race, recalling the long defeat of his people who haunt him as dying memories and evanescing ghosts. Supposedly the remnants of an archaic oral tradition, they were initially published as

---

67 For heraldry, see Alexander Nisbet, *An Essay on the Ancient and Modern Use of Armories* (London, 1718), pp. 7–8; for chivalry, see Hurd, *Chivalry and Romance*, pp. 1ff.
68 For hunting, see *The Guardian*, no. 61 (21 May 1714); for duelling, see John Cockburn, *The History and Examination of Duels* (London, 1720), pp. 133–4; and Anon., *Foreign Tales, Witty & Merry Sayings, Repartees, &c. from the Best Authors* (London, 1719), pp. 145–7 [apothegm 228]; also John Selden, *The Duello, or, Single Combat: From Antiquity Derived into This Kingdom of England* (London [1711?]), pp. 37–42; and Ambrose Philips, *The Free-Thinker: or, Essays of Wit and Humour*, 3rd edition, 3 vols (London, 1739), vol. 1 p. 64 (No. 15).
69 William King, 'Animadversions on the Pretended Account of Danmark', *Miscellanies in Prose and Verse* (London, [1709]), pp. 51–2.

fragments – *Fragments of Ancient Poetry, collected in the Highlands of Scotland, and translated from the Galic or Erse Language* (1760) – then swiftly amplified into two epic poems, *Fingal* (1761) and *Temora* (1762). Poetic genius was located in the Scottish Highlands, and so *Ossian* advanced an alternative history of the Isles – and was inevitably denounced as a forgery.

Macpherson's lines reverberate with the Burkean sublime, portraying a bleak, storm-wracked wilderness through which the wind and rain echo with the voices of the past. Hugh Blair, Professor of Belles Lettres at the University of Edinburgh, considered *Ossian* to be 'the thunder and the lightning of genius ... the offspring of nature, not of art',[70] In fact, *Ossian* reads like a derelict prototype of later Gothic literature, a failed commemoration of the thwarted Jacobite Rebellion, advocating a pragmatic political expediency that reflected the Scottish dominance of British politics at the time – which, like *Ossian* itself, was mired in questions of legitimacy and authenticity.

If there was an English Gothic response to *Ossian*, it was Thomas Percy's scholarly anthology of songs and ballads, *Reliques of Ancient English Poetry* (1765). Joseph Addison had already recognised the strengths of the 'Gothick Manner in Writing' in historical ballads such as 'Chevy-Chace', but Percy proposed a much more daring lineage: that the medieval minstrel tradition of England was descended from the Gothic Runers via the Norse skalds.[71] He saw in the popular ballad tradition a survival of an ancient national poetry in tangible textual sources, rather than the transitory nature of the oral tradition. Percy's fascination with amoral and supernatural medieval ballad narratives, his perpetual emphasis on manuscripts and the written or printed word, and his strong sense of the Gothic cultural genealogy that had helped to shape English poetry, was positioned within a state framework. According to Percy, medieval minstrels held a central role at court in safeguarding national culture – in other words, the English past was presented in Whiggish terms, according to which Gothic values of political progress were seen to be enshrined in the highest accomplishments of the arts. Moreover, Percy relentlessly hemmed his ballads with paratexts – prefaces and footnotes and cross-references and glossaries – creating layered palimpsests that would develop into the patchwork condition of later Gothic fiction.

Both Macpherson and Percy, as well as Shakespeare and the Whig cognoscenti, were signal influences on Thomas Chatterton, the precocious

---

70 Hugh Blair, *A Critical Dissertation on the Poems of Ossian, the Son of Fingal* (London, 1763), p. 68.
71 *Spectator*, vol. 1, pp. 397–8 (No. 70).

Bristol writer who died aged just seventeen. Chatterton's death – which for many years was thought to have been suicide – and his notorious reputation as a literary forger have overshadowed his bequest to the Gothic. Chatterton's Gothicism is strikingly anti-Classicist, resolutely medievalist and pioneeringly Anglo-Saxonist. It is a body of work that dramatises the archive, in which found manuscripts, translations and papers – from receipts to memoranda to maps to letters to poetry to plays – accumulate in a dizzying array. He is as much a calligrapher and orthographer as a poet, truly a crafter, a forger in the most creative sense of the word. The fifteenth-century Bristol monk and central protagonist/writer of these texts is Thomas Rowley. But histories lie within histories: Rowley translates, for example, an eleventh-century epic on the Battle of Hastings that swarms with the internecine warfare of Gothic nations: 'Dacyannes', 'Brutons', 'Normannes', 'Saxonnes', 'Scythyannes', and Welsh. Correspondingly, in Rowley's own verse the matter of English freedom is never far away in political, environmental, martial and otherworldly ways. In Rowley's play 'Goddwyn', Harold, Earl of Wessex, laments,

> Here liethe Englonde, all her drites[1] unfree,
> Here liethe Normans coupynge[2] her bie Lotte;
> Caltysnyng[3] everich native Plante to gre:[4]
> Whatte woulde I doe? I brondeous[5] wulde hem slee[6],
> Tare owte theyre sable harte bie ryghtefulle breme:[7]
> Theyre Deathe a meanes untoe Mie Lyfe shulde bee,
> Mie Spryte shulde revelle yn theyr harte-blodde streme.
> Eftsoones [soon after] I wylle bewryne[8] mie Ragefulle Ire,
>   And Goddis Anlace[9] wielde, yn furie dyre

[1] Rights Libertys [2] cutting, mangling [3] forbidding [4] grow [5] furious [6] Slay [7] Strength [8] declare [9] Sword [Chatterton's notes][72]

For Chatterton, Whig history is the raw material for inspired poetry.

   Chatterton's premature death haunted the succeeding generation of writers – so much so, that he became a powerful talisman of neglected genius. He was a daring literary innovator who had reinvented the medieval past as decisively Whiggish in every way, from artistic verve to national politics, and at the same time he was an audacious rebel who had defied the establishment. The literary canon bequeathed to Romanticism had been shaped by the political factionalism of the early eighteenth century: it essentialised

---

72 Thomas Chatterton, *Complete Works*, edited by Donald S. Taylor and Benjamin B. Hoover, 2 vols [continuously paginated] (Oxford: Clarendon Press, 1971), vol. 1, p. 299 (ll. 77–85).

originality and individualism, the imagination and the supernatural, the past and the environment. At the heart of this Whig aesthetics is the Gothic – and Chatterton was nothing less than its avatar.[73]

---

73 See Nick Groom, 'Romanticism before 1789', in David Duff (ed.), *The Oxford Handbook of British Romanticism* (Oxford: Oxford University Press, 2018), pp. 13–29.

I.3

The Literary Gothic Before Horace Walpole's *The Castle of Otranto*

DALE TOWNSHEND

Dorothy Scarborough, J. M. S. Tompkins and other Gothic scholars in the first three decades of the twentieth century were unanimous in their claim that Horace Walpole's *The Castle of Otranto* (published late 1764; dated 1765) constituted the origin and fountainhead of the Gothic tradition in literature.[1] In *The Gothic Quest* of 1938, however, Montague Summers sought both to nuance and subtly to revise this critical position, pointing in his self-proclaimed 'History of the Gothic Novel' to the existence of earlier, pre-existent French, German and British literary texts and traditions that, if not strictly 'Gothic' in themselves, certainly informed and influenced Walpole's achievements in *Otranto* and, through this, the numerous eighteenth-century Gothic fictions written and published in its wake.[2] It is when Summers turns to a consideration of what he terms the 'Historical Gothic' that his cautious, historicist interrogation of what had hitherto uniformly been taken as *Otranto*'s originary status becomes especially pronounced. Having drawn attention to a tradition of historical fiction that flourished in England from the reign of Charles II through to the early eighteenth century, Summers settles on the case of Thomas Leland's *Longsword, Earl of Salisbury: An Historical Romance* (1762), a text that he enthusiastically lauds as 'The first work in English which can fairly claim to be a Historical Novel'.[3] At this crucial moment in his study, Summers is emphatic that Leland's fiction does not belong to the same generic 'family' as that instantiated by Walpole: 'it is', he writes, 'of an entirely different kind from and the progenitor of quite

---

1 See, for example, the construction of Horace Walpole as the 'father' of the Gothic tradition in literature in Dorothy Scarborough, *The Supernatural in Modern English Fiction* (New York and London: G. P. Putnam's Sons, 1917), p. 6 and J. M. S. Tompkins, *The Popular Novel in England: 1770–1800* (London: Methuen & Co., 1932), p. 243.
2 See Montague Summers, *The Gothic Quest: A History of the Gothic Novel*, 2nd edition (London: The Fortune Press, 1968), pp. 106–52.
3 Summers, *The Gothic Quest*, p. 158.

another family than *The Castle of Otranto*', and while at certain points the 'two genera meet and contact', they are 'essentially separate and diverse'.[4] The difference between these two literary modes, he continues, 'must be emphasized, and needs to be urged, since certain ill-equipped and superficial sophomores have devoted long otiose pages to dilating upon their preconceived fancies, and expanding notions, which are in fine the effects of too little reading and unripened judgement'.[5]

As the defensiveness of Summers's tone indicates, it is clear that, in locating the origins of the 'Historical Gothic' in *Longsword*, a fiction by an Irish writer that precedes *The Castle of Otranto* by more than two years, the early twentieth century's most passionate scholar of English Gothic finds himself in a potentially compromising position. His reaction is one of partial retraction, qualification and defence: to Walpole's text, he claims, 'we owe nothing less than a revolution in public taste, and its influence is strong even at the present day'; '*The Castle of Otranto*', he reiterates, 'is, in fine, a notable landmark in the history of English taste and English literature'.[6] Nonetheless, as Summers himself has only just speculated, the possibility remains that the Gothic tradition in literature might be traced back to a different and not exclusively English source. Disconcerted by the prospect, he eventually settles the matter in *The Gothic Quest* via a compromise of sorts, claiming that '*The Castle of Otranto* is of immense importance and influence, but it certainly was not the only factor in the development of the Gothic Novel, and of the Historical Novel it was not the parent and the source.'[7]

It is true that Gothic scholars in more recent years have been far less reluctant to engage with, and confront, the question of Gothic literature before *The Castle of Otranto*. One thinks here of the work of several contemporary critics who have advanced robust arguments in favour of regarding Leland's *Longsword* as an early, if not the earliest, Gothic fiction in the history of literature. For Nick Groom, for instance, the year 1762 saw 'the first eighteenth-century Gothic novel: Thomas Leland's unjustly neglected *Longsword, Earl of Salisbury: An Historical Romance*', a narrative that he reads as 'an illustrated conduct book of the Gothic virtues and a paean to national identity and the "triumphs of British valour"'.[8] As Groom has put it elsewhere, 'Gothic literature in English did not begin in December 1764 with the publication of *The Castle of Otranto*', and that 'Thomas Leland's *Longsword*,

---

4 Summers, *The Gothic Quest*, p. 162.   5 Summers, *The Gothic Quest*, p. 162.
6 Summers, *The Gothic Quest*, p. 179.   7 Summers, *The Gothic Quest*, p. 162.
8 Nick Groom, *The Gothic: A Very Short Introduction* (Oxford: Oxford University Press, 2012), p. 71.

published in 1762, is arguably the first eighteenth-century Gothic novel.'⁹ Though motivated by more legible nationalist agendas, scholars of eighteenth-century Irish Gothic have often reached similar conclusions. Jarlath Killeen, for example, has described *Longsword* as at least 'unproblematically a Gothic novel' as Reeve's *The Old English Baron* (1778), not least in the Gothic or 'medieval' affinities that it shares with both Walpole's and Reeve's narratives, and it is in this respect that Leland's fiction might be construed as 'an important beginning to Irish Gothic fiction'.¹⁰ More circumspect in its approach, Christina Morin's *The Gothic Novel in Ireland, c. 1760–1829* (2018) has recently argued that Summers's distinction between the 'historical novel' of Leland and the 'Gothic novel' of Walpole is a false one, and that when we are attuned to the connections and similarities between the two modes, both *Longsword* and *Otranto* together have much to teach us about 'the origins of British gothic literature'.¹¹

I shall return in the conclusion to this chapter to the issue of Leland's *Longsword* and its place in the Gothic tradition in fiction. For the moment, though, I want to argue that we might approach the question of Gothic literature before Horace Walpole in at least two ways. First, we might seek to identify traces of a pre-*Otranto* Gothic aesthetic in the fashion that the critics mentioned above have done – that is, simply through pointing to the apparent thematic and atmospheric parallels, continuities and connections between earlier texts, *Longsword* among them, and the form that Gothic literature took from 1765 onwards. This is a critical gesture that depends ultimately upon hindsight and a working knowledge of the conventions that, in time, would sediment, and critically come to be recognised as, 'the Gothic'. It was the work of the cultural and architectural historian Kenneth Clark that inaugurated this particular approach to the issue, arguing in his influential *The Gothic Revival: An Essay in the History of Taste* (1928) that, before it assumed its more familiar architectural forms, the Gothic Revival in England was a largely literary phenomenon. Citing key passages from Edmund Spenser's *The Faerie Queene* (1590–6), John Milton's 'Il Penseroso' (1646), Alexander Pope's *Eloisa to Abelard* (1717), John Dryer's 'Grongar Hill' (1726), David Mallet's *The Excursion* (1728) and select poems of the so-called Graveyard

---

9 Nick Groom, 'Eighteenth-Century Gothic before *The Castle of Otranto*', in Joanne Parker (ed.), *The Harp and the Constitution: Myths of Celtic and Gothic Origin* (Leiden: Brill, 2016), pp. 26–46 (pp. 26, 44).
10 Jarlath Killeen, *The Emergence of Irish Gothic Fiction: History, Origins, Theories* (Edinburgh: Edinburgh University Press, 2014), pp. 174–8.
11 Christina Morin, *The Gothic Novel in Ireland, c. 1760–1829* (Manchester: Manchester University Press, 2018), p. 29.

school in support of his claims, Clark argued that the melancholic and imaginative responses to Gothic architecture that we witness in such poems might be called 'the true starting-point of the Gothic Revival'.[12] Notably, each of Clark's examples chronologically predates *The Castle of Otranto*, and any one of them, in turn, might be cited as evidence for the existence of a quasi- or proto-Gothic literary tradition that existed several decades if not centuries before Walpole's literary experiment of the mid-1760s. Accordingly, and seemingly under Clark's influence, several Gothic scholars in the first few decades of the twentieth century regularly identified adumbrations of the Gothic in the Graveyard verse of the 1740s and early 1750s. In *The Gothic Flame* (1957), for example, Devendra P. Varma argued that, if not actually originating there, the Gothic was certainly the successor to the 'sensational touch of supernatural horror' to be found in the earlier Graveyard poetry of Thomas Parnell's *A Night-Piece on Death* (1722); Edward Young's *The Complaint; or, Night-Thoughts on Life, Death, & Immortality* (1742–5); Robert Blair's *The Grave* (1743); and Thomas Gray's *An Elegy Wrote in a Country Churchyard* (1751).[13] More recently, critics such as David Punter, Fred Botting and Vincent Quinn have argued along similar lines.[14] Other contemporary scholars have traced back the origins of the Gothic to even more chronologically remote sources and periods, some seeing in the plays of William Shakespeare, Ben Jonson, Francis Beaumont and John Fletcher, John Ford, Thomas Middleton, John Webster and other early modern dramatists clear evidence of a 'premodern', 'early modern' or 'Renaissance Gothic' literary tradition, with others identifying adumbrations of the Gothic even as far back as the writings of the fourteenth-century scholastic philosopher, theologian and biblical exegete John Wyclif and in John Foxe's *Actes and Monuments* (1563).[15]

12 Kenneth Clark, *The Gothic Revival: An Essay in the History of Taste*, 2nd edition (Harmondsworth: Penguin Books, 1962), p. 16.
13 Devendra P. Varma, *The Gothic Flame: Being a History of the Gothic Novel in England* (London: Arthur Baker Ltd, 1957), pp. 27–8.
14 See David Punter, *The Literature of Terror: A History of Gothic Fictions from 1765 to the Present Day*, revised edition, 2 vols (London: Pearson Education Ltd, 1996), vol. 1, pp. 30–7; Fred Botting, *Gothic*, 2nd edition (Abingdon: Routledge, 2014), pp. 30–3; and Vincent Quinn, 'Graveyard Writing and the Rise of the Gothic', in Angela Wright and Dale Townshend (eds), *Romantic Gothic: An Edinburgh Companion* (Edinburgh: Edinburgh University Press, 2016), pp. 37–54 (p. 37).
15 See John Drakakis and Dale Townshend (eds), *Gothic Shakespeares* (Abingdon and New York: Routledge, 2008); Christy Desmet and Anne Williams (eds), *Shakespearean Gothic* (Cardiff: University of Wales Press, 2009); Elisabeth Bronfen and Beate Neumeier (eds), *Gothic Renaissance: A Reassessment* (Manchester: Manchester University Press, 2014); and Alison Milbank's argument in *God and the Gothic: Religion, Romance, and Reality in the English Literary Tradition* (Oxford: Oxford University Press, 2018).

To talk of the Gothic before *The Castle of Otranto*, then, is to point to the relatively superficial similarities in theme, subject-matter, characterisation, narrative patterning, atmosphere and tone between a selection of pre- and post-Walpolean texts, prose-based and otherwise. There is undoubtedly a degree of merit in this. For instance, continuously citing, reworking and adapting the most ghostly and ghastly aspects of his plays, eighteenth- and early nineteenth-century Gothic writers clearly identified in Shakespeare a source for their own horrors and terrors. With its evocative references to the 'antique pillars', 'high embowed roof' and the 'dim religious light' refracted by a stained-glass window in a Gothic cathedral, Milton's 'Il Penseroso' profoundly influenced later Gothic writers' melancholic responses to architecture, just as the Catholic Pope's tragic vision of monastical existence in *Eloisa to Abelard* fired the anti-Catholic sentiments of many a later Gothic poet and novelist, including those of Walpole himself. Similarly, portions of Mallet's *The Excursion* comprise reflections on moonlight, melancholy, death, the supernatural and the stirring imaginative effects of Gothic architecture that would not be out of place in the Gothic romances of Ann Radcliffe, while Matthew Gregory Lewis, for his part, directly drew upon the horrors of Graveyard verse when he cited lines from Blair's *The Grave* in his own rendition of the horrors beneath the sepulchre of St Clare in *The Monk* (1796).

A second, alternative approach to the problem, however, and one that is arguably more complex and more historically refined, consists in attempting to understand precisely how British culture from the late seventeenth century onwards viewed, conceptualised and responded to its own 'Gothic' literary heritage, a gesture that relies less upon the retrospective identification of post-Walpolean Gothic impulses in pre-1764 texts than a refined understanding of the aesthetic implications of the term 'Gothic' in earlier periods. It is to an account of this that I now turn, articulating as I do so the historical grounds upon which we might begin to talk about Gothic literature before *The Castle of Otranto*.

Politics, Poetry and Conflict, 1690–1712

As Samuel Kliger has shown, the term 'Gothic' first assumed currency in Britain not in aesthetic discourse but in late seventeenth-century political circles, when Whig statesmen, politicians and historiographers made regular appeal to a system of ancient 'Gothic' liberties as a means of counteracting the absolutism of the Stuart line of kings.[16] By this way of reasoning, the Glorious Revolution of 1688 marked the reinstatement and consolidation of a free and anti-authoritarian political system that, as the argument went, had been brought to England with the arrival of the Saxons or 'Goths' in c. AD 449. Such ideological and highly politicised versions of history circulated throughout the period in such forms as Richard Verstegan's early and foundational *A Restitution of Decayed Intelligence* (1605); Nathaniel Bacon's *An Historicall Discourse of the Uniformity of the Government of England* (1647–51); in William Temple's essay 'Of Heroick Virtue' (1690) and *An Introduction to the History of England* (1695); and in James Tyrrell's *Bibliotheca politica* (1692–4) and *The General History of England* (1698). As David Womersley and Abigail Williams have pointed out, literature was crucial to this Whiggish understanding of the nation's political past: from the 1680s onwards, self-identifying Whig poets saw in such historical events as the Exclusion Crisis (1679–81), the Glorious Revolution and the War of Spanish Succession (1701–14) not only occasion for the celebration of English military victories, but the recuperation and reformation of English letters and the articulation and defence of a distinctly Whiggish conceptualisation of literary aesthetics too.[17] Just as they were in the political or historical sense, notions of 'Gothic' were crucial to this aesthetic tradition, particularly in the work of William Temple, John Dennis and Anthony Ashley Cooper, 3rd Earl of Shaftesbury, though as I show below, the extent to which they promoted and celebrated this literary strain varied considerably. Nevertheless, it is in the writings of these three figures that, even if in some instances only negatively, we first see the emergence of a sense of the 'Gothic' as a distinctive and singular literary impulse, one that, as in contemporary political discourse, was perceived as running counter to the political and aesthetic principles of ancient Greek and Roman Classicism.

As British Ambassador to the Netherlands, a close personal friend of William of Orange and an influential figure behind William's marriage to James II's daughter Mary, Sir William Temple's political Whiggism was clearly established. In such publications as the essay 'On Heroick Virtue' from the second part of his *Miscellanea* and his historical study of the nation in *An Introduction to the History of England*, Temple perpetuated the familiar

---

16 See Samuel Kliger, *The Goths in England: A Study in Seventeenth- and Eighteenth-Century Thought* (Cambridge, MA: Harvard University Press, 1952).

17 See David Womersley (ed.), *Augustan Critical Writing* (London: Penguin Books, 1997) and Abigail Williams, *Poetry and the Creation of a Whig Literary Culture, 1681–1714* (Oxford: Oxford University Press, 2005).

'Gothic' version of history, tracing the advent of English liberty back through time to the Anglo-Saxons or 'Goths' and tracking its developments throughout subsequent historical events. But Temple's interests in *Miscellanea* are as aesthetic as they are historical and political, to the extent that it is impossible to distinguish clearly between the two. In 'An Essay Upon Ancient and Modern Learning', the discourse that Jonathan Swift would subsequently identify as the originating moment of the 'Battle of the Books' in his 1704 satire of that name, Temple advanced a strong argument in favour of Classical literary precedent and imitation. In his essay 'Of Poetry' from the same collection, however, he tempered this Classicism with an extended and generally enthusiastic account of what he termed 'Gothick Genius' or 'wit', the term 'wit' itself here strategically wrested back from its associations with French neoclassicism and returned to what Temple took to be its linguistic and discursive roots in ancient 'Gothick' or Saxon culture. In a characteristically anti-French turn, Temple in 'Of Poetry' accuses the 'Modern *French Wits* (or Pretenders)' – the opprobrious name itself connoting Jacobitism, yet primarily referring here to the seventeenth-century French dramatists Pierre Corneille and Jean Racine – of having been 'very severe in their Censures, and exact in their Rules, I think to very little Purpose', a tacit assertion of poetic liberty against the strictures of rule-bound composition that becomes more explicit in such claims as the following: 'The Truth is, there is something in the *Genius* of Poetry, too Libertine to be confined to so many Rules, and whoever goes about to subject it to such Constraints, loses both it's [sic] Spirit and Grace, which are ever Nature, and never learnt even of the best Masters.'[18] Temple's references to 'rules', of course, pertain primarily to Aristotle's *Poetics* (*c*. 335 BC) and Horace's *Ars Poetica* (*c*. 19 BC), English translations of which, and commentaries upon, had long furnished the Classical tradition in French and English poetry and drama with a system of precepts to be respected, employed and rigorously adhered to. Though he remains generally admiring of the Classical rules, maintaining that he knows of no modern poet or dramatist who, since Aristotle and Horace, has managed to outdo them, Temple in 'Of Poetry' nonetheless turns his attention to the spirit of Gothick genius or wit that, as he argues, put paid to ancient Classical poetry with the Goths' sacking of Rome in 410 AD.

Disregardful of the rules of Classical composition, the poetry of Gothick 'Runers' or 'Rhymers', he claims, was essentially untrammelled and free, and

---

18 William Temple, 'Of Poetry', in *Miscellanea. The Second Part. In Four Essays*, 2nd edition, corrected and augmented (London, 1690), pp. 1–63 (pp. 20–1).

while it demonstrated elements of roughness and barbarism, it bore strong traces of untutored genius, natural inspiration and 'Poetical Fire', the latter no doubt a reference to the 'Muse of fire' invoked in the Prologue to Shakespeare's *The Life of King Henry the Fifth*:

> The common Vein of the Gothick Runes was what is Termed *Dithyrambick*, and was of a raving or rambling sort of Wit or Invention, loose and flowing, with little Art or Confinement to any certain Measures or Rules; yet some of it wanted not the true Spirit of Poetry in some degree, or that natural Inspiration which has been said to arise from some spark of Poetical Fire, wherewith particular Men are Born.[19]

Passionate and unregulated though it was, Gothick verse was distinguished by its use of rhyme, for as Temple reasoned, it lacked the sophistication of the Classical languages and was unable, as such, to furnish and sustain 'such Feet and Measures, as were in use among the *Greeks* and *Latins*'.[20] By 1690, the associations between the conquering Gothic tribes and somewhat infantile forms of rhyming verse were commonplace, and went at least as far back as Roger Ascham's complaint in *The Scholemaster* (1570) that crude and barbaric rhyme was in danger of corrupting the pure spirit of schoolboy Latin. For Temple, the runic poetry of the Goths, though it retained aspects of 'true Ancient' Greek and Latin poetry, was, in its very freeness, largely distinct from the Classical tradition, and comprised records of bold martial actions; praise of valiant men; and songs and ballads to be sung at feasts.

An equally significant component of its makeup was its penchant for supernatural enchantment, an aspect of Temple's conceptualisation of 'Gothick' poetry that accords remarkably well with the ways in which the term 'Gothic' is used in literary criticism today. As he argues, 'Gothick Runers' introduced enchantment as a way of compensating for the loss of the sublime and the marvellous in the Classical verse that, through their military conquest of Rome, the Goths themselves had laid to waste:

> The *Gothick Runers* to Gain and Establish the Credit and Admiration of their Rhymes, turned the use of them very much to Incantations and Charms, pretending by them, to raise Storms, to Calm the Seas, to cause Terror in their Enemies, to Transport themselves in the Air, to Conjure Spirits, to Cure Diseases, and Stanch [sic] Bleeding Wounds, to make Women kind or easy, and Men hard or invulnerable; as one of their most antient Runers, affirms himself and his own Atchievements [sic], by Force of these Magical Arms. The Men or Women who were thought to perform such Wonders or

19 Temple, 'Of Poetry', p. 40.   20 Temple, 'Of Poetry', p. 46.

Enchantments, were from *Vüses* or *Wises*, the Name of those *Verses* wherein Charms were conceived, called Wizards or Witches.[21]

Ancient Gothick poetry is the verse of incantation, conjuration, wonder and terror, an aesthetic strain that persists throughout 'all the visionary Tribe of *Fairies*, *Elves*, and *Goblins*, of *Sprites* and *Bul-baggers*' invoked in the servant girl's orally transmitted 'Stories of Fairies, Sprites, Witchcraft, and Enchantments', tales that terrify their child listeners into obedience and which are still capable of instilling fear in later, adult life.[22] Without naming it as 'Gothick' though patently under Temple's impulse, John Locke, the key philosopher behind the libertarian Whig agenda, would invoke the deleterious effects of the same supernatural tradition in oral storytelling his *An Essay Concerning Humane [sic] Understanding* (1690) of 1700, as well as in the expanded edition of *Some Thoughts Concerning Education* (1693) that was posthumously published in 1705.

In its best possible forms, the impulses of Gothick poetry for Temple survived and persisted in the hands of its first Continental and British refiners, namely Petrarch, Pierre de Ronsard, Spenser, Ludovico Ariosto and Torquato Tasso, achieving in these writers at least some measure of the charm, grace and sweetness of the Classical tradition. For the rest, and recalling his argument in 'An Essay Upon Ancient and Modern Learning', Temple maintained that modern poetry – ostensibly any literary composition, both dramatic and poetic, more recent than Classical Roman and Greek epics and tragedies – was corrupt. 'In such poor wretched Weeds as these', he opines, 'was Poetry clothed during those shades of Ignorance that overspread all *Europe*, so many Ages after the Sun-set of the Roman Learning and Empire together, which were Succeeded by so many New Dominions, or Plantations of the Gothick Swarms, and by a New Face of Customs, Habit, Language, and almost of Nature.'[23] Though, in this comment, Temple seems dismissive of 'Gothick' political and literary culture, his claim in 'Of Poetry' is that if the spirit of ancient literature were to be revived at all, this could only be achieved through the traces of it that survived in the free, runic verse of the barbarian Goths, an argument that made of his apparently Classicist essay an influential yet unwitting defence of Gothick aesthetics.

A committed, yet independent, Whig who celebrated the Glorious Revolution and who wrote in support of the War of Spanish Succession, the English dramatist and critic John Dennis gave clear literary expression to

---

21 Temple, 'Of Poetry', p. 42.   22 Temple, 'Of Poetry', pp. 42–3.
23 Temple, 'Of Poetry', p. 45.

his political sentiments and affiliations throughout his *oeuvre*. In *The Nuptials of Britain's Genius and Fame* (1697), for instance, he celebrated the English military achievement in the Nine Years' War (1688–97), the conflict between Louis XIV of France and the Grand Alliance, a coalition of the Holy Roman Empire, the Dutch Republic, Spain, England and Savoy. Following his tribute to the Grand Alliance and the Duke of Marlborough's victory at the Battle of Blenheim in August 1704 in *Britannia Triumphans* (1704), Dennis was appointed to the sinecure of the Queen's Waiter at the Port of London through the assistance of Marlborough himself. Further praise for Marlborough, British military success abroad and Whiggish party politics followed in his poem *The Battle of Ramillia; or, The Power of Union* (1706), a commemoration of the victory of the Grand Alliance in the Battle of Ramillies in May 1706. At first sight, there is little in Dennis's drama, poetry or critical work that suggests a preoccupation with what William Temple had called 'Gothick' genius or wit. Indeed, his poems are resolutely Classicist in form and in the Preface to *Britannia Triumphans*, Dennis includes a vociferous attack upon rhyme in general and the rhyming tendencies of English tragedy and poetry in particular, a distinguishing formal feature, as I have argued, in the conceptualisation of the Gothic literary tradition in the period.[24] Dennis's aesthetic treatise in *The Advancement and Reformation of Modern Poetry* (1701), moreover, reads as a standard if not orthodox assertion of Classical literary values. Sophocles's tragedies, he claims, are far superior to even the Roman plays of Shakespeare, since while a drama such as *Oedipus Rex* is 'exactly Just and Regular', *Julius Caesar* is 'very Extravagant and Irregular'; 'Secondly', he continues, 'the Oedipus is very Religious, and the Julius Cæsar is Irreligious'.[25] A strict adherence to Aristotelian and Horatian rules of composition, it soon becomes clear, serves as Dennis's benchmark of aesthetic achievement and the primary means of 'attaining a perfection in Poetry'.[26] Since Nature, itself, is ordered, beautiful and harmonious, these should be qualities to which all art aspires. 'In fine', he argues, 'whatever is Irregular, either in the Visible or Invisible World, is to the person who thinks right, except in some very extraordinary cases, either Hateful and Contemptible.'[27] If, in comments such as these, we witness Dennis's forthright rejection of the

24 See the unpaginated Preface in John Dennis, *Britannia Triumphans; or, The Empire Sav'd, and Europe Deliver'd. By the Success of her Majesty's Forces under the Wise and Heroick Conduct of his Grace the Duke of Marlborough. A Poem* (London, 1704).
25 John Dennis, *The Advancement and Reformation of Modern Poetry. A Critical Discourse, in Two Parts* (London, 1701), no. pag.
26 Dennis, *The Advancement and Reformation of Modern Poetry*, no. pag.
27 Dennis, *The Advancement and Reformation of Modern Poetry*, no. pag.

same Gothic rulelessness that Temple had praised, he further marks his distaste for this vernacular English tradition by celebrating the genius of French neoclassicism – Molière, Corneille, Racine, Boileau – over the achievements of Spenser, Milton, Ben Jonson and even Shakespeare: while the French poets are universally known and admired, the latter 'are strangers as it were to all the world, excepting the Subjects of Great Britain'.[28]

Despite these overwhelmingly Classicist leanings, Dennis in *The Advancement and Reformation of Modern Poetry* nonetheless provides subtle but clear validation of the Gothic through at least two means. First, he suspends the well-established tendency in post-Renaissance culture to denounce Gothic architecture, art and poetry as the very embodiment of bad taste by emphasising that these remained, after all, native English forms, countering habitual claims to their 'Indecent, Immoral, Unjust, Unreasonable, Unnatural' nature with the more moderate charge of 'irregularity':

> [I]f we are not shock'd at our own Irregularity [in art and poetry], 'tis because it has the advantage of long Habitude, for we have been us'd to it from our Infancy; but that to our Neighbours [in France], who have constantly been us'd to Art and Conduct, it must seem as awkward and as disagreeable, as our Gothick Cathedrals would to those Italians who have always frequented St Peter's; and that what I barely call irregular here, would be term'd by them Indecent, Immoral, Unjust, Unreasonable, Unnatural.[29]

Acknowledgment of the sheer familiarity of Gothic forms in England, in other words, did much to ameliorate the harshness of neoclassical censure. Second, and more crucially, Dennis, both here and in the later *The Grounds of Criticism in Poetry* (1704), was at pains to valorise what, in time, would become crucial to the literary Gothic aesthetic: the primacy of the supernatural, and the sublime, imaginative effects that it engendered. The inclusion of religious themes and content in verse, he argued, was the only sure means of ensuring poetry's sublimity and its passion; without religion, he reasoned, poetry was indistinguishable from mere 'enthusiasm'. But what is crucial to Dennis's conceptualisation of the function of religious theme and content is that it incorporated what Temple before him had explicitly located within the tradition of Gothic wit, namely wonder, enchantment and the supernatural, as well as the affective responses of astonishment, horror and terror. 'Religion adds to the Terror, encreases [*sic*] the Astonishment, and augments the Horror', he writes, and through this, sacred verse is capable of making an

---

28 Dennis, *The Advancement and Reformation of Modern Poetry*, no. pag.
29 Dennis, *The Advancement and Reformation of Modern Poetry*, no. pag.

approach upon the sublime.[30] This is particularly the case when poetry engages with the supernatural, such as in the state of continuous revelation that we encounter in Classical verse and civilisation by means of 'Oracles, Visions, Dreams, Apparitions, and a thousand Fantastick Miracles'.[31] If earlier in his argument Dennis had come out strongly in favour of the ancients, he now concedes that the divine verse of 'the Moderns' might match and even exceed these examples, not least in the case of Milton's *Paradise Lost* (1667; 1674). Christianity, after all, was more amenable to poetry than Classical paganism. Even as he believed it to be epitomised by the religious poetry of ancient Greece and Rome, Dennis thus tacitly promoted a passionate, sublime, supernatural and emotionally affective form of writing that, as Temple had shown, was, and long after would remain, central to the Gothic literary aesthetic.

The grandson of one of the first Whig politicians and a key figure in the Exclusion Crisis, Anthony Ashley Cooper, 3rd Earl of Shaftesbury, was a staunch Whig and a member of the Country opposition during the 1690s, a movement that sought to promote the entire nation (or 'country's') interests against the insular policies of the London-based Court politicians. Though his political ambitions were quashed in the early eighteenth century by the accession of Queen Anne, Shaftesbury gave clear expression to his Whiggish politics in, among other places, his 'Soliloquy: or Advice to an Author' from the three-volume *Characteristicks of Men, Manners, Opinions, Times* (1711). In such passages from 'Advice to an Author' as the following, he bestows fulsome praise upon what, in other contemporary Whig writers, was unproblematically described as England's 'Gothic' system of government, a political settlement founded upon the principles of liberty, the casting off of the 'Norman Yoke' and the establishment of the so-called 'Gothic balance' – the equitable distribution of power between Parliament and the sovereign – brought about by the Glorious Revolution:

> 'Tis scarce a quarter of an Age since such a happy Ballance [*sic*] of Power was settled between our Prince and People, as has firmly secur'd our hitherto precarious Liberty, and remov'd from us the Fear of Civil Commotions, Wars and Violence, either on account of Religion and Worship, the Property of the Subject, or the contending Titles of the Crown. But as the greatest Advantages of this World are not to be bought at easy Prices; we are still at

---

30 Dennis, *The Advancement and Reformation of Modern Poetry*, p. 45.
31 Dennis, *The Advancement and Reformation of Modern Poetry*, p. 92.

this moment expending both our Blood and Treasure, to secure ourselves this inestimable Purchase of our *Free Government* and *National Constitution*.[32]

If Shaftesbury here makes no use of the term 'Gothick', it is because he is all too aware of the many negative connotations with which the word had been freighted from the Renaissance onwards, when writers as diverse as Raphael and Baldassare Castiglione, Giorgio Vasari and John Evelyn had employed it as an epithet to express their distaste for all 'German', medieval, non-Classical forms of architecture and art.[33] Indeed, throughout the *Characteristicks*, 'Gothick' serves Shaftesbury, as it did for many of his contemporaries, as a synonym for uncouthness and for a troubling spirit of barbarousness in architecture, poetry and culture more generally. His Whiggish, implicitly 'Gothic' politics, however, is no less pronounced, and much of the 'Advice to an Author' consists of passionate appeals to liberty against the forces of political and poetic absolutism in ways that recall Temple's account of Gothick genius and wit in 'Of Poetry'.

Indeed, though he studiously avoids the word, it is clear that the literary aesthetic that Shaftesbury, in *Characteristicks*, wishes to promote is 'Gothic' in all but name. His point of departure in 'Advice to an Author' is that 'The British Muses' – a category by which he means the nation's autochthonous literary traditions – 'lie abject and obscure' during 'this Dinn of Arms' that is the historical present, in 1711 a reference no doubt to Britain and the Grand Alliance's ongoing conflict with the Bourbons of France and Spain during the War of Spanish Succession.[34] These native literary traditions, he continues, 'have hitherto scarce arriv'd to any thing of Shapeliness or Person'; instead, they 'lisp as in their Cradles', while their 'stammering tongues, which nothing but their Youth and Rawness can excuse, have spoken in wretched Pun and Quibble'.[35] Already it is clear that Shaftesbury is far more ambivalent towards British Gothick verse than Temple had been. His reservations become especially pronounced in his claim that traces of this false, crude and unpolished literary style have regrettably persisted even in the works of 'Our *Dramatick* SHAKESPEAR [sic], our [John] FLETCHER, [Ben] JOHNSON [sic], and our *Epick* MILTON'.[36]

---

32 Anthony Ashley Cooper, Earl of Shaftesbury, *Characteristicks of Men, Manners, Opinions, Times*, 3 vols (London, 1711), vol. 1, p. 216.
33 For an account of how the term 'Gothic' circulated negatively in early modern architectural discourse, see E. S. de Beer, 'Gothic: origin and diffusion of the term; the idea of style in architecture', *Journal of the Warburg and Courtauld Institutes* 11 (1948): 143–62
34 Shaftesbury, *Characteristicks*, p. 217.   35 Shaftesbury, *Characteristicks*, p. 217.
36 Shaftesbury, *Characteristicks*, p. 217.

And yet, he continues, such 'reverend Bards', rude as they are, are to be commended for having provided the English nation with its 'richest Oar [sic]' or treasure. Though inevitably bound by the constraints of the dark and barbaric ages in which they lived, these writers successfully managed to cast *off* the constraints of 'Gothick' poetry in order to assert the principles of aesthetic freedom:

> To their eternal Honour they have withal been the first of EUROPEANS, who since the GOTHICK *Model* of Poetry, attempted to throw off the horrid Discord of jingling Rhyme. They have asserted antient *Poetick Liberty*, and have happily broken the Ice for those who are to follow 'em; and who treading in their Footsteps, may at leisure polish our Language, lead our Ear to finer Pleasure, and find out the true *Rhythmus*, and harmonious Numbers, which alone can satisfy a just Judgment, and Muse-like Apprehension.[37]

For Temple, Gothick literature was that native English poetic tradition that, though characterised by distracting and over-regulated rhyme, defiantly and laudably asserted aesthetic liberty in the face of Classical strictures. For the more cautious and sceptical Shaftesbury, by contrast, native English poetry is equally libertarian in spirit, yet, given the negative associations of the term, not to be designated as 'Gothick' though still expressing its resistance to regulation by throwing off the 'horrid Discord of jingling Rhyme' through its characteristic use of blank verse. For Temple, 'Gothick' ambivalently signified that which was natively English; for Shaftesbury, 'Gothick' is the name for that rude and unpolished form of literature against which the blank verse of Shakespeare's tragedies and Milton's *Paradise Lost* exerted itself. Despite their different uses of the term, both theorists enumerate the same virtues of an indigenous 'Gothick' or English literary tradition that was infused with, to the extent that it incarnated, the Whiggish principle of liberty. Indeed, the poetic values that Shaftesbury's essay praises are all a part of what Temple had designated as 'Gothick' genius or wit: '[O]ur natural Genius', he writes, 'shines above the airy neighbouring Nations' in the same way that, for Temple, English tragedy surpassed the work of the French 'Pretenders', Corneille and Racine.[38] And unlike the restrictive spirit of tragedy that presides on the Continent, this is the writing of imaginative and formal freedom, the advantageous prerogative of the British Muses that, in time, he hopes, will establish corresponding forms of 'Liberty' in 'every thing that relates to Art'.[39] Shaftesbury, in fact, tellingly ends his essay on a ghostly call to arms,

37 Shaftesbury, *Characteristicks*, pp. 217–18. 38 Shaftesbury, *Characteristicks*, p. 218.
39 Shaftesbury, *Characteristicks*, p. 219.

enlisting the supernaturalism of the Gothick imagination against the 'demonic' prejudices of prevailing neoclassical critical bias while claiming that 'we' – the English writers composing under the influence of the British Muses – are 'not altogether so *barbarous* or *Gothick* as they pretend'.[40] Not even Shakespeare, with his 'natural Rudeness, his unpolish'd Stile, his antiquated Phrase and Wit, his want of Method and Coherence, and his Deficiency in almost all the Graces and Ornaments of this kind of Writing' is beyond the powers of recuperation; on the contrary, the morality, the aptness of description and the natural turn of character that we witness in *Hamlet*, together with the 'moral genius' of Milton in *Paradise Lost*, all suggest that English letters have been built on a solid 'Gothick' foundation that may only be improved with time.[41]

As Temple, Dennis and Shaftesbury conceptualised it, then, the Gothic was an imaginative poetical strain that, sometimes rhyming and sometimes written in blank verse, comprised certain distinctive elements, including the supernatural, the sublime frisson of horror and terror and the equally intense responses of marvel, wonder and enchantment. Embodying through its resistance to the Classical rules the ancient principles of political liberty, the Gothic aesthetic was, as Kliger has argued, a largely Whiggish mode.[42] As Christine Gerrard has shown, however, the category of 'Whig' was by no means a monolithic one, and, in the period 1725–42, the claim to the nation's political Gothic origins was, under the influence of the Tory Henry St John, 1st Viscount Bolingbroke, most enthusiastically championed by those so-called 'Patriot' Whigs who opposed the policies of the Whig Prime Minister, Robert Walpole.[43] Furthermore, it is important to remember that the links between Gothic and Whig were neither inevitable nor insuperable, for many later Whig poets, particularly in the early-to-mid decades of the eighteenth century, remained deeply suspicious of the Gothic, seeing in it, as Shaftesbury had done, the vestiges of a dark and barbaric 'Gothick' past from which the implacable march of progress had mercifully delivered Britain. The stalwart Whig Joseph Addison, for example, was no champion of the Gothic, and in *Remarks on Several Parts of Italy* (1705), in certain essays published in *The Spectator* in 1712 and in his celebrated drama *Cato, A Tragedy* (written 1712; performed 1713), he expressed, invariably at the Gothic's expense, his

---

40 Shaftesbury, *Characteristicks*, p. 274.   41 Shaftesbury, Characteristicks, pp. 275–6.
42 See Samuel Kliger, 'Whig aesthetics: a phase of eighteenth-century taste', *ELH* 16:2 (June 1949): 135–50.
43 Christine Gerrard, *The Patriot Opposition to Walpole: Politics, Poetry, and National Myth, 1725–1742* (Oxford: Clarendon Press, 1994), pp. 108–3.

enthusiasm for Classical literary and architectural forms.[44] Later, in his influential poem *The Pleasures of Imagination* (1744), the Whiggish poet Mark Akenside would draw upon the work of Addison in order to call for an outright rejection of the Gothic imagination in favour of the order and the regularity of Classicism, urging his readers to 'tune to Attic [i.e. ancient Greek] themes, the British lyre' and calling for a turn away from 'the reluctant shades of Gothic night' embodied in the ghostly oral tales of servants and old wives so as to embrace the order and regularity of Classical literary and architectural forms.[45] Such anti-Gothic tendencies were present in Whiggish conceptualisations of the Gothic from the very start, for, as I have shown, the accounts of Temple, Dennis and Shaftesbury were all hedged about with ambivalence and reservation, and, with the possible exception of Temple, hardly amounted to unequivocal defences of the Gothick strain in English poetry and drama.

The Gothic could also be deployed by Tory writers of the period, even by so unlikely a critic, poet and playwright as John Dryden. Though born to a Puritan family, Dryden would later convert to Catholicism, expressing throughout his *oeuvre* his distaste for republicanism and his allegiance to the Royalist cause. A keen supporter of the restoration of the monarchy, Charles II and the House of Stuart, Dryden would be appointed Poet Laureate in April 1668 and Historiographer Royal in August 1670. In the Exclusion Crisis of the early 1680s, Dryden, like other Tories, predictably took the side of the king, further expressing his loyalties to Charles II in his satirical *roman-a-clèf, Absolom and Achitophel* (1681). Reluctant to swear allegiance to the new sovereigns William and Mary, however, Dryden after the Glorious Revolution found himself in a particularly compromising position, when, in addition to being a member of the Catholic, Tory, Royalist minority in an otherwise Protestant, Whiggish regime, he lost his position as Poet Laureate and was increasingly forced thereafter to rely on the financial support provided by a number of influential patrons. Though he remained a Classicist at heart, Dryden in later years also worked in what we would now describe as the Gothic mode, particularly in *King Arthur; or, The British Worthy*, a short operatic piece, with music by Henry Purcell, that was first staged at the Queen's Theatre, London, in May or June 1691 and almost

---

44 For more on Addison's rejection of the Gothic, see Dale Townshend, *Gothic Antiquity: History, Romance, and the Architectural Imagination, 1760–1840* (Oxford: Oxford University Press, 2019), pp. 47–52.

45 Mark Akenside, *The Pleasures of Imagination. A Poem in Three Books* (London, 1744), Book I, l. 604. See, too, Townshend, *Gothic Antiquity*, chapter 1.

immediately printed. Though *King Arthur* had been written for Charles II seven years earlier, the king, dying in 1685, never saw it performed; in its published form, Dryden – as he did for his earlier theatrical pieces – dedicated the piece to the statesman and writer George Savile, 1st Marquess of Halifax – whose wit he had praised in *Absolom and Achitophel* – and his patron, Anna Scott, Duchess of Monmouth and Duchess of Buccleuch.

It is Dryden's reference in the Dedicatory Epistle of *King Arthur* to what he refers to as the Duchess of Monmouth's taste for 'the Airy and Earthy Spirits, and that Fairy kind of writing' that is of particular significance here, a literary mode the precise nature of which becomes apparent as the opera proceeds.[46] With one or two important modifications, the action of *King Arthur* recounts what, by the time of its composition during the 1680s, were the standard features of seventeenth century 'Gothic' historiography: the arrival of the Saxons or 'Goths' in Kent and their early interaction with the native Britons. In the histories of Verstegan, Bacon, Temple and other Whigs, it was held that the Goths, under the leadership of the brothers Hengist and Horsa, had entered Britain at the invitation of Vortigern, the king of the ancient Britons – a nation who, made vulnerable by the recent withdrawal of the Romans, was subject to the continuous tides of violence inflicted by the Picts and the Scots who had settled north of Hadrian's Wall. In such accounts, the Goths were heralded as the British nation's veritable deliverers, the nation who successfully drove Britons' belligerent neighbours into the western and southernmost points of the island and established their Gothic systems of freedom and democracy across the seven kingdoms of the Anglo-Saxon heptarchy.

In the Tory Dryden's version, though, the initial relationship between the native Britons, united under the leadership of the mythological King Arthur, and the Saxons, under Oswald, the son of Hengist, is anything but peaceful and cooperative: far from entering Britain by invitation, Dryden's Saxons are presented as marauding invaders, with each nation representative of different if not entirely incompatible cultural systems and worldviews. Throughout, in fact, Arthurian myth and standard Gothic political myths of national origins are starkly juxtaposed. While Arthur and the Britons, for instance, are Christian, the Saxons are resolutely heathen, making characteristic appeal in the course of the action to a panoply of gods that includes Woden, Thor

---

46 John Dryden, *King Arthur; or, The British Worthy* (London, 1691), Dedicatory Epistle.

and Freya. True to late seventeenth-century perceptions of Gothick poetry, moreover, the Saxons and their gods are said to speak in 'Sacred Runick Rhymes', while the dialogue of the Britons is written in blank verse.[47] Arthur and Oswald, Briton and Saxon, are also rivals for the love of the blind Emmeline, Arthur's beloved whom he, by the end of the action, eventually manages to secure as his own. Each nation and its army, furthermore, is assisted by supernatural means, with the Saxons attended by the 'earthy spirit' Grimbald and the Britons by the 'famous Inchanter [sic]' Merlin and the 'airy spirit' Philidel.[48] Nothing less than supernatural warfare ensues between the two sides, with Merlin and Philidel mobilising benevolent forms of magic and Grimbald all manner of 'dire Inchantments' that include, in Act IV, such horror-inducing tropes as a bleeding tree in a 'Hell-haunted Grove'.[49] Allusions to *A Midsummer Night's Dream*, *The Tempest* and Milton's *Comus* feature throughout. Even though *King Arthur* does not employ the word, it is clear that Dryden's 'fairy kind of writing' is the same strain that Temple in 'Of Poetry' only one year before had identified as 'Gothick': the poetry of horror, terror and wonder, the imaginative and sublime writing of supernatural agency, all closely tied here, as in other writers, into the English nation's political 'Gothic' past.

When King Arthur secures victory over the Saxons, he responds to Oswald with a politically revealing rejection of the Whiggish myth of Gothic political origins:

> Thy Life, thy Liberty, thy Honour Safe,
> Lead back thy Saxons to their Antient Elb:
> I wou'd Restore thee fruitful *Kent*, the Gift
> Of *Vortigern* for *Hengist's* ill bought aid,
> But that my Britain's brook no Foreign Power,
> To Lord it in a Land, Sacred to Freedom;
> And of its Rights, Tenacious to the last.[50]

According to Arthur's Tory logic, Britain is a natively free land that requires neither deliverance nor political intervention by the invading Goths. But if the Britons' rejection of the Gothic bequest of Hengist and Horsa opens up a fissure at the nation's ancient origins, it is one that Dryden in the final moments of *King Arthur* will labour to breach. Indeed, having been conquered, the Saxons are swiftly incorporated into a composite sense of Britishness in the play's closing scene. As Merlin says to Oswald, 'Nor though,

---

47 Dryden, *King Arthur*, p. 6.   48 Dryden, *King Arthur*, Dramatis personae.
49 Dryden, *King Arthur*, pp. 24, 39.   50 Dryden, *King Arthur*, p. 44.

brave Saxon Prince, disdain our Triumphs; Britains and Saxons shall be once one People; / One Common Tongue, one Common Faith shall bind / Our Jarring Bands, in a perpetual Peace.'[51] With the entrance of the figure of Britannia and the raising of toasts to Saint George and the honour of Old England, the opera ends upon a note of unity. In the process, however, Dryden's 'fairy kind of writing' – the 'Gothick' literature of horror, terror, enchantment, magic and the supernatural – is installed at the heart of national British aesthetics, albeit here through a Tory historical vision.

In a surprising suspension of his Classicist biases, the ardently Whiggish Joseph Addison turned in an essay published in *The Spectator* on 1 July 1712 to reflect upon, and pay warm tribute to, Dryden's 'fairy kind of writing', this particular essay in his influential 'Taste and the Pleasures of the Imagination' series a continuation of his positive assessment of the work of Milton that he had published in *The Spectator* earlier. 'There is a kind of writing', Addison observes, 'wherein the poet quite loses sight of nature, and entertains his reader's imagination with the characters and actions of such persons as have many of them no existence, but what he bestows on them.'[52] Such imaginary beings, he explains, include the fairies, witches, magicians, imaginary beings and departed spirits or ghosts that Dryden in *King Arthur* had designated as 'the fairy way [sic] of writing', a mode that requires of the poet who employs it 'a very odd turn of thought' or 'a particular cast of fancy, and an imagination naturally fruitful and superstitious'.[53] In addition to this, writers who dabble in this supernatural, highly imaginative aesthetic ought to be well versed in traditional legends, fables and romances, as well as in the oral tales of nurses and old women – that is, in the stories of those who had been identified as the primary vanguards of the 'Gothick' imagination in the work of Temple and Locke, and whom Akenside would similarly invoke in *The Pleasures of Imagination*. 'These descriptions', Addison continues, 'raise a pleasing kind of horror in the mind of the reader, and amuse his imagination with the strangeness and novelty of the person who are represented in them', the very fact of their ability to evoke memories of 'the stories we have heard in our childhood' said to be the primary source of their pleasure.[54] But whereas, for John Dennis, this tendency towards sublime otherworldliness was epitomised by the poetry of ancient Greece and Rome, Addison locates it

---

51 Dryden, *King Arthur*, p. 45.
52 Joseph Addison, 'Essay No. 419, Tuesday 1 July 1712', in Donald F. Bond (ed.), *Critical Essays by Joseph Addison, with Four Essays by Richard Steele* (Oxford: Clarendon Press, 1970), pp. 199–202 (p. 199).
53 Addison, 'Essay No. 419', p. 200.   54 Addison, 'Essay No. 419', p. 200.

squarely in a non-Classical, natively English tradition – one that, in his reference to 'the darkness and superstitions of later ages', is also historically medieval or 'Gothic':

> The Ancients have not much of this poetry among them, for, indeed, almost the whole substance of it owes its original to the darkness and superstitions of later ages, when pious frauds were made use of to amuse mankind, and frighten them into a sense of their duty. Our forefathers looked upon Nature with more reverence and horror, before the world was enlightened by learning and philosophy, and loved to astonish themselves with the apprehensions of witchcraft, prodigies, charms and enchantments.[55]

At work here is that familiar eighteenth-century conceptualisation of the Catholic Middle Ages as a particularly dark and superstitious period in national history, the horrors and terrors, enchantments and wonders of its literary forms all perceived as clear expressions of this fundamental barbarism. Even so, the supernatural excesses of the mode are to a large extent explained and justified by the recognition of the historical period in which they took form, for then, Addison explains, 'There was not a village in England that had not a ghost in it': the churchyards all were haunted, all shepherds claimed to have seen a ghost and every large common in the country was thought to contain a fairy circle.[56] As does the Tory Dryden in *King Arthur*, the Whiggish Addison figures the Gothic as the nation's indigenous, most natural form of creative expression, for 'the English are naturally fanciful, and very often disposed by that gloominess and melancholy temper, which is frequent in our nation, to many wild notions and visions, to which others are not so liable'.[57] In by-now predictable terms, the essay concludes with a tribute to the manifestations of the fairy way of writing in the untutored genius of Shakespeare, as well as in the allegorical supernaturalism of Milton and Spenser.

The Gothic Revival of the 1760s

Even if they did not always name it as such, British political theorists, poets, critics and aestheticians had thus articulated by the second decade of the eighteenth century a clear sense of the 'Gothick' literary aesthetic, an autochthonic and resolutely non-Classical English tradition of sublime and supernatural poetry and dramatic verse that distinguished itself through the

---

55 Addison, 'Essay No. 419', p. 201. 56 Addison, 'Essay No. 419', p. 201.
57 Addison, 'Essay No. 419', p. 201.

responses of horror and terror, enchantment and wonder. However, though the writers of the period 1690–1712 that I have addressed above all variously theorised, reflected upon and shared a remarkably consistent understanding of this literary strain, not one of them could legitimately be described as a 'Gothic Revivalist', particularly if by this term we mean one who actively desires to revivify and resurrect the literary and architectural art-forms of the Middle Ages in the modern, Enlightenment present. To employ a concept that Clark had influentially coined in *The Gothic Revival*, and which has structured several accounts of the 'Gothic Revival' in architecture ever since, Temple, Dennis, Shaftesbury, Dryden and Addison were, at best, impartial commentators on 'Gothic Survival', that is, on that 'tiny stream of the Gothic tradition [that] was never lost', but which flowed, virtually unbroken, from the medieval period through to the sixteenth and seventeenth centuries.[58] While these writers reflected, for the most part positively, on the poetry of the ancient Goths and the legacy that it was said to have left in the work of Shakespeare, Fletcher, Jonson, Spenser and Milton in the English tradition, and Petrarch, Ariosto, Tasso and others in the European, they never went so far as actively to endorse the 'Revival' of Gothic forms in their own day, remaining, in the end, far too closely wedded to the proportion, regularity and symmetry of Classicism to countenance this.

Instead, it is to the 1760s, the decade that witnessed the writing and publication of *The Castle of Otranto*, that we should look for the more immediate cultural impetus behind Walpole's fiction and the Gothic Revival in literature more broadly. In 1762, the Reverend Richard Hurd, later Bishop of Worcester, published *Letters on Chivalry and Romance*, a treatise that, despite Walpole's marked personal and political differences from Hurd, would exert considerable influence over the conceptualisation and writing of *Otranto* some two years later. A moderate Tory who had published an edition of *Ars Poetica* in 1749 and an edition of Horace's *Epistola ad Augustum* in 1751, Hurd, on first impressions, seems an unlikely candidate for the defence of the largely Whiggish, non-Classical Gothic aesthetic, yet *Letters on Chivalry and Romance* is clearly a continuation of the interest in the art and politics of the Gothic past that he had explored earlier in *Moral and*

---

58 Clark, *The Gothic Revival*, p. 1. For a sense of how Clark's distinctions between 'Gothic Survival' and 'Gothic Revival' have been appropriated and revised by other historians of the Gothic Revival in architecture, see H. M. Colvin, 'Gothic survival and gothick revival', *The Architectural Review* 103 (1948): 91–8; and Giles Worsley, 'The origins of the gothic revival: a reappraisal: the Alexander Prize essay', *Transactions of the Royal Historical Society* 3 (1993): pp. 105–50.

Political Dialogues (1759). What follows in the *Letters* is a nuanced revision of the long-held assumption that the Gothic period of the Middle Ages was a particularly 'barbarous' period in human history, and a daring assertion of the spirit of 'Gothic CHIVALRY' and the traces of it that persisted in the annals of ancient 'ROMANCE'.[59] 'The spirit of Chivalry', he, in a particularly memorable passage, argues, 'was a fire which soon spent itself: But that of *Romance*, which was kindled at it, burnt long, and continued its light and heat even to the politer ages.'[60] The epic romances of Tasso's *La Gerusalemme liberata* (1581) and Ariosto's *Orlando Furioso* (1516) in Italy and Spenser's *The Faerie Queene* and select works by Shakespeare and Milton in England were all 'charmed by the Gothic Romances', to the extent that we might deduce that there is 'something in the Gothic Romance [that is] particularly suited to the views of a genius, and to the ends of poetry'.[61] Spenser, that is, revived 'the magic of old romances' that was first glimpsed in Chaucer's 'Sir Thopas' from *The Canterbury Tales* and continued in such European romances as the *Amadis of Gaul* narrative, but which was sadly 'dissolved' in Milton's defection to the Classicist camp in his use of Roman and Greek epic forms in *Paradise Lost*.[62]

Central to Hurd's reassessment of the art and literature of the Middle Ages is the assertion of the principle of aesthetic relativism, or the claim that Gothic forms, though long maligned by Classical and neoclassical aesthetics, ought to be judged and assessed on criteria that are peculiar to themselves:

> When an architect examines a Gothic structure by Grecian rules, he finds nothing but deformity. But the Gothic architecture has it's [sic] rules, by which when it comes to be examined, it is seen to have it's [sic] merit, as well as the Grecian. The question is not, which of the two is conducted in the simplest or truest taste: but, whether there be not sense and design in both, when scrutinized by the laws on which each is projected.[63]

As in architecture, so in poetry: when judged by Aristotelian and Horatian standards, *The Faerie Queene* might well appear to be disordered, but when considered 'with an eye to it's [sic] Gothic original', it is remarkably unified, regular and simple in content and form.[64] His point is directly aimed at Thomas Warton's occasionally negative assessment of *The Faerie Queene* in his expanded and revised edition of

---

59 Richard Hurd, *Letters on Chivalry and Romance* (London, 1762), p. 1.
60 Hurd, *Letters on Chivalry and Romance*, pp. 3–4.
61 Hurd, *Letters on Chivalry and Romance*, p. 4.
62 Hurd, *Letters on Chivalry and Romance*, pp. 108–18.
63 Hurd, *Letters on Chivalry and Romance*, p. 61.
64 Hurd, *Letters on Chivalry and Romance*, pp. 61–2.

Observations on the Fairy Queen of Spenser (1754; 1762) that was published earlier that same year, and in which Warton had argued that Spenser's poetic romance ultimately failed to conform to the unity and coherence demanded by the Classical rules. Proceeding along familiar lines to juxtapose 'Gothic' verse with the poetry of Classical Greece and Rome, Hurd argues not only that the literature of Greek antiquity 'very much resembles the Gothic', but also, and rather more audaciously, that the imaginative richness of the Gothic far exceeds that of the Classical: 'the *gallantry*, which inspired the feudal times, was of a nature to furnish the poet with finer scenes and subjects of description in its every view, than the simple and uncontrolled barbarity of the Grecian'.[65] Unlike the more cautious assessments of the mode in the work of Dennis and Shaftesbury, Hurd here promotes the Gothic as being infinitely superior to the Classical, its superlative imaginative capacity alone sufficient grounds for its reassessment and revival in contemporary England. Echoing and revising Dennis's views on the religious contents of Classical verse, he claims that the '*religious machinery*' of the Gothic poets 'had something in it more amusing, as well as more awakening to the imagination' than the Classical; equally, the 'popular tales of Elves and Fairies', the negative effects of which earlier theorists such as Temple and Locke had feared, 'were even fitter to take the credulous mind, and charm it into a willing admiration of the specious miracles' than 'those of the old traditionary rabble of pagan divinities'.[66] With reference to scenes of witchcraft and incantation in both traditions, he writes that 'the horrors of the Gothic were above measure striking and terrible': while the 'mummeries of the pagan priests' were 'childish', the 'Gothic Enchanters' powerfully 'shook and alarmed all nature'.[67] As Hurd concludes, verse, on the whole, is 'more poetical for being Gothic', a point that he illustrates through reference to the terrors, the witcheries and the supernatural enchantments of Shakespeare, Spenser and Milton.[68]

The imaginative richness of the Gothic, the unusual beauties of Gothic architecture, and the tradition of 'Gothic story' that he identified in Chaucer, Tasso, Ariosto and Spenser, as well as in select works by Shakespeare and Milton: Hurd's *Letters on Chivalry and Romance* takes us directly into the same

---

65 Hurd, *Letters on Chivalry and Romance*, pp. 31, 46.
66 Hurd, *Letters on Chivalry and Romance*, p. 48.
67 Hurd, *Letters on Chivalry and Romance*, pp. 48–9.
68 Hurd, *Letters on Chivalry and Romance*, p. 55.

cultural terrain that Horace Walpole would occupy in *The Castle of Otranto*. The fiction itself, as Walpole famously wrote to William Cole in March 1765, was inspired by a dream, a 'very natural dream for a head filled like mine with Gothic story'.[69] If Walpole did not include the phrase 'Gothic Story' in the first edition of *The Castle of Otranto* of late 1764, choosing instead the subtitle 'A Story', this was because, as I have shown in this chapter and as Walpole himself well knew, 'Gothic' as a category of literary description was largely a retrospective critical invention of the late seventeenth and eighteenth centuries, and could thus not be included in a text that was purportedly written sometime between 1095 and 1243 and printed in Naples in 1529 without the courting of glaring anachronism. The word 'Gothic', in fact, would have immediately disclosed the text's status as a literary hoax engineered by a contemporary writer, and it is for this reason that Walpole studiously excluded it from the first edition, even in the descriptions of those architectural features that are patently 'Gothic' in style. But having disclosed his authorship in the second edition of 1765, Walpole was now free to make use of the term, thus aligning himself with an established line of Whiggish political and aesthetic thought that ran from Temple onwards, including in the second Preface a clear statement of his fiction's motivation and rationale. All of these, it is clear, were 'Gothic' in the sense in which I have explored it here. In the guise of the translator William Marshal, Walpole in the first Preface had anxiously gestured towards the seemingly inappropriate inclusion of the servants in the narrative, their trademark simplicity, naïveté and humour apparently at odds with the sublime heights of terror and pity and a clear infringement of the Classical rules on tragedy. But in the second Preface, the inclusion of what Walpole now terms the 'deportment of the domestics' is revealed to be a deliberate and politically informed choice, an insouciant and deliberate violation of Classical strictures that, he claims, was licenced by none other than 'That great master of nature, Shakespeare' himself, particularly the gravediggers in *Hamlet*, and the plebian mob in *Julius Caesar*.[70] While Shakespeare defends Walpole's aesthetic choices, it is also Shakespeare, the second Preface continues, to whose defence Walpole in writing *The Castle of Otranto* has sprung. In his twelve-volume edition of the works of Corneille in *Le Théâtre de Pierre Corneille avec des commentaires* (1763) and elsewhere,

---

69 Horace Walpole to William Cole, 9 March 1765, in W. S. Lewis (ed.), *The Yale Edition of Horace Walpole's Correspondence*, 48 vols (New Haven: Yale University Press, 1937–85), vol. 1, p. 88.
70 Horace Walpole, *The Castle of Otranto*, edited by Nick Groom (Oxford: Oxford University Press, 2014), p. 10.

Voltaire had criticised Shakespeare for his intermingling of coarse humour and sublime heroism, unfavourably comparing his work with that of the French dramatist. Beyond this particular example, the French wits of the eighteenth century routinely denounced Shakespeare for his barbarity, his roughness and for his apparent refusal of the rules of Classical composition, invariably expressing a preference for the neoclassicism of Corneille and Racine over the works of England's 'Gothic bard'.[71] Sheltering his own daring beneath 'the cannon of the brightest genius' that the nation has ever produced, however, Walpole engages in *Otranto* in a form of cultural warfare: enchanted, irregular and supernatural to boot, the text is a politically acute assertion of ancient Gothic literary values, an exercise in the splendid liberties of Addison's 'fairy way of writing' and a throwing off of the 'fetters', Walpole claims, that have 'cramped' and confined the French.[72] As Angela Wright has observed, these gestures appear to re-enact, at least on the surface, contemporary hostilities between France and Britain during the Seven Years' War (1756–63), a context that makes of *Otranto* as strident an assertion of cultural Whiggism as the poems and aesthetic treatises of Temple, Dennis and Shaftesbury.[73] Though such conceptualisations of the Gothic had been current in English Whiggish culture since the late seventeenth century, Walpole nevertheless distinguished *The Castle of Otranto* through a major formal innovation: the deliberate introduction of what was essentially an ancient poetic mode into prose, constructing a 'new species of romance' – what we now term 'Gothic fiction' – through the fusion of ancient romance, in which 'all was imagination and improbability', and the modern novel, in which 'the great resources of fancy have been dammed up, by a strict adherence to common life'.[74] Taken out of the realm of aesthetic abstraction, the Gothic Revival, for which Hurd in *Letters on Chivalry and Romance* had called, had commenced.

The year 1765 was a particularly notable one for the revival of interest in the literary remains of England's ancient Gothic past: as Groom in his chapter in this volume and elsewhere has observed, the same year in which *The Castle of Otranto* was dubbed 'A Gothic Story' also saw the

---

71 For a more detailed account of this, see Dale Townshend, 'Gothic and the Ghost of Hamlet', in John Drakakis and Dale Townshend (eds), *Gothic Shakespeares* (Abingdon and New York: Routledge, 2008), pp. 60–97; and Angela Wright, *Britain, France and the Gothic, 1764–1820: The Import of Terror* (Cambridge: Cambridge University Press, 2013), pp. 18–22.
72 Walpole, *The Castle of Otranto*, p. 13.
73 Wright, *Britain, France and the Gothic*, pp. 22–3.
74 Walpole, *The Castle of Otranto*, p. 9.

publication of Thomas Percy's *Reliques of Ancient English Poetry* (1765) and Samuel Johnson's *Mr Johnson's Preface to His Edition of Shakespear's [sic] Plays* (1765), both examples of the literary antiquarianism of the second half of the century and both publications in which notions of 'Gothic' played a significant role.[75] Percy's three-volume collection of English poems, songs, ballads and metrical romances sought to collect, preserve and showcase 'select remains of our ancient English Bards and Minstrels', 'the first efforts of ancient genius' and the work of 'unlettered warriors' that had survived in the musical poetry of the English minstrels, themselves the successors of the bards of the ancient Britons and the scalds of the 'Our Saxon ancestors', the Goths.[76] As in Temple earlier, this Gothic verse for Percy was largely composed in rhyme, to the extent that it often appeared artificial and strained when transcribed, written down or printed. The contents of this poetry are 'Gothick' in the sense in which Temple, Shaftesbury, Dennis, Dryden and Addison had understood the term, too, including, say, the supernaturalism of 'Admiral Hosier's Ghost' and 'The Lunatic Lover' from volume I, or in such selections as 'Fair Margaret and Sweet William', 'Sweet William's Ghost', 'The Witches' Song' and other texts in volumes II and III. In the essay 'On the Ancient Metrical Romances' in volume III, Percy advanced an influential argument for the 'Gothic' origins of romance, claiming that this spectacular and imaginative literary form originated in the histories of the scalds, England's Gothic ancestors, an argument that Thomas Warton would later challenge with his emphatic assertion of romance's Eastern origins in *The History of English Poetry* (1774–81). Once replaced by prose-based forms of historiography, these marvellous fictions for Percy became the stuff of pure embellishment or entertainment, and thus began 'stories of adventures with giants and dragons, and witches and enchanters, and all the monstrous extravagances of wild imagination, unguided by judgment, and uncorrected by art'.[77] Tales of fairies, of chivalrous combat with monsters and dragons, stories of ghouls, of giants and of dwarves: Percy assembles in the *Reliques* 'surviving' fragments of the same Gothic imagination that Walpole in *Otranto* that same year sought to 'revive'. Johnson's *Preface* resonated strongly with Walpole's

---

75 See Groom, 'Eighteenth-Century Gothic'.
76 Thomas Percy, *Reliques of Ancient English Poetry: Consisting of Old Heroic Ballads, Songs, and Other Pieces of Our Earlier Poets, (Chiefly of the Lyric Kind). Together with Some Few of Later Date*, 3 vols (London, 1765), vol. 1, pp. xi, vi, viii.
77 Percy, *Reliques*, vol. 3, p. iii.

endeavours in *The Castle of Otranto*, too, for not only did it constitute, against the criticisms of Voltaire and others, a robust nationalistic defence of Shakespeare's flouting of the Aristotelian Unities, his transgressive mixing of servants and kings, of comic and tragic modes, but his deployment of 'the *Gothick* mythology of fairies' too.[78]

Conclusion: The Case of *Longsword, Earl of Salisbury*

By way of conclusion to this chapter, I wish to return to the case of Thomas Leland's *Longsword* of 1762, reflecting on its relation to the Gothic through the two approaches that I outlined above. At the level of plot and characterisation, the text certainly contains elements that, from 1765 onwards, would cohere into the recognisable conventions of Gothic romance. Set during the reign of Henry III, the narrative makes loose historical reference to the Crusades and to other feats of chivalrous action, thus locating itself in the epoch that later Gothic writers such as Reeve would specifically refer to as 'Gothic' times. Earl William, the eponymous hero, is based on the historical figure of William Longespée, 3rd Earl of Salisbury and illegitimate son of Henry II, who is pitted against the machinations of Lord Raymond and his accomplices when William returns from battle in France. If Longsword is an early version of the wronged, returning hero of later Gothic romance, then Raymond and his supporters, including the crafty, vengeful Hubert and the wily and manipulative Grey, are all proto-Gothic villains the likes of Signor Montoni and his corrupt band of allies in *The Mysteries of Udolpho* (1794). Like *Otranto*, *The Old English Baron* and numerous other Gothic fictions, moreover, this is a story of illegitimacy and usurpation, for during William's absence from England Raymond has unlawfully taken possession of the Castle of Salisbury. Consequently, as in *Otranto*, it is a Gothic castle and the political legacy for which it stands that lies at the heart of the action; elsewhere in the narrative, as in those portions set in the nearby Cistercian abbey, Gothic architecture serves an equally determining and atmospheric function. Here, of course, resides the hypocritical monk Reginald, the brother of the nefarious Grey and a would-be murderer and sexual philanderer in the spirit of Lewis's infamous Father Ambrosio. Sexual indiscretion is detailed in other portions of the narrative, too, not least in the novel's account of Raymond's unwelcome, passionate advances upon Lady Ela, William's wife and mother

---

[78] Samuel Johnson, *Mr Johnson's Preface to His Edition of Shakespear's [sic] Plays* (London, 1765), p. xxxi.

of his only son. Adulterous to the point of being bigamous, the villain's sexual desire, as in *Otranto*, is used as a means of securing tenuous political power. Lady Ela's story, consequently, anticipates the turn of many a later Gothic heroine, including, as it does, scenes of physical incarceration and gruelling forms of psychological torture. The fiction is, indeed, replete with the language of horror and terror, not only in its sympathetic account of the plight of Lady Ela, but also in the passions and phantasms that plague the mind of William. At the end of the narrative, however, order is eventually restored. With all past wrongs redressed and justice duly dispensed, the legitimate hero may once again occupy the Gothic castle and preside there, as in so many later Gothic romances, over the marriages of the younger generation.

When John Langhorne reviewed the first edition of *The Castle of Otranto* in the *Monthly Review* in February 1765, he made pointed and telling use of a term that he would not have encountered anywhere in Walpole's fiction: 'Those who can digest the absurdities of Gothic fiction, and bear with the machinery of ghosts and goblins, may hope, at least, for considerable entertainment from the performance before us.'[79] If *Otranto* for Langhorne was 'Gothic', this was partly because it contained 'the machinery of ghosts and goblins', that crucial element, as I have shown, in critical conceptualisations of the Gothic aesthetic from the late seventeenth century onwards. Contemporary reviews of *Longsword*, by contrast, mentioned nothing of the sort. If Leland's novel did constitute what the reviewer in *The Critical Review* referred to as 'a new and agreeable species of writing', this was primarily because it brought together 'the beauties of poetry' with 'the advantages of history', the text remaining quite distinct, in this respect, from the 'hyper-fictionality' of *The Castle of Otranto* – Walpole's fusion of ancient poetic romance and the modern novel.[80]

But *Longsword* failed to conform in other ways to what Richard Hurd in the same year called 'Gothic story', too. Seemingly unmotivated by more than a desire to supplement and enrich the work of 'the antient English historians' with the liberties of imaginative fiction, *Longsword* did not participate in that lively culture of Whiggish politics that I have outlined in this chapter. It was not, in other words, an assertion of British aesthetic liberties against the strictures of Classical and neoclassical composition, and by no means a

---

79 This review is reprinted in Peter Sabor (ed.), *Horace Walpole: The Critical Heritage* (London and New York: Routledge & Kegan Paul, 1987), pp.70–1 (p. 70).
80 Review of *Longsword, Earl of Salisbury*, in *The Critical Review; or, Annals of Literature* 13 (1762): 252–7 (p. 252).

concerted, highly politicised revival of this native tradition of sublime literature even remotely approaching that undertaken by Walpole in *The Castle of Otranto*. Unlike the writers I have explored above, it did not emerge in an immediate context of cultural and political conflict. Most crucially, perhaps, it lacked all reference to the delights and enchantments of the fairy way of writing, that definitive aspect of the Gothic bequest that writers as diverse as Temple, Dennis, Shaftesbury, Dryden, Addison and Hurd had consistently foregrounded: other than the 'dreadful' presentiments that plague the consciences of the guilty Grey and Raymond, there is no intimation of the supernatural in *Longsword*. If we are to speak of Leland's fiction as an instance of pre-Walpolean Gothic at all, then, we might only do so in a very qualified sense, resting our claims on a form of historical presentism while rather overlooking the specific ways in which eighteenth-century Britain conceptualised its own literary 'Gothick' tradition.

I.4

Gothic Revival Architecture Before Horace Walpole's Strawberry Hill

PETER N. LINDFIELD

Strawberry Hill, the Gothic villa of Horace Walpole (1717–97), was constructed within sight of the River Thames in Twickenham in the mid-to-late eighteenth century, and stands today as one of the most important landmarks of eighteenth-century British architecture and design.[1] We know more about the building and its contents than about almost any other structure that was realised in the Gothic mode in the mid-Georgian period. Walpole wrote extensively about the house and its construction to friends, correspondents and designers; numerous executed and rejected designs survive for Strawberry Hill's exterior, interior and furniture; and the house's art collection, as well as attributions and sources for the house's various parts, from ceilings to chimneypieces, are documented in an official 'catalogue', 'description', or 'guide' that Walpole wrote and had printed at his private press: *A Description of the Villa of Mr. Horace Walpole* (1774, 1784).[2] In 1842, Strawberry Hill's contents were put up for auction by George Robins in a spectacular 24-day sale; the sale catalogue is another monument to Walpole's collection and his villa, even if Robins's auction effectively dismantled Strawberry Hill and dispersed the collections that Walpole had amassed largely at and for his house.[3] Thereafter, Strawberry Hill was transformed into a bare skeleton, stripped of its historicising, antiquarian and contemporary collection of objects and paraphernalia. But not all was lost: shortly after his graduation from Yale University in 1918, the redoubtable twentieth-century American scholar Wilmarth Sheldon Lewis energetically began to

---

[1] See Michael Snodin, with Cynthia Roman (eds), *Horace Walpole's Strawberry Hill* (New Haven and London: Yale University Press, 2009) and Clive Wainwright, *The Romantic Interior: The British Collector at Home, 1750–1850* (New Haven and London: Yale University Press, 1989), pp. 71–106.

[2] See Stephen Clarke, *The Strawberry Hill Press & Its Printing House: An Account and an Iconography* (New Haven and London: Yale University Press, 2011), pp. 26–7.

[3] George Robins and Dudley Costello, *A Catalogue of the Classic Contents of Strawberry Hill Collected by Horace Walpole* (London, 1842).

buy, collect and amass all manner of Walpoliana at his home at Farmington in rural Connecticut, eventually going on to edit the capacious 48-volume *The Yale Edition of Horace Walpole's Correspondence* (1937–83), and indefatigably promoting for the rest of his life Walpole as a rich topic for study. For all of these reasons, together with the fact that Lewis helpfully sought out and brought together so much of Walpole's Library and objects from the villa, especially furniture, Strawberry Hill has been reconstructed, even if the house and the objects in the Lewis Walpole collection are separated from one another by the Atlantic. Strawberry Hill has consequently been elevated, especially during the twentieth century, from what was strictly a modest, if idiosyncratic, eighteenth-century Gothic villa to the pre-eminent example of mid-Georgian Gothic Revival architecture.[4] Walpole's status as a prolific eighteenth-century correspondent, historian, writer on art and architecture, and the son of Britain's first Prime Minister, as well as Lewis's collection of Walpoliana, helped substantiate the villa's pre-eminence.

Michael McCarthy's landmark publication on the Gothic Revival in eighteenth-century Britain, *The Origins of the Gothic Revival* (1987), is based heavily upon Lewis's Walpoliana, and the monograph reproduces the bulk of the Strawberry Hill-related manuscript designs and correspondence in the collection. As his book's title suggests, McCarthy seeks to address the beginnings of the Gothic Revival in Britain. He opens by claiming that 'this book is born of the conviction that the beginnings of the gothic revival in architecture have hitherto been presented to the public in an incomplete and therefore mistaken manner'.[5] McCarthy continues by assessing Walpole's place in the reawakened interest in the medieval or 'Gothic' past in the eighteenth century by arguing that the mastermind behind Strawberry Hill, with good reason, 'played such a large part in the revival that he cast himself in the role of its originator'.[6] The emphasis that McCarthy places upon the Gothic *milieu* around Walpole perpetuates the notion of Strawberry Hill as the pioneering work in the style, and Walpole as Gothic's standard-bearer. This assessment corresponds with the first historical study of the Gothic Revival, Charles Locke Eastlake's *History of the Gothic Revival* (1872), which introduced eighteenth-century Gothic design by framing Strawberry Hill as the foremost building emerging from a period 'more distinguished than

---

4 See Wilmarth Sheldon Lewis, *Collector's Progress* (New York: Knopf, 1951).
5 Michael McCarthy, *The Origins of the Gothic Revival* (New Haven and London: Yale University Press, 1987), p. 1.
6 McCarthy, *The Origins of the Gothic Revival*, p. 1.

another for its neglect of Gothic'.[7] Kenneth Clark's *The Gothic Revival: An Essay in the History of Taste* (1928), the first twentieth-century work to approach the Gothic Revival with any level of seriousness, similarly places Walpole and his villa at the heart – although not the forefront – of the architectural mode, in particular the Rococo Gothic, and, perhaps because of this, Clark believed that Walpole's villa 'has been studied at least as much as it deserves'.[8] The touring exhibition curated by Michael Snodin, *Horace Walpole's Strawberry Hill*, at the Yale Center for British Art, New Haven, Connecticut, and the Victoria and Albert Museum, London (2009–10), together with the exploration of Walpole's sexuality and its theorised impact upon his aesthetic choices, have enshrined the centrality of Walpole and Strawberry Hill to any understanding of the Gothic Revival in Georgian Britain.[9] Marion Harney's *Place-Making for the Imagination* (2013) continues to assert the importance of the villa and Walpole to eighteenth-century British aesthetics, and helpfully brings together a large proportion of Walpole's writings about the house and its garden.[10]

While it is impossible to deny the importance of Walpole and Strawberry Hill to eighteenth-century Gothic design, Walpole's villa is far from being the first or, indeed, the most significant example of Gothic Revival design from the period. This is especially the case if one considers the important distinction between two very different types of post-medieval/Tudor Gothic: Gothic *Survival* and Gothic *Revival*. Sir Howard Colvin articulated cogently the difference between these two kinds of Gothic in his landmark 1948 essay, 'Gothic Survival and Gothick Revival', most recently republished in 1999.[11] Referring to the lingering tradition of Gothic in post-medieval English building, Colvin writes that the style:

---

7 Charles Locke Eastlake, *A History of the Gothic Revival* pp. 42, 43–9.
8 Kenneth Clark, *The Gothic Revival: An Essay in the History of Taste*, 2nd edition (London: Murray, 1962), pp. 46, 57–62.
9 Snodin, with Cynthia Roman (eds), *Horace Walpole's Strawberry Hill*; George E. Haggerty, *Men in Love: Masculinity and Sexuality in the Eighteenth Century* (New York: Columbia University Press, 1999), pp. 152–57; Haggerty, 'Queering Horace Walpole', *Studies in English Literature 1500–1900* 46:3 (2006): 543–61; and Matthew M. Reeve, 'Gothic architecture, sexuality and license at Horace Walpole's Strawberry Hill', *Art Bulletin* 95:3 (September 2013): 411–39.
10 Marion Harney, *Place-Making for the Imagination: Horace Walpole and Strawberry Hill* (Farnham: Ashgate, 2013), pp. 1–28, 129–218.
11 Howard Colvin, 'Gothic Survival and Gothick Revival', in Howard Colvin, *Essays in English Architectural History* (New Haven and London: Yale University Press, 1999), pp. 217–44.

is essentially a mason's architecture (what carpenter's Gothic could be like Batty Langley was soon to demonstrate), and its survival was bound up with the survival of the mason as an independent craftsman. In eighteenth-century London the mason was losing ground as a designer to the new profession of the architect, and as a builder to the expanding trade of bricklayers, neither of which understood Gothic traditions. And so Gothic retreated with the masons to the stone districts of the Midlands, the West and the North.[12]

The exact genesis of the Gothic Revival is, consequently, difficult to pinpoint with any precision given that the style had not entirely fallen out of practice since the medieval period. Local builders and masons who worked in historical ways and styles well into the seventeenth century and beyond were practitioners of 'traditional' medieval Gothic too.

When, then, was the Gothic revived? This is a challenging question, and Colvin, for one, shows that the Gothic style was very much alive in the seventeenth century and even in the early Georgian period, an age that adopted and followed, almost universally, Classical architecture's forms and motifs.[13] He writes that there were 'parts of the country where the tradition of Gothic masoncraft had survived both the Reformation and Civil War and was alive in the early eighteenth century'.[14] This tradition, however, is very different from what we think of today as Gothic Revival architecture and design, which is markedly different in form, appearance, construction and syntax from the conservatively and traditionally practiced 'Gothic Survival'. The Gothic Revival can be separated quite easily in formal and visual terms simply by considering the practitioner's background: an insular, historically trained mason (Survival), or a 'professional' architect lacking any understanding of the style (Revival) who bases his work – perhaps just superficially imitative – upon what was often only a limited understanding or comprehension of medieval architectural forms and motifs.

The Gothic Revival, then, was spearheaded not by builders who continued to work in traditional ways but by a new generation and distinct group of professional architects who were not schooled in, and who had little understanding of, medieval buildings, including their form, ornament and constructional logic. This gap in knowledge and lack of expertise meant that these Gothic architects, when called upon, created Gothic structures – either

12 Colvin, 'Gothic Survival', p. 223.
13 See, for example, Giles Worsley, *Classical Architecture in Britain: The Heroic Age* (New Haven and London: Yale University Press, 1995), pp. 1–174, 197–288.
14 Colvin, 'Gothic Survival', p. 218.

real or imaginary, as in the case of book illustrations – that, at best, only *attempted* to mirror, recreate, hint at or reference some aspect or aspects of the medieval style. Their works, consequently, were systematically different from the output of medieval masons and those keeping centuries-old building techniques and stylistic formalities alive and in place outside of the metropolis.[15] This definition of the Gothic Revival ably describes Strawberry Hill, even though its appearance moved swiftly away from the overtly whimsical to a far more sober 'antiquarian' design as the process of construction unfolded. It also characterises other examples of Georgian Gothic architecture and design that predate even the earliest work at Strawberry Hill by at least half a century; there is a rich and important genealogy of Gothic *Revival* – as opposed to Gothic *Survival* – design before Strawberry Hill in Britain that is easily and repeatedly overlooked when considering Georgian and Victorian Gothic as a whole. Walpole's villa was not the fountainhead of the Gothic Revival and representing it as such is to misunderstand the style's history.

Aesthetic Schism: The beginnings of the Gothic Revival

During the seventeenth and eighteenth centuries, high-profile professional and amateur architects, including Sir Christopher Wren (1632–1723), Nicholas Hawksmoor (*c.* 1662–1736), Sir John Vanbrugh (1664–1726), William Kent (*c.* 1686–1748) and Batty Langley (1696–1751), followed the mainstream aesthetic of Classicism. Others, such as Sanderson Miller (1716–80), worked largely in the medieval-inspired style, but Miller was the exception rather than the rule. Not one of these Classical architect-designers could avoid the Gothic. Some, such as Vanbrugh, embraced it actively; Langley published a highly influential Gothic pattern-book, while Kent's limited foray into pointed-arch architecture had a significant impact upon eighteenth-century Gothic buildings, interior plasterwork and furniture. Irrespective of their limited or more protracted engagement with the Gothic, these six 'Classicists', along with traditionally skilled craftsmen who were more insulated from leading London fashions, helped preserve an unbroken tradition of Gothic design that ran from the medieval period through to the eighteenth century. Their use of Gothic forms, however, fundamentally reformed the style's visual identity away from its medieval origins to create a new, distinctively modern

---

15 Colvin, 'Gothic Survival', pp. 217–18.

Gothic idiom that largely followed the seventeenth- and eighteenth-century fashion for Classical, Palladian simplicity. The discussion below considers select works and designs by each architect, from Wren to Langley, illustrating the vibrant and sustained tradition of Gothic design before Walpole leased 'Chopp'd-Straw-Hall' in 1747, the unassuming tenement that, after he purchased it in 1748, was transformed and enlarged to become Strawberry Hill over the next three decades.

Sir Christopher Wren

Wren is known primarily for his Classical structures, including The Sheldonian Theatre, Oxford (1664–69); The New Library at Trinity College, Cambridge (1676–84); and his most prominent work, St Paul's Cathedral, London (1674–1710). The precise mathematical qualities and underlying simplicity of Classical architecture clearly appealed to Wren, who was a scientist and mathematician by training and eventually appointed Professor of Astronomy at Gresham College, London, in 1657. Wren's leaning towards Classicism, articulated by his most well-known structures, is also expressed in his memoires, *Parentalia*, compiled by his son and published posthumously in 1750. Writing about English architecture, Wren here maintained that 'almost all the Cathedrals of the *Gothick* Form are weak and defective in the Poise of the Vault of the Aisles'; as instances of 'unbounded Fancies', their tracery 'induced too much mincing of the Stone into open Battlements and spindling Pinnacles, and littler Carvings without Proportion of Distance', even to the extent that 'the essential Rules of good Perspective and Duration were forgot'.[16] Instead, Wren preferred and cherished the mathematics of Classicism, including 'Regularity and good Proportion ... of Columns, Entablatures, &c.'[17]

Nevertheless, Wren himself made occasional recourse to medieval forms. His most significant work in the Gothic mode, a style that he referred to with at least a little contempt as '*Saracenick Architecture*',[18] is collegiate: he erected Tom Tower over the main entrance to Christ Church, Oxford (1681–2). The entrance tower's construction had been abandoned just above the height of the portal; Wren only had the

---

16 Christopher Wren, *Parentalia; or, Memoirs of the Family of the Wrens: Viz., of Matthew, Bishop of Ely, Christopher, Dean of Windsor, Etc. But Chiefly of Sir Christopher Wren in Which Is Contained, Besides His Works, a Great Number of Original Papers and Records* (London, 1750), pp. 305, 307.
17 Wren, *Parentalia*, p. 306.   18 Wren, *Parentalia*, p. 306.

college's existing fabric, and other Gothic towers, to follow as models. Wren also inserted a door (1669) into the fifteenth-century Perpendicular Gothic Divinity School, Oxford, to align with the processional entrance to his newly built Classical Sheldonian Theatre (1664–9), the University's graduation auditorium. In each instance, Wren adopted Gothic forms so that his additions would harmonise with the pre-existing structures: for Tom Tower he 'resolved it ought to be Gothick to agree with the Founder's Worke'.[19] A Classical tower on the college's St Aldate's façade, like a pedimented doorway inserted into the fifteenth-century rigidly Perpendicular Gothic Divinity School, would have jarred with the existing architecture. Both of Wren's additions to these Oxford fabrics, the tower and door, are identifiably Gothic, but certain aspects of each addition do not accord with the traditions of medieval architecture exhibited by the existing structures. What are meant to be buttresses on Tom Tower, for example, are not treated with any sympathetic appreciation of medieval forms; instead, they are essentially Classical pilasters. The reticulations in the tower's two-light openings are cusped, but the cusping is too numerous and stilted in comparison with the Tudor cusped panelling below. Wren's Divinity School door is an equally distinctive re-composition of medieval forms, most noticeably the combination of a Tudor, four-centred arch with two isolated cusps placed beneath a heavily moulded ogee-flip and oversized finial. The fusion of Gothic motifs indicates Wren's assimilation of the Gothic style, but their re-composition is hardly in keeping with the rest of the structure. This was not an unthinking concession to tradition, an impulse which can be seen in the University's Schools Quadrangle and Convocation House,[20] but rather for the purpose of coherence, even if this coherence is, at best, superficial.

Although only minor additions to existing structures and isolated examples within Wren's larger *oeuvre*, the tower and doorway demonstrate his embrace and deployment of Gothic forms as and when appropriate. Despite wanting to preserve the aesthetic unity of these buildings, his lack of understanding of, and inexperience in working with, Gothic architecture in comparison with the Classical meant that his additions were far from convincing recreations of the medieval

19 Christopher Wren, 'Tom Tower, Christ Church, Oxford (1681–2)', *The Wren Society* 5 (1928): 17–23 (p. 17).
20 John Newman, 'The Architectural Setting', in Nicholas Tyacke (ed.), *The History of the University of Oxford*, Vol. 4 (Oxford: Clarendon, 1997), pp. 135–78 (p. 169).

style: though they were meant to 'agree with the Founder's Worke', they do not do so in very strict or accurate terms.[21] This is at least partially understandable given that, unlike Classical architecture, there was no nucleus of professional architects working exclusively in the Gothic style, or, indeed, treatises published on its forms, ornament or proportions in the late seventeenth century. Consequently, and save the buildings themselves, Wren had very little to go on when designing these Gothic additions. Walpole, writing about Tom Tower, observes and records Wren's failure to grasp completely and execute convincingly these medieval forms, differentiating as he does so between actual and revived instances of the Gothic style: 'the great Campanile at Christ-church Oxford is notable, and though not so light as a gothic architect would perhaps have formed it, does not disgrace the modern'.[22] In Walpole's pro-Gothic eyes, it does not disgrace the modern because it attempted to embrace the medieval style, even if it failed ultimately to realise the Gothic's 'lightness'. Walpole may well not have possessed the visual knowledge necessary to articulate the irregularities of Tom Tower, but he could certainly differentiate between Wren's contribution and that of the original Tudor fabric, or between modern utilisations of the mode and medieval Gothic architecture in general.

Although unrealised, Wren's Warrant Design (1675) for St Paul's Cathedral also embraced Gothic forms. After the rejection of the unconventional Great Model (1763-4), Wren offered the cathedral's Chapter a far more traditional, medieval-structured building with a tall nave flanked by lower side aisles.[23] What would be formed from pointed arches (vaulting and window openings) in a Gothic Cathedral were instead rendered in a Classical manner and replaced with round-headed variants, pilasters substituting the high vault's responds. Wren's conservative design, consequently, was essentially a Gothic cathedral completely rewritten in Classical form and ornament. Although this design was not executed, the realised fabric makes use of flying buttresses – that

---

21 Wren, 'Tom Tower', p. 17.
22 Horace Walpole, *Anecdotes of Painting in England; with Some Account of the Principal Artists; and Notes on Other Arts; Collected by G. Vertue, and Now Digested from His MSS*, 3rd edition, 4 vols (London: Printed for J. Dodsley, 1782), vol. 3, pp. 167–8.
23 Oxford, All Souls College, II.14. See Kerry Downes, *Sir Christopher Wren: The Design of St Paul's Cathedral* (London: Trefoil in association with Guildhall Library, 1988) and Anthony Geraghty, *The Architectural Drawings of Sir Christopher Wren at All Souls College, Oxford: A Complete Catalogue* (Aldershot: Ashgate, 2007), pp. 62–3.

distinctive feature of the great Gothic churches – while keeping them hidden behind Classicised screen walls. Wren's most well-known Classical essay, is, consequently, indebted to medieval architectural forms and structures obfuscated by a Classical veneer. Despite its limited scale, Wren's Gothic output reveals that it was not inconceivable for a thoroughly Classical architect to embrace the Gothic, even if it was not considered a valuable and tasteful architectural style.

Nicholas Hawksmoor

Hawksmoor, Wren's pupil, worked in his mentor's Classical-Gothic hybrid style, and similarly completed medieval structures. His most significant work is a range of buildings forming the North Quadrangle (Fig.4.1) at All Souls College, Oxford (1708–30). Of the additions, the pair of towers in the quadrangle and the copula over the Radcliffe Square gate are the most significant. Together, they illustrate Hawksmoor's understanding of medieval architectural forms, but also his persistent use of these motifs within the Classical frameworks of proportion and ornament. His unexecuted 1708–9 design for the college's High Street façade, replete with Gothic forms including crenellations, crocketed pinnacles, aedicular niches, buttresses, registers of trefoil-cusped lancets and ogee-flip crestings, is entirely symmetrical and regimented by round-headed windows.[24] An unexecuted proposal for the North Quadrangle's square-plan towers in perspective shows the buttresses terminating just above the main register's recessed window openings, and the level above is left plain, save for a trio of narrow early English-style lancet windows on each face, above which rises a two-story embattled and buttressed octagon on each tower.[25] The towers, as executed, are more ornamentally ambitious and coherent, yet they retain this design's inconsistent application of buttresses and simplified, even plain, surface treatment. Perhaps the most incongruous piece of executed work from this programme is the entranceway from Radcliffe Square. The late-Gothic, Perpendicular-style onion dome akin to those on the buttresses of King's College, Cambridge, and Henry VII's Chapel, Westminster Abbey, is not finished with a suitably Gothic finial as seen in these Tudor examples, but with a Corinthian capital. A 1720 proposal for the Radcliffe Square façade and tower[26] that, like the High Street façade,[27] mixes round-headed windows among Gothic buttressing and pinnacles, does

24 Oxford, Worcester College, YD4, f. 131. 25 Oxford, Worcester College, YD4, f. 2.
26 Oxford, Worcester College, YD4, f. 127. 27 Oxford, Worcester College, YD4, f. 131.

Fig.4.1: Nicholas Hawksmoor, *North Quadrangle towers and east range, All Souls College, Oxford*. Author's photograph.

not include this Corinthian capital; instead the dome is finished with a sphere, and even his Classically-styled screen and dome does not include this Corinthian capital,[28] though it is perhaps hinted at in his perspective rendering of the North Quadrangle in red.[29] This blatant mixture of Classical and Gothic forms within one apparently coherent scheme is not unusual in Hawksmoor's corpus, and a Corinthian capital can be found serving as a finial to the dome that he projected for Westminster Abbey's crossing tower.[30]

Equally notable are Hawksmoor's additions to and completion of Westminster Abbey's western towers, which, much like Christ Church's tower, had been left unfinished in the medieval period. In 1712 Wren wrote that 'the two West-towers [at the Abbey] were left incomplete, … one much higher than the other, though still too low for Bells … they ought certainly to be carried to an equal Height, one story above the Ridge of the Roof, still

28 Oxford, Worcester College, YD4, f. 5. 29 Oxford, Worcester College, YD4, f. 11.
30 London, Westminster Abbey Archives, Hawksmoor Drawings, no. 4.

continuing in the Gothick Manner, in the Stone-work, and Tracery'.[31] The northern tower was significantly lower, carried only up to just above the side aisle, whereas the southern tower was at the level of the high vault apex. Hawksmoor resolved the towers' design in 1734. However, the additions above the top of the western window were not universally consistent with the medieval forms and ornament below. Hawksmoor's towers above an entablature, complete with Classical piercings, are divided into bold horizontal registers that, most noticeably over the clock and corresponding oculus, are framed by round pediments. The towers' louvred openings, while loosely mirroring tracery windows, are composed from simplified lancet shapes and reticulations that are noticeably lacking cusps in contradiction to the remainder of the structure below. Each opening's ogee-flip cresting is also finished uncomfortably with Corinthian-like capitals akin to that on the tower of All Souls' Radcliffe Square screen. Hawksmoor's mixture of Classical and Gothic elements in the western towers, and the resultant contradiction with the earlier medieval fabric, did not go unnoticed: as one commentator put it, it was 'not conformable and pursuant to the old'.[32]

Hawksmoor wrote about the Abbey's Gothic architecture in Classical terms: referring to the façade's gable, he claimed that 'as soon as the mason can get stone he will put on the Crockets (or Calceoli) at the West end on the pediment'.[33] This mixture of Gothic and Classical forms could have expanded beyond the abbey's western towers to encompass the entire fabric. A *c.* 1724 design reveals his plan to encase the structure's exterior in a form of simplified Gothic, with a Classical entablature suitably Gothicised and running above each of the three windows' levels.[34] Another of Hawksmoor's proposals for the towers places a Corinthian capital at the top of each tower's proposed spire, with flying buttresses almost in the form of volute-scrolls and pedimented-tops to the upper panelling.[35] Hawksmoor's additions to the Abbey, consequently, reflect his predilection for mixing Classical and Gothic architectural forms, albeit on a scale much more restrained than he had envisioned at one point.

Because of his work in Oxford and London, Hawksmoor, much like Wren, clearly perpetuated medieval forms, but in a manner quite different from the

---

31 Kerry Downes, *Hawksmoor* (London: A. Zwemmer, 1959), p. 283.
32 Quoted in Vaughan Hart, *Nicholas Hawksmoor: Rebuilding Ancient Wonders* (New Haven and London: Yale University Press, 2002), p. 62.
33 Quoted in Hart, *Nicholas Hawksmoor*, p. 62.
34 London, Westminster City Archives, Gardner Box 53 ff. 6–7.
35 London, Westminster Abbey Archives, Hawksmoor Drawings, no. 17.

local masons in the seventeenth and eighteenth centuries that Colvin framed as the exponents of Gothic Survival. Hawksmoor's Gothic works reinterpreted and re-composed medieval motifs and structural forms in a way that was never seen in the medieval period. Thus, although his Gothic works perpetuated the unbroken lineage of Gothic design in Britain, it was in a new, rejuvenated form that he responded to the prevailing and accepted architectural aesthetic of Classicism.

Sir John Vanbrugh

Vanbrugh, even more so than Wren, had a varied career. Well known today as a playwright (his *The Relapse* ran in London from 1696, and a second comedy, *The Provok'd Wife*, opened in 1697), he initially worked for William Matthews, a paternal cousin, in the London wine business, and then as a factor in the East India Company. His first architectural commission was a palatial and highly influential one: Castle Howard, Yorkshire, for Charles Howard (1669–1738), 3rd Earl of Carlisle, and fellow member of the Kit-Cat Club that Horace Walpole believed contained 'the Patriots that saved Britain'.[36] Like the bulk of Wren's and Hawksmoor's architecture, Castle Howard is Classical. A good number of Vanbrugh's country houses, on the other hand, make repeated concessions to the medieval. While this may not be articulated as consistently as it was by Walpole at Strawberry Hill – indeed Walpole's villa is an essay recording his and his designers' increasingly rigorous comprehension and command of medieval architectural motifs – his use of the Gothic deliberately courted association with the historic, the chivalric and the masculine.[37] This is what Vanbrugh referred to as the 'castle air'. As its name suggests, the 'castle air' created the impression of a robust medievalist fortification conveyed through a select range of architectural forms, including crenellations, machicolations, arrow-slits and massy walls. Vanbrugh's proposals for Inveraray Castle, Argyll, make use of all of these motifs to create a new-old medievalist country house (Fig.4.2).[38] The preparatory sketch of *c.* 1720 illustrates the importance of all of these motifs, together with massy round-towers; however, the

---

36 James Caulfield, *Memoirs of the Celebrated Persons Composing the Kit-Cat Club: With a Prefatory Account of the Origin of the Association* (London, 1821), title page.
37 Vaughan Hart, *Sir John Vanbrugh: Storyteller in Stone* (New Haven and London: Yale University Press, 2008), pp. 45–81.
38 Victoria and Albert Museum, London, E.2124:79–1992 and E.2124:138–1992.

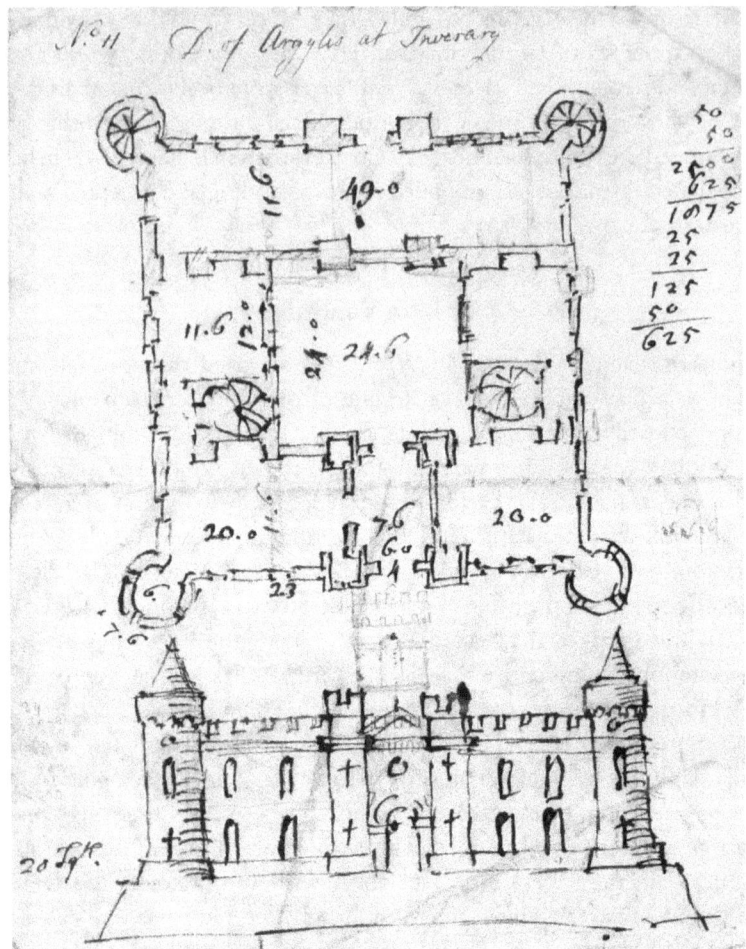

Fig.4.2: Sir John Vanbrugh, *Sketch plan and elevation of Inveraray Castle, Argyll.* c. 1720. E.2124:79–1992. © Victoria and Albert Museum, London.

large round-headed windows and symmetrical façade contradict this medievalist style.[39] A presentation design for the house makes a rare concession in his *oeuvre* to the pointed arch by incorporating two Gothic relieving arches above the portal.[40]

39 Victoria and Albert Museum, London, E.2124:79–1992.
40 Victoria and Albert Museum, London, E.2124:138–1992.

At Kimbolton Castle, Cambridgeshire, Vanbrugh was employed by Charles Montagu (c. 1662–1722), 1st Duke of Manchester, to repair the house following the collapse of the garden (south) façade. This fabric, in need of attention, played directly into Vanbrugh's predilection for creating castellated allusions. Writing to the Countess of Manchester in 1707, Vanbrugh indicates his interest in restoring the house and incorporating references to the medieval – the house, after all, was medieval at heart and the medievalising refurbishment would thus not be too inappropriate: 'As to the Outside, I thought 'twas absolutely best, to give it something of the Castle Air, tho' at the Same time to make it regular. And by this means too, all the Old Stone is Serviceable again; which to have had the new would have run to a very great Expense.'[41] Sensitive to the proposal's mixture of Gothic and Classical architectural components, Vanbrugh convincingly acknowledges his reinterpretation of medieval design and his deviation from orthodox Classical architecture: 'I hope your L^{d}ship won't be discourage'd, if any Italians you may Shew it to, shou'd find fault 'tis not Roman, for to have built a Front with Pillasters, and what the Orders require cou'd never have been born with the Rest of the Castle'.[42] The façade designs, orchestrated according to regular proportion and dominated by round-headed windows, are crowned with crenellations to convey the castle air.[43] This repertoire is also found on a façade proposal for an unknown house, illustrating the repeated use of this aesthetic trope.[44]

In his c. 1718–23 proposal for Sir William Saunderson's House, Greenwich, the castle air is confined to the *faux* machicolations.[45] This deployment contradicts directly the Venetian window inserted into the second story. A similar repertoire of ornament was applied to Vanbrugh's own house, Vanbrugh Castle, Greenwich, a massy brick structure dominated by a circular staircase.[46] Vanbrugh, in the same manner as the architects considered already, advanced a style of Gothic architecture that was personal to his own interpretation. Vanbrugh's Gothic – the castle air – consequently offered a new and distinctly Georgian reinterpretation of the medieval that, like the Gothic of Wren and Hawksmoor, owed a considerable debt to the forms and principles of prevailing Classical design.

41 Bonamy Dobrée and Geoffrey Webb (eds), *The Complete Works of Sir John Vanbrugh*, Vol. 4 (London: Nonesuch Press, 1928), p. 14.
42 Dobrée and Webb (eds), p. 14.
43 Victoria and Albert Museum, London, D.97-1891; D.109-1891; D.112-1891.
44 Victoria and Albert Museum, London, E.2124:149-1992.
45 Victoria and Albert Museum, London, E.2124:129-1992.
46 Hart, *Nicholas Hawksmoor*, pp. 213–41.

William Kent

The same mixture of styles emerges in the work of William Kent, a painter, designer and architect who was 'discovered' by Richard Boyle (1694–1753), 3rd Earl of Burlington and 4th Earl of Cork, and referred to by Horace Walpole as 'a proper priest' to Burlington's 'Apollo of Arts'.[47] Kent's work is overwhelmingly Classical – unsurprisingly so, given his decade-long Italian sojourn – but he can nevertheless be connected firmly to several significant examples of Gothic Revival design between c. 1729 and 1741. These range in scale from modest cartoons for book illustrations,[48] through to country house architecture and interiors,[49] and perhaps even a Herefordshire church in 1748 (the year of his death) for a friend and correspondent of Walpole's, Dickie Bateman (c. 1705–74).[50]

A number of Kent's book illustrations, executed perhaps as early as 1729 for the 1751 edition of Edmund Spenser's metrical romance *The Faerie Queene* (1590–6), demonstrate the breadth and complexity of his style. They confirm that he was interested in creating a Gothic effect without actually attempting to recreate the exact form, appearance and structure of medieval English architecture. As I have written elsewhere, his illustration of *The Redcross Knight Introduced by Duessa to the House of Pride* (Fig.4.3) sets a relatively convincing Gothic hall in the background, in front of which appears confused foreground architecture comprising what is effectively a Classical Ionic colonnade and gatehouse peppered with Gothic ogee arches, quatrefoils and trefoil-cusped arches.[51] His illustration of the Italianate castle in *Arthegal*

---

47 Horace Walpole, *Anecdotes of Painting in England; with Some Account of the Principal Artists; and Notes on Other Arts; Collected by G. Vertue, and Now Digested from His MSS*, 4 vols (Strawberry Hill: Printed by Thomas Farmer, 1762–71[i.e. 1780]), vol 4, p. 111. See Susan Weber (ed.), *William Kent: Designing Georgian Britain* (New Haven and London: Yale University Press, 2013), pp. 27–181.
48 Nicholas Savage, 'Kent as Book Illustrator', in Weber (ed.), *William Kent*, pp. 412–47.
49 Julius Bryant, 'From "Gusto" to "Kentissime": Kent's Designs for Country Houses, Villas, and Lodges', in Weber (ed.), *William Kent*, pp. 183–241.
50 See Matthew M. Reeve, 'Dickie Bateman and the gothicization of Old Windsor: architecture and sexuality in the circle of Horace Walpole', *Architectural History* 56 (2013): 97–131; Howard Colvin, 'Henry Flitcroft, William Kent and Shobdon Church, Herefordshire', in David Jones and Sam McKinstry (eds), *Essays in Scots and English Architectural History: A Festschrift in Honour of John Frew* (Donington: Shaun Tyas, 2009), pp. 1–8; Peter N. Lindfield, *Georgian Gothic: Medievalist Architecture, Furniture and Interiors, 1730–1840* (Woodbridge: Boydell and Brewer, 2016), pp. 71–8; and Roger White, 'William Kent and the Gothic Revival', in Susan Weber (ed.), *William Kent*, pp. 247–69 (p. 264).
51 London, Victoria and Albert Museum, E.876–1928. See Peter N. Lindfield, '"Hung Round with the Helmets, Breast-Plates, and Swords of Our Ancestors": Allusions to Chivalry in Eighteenth-Century Gothicism?', in Barbara Gribling and Katie Stevenson

Fig.4.3: William Kent, *Cartoon of The Redcross Knight Introduced by Duessa to the House of Pride. c.* 1729–40. E.876–1928. © Victoria and Albert Museum, London.

Fights the Sarazin Pollente is made overtly Gothic by the overabundance of arrow-slits, and domestic rather than militaristic ogee and Tudor windows and doorways.[52] Even when attempting to recreate extant architecture, such as Hampton Court Palace's interior and exterior, Kent exercised significant 'artistic license' in reconfiguring the historic Gothic architecture. His depiction of *Henry VIII Receiving Montmorency, the French Ambassador, at Hampton Court* replaces the rigidly Perpendicular tracery patterns of the Great Hall's west window with a far more Decorated – and typically Kentian – type of tracery found in numerous other examples of his Gothic work, in which a quatrefoil is 'punched' though a piece of masonry (plate tracery from the twelfth century) at the window's head, and the remainder of the window is made from *circa* fourteenth-century bar tracery.[53] Kent also substituted the

(eds), *Chivalry and the Vision of the Medieval Past* (Woodbridge: Boydell and Brewer, 2016), pp. 74–6.
52 London, Victoria and Albert Museum, E.892–1928.
53 London, British Museum, 1927-7-21-4.

hammer beam roof in Hampton Court Palace's Great Hall with a type of pendant vaulting more akin to that found in the Palace's Chapel Royal.

Similar artistic liberties were taken with his rendering of Hampton Court Palace from the outside. Kent's *capriccio* landscape for Michael Drayton's 'Poly-Olbion' depicts Hampton Court Palace to the left of the scene, although he significantly enlarged the scale of the Palace's Great Hall, completely rewrote its main western window's tracery again, and apparently combined the Entrance and Clock towers into one, or omitted the Entrance façade and court entirely.[54] This depiction is, at best, only a vague representation rather than an accurate depiction of the Palace. Kent's artistic liberty did not extend, on the other hand, to his rendition of Esher Place, a country house that he designed, to the right of this landscape. Kent designed and executed the house in the Gothic mode in *c.* 1730–3 for Henry Pelham (1694–1754), a future prime minister, around the time that he partially remodelled the Clock Court tower at Hampton Court Palace.[55] But unlike his modest remodelling of the Clock Court tower, Esher Place is his most significant, though now largely demolished, work in the style (Fig.4.4). Despite the scale and importance of the structure to his admittedly limited Gothic *oeuvre*, the exact genesis and nature of the commission is far from certain. A number of Kent's designs for the house's exterior and interior reveal important aspects not only of the house, but also of his Gothic 'style'.[56] One indicates that the house would have been a modest square-plan Palladian pile with pavilions on a knoll.[57] Kent's drawing sets the Classically styled house in front of a gatehouse serving as a folly; this gatehouse was all that remained of the medieval house erected *c.* 1480 by William Waynflete (1398–1486), Bishop of Winchester. For some reason, Kent's designs shifted to embrace the Gothic, and instead of employing Waynflete's tower as a folly, the medieval fragment became the centre of the new house.[58] His proposal for Esher, exhibiting Palladian simplicity, proportion and geometry, is replete with medieval-derived motifs applied to the façade to articulate a Gothic appearance with the gatehouse at its centre. A design by Kent for Esher's octagonal room demonstrates how he Gothicised a standard pedimented (Classical) door-surround as found, for example, in his interiors at Houghton Hall, Norfolk, by replacing the

54 London, British Museum, 1927, 0721.5
55 Juliet Allan, 'New light on William Kent at Hampton Court Palace', *Architectural History* 27 (1984): 50–8.
56 John Harris, 'A William Kent Discovery: Designs for Esher Place, Surrey', *Country Life* (14 May 1959): 1076–8 and Harris, 'Esher Place, Surrey', *Country Life* (2 April 1987): 94–7.
57 London, Victoria and Albert Museum, E.360-1986.
58 London, Victoria and Albert Museum, E.361-1986.

Fig.4.4: After Luke Sullivan, *Detail of A View of Esher in Surrey, the Seat of the Rt. Hon. Henry Pelham Esq.* 1759. B1978.43.1075. Yale Center for British Art, Paul Mellon Collection.

entablature with an ogee arch, while the window exhibits his anachronistic combination of plate and bar tracery as found in his drawing of *Henry VIII Receiving Montmorency*.[59] An engraved record of one chimneypiece by Kent for Esher was included by John Vardy's *Some Designs of Mr. Inigo Jones and Mr. Wm. Kent* (1744), which demonstrates perhaps Kent's most limited additions of Gothic forms in the entablature (ogee-quatrefoils) to an otherwise exclusively Classical chimneypiece to give it a medievalist tincture.

Kent's two screens – for The Court of King's Bench in Westminster Hall, 1739, and Gloucester Cathedral, 1741 (Fig.4.5) – are similarly Classical-Gothic hybrids.[60] Certain aspects of these two screens are particularly significant for the way in which overtly Classical forms, such as entablatures, columns and pilasters, are not only made fit for Gothic designs, but also modified subtly to become Gothic themselves. On both screens, the entablatures are staffed by a repeated gallery of blind cusped arcades, and the blind pedimented doorway on the upper register of the Gloucester screen is made 'medieval' by converting the rectilinear pediments into ogee arches. This, as seen in the next section on Batty Langley, had a significant impact upon eighteenth-century Gothic Revivalist architecture. Another of Kent's commissions, his work at

---

59 London, Victoria and Albert Museum, E.368–1986.
60 William Kent and Inigo Jones, *Some Designs of Mr. Inigo Jones and Mr. Wm. Kent* (London, 1744), pls. 48–9.

Fig.4.5: William Kent, *A Screen Erected before the Choir in the Cathedral Church of Gloucester*, 1741. Plate 49 from John Vardy, *Some Designs of Mr. Inigo Jones and Mr. Wm. Kent* (1744). Folio A N 63. Yale Center for British Art, Paul Mellon Collection.

York Minster in 1741, offers a second, distinct strand of Gothic that also had a significant impact upon Georgian Gothic design, including a cabinet for Henrietta Louisa (1698–1761), Countess of Pomfret, and the furniture for Shobdon Church, Herefordshire.[61] Whereas the majority of Kent's Gothic designs were largely Classical in form and structure, his contributions to the Minster were, on the other hand, overwhelmingly Gothic: the pulpit and stalls, which, in comparison with his additions to Westminster Hall and Gloucester Cathedral, were sympathetic to their location in the Minster's Gothic Choir.

Despite offering only a limited range of designs for houses and furniture, Kent had a significant impact upon Gothic design until the 1760s, in part due to Vardy's *Some Designs* of 1744. Walpole certainly did not

---

61 Terry Friedman, 'The transformation of York Minster, 1726–42', *Architectural History* 38 (1995): 69–90 (pp. 81–3). See Peter N. Lindfield, 'The Countess of Pomfret's gothic revival furniture', *The Georgian Group Journal* xxii (2014): 77–94 and Lindfield, *Georgian Gothic*, pp. 71–7.

approve of Kent's Gothic, reflecting in September 1753 that 'Kent designed the screen [at Gloucester Cathedral]; but he knew no more there than he did anywhere else how to enter into the true Gothic taste.'[62] His disapproval of Kent's Gothic, especially at Gloucester Cathedral, did not stop the architect William Robinson reproducing, quite closely, Kent's Esher chimneypiece as illustrated by Vardy in his *Some Designs* for the Breakfast Room at Strawberry Hill. Walpole and his designers moved away from Kent's style of Gothic in the 1750s, though, reviewing the house on 5 June 1788 in a letter to Thomas Barrett of Lee Priory, Kent, Walpole claimed that 'neither Mr. Bentley nor my workmen has studied the science [of Gothic], and [that ...] My house therefore is but a sketch by beginners'.[63] Kent's Gothic certainly falls short of Walpole's later 'scientific' understanding and application of medieval forms, but Kent was nonetheless an important designer for promoting a distinct type of Gothic that was suitable across many different contexts, both domestic or ecclesiastical, and for the remodelling of medieval architecture to create a new country house.

Batty Langley

Of all the early Georgian Gothic designers, Langley is, without doubt, the most well known but also the most notorious. This arises partly from Walpole's assessment of the Twickenham-based amateur architect and garden designer. His best-known contribution to eighteenth-century design is his pattern-book, *Ancient Architecture: Restored and Improved* (1741–2), which he reissued in 1747 as *Gothic Architecture, Improved by Rules and Proportions*. The book's designs advocate, principally through five Gothic 'Orders', a style of Gothic that is articulated through motifs frequently applied to Classical frameworks. Rather than proposing designs based upon the forms and structures of medieval architecture, Langley promoted a style founded upon Classical architecture: its Orders, framework of columns, entablatures, colonnades and Vitruvian proportions. Langley's re-presentation and theorisation of medieval architecture was designed to achieve a personal goal, namely to elevate Gothic architecture from a degraded and insular style lacking the intellectual

---

62 W. S. Lewis (ed.), *The Yale Edition of Horace Walpole's Correspondence*, 48 vols (New Haven and London: Yale University Press, 1937–83), vol. 35, p. 154.
63 Horace Walpole, *The Works of Horatio Walpole, Earl of Orford*, 5 vols (London: Printed for G. G. and J. Robinson and J. Edwards, 1798), vol. 5, pp. 668–9.

rigour and prestige of Classicism.[64] This is evident in Wren's assessment of Classical and Gothic architecture, but these opinions can also be found in the work of other writers such as John Evelyn.[65] Walpole also articulated the intellectual and emotional differences separating these two styles on a number of occasions, perhaps the most concise being in the fourth volume of his *Anecdotes of Painting* (1762):

> one must have *taste* to be sensible of the beauties of Grecian architecture; one only wants *passions* to feel Gothic. In St. Peter's one is convinced that it was built by great princes. In Westminster abbey, one thinks not of the builder; the religion of the place makes the first impression—and though stripped of its altars and shrines, it is nearer converting one to popery than all the regular pageantry of Roman domes. Gothic churches infuse superstition; Grecian, admiration.[66]

This critical distinction between the Classical and the Gothic styles was widely held at the time, and structured much eighteenth-century architectural thought, aesthetics and practice.

Attempting to overturn received opinion, Langley proposed in the dedication of *Ancient Architecture* to Charles, Duke of Richmond, that it is a 'Specimen (or Attempt) to restore the *Rules* of the ANCIENT SAXON ARCHITECTURE, (vulgarly, but mistakenly called *Gothic*) which have been lost to the Public for upwards of seven hundred Years past'.[67] In the pattern-book's second dedication, here to the Dean and Chapter of Westminster Abbey, he similarly underscored the originality of his publication, spuriously claiming that it sought to recover those aspects of medieval architecture that made it intellectually respectable:

> by strict Researches, I have discovered many of the Rules by which its principal Parts are proportioned and adorned, whose Result commands the *Admiration* and *Attention* of all Beholders: And as, by great Variety of Examples, I have Illustrated their Uses, in the Formation, Ornamenting of

---

64 Eileen Harris, 'Batty Langley: a tutor to freemasons (1696–1751)', *Burlington Magazine* 119:890 (1977): 327–35.

65 John Evelyn, *An Account of Architects and Architecture, Together, with an Historical, Etymological Explanation of Certain Terms, Particularly Affected by Architects* (London, 1706), pp. 9–10. See Peter N. Lindfield, '"Serious gothic" and "doing the ancient buildings": Batty Langley's Ancient Architecture and Principal Geometric Elevations', *Architectural History* 57 (2014): 141–73.

66 Horace Walpole, *Anecdotes of Painting in England*, vol. 4, pp. 114–15.

67 Batty Langley and T. Langley, *Ancient Architecture: Restored, and Improved, by a Great Variety of Grand and Useful Designs, Entirely New in the Gothick Mode for the Ornamenting of Buildings and Gardens Exceeding Every Thing That's Extant* (London, 1741–2), Dedication 1.

private Buildings, in the same *Mode*, which never was done, or attempted before; and as such may justly be esteemed an Improvement in the *Noble Art of Building*.[68]

Langley's pattern-book was criticised, not least by Horace Walpole. In a letter from 5 July 1755 to Richard Bentley, one of the designers of Strawberry Hill, Walpole writes of Latimers, Chesham, Buckinghamshire, that 'the house has undergone the Batty Langley-discipline: half the ornaments are of his bastard Gothic ... I want to write over the doors of most modern edifices, *Repaired and beautified, Langley and Hallet churchwardens*'.[69] In *Anecdotes of Painting*, Langley's Gothic is equally derided: he 'endeavoured to adapt Gothic architecture to Roman measures', Walpole writes, 'as Sir Philip Sidney attempted to regulate English verse by Roman feet. Langley went farther, and (for he never copied Gothic) *invented* five orders for that style'.[70] Later, in 1872, Charles Locke Eastlake pronounced that,

> Gothic architecture has had its vicissitudes in this country. There was a time when its principles were universally recognised; there was a time when they were neglected or forgotten. But in the days of its lowest degradation, it may be questioned whether it would not have been better that the cause should have remained unexposed than have been sustained by such a champion as Batty Langley.[71]

Despite this criticism, Langley's Gothic was, in fact, rather influential, not least because he produced the first Georgian pattern-book to advance designs for architecture relevant to the eighteenth century. His plates included proposals for garden buildings, including pavilions and umbrellos, windows, chimneypieces and fireplaces.

While there is no evidence to indicate that Langley ever executed any of his designs,[72] his plates had significant impact upon mid-Georgian Gothic, especially on pieces executed by local builders. William Porden, writing about a chimneypiece design for Eaton Hall, Chester, on 28 December 1804, indicates the wide popularity and uptake of Langley's proposals: 'I have only to object that it has been executed in every Gothicised Cottage

---

68 Langley and Langley, Dedication 2.
69 Walpole, in Lewis, *Horace Walpole's Correspondence*, vol. 35, p. 233.
70 Walpole, *Anecdotes of Painting*, vol. 4, pp. 106–7.
71 Charles Locke Eastlake, *A History of the Gothic Revival*, p. 54.
72 Timothy Mowl and Brian Earnshaw, *An Insular Rococo: Architecture, Politics and Society in Ireland and England, 1710–1770* (London: Reaktion, 1999), p. 99. See also Roger White, 'The Influence of Batty Langley', in J. Mordaunt Crooke (ed.), *A Gothick Symposium at the Victoria and Albert Museum* (London: Victoria and Albert Museum, 1984), no. pag.

these 50 years and was originally designed by Batty Langley. In short, it was only what was called a modern Chimney piece before the present French fashion became prevalent with the usual gothic ornament instead of the Grecian patera.'[73] Indeed, a chimneypiece added to the Family Pew at Shobdon Church, Herefordshire, c. 1755, exactly reproduces Plate XLIII from Langley's *Ancient Architecture* (1741–2). The Gothic Temple at Bramham Park, Yorkshire (1750), duplicates Plate LVII in *Ancient Architecture*, and the umbrello at Great Saxon Hall, Suffolk (c. 1801–15), reflects the structure and many of the motifs found on Plates XXXI and LII of the same volume.[74] Although Porden's assessment of Langlean Gothic is hyperbolic, the designs' influence cannot be understated. Langley created a formal and fully illustrated repertoire of Gothic ornament that had practical application: combined with one another, applied to architecturally unrelated surfaces and structures, and in whatever way that the designer wished. With Langley, Gothic Orders supporting an entablature, modelled directly upon a Classical colonnade, were, for the first time, a possibility.

Part of Langley's apparently unbridled influence stems from the fact that his designs were copied, imitated and paraphrased in the 1750s. Each of William Pain's editions of *The Builder's Companion and Workman's General Assistant* (1758, 1765, 1769), for instance, offered a version of Langley's five Gothic Orders and his other designs.[75] Pain's Gothic Orders follow roughly those developed by Langley, although their sequence is re-arranged as follows: 1, 3, 5, 2, 4. Pain also offered some designs in Langley's Classical-Gothic style, but of his own inventions. Plate 80, *Four Gothick Frontispieces for outside Work*, is a synthesis of Gothic Frontispieces from *Ancient Architecture*, but the shafts rise to support an entablature, upon which sit crenellations, a pediment or a Chinese Pagoda. Indeed, all four designs on Plate 80 feature square- headed doors, upon which token tracery details are added. *Gothick Frontispieces for the Inside of Rooms*, Plate 82, illustrates the flexibility of Gothic's appearance: the only parallel between the designs and medieval architecture is the arched decoration cut into some of the moulding patterns and panels either side of the jamb mouldings. Langley's style of Classical-Gothic architecture was, consequently, promoted by other designers and

---

73 Chester, Eaton Hall Archive, 9/278 28 December 1804, fol. 1r.
74 See Gwyn Headley, *Follies, Grottoes & Garden Buildings* (London: Aurum, 1999), pp. 550–1.
75 Alistair John Rowan, 'Batty Langley's Gothic', in Giles Robertson and George Henderson (eds), *Studies in Memory of David Talbot Rice* (Edinburgh: Edinburgh University Press, 1975), pp. 197–215 (p. 208).

pattern-book authors keen to offer designs according to mid-eighteenth-century fashion. A letter in *The World* from 1753 highlights Gothic's popularity at the time particularly well:

> FROM a thousand instances of our imitative inclinations I shall select one or two, which have been, and still are notorious and general. A few years ago everything was Gothic; our houses, our beds, our book-cases, and our couches, were all copied from some parts or other of our old cathedrals. The Grecian architecture ... which was taught by nature and polished by the graces, was totally neglected.[76]

Numerous pattern-books supplied this fascination with the Gothic, though because Langley's came first, its place in the Gothic Revival has surpassed that of, for example, the prolific and influential work of William and John Halfpenny in their 1752 publications, *Rural Architecture in the Gothick Taste* and *Chinese and Gothic Architecture Properly Ornamented*.

Coda

Important though it was, Walpole's Strawberry Hill cannot be seen as the only or the most prominent example of 'new', or 'modern' Gothic architecture in eighteenth-century Britain. As this essay has shown, numerous examples were imagined, designed and realised by such figures as Wren, Hawksmoor, Vanbrugh, Kent and Langley, albeit often in hybrid, Classical-Gothic forms. While it is clear that Strawberry Hill witnessed and attested to an evolution in the Gothic style, particularly in Walpole's later turn towards archaeological and antiquarian precision, it cannot be taken to represent the genesis of the Gothic Revival of the eighteenth century in its entirety.

---

76 H. S. [William Whitehead], 'Number 12. Thursday 22 March 1753', *The World*, pp. 67–72 (p. 68).

1.5
Horace Walpole and the Gothic

STEPHEN CLARKE

Walpole's 'little play-thing-house' at Strawberry Hill

The Gothic castle of Strawberry Hill created by Horace Walpole (1717–97) was an irregular confection of pinnacles, gables and ogee arches. It contained a succession of, mostly, moderately sized rooms with exotic chimneypieces and elaborate plasterwork, and those rooms housed a collection densely hung with portraits and miniatures, the surfaces rich in sculpture, porcelain, antiquities and curiosities. The pictures ranged from drawings by Jean and François Clouet, miniatures by Hans Holbein the Younger, and paintings by Peter Paul Rubens, Anthony Van Dyck and Joshua Reynolds to the works of 'female genius', the coterie of amateur artist friends whose productions Walpole loved to praise. Among those, on the walls of the Red Bedchamber, was 'A young lady reading the Castle of Otranto to her companion; a graceful and expressive drawing, done for a present to Mr. W. by Lavinia Bingham, eldest daughter of Lady Lucan the celebrated copyist.' At the other end of the house were displayed 'seven incomparable drawings of lady Diana Beauclerk for Mr. Walpole's tragedy of The Mysterious Mother', which shared a specially constructed hexagonal room a mere 8 feet across with nine other pictures, furniture, antiquities, porcelain, cameos, and a locket of the hair of Mary Tudor, Queen of France.[1]

---

1 Walpole's accounts of the drawings from *The Castle of Otranto* and *The Mysterious Mother* are from Horace Walpole, 'A Description of the Villa of Mr. Horace Walpole, at Strawberry-Hill Near Twickenham', in Horace Walpole, *The Works of Horatio Walpole, Earl of Orford*, 5 vols (London: Printed for G. G. and J. Robinson and J. Edwards, 1798) vol. 2, pp. 394–516 (pp. 438, 503). For the most detailed overview of Walpole's collection see Michael Snodin, with Cynthia Roman (eds), *Horace Walpole's Strawberry Hill* (New Haven and London: Yale University Press, 2009); and more recently Silvia Davoli, *Lost Treasures of Strawberry Hill: Masterpieces from Horace Walpole's Collection* (London: Scala, 2018). For Walpole and 'female genius' see Cynthia Roman, 'The Art of Lady Diana Beauclerk: Horace Walpole and Female Genius', in Snodin, with Roman (eds), *Horace Walpole's Strawberry Hill* pp. 155–69.

Horace Walpole and the Gothic

Thus Walpole celebrated his two Gothic fictions, *The Castle of Otranto* (published 24 December 1764; dated 1765) and his play *The Mysterious Mother* (1768), on the walls of the house that famously inspired the first of them, the house in which 'I waked one morning ... from a dream, of which, all I could recover was, that I had thought myself in an ancient castle (a very natural dream for a head filled like mine with Gothic story), and that on the uppermost bannister of a great staircase I saw a gigantic hand in armour.'[2] How closely that staircase can be identified with the stairs at Strawberry Hill has been much debated, though Walpole was clear that the idea of the picture walking out of its frame in *The Castle of Otranto* was suggested by his portrait of Henry Cary, Lord Falkland, dressed in white, which hung in the Gallery.[3] But what connects Walpole hailing Beauclerk's 'sublime drawings, the first histories she ever attempted ... all conceived and executed in a fortnight', the historical portraits such as that of Lord Falkland, the labyrinthine interiors of the house and the Gothic world that both house and fictions evoked, was Walpole's historically informed but archaeologically unrestrained imagination.

It has often been remarked that the Gothic style and small scale of Strawberry Hill reflected Walpole's position in relation to his father: letter-writer and sinecure-holder rather than prime minister, master of Strawberry Hill rather than of the Palladian palace of Houghton, collector of miniatures and historical English portraits rather than of Old Masters – though despite early antagonism, after his father's fall from power in 1742 and beyond his father's death in 1745, Walpole increasingly idolised him. But as a young man, brought up largely by his mother (who died when he was at Cambridge), Walpole was, in the words of his close friend and cousin Henry Seymour Conway, 'buried in romances and novels; I really believe you could have said all the *Grand Cyrus's*, the *Cleopatra's*, and the *Amadis's* in the world by heart, nay, you carried your taste for it so far that not a fairy tale escaped you'.[4] That taste he retained in his continuing admiration for Ludovico Ariosto's *Orlando Furioso* (1532) and Torquato Tasso's *La Gerusalemme liberata* (1581) and his love of Shakespeare, whom he

---

2 Horace Walpole to William Cole, 9 March 1765, in W. S. Lewis (ed.), *The Yale Edition of Horace Walpole's Correspondence*, 48 vols (New Haven and London: Yale University Press, 1937–83), vol. 1, p. 88. For a selection of Walpole's letters see Stephen Clarke (ed.), *Horace Walpole: Selected Letters* (New York, London and Toronto: Everyman's Library, 2017).
3 Walpole, *Works*, vol. 2, p. 466.
4 Henry Seymour Conway to Horace Walpole, 18 April 1745, *Correspondence*, vol. 37, p. 189.

championed against what he considered to be the irrelevant restrictions of seventeenth-century French neoclassicism.[5]

As a young man, having in September 1741 returned alone from the Grand Tour that he had commenced with the poet Thomas Gray, Walpole took his place in Parliament and in London society. In the summer of 1747, he rented from Mrs Chenevix Chopp'd Straw Hall, a tenement house near Twickenham that came with 5 acres of land, in a fashionable area and with a view of the Thames and Richmond Hill. Two years later, he acquired the freehold to the property, and the first major building campaign took place in 1752–4, with Walpole forming a 'Committee' with John Chute, talented amateur architect and owner of The Vyne in Hampshire, and Richard Bentley, wayward but original designer son of the great Classicist of the same name.[6] Walpole's choice of style was Gothic: as he announced to his correspondent Horace Mann in January 1750, 'I am going to build a little Gothic castle at Strawberry Hill.'[7] That choice was not in itself unduly radical. The journal *The World* in 1753 noted how 'A few years ago every thing was Gothic; our houses, our beds, our book-cases, and our couches, were all copied from some parts or other of our old cathedrals.'[8] Walpole's use of Gothic was initially decorative rather than structural, and in the early years owed more to the 'bastard Gothic' of designers such as Batty Langley and William Hallett than he might have cared to acknowledge.[9] But Chute's

---

5 See W. S. Lewis (ed.), *Notes by Horace Walpole on Several Characters of Shakespeare* (Farmington: privately printed, 1940), and Walpole's exchange of letters with Voltaire, *Correspondence*, vol. 41, pp. 146–59.
6 For Chute's architectural work see the entry in Howard Colvin, *A Biographical Dictionary of British Architects 1600–1840*, 4th edition (New Haven and London: Yale University Press, 2008); for Bentley see the entry in Colvin and see Loftus Jestin, *The Answer to the Lyre: Richard Bentley's Illustrations for Thomas Gray's Poems* (Philadelphia: University of Pennsylvania Press, 1990), pp. 83–130.
7 Horace Walpole to Horace Mann, 10 January 1750, *Correspondence*, vol. 20, p. 111.
8 H. S. [William Whitehead], 'Number 12. Thursday 22 March 1753', *The World*, pp. 67–72 (p. 68).
9 Horace Walpole to Richard Bentley, 5 July 1755, *Correspondence*, vol. 35, p. 233. For the architectural development of Strawberry Hill see Paget Jackson Toynbee, *Strawberry Hill Accounts: A Record of Expenditure in Building Furnishing, &c Kept by Mr Horace Walpole From 1747 to 1795* (Oxford: Clarendon Press, 1927); W. S. Lewis, 'The genesis of Strawberry Hill', *Metropolitan Museum Studies* 5:1 (June 1934): 57–92; Michael McCarthy, *The Origins of the Gothic Revival* (New Haven and London: Yale University Press, 1987), pp. 63–91; Peter Guillery and Michael Snodin, 'Strawberry Hill: building and site', *Architectural History* 38 (1995):102–28; Michael Snodin, 'Going to Strawberry Hill', and Kevin Rogers, 'Walpole's Gothic: Creating a Fictive History', both in Michael Snodin, with Cynthia Roman (eds), *Horace Walpole's Strawberry Hill*, pp. 14–73; Marion Harney, *Place-Making for the Imagination: Horace Walpole and Strawberry Hill* (Farnham: Ashgate, 2013); and Peter N. Lindfield, *Georgian Gothic: Medievalist Architecture, Furniture and Interiors, 1730–1840* (Woodbridge: Boydell and Brewer, 2016), pp. 145–61.

casing of the building in white-painted, parapet-topped walls punctuated with ogee-headed windows, and Bentley's design for the hall and main staircase at the rear and the Great Refectory and Library beyond the stairs, were between them wholly original as a heady mixture of fantasy and atmosphere. Walpole wrote in a note on the manipulation of light and colour in the interior of Strawberry Hill how striking was the gloom of the entrance hall (lit only by two lancet windows filled with stained glass), from which the staircase (which was top-lit) opened upwards to greater light.[10] The walls were stone-coloured, 'hung with gothic paper, painted by one Tudor, from the screen of prince Arthur's tomb in the cathedral of Worcester'.[11] The staircase was based loosely on a Jacobean form, with Walpole's armorial supporters of an antelope holding a shield on each of the newel posts, and with the balustrade copied by Bentley from a staircase at Rouen Cathedral. At night it was lit by a single candle in a stained glass lantern suspended from the ceiling; on a vaulted landing was an Armoury, a confection of plausible antique and Eastern armour arranged for scenic effect, an effect heightened when in 1771 Walpole acquired the parade armour that he believed had belonged to Francis I, and inserted it in a niche overlooking the stairs. It was, as Michael Snodin has written, pure theatre.[12]

Beyond the Armoury lies the Library that was added in 1754, with hinged Gothic bookcase arches rippling round the room (designed by Chute from the side doors of the screen of Old St. Paul's), an armorial ceiling of Walpolian genealogy, and a highly ornate chimneypiece incorporating elements from the tombs of John of Eltham at Westminster Abbey and the Duke of Clarence at Canterbury Cathedral. There was a late fifteenth-century painting that Walpole believed showed the marriage of Henry VI, 'stuck in a thicket of pinnacles' over the chimneypiece, together with stained glass, family portraits, miniatures, and the famous gilt metal clock bearing the arms and initials of Henry VIII and Anne Boleyn.[13] Beneath the Library, the Great Refectory was given by Bentley a fantastical chimneypiece that is Gothic to the extent that it employs crockets, niches and distorted quatrefoils, but is as wilful a play on Gothic as could be imagined. Yet otherwise the room was furnished (along with some Gothic chairs and a table also designed by Bentley) with sofas and family portraits.

10 MS13–1947, Fitzwilliam Museum, transcribed in Michael Snodin, with Cynthia Roman (eds), *Horace Walpole's Strawberry Hill*, p. 348.
11 Walpole, *Works*, vol. 2, p. 401.
12 Snodin, with Cynthia Roman (eds), *Horace Walpole's Strawberry Hill*, p. 34.
13 Horace Walpole to Richard Bentley, 19 December 1753, *Correspondence*, vol. 35, p. 158.

Further and more extensive building campaigns were to follow: in 1758–9 the Holbein Chamber, arguably the first museum room in England, which was a recreation of the Tudor Court; and in the early 1760s the major extension of The Gallery, the Oratory, and the Round Tower. The Gallery, part-Tudor Long Gallery and part-European Baroque *galerie*, was the largest and the most ornate room in the house, with fan vaulting copied from Henry VII's chapel and recesses along the walls taken from Archbishop Bourchier's tomb at Canterbury. Thomas Gray, writing to Thomas Warton, described it as 'all Gothicism, & gold, & crimson, & looking-glass', whereas Walpole revealed his engaged enthusiasm in a letter proposing a visit to Northamptonshire to see his correspondent George Montagu:

> I quit the Gallery almost in the critical minute of consummation. Gilders, carvers, upholsterers, and picture-cleaners are labouring at their several forges, and I do not love to trust a hammer or a brush without my own supervisal ... Well! but I begin to be ashamed of my magnificence; Strawberry is growing sumptuous in its latter day ...[14]

That sumptuousness extended to the Tribune (otherwise described by Walpole as the Chapel, or Cabinet), a Gothic vaulted square space with apsed projections in all four walls, a cross between a Cathedral chapter house and the Tribuna of the Uffizi Palace. It was protected by a grated door and reserved for the finest miniatures, small paintings, antiquities and precious objects. The Round Tower beyond the Gallery was, despite a Gothic ceiling based on the rose window of Old St Paul's and a scagliola chimneypiece adapted from the tomb of Edward the Confessor (both designed by Robert Adam), a more modern room with French seat furniture, a Boulle coffer and a widely spaced hang of paintings. The Great North Bedchamber, which followed in 1771, was part Gothic, with a chimneypiece copied from the tomb of William Dudley, Bishop of Durham, in Westminster Abbey, and part a recreation of a state bedchamber from an English country house, hung predominantly with English and French portraits of the seventeenth and eighteenth centuries.

It is not possible to more than hint at the variety of the interiors of Strawberry Hill, which served in part as a form of casket to display the riches of Walpole's extraordinary collection. But certain themes do emerge. First,

---

14 Thomas Gray to Thomas Warton, 5 August 1763, in Paget Toynbee and Leonard Whibley (eds), *Correspondence of Thomas Gray*, 3 vols (Oxford: Clarendon Press, 1935), vol. 2, p. 805; Horace Walpole to George Montagu, 1 July 1763, *Correspondence*, vol. 10, p. 84.

the building cannot be understood in isolation from the collection that it was designed to house. Second, the initial symmetrical Chute design, at least on the south front, was soon replaced by a series of irregular accretions that gave the impression of 'the castle (I am building) of my ancestors'.[15] Third, the use of medieval architectural precedents, however out of context (typically, the design of a tomb adapted to a chimneypiece), developed and matured as the building progressed. Fourth, there was a conscious manipulation of light and shade and scale to heighten visitors' experience, the house being accessible to visitors by ticket, and attracting during the period 1784 to 1796 covered by Walpole's 'Book of Visitors' an average of between sixty and one hundred parties a year.[16] Fifth, Walpole himself announced that 'I did not mean to make my house so Gothic as to exclude convenience, and modern refinements in luxury. The designs of the inside and outside are strictly ancient, but the decorations are modern.'[17] It is no coincidence that for all the copious illustrations of the interior of the house, not merely in the prints to the 1784 edition *of A Description of the Villa of Mr Horace Walpole* that Walpole wrote to record Strawberry Hill and his collection but also in the numerous watercolours and drawings commissioned by Walpole and his circle, there are no general views of any of the smaller and more private rooms, which contained bright, modern wallpaper and comfortable upholstered seat furniture.

Walpole and the Aesthetics of Association

What was the role of Gothic at Strawberry Hill? It was not just the Gothic detailing of the interiors that was insistent, but the dense and claustrophobic presentation of the collection – there were 670 pieces of china in the China Closet, a small room about 12 foot by 9 foot, and about 150 paintings and other items were displayed in the equally small space of the Green Closet immediately above it. These rooms had ogee-headed windows and heraldic chimneypieces, but were essentially collectors' cabinets. Gothic and the medieval sources for Walpole's designs provide an anecdotal thread throughout the building – not a chimneypiece or papier-maché ceiling without a story to tell. Similarly, many of the works of art were memorialised, like the

---

15 Horace Walpole to George Montagu, 11 June 1753, *Correspondence*, vol. 9, p. 149.
16 Walpole's Book of Visitors is printed in *Correspondence*, vol. 12, pp. 217–52. For an account of visitors' responses to the house and the evolution of Walpole's *Description* of Strawberry Hill, see Stephen Clarke, '"Lord God! Jesus! What a house!": describing and visiting Strawberry Hill,' *Journal for Eighteenth-Century Studies* 33:3 (September 2010): 357–80.
17 Walpole, *Works*, vol. 2, p. 397.

portrait by John Opie of Mary Delany, whose heavily carved frame was designed by Walpole to display and recount her virtues and accomplishments; or the china vase in which his cat had drowned, for which Walpole printed a label at the Strawberry Hill Press to record the fact that this was the very vase where pensive Selima had reclined, as immortalised by Gray's 'Ode on the Death of a Favourite Cat, Drowned in a Tub of Gold Fishes' (1748).

This is precisely the point made by Thomas Babington Macaulay in his famous *Edinburgh Review* article on Walpole of 1833, in which he claimed that 'In his villa, every apartment is a museum, every piece of furniture is a curiosity; there is something strange in the form of the shovel; there is a long story belonging to the bell-rope.'[18] What interested Walpole was anecdote, and the way that history and romance were interwoven. His house was full of portraits, as a real portrait 'calls up so many collateral ideas, as to fill an intelligent mind more than any other species'.[19] He saw history and romance as inevitably intertwined, and a number of times noted that 'History in general is a Romance that is believed, and that Romance is a History that is not believed.'[20] He found letters and memoirs more entertaining than other historical records ('nothing gives so just an idea of an age as genuine letters; nay, history waits for its last seal from them') and his love of story, and of the references and associations implicit in objects, applies to the Gothic detailing of Strawberry Hill as it does to the items in the collection that it housed.[21]

Marion Harney and others have written on Walpole's associationist aesthetic, his investing buildings and works of art with their own history, as if they were animated participants rather than inanimate relics.[22] One element of this is his fascination with provenance, the hands through which objects in his collection had passed. Another is his immersing himself imaginatively in the past, as in a summer evening in 1778 when, walking with his nieces in the gardens of Hampton Court, they joined a party, one of whom sang for the company.

---

18 Thomas Babington Macaulay, review of Walpole's letters to Horace Mann, *Edinburgh Review* 58 (October 1833): 227–58, reprinted in Peter Sabor (ed.), *Horace Walpole: The Critical Heritage* (London: Routledge & Kegan Paul, 1987), pp. 311–31 (p. 323).
19 John Pinkerton (ed.), *Walpoliana*, 2 vols (London, 1799), vol. 1, p. 26.
20 Horace Walpole to Robert Henry, 15 March 1783, *Correspondence*, vol. 15, p. 173.
21 Horace Walpole to Sir David Dalrymple, 30 November 1761, *Correspondence*, vol. 15, p. 73.
22 See in particular Harney, *Place-Making for the Imagination*; Stephen Clarke, 'Horace Walpole's Architectural Taste', in Peter Sabor (ed.), *Horace Walpole: Beyond the Castle of Otranto*, special feature in *1650–1850 Ideas, Æsthetics, and Inquiries in the Early Modern Era* 16 (2009): 223–44; and Dale Townshend, *Gothic Antiquity: History, Romance, and the Architectural Imagination, 1760–1840* (Oxford: Oxford University Press, 2019).

> It was moonlight and late, and very hot, and the lofty facade of the palace, and the trimmed yews and canal, made me fancy myself of a party in Grammont's time—so you don't wonder that by the help of imagination I never passed an evening more deliciously. When by the aid of some historic vision and local circumstance I can romance myself into pleasure, I know nothing transports me so much.[23]

Notable, here, is the fact that for Walpole's imagination to be engaged, the historical references did not have to be Gothic: despite his architectural preferences, the courts of the Renaissance and of Charles II or Louis XIV and their personalities held as much magic for him as the medieval past. His response to country houses was equally personal. He travelled in England in the summers of the 1750s and 1760s, visiting old houses as well as old churches, and recording detailed and evocative accounts in his correspondence and his Books of Materials.[24] For example, he wrote to Bentley of his visit to Welbeck Abbey: 'such a Gothic hall, with pendent fretwork in imitation of the old, and with a chimney-piece extremely like mine in the library! Such water-colour pictures! such historic fragments! In short, such and so much of everything I like, that my party thought they should never get me away again.'[25]

Walpole defined his imaginative and associational response to architecture as follows:

> If (which but few have) one has any partiality to old knights, crusadoes, the wars of York and Lancaster, &c., the prejudice in favour of Grecian buildings will be balanced ... I, who have great difficulty of not connecting every inanimate thing with the idea of some person, or of not affixing some idea of imaginary persons to whatever I should see, should prefer that building that furnished me with most ideas, which is not judging fairly of the merit of the buildings abstractedly. And for this reason, I believe, the gloom, ornaments, magic of the hardiness of the buildings, would please me more in the Gothic than the simplicity of the Grecian.[26]

---

23 Horace Walpole to Lady Ossory, 11 August 1778, *Correspondence*, vol. 33, p. 42.
24 The notes on country houses in the two Books of Materials dated 1759 and 1771 are published in Paget Jackson Toynbee, 'Horace Walpole's journals of visits to country seats &c.', *Walpole Society* 16 (1927–8): 8–80. The third Book of Materials of 1786–95 has been published as Lars E. Troide (ed.), *Horace Walpole's Miscellany, 1786–1795* (New Haven: Yale University Press, 1978). Further selections on the arts from the three Books of Materials are collected in F. W. Hilles and P. B. Daghlian (eds), *Anecdotes of Painting in England [1760–1795] With some Account of the Principal Artists; And incidental Notes on other Arts; Collected by Horace Walpole ... Volume the Fifth* (New Haven: Yale University Press, 1937).
25 Horace Walpole to Richard Bentley, August 1756, *Correspondence*, vol. 35, p. 271. See also Walpole's account of Drayton House, *Correspondence*, vol. 10, pp. 89–90.
26 F. W. Hilles and P. B. Daglian, *Anecdotes of Painting in England [1760–1795] Volume the Fifth*, pp. 158–9.

He expanded on the contrasting impact of Gothic and Classical architecture in an equally telling and much-quoted passage from his account of the 'State of Architecture to the end of the Reign of Henry VIII' in the first volume of his *Anecdotes of Painting* (1762):

> It is difficult for the noblest Grecian temple to convey half so many impressions to the mind, as a Cathedral does of the best Gothic taste—a proof of skill in the architects and of address in the priests who erected them. The latter exhausted their knowledge of the passions in composing edifices whose pomp, mechanism, vaults, tombs, painted windows, gloom and perspectives infused such sensations of romantic devotion; and they were happy in finding artists capable of executing such machinery. One must have taste to be sensible of the beauties of Grecian architecture; one only wants passions to feel Gothic.[27]

Both passages, well known as they are, remain rich in meaning. They are part of a tradition of comparisons of the imaginative effect of Gothic and Classical architecture that goes back to John Evelyn and Joseph Addison, and continues beyond Walpole to Sir John Soane – Evelyn and Addison claiming that imagination was far more satisfied by Classical than by Gothic buildings, while Soane, though a committed Classicist, reflected the changing sensibility of the late eighteenth century in acknowledging how Gothic cathedrals and churches were 'so well calculated to excite solemn, serious, and contemplative ideas, that it is almost impossible to enter such edifices without feeling the deepest awe and reverence'.[28] Walpole's aesthetic response was the reverse of that of Evelyn and Addison, both a reflection of their respective frames of reference – though for Walpole, engagement with the Gothic co-existed with an untroubled acknowledgement of the majesty and decorum of Classical architecture, with buildings such as Henry Holland's Carlton House and James Wyatt's Pantheon, London, receiving his unqualified praise. For all his enjoyment of Gothic, he did not accept the theory of Archibald Alison that beauty and sublimity in objects were inevitably filtered through the viewer's imagination rather than being innate, claiming that that was to confuse '*the effects* of taste for *the principles of* taste'.[29]

---

27 Horace Walpole, *Anecdotes of Painting in England*, 4 vols (Strawberry Hill: Printed by Thomas Farmer, 1762–71 [i.e. 1780]), vol. I, pp. 107–8.
28 William Upcott (ed.), *The Miscellaneous Writings of John Evelyn, Esq. F.R.S* (London, 1825), p. 366; *The Spectator* 415 (26 June 1712); John Soane, *Plans, Elevations and Sections of Buildings* (London, 1788), p. 9.
29 See Clarke, 'Horace Walpole's Architectural Taste', pp. 239–44, and Walpole's letter to Mrs. Archibald Alison, 18 February 1790, *Correspondence*, vol. 42, p. 273.

For Walpole, taste remained paramount: he was not antiquary enough to have any interest in the rude origins of art. As he acknowledged to William Cole, 'I know I am but a fragment of an antiquary, for I abhor all Saxon doings, and whatever did not exhibit some taste, grace or elegance, and some ability in the artists.'[30] He contrasted the 'peculiar ugliness' of Saxon and Norman building with Gothic architecture, which he described in contrast as 'a species of modern elegance'. What he thought of as Saxon churches that were 'so dark, so ugly, so uncouth' did not inspire him with visions of a storied medieval past, unlike the grace and taste that he saw in the Gothic, whose buildings he tellingly described as 'magnificent, yet genteel, vast, yet light, venerable and picturesque' – gentility being surely the quality of some of the historical figures whom he could imagine using those buildings.[31] It is consistent with the biographical concept of his *Anecdotes of Painting in England* (1762–71) that his account of Gothic architecture should consist of a lament that the names of medieval architects are largely unknown. There is hardly any historical stylistic analysis: at Gloucester Cathedral, for example, he explained away the contrast between the Norman nave and Perpendicular exterior in the phrase, 'The outside of the cathedral is beautifully light; the pillars in the nave outrageously plump and heavy.'[32] His overall view of Gothic architecture, judging from 'the delicacy, lightness, and taste of it's [sic] ornaments', was that it reached its perfection about the reign of Henry IV (1399–1413), before being corrupted with ill-understood elements of Classical architecture that resulted in the bastardised and confused mixture of styles and the 'mungrel species' of Jacobean architecture.[33] When he was asked by Cole to advise the Cambridge architect and antiquary James Essex on the preparation of a history of Gothic architecture, his analysis was little more detailed, though he did recommend that Essex should study stylistic development as well as considering building methods and costs.[34] There is a clear contrast here between Walpole, who loved Gothic for its decorative profusion and allusive richness, and the researches of Gray and Thomas Warton, who filled the pages of their respective commonplace books with descriptions and analysis and chronology of the cathedrals and churches they had studied.[35]

---

30 Horace Walpole to William Cole, 15 February 1782, *Correspondence*, vol. 2, p. 301.
31 Walpole, *Anecdotes of Painting*, vol. 1, pp. 106–7.
32 Walpole to Richard Bentley, September 1753, *Correspondence*, vol. 35, p. 153.
33 Walpole, *Anecdotes of Painting*, vol. 1, pp. 113, 114.
34 Horace Walpole to William Cole, 11 August 1769, *Correspondence*, vol. 1, pp. 190–2.
35 Barrett Kalter, 'DIY gothic: Thomas Gray and the medieval revival', *ELH* 70:4 (2003): 989–1019 (pp. 999–1000); and Winchester College, Fellows' Library, Warton Papers, *Itinerarium* and *Observations*, being twelve notebooks, call no. MS 109, Shelf 12–5.

Returning to the two quotations above in which Walpole compared Gothic and Classical architecture, the first passage speaks of animating Gothic buildings with his ideas of people, and the magic inherent in them; the second refers to priests who used their knowledge of the passions in designing buildings to create sensations of romantic devotion; both introduce the concept of gloom. And priests, animated buildings, the exercise of passion and imagination, the presence of magic and the prevalence of gloom are all qualities that permeate Walpole's Gothic fictions.

Gothic Fictions and Gothic Excess

The Castle of Otranto was published on Christmas Eve 1764 by Thomas Lowndes. Walpole's fear of ridicule was such that the book was published 'not boldly with my own name', as he explained to Cole, but under the conceit of its having been translated from a copy of an Italian text, printed in Naples in 1529, that had been 'found in the library of an ancient catholic family in the north of England'.[36] The Preface to the first edition is a delightful exercise in parody, enriched by Walpole's own considerable attainments as an antiquary, the author of a seminal work of art history in the *Anecdotes of Painting* and editor of miscellaneous antiquarian tracts.[37] In the guise of translator he speculates on the date and circumstances of the original composition, laments the shortcomings of the translation, and even offers, if encouraged, to publish the 'original' Italian text.

Within four months a second edition was called for and, assured of the success of his experiment, Walpole adjusted the title, replacing the claim that the story was translated with the simple subtitle 'A Gothic Story.' He provided a new Preface, acknowledging his authorship, and explaining his intentions, namely 'to blend the two kinds of romance, the ancient and the modern' and to make his characters 'think, speak and act, as it might be supposed mere men and women would do in extraordinary positions'. He used Shakespeare as his model when justifying his use of humour and incomprehension among the servants (Nick Groom has commented that

---

36 Horace Walpole to William Cole, 28 February 1765, *Correspondence*, vol. 1, p. 85; Walpole, *The Castle of Otranto*, edited by Nick Groom (Oxford: Oxford University Press, 2014), p. 5.

37 For Walpole as antiquary, see W. S. Lewis, 'Horace Walpole, Antiquary', in Richard Pares and A. J. P. Taylor (eds), *Essays Presented to Sir Lewis Namier* (London: Macmillan & Co., 1956), pp. 178–203.

'*Otranto* is drenched in Shakepearean allusion') and challenged Voltaire in his criticism of Shakespeare for these assumed faults.[38]

We do not know how many of *The Castle of Otranto*'s earliest readers had been misled by Walpole's deception. The *Monthly Review*'s account of the first edition was written 'on the supposition that the work really is a translation, as pretended', and then complained of the second edition that although it had been dubious of the antiquity of the work, 'While we considered it [a translation] we could readily excuse its preposterous phenomena, and consider them as sacrifices to a gross and unenlightened age.' The *Critical Review* had described the first edition as 'very curious', adding that it was unclear 'whether [the translator] speaks seriously or ironically'), but complained strongly of the supernatural absurdities of the story.[39]

Among Walpole's friends, only William Mason admitted to having been deceived, though the modern cast of the dialogue was pointed out to him by a friend to whom he had recommended the book.[40] Certainly for modern readers, the flowing dialogue, free indirect speech, psychological awareness and tender exchanges of female sympathies are transparently modern, but part of the problem of understanding *Otranto's* contemporary reception is the difficulty in stripping away the awareness of the succeeding 250 years of Gothic fiction – as challenging as it is for readers of Laurence Sterne's *A Sentimental Journey* (1768) to block out the tidal wave of sensibility that followed in that novel's wake. It is interesting that, despite having claimed to have discovered a text of medieval origins, Walpole, on drawing aside the veil and revealing his authorship, attracted none of the opprobrium of the forgers James Macpherson or Thomas Chatterton. His deception, not undertaken for gain and promptly acknowledged, had no effect on the novel's success, and seems no more to have offended the public than the fact that contemporary epistolary novels were not made up of real letters.

Offending the public was also a concern with Walpole's other major piece of Gothic writing, the tragedy of *The Mysterious Mother* (1768). In his Postscript to the play he claimed that 'From the time that I first undertook the foregoing scenes, I never flattered myself that they would be proper to appear on the stage', and the well-known shocked response of Frances Burney ('Dreadful was the whole! Truly dreadful!') when she read it at Court in 1786, claiming to

---

38 Walpole, *The Castle of Otranto*, p. xxvi.
39 *Monthly Review* 32 (February 1765): 97–99, and *Monthly Review* 32 (May 1765): 394; *Critical Review* 19 (January 1765): 50–51; all reprinted in Sabor, *Horace Walpole: The Critical Heritage*, pp. 68–72.
40 William Mason to Horace Walpole, 14 April 1765, *Correspondence*, vol. 28, p. 5.

feel ill-used in being exposed to it, bore out his concerns.[41] Incest is central to both tales: in *Otranto*, the parent–adoptive-child incest plotted by Manfred, Prince of Otranto, in his desperate quest for a plausible male heir to preserve his House, and in *The Mysterious Mother* the double incest by which the Countess of Narbonne knowingly seduces her own son, only to find that he, in due course, has married the innocent fruit of their unlawful union. Walpole explained in his Postscript to *The Mysterious Mother* that his intention was to display the tragedy as it operated the essential springs of Terror and Pity, and the central figure in this regard is the Countess, locked in a life of prayer and charity and contrition, but never relieved from the full horror of her guilt. It is telling that Walpole politely acknowledged but firmly rejected the amendments proposed by Mason, which in a few lines would have made the Countess's incest with her son inadvertent rather than intentional, and so mollified her crime as to make the play capable of public performance.[42] Walpole realised that the play was more effective as an unactable closet drama that concentrated on the Countess's unbearable burden of guilt.

The Countess is as compelling as Manfred, the tyrant of *Otranto* driven by the need to avert the doom awaiting his family for the usurpation committed by his grandfather. Walpole's other main female characters in the novel and the play are studies in piety and duty – Manfred's long-suffering wife Hippolita and daughter Matilda in *Otranto*, and the Countess's ward / daughter Adeliza in *The Mysterious Mother*. Only Isabella, the object of Manfred's dynastic lust in *Otranto*, has glimpses of personality: otherwise her role is that of Gothic fiction's first trapped and hunted female victim, desperately seeking through gloomy subterranean passages and vaults to evade the gross designs of her male aggressor. The modern reader may find their suspension of disbelief challenged by the deferential unquestioned obedience and propriety of the female characters, while the young men, as innocent and as wooden as the daughters of the household they aspire to, are marked by a sense of exquisite decorum: the hero Theodore in *Otranto*, for example, then in the guise of a peasant, has lines such as 'I fear no man's displeasure … when a woman in distress puts herself under my protection', and when arbitrarily and unjustly condemned to death because of the inadvertent error of his father, declares to him 'let me die a thousand deaths, rather than stain thy conscience'.[43] Such expressions, along with the exchanges of sentiment

---

41 Walpole, *Works*, vol. 1, p. 125; Peter Sabor (ed.), *The Court Journals and Letters of Frances Burney, Volume I* (Oxford: Clarendon Press, 2011), pp. 267–71.
42 See *Correspondence*, vol. 28, pp. 9–17 and 445; and vol. 35, p. 493.
43 Walpole, *The Castle of Otranto*, pp. 50, 54.

between Matilda, Isabella and Hippolita, can distance the modern reader from the raw shock of the novel's supernatural interventions and overpowering setting.

It has been often remarked that the setting of *The Castle of Otranto*, the fortified building itself, is in some respects more animated than the characters, and that 'the buildings seem to acquire a personality ... of their own'.[44] That animation is the manifestation of the supernatural, which is essential to the plot development of the novel. Throughout its course, the doomed fate of Manfred's line is intimated by a succession of miraculous events – the enormous helmet that crushes his son, the giant armour-clad leg and foot glimpsed by two servants, the huge armoured hand on the banister of the great stair, the portrait that walks from its frame, the statue that drops blood when Manfred discloses his perfidious designs and the ghostly skeleton that upbraids Count Frederic for his unwonted desires for Matilda. As Devendra Varma noted many years ago, 'There is hardly a feature of Gothic romance that was not employed by Walpole in *The Castle of Otranto*.'[45] The oppressive atmosphere of gloom and horror, the creative use of darkness, the tyrannical father figure, the pursued and bartered virgin, the vaults and trapdoors, the pall of unnamed crime and the shock of the supernatural, all emerge, like the phoenix, fully formed in Walpole's Gothic story.

The miraculous is merged with the magnificent when Count Frederic first enters the castle with his train, in a passage that displays the flamboyance of Walpole's Gothic imagination. He lovingly describes the cavalcade of harbingers, heralds, footguards, horsemen, footmen, knights, squires, and supporting gentlemen and pages, precisely numbering an improbable 470 of them. One hundred of the gentlemen carry the enormous sword whose burial place had been revealed to Frederic by a dying hermit in the Holy Land, the sword then jumping from their hands to lie by the giant helmet that had crushed the hapless Conrad. The colour and animation, the chivalric and heraldic splendour of the scene was captured for Walpole in a large watercolour entitled *The Entry of Frederick [sic] into the Castle of Otranto* by John Carter, the architect and architectural draftsman. Carter was a polemicist for the preservation of Gothic architecture in the *Gentleman's Magazine*, and an

---

44 Montague Summers (ed.), *The Castle of Otranto and The Mysterious Mother* (London: Constable, 1924), pp. xix–xxi.
45 Devendra P. Varma, *The Gothic Flame: Being a History of the Gothic Novel in England* (London: Arthur Baker Ltd, 1957), p. 57.

artist who worked for Walpole at Strawberry Hill.[46] Peter N. Lindfield has explained how Carter used this picture to present an animated fantasia of medieval pageantry, crowded with incident (Fig.5.1).[47] The grandiose architectural setting for the scene bears no relation to the generally spare description of the Castle that the novel affords, Lindfield noting elements of Bath Abbey and of the Cathedral and the Gothic cross at Winchester. It is a riot of imaginative excess, a stage set for a theatrical spectacle, and in hanging it in the modest setting of the Little Parlour at Strawberry Hill, Walpole underlined the gulf that separated the visionary creation of Otranto and the more modest reality of his own house.

Carter also produced a second watercolour from the novel, *The Death of Matilda*, recording the moment where Manfred realises that he has stabbed to death his own daughter (Fig.5.2). The setting of a magnificent Cathedral choir with apse, rich with chantry chapels, carved stonework and ornate church furnishings, reflects Walpole's love of Gothic decoration and includes, as Lindfield has noted, repeated use of Walpole's own coat of arms. The impact of the tragic moment is all but lost in the sumptuous, almost erotic celebration of Gothic excess.

The sexual charge inherent in Gothic, the deep and often forbidden emotions that Gothic fiction explores, and what would now be described as the queer milieu out of which Walpole both designed his house and devised his Gothic fictions, have from the late twentieth century been the subject of exhaustive scholarly enquiry. George Haggerty quotes Walpole's description of Isabella's flight through the dark subterranean passage that linked the castle to the sanctuary of the church of St Nicholas:

> The lower part of the castle was hollowed into several intricate cloisters; and it was not easy for one under so much anxiety to find the door that opened into the cavern. An awful silence reigned throughout those subterraneous regions, except now and then some blasts of wind that shook the doors she had passed, and which grating on the rusty hinges were re-echoed through that long labyrinth of darkness.

Haggerty notes that 'In a single image [Walpole] combines the sexual anxiety of a victimized female, the incestuous desire of a libidinous male, the use of the actual physical features of the castle to represent political and sexual

---

46 For Carter see J. Mordaunt Crook, *John Carter and the Mind of the Gothic Revival* (London: The Society of Antiquaries of London, 1995).

47 Peter N. Lindfield, 'Heraldry and the architectural imagination: John Carter's visualisation of *The Castle of Otranto*', *The Antiquaries Journal* 96 (2016): 291–313.

Fig.5.1: John Carter, *The Entry of Prince Frederick [sic] into the Castle of Otranto* (1790). Courtesy of the Lewis Walpole Library, Yale University, lwlpr15827.

entrapment, and an atmosphere deftly rendered to produce terror and gloom.'[48] The overpowering sense is of the fear engendered by the threat of patriarchal sexual aggression, and the driver for that aggression is the preservation of insecurely held property rights. As E. J. Clery has

---

48 George E. Haggerty, *Queer Gothic* (Urbana and Chicago: University of Illinois Press, 2006), p. 22.

Fig.5.2: John Carter, Unpublished illustration of 'The Death of Matilda' from Horace Walpole's *The Castle of Otranto* (1791). RIBA Collections.

commented, in *Otranto* as in *Macbeth*, the function of the supernatural is to reassert rights to property and succession.[49]

Unlike *Otranto*, *The Mysterious Mother* does not depend upon the supernatural to drive the action. The defaced cross erected by the Countess to her

49 E. J. Clery, *The Rise of Supernatural Fiction, 1762–1800* (Cambridge: Cambridge University Press, 1995), p.72.

dead husband has been struck by lightning, and the deep-toned voice 'Forbear' that disturbs the plotting friars in Act 4, scene 1 turns out to come from a procession of chanting friars. But the succession to the lands and estate of Narbonne is the underlying thread to the story, and the Countess's unnatural sin fatally compromises that succession, with the fruit of her guilt being realised when her son and heir Edmund declares in the last speech of the play his determination to abandon Narbonne and seek death and oblivion in the wars. The play uses its Gothic setting of medieval France to provide an atmosphere of threat and unease, opening as it does with the lines 'What awful silence! how these antique towers / And vacant courts, dull the suspended soul, / Till expectation wears the cast of fear', and introducing what was to become the stock Gothic figures of scheming friars, providing an odour of anti-Catholicism to the mystery of the Countess's nameless crime. But it should be remembered that Walpole's own response to Catholicism was nothing if not nuanced. As he wrote to Cole, 'I like Popery, as well as you do, and have shown I do. I like it as I do chivalry and romance. They all furnish one with ideas and visions ... A Gothic church or convent fill one with romantic dreams.'[50]

Neither the novel nor the play portray overt homosexual desire, but much work has been done on the elements of transgressive sexuality that underlie them and inform the flood of Gothic fiction that followed.[51] Walpole's fictions are only the starting point of a genre rich with innuendo, laced with the unsettling and the suggestive: but they also spring, and are celebrated by Walpole as springing, from the Gothic soil of Strawberry Hill.

Alongside the formal architectural accounts of the design of the house noted at the beginning of this chapter, there is a considerable critical literature on Walpole's own sexual orientation, and the sexual narratives implicit in his house and collection. Walpole enjoyed conflating his roles as a private gentleman, while also portraying his house as 'the fantastic fabric ... a very proper habitation of, as it was the scene that inspired, the author of the Castle of Otranto'.[52] As he wrote playfully to Lady Ossory in 1771, having just acquired from the Crozat collection the armour he believed had belonged to Francis I:

50 Horace Walpole to William Cole, 12 July 1778, *Correspondence*, vol. 2, p. 100.
51 Jill Campbell, '"I am no giant": Horace Walpole, heterosexual incest, and love among men', *Eighteenth Century* 39:3 (1998): 238–60; Haggerty, *Queer Gothic*; and William Hughes and Andrew Smith (eds), *Queering the Gothic* (Manchester: Manchester University Press, 2009).
52 Walpole, *Works*, vol. 2, p. 398.

the armour ... is actually here, and in its niche, which I have had made for it on the staircase; and a very little stretch of the imagination will give it all the visionary dignity of the gigantic hand in armour that I dreamt of seeing on the balustrade of the staircase of Otranto. If this is not realizing one's dreams, I don't know what is.[53]

It is significant that Walpole refers here to the staircase of Otranto, not of Strawberry Hill. Having claimed, among the snares laid for the readers in the Preface to the first edition, that 'The scene is undoubtedly laid in some real castle' and that there are 'strong presumptions that the author had some certain building in his eye', he would in later years refer to himself as 'the Abbot of Strawberry' and playfully on one occasion as the master of a castle whose office holders included a senechal.[54] W. S. Lewis influenced a generation of scholars in identifying Strawberry Hill with the Castle of Otranto, claiming that 'It is something more than a cliché of criticism to say that the Castle of Otranto and Strawberry Hill are one and the same.'[55] But Walpole acknowledged that Trinity College, Cambridge, also contributed to his castle setting, and simply to conflate his house and the scene of his novel is to oversimplify the richness of his imaginative vision, of which both are related but differing expressions.[56] As Dale Townshend has argued compellingly, Strawberry Hill, with its fluid references to castle and to abbey, and Otranto, the castle with its adjoining great church or cathedral of St Nicholas, are imaginatively related but architecturally distinct.[57]

What they share in common, nonetheless, is a richness of allusion, a sense of imaginative surfeit. Carter catches this in his two Otranto watercolours, in which the sparse architectural description of castle and church in the novel is supplanted by an impossibly rich fantasy of architectural decoration, an orgy of crockets and carved statues and niches. A recurrent response to Strawberry Hill was that of claustrophobic satiety. The novelist Sydney Owenson, Lady Morgan, visiting the house after Walpole's death but before the sale of the collection in 1842, described how, having toured the rooms crowded with works of art, 'attention is exhausted, eyes are dazzled, and expectation

---

53 Horace Walpole to Lady Ossory, 4 December 1771, *Correspondence*, vol. 32, p. 66.
54 Horace Walpole to George Montagu, 18 June 1764, *Correspondence*, vol. 10, p. 127; and 'The Master of Otranto to the Fairy Blandina', verses by Walpole printed at the Strawberry Hill Press, 1772, as cited in Allen T. Hazen, *A Bibliography of the Strawberry Hill Press* (New Haven: Yale University Press, 1942), pp. 204–8.
55 Lewis, 'The genesis of Strawberry Hill', p. 90.
56 Walpole to Mme. du Deffand, 27 January 1775, *Correspondence*, vol. 6, p. 145; and Harney, *Place-Making for the Imagination*, p. 110.
57 Townshend, *Gothic Antiquity*, pp. 89–130.

satiated ... and it is with a pleasure unspeakable, that one passes ... into the refreshing grounds and gardens'.[58] The idea of Walpole realising his dreams can be seen not only in the densely dressed interiors of the house, but in his use of them as stage set for social events, such as the Watteauesque *fêtes champêtres* he mounted for French and other aristocratic visitors in 1764 and again in 1769. At the former, there was a pastoral idyll of syllabub, milked from cows on the terrace before the house; at the latter, Walpole flamboyantly welcomed his guests 'dressed in the cravat of Gibbins's carving, and a pair of gloves embroidered up to the elbows that had belonged to James I'. At both, there were complementary verses fresh from the Strawberry Hill Press, a hidden band of French horns and clarinets playing at appropriate moments, and a wholly theatrical ambience.[59] The mind that designed these entertainments was the same mind that devised the climax to *The Castle of Otranto*, in which the giant ghost of Alfonso, having destroyed the walls of the castle and announced the restoration of the true heir, to the accompaniment of a clap of thunder 'ascended solemnly towards heaven, where the clouds parting asunder, the form of Saint Nicholas was seen; and receiving Alfonso's shade, they were soon wrapt from mortal eyes in a blaze of glory'.[60]

Haggerty has written extensively on the homosocial setting of Strawberry Hill and of Walpole's friendship circle, challenging Lewis's somewhat sanitised version of Walpole, while Matthew M. Reeve has written insightfully on the queer implications both of Walpole's house and his fiction.[61] Any assessment of Walpole that ignores these elements is inevitably partial, but while they may enrich, they should not restrict our view of Walpole and the Gothic. Inevitably, he himself wrote the most eloquent exposition of his imaginative and creative drive. In a passage that evolves out of a fantasy of his friend Montagu as Robin

---

58 'Strawberry Hill.—By Lady Morgan', *New Monthly Magazine* 17 (August 1826): 121–8, and September 1826, pp. 256–67 (p. 266).
59 Horace Walpole to George Montagu, 18 June 1764 and 11 May 1769, *Correspondence*, vol. 10, pp. 126–7 and 277–80.
60 Walpole, *The Castle of Otranto*, p. 103.
61 George E. Haggerty, 'Walpoliana', *Eighteenth-Century Studies* 34:2 (Winter 2001): 227–49; 'Queering Horace Walpole', *Studies in English Literature, 1500–1900* 46:3 (Summer 2006): 543–62; *Horace Walpole's Letters: Masculinity and Friendship in the Eighteenth Century* (Lewisburg: Bucknell University Press, 2011); and *Queer Gothic*, particularly chapters 2 and 4; Matthew M. Reeve, 'Gothic architecture, sexuality, and license at Horace Walpole's Strawberry Hill', *Art Bulletin* 95:3 (September 2013): 411–39; and '"A Gothic Vatican of Greece and Rome"': Horace Walpole, Strawberry Hill, and the Narratives of Gothic', in Matthew M. Reeve (ed.), *Tributes to Pierre du Prey: Architecture and the Classic Tradition from Pliny to Posterity* (London: Harvey Miller Publishers, 2014), pp. 185–209.

Hood, 'in a green frock with your rosy hue, grey locks and comely belly', he wrote:

> Visions, you know, have always been my pasture; and so far from growing old enough to quarrel with their emptiness, I almost think there is no wisdom comparable to that of exchanging what is called the realities of life for dreams. Old castles, old pictures, old histories, and the babble of old people make one live back into centuries that cannot disappoint one. One holds fast and surely what is past.

The passage is as familiar as it is revealing, epitomising as it does Walpole's intuitively imaginative response to Gothic and to history. It has often been quoted, but less often quoted is the concluding sentence of the paragraph in which it appears: 'I don't know but the idea may produce some other *Castle of Otranto*.'[62]

---

[62] Horace Walpole to George Montagu, 5 January 1766, *Correspondence*, vol. 10, p. 192.

1.6
Shakespeare's Gothic Transmigrations

ANNE WILLIAMS

'Transmigration' in contemporary usage usually refers to what Pythagoras called 'metempsychosis', the passage at death of the soul into another body.[1] The *OED* cites this meaning for the first time in 1594. Surprisingly, however, the word appears in English as early as 1297, as an obsolete term for physical movement, 'The removal of the Jews into captivity at Babylon.' By the sixteenth century, the *OED* continues, it had become more generally used to describe 'Passage or removal from one place to another, especially from one country to another.' 'I ... know her To be a woman-Woolfe by transmigration', writes John Fletcher in *The Woman's Prize* in 1524, and in 1643 Sir Thomas Browne refers in *Religio Medici* to 'Those strange and mysticall transmigrations that I have observed in Silkworms', presumably referring to the stages that transform the insect into a creature that is capable of spinning silk thread. Evidence of 'transmigration' may thus be visible or merely implicit.

This word's double meaning suggests a useful metaphor for Shakespeare's multifaceted presence in British culture from the Restoration of 1660 to 1765, when Horace Walpole published the second edition of *The Castle of Otranto* with its notorious subtitle, *A Gothic Story*. During these years, the playwright's presence became increasingly public and material, as the statue erected in the Poet's Corner in Westminster Abbey in 1741 attests. But many different aspects of Shakespeare were to be reincarnated in the burgeoning body of 'Gothic' writings published between 1765 and approximately 1830, by which time Walpole's original fantasy of a castle haunted by family secrets had become all too familiar a trope. Following his example, authors

---

[1] I dedicate this essay to the memory of Christy Desmet, my colleague and friend for more than three decades. We were to co-author it, but, before we had begun, Christy died in July 2019. I hope she would have been pleased, though all the mistakes are, of course, my own.

began to tell new stories suggested by this new locus of human horrors and in inventing a new species of romance, Walpole claimed to be Shakespearean: 'to shelter my own daring under the canon of the brightest genius this country, at least, has produced'.[2] By 1765, this claim could qualify as something of a cliché – and the reader should beware of taking Horace at his word in his Prefaces to the first and second editions of *Otranto*. But this new species of romance – what we now call Gothic romance – is predetermined, overdetermined, even *haunted* by Shakespeare. The chapter to follow explores Horace Walpole's enduring fascination and imaginative engagement with 'the brightest genius of this country'. While Ann Radcliffe became the author later known as 'the Shakspear [sic] of Romance writers', this chapter examines Walpole's transmigration of the Bard through his unique figurations of his works through plotlines, scenes and names.[3]

Horace Walpole's Patron Saint

Michael Dobson's *The Making of the National Poet: Shakespeare, Adaptation, and Authorship, 1660–1769* (1992) has traced the playwright's growing cultural presence and prestige after the Restoration of the monarchy. Dobson argues that 'Shakespeare' as he evolved from the Restoration to Garrick's Jubilee in 1769 was essentially 'a construction of the Restoration and eighteenth century, a ghost raised by the dubious powers of nascent capitalism ... and pressed into the national consciousness as the (literally) authoritarian father of a problematically wanton body of texts'.[4] In public discourse, Shakespeare was increasingly seen as a secular saint. His works had, after all, effectively died when the Puritans closed the theatres in 1642, making him a symbolic martyr to religious fanaticism.

With the Restoration, however, the once dead author miraculously rose again. As Gary Taylor suggests, part of Shakespeare's immediate prominence was due to the fact that the theatres, reopened in 1660, now needed plays, and there were very few playwrights to provide the scripts, which had once

---

2 Horace Walpole, *The Castle of Otranto and The Mysterious Mother*, edited by Frederick S. Frank (Peterborough, Ont.: Broadview Press, 2003), p. 70. All further references to both *The Castle of Otranto* and *The Mysterious Mother* are taken from this edition, with citations from the play indicated in the text by act, scene and line numbers.
3 See Nathan Drake, *Literary Hours; or, Sketches Critical and Narrative* (London, 1798), p. 249.
4 Michael Dobson, *The Making of the National Poet: Shakespeare, Adaptation, and Authorship, 1660–1769* (Oxford: Clarendon Press, 1992), p. 1.

largely been treated as highly disposable.[5] Furthermore, the incipient saint had left relics, including the various quartos and the First Folio of 1623, but like many such relics they were ambiguous and subject to interpretation. Joseph P. Hart, a nineteenth-century sceptic, imagined the first step towards sanctification as follows: 'Betterton the player, and Rowe the writer, made a selection from a promiscuous heap of plays found in a garret, nameless as to authorship ... "I want an author for this collection of plays!" said Rowe. "I have it" said Betterton; "call them Shakespeare's!"'[6] Like many a Gothic novel, including Walpole's own, 'Shakespeare's' history begins with 'found' texts.

As 'relics', Shakespeare's plays facilitated his increasingly material presence on the stage and in print. Rowe published the first attempt at a scholarly edition in 1709, which included his dubious biographical fantasy about the young poet as a wild boy poaching deer; as hagiography has long taught us, after all, the lives of saints are prone to accruing legends. Despite the impressive scholarship of critics such as Samuel Schoenbaum and Stephen Greenblatt, we have, even today, very few concrete clues to the poet's youthful self. Rowe's edition was followed by those of Alexander Pope (1725), Lewis Theobald (1733), William Warburton (1747) and Samuel Johnson (1765). All but the last of these would have been available to Walpole before he conceived *Otranto*, and as Walpole's tribute to Shakespearean authority in the second Preface to the novel implies, throughout the eighteenth century a growing number of English literary critics deemed the writer whom Elizabeth Montagu dubbed the 'Gothic Bard' worthy of their attention, including John Dryden, John Dennis, Joseph Addison, Pope and Johnson.

David Garrick's Jubilee at Stratford in 1769 consummated Shakespeare's canonisation as the supreme English author. The three-day celebration (6–8 September) included music composed specifically for the occasion, a masquerade ball, a parade of Shakespearean characters and Garrick's declamation of his 'Ode on Shakespeare'.[7] Though hampered by torrential rains and ironically involving no actual performances of any plays, the Jubilee was sensationally a commercial boon for Stratford. Food, lodging and souvenir trinkets were sold at extortionate rates. The mulberry tree that had supposedly grown near the

---

5 Gary Taylor, *Reinventing Shakespeare: A Cultural History from the Restoration to the Present* (Oxford: Oxford University Press, 1989), p. 16.
6 Quoted in Dobson, *National Poet*, p. 1.
7 Andrew McConnell Stott, *What Blest Genius? The Jubilee that Made Shakespeare*, 2nd edition (New York: W.W. Norton, 2019), p. 131.

church in Shakespeare's time had been felled in 1756, and most of its timber sold. Thomas Sharp had bought part of it for firewood, but retained a portion, which he began to sell as relics, 'earning at least three hundred pounds by turning out chairs, toothpick and needle cases, ladles, nutmeg graters, and other kinds of Birmingham-inspired toy works'.[8] There were as many souvenirs purporting to be fragments of Stratford's mulberry tree as medieval splinters of the True Cross. The most startling episode in the affair occurred when 'Lord Grosvenor reverentially raised a mulberry cup, treating the "blest relic" as if were a chalice filled with communion wine.'[9]

The climax of the festival, however, was Garrick's declamation of his 'Ode', accompanied by the orchestra:

> Who Avon's flow'ry margin trod,
> While sportive *Fancy* round him flew,
> Where *Nature* led him by the hand,
> Instructed him in all she knew,
> And gave him absolute command!
> 'Tis he! 'Tis he!
> 'The god of our idolatry!'[10]

Garrick's canonisation ceremony even included a devil's advocate. As the music continued to play, Garrick asked, 'Now, Ladies and Gentlemen will you be pleased to say anything *for* or *against* Shakespeare?' As Andrew McConnell Stott continues,

> a ... man stood up, taking off his great coat to reveal a blue suit embroidered with silver frogs (an audaciously Parisian style), he approached the orchestra and began to complain that Shakespeare was an ill-bred, vulgar author ... He accused Shakespeare of being a debaucher of minds, when, he said, 'the chief excellence of man, and the most refined sensation was to be devoured by ennui, and only live in a state of insensible vegetation!'[11]

But the joke fell flat, for the audience began to realise that the man parodying the anti-Shakespearean French critic Voltaire was Tom King, a Drury Lane comedian and one of Garrick's favourite players.[12]

---

8 McConnell Stott, *What Blest Genius?*, p. 134.
9 McConnell Stott, *What Blest Genius?*, p. 194.
10 This music has recently been recorded by Retrospect Opera: *Charles Dibdin & David Garrick: The Jubilee, with Queen Mab and Datchet Mead.*
11 Garrick's Ode is reprinted in Kristina Straub, Misty G. Anderson and Daniel O'Quinn (eds), *The Routledge Anthology of Restoration and Eighteenth-Century Drama* (New York and London: Routledge, 2017), pp. 675–78.
12 McConnell Stott, *What Blest Genius?*, pp. 150–3.

The transmigration of Roman Catholic ritual into the Jubilee's secular canonisation is, in historical context, remarkable indeed. Though Garrick's wife Eva was Catholic, and while Stratford had once been infamous as a nest of recusants, two centuries of Protestantism had struggled to banish the saints from England and destroy their shrines. Bitter religious conflicts had racked England since Henry VIII had broken with Rome in 1531, offering the populace a public theatre of hangings, burnings and beheadings as the two sides struggled for supremacy. Shakespeare as secular saint, however, implied a compromise between that old world and the new. When the Puritans beheaded Charles I, they rejected the ancient Christian culture in which the divine right of kings was vested by the sacred authority of a universal church. Thus Shakespeare's installation as a secular saint could be read as further evidence of the process that Terry Castle has described in *Masquerade and Civilization* (1986): a demonstration that Enlightenment assumptions were gradually permeating the culture at large, one characterised by 'a desire for firm conceptual boundaries ... [and] a world made up of discrete forms, of rigid categories, and hygienically polarized opposites'.[13]

For the Restoration of Charles II had not restored everything; the increasingly powerful Whigs were intent on establishing a constitutional monarchy, in which the king was subject to the will of an elected parliament. But 'Saint Shakespeare', while still implying an atavistic desire to worship a quasi-divine human ideal, was gratifyingly a native Englishman whose miracles were cultural and aesthetic. Furthermore, he implied a native English political tradition that was satisfyingly seen as running counter to French absolutism. Shakespeare's plays, especially the history plays, provided a heroic if brutal English story of origins, but relegated violence and treachery to the distant past. The Glorious Revolution of 1688, when the Protestant William of Orange and Mary deposed Charles II's rightful heir, his Catholic brother James II, showed that power could be transferred without a Battle of Bosworth or Mary Tudor's burnings at Smithfield. When Queen Anne, the last of the Protestant Stuarts, died, the Whigs, by a genealogical sleight of hand, replaced her with the safely Protestant George of Hanover, a great-grandson of James I. James II's exile had in a sense 'hygienically' removed the Catholic threat to the continent, but fears of a Jacobite invasion haunted English politics until 1746, when Charles Edward Stuart, the so-called Young Pretender and James II's grandson, was defeated at the Battle of Culloden.

---

13 Terry Castle, *Masquerade and Civilization: The Carnivalesque in Eighteenth-Century Culture and Fiction* (Stanford, CA: Stanford University Press, 1989), p. 102.

And yet, though exiled, the dark, mysterious practices (and medieval architecture) of Roman Catholicism would provide a rich matrix for Gothic novelists from Walpole onwards.[14]

One might argue that when Shakespeare returned to the English stage his plays offered theatrical audiences the same pleasures that, after *Otranto*, would be supplied by Gothic novelists. He was, after all, Gothic in the sense of 'uncivilised', 'uncouth' or 'medieval', and as the French critics so often proclaimed, his plays were 'barbarous', not only ignoring neoclassical aesthetic rules, but portraying on the stage battles, betrayals, cruelty, murder, war, ghosts and witches. Restoration producers' notorious carelessness with Shakespeare's texts was, among other things, simply practical. They aimed to sell tickets: change the archaic words; omit the scenes that offend contemporary sensibilities; let Cordelia live happily ever after; transform *The Tempest* into a popular opera, as in John Dryden and William D'Avenant's *The Tempest; or, The Enchanted Island* (1667). Shakespeare offered English audiences a violent journey towards contemporary English identity, an opportunity to explore past horrors safely ensconced in a much less violent present. Taylor quotes Robert Gould's tantalisingly Gothic response to Shakespeare in 1689:

> When e'r I *Hamlet* or *Othello* read,
> My *Hair* starts up, and my *Nerves* shrink with dread:
> *Pity* and *Fear* raise my concern still higher,
> Till, betwixt both, I am ready to expire!'[15]

But Restoration responses to *Hamlet* also adumbrate Shakespeare's future transmigration into the realm of 'Gothic Story'. According to Taylor, Anthony Ashley Cooper, 3rd Earl of Shaftesbury, called it 'that piece of [our old dramatic Poet], which seems to have most affected *English* Hearts, and has perhaps been oftenest acted of any that have come upon our Stage'.[16] Taylor notes that, 'In addition to the collected editions of 1664 and 1683, [*Hamlet*] was separately published in five quarto editions (two in 1676, others in 1683, 1695, and 1709).'[17] Davenant's popular production was somewhat unusual in making relatively few changes to the text, aside from modernising the language and eliminating some oaths and profanities. Taylor speculates

---

14 See Diane Long Hoelever, *The Gothic Ideology: Religious Hysteria and Anti-Catholicism in British Popular Fiction, 1780–1880* (Cardiff: University of Wales Press, 2014).
15 Quoted in Taylor, *Reinventing Shakespeare*, p. 46.
16 Quoted in Taylor, *Reinventing Shakespeare*, p. 46.
17 Taylor, *Reinventing Shakespeare*, p. 46.

that *Hamlet* in particular reassured the public about the validity of the Restoration itself: the play 'is about a wicked usurper who had murdered the true king ... This usurper also tries to murder the old king's son, and punishes the villain.' A patent in 1660 had required that plays be edited so as not to offend the pious. In a scenario that so inevitably elicits parallels with English politics from 1642 to 1660, the hero must be made as 'straightforward, godly and admirable as possible'; '"The pious" had, after all recently 'closed the theatres and executed Charles I.'[18]

Due to the fact that, since the death of Charles II, there had been two kings with equal claims to the throne in terms of birth, audiences could either conveniently find reassurance that the Restoration had restored a rightful king, or, along with the Jacobites, observe the tragic consequences of violating God's law of legitimate succession. Shakespeare's ambiguity as well as his 'Englishness' thus facilitated the cultural impulse towards 'canonisation'. In *Will in the World* (2004) Stephen Greenblatt reminds us that in Shakespeare's youth, Jesuit missionaries and spies were being hanged, drawn and quartered. He notes, too, the considerable evidence that suggests that John Shakespeare, William's father, had practised – or was at least sympathetic to – the Old Religion, but concludes that this youthful experience may well have contributed to what he calls Shakespeare's 'double consciousness'. While not expressing any explicit doctrines, the plays liberated audiences to project their own biases, conscious or unconscious.[19]

During the decades that progressed towards Garrick's Jubilee, however, Shakespeare's barbarously 'Gothic' aspects were increasingly less emphasised. As Dobson writes, 'the Shakespeare of the mid eighteenth century is imagined and rewritten as an author at once domestic, national, and moral, and in all of these respects, which spectacularly converge on the Jubilee, he is rapidly escaping from the stage altogether'.[20] He was now regarded 'as a writer of unimpeachable respectability', his plays 'unobtrusively rewritten to endorse mid-eighteenth century views of both the family and the stage'. Primarily considered as a text for reading, editions were published that rendered 'what we call the essence of SHAKESPEARE, more instructive and intelligible, especially to the ladies and to youths; glaring indecencies being removed'.[21] In cultural practice, Shakespearean drama was becoming as much read in private as staged in public. His works certainly remained

---

18 Taylor, *Reinventing Shakespeare*, pp. 47–8.
19 Stephen Greenblatt, *Will in the World: How Shakespeare Became Shakespeare* (New York: W. W. Norton, 2004), p. 103.
20 Dobson, *National Poet*, p. 186.   21 Dobson, *National Poet*, p. 109.

'Gothic' in the sense of 'antediluvian', but his Gothic barbarities were increasingly elided, even emasculated. While Samuel Johnson proclaimed that Shakespeare is 'the poet that holds up to his readers a faithful mirror of manners and of life', he nevertheless approved of Nahum Tate's happy ending for Cordelia in *The History of King Lear* (1681).[22]

Johnson might not have lamented with Walpole that 'The great resources of fancy have been damned up', as proclaimed in the second Preface to *Otranto*.[23] But in writing the first 'Gothic story', Horace inadvertently (or, to coin a Walpolean term, serendipitously) turned the mirror inwards and reflected what Sigmund Freud would later call 'dream work' – mysterious images evoking intense emotions, the private world of the nightmare and the wish-fulfilment of dream. Indeed, Walpole appears to have stumbled upon the process of Freudian psychoanalysis long before the event. Awakened by his terrifying vision of the gigantic, armoured hand, he wrote *The Castle of Otranto* through an exercise in free association; 'I sat down and began to write without knowing in the least what I intended to say.'[24] It is tempting to ask what was so terrifying about this nightmare to Horace. While it was unique to him, what is equally curious is the fact that story that the dream inspired awakened an insatiable public taste for tales about haunted castles set in distant times and faraway places. Walpole's conscious and unconscious reading of Shakespeare supplies the link. While his invocation of Shakespeare would justify generations of writers in their creation of historical fictions that incorporated the supernatural, his personal reading of *Hamlet* informs the trilogy of Shakespearean works that he produced between 1764 and 1768: *Historic Doubts on the Life and Reign of Richard the Third* (1768) and *The Mysterious Mother* (1768). Read as a sequence, they suggest that at the age of 47 – rather late to be fantasising a family romance – Walpole began working, via Shakespeare, through the essential terror of his life: the knowledge or the fear that he was illegitimate.

In all the conflicts of English history about who should inherit the throne, one principle was never challenged: that the new ruler should be related by

---

22 Samuel Johnson, *Dr Johnson: Poetry and Prose*, edited by Mona Wilson (Cambridge, MA: Harvard University Press, 1967), p. 491.
23 Horace Walpole, *The Castle of Otranto*, p. 65.
24 Horace Walpole to William Cole, 9 March 1765, in W. S. Lewis (ed.), *The Yale Edition of Horace Walpole's Correspondence*, 48 vols (New Haven: Yale University Press, 1937–83), vol. I, p. 88.

blood to the one that he or she succeeded. W. S. Lewis, Horace's greatest twentieth-century editor and champion, vigorously resisted two eighteenth-century rumours about his favoured subject: that he was homosexual and that he was illegitimate, the result of Lady Walpole's affair with Carr, Lord Hervey (the elder half-brother of Pope's 'Sporus'). Lewis's discovery and publication of Walpole's letters to his Eton friend Lord Lincoln challenged his denial of the first rumour, and Timothy Mowl's *Horace Walpole: The Great Outsider* (1996) effectively, if not sympathetically, 'outed' him. Lewis's insistence that Horace was Sir Robert's son, however, remains the received opinion.[25]

Any work that, like *Otranto*, concludes with an armoured ghost 're-membered' inevitably invokes *Hamlet*. Dale Townshend, who emphasises that the play portrays inadequate rituals of mourning, cites a remarkable number of early Gothic novels that narrate a similar impulse.[26] Robert B. Hamm, Jr has discussed the ways that Garrick and others enacted 'terror' in *Hamlet*'s scenes with his father's ghost, showing how *Otranto* is replete with allusions to the play.[27] Indeed, of all of Shakespeare's plays, Walpole mentions *Hamlet* most frequently in his correspondence, and he wrote a proto-Freudian argument defending the graveyard scene in response to Garrick's choice to omit it in one production:

> The ... skull of Yorick and the accounts of his jests could have no effect but to recall fresh to the Prince's mind the happy days of his childhood, and the court of the King his father, and then make him [see] his uncle's reign in a comparative shew that must have rendered the latter odious to him ... consequently the scene serves to whet *his almost blunted purpose*. Not to mention that the grave before him was destined to his love Ophelia. What incident in this scene but tends to work on his passions?[28]

Notably, the phrase 'almost blunted purpose', which Walpole here italicised, does not belong in this scene; rather, it is spoken by the ghost who reappears, and for the last time, when Hamlet is preparing to berate Gertrude, as the

---

25 See Michael Snodin, with Cynthia Roman (eds), *Horace Walpole's Strawberry Hill* (New Haven and London: Yale University Press, 2009), p. 1. For a summary of Lewis's denials, see R. W. Ketton-Cremer, *Horace Walpole: A Biography*, 3rd edition (London: Methuen & Co, 1964), pp. 26–9.
26 Dale Townshend, 'Gothic and the Ghost of *Hamlet*', in John Drakakis and Dale Townshend (eds), *Gothic Shakespeares* (Abingdon: Routledge, 2008), pp. 60–97.
27 Robert B. Hamm, Jr, '*Hamlet* and Walpole's *The Castle of Otranto*', *Studies in English Literature 1500–1900* 49:3 (Summer, 2009): 667–92.
28 Horace Walpole, 'Notes by Horace Walpole on Several Characters of Shakespeare', in Wilmarth Sheldon Lewis (ed.), *Miscellaneous Antiquities* (Windham, CT: Hawthorne House, 1940), pp. 5–7.

ghost had instructed him to (3.4.100), for having married her brother-in-law Claudius.[29] Critics interested in the play's Gothic progeny have understandably focused on the opening conversation between father and son. But Walpole's confusion regarding the place of 'almost blunted purpose' implies that the most powerful scene for him occurs in Gertrude's closet. He shares the father's and son's misogynistic disgust of the 'seeming-virtuous queen': 'So Lust, though to a radiant angel linked / Will sate itself in a celestial bed / And prey on garbage' (1.5.55–6). Hamlet's brief soliloquy before he enters Gertrude's closet is fraught with Gothic imagery: "Tis now the witching time of night / When churchyards yawn, and hell itself breaths out / Contagion to the world' (3.2.377–9). He concludes with a resolution that obeys the ghost's demand that he not harm his mother physically: 'Let me be cruel, not unnatural: / I will speak daggers to her but use none' (3.2.385–6). As R. W. Ketton-Cremer observes, Horace's 'love for his mother was the most powerful emotion of his entire life'.[30] But if he knew or feared that Sir Robert was not his father, then his beloved mother was what is euphemistically called a fallen woman – another Gertrude.

Of course, the views of female sexuality expressed by the ghost and by Hamlet are inherent in patriarchy, in which mothers are both necessary and frightening, giving death as well as birth. Janet Adelman has argued that Shakespearean confrontations with the maternal body appearing within this symbolic order are inevitably tragic, and that Shakespeare wrote tragedies when he began to address this problem:

> [If] Hamlet attempts both to remake his mother as an enclosed garden in 3.4 and to separate the father he idealizes from the rank place of corruption, Shakespearean tragedy and romance will persistently work toward the desexualization of the maternal body and the recreation of a bodiless father, untouched by her contamination.[31]

Hamlet's loathing of his mother's sin, in which he includes incest, is passionately intense. His dagger-like words are sharp indeed: 'Nay, but to live / In the rank sweat of an enseamed bed / Stewed in corruption, honeying and making love / Over the nasty sty' (3.4.81–4). And they inflict emotional if not

---

29 William Shakespeare, *Hamlet: The Texts of 1603 and 1623*, The Arden Shakespeare, edited by Ann Thompson and Neil Taylor (London: Bloomsbury, 2006). All citations are taken from this edition and will be indicated in the text by act, scene and line numbers.
30 R. W. Ketton-Cremer, *Horace Walpole*, p. 44.
31 Janet Adelman, *Suffocating Mothers: Fantasies of Maternal Origin in Shakespeare's Plays, Hamlet to the Tempest* (New York and London: Routledge, 1992), p. 18.

physical violence. As Gertrude exclaims, 'These words like daggers enter into mine ears' (3.4.86).

Elsinore on the Thames

Lady Walpole died in 1737, when Horace was 20, and Sir Robert, who almost immediately married his mistress (who died in childbirth six months later), died in 1745 on the best of terms with his son. In 1753, Horace erected a monument to his mother in Westminster Abbey, engraved with a lengthy encomium to her many virtues and adorned with a statue of Modesty, a quality that, according to Hamlet, Gertrude singularly lacked: 'Such an act / That blurs the grace and blush of modesty' (3.4.41). Lewis argues that if Horace had had any idea of his mother's reputation, he could never have praised her in these terms. But one might read the monument as his first effort to reconcile his love for this mother with his knowledge of her sexual guilt: simply by denying it, in ways that uncannily recall Hamlet's barbed quip to his mother, 'Assume a virtue if you have it not' (3.5.151). It was not until the nightmare of 1764 that Walpole began to work out the paradox of his existence by turning to words, using Shakespeare as his model for three different genres: prose fiction, scholarly discourse and closet drama.

Otranto manifestly describes a failed Oedipal crisis; Manfred's castle collapses when he learns that he is not the rightful heir. But the story inspired by the nightmare of the gigantic hand suggests a latent meaning that is congruent with his experience of Hamlet and his mother. In *The Psychopathology of the Gothic Romance* (2010), Ed Cameron usefully surveys various psychoanalytic readings of Walpole's novella, reading *Otranto* as an example of 'perversion': because the son cannot symbolise the mother's desire, a necessary step in negotiating the Oedipal stage, he remains inadequately separated from her. Cameron cites Lacan in order to argue that this situation occurs when the Law of the Father is too weak.[32] Hamlet so powerfully wields his symbolic daggers in naming the desire of the mother. But in *The Castle of Otranto*, Walpole symbolises the mother's desire while disguising it by the plot and setting.

The Castle of Otranto is *Hamlet* without a Gertrude. Horace was christened Horatio, named after one of Sir Robert's younger brothers; he disliked the name and preferred 'Horace' instead. But Horatio is one of the 'attendant

---

32 Ed Cameron, *The Psychopathology of the Gothic Romance: Perversion, Neuroses and Psychosis in Early Works of the Genre* (Jefferson, NC: McFarland, 2000), p. 65.

lords' in T. S. Eliot's 'The Love Song of J. Alfred Prufrock' (1915), one who both leads Hamlet to his father's ghost and who lives to tell the tale. The initially anonymous Horace recounts the fall of Manfred as Hamlet's Horatio, an invisible and omniscient observer/narrator who both shows and tells. One might describe the characteristic nesting of frame narratives that comprise *Otranto* as modes of psychoanalytic displacement, but here it is tempting to feel that they might be compared to the layers that confine and preserve the body of the mummy: anonymously published as the translation of an ancient Italian text found in the possession of a Catholic family by Onuphrio Muralto, Canon of the Church of St Nicholas at Otranto, and probably composed in the twelfth century.

In *Otranto* the dangers and destructive potential of the female principle are marginalised. Denied the supreme patriarchal virtue of motherhood, Walpole's women are interesting, if young, as objects of pursuit (Isabella) or as victims (Matilda). Manfred rejects his wife Hippolita as 'past the age of childbearing'; his daughter Matilda is declared a virgin in the first sentence, and Isabella is the elusive 'other' whose flight is always successful. And yet they are all named for warrior queens: Hippolita was Queen of the Amazons, though in *A Midsummer Night's Dream* she is about to marry, submitting herself thus to domesticity. William the Conquerer's queen was called Matilda, but perhaps more relevant here is Matilda, daughter of Henry I and widow of a Holy Roman Emperor, who returned to England to claim the throne and fomented a civil war. Isabella was the warrior queen of Castile, mother of Katherine of Aragon (who shared Hippolita's infertility), Edward II's queen, known as 'the she-wolf of France', or the devout Isabella of *Measure for Measure*. Male heirs in *Otranto* are sickly or non-existent, and Manfred's misdirected desire for his dead son's fiancée results in his accidental stabbing of his daughter, doomed like Polonius to misdirected rage that is impelled by sexual turmoil.

The most impressive and influential representation of the female according to patriarchy must surely be the Castle of Otranto itself. It is an enclosed space – dark, mysterious, dangerous, unknowable, replete with secrets that are organised around questions of legitimacy. In Walpole's imagination, the castle encloses the uncanny, a space that, in *Hamlet*, is described as 'disjoint and out of frame' (1.2.20). The appearances of Alphonso's disjointed armour drive the plot, and the portrait of Manfred's grandfather, the usurper Ricardo, steps out of his frame, an early foreshadowing of the narrative denouement. But an embodiment of the culturally female is also inherent in Gothic architecture – dark, complex, overwhelming. As Peter Fingesten has pointed out, the great Gothic cathedrals of the fourteenth century (almost always dedicated to 'Notre Dame') symbolise the Virgin's womb, that repository of irrational mysteries.[33] Adelson notes that fantasies of a disjointed body are characteristic of infantile fantasies because they echo early experience of the mother's body.[34] From this perspective, Walpole's complaint in the first Preface appears as somewhat of an alibi: 'I could wish he had grounded his plan on a more useful moral than this, that *the sins of the fathers are visited on their children to the third and fourth generations*'. In *The Castle of Otranto*, rather, it is the sin of the mother that compels him.

Over the next four years, Walpole turned to two other Shakespearean projects that unconsciously address the familial issues implied in *Otranto*. Having exposed his fear of illegitimacy, and its implicit accusation of maternal perfidy, he turns to the figure of his supposed father: Sir Robert Walpole. *Historic Doubts on the Life and Reign of Richard the Third* was published commercially by Dodsley in 1768 in an edition of 1,250 copies. To the surprise of both author and publisher, they immediately sold out and another 1,000 copies were printed.[35] In this work Walpole implicitly challenges Shakespeare, the 'authoritarian father' of English literature on his own ground: English history. *Otranto* was spurred by emotion; *Historic Doubts* is a work of reason, based on empirical evidence and presented as a scholarly treatise: 'I did not take Shakespeare's tragedy for a genuine representation.'[36] Legitimacy is still a controlling issue, however. Richard was vilified above all for having murdered his nephews, supposedly England's rightful heirs, as he, like Manfred's grandfather, seized a throne that was not his. Walpole was one of the earliest to defend Richard III, though nowadays historians tend to assume that Shakespeare's play is primarily Tudor propaganda.[37]

In his antiquarian researches, Walpole had discovered a document that he believed to be Richard's Coronation Roll, which included the name of the elder son of Edward IV, one of the 'Princes in the Tower' that Richard had supposedly murdered. If he were alive and attending Richard's coronation, Walpole reasoned, he could not have been murdered by his uncle. Like many

---

33 Peter Fingesten, 'Topographical and anatomical aspects of the gothic cathedral', *The Journal of Aesthetics and Art Criticism* 20:1 (Autumn, 1961): 3–23 (p. 20).
34 Adelman, *Suffocating Mothers*, p. 4.
35 Horace Walpole, *Historic Doubts on the Life and Reign of Richard the Third*, edited by P. W. Hammond (Gloucester: Alain Sutton, 1987), p. vii.
36 Walpole, *Richard the Third*, p. 9.
37 For a fascinating account of the discovery of Richard's skeleton and a contemporary account of his life, see Philippa Langley and Michael Jones, *The King's Grave: The Search for Richard III* (New York: St. Martin's Press, 2013).

a Gothic novel, Walpole's treatise is inspired by an ancient found document; ironically, it was not what he believed it to be.[38] More significant, however, is Walpole's apparent investment in this project, suggested by the vigour with which he defended his treatise after it was published.[39] As a version of *Hamlet*, it implicitly presents a situation in which both Hamlet's father, the good king, and Claudius, the evil one, co-exist in the real world.

There is no doubt that Sir Robert, in public Horace's father, was a monster, at least to his political enemies, who were legion. Unfortunately for him and the Whig Party, all the best writers of the period seemed to be Tories – Pope, Jonathan Swift, Johnson, John Gay, Henry Fielding. In *The Great Man: Sir Robert Walpole: Scoundrel, Genius, and Britain's First Prime Minister* (2011), Edward Pearce explores some of the many authors who satirised and excoriated him – most memorably, perhaps, as a thief in Gay's *The Beggar's Opera* (1728) and the rope-dancing Prime Minister of Lilliput from Swift's *Gulliver's Travels* (1726).[40] Their disdain was rooted in their conservative view that the Whigs had erred in denying James II his throne while they crowned a foreigner, William of Orange, as King of England. Sir Robert remained in power for 20 years. Though a supremely astute politician, he was also corrupt even by the standards of the time. His massive Palladian mansion in Norfolk, Houghton Hall, was not financed by his private income as a country squire. Early eighteenth-century political discourse was vicious, and papers such as *The Craftsman* existed merely to excoriate Sir Robert.

And yet, Horace knew another side of him, a genial and generous man who sheltered him and his mother from the opprobrium of bastardy. Sir Robert was apparently easy-going and good-natured. For years, he and Lady Walpole lived more or less separate lives. Sir Robert had an acknowledged mistress and an illegitimate daughter. Thus, when Horace was born eight years after the last of Sir Robert and Catherine's unquestionably legitimate children, the baby was baptised as a Walpole, and named after Sir Robert's younger brother Horatio, though the birth was not announced in the newspapers. According to Lady Louisa Stewart, Sir Robert ignored the child until after he finished Eton, when he showed signs of intellectual precocity.[41] That

---

38 Walpole, *Richard the Third*, p. 65.
39 Walpole's numerous responses to criticisms of *Historic Doubts on the Life and Reign of Richard the Third* are included in Walpole, *Richard the Third*, pp. 124–225.
40 Edward Pearce, *The Great Man: Sir Robert Walpole: Scoundrel, Genius and Britain's First Prime Minister* (London: Jonathan Cape, 2007), pp. 331–63.
41 Lady Louisa Stewart inherited Lady Mary Wortley Montagu's papers with instructions to burn them. She read them first, however, and published a summary containing the juicy gossip. Lewis discounted this evidence because Horace had loathed Lady Mary.

Horace in *Richard the Third* was working though the ambiguities of his paternity offers insight into two puzzling episodes in his life. Shortly after arriving at Eton at the age of nine, Horace pleaded with Sir Robert to arrange an audience for him with the king. Sir Robert did so, and the child met King George I shortly before he died. Why would a 9-year-old make so improbable a request? One possible explanation for this might be that when he arrived at Eton, his schoolmates, confronted with the 'son' of the Prime Minister, mocked him by repeating the popular gossip about his birth; Horace's childish response was to prove himself by showing that his 'father' could arrange a royal meeting.

The second mystery concerns Walpole's bitter quarrel with Thomas Gray at the end of their two-and-a-half-year Grand Tour (1739–41). The two men had spent much of that time in Florence as guests of Sir Horace Mann, a distant Walpole cousin who served as British envoy. During their long sojourn in France and Italy, however, Horace and Gray had become increasingly incompatible. Horace was sociable and relished his position as son of Sir Robert; Gray, by contrast, was a serious scholar. As they began their journey homeward, the two quarrelled bitterly. Timothy Mowl speculates that since they had encountered Lord Lincoln, Walpole's possible lover, in Reggio, the cause was a lover's tiff.[42] Gray went to Venice and Horace returned to London, having destroyed the letters to Mann about the episode. It is tempting to surmise that Gray had become increasingly irritated with Horace's pretentions, and finally confronted Walpole with the aspersion concerning his illegitimacy. As Horace revealingly answered William Mason's inquiry about the quarrel, 'I was too young, too fond of my own diversions ... too much intoxicated by ... the insolence of my situation as a Prime Minister's son ... [Gray] freely told me of my faults.'[43] When Horace returned to England, Sir Robert apparently assured him that he would never disown him. After his return, Horace grew close to his father, visiting him regularly at Houghton Hall though not showing any interest in hunting, Sir Robert's favoured activity. He published *Aedes Walpoliana* (1743), a catalogue of his father's paintings at Houghton, wrote political pamphlets defending his policies, and to the end of his life nostalgically recalled Sir Robert as presiding

---

But she had been a friend of Sir Robert and his sister in his youth, so she most undoubtedly knew the truth about Horace's birth.
42 Timothy Mowl, *Horace Walpole: The Great Outsider* (London: Faber & Faber, 2010), pp. 83–91.
43 Ketton-Cremer, *Horace Walpole*, p. 71.

over a peaceful and prosperous kingdom. Horace was eventually reconciled with Gray in December 1745, eight months after Sir Robert's death.

Anxiety about mothers and the question of legitimacy creeps into Horace's arguments about Richard III. He repeatedly expresses incredulity that Richard might have, as rumoured, claimed that he was the only legitimate son of York, since his brothers were the result of his mother's liaison with a commoner: 'What man of common sense can believe, that Richard went so far as publicly to asperse the honour of his own mother?' As he rhetorically continues,

> Is it, can it be credible, that Richard activated a venal preacher to declare to the people ... that his mother had been adulteress and that her two eldest sons ... were spurious ... Ladies of the least disreputable gallantry generally suffer their husbands to beget his heir; and if doubts arise on the legitimacy of their issue, the younger branches seem most likely to suspicion.[44]

As Horace rather tellingly concludes, 'In Richard's case, the imputation was beyond measure atrocious and absurd. What! Taint the fame of his mother to pave the way to the crown!'[45]

Near the end of *Historic Doubts*, Walpole oddly ventures into a dubious and original speculation about another play by Shakespeare, *The Winter's Tale*, which he calls *The Winter Evening's Tale*. He argues that it may be ranked among Shakespeare's histories, and intended as a 'compliment to queen Elizabeth as an indirect apology for her mother Anne Boleyn'.[46] He believes that Leontes's 'unreasonable jealousy and his violent conduct in consequence' is 'a true portrait of Henry the Eighth, who generally made the law the engine of his boisterous passions', a figure not unlike Manfred in *Otranto*. Furthermore, Walpole reads Hermione's lines (—for honour, / 'Tis a derivative from me to mine, / And only that I stand for') as an allusion to a letter that Anne Boleyn wrote to the king before her execution. As he concludes, *The Winter Evening's Tale* was therefore in reality a second part of *Henry the Eighth*.[47] Anne Boleyn was convicted of adultery, treason, incest and witchcraft. Having convinced himself that Richard III was not a monster, Horace could believe more assuredly in the Sir Robert that he knew as kind and generous. But his digression on Anne Boleyn implies that in this project, too, he is close to confronting the desire of his mother who betrayed such a man. Sir Robert's kindness, however, had also condemned Horace to a life masquerading as a Walpole. The armoured hand on the bannister is Sir

---

44 Walpole, *Richard the Third*, pp. 42–3.   45 Walpole, *Richard the Third*, p. 43.
46 Walpole, *Richard the Third*, p. 108.   47 Walpole, *Richard the Third*, p. 108.

Robert's, a symbol of the legal concept of 'mortmain', a term in British common law indicating the power of the dead to control the inheritances of the living. According to Pearce, Parliament debated the concept in 1737, the year that Lady Walpole died; the law, dating from the Middle Ages, permitted the 'alienating of wealth outside the family line', so that monasteries could inherit.[48] Horace's nightmare implies that he knew at some level that he had no right to the sinecures inherited from Sir Robert, money that built Strawberry Hill, the 'castle' he had constructed to please himself. And yet the heavy hand of the father who was not a father prevailed.

Finally, Walpole confronted in dramatic form the hitherto unspeakable 'desire of the mother', his unconscious motivation for writing *The Castle of Otranto* and his unconscious impulse for challenging Shakespeare's authoritative portrait of a monstrous political leader. In 1768 he had printed at Strawberry Hill fifty copies of his Shakespearean drama *The Mysterious Mother*, which he distributed only among intimate friends. In writing *Historic Doubts*, Walpole sheltered under the conventions of scholarly discourse, supporting and concealing his emotional impulses with rational arguments based on empirical evidence. To write his closet drama, however, he dons a full suit of Shakespearean armour, appropriating his precursor's tragic genre, poetic technique and literary conventions: the plot hinges on a bed trick that, though ultimately tragic, is not unlike those found in *Measure for Measure* and *All's Well That Ends Well*. The play contains a catalogue of Gothic horrors: unregulated lust, madness, betrayal, murder, family quarrels over inheritance, conniving priests, double incest and suicide. As the play begins, Edmund, the Countess of Narbonne's son, returns from his 16-year exile, mysteriously commanded by his mother immediately after the death of his father. At once, one is struck by the resonances of the characters' names: the bastard in *King Lear* is named Edmund, and Lady Walpole, had she lived until Sir Robert was created Earl of Orford in 1742, would have become a countess. Edmund has spent the years of exile as a soldier of fortune, but he is weary of fighting the Turks and wants to reclaim his lands. Father Benedict, who resents the Countess's resistance to the Church of Rome, has told her that her son is dead.

The Countess, meanwhile, has led a life of oppressive virtue, succouring orphans and raising her 16-year-old 'ward' Adeliza. But Edmund meets Adeliza and they fall in love. Benedict, who has learned that the Countess broods over some terrible guilt, marries the couple in secret. When she learns

---

48 Pearce, *The Great Man*, p. 179.

of the marriage, the Countess confesses that she herself is Adeliza's mother. On the day of her husband's unexpected death in a hunting accident, she substituted herself for the maid Beatrice, with whom Edmund had an assignation. Upon hearing of her son's marriage to his sister/daughter, the Countess confesses. Filled with rage, Edmund threatens to kill her, but she seizes his dagger and stabs herself. Edmund declares that Adeliza will take the veil and he himself returns to the battlefield, hoping to die.

Though the play describes the desire of the mother that was literally unspeakable in *Otranto*, Walpole shares Hamlet's view of female sexuality as vile and dangerous. The horrific conclusion is foreshadowed throughout. When the Countess speaks, she hints at the terrible secret that she harbours: 'Death alone ... can slake my torments' (4.4.58); 'Be known my crimes! / Let shame anticipate the woes to come' (3.2.28–9); 'I know that guilt is torture' (4.4.58); 'Avoid the Scorpion pleasure; / Death lurks beneath the velvet of his lip'(4.4.51–2); 'Her sex', she says, 'when gratified are frail; / When check'd a hurricane of boundless passion'(1.3.12); 'Artful woman! / Thou subtle emblem of thy sex composed of madness and deceit' (5.4.81–2). Like the insanity that plagues such Shakespearean characters as Ophelia and Lady Macbeth, Walpole also inflicts madness upon his Countess.

Horace's use of Shakespearean conventions distances himself from the rage that he indirectly expresses through the Countess. Edmund is an innocent victim, and his mother's monstrous passion is confined to one episode sheltered within the conventional bed trick. Here, Hamlet's verbal dagger has become a real one, and the countess stabs herself, in contrast to the accidental stabbings of Polonius and Matilda. This conclusion expresses vicarious rage at the mother who remains 'mysterious' – outwardly virtuous, inwardly sharing the qualities that Hamlet loathes in Gertrude. 'Execrable woman!' he exclaims. But he refrains from murdering her himself: 'I dare not punish what you dared commit!' (5.6.78).

Even here, at the climax of this family romance, the play suggests that Edmund has never fully separated himself from his mother. That mother/son incest constitutes the mother's heart of darkness offers one insight into Walpole's unconscious. He defended his choice of theme by invoking Sophocles, an anecdote told by Archbishop Tillotson and an episode in Marguerite of Navarre's *Heptameron* (1558).[49] But one may guess at a more immediate reason why this tale of guilt, incest and female sexuality attracted him. In 'A Special Type of Object Choice Made by Men' (1910), Freud writes

---

49 Horace Walpole, *The Mysterious Mother*, pp. 251–2.

that a dimension of the family romance may consist of the child's fantasy of rescuing his parent, both to repay them for the gift of life and to escape the burden of indebtedness:

> Rescuing the mother acquires the significance of giving her a child or making one with her—one like himself, of course ... in the rescue fantasy he identifies completely with the father. All the instincts, the loving, the grateful, the sensual, the defiant, the self-assertive and independent—all are grafted in the wish to be the father of himself.[50]

The Countess's dying words to her son are 'Peace! And conceal our shame – quick frame some legend ...' Walpole's invention of 'Gothic Story' was one aspect of his lifelong project to create an identity for himself. *The Mysterious Mother* is the last of Walpole's major literary creations. His friend Lady Diana Beauclerk created a series of illustrations for the play, which Walpole admired so much that in 1776 he added one last feature to Strawberry Hill: a bespoke closet to house the drawings.

As Adelman notes, 'Characteristically in Shakespeare, the site of blessing and of cursedness is the family, their processes psychological.'[51] Horace Walpole intuited this insight and effected the transmigration of Shakespeare through a coincidence of birth: wealthy, highly educated, extremely fond of the theatre, yet always knowing that he played the role of 'Horace Walpole'. His life (1717–97) corresponded with Shakespeare's rise to prominence as the supreme English poet. But Hamlet's confrontation with his mother Gertrude offered him a kind of Freudian primal scene, the locus of the intense anxieties aroused by his knowledge or fear that his beloved mother desired men other than her husband. In *Hamlet*, Shakespeare implicitly authorised his fascination with the violent, forbidden passions residing within the structure of the patriarchal family. In naming 'Gothic' fiction, Walpole thus represented family structure as a haunted house. Though the French critics complained that Shakespeare disregarded the unities of time, place and action, the action of *Hamlet* is almost entirely enclosed within the haunted, indeterminate spaces of Elsinore. His interpretation of his nightmare is also a psychoanalysis of Strawberry Hill, his fantasy of a Gothic castle. Though the building is playful, theatrical, light and colourful, Otranto, its latent shadow, is dark, mysterious and ruled inexorably by the Law of the

---

50 Sigmund Freud, 'A Special Type of Object Choice Made by Men', in *The Standard Edition of the Complete Psychological Works of Sigmund Freud, Vol. XI: Five Lectures on Psycho-Analysis, Leonardo da Vinci and Other Works* (London: The Hogarth Press, 1910), pp. 163–76 (p. 173).
51 Adelman, Janet, *Suffocating Mothers*, p. 318, n. 20.

Father. Walpole's reading of *Hamlet* created in *Otranto* a new archetype – the haunted castle as a symbol of the family and the self. This image resonated so profoundly with his contemporaries that for several generations the haunted castle was virtually synonymous with Gothic fiction itself. In introducing her 'Index of Gothic Motifs', Ann B. Tracy notes that she omitted listing this convention because 'Castles are so pervasive a device that no purpose can be served by the recitation of two hundred novels that have them.'[52] Indulging his architectural fantasies, and informed by his reading of Shakespeare, Horace Walpole constructed his own Elsinore in the affluent London suburb of Twickenham.

52 Ann B. Tracy, *The Gothic Novel, 1790–1830: Plot Summaries and an Index to Motifs* (Lexington: University Press of Kentucky, 1981), p. 195.

I.7
Reassessing the Gothic/Classical Relationship

JAMES UDEN

Periods of contest between antiquity and modernity are, in the words of Hans Robert Jauss, 'a literary constant, as normal and natural in the history of European culture as the alternation of generations is in biology'.[1] Each periodic break with history is expressed less in the redefinition of the self than in the redefinition of the past, the selective characterisation of previous generations or centuries as allies or enemies to current cultural concerns. The English Gothic novel emerged out of just such a process of historical redefinition. The eighteenth century saw the production of a new, English antiquity. Writers and artists rediscovered the Middle Ages as an enchanted era of imagination, canonised vernacular authors (Shakespeare, Spenser, Milton) as classics worthy of learned commentary and looked to the so-called 'Gothic Constitution' as a source of native political values of liberty and virtue. A new, expanded print readership fed a demand for English-language texts that explored the legacy of that history.[2] The authority of the Classical world as a political and literary model accordingly declines, transforming (in very broad terms) from 'an emulatable model to a historical antitype'.[3] In most Gothic texts, the 'ancient' is quite deliberately not the world of ancient Greece or Rome, but an imagined world of chivalry or romance, the Middle Ages or later. Yet rather than the Gothic simply erasing or omitting the Classical, we can read Gothic literature as one of the cultural forms in which the meaning and influence of antiquity for modernity is most keenly contested. If the Gothic encodes in its very name an opposition to the Greek and Latin legacy – it preserves the memory, however faint, of the people who legendarily sacked Rome – then the appearance of traces of that legacy in

---

[1] Hans Robert Jauss, 'Modernity and literary tradition', trans. by Christian Thorne, *Critical Inquiry* 31 (2005): 329–64 (p. 330).
[2] Jonathan Brody Kramnick, *Making the English Canon: Print-Capitalism and the Cultural Past, 1700–1770* (Cambridge: Cambridge University Press, 1999).
[3] Jauss, 'Modernity and Literary Tradition', p. 352.

Gothic texts testifies to an inability truly to repress or control the past. The unexpected re-emergence of Classical antiquity in such texts is, ironically, a quintessentially Gothic motif.

The three sections of this chapter briefly trace three stages in the imagined relationship between the Gothic and the Classical in England in the eighteenth and early nineteenth centuries.[4] First, the authority of the Classical was challenged by mid-century authors as part of the investment of literary and political value in the post-Classical world. Yet writers of the period do not merely omit or ignore the Classical: they polemically reframe Classical works so that they no longer seem like models of virtue or propriety, but more distant examples of supernatural fancy and, curiously, the Gothic imagination. Horace Walpole's *The Castle of Otranto* (1764) makes a spectacle out of the fragmentation and displacement of Classical authority through the scrambling of ancient texts and myths. The second stage is a reaction against that irreverence towards the past. The most significant – and underappreciated – author in this respect is Clara Reeve, whose Gothic romance *The Old English Baron* (1778) mimics the virtue discourse and exemplary moralism of the Classical historians, beloved of the Whig tradition, whom she saw as foundational for both literary activity and political life. Finally, writers of the Romantic era see the city and legacy of Rome through a Gothic lens, expressing both attraction to, and repulsion from, ancient examples. Romanticism separates what had now been cast as 'neoclassical' rules and standards from a free, original ancient spirit in harmony with their own ideas. Mary Shelley's *Frankenstein; or, The Modern Prometheus* (1818) suggests at once a desired closeness to Greek and Roman texts and an irremediable alienation from the world upon which the present had long modelled itself.

A Giant's Influence: Breaking the Ancient Analogy

> *Rome* was a powerful Ally to many States; antient Authors are our powerful Allies; but we must take heed that they do not succour, till they enslave, after the manner of *Rome*. Too formidable an Idea of their Superiority, like a Spectre, would fright us out of our Wits; and dwarf our Understanding, by making a Giant out of theirs.

So Edward Young describes the oppressive influence of Classical authors in his *Conjectures on Original Composition* (1759), employing an image – the

---

4 I examine many of the texts in this chapter in greater detail in *Spectres of Antiquity: Classical Literature and the Gothic* (New York: Oxford University Press, forthcoming).

ancestor as terrifying, ghostly giant – that would be indelibly imprinted as Gothic in *The Castle of Otranto*.[5] Young takes explicit aim at what he casts as the idolatry of Greek and Roman writers, and particularly at Alexander Pope, whose Catholicism left him open to Young's unfair charges of obeisance to continental authority. Pope's respect for the Ancients has in its background a broader discourse that connected England and Rome. Works such as Addison's *Cato* (1713) – for which Pope wrote a prologue – encouraged an analogy between Republican Romans and contemporary politicians that stood to flatter the sympathies of both Whigs and (less commonly) Tories; Pope wrote memorably that the play elicited 'Roman drops from British eyes'.[6] If much of Pope's work undoubtedly took inspiration from Latin literary works and genres, we should be wary of accepting at face value characterisations of early eighteenth-century literary culture as a period of uncritical imitation of Classical literary precedent.[7] As Larry Norman has emphasised, it is precisely the partisans of the Ancients in the later seventeenth-century French *Querelle des Anciens et des Modernes* who stressed the distance between the ancient and the modern, in order to defend the alien moral values that readers found in Homer and Virgil; in doing so, they began to articulate, in his words, 'nothing less than a literary paradigm of historical realism'.[8] Identification with Classical models had never been easy or unproblematic, but a sense of the alterity of the ancient became more marked in England throughout the eighteenth century.

Another reason for that alterity was a change in the knowledge of Latin and Greek. Benedict Anderson's claim that by 1700 Latin had largely ceased to be spoken, and that 'even fewer, one imagines, dreamt in it', is too simplistic.[9] For some eighteenth-century writers, at least, the distant language of Rome seems to have encouraged the taking of certain personal and imaginative

---

5 Edward Young, *Conjectures on Original Composition* (London, 1759), p. 25.
6 Alexander Pope, *Minor Poems*, edited by Norman Ault and John Butt (London: Methuen, 1964), pp. 96–8. On the political analogy between England and Rome, see Philip Ayres, *Classical Culture and the Idea of Rome in Eighteenth-Century England* (Cambridge: Cambridge University Press, 1997). Ayres (p. 49) cites Voltaire, who begins his 'Letter VIII' on England by saying: 'The members of the English parliament are fond of comparing themselves to the old Romans.' See Voltaire [François-Marie Arouet], *Letters Concerning the English Nation* (London, 1778), p. 44.
7 On the 'preromantic' and Romantic mischaracterisation of Pope as a poet concerned only with imitation, order and decorum, see Robert J. Griffin, *Wordsworth's Pope: A Study in Literary Historiography* (Cambridge: Cambridge University Press, 2005).
8 Larry F. Norman, *The Shock of the Ancient: Literature and History in Early Modern France* (Chicago: University of Chicago Press, 2011). p. 210.
9 Benedict Anderson, *Imagined Communities: Reflections on the Origin and Spread of Nationalism* (London: Verso, 1983), p. 38.

liberties – encouraged them, we might say, to dream.[10] Yet it is true that the ability to read Latin and Greek depended on the resources to attend schools, or the opportunity to be tutored by a family member capable of doing so, and it was no longer to be assumed that the Classical languages formed the core of a school's curriculum. Dissenting academies promoted the importance of modern languages over ancient ones, and the utility of Classical learning for the working and middle classes was increasingly questioned.[11] One pamphlet, by the father of the novelist Elizabeth Gaskell, argued that Classical languages be removed from a system of general education altogether, maintaining that 'every branch of natural history and philosophy' afforded greater utility and pleasure than 'the ability to read, write, and talk the languages of Greece and Rome'.[12] The Romantic call to expression and sensation over mimesis, according to Paul Fry, was driven partly by these changes in education. Mental recourse to Classical texts and ideas was now less universal, less natural, less instinctive. 'For a Wordsworth or Keats', he writes, 'the effort of suppression – at least of ancient poets, and still more, of ancient critics – need not have been as exhausting.'[13]

Edward Young's call to exorcise the spectral influence of Horace or Virgil, however, was founded on neither pleasure nor utility. Its context was instead the mid-century effort to distill a pure poetry associated with 'fancy' and the imagination. As the simile of the giant ghost suggests, this strain of literary activity was strongly associated with the newly valorised world of romance. Richard Hurd's *Letters of Chivalry and Romance* (1762) is typically cited for this contrast between Classical literature and the Gothic. Unlike Young, though, Hurd does not struggle to expel the Classical. Rather, he refashions the ancient works in the image of romance:

> Now in all these respects *Greek* antiquity very much resembles the *Gothic*. For what are Homer's *Laestrigons* [sic] and *Cyclops*, but bands of lawless savages, with, each of them, a Giant of enormous size at their head? And

---

10 Thomas Gray's exuberant early Latin poem about living on the moon (*Luna Habitabilis*) is a good example; it bears the influence of Johannes Kepler's popular Latin moon-voyage text entitled *Somnium* ('The Dream'). See Estelle Haan, *Thomas Gray's Latin Poetry* (Brussels: Latomus, 2000), pp. 168–73.
11 For a concise overview, see Penny Wilson, 'Classical Poetry and the Eighteenth-Century Reader', in Isobel Rivers (ed.), *Books and their Readers in Eighteenth-Century England* (New York: St. Martin's Press, 1982), pp. 69–96 (pp. 72–5).
12 William Stevenson, *Remarks on the Very Inferior Utility of Classical Learning* (London, 1796), p. 34.
13 Paul H. Fry, 'Classical Standards in the Period', in Marshall Brown (ed.), *The Cambridge History of Literary Criticism, Vol. 5: Romanticism* (Cambridge: Cambridge University Press, 2000), pp. 7–28 (p. 14).

what are the Grecian Bacchus and Hercules, but Knights-errant, the exact counterparts of Sir Launcelot and Amadis de Gaule?'[14]

Classical texts, he shows, are equally populated with monsters, giants and knights. Hurd goes on to argue that the Classical works are inferior in evoking terror, but the very comparison suggests a rather particular vision of the Classical, not as a source of examples of public virtue but equally a charmed world of fancy and the supernatural. The influential *A Philosophical Enquiry into the Origin of Our Ideas of the Sublime and Beautiful* (1757) by Hurd's contemporary Edmund Burke similarly reframes rather than rejects or ignores Classical literature in order to satisfy a contemporary desire for what was dark, imaginative and terrifying. The most frequently cited author in the treatise is Virgil, and Burke evokes with emotive force the immersive experience of the Underworld for Aeneas in book 6, which becomes the experience of the reader, too: 'Now some low, confused, uncertain sounds, leave us in the same fearful anxiety . . . a light now appearing, and leaving us, and so off and on, is more terrible than total darkness.'[15] For Burke and Hurd, the Classical is not the paradigm of order or virtue, but a dimmer and more distant source of terror in the present.

If these influential texts reframe rather than reject the Classical, the first canonical Gothic novel is more direct in its challenge to ancient authority. *The Castle of Otranto, A Gothic Story* – to give the work its full title in its second edition in 1765 – is 'Gothic' at least in part because of its irreverent desire to fragment, marginalise and undermine the Classical texts to which it alludes. As a number of recent authors have observed, the second edition begins by exerting some textual vandalism on one of the holy texts of classicizing aesthetics.[16] The novel begins with an untranslated quotation from Horace's *Ars Poetica*:

>   . . . vanae
> fingentur species, tamen ut pes et caput uni

---

14 Richard Hurd, *The Works of Richard Hurd*, 8 vols (London, 1811), vol. 4, p. 266.
15 Edmund Burke, *A Philosophical Enquiry into the Origin of Our Ideas of the Sublime and Beautiful*, edited by Paul Guyer (Oxford: Oxford University Press, 2015), p. 69.
16 Horace Walpole, *The Castle of Otranto*, edited by W. S. Lewis (Oxford: Oxford University Press, 1996). Walpole's manipulation of these lines, and their significance for the novel as a whole, has received detailed analysis recently in H. Christian Blood, *Some Versions of Menippea*, unpublished PhD dissertation, University of California, Santa Cruz, 2011, pp. 158–62; see also Brett M. Rogers and Benjamin Eldon Stevens (eds), *Classical Traditions in Modern Fantasy* (New York: Oxford University Press, 2017), pp. 1–7, and James Uden, 'Horace Walpole, gothic classicism, and the aesthetics of collection', *Gothic Studies* 20:1 (2018): 44–58.

>   *reddantur formae* . . .   - HOR.
>   [. . . vain images will be invented, yet in such a way that
>   foot and head are restored to a single shape . . .].

Since few of us know the Latin poets as intimately as Walpole, Gray and his elite milieu did, it is difficult for us to recover the sense from simply reading these lines that something is awry. Yet, in the novel's first instance of the uncanny, the reassuringly familiar quotation from one of the Classical tradition's best-known poems has had its wording altered and its meaning reversed. The more familiar version of these lines reads:

>   . . . *vanae*
>   *fingentur species; ut nec pes, nec caput uni*
>   *reddatur formae* . . .   (*Ars Poet.* 7–9)[17]
>   [. . . vain images will be invented, in such a way that
>   neither foot nor head are restored to a single shape . . .].

In the original passage, Horace is arguing for artistic unity. An artwork can never be satisfactorily unified, he claims, if it has been forced together from mismatched elements. What would result, he says, is the monster described in the *Ars Poetica's* opening lines: a grotesque, laughable, Scylla-like creature with animal and human limbs 'collected together from every place' (*undique collatis membris*, line 3). Such art would 'resemble a sick man's dreams' (*velut aegri somnia*, line 7). Walpole rewrites the Latin while maintaining the metre, replacing *ut nec . . . nec* with *tamen ut . . . et*, so that it makes a positive rather than negative statement. The venerable Roman now appears to argue that one can and should achieve artistic unity by reassembling mismatched parts. This is, of course, precisely what Walpole does in *The Castle of Otranto*: he combines mismatched elements of the 'ancient and modern' in a novel that had its origins, he claimed, in a 'feverish dream'.[18]

Echoes of this opening passage recur throughout in the images of the giant detached feet and limbs of Alfonso's ghost, which appear to the characters in the castle and will indeed come together at the novel's conclusion when the spectre appears in its final form.[19] So too are there reminiscences of Classical myth in the novel, but they appear similarly fragmented and disoriented. The

---

17 I print the text and punctuation from Richard Bentley (ed.), *Q. Horatius Flaccus, ex recensione & cum notis atque emendationibus Richardi Bentleii* (Cambridge, 1711), p. 293.

18 W. S. Lewis (ed.), *The Yale Edition of Horace Walpole's Correspondence*, 48 vols (New Haven: Yale University Press, 1937–83), vol. 1, p. 188.

19 Walpole, *The Castle of Otranto*, p. 112.

name Hippolita recalls the character of Hippolyta in Shakespeare's *A Midsummer Night's Dream*, but also, in a broader sense, the Classical myth of Hippolytus, in which a son is dashed to pieces after being accused of an incestuous affair with his stepmother. Here, the myth itself is scrambled: in *Otranto*, the son is dashed to pieces at the beginning of the story, the name Hippolita is transferred to a virtuous rather than a scheming mother and the incestuous passion is transferred to the father, Manfred. In Walpole's Gothic drama *The Mysterious Mother* (1768) there is also striking manipulation of Classical sources. In one egregious example, Walpole has the play's impious mother, who has consciously committed incest with her son, declaim lines originally spoken by the virtuous Cato in Lucan's epic poem *Bellum Civile* – a shocking juxtaposition with Addison's Roman hero, and a parodic recontextualisation of a passage that enjoyed particular fame in the period. (Lines from the same scene are quoted, for example, on the title page of book 3 of Hume's *A Treatise of Human Nature*).[20] In the Preface to *Hieroglyphic Tales*, which Walpole began to write between *Otranto* and *Mysterious Mother* but only printed in six copies at Strawberry Hill in 1785, he imagined forging a work of history that would debunk the claims to virtue of Republican Roman heroes, intending to 'ridicule, detect and expose, all ancient virtue, and patriotism'.[21] This direct assault on a British culture of Roman analogising was never written. But his Gothic works nonetheless undermine any direct link between contemporary British culture and the Classical past, confronting their giant influence through fragmentation, dismemberment and misuse.

Challenging Genre and Gender Prejudice: Classics and Romance

The Gothic novel and Classical literature occupied opposite poles of literary respectability in the eighteenth century, and the values accorded to each carried implications of gender and class difference. Knowledge of Greek and Latin was consistently coded as elite and male, whereas novel-reading, especially towards the end of the century, was coded as middle class and female. Jacqueline Pearson, in her study of women's reading in the eighteenth century, quotes Lady Mary Wortley Montagu warning her granddaughter to conceal

---

20 Paul Baines and Edward Burns (eds), *Five Romantic Plays, 1768–1821* (Oxford: Oxford University Press, 2000), pp. 15–16 (= Lucan, *Bellum Civile* 9.565–84); David Hume, *A Treatise of Human Nature*, edited by L. A. Selby-Bigge (Oxford: Clarendon Press, 1888), p. 455.
21 Horace Walpole, *Hieroglyphic Tales* (Twickenham, 1785).

any learning she has attained as if it were 'crookedness or lameness'.[22] Despite the celebrity of the so-called Bluestocking circle, a woman proficient in Classical languages typically provoked suspicion and even mockery in the eighteenth century.[23] Yet the writing of novels was increasingly a means for women to achieve recognition and independence, as well as a mode through which they could assert their learning. Clara Reeve claims particular attention here as a writer who challenged the boundaries between the sorts of literary activity that were judged proper for middle-class women. In a letter preserved by Walter Scott, Reeve claims to have read 'the Greek and Roman Histories, and Plutarch's *Lives* . . . at an age when few people of either sex can read their names'. Scott himself quipped that her Gothic novel, *The Old English Baron*, showed evidence of greater familiarity with the Greek historian Plutarch than with the period in which the novel is set.[24] Deliberately so: *The Old English Baron*, often dismissed as a tame and overly sober successor to Walpole's outré Gothic fantasy, should be read instead as a meld of Plutarchan moralism and contemporary narrative form, a consciously Classicising text that destabilises the arbitrary prejudice that accorded value to one mode of literature and learning over the other.

Prejudice is a key term in Reeve's writing. In her first work, *Original Poems on Several Occasions* (1769), published when she was already 40 years of age, she declares in her opening address to the reader:

> I formerly believed, that I ought not to let myself be known for a scribbler, that my sex was an insuperable objection, that mankind in general were prejudiced against its pretensions to literary merit; but I am now convinced of the mistake, by daily examples to the contrary.[25]

The second poem in Reeve's collection addresses a contemporary female writer's argument for equality of the sexes and includes a long parody of Classical imagery of the Muses. In his grandiloquent *Feminiad* (1754), John Duncombe praised the learned women of Britain by casting them in Classical dress, describing them as 'British nymphs' and 'sister

---

22 Jacqueline Pearson, *Women's Reading in Britain 1750–1835: A Dangerous Recreation* (Cambridge: Cambridge University Press, 1999), p. 70; Lady Mary Wortley Montagu, *The Selected Letters of Lady Mary Wortley Montagu*, edited by Robert Halsband (Harmondsworth: Penguin Books, 1986), p. 237.
23 Jane Stevenson, *Women Latin Poets: Language, Gender, and Authority from Antiquity to the Eighteenth Century* (Oxford: Oxford University Press, 2005), pp. 387–94.
24 'Clara Reeve', in Ioan Williams (ed.), *Sir Walter Scott on Novelists and Fiction* (London: Routledge & Kegan Paul, 1968), pp. 94–101 (p. 98): 'Clara Reeve, probably, was better acquainted with Plutarch and Raptin, than with Froissart or Olivier de la Marche.'
25 Clara Reeve, *Original Poems on Several Occasions* (London, 1769), p. xi.

Muses'.²⁶ Later, in the 1770s, the painter Richard Samuel would paint the Bluestocking circle in his *Portraits in the Characters of the Muses in the Temple of Apollo* (*The Nine Living Muses of Great Britain*), though one of the women depicted, the Classicist and poet Elizabeth Carter, complained that the image was so idealised that it was impossible to tell who was who.²⁷ When Reeve refers to the 'daily examples' of celebrated female authors in her *Collected Poems*, it is likely that she has the Bluestocking circle in mind, but the conservative Reeve, who spent her entire life in provincial Ipswich, seems to have felt marginalised from these other literary women. She argues in fact *against* claims for the equality of the sexes but indignantly demands that her own works be treated without prejudice. When she writes of her own efforts, images of poetic failure predominate: she describes 'the laurel wreath blasted on my brow', of the female poet as 'a muse conceal'd', of the 'fear' that 'restrains' the impoverished author.²⁸ *Spes incerta futuri*, 'an uncertain hope for the future', words uttered by Evander in the *Aeneid* about his son Pallas doomed to die, is the gloomy motto attached to the title page of this literary debut. Reeve's earliest work offers a vision of female authorship in the period, satirising its incipient mythology, lamenting its injustices and limitations. She resentfully portrays herself as an outsider to more celebrated instances of female learning, as a gadfly biting at the Muses of the metropolis.

The complaints about prejudice in her earliest work offer a background for understanding her important two-volume work of literary history, *The Progress of Romance* (1785).²⁹ This imagined dialogue between two principal characters, 'Euphrasia' and 'Hortensius', provocatively collapses literary categories. Rather than separating the Greco-Roman tradition from the medieval, Reeve argues that Homer and Virgil were themselves authors of romance. They too wrote works of supernatural fancy, she argues, and their poems form the earliest parts of a tradition stretching through the Middle Ages and Renaissance to the eighteenth century, from the 'ruins' of which the

---

26 John Duncombe, *The Feminiad, a Poem*, edited by Jocelyn Harris (Los Angeles: Williams Andrew Clark Memorial Library, 1981), pp. 8, 9.
27 Montagu Pennington (ed.), *Letters from Mrs. Elizabeth Carter, to Mrs. Montagu, between the years 1755 and 1800* (London, 1817), pp. 47–8, cited by Shearer West, 'Roles and Role Models: Montagu, Siddons, Lady Macbeth', in Elizabeth Eger (ed.), *Bluestockings Displayed: Portraiture, Performance and Patronage, 1730–1830* (Cambridge: Cambridge University Press), pp. 164–86 (p. 164).
28 Reeve, *Original Poems on Several Occasions*, 3, 18, 79.
29 Clara Reeve, *The Progress of Romance, through Times, Countries, and Manners*, 2 vols (Colchester, 1785).

novel was sprung. This is less an argument about literary history than it is about cultural capital. Because the Classical epics share the same divine machinery and outlandish fancy as the romance, there is no reason, she maintains, for one type of literature to be accorded prestige and the other not. Despite the title of the work, Reeve has little time for teleological notions like progress, and is generally indifferent to genre or historical context. It is only prejudice, she asserts, that has prevented readers from discerning 'a striking resemblance between works of high and low estimation'.[30] If Walpole aimed in *Otranto* to blend the 'ancient and modern' romance, and thereby to draw from the more fantastic themes that Hurd and others had opposed to the Classical, Reeve claims that the distinction between the two is merely ideological:

> *Euphrasia*: It is astonishing that men of sense, and of learning, should so strongly imbibe prejudices, and be so loath to part with them. — That they should despise and ridicule Romances, as the most contemptible of all kinds of writing, and yet expatiate in raptures, on the beauties of the fables of the old classic Poets, —on stories far more wild and extravagant, and infinitely more incredible.[31]

While prejudice is here used mostly in its old empiricist sense of 'prejudgement', there are conscious social implications to Reeve's argument. The prose romances that the work as a whole seeks to defend were pervasively considered women's reading and, as such, less socially elite. Even the names of characters in *The Progress of Romance* are significant: Hortensius suggests soundly Classical Roman learning, while Euphrasia, a sort of pseudo-Greek name, suggests the timeless, Hellenising world of the French heroic romance. But Reeve self-consciously challenges these stereotypes: she makes Euphrasia, the 'bookish heroine', both learned about romance *and* superior to the man in her knowledge of the Classics, and he repeatedly asks for translations of works that Euphrasia has read in the original languages.[32] Moreover, despite Reeve's conservatism and advocacy elsewhere for social order, she is entirely self-conscious about the way in which her ideas challenge accepted ways of reading. When Euphrasia compares Homer to the *Arabian Nights' Entertainments*, Hortensius complains that 'you can't be earnest in this comparison', and then twice later says 'you've staggered my

---

30 Reeve, *Progress of Romance*, vol. 1, p. 24.
31 Reeve, *Progress of Romance*, vol. 1, p. 21; cf. Walpole, *The Castle of Otranto*, p. 9.
32 Reeve herself read Latin well; her second work (*The Phoenix*, 1772) was a translation of the Neo-Latin novel *Argenis* (1621) by John Barclay.

opinions'.³³ In the second volume, when Hortensius has given in to most of Euphrasia's points, he still resentfully refers to 'Homer and Virgil, whose works you have as I think degraded by base comparison'. Again, in this section, Euphrasia resists the 'prejudice' that accords Homer and Virgil the first rank and casts all other epic poets as imitators. 'You think I have a prejudice of the same kind?', asks Hortensius angrily; 'According to your account, Epic poets are as plentiful as mushrooms.'³⁴ Yet 'epic' – and indeed 'Classical' – are for Euphrasia terms of misplaced approbation rather than truly being descriptions of a specific historical tradition or a metrical or linguistic form. In a more explicit version of a tendency that is present in Hurd's treatise, Reeve reassesses the distinction between the Gothic and the Classical by making the two look surprisingly alike.

This literary-critical project also helps to illuminate the Gothic novel for which she is best known, *The Champion of Virtue* (1777), which was republished in a revised form a year later as *The Old English Baron: A Gothic Story*.³⁵ The novel concerns a poor son of a peasant, Edmund; a haunted castle where apparitions seem to hold the key to the murder of his real parents and the secret of his noble birth; and a series of paternal figures who act on Edmund's behalf to restore him, by the end of novel, to his true title of Lord Lovel. Modifying an older critical model that suggested Reeve had initiated a genre of 'female Gothic', James Watt argues that Reeve instead wrote 'loyalist romance', a literary type set not in faraway or exotic lands but in England, and which imagines the past not as the source of pre-Enlightenment irrationality and terror but as the source of the traditions and models that legitimate political arrangements in the present.³⁶ The supernatural elements in *The Old English Baron* are muted and subdued; Walter Scott called it 'tame and tedious', and mocked the contrived gentility of all involved, even the ghosts. But this gentility in Reeve's novel is part of her sustained attempt to subvert the generic hierarchy and the prejudices underlying it.

Much of the behaviour of the characters in Reeve's novel can be read as an attempt to subvert the expectations – even the prejudices – imposed by Walpole's wildly popular novel. Reeve replaces the emotional extremes of *Otranto* with exemplary virtue. In contrast to the feverish confusion and

33 Reeve, *Progress of Romance*, vol. 1, pp. 22, 28.
34 Reeve, *Progress of Romance*, vol. 1, vol.2, 68, 69.
35 Clare Reeve, *The Old English* Baron, edited by James Trainer, intro. by James Watt (Oxford: Oxford University Press, 2003).
36 James Watt, *Contesting the Gothic: Fiction, Genre and Cultural Conflict, 1764–1832* (Cambridge: Cambridge University Press, 1999), pp. 42–69.

frantic accidents of *Otranto,* Reeve's characters are preternaturally knowing, moving swiftly and adroitly through the plot:

> I perceive, said Oswald, that some great discovery is at hand. – God defend us! said Edmund, but I verily believe that the person that owned this armour lies buried under us. Upon this, a dismal hollow groan was heard as if from underneath.[37]

The prose struggles to keep ahead of its characters. Nocturnal visitations are without mystery or ambiguity: Edmund 'perfectly remembered his dreams'.[38] Guesses by characters are unerringly correct: 'do you think it possible that he should be of either birth or fortune?', postulates one character about the central mystery, less than halfway through.[39] 'I have no doubt that Edmund is at the bottom of this business', presciently declares another character, and then, later in the same paragraph, 'my conjecture was too true'.[40] The Preface to the first version of the novel combatively addresses the sort of reader represented later by Hortensius in *The Progress of Romance*, one who 'delights in the fables of the ancients, the old poets, or story-tellers', but who dislikes or despises the 'ancient romance and the modern Novel'.[41] By deliberately stripping her story of the cheerful absurdities of Walpole's model, Reeve attempts to rebut the assumption that her chosen form is beneath the dignity of serious literature.

More specifically, I suggest, Reeve crafts her Gothic novel through conscious evocation of a particular Classical author. In the Preface to one of her last works, the reactionary and anti-Revolutionary historical novel *Memoirs of Sir Roger de Clarendon* (1793), she argues that historical writing should be a source of examples for ethical imitation. The pre-eminent exponent of this sort of moral historiography, she says, is Plutarch, the 'prince of historians', and she quotes from the Preface to his *Life of Aemilius Paulus:* 'the virtues of these illustrious men are to me as a mirror, by which I learn to regulate my own life and conduct'.[42] Reeve explicitly casts that later novel as an attempt to 'enforce the lesson of the excellent Plutarch', relating the lives of famous Englishmen as intended objects of moral aspiration. There is no explicit mention of Plutarch in *The Old English Baron*, but there is a pronounced emphasis on exemplary

---

37 Reeve, *The Old English Baron*, p. 46.   38 Reeve, *The Old English Baron*, p. 39.
39 Reeve, *The Old English Baron*, p. 72.   40 Reeve, *The Old English Baron*, pp. 97–8.
41 Reeve, *The Old English Baron*, p. 137 (in an appendix of the Oxford edition of the novel).
42 Clara Reeve, *Memoirs of Sir Roger de Clarendon, The Natural Son of Edward Prince of Wales, Commonly Called the Black Prince; with Anecdotes of Many Other Eminent Persons of the Fourteenth Century* 3 vols (London, 1793), vol. 1, pp. vi–vii.

ethics and the imitation of character, which are signature Plutarchan themes:

> Oh what a glorious character! said Edmund: how my heart throbs with wishes to imitate such a man! Oh that I might resemble him, though at ever so great a distance! Edmund was never weary of hearing the actions of this truly great man . . .[43]

Plutarch's *Lives*, as Gary Kelly has argued, were part of the standard reading of the Old Whig tradition, and the association between Plutarch's Greek and Roman heroes and the values of civic service and individual liberties spoke loudly to their political nostalgia.[44] Scott's quip about Reeve's excessive fondness for Plutarch contains more than a grain of truth. Her novel not only encourages a new and more conservative vision of the 'Gothic' past; it also attempts to subvert prejudices about what people 'of either sex' write and read. *The Old English Baron* combines male-oriented history and Classical literature with female-oriented romance and challenges the distinction between the two.

Gothic Visions of Antiquity in the Romantic Age

> With all his senses about him, he heard a noise at the door of his tent, and looking towards the light, which was now burnt very low, he saw a terrible appearance in the human form, but of prodigious stature, and the most hideous aspect. At first, he was struck with astonishment; but when he saw it neither did nor spoke any thing to him, but stood in silence by his bed, he asked 'who it was?' The spectre answered, 'I am thy evil genius, Brutus; thou shalt see me at Philippi'. Brutus answered boldly, 'I'll meet thee there'; and the spectre immediately vanished.

In this passage, we see a concatenation of eighteenth-century Gothic tropes. A noise startles a hero or heroine in the darkness. A candle or lamp offers flickering, dying light. The hero peers out to see a spirit dilated to giant size (as in *Otranto*); the spirit appears above or beside a bed (as in the haunted chamber of the late Marchioness de Villeroi in Ann Radcliffe's *The Mysteries of Udolpho*); it hounds the protagonist for a horrific crime he has perpetrated (as

---

43 *The Old English Baron*, 73; cf. at 134–5: 'Sweet is the remembrance of the virtuous, and happy are the descendants of such a father! they will think on him and emulate his virtues; they will remember him, and be ashamed to degenerate from their ancestor.'
44 Gary Kelly, 'Clara Reeve, Provincial Bluestocking: From the Old Whigs to the Modern Liberal State', in Nicole Pohl and Betty A. Schellenberg (eds), *Reconsidering the Bluestockings* (San Merino: Huntington Library, 2002), pp. 105–25.

in Matthew Gregory Lewis's *The Monk*). Only when we see the names at the end of the excerpt is the truth revealed. This is not in fact an excerpt from a Gothic novel or short story, but a passage from John and William Langhorne's 1778 translation of Plutarch's *Lives*, describing Brutus hounded by terrors after his assassination of Julius Caesar, a scene that was familiar in a different form to eighteenth-century readers from Shakespeare's *Julius Caesar* (Act IV, scene 3).[45] We might instinctively look to the influence of Walpole's *Otranto* on the Langhornes' rendering of Plutarch; and sure enough, just five years before the first edition of the Plutarch translation, John Langhorne himself wrote reviews of the first and second editions of *The Castle of Otranto* in the *Monthly Review*, praising, at least in the first of these, the novel's 'great dramatic powers'.[46] But attributing the supernatural elements to the influence of Walpole underestimates the extent to which Greek and Roman literature was itself viewed as a source of terror and the supernatural, despite Joseph Addison's specious claim at the beginning of the century that antiquity lacked stories of this type.[47] Ghosts were not the exclusive property of any period or genre. Classical literature could be viewed through Gothic eyes, and this anecdote in particular fits with current trends. When the publisher James Fletcher Hughes published a collection entitled *Terrific Tales* in 1804, one of the stories included was this one, here under the title 'The Ghost of Brutus appearing to him before his death'. The probably pseudonymous author Isabella Lewis expands on the description of the spectre ('a monstrous and hideous figure of a human body emaciated, withered, horrible'), appends a brief account of Brutus's subsequent suicide at the Battle of Philippi and even cites actual Greek texts as sources for the tale.[48]

Gothic elements are identifiable in other Classical translations of the Romantic era. Stuart Gillespie has remarked upon the 'Gothic cast' (or perhaps Gothic parody) in an early imitation of Juvenal's eighth *Satire* by William Wordsworth and Francis Wrangham, who transform the Roman

---

45 John and William Langhorne, *Plutarch's Lives, translated from the original Greek*, 6 vols, 3rd edition (London, 1778), vol. 4, p. 402. The translation was first published in 1770, but this section was expanded and made considerably more dramatic in this third edition.
46 Peter Sabor (ed.), *Horace Walpole: The Critical Heritage* (London and New York: Routledge & Kegan Paul, 1987), pp. 70–2.
47 'The Ancients have not much of this Poetry among them, for, indeed, almost the whole Substance of it owes its Original to the Darkness and Superstition of later Ages ...': Joseph Addison, no. 419, July 1, 1712 in Donald F. Bond (ed.), *The Spectator*, 3 vols (Oxford: Clarendon Press, 1965), vol. 3, p. 572.
48 Isabella Lewis, *Terrific Tales* (Chicago: Valancourt Books, 2006), p. 25. On this text, see Diane Long Hoeveler, *Gothic Riffs: Secularizing the Uncanny in the European Imaginary, 1780–1820* (Columbus: Ohio State University Press, 2010), pp. 197–8.

poet's scene of an atrium adorned with ancestral busts into a gloomy English castle in which a 'grim warrior train' of knights' has 'frown'd on time and hostile brooms in vain'.[49] Matthew Gregory Lewis begins *The Monk* (1796) with a poetic imitation of Horace's *Epistles* 1.20, the Roman poet's jealously erotic address to his book as a beloved male slave; the gender of the book in Lewis's version is deliberately obscured, but the imitation communicates strongly the Gothic author's own anxieties about the consequences of his sensationalistic novel, 'doomed', he says, 'to suffer public scandal'.[50] Perhaps the most extended and notable Classical translation by a major Gothic author is Lewis's later *The Love of Gain* (1799), a highly Gothicising and much-expanded translation of Juvenal's thirteenth *Satire*. Juvenal's original poem (written soon after 127 AD) explores the terrors of conscience on the guilty and oscillates unnervingly between brash expressions of divine defiance and nightmarish evocations of supernatural retribution. It is easy to see its appeal.[51] Lewis frequently deviates from the Latin original to incorporate scenes reminiscent of *The Monk* and his melodrama *The Castle Spectre*, so that the Classical imitation becomes an implicit commentary on his own Gothic literary works. Like Reeve and other earlier writers, Lewis shows that Gothic images of the supernatural were already evident in Classical writers, confuting a literary-historical narrative that saw a breach between the two. He also highlights the hypocrisy of his conservative critics, who fulminate against *The Monk* for its alleged impiety and corrupting influence but continue to embrace Juvenal as a trusted favourite, praising him for putting, in William Gifford's words, 'the deformity and horror of vice, in full and perfect display'.[52]

The imagery of ghosts and haunting is also part of the Classical/Gothic intersection in the Romantic era. Jonathan Sachs has described what he has called the 'internally differentiated classicism' of the period, the divergence of the cultural associations of ancient Greece from ancient Rome in British culture during and after the French Revolution.[53] While the philhellenic strain in the second-generation Romantics – most famously exemplified by

---

49 Stuart Gillespie, *English Translation and Classical Reception: Towards a New Literary History* (Malden: Wiley-Blackwell, 2011), p. 133.
50 Matthew Gregory Lewis, *The Monk*, edited by D. L. Macdonald and Kathleen Scherf (Peterborough, Ont.: Broadview, 2004), p. 35.
51 Lines from the poem also appear on the title page of John Moore's influential *Zeluco* (1789). See John Moore, *Zeluco*, edited by Pamela Ann Perkins (Kansas City: Valancourt Books, 2008), p. 1.
52 William Gifford, *The Satires of Decimus Junius Juvenalis* (London, 1802), p. li.
53 Jonathan Sachs, *Romantic Antiquity: Rome in the British Imagination, 1789–1832* (Oxford: Oxford University Press, 2010), p. 11.

Percy Shelley's cry that 'We are all Greeks' – identified Greece with unfettered originality and artistic freedom, the Roman Republic became a model of renewed importance for understanding contemporary political upheavals. With a heightened awareness of the transience of political forms, post-Revolutionary Romantic writers looked upon Rome as an earlier paradigm of a civilisation that had fallen and tended to employ Gothic tropes in describing the city. They imagined it as deserted and decayed, yet still capable of exerting a powerful, even supernatural, force upon visitors. It was, in short, a haunted city.[54] The imagery of ghosts and spectres, often dismissed by Romantic poets in their later works as childish or too closely connected with popular fiction, was unapologetically part of the Romantic imaginary when describing the Classic ground of Rome.[55]

Gothic writers and texts also contributed to this cultural representation of the Eternal City as unnervingly undead. When the lonely Lionel wanders around a desolate Rome as the last man alive in Mary Shelley's post-apocalyptic *The Last Man* (1826), he remembers 'the dark monk, and floating figures of "The Italian", and how my boyish blood thrilled at the description'.[56] Indeed, Ann Radcliffe's novels are notable for their repeated association of the Classical with what is empty, ruined or sinister: consider, for example, the busts of ancient authors in the threatening, cavernous hall of the Marquis in *The Romance of the Forest* (1791); the poem describing an attack on a trader on the site of the neglected ruins of Troy in *The Mysteries of Udolpho* (1794); and the description of Roman monuments in *The Italian* (1796–7) as 'gigantic skeletons, which once enclosed a soul'.[57] In 'The Vampyre' (1819), the first extended example of prose narrative of a vampire in English, John Polidori similarly describes Rome as 'another almost deserted city', and

---

54 Jerome J. McGann, *The Beauty of Inflections: Literary Investigations in Historical Method and Theory* (Oxford: Oxford University Press, 1988), pp. 313–33; Timothy Webb, 'Haunted City: The Shelleys, Byron, and Ancient Rome', in Timothy Saunders, Charles Martindale, Ralph Pite and Mathile Skoie (eds), *Romans and Romantics* (Oxford: Oxford University Press, 2012), pp. 203–24.

55 On the contested relationship between 'high' Romanticism and the Gothic in the eighteenth and early nineteenth centuries and in contemporary scholarship, see Dale Townshend and Angela Wright, 'Gothic and Romantic: An Historical Overview', in Angela Wright and Dale Townshend (eds), *Romantic Gothic: An Edinburgh Companion* (Edinburgh: Edinburgh University Press, 2016), pp. 1–34.

56 Mary Shelley, *The Last Man*, edited by Morton D. Paley (Oxford: Oxford University Press, 1994), p. 462.

57 Ann Radcliffe, *The Romance of the Forest*, edited by Chloe Chard (Oxford: Oxford University Press, 1986), p. 156; Radcliffe, *The Mysteries of Udolpho*, edited by Bonamy Dobrée with notes and intro. by Terry Castle (Oxford: Oxford University Press, 1998), pp. 206–8; Radcliffe, *The Italian*, edited by Robert Miles (London: Penguin Books, 2000), pp. 226–7.

the story takes place in large part in Athens, where the central character haplessly follows archaeological trails and attempts to decipher inscriptions with the ancient travel writer Pausanias in hand.[58] Mary Shelley herself contributed to the theme in a story fragment unpublished in her lifetime, 'Valerius, the Reanimated Roman' (generally dated to 1819), in which English travellers encounter a Republican-era Roman who was 'like a statue of one of the Romans animated to life'. But the story records disillusionment on all sides. Valerius is dismayed that the monuments of his own Republican period in Rome have been effaced by the gaudy structures of the later Emperors, such as the Colosseum. Meanwhile, Shelley describes the unease felt by the modern traveller in the presence of this antique figure ('I cannot call it dread, yet it had something allied to that repulsive feeling'). Ultimately, the story expresses Shelley's sense of the unbridgeable gulf between modern, post-Revolutionary Britons and the Roman characters who were once models for British culture.[59]

Perhaps the best-known Gothic adaption of Classical themes in the Romantic period is Shelley's *Frankenstein; or, the Modern Prometheus* (1818), the very subtitle of which suggests the revival of ancient ideas.[60] We know from Mary Shelley's diary that she was reading Ovid's *Metamorphoses* in 1815, which describes in its first book Prometheus's fashioning of human beings from clay (1.80–7), and Percy read Aeschylus's *Prometheus Bound* to her in 1816. The novel of course concerns Victor's desire to 'renew life where death had apparently devoted the body to corruption', a project connected to contemporary notions of 'life-function' in biology and chemistry, but which is identified within the text as a revival of the premodern ideas of alchemical writers in the Renaissance. Yet this text too suggests the barrier between ancient and modern, an ambivalence about the Classical inheritance and a scepticism about the capacity to revive it. In a scene mocked by contemporary reviewers for its incongruity, the monster undergoes a liberal education

---

58 John Polidori, *The Vampyre and Ernestus Berchtold; or, the Modern Oedipus*, edited by D. L. Macdonald and Kathleen Scherf (Peterborough, Ont.: Broadview, 2008), p. 43; James Uden, 'Gothic Fiction, the Grand Tour, and the Seductions of Antiquity: Polidori's *The Vampyre* (1819)', in Roberta Micallef (ed.), *Illusions and Disillusionment: Travel Writing in the Modern Age* (Boston: Ilex Foundation, 2018), pp. 58–77.
59 Charles E. Robinson (ed.), *Mary Shelley: Collected Tales and Stories* (Baltimore: Johns Hopkins University Press, 1992), pp. 332–44.
60 Mary Shelley, *Frankenstein: The 1818 Text*, edited by Marilyn Butler (Oxford: Oxford University Press, 1993). For the fullest account of Shelley's transformation of Classical materials in *Frankenstein*, see Jesse Weiner, Benjamin Eldon Stevens and Brett M. Rogers (eds), *Frankenstein and its Classics: The Modern Prometheus from Antiquity to Science Fiction* (London: Bloomsbury, 2018).

and, in particular, reads the first volume of Plutarch's *Lives*. Shelley, in the persona of the monster, echoes the conventional claims that reading the Greek historian can lead one to 'admire and love the heroes of past ages', but the description of the lesson offered by the ancient writer is far from uniformly positive:

> I read of men concerned in public affairs governing or massacring their species. I felt the greatest ardour for virtue rise within me, and abhorrence of vice ... Induced by these feelings, I was of course led to admire peaceable law-givers, Numa, Solon, and Lycurgus, in preference to Romulus and Theseus.[61]

The example of the Romans is double-edged, comprised of men who both governed and massacred their species. The monster regards the very founder of Rome, Romulus, as less admirable than his pacifistic successor, Numa. The Classical analogies offer at best an ambivalent pattern for modern life – and indeed the central character, Victor Frankenstein himself, corresponds very imprecisely with his ancient model. William Godwin, Mary's father, described Prometheus's creation of human beings in his guide to mythology in this way: 'The man of Prometheus immediately moved, and thought, and spoke, and became everything that the fondest wishes of his creator could ask.'[62] This sounds nothing like Victor's own experience with his creation, and as the novel progresses, he degenerates further and further from his Classical paradigm. He is at best a very approximate – at worst, a disappointing and destructive – modern version of the ancient Prometheus. Despite the implied equivalence in the subtitle, Shelley's novel describes a grotesque, failed revival, rather than an intimate communion, between modernity and antiquity.

The ambition of Romantic-era authors to reanimate aspects of the Classical in the Gothic would have seemed counterintuitive in the mid eighteenth century, when the Gothic emerged as part of a desire to elaborate a political and cultural alternative to the predominance of the Classical. Yet the effort in any era to redefine its relationship to the Classical past raises the more basic question of what counts as 'Classical' at all. Is the word a chronological descriptor, a marker of value, an aesthetic designation? It can mean any and each of these, according to ideological needs.[63] For most

---

61 Shelley, *Frankenstein*, p. 104.
62 Edward Baldwin [William Godwin], *The Pantheon; or, Ancient History of the Gods of Greece and Rome*, 2nd edition (London, 1809), p. 77.
63 James I. Porter, 'What is "Classical" about Classical Antiquity?', in James I. Porter (ed.), *Classical Pasts: The Classical Traditions of Greece and Rome* (Princeton, NJ: Princeton University Press, 2006), pp. 1–68.

contemporary readers of Greek and Roman literature, I suspect, the idea of seeing affinities with the Gothic is far from outlandish or perverse. Many of the aspects of ancient literature and culture that claim attention today in Classics classrooms and studies – the violence and female subjectivity of the *Bacchae* or *Medea*; the surreal fantasies of Aristophanic comedy; the graphic horror of Lucan or Senecan tragedy; the curse tablets and ghost stories of everyday ancient life – bear the qualities that the eighteenth century recognised as Gothic: an attraction to the irrational, a fascination with grotesquerie and violence, the seduction of the supernatural. 'Gothic Greece and Rome' sounds less paradoxical now than ever.[64] If wrestling with the meaning of the past for modernity is part of the cultural work of Gothic literature, allusions to Classical texts by Gothic authors draw attention to aspects of ancient literature that exceeded artificial rules of propriety and evoked a chaotic space of disturbing violence and emotion. To see the Classical displaced from cultural centrality, relegated to the margins and yet returning as a spectral presence, is to see antiquity through Gothic eyes. Many of us see with those eyes still.

64 On ghost stories within Classical literature, see especially D. Felton, *Haunted Greece and Rome: Ghost Stories from Classical Antiquity* (Austin: University of Texas Press, 1999) and Antonio Stramaglia, *Res inauditae, incredulae: Storie di fantasmi nel mondo greco-latino* (Bari: Levante editori, 1999).

1.8

'A World of Bad Spirits': The Terrors of Eighteenth-Century Empire

RUTH SCOBIE

In December 1785, John O'Keeffe and William Shields's Covent Garden pantomime *Omai; or, A Trip Round the World* opened with the scene of a vigil in a moonlit tomb. After a lone watcher in the darkness invoked his dead ancestors, a looming supernatural figure appeared in a blaze of fire. 'My quiv'ring flesh, my limbs bedew'd all o'er', cried the watcher, 'Each feeble sense – my eyes – my voice – no more!' – and he fell to the ground. Designed by Philippe-Jacques de Loutherbourg, the master of European theatrical Gothic, this scene was set not in an English graveyard or beneath an Italian castle, but in '*A Morai*', or sacred place, in Tahiti. Loutherbourg borrowed heavily from recently published accounts of British and French voyages in Oceania to conjure a Gothic scare out of the figure of 'Towha, the Guardian Genius of Omai's Ancestors, and Protector of the legal Kings of Otaheite', whom he dressed in a Tahitian *heva*, or chief mourner's dress.[1]

The *heva* had struck Joseph Banks, on his 1769 visit to Tahiti, as 'fantastical' and a 'dreadfull [sic] apparition'.[2] Loutherbourg's costume sketch for Towha does not depart far from the models he would have found in museums and the illustrations to Banks's voyage.[3] Made to be worn by a ceremonial lead mourner in high-status Tahitian funeral rituals, the *heva* had always been designed to prompt reverence. Long robes and a feather cloak were draped around the mourner's body, pearl shells glittered in an intricate mail breastplate and feathers extended in tall spikes from a headdress, while

---

1 John O'Keeffe, *A Short Account of the New Pantomime called Omai; or, A Trip Round the World* (London, 1785), pp. 1–3.
2 Joseph Banks (10 June 1769), *The Endeavour Journal of Joseph Banks, 1768–1771*, edited by J. C. Beaglehole, 2 vols (Sydney: Public Library of New South Wales, 1962), vol. 1, p. 288; Banks, 'Manners & customs of S. Sea Islands', *The Endeavour Journal*, vol. 1, p. 378.
3 See Philippe-Jacques de Loutherbourg, *Chief Mourner Otaheite*. Watercolour, 1785. National Library of Australia.

the face was hidden behind a large, blank mask.[4] The resulting figure, John Trusler explained, was 'such a one as in England would convey the idea which nurses affix to a ghost or goblin'.[5] Such eeriness in English eyes – related but certainly not identical to the fear experienced by Tahitian onlookers – made it easy for Loutherbourg to appropriate and resignify the *heva* in terms of the familiar aesthetics of the Western supernatural. This scene of exotic Gothic opened a pantomime that allegorised and encouraged future British colonialism, as many critics have observed.[6] In *Omai's* finale, Towha returns to the stage to hear Britannia announce that it is her sons who will 'protect and humanize' the 'new-found world' of Oceania. The presence, and implicit assent, of Tahiti's ancestral 'Guardian Genius' during the symbolic surrender of Oceania to the 'sign of British love, this British sword' affirms British conquest as legitimate inheritance, of course.[7] Yet, as a specifically Gothic apparition, faceless, 'fantastical' and evoking death and terror, Towha can also be seen as haunting *Omai's* confident conclusion by eliciting a continued uncanniness that resists easy incorporation. On the one hand, then, late eighteenth-century Gothic could be a means of discursively containing the extraordinary diversity of human cultural difference experienced up-close by Britons in their encounters with other cultures, and of transforming this difference into colonial commodity or even propaganda. On the other, as this chapter will suggest, the Gothic mode also allowed British writers in this period to register the unassimilable strangeness not just of other societies, but of their own new and alarmingly global empire, as a potential source of pleasure, fear, astonishment, guilt or revulsion.

This 'doubleness' was possible in part because of the Gothic's roots in an older rhetoric of national identity that defined Britishness in terms of its difference from, and resistance to, empire. To be sure, in the opening years of the eighteenth century, 'Britain' itself was the product of Anglophone Protestant expansion and exploitation in Wales, Ireland and Scotland, as well as the Caribbean and North America. Nevertheless, very few early eighteenth-century inhabitants of England thought of themselves as belonging to a conquering power. Indeed, many English, and later British, people

---

4 See Paul Turnbull, 'The Chief Mourner's Costume: Religion and Political Change in the Society Islands, 1768–73', in Michelle Hetherington and Paul Morley (eds), *Discovering Cook's Collections* (Canberra: National Museum of Australia, 2009), pp. 41–57.
5 John Trusler, *A Descriptive Account of the Islands Lately Discovered in the South-Seas* (London, 1778), p. 32.
6 See Daniel O'Quinn, *Staging Governance: Theatrical Imperialism in London, 1770–1800* (Baltimore: The Johns Hopkins University Press, 2005), pp. 74–114.
7 O'Keeffe, *Omai*, p. 23.

enthusiastically identified themselves with what Laura Doyle labels the 'postcolonial discourse' of British national origins. This centred on a genealogy of native English/ British liberty, oppressed first by the Roman empire and then by Norman conquest.[8] Thus, in 'Rule Britannia', sung in a 1740 masque depicting the ninth-century English struggle against Viking occupation, the Lowland Scot James Thomson could proclaim that resistance to 'haughty tyrants' was the defining characteristic of Britons and the reason they never would be slaves.[9]

At the same time, many Britons perceived themselves, often in urgent, material ways, as precisely still vulnerable to the threats of Catholic despotism or Barbary Coast slavery, forces that they associated with more recent territorial empires. Images that would be reused in later Gothic, in particular, were established through retellings of what has come to be known as the Protestant 'Black Legend' of the sixteenth- and seventeenth-century Spanish and Portuguese conquests in South America. Catholic conquistadors, nobles and priests, the Black Legend went, had been guilty of massacres, torture, enslavement and destruction on a vast scale, wallowing in gold, luxury and unlimited, illicit power. They introduced to indigenous societies the bigotry of the Inquisition and manipulated the ignorant through superstition and terror. Daniel Defoe's protagonist Robinson Crusoe, for example, offers as a paradigm of the colonial aggression forbidden by his Protestant conscience 'the Conduct of the *Spaniards* in all their Barbarities practis'd in *America*'. He recalls that this invasion:

> is spoken of with the utmost Abhorrence and Detestation, by even the *Spaniards* themselves, at this Time; and by all other Christian Nations of *Europe*, as a meer Butchery, a bloody and unnatural Piece of Cruelty, unjustifiable either to God or Man; and such, for which the very Name of a *Spaniard* is reckon'd to be frightful and terrible to all People of Humanity, or of Christian Compassion.[10]

In the British imagination, such instances of overt imperialism were understood as symptoms of 'frightful and terrible' foreign tyranny: if not Roman, Viking or Catholic, then Ottoman, Persian Safavid or Mughal. As such, the moralists of the Graveyard School placed imperial victories among the vanities and cruelties that an enlightened modern Protestant would recognise

---

8 Laura Doyle, *Freedom's Empire: Race and the Rise of the Novel in Atlantic Modernity, 1640–1940* (Durham, NC: Duke University Press, 2008), p. 3.
9 James Thomson, *Alfred: A Masque* (London, 1740), p. 42.
10 Daniel Defoe, *Robinson Crusoe*, edited by Thomas Keymer (Oxford: Oxford University Press, 2007), p. 145.

as ephemeral. In 1743, Robert Blair would not have been consciously referring to English 'Wantonness of Power' when he imagined the posthumous infamy of 'the mighty Troublers of the Earth, / Who swam to Sov'reign Rule thro' Seas of Blood' as a kind of ghostly revenge:

> Th' oppressive, sturdy, Man-destroying Villains!
> Who ravag'd Kingdoms, and laid Empires waste,
> And in a cruel Wantonness of Power
> Thinn'd States of half their People, and gave up
> To Want the rest: Now, like a Storm that's spent,
> Lye hush'd, and meanly sneak behind thy Covert.
> Vain Thought! to hide them from the general Scorn,
> That haunts and doggs them like an injur'd Ghost
> Implacable.[11]

Instead, when writers in the first half of the eighteenth century spoke of a *British* empire, what they often had in mind was a metaphor for global trade. Britain's expanding global presence, regulated and promoted by a series of Navigation Acts from the late seventeenth century, was supposed to be 'maritime, commercial and free': an empire that ruled the waves but not the people of far-flung regions, driven by private entrepreneurship, not state ambition.[12] However, the most fervent proponents of Britain's native liberty usually agreed that its 'commercial and free' dominion needed to be secured by military force against European rivals and indigenous resistance. With this agreement went a widespread, though mostly tacit, consensus that profitable global trade necessarily involved enslaved labour. It did not escape every observer that these early forms of 'war capitalism'[13] often bore a disturbing resemblance to the stories that Britons told themselves about 'oppressive, sturdy, Man-destroying' foreign enemies. Defoe's Crusoe, for example, wishes to distinguish himself from the 'bloody and unnatural' Spanish, but since his denunciation comes as he is crouching with a loaded gun, fantasising about shooting or enslaving the native people who land on 'his' island, it is easy for the reader to suspect that his Protestant empire building might be just as 'bloody and unnatural' as that of the conquistadors.[14]

---

11 Robert Blair, *The Grave. A Poem*, 2nd edition (London, 1743), p. 15.
12 David Armitage, *The Ideological Origins of the British Empire* (Cambridge: Cambridge University Press, 2000), p. 8.
13 The term 'war capitalism' is coined in Sven Beckert, *Empire of Cotton: A Global History* (New York: Vintage, 2014), pp. xv–xvi.
14 Defoe, *Robinson Crusoe*, p. 145.

In the second half of the century, these suspicions became much more obtrusive. With the global redistribution of territory at the end of the Seven Years War (1756–63) and a string of unexpected victories for the East India Company, British men and women reading their newspapers found themselves part of a sizeable, culturally diverse yet nominally unified 'nation' which included large populations in North America and India, as well as new Caribbean islands: a 'nation', in other words, which began to look remarkably like an old-fashioned empire, despite its lack of consistent central control. The loss of many American colonies in the early 1780s, in a revolution which made noisy use of the 'postcolonial' rhetoric of native liberty, made the concept of dominion through free trade seem still more implausible. And just a few years later, there were disturbing revelations about the consequences of the East India Company's corruption in Bengal, where reckless profiteering had, as Blair might have predicted, 'ravaged kingdoms', dispossessing, plundering and leaving famine in its wake. Finally, British domination of the transatlantic slave trade became more and more troubling to the British public as abolitionist campaigns intensified, and repeatedly failed, from the 1770s. 'My ear is pain'd, / My soul is sick', William Cowper wrote in 1785, 'with ev'ry day's report / Of wrong and outrage with which earth is fill'd'.[15] Recent historians have described a pervasive 'sense of shock' among British writers during this period, confronted with glaring evidence of their own re-enactment of the horrors of foreign empire.[16] This resemblance, though, was frequently explained or reinscribed as a sign not that the rhetoric of British natural liberty had been unfounded, but that contact with the foreign had corrupted the national character.

Orientalist Empires

William Beckford's *Vathek* – Samuel Henley's unauthorised English translation of Beckford's French Oriental fiction of 1782 that was published in 1786 as *An Arabian Tale, from an Unpublished Manuscript* – is set in the Abbasid empire and reacts both to the new presence of Indian, Persian and Arab artefacts in Britain, and to the news of British despotism in India, constructing the Orient

---

15 William Cowper, *The Task* Book 2: 'The Time-Piece', in *The Poems of William Cowper*, edited by John D. Baird and Charles Ryskamp (Oxford: Oxford University Press, 1995), pp. 139–60 (ll. 5–7.)

16 Jack P. Greene, *Evaluating Empire and Confronting Colonialism in Eighteenth-Century Britain* (Cambridge: Cambridge University Press, 2013), p. xiii. See also Nicholas B. Dirks, *The Scandal of Empire: India and the Creation of Imperial Britain* (Cambridge, MA: Harvard University Press, 2006).

as both the agent and the object of sublime power. This depiction is intensified by what Eve Kosofsky Sedgwick calls the fiction's 'strong Gothic influences', which act as a selecting and ordering principle for Beckford's mass of Orientalist imagery, shaping it into scenes recognisable enough to entertain but also electrify the European reader.[17] Beckford borrows from Antoine Galland's *Arabian Nights Entertainments*, for example, an episode in which the young female protagonist, the princess Nouronihar, travels by night to a hidden treasure cave. The novel adds atmospheric cliché and imagines Nouronihar's psychological suspense to create a Gothic scene not unlike the one that had opened *Omai* a year earlier:

> She stopped, a second time: the sound of water-falls mingling their murmurs; the hollow rusting among the palm-branches; and the funereal screams of the birds from their rifted trunks: all conspired to fill her soul with terror. She imagined, every moment, that she trod on some venomous reptile. All the stories of malignant Dives and dismal Goules thronged into her memory: but, her curiosity was, notwithstanding, more predominant than her fears.[18]

Briefly acting as a virtuous Gothic heroine (although soon to be corrupted), Nouronihar provides substitute eyes and ears for *Vathek*'s fearful, curious readers. The man-eating *ghūl* was an Arab myth, freely adapted by Galland in combination with Greek, Turkish and French folklore to produce the graveyard-dwelling apparitions of his *Arabian Nights*.[19] 'Dismal Goules', Henley's footnotes to *Vathek* duly explain, are monsters 'supposed to haunt forests, cemeteries, and other lonely places; and believed not only to tear in pieces the living, but to dig up and devour the dead'.[20] Not quite *ghūl* and not quite ghost, Beckford's Orientalist 'Goules' live in tombs, feast on corpses, reveal secrets and even 'form ... tender connexions' with living women. In this scene, in particular, they also seem akin to Gothic's internal, psychological spectres, 'throng[ing] into' minds made vulnerable by superstitious 'stories' and overcharged imagination.[21] In moments like this, the Gothic mode repackages cultural difference for metropolitan readers as a source of metropolitan sensation. As such, the novel has been read by many postcolonial

---

17 Eve Kosofsky Sedgwick, *The Coherence of Gothic Conventions* (New York: Arno Press, 1980), p. 19.
18 William Beckford, *Vathek with The Episodes of Vathek*, edited by Kenneth W. Graham (Peterborough, Ont.: Broadview Press, 2001), p. 105.
19 See Ahmed K. Al-Rawi, 'The Arabic ghoul and its Western transformation', *Folklore* 120:3 (2009): 291–306.
20 William Beckford, *An Arabian Tale, from an Unpublished Manuscript: With Notes Critical and Explanatory*, edited and translated by Samuel Henley (London, 1786), note to p. 124.
21 Beckford, *Vathek*, pp. 124, 105.

critics as participating in a wider Orientalist 'cultural fantasy' of the East as always and inherently 'supine, infantile, inviting' to the pleasure-seeking European consumer.[22]

Vathek's mythical setting, though, also acts as an alibi for Beckford's engagement with topical debates about the East India Company. Beckford – as MP, avid collector of artworks looted from Indian courts and the son of a leading political opponent of Company monopolies – was familiar with, though somewhat ambivalent towards, the issues and language of these discussions. From British merchants' acquisition of the island of Bombay in the 1660s until the mid-century, British activities in India had been rapacious but limited to private trade. Maintaining and increasing shareholders' profits continued to motivate the Company's strategies throughout the century, but after 1750 a series of ambitious officers aimed to secure these through military dominance, installing puppet rulers and hiring out an enormous mercenary army. Led by the 'unstable sociopath' Robert Clive, the Company bullied its way into de facto control of Bengal, and by the 1780s a population of tens of millions and an army of tens of thousands were controlled directly from the Company's small offices in Leadenhall Street, London.[23] The powerful and unaccountable Company had always been, as Jon Wilson writes, 'controversial' in Britain, with some political commentators worrying that it 'wielded an abstract, inhuman and unaccountable kind of power, acting like a tyrant rather than a trader'.[24] Clive, rich and fêted after his military successes, attempted to enter British politics, but was haunted by rumours of corruption and brutality. In 1769, news arrived in Britain of millions killed in a famine in Bengal, exacerbated by Company over-taxation and hoarding. Reports of dogs and vultures eating the dead, and even of human cannibalism, cemented Clive's reputation as a ruthless tyrant or 'nabob', a term derived from the Urdu title *nawāb*, which would be applied to many future generations of wealthy British colonial officers.

---

22 Alan Richardson, 'Introduction', in *Three Oriental Tales: Complete Texts with Introduction, Historical Contexts, Critical Essays*, edited by Alan Richardson (Boston: Houghton Mifflin, 2002), pp. 1–14 (p. 10).
23 William Dalrymple, 'The East India Company: The original corporate raiders', *The Guardian* (4 March 2015). <www.theguardian.com/world/2015/mar/04/east-india-company-original-corporate-raiders> (last accessed 27 March 2019).
24 Jon Wilson, *India Conquered: Britain's Raj and the Chaos of Empire* (London: Simon & Schuster, 2016), pp. 33–4.

Nabobs were visible embodiments of the Company's power, and thus, in Tillman Nechtman's words, 'empire's hobgoblins': they could be depicted as exotic villains who threatened to invade and destabilise British liberty and peace.[25] In Samuel Foote's comedy *The Nabob* (first performed in 1772), the corrupt, predatory Sir Matthew Mite, a Company man who 'owes his rise to the ruin of thousands', plots to use his power and 'cunning' to force an innocent English girl into marriage. His Gothic persecution of Sophy Oldham, whom he threatens with imprisonment in a seraglio guarded by 'three blacks from Bengal', is only averted by the play's comic conclusion – and by a more honest white British merchant, whose unpolluted 'commercial and free' wealth saves the day. Foote equates Mite's would-be domestic tyranny explicitly with the Company's oppression of the 'innocent Indian'.[26] However, while such figures of bejewelled, voracious and seraglio-owning nabobs satirised Company abuses in India, they did so through a discourse of Eastern despotism elsewhere energetically deployed in defence of Company colonialism. Advocates for men like Clive argued that many of the rulers they had deposed or subjugated in India were themselves foreign to the lands in question. Many were Muslim and had acquired their power over majority-Hindu populations more or less directly from the Mughal empire. The people of Bengal, a pamphlet by a British merchant reassured British readers, had thus experienced from the Company not 'a conquest' but 'simply a change of masters', the free and fair British supplanting the earlier 'indolent, pusillanimous Asiatic despot' who had 'stripped them of every thing acquired by their industry'.[27] If there was any oppression in 'Indostan', Clive himself insisted in a speech to the House of Commons in 1772, it had not arrived with him, but was endemic to a region whose 'superior' classes had always been 'luxurious, effeminate, tyrannical, treacherous, venal, cruel'.[28] In this context, the villainy ascribed to the nabob by the often overtly racist Foote lies not so much in his previous occupation of India as in his presence, 'tinged by the East', at home.[29]

---

25 Tillman W. Nechtman, *Nabobs: Empire and Identity in Eighteenth-Century Britain* (Cambridge: Cambridge University Press, 2010), p. 15.
26 Samuel Foote, *The Nabob; A Comedy* (London, 1778), pp. 11, 37–8, 5. See O'Quinn, *Staging Governance*, pp. 34–43.
27 Joseph Price, *Five Letters, from a Free Merchant in Bengal, to Warren Hastings, Esq* (London, 1778), pp. 4, 91.
28 Robert Clive, *Lord Clive's Speech in the House of Commons, 30th March, 1772* (London, 1772), p. 42.
29 Foote, *The Nabob*, p. 5.

Similarly, Beckford's Gothic depiction of power channels both pro- and anti-Company rhetoric about India. Vathek, as Abbasid Caliph, enjoys unimaginable wealth and absolute rule over a global empire, including parts of India. His possessions, for example, anachronistically include Masulipatan, a French trading fort on the Bay of Bengal, which had been seized by the Company in 1759. That his government of Masulipatan consists essentially of plunder can be read as a satirical jab at recent Company nabobery: after his soldiers 'confiscate' and 'strip' the property of his subjects, the town is left without 'a single piece of chintz', a major modern commodity. Vathek's European mother and his education in Greek 'sciences and systems', the narrator explains, alienate him from his Muslim subjects' faith and culture, leaving only a predatory interest in their material goods and sensory pleasures. At the same time, Vathek clearly enacts the stereotype of the Eastern as well as Western despot, *nawāb* as well as nabob. 'Tinged by the east' in his decadence and power, and asserting Islamic authority over the Indian Giaour (whose name means 'non-Muslim'), the Caliph also represents Orientalist ideas of Mughal rulers in India.[30] Then again, the Giaour is not native to the lands in which the novel is set, but a 'horrible stranger' whose real motives and powers are initially hidden behind the 'rarities' and 'merchandise' he offers Vathek. These jewel-encrusted, 'magical gew-gaws' recall James Cox's automata and clockwork novelties, imported by the Company to court Mughal leaders in the 1760s and 1770s. This echo might prompt an alternative reading of the Giaour's progress from supplicant merchant to 'voracious ... guest', and finally bloodthirsty parasite, as an allegory of Britain's career in India. Like the Company in Indian states, the Giaour provokes chaos and leaves devastation, with the Abbasid capital left 'like a city taken by storm, and devoted to absolute plunder', and its ruling dynasty destabilised and eventually overthrown.[31] The Giaour, then, may stand in simultaneously for Hindu subject and British imperialist, and Vathek for British imperialist and Muslim monarch. Their fractious, absurd relationship suggests the awkward paradox of British readers' imagined relationship to global empire: the fear of subjugation and the shock of complicity. In other words, *Vathek*'s ambiguous doublings and power struggles replicate the tangled nature of contemporary

---

30 Beckford, *Vathek*, pp. 78, 52, 57.
31 Beckford, *Vathek*, pp. 49, 60, 59, 62. For a discussion of Cox's 'magical gew-gaws', see Marcia Pointon, 'Dealer in magic: James Cox's jewelry museum and the economics of luxurious spectacle in late-eighteenth-century London', *History of Political Economy* 31 (1999): 423–51.

debates about British presence in India, without pledging the novel to any clear or stable political position.

For Beckford's fellow MP Edmund Burke, on the other hand, Gothic tropes were a means of expressing and inducing shock in order to jolt a distant but implicated British readership to support a specific course of action in India. In a series of speeches and pamphlets in the 1780s, Burke argued for state regulation and supervision of the Company, and for the impeachment of one of Clive's successors in the government of Bengal, Warren Hastings. Hastings's highly publicised, drawn-out trial ended in acquittal, but between 1788 and 1795 it provided Burke and others with a stage in the House of Lords from which they attacked the Company. Prosecution speeches became a source of 'X-rated entertainment', as Burke told graphic – critics claimed, exaggerated – stories of corruption, sadistic violence, famine and rape.[32] In the excoriated figure of Hastings, the comic nabob or fantasy Caliph became a fully developed Gothic villain with 'a heart dyed deep in blackness', ruthlessly pursuing wealth through increasingly convoluted and corrupt schemes.[33] Indeed, the strong sense of this character as a stock element in romance and fiction may have contributed to the ultimate failure to convince the House of Lords of the reality of Hastings's crimes. The trial became a popular London spectacle, with ticket-holding audiences responding to testimony in the terms of sensation and sensibility that they had learned from novels and theatre. Famously, at the climax of Burke's description of 'horrid scenes', on the third day 'a convulsive sensation of horror, affright, and smothered execration, pervaded all the male part of his hearers, and audible sobbings and screams, attended with tears and faintings, the female'.[34] Burke's later use of a discourse of the Gothic sublime in his accounts of the French Revolution, Ronald Paulson influentially argues, was a means of making comprehensible the Revolution's incomprehensibility.[35] For Burke in the 1780s, the recent history of the British in India posed equivalent

---

32 Michael J. Franklin, 'Accessing India: Orientalism, Anti-"Indianism" and the Rhetoric of Jones and Burke', in Tim Fulford and Peter J. Kitson (eds), *Romanticism and Colonialism: Writing and Empire, 1780–1830* (Cambridge: Cambridge University Press, 1998), pp. 48–66 (p. 55). See also Frans de Bruyn, 'Edmund Burke's gothic romance: the portrayal of Warren Hastings in Burke's writings and speeches on India', *Criticism* 29:4 (1987): 415–87.

33 Edmund Burke, 'Speech on Opening of Impeachment', 15 February 1788, in *The Writings and Speeches of Edmund Burke*, Vol. VI, edited by P. J. Marshall and William B. Todd (Oxford: Oxford University Press, 1991), pp. 269–312 (p. 275).

34 James Prior, *Memoir of the Life and Character of the Right Hon. Edmund Burke*, 2nd edition, 2 vols (London: Baldwin, Cradock and Joy, 1826), vol. 1, p. 494.

35 Ronald Paulson, *Representations of Revolution, 1789–1820* (New Haven and London: Yale University Press, 1983).

representational problems, since the immense scale involved was impossible to grasp. Turning to the Speaker of the House of Commons during an earlier proposal for a regulatory 'India Bill', he had commented,

> It is impossible, Mr. Speaker, not to pause here for a moment, to reflect on the inconstancy of human greatness, and the stupendous revolutions that have happened in our age of wonders. Could it be believed, when I entered into existence, or when you, a younger man, were born, that on this day, in this House, we should be employed in discussing the conduct of those British subjects who had disposed of the power and person of the Grand Mogul? This is no idle speculation. Awful lessons are taught by it.[36]

The spectacle of empire stunned the British onlooker, this suggested, into an astonishment that Burke had defined in his earlier treatise on the sublime as 'that state of the soul in which all its motions are suspended, with some degree of horror'.[37] Communicating the 'awful lessons' to be found in 'the inmost recesses and labyrinths of the Indian detail' was yet more challenging than telling the story of the French Revolution, since the unfamiliarity of Indian victims, their cultures and even their languages made it 'very difficult for our sympathy to fix upon these objects'.[38] As a result, he complained, any expression of the 'foul enormities, which had deluged the Indies in poverty and blood' would sound, to a white British audience, 'harsh and dissonant, ... violent and unaccountable'.[39] Burke stressed that it was the history of India, that 'catalogue of the blackest crimes', that was inherently Gothic, and not the style of his own retelling. He recalled becoming aware of 'the facts' of these crimes as an experience almost indistinguishable from that of the extremes of horrid fiction-reading. 'The facts related in papers, which, under the direction of Parliament, he was obliged to read, had left on his mind such an impression of horror, as had frequently deprived him of sleep', he explained. 'The most savage or hardest heart could scarcely read' this history, he claimed, 'without shuddering'.[40]

---

36 Edmund Burke, 'Speech on Fox's India Bill', 1 December 1783, in P. J. Marshall and William B. Todd (eds) *Writings and Speeches of William Burke, Vol V*, pp. 378–451 (p. 392).
37 Burke, 'Fox's India Bill', p. 430; Edmund Burke, 'A Philosophical Enquiry into the Origin of Our Ideas of the Sublime and Beautiful' (1757), in *The Writings and Speeches of Edmund Burke, Vol. I*, edited by T. O. McLoughlin, James T. Boulton and William B. Todd (Oxford: Oxford University Press, 1991), pp. 185–320 (p. 230).
38 Burke, 'Fox's India Bill', pp. 383, 404.
39 Burke, 'Speech on Almas Ali Khan', 30 July 1784, in Marshall and Todd (eds)*Writings and Speeches, Vol. V*, pp. 460–78 (p. 461). Burke, 'Fox's India Bill', p. 404.
40 Burke, 'Almas Ali Khan', pp. 462, 471.

Abolitionist Gothic

Similar problems troubled contemporary attempts to represent for British readers the transatlantic slave trade. The extremities of suffering caused by the trade 'were such as exhausted all powers of description', the abolitionist politician William Wilberforce despaired. The vast global scale of this 'mass of misery' could never be adequately communicated or understood. 'Our organs are not fitted for the contemplation of it', he went on, 'our affections are not suited to deal with it; we are lost in the immensity of the prospect'.[41] Captured and enslaved African people had supplied European colonies in America and the Caribbean with labour since the fifteenth century, but only in the eighteenth had British merchants overtaken the Spanish and Portuguese to dominate the trade, which expanded unimaginably. By the 1760s, British ships carried tens of thousands of enslaved people a year from the west of Africa across the Atlantic. Organised campaigns to ban or at least regulate the transatlantic slave trade only began in the 1770s, and revelations of the brutalities specific to contemporary transatlantic chattel slavery, its devastating impact on many African societies, and the unprecedented numbers of enslaved and dead were initially received with disbelief. Like Burke's India, they demanded recognition of the supposedly freedom-loving white British self as complicit in imperial tyranny. 'Is it not utterly astonishing', Wilberforce wondered, 'that Great Britain should have been the prime agents in carrying on this trade of blood? Posterity will scarcely believe it. We, the happiest, render the Africans the most miserable of mankind!'[42] In his abolitionist tract *Thoughts and Sentiments on the Evil of Slavery* (1787), Ottobah Cugoano, a formerly enslaved Fante man living in London, explicitly equates the slave-trading British 'haughty tyrant' with the conquistador Hernán Cortés.[43] The British reader might struggle against the 'discovery and knowledge of such an enormous evil', Cugoano suggests, because they would reveal 'the great and opulent banditti of slave-holders' to be not foreign enemies, but 'his friends'.[44]

Scholars have discussed in detail the British abolitionist campaign's use of literary genres and traditions to influence the reading public. As Brycchan Carey notes, polemics 'couched in the language of reason', and bristling with statistics, were complemented by texts of sensibility and 'emotional

---

41 William Wilberforce, *A Letter on the Abolition of the Slave Trade* (London, 1807), pp. 98, 340.
42 Wilberforce, *Letter on Abolition*, p. 345.
43 Ottobah Cugoano, *Thoughts and Sentiments on the Evil of Slavery* (London, 1787), p. 17.
44 Cugoano, *Thoughts and Sentiments*, pp. 19, 16.

response', especially poetry and, later, prose fiction.[45] The result was a vast literature in which, as Marcus Wood's anthology *The Poetry of Slavery* demonstrates, slavery 'was manifested as a set of fictive literary constructs'.[46] One of the foundation texts of this literature, Thomas Day and John Bicknell's 1773 poem *The Dying Negro*, repeatedly resorts to Gothic conventions to express the sublimely inexpressible scale of imperial horror. Indeed, the introductory dedication to the third edition anticipates Burke by placing the poem within a wider project to 'Astonish and instruct posterity by the dreadful spectacle of human crimes'.[47] Lines added to later editions made the 'dreadful spectacle' of *The Dying Negro* increasingly Gothic. The speaker's sentimental account of his lost love comes to be overshadowed by threats of vengeance, drawing on Walpolean images of captivity and supernatural catastrophe as well as older narratives (like that of *The Grave*) about the spectral revenge of dead victims against tyranny. By the third edition in 1775, the speaker is no longer reconciled to his situation by death's 'kind pass-port' as in the first edition, but imagines himself 'Arm'd' by death's 'dreadful mercy'.[48] Similarly, later versions of the speaker close the first stanza not with the resignation of the first, who sighs that 'the world and I are enemies no more', but with an insistence that he can never 'forgive' the country which enslaved him.[49] In place of the original 'shame and anguish', his fellow slaves are described as burning with 'rage and shame', and new stanzas express the speaker's contempt for the 'feeble soul' of British 'pallid tyrants', assuring the reader that he is 'resistless in his hate'. Chained and bleeding, the speaker curses Britain and interprets 'flashing lightning' and 'involving night' as omens of a doom glimpsed in increasingly lurid and apocalyptic visions:

> I see the flames of heav'nly anger hurled,
> I hear your thunders shake a guilty world.
> The time shall come, the fated hour is nigh,
> When guiltless blood shall penetrate the sky.

---

45 Brycchan Carey, *British Abolitionism and the Rhetoric of Slavery: Writing, Sentiment, and Slavery, 1760–1807* (Basingstoke: Palgrave Macmillan, 2005), p. 74.
46 Marcus Wood, 'Introduction', in *The Poetry of Slavery: An Anglo-American Anthology 1764–1865*, edited by Marcus Wood (Oxford: Oxford University Press, 2003), pp. xi–xxxiv (p. xvii).
47 Thomas Day and John Bicknell, *The Dying Negro, A Poem*, 3rd edition (London, 1775), Dedication, p. v.
48 Thomas Day and John Bicknell, *The Dying Negro, A Poetical Epistle, Supposed to Be Written by a Black, (Who lately shot himself on board a vessel in the river Thames;) to His Intended Wife* (London, 1773), p. 1; Day and Bicknell, *The Dying Negro* (1775), p. 1.
49 Day and Bicknell (1773), p. 1; Day and Bicknell (1775), p. 1.

> ...
> Then the stern genius of my native land,
> With delegated vengeance in his hand,
> Shall raging cross the troubled seas, and pour
> The plagues of Hell on yon devoted shore.[50]

The Dying Negro, according to Thomas Clarkson's history of British abolitionism, 'was read extensively; and ... added to the sympathy in favour of suffering humanity, which was now beginning to show itself'.[51] As the campaign gathered momentum in the 1780s and 1790s, new editions were published alongside growing reams of verse by other writers. In diction that strategically echoed older anti-imperialist patriotism, planters and slave traders became 'tyrants', and enslaved men and women captive heroes and 'fainting', virtuous, 'lovely maids'.[52]

Often formulaic, much of this poetry repeats not just what Alan Richardson identifies as 'the dying slave topos',[53] but also Day and Bicknell's imagery of darkness, storms, shipwreck, blood, live entombment and vengeful afterlife. Hugh Mulligan's 'The Lovers, an African Eclogue' (1784) is set during a moonlit escape from a slave ship in Guinea. As the speakers cling to each other, they hear 'thunders roll' and a 'scream of woe' and see fires on board which 'gain reflected horror from the stream!' 'What fears my bosom fill!' exclaims the woman, and the poem ends as the ship explodes.[54] Edward Rushton's *West-Indian Eclogues* (1787) catalogue the sadistic violence of the 'pallid race', and predict that supernatural revenge will 'poison their days, appall their midnight hour', while Samuel Jackson Pratt (1788) portrays the slave ship as a dark 'prison and a tomb', in which the 'base tyrant' is found 'glorying' over his helpless victims. Pratt's wish, he explains, is that his account of slavery, like Hamlet's ghost, 'should "harrow up the [sic] soul"'.[55] Written the same year, Helen Maria Williams's *Poem on the Bill Lately Passed for Regulating the Slave Trade* compares the British reading public's

---

50 Day and Bicknell (1773), p. 4; Day and Bicknell (1775), pp. 4, 15, 22–3.
51 Thomas Clarkson, *The History of the Rise, Progress, and Accomplishment of the Abolition of the African Slave-Trade by the British Parliament*, 2 vols (London, 1808), vol. 1, p. 83.
52 Hugh Mulligan, 'The Lovers, an African Eclogue', in *Poems Chiefly on Slavery and Oppression* (London, 1788), pp. 23–31 (ll. 35, 87, 41).
53 Alan Richardson, 'Introduction', in *Slavery, Abolition, and Emancipation: Writings in the British Romantic Period*, edited by Debbie Lee and Peter J. Kitson, 8 vols (London: Pickering and Chatto, 1999), vol. 4, pp. ix–xxvi.
54 Mulligan, 'The Lovers', ll. 156, 149, 153, 151.
55 Edward Rushton, *West-Indian Eclogues* (London, 1787), p. 18; Samuel Jackson Pratt, *Humanity; or, the Rights of Nature, A Poem* (London, 1788), pp. 27–8, 12.

consciousness of the slave trade to a Gothic 'foul drama, deep with wrong' (in which the Middle Passage is just *'one* dire scene'). Williams depicts the spectacle of slavery haunting its audience's imaginations, transforming the ordinary sound of the wind into the groans and sighs of a 'pent victim's sinking breath'. In this poem, generic and even clichéd Gothic imagery represents an attempt to grasp the overwhelming magnitude of the *Zong* massacre, a real 1781 incident in which slave traders murdered 132 African men and women. Yet, like Burke, Williams also portrays such subjects as inherently Gothic, requiring no literary mediation to fit into its aesthetic mould:

> where the wintry tempests sweep
> In madness, o'er the darken'd deep;
> Where the wild surge, the raging wave,
> Point to the hopeless wretch a grave;
> And Death surrounds the threat'ning shore –
> Can Fancy add one horror more?[56]

Gothic depictions of slavery were not always abolitionist, despite gaining force and popularity through their circulation in abolitionist writing. While Day, Mulligan and Rushton were uncompromising abolitionists, for example, Pratt was explicitly ameliorationist, and Williams's poem ends with a self-congratulatory paean to 'lov'd Britain', celebrating the passing of a 1788 regulatory act which she expects to end the worst suffering of transatlantic slavery without outlawing the trade. Most startlingly, related images of blood, darkness, 'livid light'nings' and the supernatural 'vengeance' of 'Afric's ruthless rage' appear in poems such as 'Ode on Seeing a Negro Funeral' (*c.* 1773) by Bryan Edwards, a Jamaica planter and later the fiercest of pro-slavery advocates.[57] Nevertheless, the Afro-British abolitionist Olaudah Equiano strategically adopted Gothic among the 'myriad popular genres' of his *Interesting Narrative* (1789).[58] Equiano was a vocal fan of Pratt's poem and quotes the 'elegant and pathetic' *Dying Negro* in his own work.[59] By framing

---

56 Helen Maria Williams, *A Poem on the Bill Lately Passed for Regulating the Slave Trade* (London, 1788) (ll. 36, 34, 3–14, 345–50).
57 Bryan Edwards, 'Ode on Seeing a Negro Funeral', in Wood (ed.), *Poetry of Slavery*, pp. 70–1 (ll. 41, 30, 32).
58 John Bugg, 'The other interesting narrative: Olaudah Equiano's public book tour', *PMLA* 121:5 (2006): 1424–42 (p. 1426).
59 Equiano's open letter to Pratt is in *Morning Chronicle* (27 June 1788). Olaudah Equiano, 'The Interesting Narrative of the Life of Olaudah Equiano, or Gustavus Vassa, the African, in *The Interesting Narrative and Other Writings'*, edited by Vincent Carretta (London: Penguin, 2003), note to p. 98.

his experience of the slave trade in the familiar terms of supernatural monstrosity and darkness, Equiano renders apparently manageable to the white reader its potentially numbing enormities.

Equiano's account of his real or fictional childhood in Essaka, on the other hand, produces moments of Gothic exoticism comfortably recognisable to a British public familiar with Beckford, Burke and *Omai* as well as Day and Pratt. In his first chapter, for example, Equiano outlines Eboe belief in the good and bad 'spirits' of the dead. Switching perspectives from that of an analytical European observer ('the natives believe ... ') to the first-person experience of a child afraid of the dark, he then describes accompanying his mother at night to 'make oblations at her mother's tomb'. As perplexed and as responsive to atmosphere as any Gothic protagonist, the narrator ascribes obscurity and sensation to Eboe religious practices through the repeated terminology of the Burkean sublime:

> I have been often extremely terrified on these occasions. The loneliness of the place, the darkness of the night, and the ceremony of libation, naturally awful and gloomy, were heightened by my mother's lamentations; and these, concurring with the doleful cries of birds, by which these places were frequented, gave an inexpressible terror to the scene.[60]

Helen Thomas identifies this scene as 'an alternate paradigm of the sublime ... within an African context', arguing that Equiano deploys the language of sublimity to explore slavery's dissolution of the enslaved self.[61] These scenes also, though, signal Equiano's complex inheritance from the existing tradition of British texts presenting slavery and empire through the repetition of Gothic formulae. The episode is repeated years later in Equiano's life as explained supernatural. Staying overnight in a 'haunted' house in Montserrat, he mistakes an earthquake for 'a visitation of the spirits', and is 'thr[own] into such a tremor as is not to be described'.[62] Here, Equiano briefly writes himself into the Walpolean role of comic superstitious servant, illustrating his own progress to his final narratorial position of rational Protestant authority.

Much less dismissably, Equiano's 'inexpressible terror' also reoccurs in the narrative at key moments of encounter with the transatlantic slave trade (rather than with slavery in general, which in its African form he

---

60 Equiano, *Interesting Narrative*, p. 40.
61 Helen Thomas, *Romanticism and Slave Narratives: Transatlantic Testimonies* (Cambridge: Cambridge University Press, 2004), p. 236.
62 Equiano, *Interesting Narrative*, p. 114.

depicts as relatively mundane). His first sight of a European slave ship, he writes, 'filled me with astonishment, which was soon converted into terror, which I am yet at a loss to describe'. Equiano's child protagonist is convinced that the 'white men with horrible looks, red faces, and long hair' are magical beings or cannibals, and that the ship is 'a world of bad spirits', like those imagined more fleetingly in the tomb or the haunted house. In another repetition of a Gothic formula, he describes how, 'quite overpowered with horror and anguish', he 'fell motionless on the deck and fainted'.[63] The reader's awareness of the real 'scene of horror almost inconceiveable' to be revealed on board the slave ship undercuts any potentially ironic interpretation of this overwhelming fear as one more instance of pre-conversion superstition. Instead, Equiano characterises as instinctive and ingenuous the assumption of abolitionist poets that the transatlantic slave trade was comprehensible only in terms of supernatural menace. As Mark Stein and others point out, Equiano's child protagonist will be 'civilised' out of his superstition, but in the process will be proven essentially correct in his belief that the white slave traders are monsters who wish to 'kill and eat' him.[64] That is, just as Catherine Morland's Gothic imagination will later allow her to recognise the modern domestic tyranny concealed at Northanger Abbey in Austen's posthumously published 1818 novel, the child-Equiano's apparently naïve translation of ordinary evil into supernatural threat enables him to characterise quite accurately a system that aims at the annihilation of his personhood and the economic consumption of his body.[65] As he later 'reflect[s] with surprise', this 'first sight' of white slave-trading Britons prompts in him more terror and horror than 'any of the numerous dangers' – among them ghosts, shipwrecks, storms and violence – that he encounters as an adult. The next time he faints, many chapters later, it is as a free sailor 'overpowered' with further evidence of the extreme cruelty of slave traders, when his ship is foundering in a storm and his captain 'order[s] the hatches to be nailed down on the slaves in the hold'. Such narratives by and about slaves, Teresa A. Goddu asserts, became 'a core cultural context for the Gothic',

---

63 Equiano, *Interesting Narrative*, pp. 114, 77, 149, 55.
64 Equiano, *Interesting Narrative*, pp. 58, 65. Mark Stein, 'Who's Afraid of Cannibals? Some Uses of the Cannibal Trope in Olaudah Equiano's *Interesting Narrative*', in Brycchan Carey, Markman Ellis and Sara Salih (eds), *Discourses of Slavery and Abolition: Britain and its Colonies, 1760–1838* (Basingstoke: Palgrave Macmillan, 2004), pp. 96–107.
65 See Shinobu Minma, 'General Tilney and tyranny: *Northanger Abbey*', *Eighteenth-Century Fiction* 8:4 (July 1996): 503–18.

producing a genre which 'registers slavery as the cultural contradiction which haunts the Atlantic world's myths of freedom'.[66]

The use of supernatural terror in widely circulated texts on empire such as these was one of the factors behind the eruption of Gothic fiction in the following decades, although the moment of shock that prompted them did not seem long to survive a backlash in the 1790s that encouraged British complacency about the nation's imperial role, moral status and racial superiority. As Doyle writes, the concept of native British resistance to empire was 'ultimately recontained ... within an exclusionary Saxonist narrative'.[67] British imperialism was becoming more centralised in its administration, and more self-justifying as a national moral project. Burkean outrage at the abuses of the Company, for example, was diverted onto what were seen as barbaric Indian practices in need of British reform, such as *sati*, a new preoccupation of fictions like Robert Southey's *The Curse of Kehama* (1810). And, while the national campaign for abolition repeatedly failed to overcome entrenched financial interests, to many Britons its scale could be interpreted as reassuring evidence of the nation's benevolence and love of liberty. Many Gothic writers continued to be closely engaged in debates over empire in this period. Matthew Lewis, for example, was, like Beckford, the heir to West Indian plantations worked by enslaved labour and published fictions set in India, as well as an account of his time in Jamaica. In 1792, the Gothic novelist Clara Reeve warned that enslaved men and women in the Caribbean were 'preparing to rise against their masters, and to cut their throats', prophesying invasion and miscegenation in Britain.[68] As Maisha Wester discusses in her chapter on nineteenth-century Gothic and slavery in the second volume of this *History*, such responses to the perceived threat of slave revolt – prompted especially by the Haitian Revolution – combined with images of the French Terror to create a new Gothic genre. By the end of the century, white British readers were consoled by the belief that rebellion against British rule, not that empire itself, was the worst and most monstrous of the world's hidden terrors.[69]

---

66 Teresa A. Goddu, 'The African American Slave Narrative and the Gothic', in Charles L. Crow (ed.), *A Companion to American Gothic* (Malden: John Wiley, 2014), pp. 71–83 (p. 71).
67 Doyle, *Freedom's Empire*, p. 4.
68 Clara Reeve, *Plans of Education with Remarks on the System of Other Writers* (London, 1792), p. 96.
69 See Maisha Wester's chapter on 'Nineteenth-Century British and American Gothic and the History of Slavery' in volume 2 of *The Cambridge History of the Gothic*, pp. 394–415.

1.9

In Their Blood: The Eighteenth-Century Gothic Stage

PAULA R. BACKSCHEIDER

The origins of Gothic theatre lie deep in the soul of eighteenth-century drama. From scenes like the rebels in dark cellars and the hostage Belvidera's alleged rape in Thomas Otway's much-revived *Venice Preserved* (1682) to Lucy's attempt in John Gay's *The Beggar's Opera* (1728) to poison Polly with a ratsbane-laced cordial in dismal, dank Newgate Prison, Gothic drama had strange tragic, comic and musical roots. In *The Horror Plays of the English Restoration*, Anne Hermanson writes about a number of seventeenth-century tropes that would be notable in the Gothic theatre of the 1790s, including scenes of imprisonment and the spectacle of a woman's bleeding breast.[1] After 1780, the Gothic became a stranger and stranger creation, an established dramatic kind in its own right, and an essential part of the history of the literary Gothic. From its beginning, it was the most contradictory of genres. Almost every play quickly became popular culture while also carrying high art genes.

The epilogue to James Boaden's hit Gothic play *Fontainville Forest* (1794) touts the play's artistic legitimacy with the lines, 'Know you not, Shakspeare's petrifying pow'r / Commands alone the horror-giving hour?'[2] Matthew Gregory Lewis's much-quoted Prologue to *The Castle Spectre* (1797) lists among the essential elements in a Gothic play within which he was working (and promising his audience) 'dungeons damp, / Drear forests' and 'choosing from great Shakspeare's comic school'.[3] The Gothic comic operas were scored by the greatest musicians of the time,

---

[1] Anne Hermanson, *The Horror Plays of the English Restoration* (Farnham: Ashgate Publishing, 2014).
[2] James Boaden, 'Fontainville Forest, A Play', in *The Plays of James Boaden*, edited by Steven Cohan (New York: Garland, 1980), pp. 1–70 (p. 69).
[3] Matthew Gregory Lewis, *The Castle Spectre*, 2nd edition (London, 1798), pp. 1–99 (pp. iii–iv). All quotations are from this edition.

the most respected *opera seria* composers' music enriched Gothic tragedies, and experienced playwrights contributed pseudo-folk songs such as 'The Ballad of Poor Mary' that George Colman the Younger wrote for Boaden's *The Italian Monk* (1797). The engagement of top-notch composers and near-operatic quality singers was continuous. Farce, melodrama, horror, slapstick and tragedy miscellaneously headlined or just suddenly took over. Samuel Johnson wrote of the characters in one of John Dryden's plays what could be said of any Gothic play: 'They exhibit a kind of illustrious depravity, and majestick madness: such as, if it is sometimes despised, is often reverenced, and in which the ridiculous is mingled with the astonishing.'[4]

And the late eighteenth-century Gothic plays *are* astonishing and ridiculous. They plumb the depths of human evil, exploit the spectacular resources of the theatres and send buffoons, clowns, kings, rustics and heroic, noble women across the stage. It is hard to find an eighteenth-century Gothic play that did not have a respectable initial run and regular revivals. Given that, by the first half of the 1790s, they were held in the 3,013-capacity Covent Garden; the 3,611-seating Drury Lane; in other London venues; and in at least 100 theatres outside of London in England, Wales and Scotland, their success was truly remarkable.[5] James Cobb's *The Haunted Tower* (1789), with 84 performances in the first two seasons, was the most successful opera staged by Drury Lane in the entire century. Colman the Younger's *Blue-Beard* (1798) ran for 64 nights in its first season, the longest first run of any play produced between 1776 and 1800. His *Iron Chest* (1796), a dramatic adaptation of William Godwin's radical Gothic fiction *Things as They Are; or, The Adventures of Caleb Williams* (1794), ran almost annually until as late as 1879. As Carol Margaret Davison observes, 'it was the Gothic drama and not the Gothic novel that proliferated and drove the Gothic vogue between 1768 and 1789'.[6] The place that the Gothics came to absorb in the repertoire is arresting. Among the most successful plays of the 1794–5 season were Gothic: George Colman the Younger's *The Mountaineers* (1793); Robert Jephson's *The Count of Narbonne* (1781); Boaden's

---

4 Samuel Johnson, 'Life of Dryden', in John H. Middendorf (ed.), *Lives of the Poets*, The Yale Edition of the Works of Samuel Johnson, vols 21–3 (New Haven: Yale University Press, 2010), vol. 21, p. 382.
5 See David Thomas (ed.), *Restoration and Georgian England 1660–1778* (Cambridge: Cambridge University Press, 1989), pp. 4–5.
6 Carol Margaret Davison, *Gothic Literature 1764–1824* (Cardiff: University of Wales Press, 2009), p. 138.

Fontainville Forest (25 March, opening the season before, thirteen performances); Colman the Younger's *The Battle of Hexham* (1789; thirty-six performances in the first two seasons); and new that season, Miles Peter Andrews's *The Mysteries of the Castle* (1795) and Boaden's *The Secret Tribunal* (1795). In this decade critics complained that the Gothic drama was threatening to drive all other plays off the stage.[7]

Critics today struggle to define 'Gothic drama' as a genre. Although it is common to default to a list of 'devices', 'trappings', 'appurtenances' or 'atmospheric objects', its 'mixed', 'composite', or 'hybrid' nature has emerged as its genre-defining characteristic in critical opinion.[8] Robert L. Platzner's conception of a 'conglomerate' is a near history of English literary movements: Jacobean drama, Graveyard poetry and the 'cult of the sublime'.[9] As popular theorists have long recognised, however, it is the ways in which elements are orchestrated that make meaning and experience, and too few of us work seriously with that. Line of action is especially important.[10]

In fact, Gothic drama changed decade by decade more than has been critically recognised, and, in this chapter, I will trace trends and emphases in Gothic drama through, mostly, two decades. Because the majority of criticism on the Gothic drama focuses on the 1790s, my emphasis will be heavily on the 1780s, and I will not venture into the Romantic period. I will begin, however, rather perversely, with John Home's *Douglas* (Edinburgh 1756, London 1757), a play that I identified as 'Gothic' many years ago. From there I will move to a cluster of Gothic plays from the earliest years of the 1780s, including the astonishing rewrite of *Douglas*, Richard Cumberland's *The Carmelite* (1784).

---

7 This opening section borrows from the similar introduction in Paula Backscheider, *Spectacular Politics: Theatrical Power and Mass Culture in Early Modern England* (Baltimore: Johns Hopkins University Press, 1993), pp. 13–57. I am grateful to the press for allowing me to excerpt passages from my earlier work.

8 Essays in David Punter (ed.), *A New Companion to the Gothic* (Oxford: Wiley-Blackwell, 2012) are the best source for present discussions of possible definitions and defining characteristics. Backscheider in *Spectacular Politics* noted the genres that the playwrights themselves assigned to their plays, pp. 155–6.

9 Quoted in Angela Wright and Dale Townshend (eds), *Romantic Gothic: An Edinburgh Companion* (Edinburgh: Edinburgh University Press, 2016), p. 27.

10 On patterns or lines of action, see John G. Cawelti's ground-breaking exploration of formula art, *Adventure, Mystery, and Romance: Formula Stories as Art and Popular Culture* (Chicago: University of Chicago Press, 1976), especially pp. 80–2 and pp. 267–8. As an example, Jeffrey N. Cox notes that Gothic plays often move to affirm 'marriage' and 'traditional values'. See Cox, 'Gothic drama', in Marie Mulvey-Roberts (ed.), *The Handbook of the Gothic* (New York: New York University Press, 2009), pp. 131–5 (p. 134).

Transitional *Douglas*

Douglas was written in the company of Edinburgh intellectuals and continues to be performed today.[11] Privately and later in rehearsal, Home played young Norval; David Hume was Glenalvon; Hugh Blair Anna the wise and faithful maid; and William Robertson and Adam Ferguson Lord and Lady Randolph. After David Garrick declared the play 'totally unfit for the stage', these and other friends saw to its production at the Canongate Theatre, recently put under the management of West Digges, a versatile actor of great popularity in Scotland and notorious for his liaison with Sarah Ward.[12] He played Douglas to her Lady Randolph.[13] The scandal that followed the production was rather Gothic in itself; clerics who attended were disciplined, and Home was finally forced to resign his pastorate.[14]

The opening lines of the play are 'Ye woods and wilds, whose melancholy gloom / Accords with my soul's sadness.'[15] The mingling of these exact physical and emotional settings became an identifying characteristic of Gothic drama and captured the imagination of fiction writers as well as dramatists. An especially close relationship between Ann Radcliffe's novels and playwrights developed, as the play was the primary source for her first Gothic romance, *The Castles of Athlin and Dunbayne* (1789) and her later novels were adapted by playwrights.[16] Born in the dark winters of repressively

---

11 As might be expected, it is most popular in Scotland. Representative performances were at the Edinburgh Festival in 1950 and 1986 and at the Glasgow Citizens' Theatre in 1989.
12 James S. Malek, 'Introduction', in *The Plays of John Home*, edited by James S. Malek (New York: Garland, 1980), pp. vii–xliii (p. ix).
13 Sarah Achurch Ward was the estranged wife of Henry Ward, actor and playwright; her relationship with Digges probably began in 1752. In 1758, she signed herself 'Mrs. Digges'. See *A Biographical Dictionary of Actors, Actresses, Musicians, Dancers, Managers and Other Stage Personnel in London, 1660–1800*, edited by Philip H. Highfill, Jnr, Kalman A. Burnim and Edward A. Langhans, 16 vols (Carbondale: Southern Illinois University Press, 1973–93).
14 For a comprehensive account, see Lisa A. Freeman, *Antitheatricality and the Body Public* (Philadelphia: University of Pennsylvania Press, 2017), pp. 147–88.
15 John Home, 'Douglas: A Tragedy', in James S. Malek (ed.), in *The Plays of John Home* (New York: Garland, 1980), pp. 7–75 (p. 7).
16 Plays adapted in various degrees from fiction include Andrews's *The Mysteries of the Castle*, which drew upon *The Castle of Otranto* (1764) and Radcliffe's *The Mysteries of Udolpho* (1794); Boaden's *Fontainville Forest* adapts Radcliffe's *The Romance of the Forest* (1791), his *The Italian Monk* is from her *The Italian* (1796–7), and his *Aurelio and Miranda* (1798) from Lewis's *The Monk* (1796). The practice continued with stage adaptations following novels more quickly, with James Robinson Planché's *The Vampire; or, The Bride of the Isles* (1820), a dramatic adaptation of John Polidori's novel *The Vampyre* (1819). See Jeffrey N. Cox, 'Gothic Drama', pp. 131–5, and Diego Saglia, '"A portion of the name": Stage Adaptation of Radcliffe's Fiction, 1794–1806', in Dale Townshend and

Presbyterian Scotland, set in the medieval gloom of castles and featuring a cliff above a stormy sea and gloomy, threatening nights, it was first performed on 14 December 1756. The long nights and cold winds of Edinburgh were part of the event structure, as was the plotting to shut it down or defend it outside the theatre. At the centre of the play is Lady Randolph, whose secret marriage to the great hero Douglas ended with his death. Rather than confess to the marriage, she sends their infant son away and her existence has become one of continual mourning for Douglas and the reliving of what she imagines was the baby's death in a raging stream. With the backdrop of an invasion by the Danes and the machinations of Glenalvon, who is in competition with her new husband Lord Randolph, her son (reared as 'Norval', now also called 'Douglas') is returned by the old shepherd who has reared him.

In the Gothic, the characters always seem to be on the verge of directing violence against themselves or others. While Glenalvon and Lord Randolph plot against each other and against Norval and even Lady Randolph, she breaks gender norms and threatens Glenalvon: 'at thy peril, practice ought against [Norval]'.[17] Ambition and greed are the motives of almost all leading Gothic characters, and, as in this play, it is true of the 'good' characters as well as the villains. Lady Randolph and Norval admiringly turn the recovered family jewels in their hands and imagine the restoration of the Douglas legacy, and neither the fact that he is the rightful heir nor his plans to be a virtuous, generous lord who brings prosperity erase this scene from memory. Norval quickly claims his noble lineage, and he and Glenalvon insult and kill each other.

Douglas foregrounds plot devices that would come to predominate in Gothic drama. For example, Norval has insisted to his mother that she reveal his identity, and her keeping the secret along with the men's pride and jealousy leads to Norval's death. In the Gothic, there are always secrets – here her marriage and Glenalvon's false loyalty – and they spark the kind of tortured consciences and horrific events that are also characteristic of the Gothic stage. And as here, the consequences are usually written on the *bodies* of the heroine and on the *souls* of the villain-heroes. Glenalvon dies 'Foaming with rage and fury ... Cursing his conqueror', and Lord Randolph accepts his multiple sins from coercing Lady Randolph into marrying him to exercising his jealousy towards Norval. He says, 'Peace in this world I never can

Angela Wright (eds), *Ann Radcliffe, Romanticism and the Gothic* (Cambridge: Cambridge University Press, 2014), pp. 219–36, for surveys of adaptations.

17 Home, 'Douglas', p. 27.

enjoy.'[18] Hoping not to survive, he leaves to fight the Danes. Gothic plays pass eternal judgements, as had earlier tragedies with Gothic tones. The penalty is performed by combining regret and violent passion in a single character or by a pair of characters, one eternally tortured by conscience and one pushed into madness by failure. Jaffeir and Pierre in *Venice Preserved* rise from hell. Spectres such as these come to populate the Gothic plays as the years pass. Lord Randolph's attempt to die without the act of suicide that Jaffeir commits was more moral but equally ambiguous as a sign of redemption. Foaming and cursing like Glenalvon are the signs of being unredeemably evil and unrepentant. Glenalvon's end was described, not put on stage, but actors learned to foam and perform this state of mind. Evil was becoming increasingly spectacular.

In a series of aesthetically conceived moments, actresses from Sarah Ward and Peg Woffington (London 1757), through to Ann Barry Crawford and Sarah Siddons at the end of the century, moved from mourning, into brief joy (and plotting) with the discovery that Norval is not dead, to the final horror. Anna, the witness, reports that Lady Randolph 'flew like light'ning' up a hill, halts at the precipice, and flings herself into the waterfall. This recreates another aesthetic, desponding tableau for Lady Randolph: 'Upon the brink she stood / ... / then lifting up her head / And her white hands to heaven / ... / plung'd herself / Into the empty air.'[19] By breaking Anna's dramatic speech into two parts with an ejaculation of guilt by Lord Randolph, Home describes it twice, thereby emphasising its horror. At this point, Lady Randolph is not just despairing but mad, the formulaic destiny or tragic evolution for women such as Belvidera who have made terrible choices or who have been forced into situations in which all available options are catastrophic. In his review in the *Literary Magazine* (April 1757), the playwright Arthur Murphy seemed to regret that Lady Randolph had not died of grief, thereby providing a 'pathetic' closing.[20] This is a significant recognition, as the reduction of the pathetic is one of the contrasts between the true Gothic theatre of the 1780s and the tragic and sensibility plays that were dominating the serious repertoire at the time.

---

18 Home, 'Douglas', pp. 73–4.   19 Home, 'Douglas', p. 73.
20 Arthur Murphy, *The Literary Magazine: or Universal Review* April 1757 (15 March – 15 April, 1757), 3 vols (London, 1757), vol. 2, p. 139.

Creating Gothic Drama

It is unusual for a very small group of plays to set new directions in theatre, as three plays that were produced in the early 1780s did. Robert Jephson's *The Count of Narbonne*, John O'Keeffe's *The Castle of Andalusia* (1782) and Richard Cumberland's *The Carmelite* featured the most important conventions that developed in the 1780s. Settings and special effects, as well as character types and configurations, firmly took hold. All three men were successful playwrights. Jephson's first play, *Braganza* (1775), had been performed fifteen times in its first season, and Garrick called it 'a Tragedy of great Merit'.[21] *The Castle of Andalusia*, produced first as *The Banditti* in 1781, was O'Keeffe's thirteenth performed play, and *The Carmelite* was Cumberland's nineteenth.

The Count of Narbonne is the best known of these plays because it is an adaptation of Horace Walpole's *The Castle of Otranto* (1764).[22] It opens in an elaborate Gothic hall with a 'full-length Picture of Alphonso in Armour' at the back centre, an aspect of the stage furniture that readers of *The Castle of Otranto* would have recognised (Fig.9.1). It was extremely popular, as it was performed twenty-one times in its first season. Jephson and Walpole corresponded with one another about the play, and Walpole was delighted with Jephson's work. Because Jephson could not be in London himself, Walpole left Strawberry Hill to collaborate on the production, even loaning a costume to the priest. The great Shakespeare editor, Edmond Malone, supplied the Epilogue to the piece. In its title, the naming of the characters and in aspects of its plot, the play also suggests that Jephson was allowed to draw upon *The Mysterious Mother* (1768), Horace Walpole's Gothic closet drama of double incest that, though privately published at Strawberry Hill in a small print-run of fifty copies in 1768, was, in a common eighteenth-century practice, only shown to, and read by, a few small groups of people.[23] It appears that Richard

---

21 David Garrick to George Steevens, 16 December [1774], in David M. Little and George M. Kahrl (eds), *The Letters of David Garrick*, 3 vols (Cambridge, MA: Harvard University Press, 1963), vol. 3, p. 972.
22 On the changes Jephson made, see Jacek Mydla, 'The gothic as a mimetic challenge in two post-*Otranto* narratives', *Image & Narrative* 18:3 (2017): 80–93 (pp. 85–9).
23 *The Mysterious Mother* was only made publicly available when Walpole eventually conceded to its publication in Dublin in 1791. Jephson too used the strategy of reading his play with influential groups more than most playwrights of the time; he was accused by the envious of assuring the success of *Braganza* in this way. The novelist and playwright Frances Brooke compares Jephson's strategy with the lack of access that her heroine has to the production of her play in *The Excursion* (1777). As early as 1762, Jephson associated with Horace Walpole, Edmond Malone, Frances Sheridan and Edmund Burke; he was so close to Garrick that he uncharacteristically made Jephson an unsecured loan of £500. Temple Maynard cites sources for Jephson's practices and

In Their Blood: The Eighteenth-Century Gothic Stage

Fig.9.1: Susanna Highmore Duncombe, *Manfred Pursuing Isabella in Front of the Portrait*. A Scene from *The Castle of Otranto*. Courtesy of the Lewis Walpole Library, Yale University, 24 17 765 Copy 4.

Cumberland may have also seen Walpole's closely guarded Gothic tragedy as he composed *The Mysterious Husband. A Tragedy* (1783), a formula returning-navy-son-in-wartime play that suddenly explodes into one of the earliest Gothic plays with a story of incest, despair, haunting and suicide. A horrible curse lies over the house of Count Narbonne in Jephson's play because Narbonne's father murdered Alphonso while on a Crusade. Narbonne, the Gothic villain, intends to divorce his wife and marry his dead son's fiancée. In Cumberland's tragedy, Lord Davenant had secretly married Marianne, then tricked her into believing that he was dead, and she marries Charles Davenant, thereby entering into an incestuous, bigamous marriage.

With a desperate willingness to do anything to hang on to his illegitimate wealth and title, Jephson's Count is accused of, among other things, intending to carry out 'the law by which the tyger tears the lamb'.[24] The Countess of Narbonne is the perpetually mourning, threatened woman not unlike the figure of Home's Lady Randolph. Jephson substituted a fall from a horse as the heir's cause of death rather than stage what would have been his risible crushing by a giant helmet (of course, Narbonne gave his son the horse). Godfrey is marching towards the castle to claim the estate, since Narbonne no longer has a male heir. An unnamed peasant in the mould of Home's Norval appears. 'Awe nor fear I know not', he pronounces in the face of Narbonne's opening threats, claiming that he is 'The equal of thy birth'.[25] He, Theodore, is the rightful heir of Alphonso, has rescued Narbonne's daughter from an outlaw gang and is in love with her. Theodore, as had Norval, arouses Narbonne's dangerous jealousy and his death is planned. The major horror in the play is not the crazed and desperate Count but the threat that the curse will be enacted on the entire Narbonne lineage, including the good Adelaide. Secrets, undisclosed identities and wild rage abound. Narbonne mistakenly kills his daughter and then kills himself. The grieving Theodore eventually possesses the castle, now purged of the curse of Alphonso.

Entertainment is a legitimate purpose of art and certainly of stage plays, and perhaps Gothic drama will help us take full cognisance of that fact and study it in more sophisticated ways. *The Count of Narbonne* might be taken as

> collaborations with Walpole, including Martin S. Peterson, *Robert Jephson (1736–1803): A Study of His Life and Works* (Lincoln, NE: University of Nebraska Press, 1930) and James Prior's *Life of Edmond Malone, Editor of Shakespeare*, 2 vols (London: Smith, Elder and Co., 1860) and quotes Walpole's praise for Jephson's writing in his 'Introduction' to *The Plays of Robert Jephson* (New York: Garland, 1980), pp. vii–xxvii.
> 24 Robert Jephson, 'The Count of Narbonne', in Temple James Maynard (ed.), *The Plays of Robert Jephson* (New York: Garland, 1980), pp. 1–61 (p. 27).
> 25 Jephson, 'The Count of Narbonne', pp. 7, 29.

the first true, publicly performed Gothic drama, the bearer of the major elements in character types, line of action and settings in past times and in castles, monasteries and prison cells, with chills, thrills, horror and spectral appearances. The good, like Adelaide and her mother, are placed in sentimental, pathetic tableaux. Women live in states of sexual anxiety, but they are not objects of true sexual desire. Isabel feels no distress at the death of her fiancé and is in desperate fear of the Count's plan to marry her, knowing all too well his motive and lack of any attraction to her. As in the later Gothics, the sex that is portrayed there is a perverse fantasy, such as when Narbonne accuses the priest as follows:

> Pent in your close confessionals you sit,
> Bending your reverend ears to luscious secrets;
> While with their heaving breasts, and love-fraught eyes,
> Devoutly they sigh out each amorous wish.[26]

There are freeze-scenes for men and women, including both the Count and Countess; Adelaide is kneeling at the altar, and Theodore is dressed in his peasant garb and in Alphonso's armour. It is entertainment, composed and staged to be just that, and, as many examples of popular culture are, chosen to take advantage of a faddishly popular piece of fiction or news.

Eleven days after *Narbonne*'s first performance in November 1781, O'Keeffe's *The Banditti; or, Love's Labyrinth* with music by Samuel Arnold opened. It was an embarrassing failure; O'Keeffe and Arnold revised it as *The Castle of Andalusia*, which opened on 2 November 1782 and became the fifteenth most popular new mainpiece on the London stage between 1776 and 1800.[27] The play has two groups, a gang of marauding bandits and a stereotypically troubled noble family. The patriarch of the family is Don Scipio, the marital target of the scheming Isabella. He has banished his son, Don Caesar, and intends his daughter Victoria for Don Fernando. Don Caesar, disguised as Ramirez, has become the bandit leader. Isabella's daughter Lorenza is in love with Ramirez but disguised as Victoria, as her mother wants her to marry the richest suitor.

For the twenty-first-century reader, *Andalusia* seems more a comic opera than a Gothic drama. It features, however, all of the characteristics that would keep the *Gothic* comic opera in business. Arnold was an important composer, and Ramirez was played by Frederick Reinhold, a popular concert

---

26 Jephson, 'The Count of Narbonne', p. 27.
27 See Frederick Link, 'Introduction', in Frederick M. Link (ed.), *The Plays of John O'Keeffe*, 4 vols (New York: Garland, 1981), vol. 1, pp. vii–lxxii (pp. xxiv–xxvi).

and Covent Garden Theatre bass singer. This quality and variety of music would become an essential part of the Gothic, even in the most serious and tragic of plots. The opening scene was a shadow-marked cavern den far below the earth, 'with winding Stairs, and Recesses cut in the Rock; a large Lamp hanging in the Center'.[28] It was followed by a dark forest scene in which Don Scipio is attacked. His life is presented as being in danger, but the knight-errant type, Fernando, rescues him. The location shifts to a variety of rich spaces in the castle. Among Don Caesar's followers are the evil Sanguino and the apparently comic Spado, who quickly get into Don Scipio's house to plunder it. The action thus includes plotting by an evil woman and by bandits, two staples of the later Gothic stage. The lower-class characters in Gothic plays are, for the most part, simply drawn (although they often cause bad things to happen, as Old Norval did in *Douglas*); alternatively, they are often predatory, like the thieves and highwaymen feared by the people of the time. They continued to provide farce, however, as Hilario does in *The Mysteries of the Castle*.

Spado turns out to be the dangerous bandit but also the source of effective farce. He robs Don Scipio, and in the darkness claims to be Fernando and accepts a purse with a ring attached to it. Spado disguises himself as Fernando's father's secretary. He persuades the household that Fernando is the servant and that his man Pedrillo is Fernando. From that point on, Don Scipio amusingly mutters over a man of Fernando's position keeping the ring and purse. Don Scipio is mistaken for the butler, and there is an entertaining scene in which Pedrillo performs the role of master, orders Fernando around and wants to kick him. Spado cheats a number of characters and threatens some with his pistol. The play is the kind of comedy of mistaken identities on two levels, since the young women have exchanged identities, and Spado's actions cause the kind of class confusion in which Oliver Goldsmith, in particular, had excelled. O'Keeffe had produced two Tony Lumpkin plays, and puts the comic device to the service of Spado's greed and the thwarting of Isabella's ambition. By borrowing from hits like Goldsmith's *She Stoops to Conquer* (1773), O'Keeffe contributes to the establishment of the Gothic as a mixed form.

In September 1782, Sarah Siddons returned to the Drury Lane stage, and, in her first performance in *Isabella; or, The Fatal Marriage*, David Garrick's adaptation of Thomas Southerne's *The Fatal Marriage* (1694), she had the

---

28 John O' Keeffe, 'The Castle of Andalusia', in Frederick M. Link (ed.), *The Plays of John O'Keeffe*, 4 vols (New York: Garland, 1981), vol. 1, pp. 1–82 (p. 1).

kind of visceral, emotional impact on the audience for which she became famous. Over the next two years, with similar impact, she played Belvidera; Jane Shore in Nicholas Rowe's *The Tragedy of Jane Shore* (1715); Home's Lady Randolph (ten performances); and many similar parts. Richard Cumberland left Covent Garden for Drury Lane and wrote his only true Gothic play, *The Carmelite* (1784), for her; the play had thirteen performances that season. Siddons became, of course, a cult figure, and by the end of the season was being profusely acclaimed. Remarkably, *The Carmelite* is a rewriting of *Douglas*.[29] Matilda, the Lady of St Valori, is unhinged by 20 years of grief and has several highly dramatic scenes reminiscent of Lady Matilda Randolph in *Douglas*, some on the rocky shore of the sea. At times she contemplates a suicidal leap, 'Mad'ning I rush'd; there, from the giddy edge / Of the projecting battlements, below, / Measuring the fearful leap, I cast my eye'.[30]

Unlike Lady Randolph, she has kept her son – called Montgomeri – disguised with her, and seeing him playing stops her from following through with her suicidal intentions. He is modelled on Norval and embodies the quality of nobility. He calls Lord Hildebrand, the usurper of his estate, a 'hungry vulture' who has 'hover'd o'er thee on his felon wings' and intends to defend her: 'my great father's spirit Swells in my bosom'.[31] Hildebrand is the villain haunted by his conscience as he believes he has killed St Valori, who was actually found and nursed back to health and then held captive in the East. He and St Valori, disguised as the eponymous Carmelite, have been rescued from a shipwreck by Montgomeri. Valori soon thinks Matilda has married this lowly page and flies into a jealous rage, just as Lord Randolph had done over Norval. Neither Lord Randolph nor Hildebrand is the legitimate holder of the women's estates, and Montgomeri, like Norval, is in danger because of the men's contest for wealth and their jealousy of the young man who is loved by the widow. Alphonso in *Narbonne* assumed his grandfather's armour, and Montgomeri puts on his father's to represent Matilda's claims and 'bears the shield of great Saint Valori'. This drives St Valori to distraction, and he threatens, 'Let them beware ... / Before the lion's kill'd'.[32] In a dramatic speech Hildebrand confesses to killing St Valori and describes a vision he has

---

29 The only recognition of this fact that I have found is a brief mention in the review in 'Postscript', *St. James's Chronicle* (4 December 1784), p. 4.
30 Richard Cumberland, 'The Carmelite: A Tragedy', in Roberta F. S. Borkat (ed.), *The Plays of Richard Cumberland*, 6 vols (New York: Garland, 1982), vol. 3, pp. 1–72 (p. 21).
31 Cumberland, 'The Carmelite', p. 23.   32 Cumberland, 'The Carmelite', pp. 28–9.

just had of a secret door flying open to reveal 'the funeral trophies of Saint Valori', 'the banner of the bloody Cross', 'the Lady Widow' and Montgomeri.

At the moment in the play when St Valori is on the brink of fighting and killing his own son, Cumberland revises Home's conclusion. First, he replicates Lady Randolph by pushing Matilda towards full madness when she believes her husband is confirmed dead, and then he supplies a happy ending. Recognising what he had in Siddons, Cumberland wrote speeches that are archetypally hers. When Hildebrand confesses to her that he has killed St Valori, she exclaims, 'Ah, Scorpion! is it thou? I shake with horror – / . . . thee have I preserv'd? / . . . / Art not asham'd, O earth, to bear him yet?'[33] Siddons was a master of telegraphing noble, powerful 'lightnings of scorn'; one witness to Siddons's 1786 performance of Belvidera commented on her performance of 'great resentment' of the insults 'to a high-born Senators daughter' and contempt for 'that assembly, all made up of wretches'.[34] This interpretation perhaps was not in any other actress's repertoire, and the skill vivifies Matilda's contemptuous condemnation of Hildebrand.

Reviews, although decidedly mixed, record 'bursts of applause', while claiming that no play in living memory had been so 'loudly applauded at its conclusion', a solid approval of the happy ending. These reviews are evidence of the rise of Gothic drama and the growing enjoyment of its least respectable characteristics, especially its mixed and unrealistic aspects. The *St. James Chronicle; or, The British Evening Post*, *Critical Review* and *London Chronicle* note 'Inventions' and borrowings of comic scenes from other plays and that the plot is 'like a pantomime, when we are admitted behind the scenes'.[35] The view of the sea in a storm, the 'Gothic hall' in the castle and the painted windows in the chapel were sets singled out for praise. Even the growing effect on acting is discernible, as moments in Siddons's interpretations and Palmer's 'determination' to 'reconcile' the audience to his performance show. Consistently observed are 'improbable', even 'incredible', plot details and 'unaccountable' actions, such as St Valori choosing to disguise himself as a Carmelite. Regardless, this drama of male haunted conscience and female suffering, along with the noble youth's British character, clearly appealed.

33 Cumberland, 'The Carmelite', pp. 47–48.
34 See A Lady of Distinction, *The Beauties of Mrs Siddons* (London, 1786), pp. 4, 6; Jonathan Bate, 'Shakespeare and the Rival Muses: Siddons versus Jordan', in Robyn Asleson (ed.), *Notorious Muse: The Actress in British Art and Culture, 1776–1812* (New Haven: Yale University Press, 2003), pp. 81–103 (p. 97).
35 *The London Chronicle* (2–4 December 1784), p. 4; *The Critical Review* (February 1785), vol. 59 (London, 1785), pp. 104–5; *St. James Chronicle* (2–4 December 1784), p. 4, respectively.

Releasing Gothic Drama

As this discussion has suggested, the London theatres had been prepared for the Gothic for a long time, and the 1790s Gothic plays exploited both the times and mature stage effects fully. In this section, I will analyse some of the evolutions in this decade. Gothic plays always had spectacular elements, and they became more fully spectacle plays as the century wore on. The standard for spectacular productions was set by Dorset Garden in the last decades of the seventeenth century, and machines and engines and even entire scenes from the 1680s can be found in productions in the last half of the eighteenth century. Traps had long been used to raise spirits from the dead, and allowed invasions of plunderers, single molesters and ghosts. In Colman's innovative *Blue-Beard*, the enormous door to the Blue Chamber sinks with a crash to reveal the blood-streaked room. Painted scenes and flats were used for years and new ones added. By the 1780s, both royal theatres had enormous resources for spectacular effects and entire plays. Lighting, sets and even more elaborate machinery forged with content heightened effect and audience appeal. Scenes from tragedies such as panoramic views, sweeping landscapes, forests, palace gardens, temples and tombs often came from stock. These collections allowed affordable spectacle effects in the farces, afterpieces and minor Gothic mainpieces.

Gothic plays and the demand in other plays for more special effects contributed to a new surge in developments and combinations that, as in Colman's *Blue-Beard*, left audiences in awe. The staging of natural and manmade disasters, some with illusions of distance, increased the sense of a dangerous, unpredictable world. Flaming palaces were common and volcanoes had erupted by 1727 at Covent Garden.[36] Covent Garden had put fireworks on the stage as early as the 1770s and both theatres had expert pyrotechnics. Fire was always effective, whether within a comforting gathering-place or as the glimpse of the beginning of a conflagration of certain destruction. Sound was important, too. Waterfalls into which people could jump roared; boulders fell and rolled; avalanches' 'whumpfing' became crashes.

The rise of the Gothic inspired important advances in lighting. Much attention has been given to what critics identify as conventional sets, but the importance of sophisticated lighting technology has been less studied. The coming of night, the sudden extinguishing of all light, the picturesque

---

36 Sybil Rosenfeld, *Georgian Scene Painters and Scene Painting* (Cambridge: Cambridge University Press, 1981), pp. 53, 56–7.

nature of light filtering into ruined abbeys, passages and dark paths are major parts of these plays. Ruins, damaged or roofless rooms and partly crumbled walls variously provide ways to make light welcome or threatened and fragile. Characters reacted more fully to contexts. Adeline in *Fontainville Forest* says, as she walks through a room with grated windows in a ruined abbey, 'The waning light warns me to gain my chamber', and when she takes refuge in a secret room, she claims 'A general horror creeps thro' all my limbs ... Shut from the light of day, and doom'd to perish.' Flashes of lightning accompany the shaking of the abbey, and one of the turrets is struck by lightning and falls.[37]

Mood-altering shadows served to render people huge and made the silhouette of a weapon an arresting focal point. The development of transparencies and new kinds of lamps with better machinery to raise and lower them allowed impressive special effects. 'Silk screens of different colors working on pivots in front of bright lights' produced the effects of clouds, storms and supernatural messages as, for instance, foliage turned from green to blood colour.[38] By 1784, Argand lamps in the wings and sheets of gauze created a blue-grey haze in front of ghosts, visions and spectres. Various times of day and sudden changes could be omens, such as when the stage suddenly went dark. Different colours and textures of silk; back lighting; lights on moveable posts; stained glass in front of lamps; tints in the sky; and transitions in the darkness all developed from technical advances.[39] Covent Garden could provide a gradual and beautiful coming of day or an especially threatening falling of night. Footlights and chandeliers could be raised and lowered, or even pulled into the wings. Polished reflectors and transparencies produced startling effects, such as burning buildings and even cities and storms with added effects from 'lightning flashers'.

Of the Drury Lane theatre that opened in 1794, Boaden wrote, 'Everything that machinery could accomplish was put within the grasp of the proprietors.' Matthew Gregroy Lewis's 1801 *Adelmorn, the Outlaw* prescribes moonlight, a wall opening to show the moon turning red, a burst of thunder and strangely lighted demons.[40] Stage directions written by playwrights became

---

37 Boaden, 'Fontainville Forest', pp. 26, 38, 41.
38 Charles B. Hogan, *The London Stage: Part 5, 1776–1800: A Critical Introduction* (Carbondale: Southern Illinois University Press, 1968), pp. lxvi–lxvii.
39 Rosenfeld, *Georgian Scene Painters*, pp. 59–62; David Worrall, *Theatric Revolution: Drama, Censorship and Romantic Period Subcultures 1773–1832* (Oxford: Oxford University Press, 2006), pp. 153–6.
40 Quoted in David Francis Taylor, *Theatres of Opposition: Empire, Revolution, and Richard Brinsley Sheridan* (Oxford: Oxford University Press, 2012), pp. 195, 209 respectively.

more common. Architectural changes to the theatre, beginning in the 1780s, moved the actors back from isolation on the forestage and into close relationship with the scenery. Scenery, therefore, played a much larger part in creating the Gothic atmosphere and enhancing the characters' emotional states. Too often we are text-centred when considering the eighteenth-century Gothic stage, but imagining the performance of nature's destructive and symbolic power is an essential part of the historical reconstruction of the Gothic experience.

What had previously been described now came to be shown. In *The Count of Narbonne* the Countess describes a tower shaking, but in *Fontainville Forest*, 13 years later, the audience sees for itself the turret fall. From static image, like the portrait of Alphonso in armour, came the activation of the potential for moving dramatisation, such as mysterious entrances and disappearances. Ghosts came to be expected, and a creative range of special effects created them. By the 1820s, more was invisibly carried out, and reality and illusion techniques evolved. In James Robinson Planché's *The Vampire; or, The Bride of the Isles* (1819), the Lyceum had invented a way to make an actor instantly disappear through the use of a so-called 'Vampire Trap'.[41]

The plays of the 1780s set the mixed genre pattern, often composed, as they were, of usually incompatible elements. Music became *de rigueur*, as did pantomime and comedy roles for the great comic actors. In the opening scene of *Andalusia*, John Quick, as Spado, narrates and pantomimes his favourite robbery: 'Oh, I love to rob a fat Priest. – Stand, says I, and then I knock him down.'[42] Fifteen years later, Paullo (played by Richard Suett), in Boaden's *The Italian Monk*, is a great comic character as he defies the Inquisition as 'tipstaves for the devil's court'.[43] The music in *The Italian Monk* is more thematically interwoven than in the earlier dramas and a contrast in genre to *Andalusia*. The earlier plays drew more from English theatrical types, especially comic opera, pantomime, nursery, and fairy-tale elements and farce. Miles Peter Andrews's *The Enchanted Castle* (1786), which was basically a pantomime, morphed into James Cobb's *The Haunted Tower*, a comic opera in which Suett's character repeated, 'I wish I was in love or in liquor', and the great opera

---

41 Diego Saglia, 'The Gothic Stage: Visions of Instability, Performances of Anxiety', in Angela Wright and Dale Townshend (eds), *Romantic Gothic: An Edinburgh Companion* (Edinburgh: Edinburgh University Press, 2016), pp. 73–94 (p. 90).
42 O'Keeffe, 'The Castle of Andalusia', p. 2.
43 James Boaden, 'The Italian Monk', in Steven Cohan (ed.), *The Plays of James Boaden* (New York: Garland, 1980), pp. 1–78 (p. 37).

singer Michael Kelly performed the lead.[44] In fact, the connections between opera and Gothic theatre deepened after Richard Brinsley Sheridan and Thomas Harris, the managers of the royal theatres, purchased and began managing King's Opera House (June 1778).

As adaptations of Gothic fictions like *The Italian Monk* grew, so the percentages of material drawn from other English theatrical kinds, such as post-1670s tragedies and the she-tragedies, increased. Jeffrey N. Cox argues that with genre importation after 1800, Matthew Gregroy Lewis and a few others were attempting to convert the Gothic into tragedy; he also links Gothic plays with the rise of melodrama. The Gothic's sources cannot be fixed. For example, Cox works with Robert Maturin's *Bertram; or, The Castle of St. Aldobrand* (1816) without noticing its source: John Aikin's *Sir Bertrand, a Fragment* (1773), the short Gothic tale that accompanied his sister Anna Laetitia Aikin's essay 'On the Pleasure Derived from Objects of Terror' (1773). Walpole believed that *Sir Bertrand* was a tribute to himself as it was a Gothic tale in the mode of *The Castle of Otranto*.[45]

Orchestrating the Gothic Play

One reason why Gothic drama scholarship has not advanced in revisionary ways is that we largely ignore 'orchestration'; that is, the ways in which playwrights and managers coordinate sets, the particular cast of characters with predictable casting decisions, readable cultural icons and the dominant lines or patterns of action to create the play, the experience and the meaning. Thus, subtleties like the shifting subordination of genres with the rise of others are ignored as formulaic characteristics and 'tricks' are often tallied. This practice serves to demean the Gothic drama, as does ignoring the plays' dates of composition and performance.

In the earlier plays, the tortured, guilt-ridden man drives the action. In *The Carmelite*, Hildebrand's tortured conscience is the centre of the play, and his crazed vision is the supernatural component. As the years pass, the pending dreaded event evolves into what George E. Haggerty once observed of the

---

44 James Cobb, *The Haunted Tower* (London, [1796]), p. 4. Before this there were only editions of 'Songs, Duets, Trios, and Choruses in the Haunted Tower' in London. There was a 1790 Dublin edition of the script.
45 Walpole and others have believed that Anna Laetitia Aikin (Barbauld) wrote either the tale or the essay. See William McCarthy, *Anna Letitia Barbauld: Voice of the Enlightenment* (Baltimore: Johns Hopkins University Press, 2008), pp. 111–12.

'female Gothic': 'a range of victimization' in female characters.[46] Women in the she-tragedies raised masculine status by their beauty and superior sexuality; in the 1780s Gothic, they are adversaries desired for their wealth and are creative spectacles of victimhood. These plays feature mothers and wives more than virgins, and reflect what Mary A. Favret has identified as the affliction of the kinds of waiting characteristic of these decades: 'feelings of "dreary agitation"'.[47] This is the Gothic state of mind of Lady Randolph, Boaden's Adeline and most other Gothic heroines.

Deceptively, the trope endured but revised orchestration brought grim twists embedded more deeply in sets. Schedoni in *The Italian Monk* goes away for an extended time in order to test his wife, returns, sees her with a man and accidentally kills her instead of him. Julia in *The Mysteries of the Castle* chose an endless, hideous entombment and elected to be thought dead so as to avoid the immurement of a forced marriage. The creation of interwoven background music also developed. Lewis writes stage directions in *The Castle Spectre*, with Angela standing in front of a 'perforated door of pure Gothic'. 'A brilliant illumination suddenly took place, and the door of the oratory opened – the light was perfectly celestial.' The spirit of Angela's mother advances, and the lighting effects are enhanced by music loaded with cultural capital. Niccolò Jommelli's *Chaconne* ('his celebrated overture in three flats') accompanied the opening of the scene,[48] and, at the conclusion, a startling, sudden 'blaze of light flashes through the Oratory' as 'a full chorus of female voices chaunt "Jubilate!"'.[49]

In the 1790s, women characters are still waiting, half in hope of happiness and half in fear of the horror that is often housed in a man whom they know. In fact, both men and women alike can be killers. Anticipation is essential. The sense of expecting something terrible, even horrible, to happen to the woman exists from the opening scene of these plays. Moreover, the plays increasingly activate a collective dread of 'a threat to our assumptive world', the psychological concept referring to the assumptions and beliefs about the way the world is that ground, stabilise and make people feel secure. Angela, the brave, virtuous heroine of *The Castle Spectre*, is imprisoned by her predatory uncle Osmond who killed her mother. He begins his declaration,

---

46 George E. Haggerty, *Unnatural Affections: Women and Fiction in the Later 18th Century* (Bloomington: Indiana University Press, 1998), p. 13.
47 Mary A. Favret, *War at a Distance: Romanticism and the Making of Modern Wartime* (Princeton, NJ: Princeton University Press, 2010), pp. 74–5.
48 Backscheider, *Spectacular Politics*, pp. 173–4; quoted from James Boaden, *Memoirs of Mrs. Jordan*.
49 Lewis, *The Castle Spectre*, pp. 79–80.

'My bosom is a gulph of devouring flames! I must quench them in your arms... If you refuse and scorn my offer, force shall this instant—'.[50] A grim cat-and-mouse conflict between them begins and is carried out in a sequence of sensational sets. At the conclusion, Angela suddenly springs forward, yelling 'Die!' She, not the men around her, stabs him. The unknown and the unpredictable are always 'out there', and whatever activates an awareness of what might happen, of what human beings – even a friend or relative – might suddenly do, occurs at some point in every Gothic play.

The range of victimisation drew out frightening creativity in plots and sets and established the woman's importance. Gothic plays always used surveillance, as the men watched the Matildas jealously, but in the 1790s a sexually charged surveillance emerged, as in *The Italian Monk* and *The Castle Spectre*. Anticipation pushed beyond the reach of the imagination and into the abyss of the unpredictable and the ever-more horrible. In modern genre movies, violence against the woman is predictable – the man will stab her; grab her from behind and garrote her; or commit violent rape on the floor of her apartment. Not so in Gothic drama. As Judith Wilt explains, 'Dread is the father and mother of the Gothic. Dread begets rage and fright and cruel horror, or awe and ... a shining standfastness—all of these have human features, but Dread has no face.'[51]

At these moments, the physical and emotional settings are mingled. The majestic, spectacular sets that could quickly become dark prison cells, catacombs and small clearings in a thick forest were stock in both patent theatres; when such fixtures housed innocent virgins or characters who appeared to be wholesome, 'normal' men but who suddenly turned into victims of serial killers or monsters, they, to use Johnson's words, 'astonished' and entertained. These episodes expressed the evil that the audiences feared was in every human heart, lurking in caves and narrow, dark paths. Uniting physical and emotional settings, this kind of vision became familiar.

This mingling extended to the audience, and it began with the heroines. As early as *The Carmelite*, eye-witnesses wrote of visible and audible weeping during Siddons's most dramatic scenes.[52] Episodes were constructed to give recognisable signals of a horror to come, touching deep fears and suddenly generating *frisson*, as with the line 'Kill my father' uttered by Siddons in *Venice*

50 Lewis, *The Castle Spectre*, p. 27.
51 Judith Wilt, *Ghosts of the Gothic: Austen, Eliot and Lawrence* (Princeton, NJ: Princeton University Press, 1980), p. 5.
52 See, for example, *London Magazine* 3 (December 1784), p. 479.

Preserved. Entire scenes were built around such moments. In *Douglas*, the line was Lady Randolph's question to Old Norval about the baby whom he rescued from the water: 'Was he alive?' Eye-witnesses and reviewers testified that Ann Barry Crawford 'checked [the audiences'] breathing' with her 'instantaneous ... shriek of a mother's agonizing effort to know all', and Siddons 'sent an electric thrill through the audience.' Releasing the power of the mother persona that she had cultivated, Siddons used her 'countenance' rather than her voice as 'her whole figure displayed' 'the trembling anxiety of a mother'.[53] Gothic dramatists intended to make audiences feel and react in physical ways. In tragedies, and especially in Gothic plays, reports of members of the audience sobbing, screaming in shock, going into hysterics and even fainting increased.[54]

Critics continue to debate the extent to which Gothic drama is 'political', a space in which various ideologies or specific, short-term positions could be exhibited, supported, discredited or debated. Again, seeing Gothic plays in two decades rather than as a group explains important differences in orchestration that affect plot, settings and performance. From the beginning of the 1780s, it is possible to align individual plays and revivals almost day by day, with news in the daily press, changes in public opinion and in flare-ups of pamphlet warfare. *The Count of Narbonne* came out a year after the Gordon Riots, and it raised the possibility of mob action. Those who attempt to kidnap Adelaide are 'outlaws', and the crowd that attempts to deny Narbonne his *unjust* claim is defeated, including by the supposedly exemplary Theodore. Adelaide describes them as follows: 'The castle is beset; / The superstitious, fierce, inconstant people, / Madder than storms, with weapons caught in haste, / Menace my father's life.'[55] Mobs, gatherings of 'rabble' or robbers figured in most of the Gothic plays of the decade, beginning with

---

53 Diego Saglia, 'Staging Gothic Flesh: Material and Spectral Bodies in Romantic-Period Theatre', in Lilla Maria Crisafulli and Fabio Liberto (eds), *The Romantic Stage: A Many-Sided Mirror* (Amsterdam: Rodopi, 2014), pp. 161–84 (pp. 177–8); descriptions and quotations from Nancy E. Copeland, '"Simple art and simple nature": Sarah Siddons versus Ann Crawford', *RECTR* 2nd series 2:1 (1987): 54–61 (pp. 55–58) and Susan Staves, 'Douglas's Mother', in John. H. Smith (ed.), *Brandeis Essays in Literature* (Waltham, MA: Brandeis University Press, 1983), pp. 51–67 (pp. 59–60).

54 Boaden writes of one of Siddons's performances: '(how is it possible I should ever forget?) the *sobs*, the *shrieks*, among the tenderer part of her audiences; or those *tears*, which manhood, at first, struggled to suppress, but at length grew proud of indulging ... but the nerves of many ... gave way ... and fainting fits long and frequently alarmed the decorum of the house'. See James Boaden, *Memoirs of Mrs. Siddons*, 2 vols (London, 1827), vol. 1, p. 327.

55 Jephson, 'The Count of Narbonne', p. 44.

Douglas in which robbers attacked Lord Randolph and 'barbarians' Old Norval.[56]

David Worrall finds *The Count of Narbonne* 'deflecting' of political thought, but the play is actually a good indicator of the opinions of the lower orders at the time of the Wilkite and the Gordon Riots.[57] Walpole, Edmund Burke and others were criticising the 'exorbitance of the peers', and Narbonne's declarations of his power ('because I can') are certainly political representations.[58] Ruins spoke of the demise of entire, once great and respected families or of abbeys, and Gothic plots move reassuringly towards the restoration of legitimate ownership. *Andalusia* actually depicts a civil war, as Don Caesar, the son, has invaded and is at war with his father. 'This night shall give me possession of the castle', he proclaims, 'I'll see if terror can't restore that right of which injustice has depriv'd me.'[59] By the time that *The Carmelite* came out in 1784, Britain had lost the American War of Independence, which many Englishmen considered a civil war. *The Battle of Hexham*, by Colman the Younger, was set during the War of the Roses. Home, who had fought in the Jacobite uprising, includes moving passages against the long history of English–north Britain conflict. Oliver Goldsmith stated unequivocally of *Douglas* that a passage was 'an oblique panegyric on the Union, and contains a pleasing gradation of sentiment'.[60] That these plays commented on current and topical political events was something that the patrons and audiences of the London theatres understood.

Much Gothic criticism relates the political content of the Gothic stage to specific events in France, yet Gothic drama is consistently inseparable from British structures of feeling, events and reactions. Cox states unequivocally that there are two 'historical moments' that are key to the Gothic and the achievement of 'its full power': the fall of the Bastille in July 1789 and the fall

---

56 On the frequency and significance of 'bands' of robbers and impoverished people 'living at large' depicted in 1790s plays and representing public opinion and the fears of the common people, see Backscheider, *Spectacular Politics*, pp. 218–31.
57 David Worrall, 'The Political Culture of Gothic Drama', in David Punter (ed.), *A New Companion to the Gothic* (Chichester: Wiley-Blackwell, 2012), pp. 148–60 (p. 151). George Rudé notes the first Wilkite disturbance when 'the lower orders ... "pelted"' the Earl of Bute in 1761 preceding the Massacre of St. George's Field in 1768. See George Rudé, *The Crowd in History: A Study of Popular Disturbances in France and England, 1730–1848* (New York: John Wiley, 1964), pp. 52–7.
58 Vincent Carretta, *George III and the Satirists* (Athens, GA: University of Georgia Press, 1990), p. 47.
59 O' Keeffe, 'The Castle of Andalusia', p. 34.
60 Oliver Goldsmith, *The Monthly Review* (May 1757) in Arthur Friedman (ed.), *The Collected Works of Oliver Goldsmith*, 5 vols (Oxford: Clarendon, 1966), vol. 1, pp. 12–13.

of Napoleon at Waterloo in June 1815.[61] I would add to these the September Massacre in revolutionary Paris in September 1792, while emphasising that there is no denying the impact of events in France and of the Jacobin/ anti-Jacobin movements in England. One highly noticeable impact on the plays, for example, is the demonisation of priests. In the 1780s, as in *The Count of Narbonne* or *The Carmelite*, the priests are good men or disguised men who are not priests at all. Because the plays are often set in the Catholic times of the Middle Ages, religious denominations are largely unnoted. Later emphasis is on the gulf between what they are supposed to be and what they are, and they serve as propaganda to raise fear and resistance to Britain's greatest Catholic enemy.

The 1790s expanded that Gothic plot line. The rise of incidents of arbitrary exercises of power are as much a reaction to the rapid succession of new English acts, such as the suspension of Habeas Corpus in 1794, as to news from France. As Diane Long Hoeveler observes, 'The use of the imprisonment and rescue motif seems to have originated in the private domestic sphere and then moved to the public, political realm in works that feature male aristocrats under siege by hostile, usually "revolutionary" forces'.[62] The shadow of French events is, indeed, critical to the construction of Gothic plays, but immediate English events are at least as important. David Francis Taylor offers an example as he carefully argues for the significance of Richard Brinsley Sheridan's having been the manager of Drury Lane at the same time as he was an MP who passionately campaigned for major reforms in the mid-1790s. As he points out, we need to 'recalibrate' scenes of incarceration: 'If we read the dramaturgy of the Gothic not within an ahistorical vacuum or by means of a generalized conception of revolution / repression, but rather within the specific political contexts, spatially and temporally ... then it becomes possible to perceive the workings of and performance conditions for a radical Gothic'. Setting plays next to such details as Sheridan's visits to prisons, Taylor's identification of the 'radical Gothic' provides a firm, gripping critical technique of absolute and immediate political commentary activated through the history of English drama.[63] In a much-needed move, he goes beyond factoring in the playwright to include the influence of the theatre manager.

---

61 Jeffrey N. Cox (ed.), *Seven Gothic Dramas, 1789–1825* (Athens, OH: Ohio University Press, 1992), p. 8.
62 Diane Long Hoeveler, 'Gothic Adaptation, 1764–1830', in Glennis Byron and Dale Townshend (eds), *The Gothic World* (Abingdon: Routledge, 2014), pp. 185–98 (p. 192).
63 Taylor, *Theatres of Opposition*, pp. 205, 220, 204.

Conclusion

If we compare the plays of the Exclusion Crisis (1678–81) to eighteenth-century Gothic plays, it is hard for me to move far from what I identified in *Spectacular Politics* (1993) as the primary kind of work that Gothic drama does. The plays of the 1680s debated issues, including the nature of kingship, and were political to their core. The Gothic drama differed in degree and tilted into *popular* entertainment that quickly became mass entertainment. The theatre had become increasingly commercial as decades passed, and the respectability of entertainment grew. The Prologue to Andrews's *The Mysteries of the Castle* promises 'Music, Pantomime, and graver scenes' and the play delivers 'a mélange of timeless Gothic-comic routines'.[64]

Among the things that the audience and critics jeered at in O'Keeffe's *The Banditti* (1781) were 'lightning flashing ... through the windows of a dark room' and 'a talkative old nurse'.[65] Both became pleasurable, and the latter calls Shakespeare to mind and the collection of nurses, rustics, swains, old men and women that add resonance and depth to many Gothic plays. They delighted audiences and are instances of what scholars of Music Hall entertainment call 'the detached parts of Shakespeare'. When censured, Boaden defended his ghost with 'Hamlet's pedigree' and also quotes Shakespeare in lines that the audience could be expected to recognise: 'You mean to sanction then your own pale sprite, / By his "that did usurp this time of night"' (Epilogue). Political and entertaining. Astonishing and ridiculous. In its own time, *Douglas* was criticised as improbable and Lady Randolph's behaviour as 'preposterous'.[66] Yet it was associated with Shakespeare from the beginning, and it became a much-performed sensation and cast an extraordinarily long shadow. Lady Randolph tells her son,

> ... In me thou dost behold
> The poor remains of beauty once admir'd:
> The autumn of my days is come already;
> For sorrow made my summer haste away.[67]

This quatrain in blank verse obviously invokes Shakespeare's Sonnet 73, 'That time of year thou mayst in me behold'. How vigorously the echo of Shakespeare was discussed has been forgotten; all we recall is the shout

---

64 Worrall, 'Political culture', p. 152.
65 Quoted in Link, 'Introduction', pp. xxiv–xxv; production information from this source.
66 Daniel O'Quinn, *Entertaining Crisis in the Atlantic Imperium 1770–1790* (Baltimore: Johns Hopkins University Press, 2011), p. 182.
67 Home, 'Douglas', pp. 50–1.

from an Edinburgh audience member: 'Whaur's yer Wully Shakespeare noo!'[68] In fact, the Church controversy anticipates the institutionalised mixture of high and low cultures of subsequent Gothic dramas. Goldsmith insisted that Glenalvon 'bears a near resemblance to [Shakespeare's] Richard',[69] an impression that was only confirmed by the character being charismatically performed on the stage by the renowned Shakespearean actor David Garrick. *The Monthly Review* noticed Hildebrand's death in *The Carmelite* similarities with the death of Beaufort in *Henry VI*.

No critic today denies that the Gothic was 'the most popular and prevalent literary mode' of the 1790s.[70] Unlike today, it was both profitable and admirable to produce entertainment, and it was acceptable and even faddish to be a consumer of it. As thrilling and entertaining, and even cathartic, as terror-moments were, the audience member could look forward to high-quality music, aesthetic sets and comic moments and have faith in a conclusion that explained the apparently supernatural; supplied poetic justice; or restored a familiar, even mundane world and human relationships.

68 Malek, 'Introduction'; Home, 'Douglas', p. ix.
69 Goldsmith, *The Monthly Review* (May 1757), in Friedman, vol. 1, p. 12.
70 Dale Townshend and Angela Wright, 'Gothic and Romantic Engagements: The Critical Reception of Ann Radcliffe, 1789–1850', in Townshend and Wright (eds), *Ann Radcliffe*, pp. 3–32 (p. 17).

I.10

Domestic Gothic Writing after Horace Walpole and before Ann Radcliffe

DEBORAH RUSSELL

The Gothic literary landscape changed in 1789, the year that saw the outbreak of the French Revolution and the publication of Ann Radcliffe's first novel, *The Castles of Athlin and Dunbayne*. With Radcliffe at the forefront of a surge of interest in the Gothic, what E. J. Clery has called 'the hothouse productivity of the 1790s' has come to define eighteenth-century Gothic writing.[1] Even an early commentator like T. J. Mathias jumps directly from Horace Walpole's *The Castle of Otranto* (1764) to the threat of French influence in the post-Revolution Gothic boom:

> Have Gallick arms and unrelenting war
> Borne all her trophies from Britannia far?
> Shall nought but ghosts and trinkets be display'd
> Since Walpole ply'd the virtuoso's trade,
> Bade sober truth revers'd for fiction pass,
> And mus'd o'er Gothick toys through Gothick glass?[2]

However, the genre was also shaped by the work that appeared in the twenty-five years between the publication of Walpole's 'progenitor' text and the beginning of the career of the 'Shakspeare [sic] of Romance writers', Radcliffe.[3] Mathias's worry about the confusion of truth and fiction, for example, speaks to the fundamental intertwining of the Gothic and historical novels in this intervening period. Mathias's poem is also, of course, a carefully curated take on literary history. When he mentions Radcliffe directly, he makes a concerted attempt to insert her 'into a literary tradition that is more continental than "Gothic" or natively English' – a 'remarkable' move, as Dale

---

1 E. J. Clery, *The Rise of Supernatural Fiction, 1762–1800* (Cambridge: Cambridge University Press, 1995), p. 142.
2 T. J. Mathias, *The Pursuits of Literature. A Satirical Poem in Four Dialogues. With Notes*, 7th edition (London, 1798), p. 402.
3 Nathan Drake, *Literary Hours; or, Sketches Critical and Narrative* (London, 1798), p. 249.

Townshend and Angela Wright point out, given the meanings that the Gothic had acquired in Britain throughout the preceding century.[4] Part of the context that Mathias elides is that, in the 1770s and 1780s, Gothic writing is overwhelmingly associated with domestic, British settings. Against the backdrop of the American Revolution, conflict with France and Spain, domestic unrest in the form of anti-Catholic riots and the growing abolition movement, early Gothic texts participate in a sustained re-examination of British history and identity.

While these decades remain underexplored in modern criticism on the Gothic, there is widespread acknowledgement that two authors writing at this time provide influential models for the subsequent development of the genre. Both Clara Reeve's *The Old English Baron* (1778; first published as *The Champion of Virtue* in 1777) and Sophia Lee's *The Recess* (1783–5) have received some critical attention, particularly in studies of women's Gothic writing.[5] Reeve and Lee were not, however, writing in isolation. This chapter will situate their novels not in terms of their legacy, but rather within a first wave of Gothic-inflected texts that are overwhelmingly concerned with Britain's Gothic heritage. Such writing aims to supplement and interrogate non-imaginative approaches to the nation's past, emerging from the same context that produces works such as William Blackstone's *Commentaries on the Laws of England* (1765–9), Oliver Goldsmith's *The History of England* (1771), Catharine Macaulay's *The History of England* (1763–83) and Thomas Warton's *The History of English Poetry* (1774–81).

Satirical Gothic

That there are more than a few isolated examples of Gothic writing in this period is indicated by the appearance at the end of the 1780s of several texts that offer a self-aware, ironised take on established Gothic trends. The best known of these is James White's satirical Gothic novel, *Earl Strongbow* (1789). Here, a frame narrative of an antiquary's visit to Chepstow Castle leads into a 'manuscript' describing encounters between a seventeenth-century prisoner

---

4 Dale Townshend and Angela Wright, 'Gothic and Romantic Engagements: The Critical Reception of Ann Radcliffe, 1789–1850', in Dale Townshend and Angela Wright (eds), *Ann Radcliffe, Romanticism and the Gothic* (Cambridge: Cambridge University Press, 2014), pp. 3–32 (p. 16).
5 For discussions of Reeve and Lee, see, for example: E. J. Clery, *Women's Gothic: From Clara Reeve to Mary Shelley* (Tavistock: Northcote House, 2000); Donna Heiland, *Gothic and Gender: An Introduction* (Oxford: Blackwell, 2004); and Angela Wright, *Britain, France and the Gothic, 1764–1820: The Import of Terror* (Cambridge: Cambridge University Press, 2013).

of Charles II and the twelfth-century ghost of the eponymous earl, Richard de Clare. The conventions of the Gothic are treated with irreverent deflation in this 'mock-Gothic ridicule of the Gothic', as Frederick S. Frank describes it.[6] The earl explains, for example, that ghosts are mainly motivated by a quest for gossip to relieve the boredom of being dead: 'Sometimes ... we are allowed, by a particular indulgence, to send some of the members of our society in quest of news to these supernal regions, and the account of the various fashions and fantastic changes which take place in the manners and customs of the living, amuse our minds'.[7] Fiona Price reads *Earl Strongbow* as 'us[ing] the gothic to generate a comic unease with history', undercutting national pride alongside any grandeur associated with historical enquiry.[8] In James Watt's view, however, 'the pseudo-historical setting ... also allowed explicit criticisms of the present by way of an idealizing appeal to the same past realm'.[9] Indeed, some reviewers seem to have overlooked the satirical elements entirely: Mary Wollstonecraft's review praises the novel's 'just sentiments and lively descriptions', expostulating, 'How far preferable are these histories of deeds of chivalry to the insipid love tales daily offered to the public, which ... instead of inspiring a taste for virtue, by exalting the first impulses of nature, debase the expanding mind.'[10] White's 'heterogenous' mingling of history, romance and burlesque (in the words of another reviewer) thus produces a multi-faceted engagement with the nation's Gothic past, enabling productive ambivalence about the relationship between that past and the present.[11]

Indeed, ambivalence about the comparison with the past is a central feature of two more comic Gothic novels published around this time: the anonymously authored *Powis Castle* (1788) and Mr Nicholson's *The Solitary Castle* (1789). Both of these texts are set in the eighteenth-century present. In *The Solitary Castle*, the central character ('a portrait of *Superstition*', as the Preface has it) has become 'disgusted with the world', retiring to a gloomy

---

6 Frederick S. Frank, *The First Gothics: A Critical Guide to the English Gothic Novel* (New York and London: Garland Publishing, 1987), p. 410.
7 James White, *Earl Strongbow: The History of Richard de Clare and the Beautiful Geralda*, 2 vols (London, 1789), vol. 1, p. 66.
8 Fiona Price, *Reinventing Liberty: Nation, Commerce, and the Historical Novel from Walpole to Scott* (Edinburgh: Edinburgh University Press, 2016), p. 113.
9 James Watt, *Contesting the Gothic: Fiction, Genre, and Cultural Conflict, 1764–1832* (Cambridge: Cambridge University Press, 1999), p. 43.
10 [Mary Wollstonecraft], 'Article XXI', *Analytical Review; or, History of Literature, Domestic and Foreign* 3 (March 1789): 343–4 (p. 343).
11 Anon., review of White's *The Adventures of King Richard Coeur-de-Lion*, *Monthly Review; or Literary Journal* 6 (October 1791): 230–1 (p. 231).

castle that he can decorate as he pleases: 'Seven niches were scooped in the walls round the hall, in which seven Kings of England ... frowned in marble: and to render the appearance of these statues perfectly terrible, the Captain had dressed them all in suits of real and complete armour'.[12] A retreat into the glories of the national past is thus framed as superstitious folly, particularly when it becomes clear that those 'perfectly terrible' suits of armour are riddled with rust. Modernity collides with the Gothic mindset in dramatic fashion when a hot-air balloon makes an unplanned descent into the castle grounds; the Captain and his daughter Margaret are unable to interpret this vision as anything other than a 'phantom' or 'demon of darkness' – until the fallen aeronaut emerges bedraggled and thorn-scratched from a hedge.[13] When the Gothic appears overtly in this text, then, it is connected with ludicrous eccentricity or largely drained of meaning (as in the vapidly fashionable entertainments that Margaret enjoys later in the novel). The narrative voice is also clearly invested in satirical modernity, making direct reference to Henry Fielding and offering a visual image of the heroine's heart, divided into such arterial components as virtue, ignorance, innocence and enthusiasm, that is reminiscent both of Laurence Sterne's experimentation with the printed page and of the subject of *The Spectator* 281, the dissection of a coquette's heart (Fig.10.1).

However, the division between Gothic superstition and modern reality is deliberately complicated as the novel proceeds. As the modern world intrudes into the life of the solitary castle, it brings with it some remarkably Gothic scenarios: attempts at seduction followed by abduction; capture by a band of robber gypsies; wrongful arrest and a close brush with a ducking stool; a near-miss with incestuous rape; and the discovery of an estranged brother/son. In the course of this narrative, the operations of the law are revealed to be corrupt, foolish and arcane, while the behaviour of army and navy officers undercuts any attempt to view these institutions with pride. The tone remains light-hearted, but the novel retains ambiguity about whether it is tracing comparisons or connections with the Gothic past evoked by the 'seven Kings of England' or the narrative poem that Margaret's suitor reads, 'Saint Genevieve of the Woods'.[14] Both possibilities engender mockery of the modern nation.

---

12 Mr Nicholson, *The Solitary Castle: A Romance of the Eighteenth Century*, 2 vols (London, 1789), vol. 1, pp. i, 15, 22.
13 Nicholson, *Solitary Castle*, vol. 1, pp. 69, 76.
14 Nicholson, *Solitary Castle*, vol. 2, pp. 128–39.

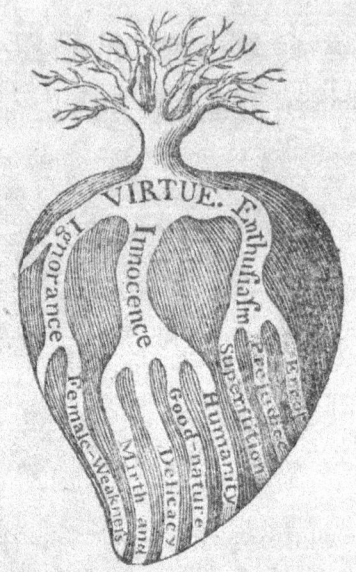

Fig.10.1: Anatomy of the heroine's heart from Nicholson's *The Solitary Castle* (1789). The British Library Board © British Library Board. All Rights Reserved/Bridgeman Images 12611.a.23, vol.1, p. 52.

Powis Castle, although less overtly satirical and more sentimentally comic in tone, offers a similar ambivalence about the place and relevance of the Gothic in the modern world. The hero, Sir Walter, scion of the 'Ancient Family' of the novel's subtitle, is left struggling with the upkeep of 'the finest piece of Gothic architecture extant in England', which has 'gone terribly into decay' as a result of his father's fondness for 'the expensive pleasures of the age'.[15] Repeated intrusions by a vulgar, wealthy neighbour, secure in his 'snug villa', ensure that the contrast between traditional values and mercenary systems is emphasised.[16] The Gothic castle is thus simultaneously a costly burden and a marker of Sir Walter's genuine status and merit. There is a noble family history to be proud of, but that history may be a sterile one in the modern world; the financial precariousness linked to the castle prevents Sir Walter from declaring his feelings for his cousin, Lady Julia. When these objections are overcome and the couple are united, Lady Julia's wealth revivifies the estate and 'the very portraits of his family seemed to eye him with a smile of satisfaction'.[17] The castle grounds are now repeatedly described as a 'paradise'[18] – only for the novel to turn Gothic in more than setting as this Eden is invaded by the satanic figure of the perfidious Italian Count Parmeni. The comedy falters as Parmeni sows marital discord as part of a scheme of seduction. The damage done by jealousy, particularly when inspired by the promptings of a treacherous advisor, is recognisable as a theme of Gothic historical tales; it is the main subject of the poem 'Saint Genevieve' in *The Solitary Castle*, for example. Suddenly, then, the darker side of the Gothic past seems all too relevant to modern manners.

Sentimental Gothic

In *Powis Castle*, Count Parmeni meets a suitably Gothic end in a shipwreck, a fate that emphasises that the source of corruption and disorder is not native. With the removal of the count's foreign influence, the harmony of the domestic setting is restored, and its evocation of an illustrious heritage stabilised. In other texts, however, the instability lingers; similarly Gothic-marked scenes that centre on seduction and jealousy appear in a number of novels of sensibility in this period. The heightened emotions of sensibility provided fertile soil for the Gothic, of course, particularly given their shared interest in evocative settings; the Bedlam scenes of Henry Mackenzie's *The*

---

15 Anon., *Powis Castle, or, Anecdotes of an Ancient Family*, 2 vols (London, 1788), vol. 1, pp. 22, 11.
16 *Powis Castle*, vol. 1, p. 27.   17 *Powis Castle*, vol. 2, p. 26.   18 *Powis Castle*, vol. 2, p. 36.

Man of Feeling (1771) or 'The Captive' episode of Sterne's *A Sentimental Journey* (1768) exemplify this overlap. The Gothic is not always a central presence in such texts, but its tropes repeatedly appear in scenes that focus on the dangers of seduction or domestic cruelty, indicating a specific anxiety about the legacies of Gothic manners in the realm of gender relations. After all, such dynamics could be seen as a measure of national character and progress, as William Alexander argued in 1779: 'in any country ... were their history entirely silent on every other subject, and only mentioned the manner in which they treated their women, we would, from thence, be enabled to form a tolerable judgement of the barbarity, or culture of their manners'.[19]

Harriet Meziere's *Moreton Abbey* (1785), for example, is set in a seemingly rational, civilised modern Britain, but the amatory relationships it depicts are deeply disordered. Women are repeatedly figured as victims of male possessive irrationality: the central narrative depicts a marriage destroyed by jealousy, with an inset plot involving emotional coercion and bigamy. In both cases, the men's chivalric passions drive them to madness, make them ill and lead to tragedy. The novel's epistolary form ensures that the misery of the central characters is juxtaposed with the wit and rationality of their respective correspondents, who repeatedly extol modern values of moderation, reason, self-control and sympathetic communication, to no avail. The Gothic resonances of the damaging gender relations are reinforced by the inclusion at the centre of the novel – in the hinge between the first and second volumes – of an incidental scene in a 'deep, gloomy' forest, in which a 'mouldering' castle houses a dying victim of seduction.[20]

In Charlotte Smith's first novel *Emmeline* (1788), meanwhile, the resonances of Mowbray Castle are largely positive: it is depicted as 'frowning in gothic magnificence', but the local peasantry associate its 'venerable towers' with 'the race of their ancient benefactors'.[21] This heritage is endangered by the schemes of parvenu lawyers in concert with the gendered perils of pursuit, seduction and suspicion; the castle can only be recovered once such threats are overcome. The Gothic means slightly different things in these two texts, then, but in each case Gothic markers function to connect the two senses of 'domestic', linking the experience of the home to national

---

19 William Alexander, *The History of Women, From the Earliest Antiquity, to the Present Time*, 2 vols (London, 1779), vol. 1, p. 103.
20 Harriet Meziere, *Moreton Abbey; or, The Fatal Mystery*, 2 vols (Southampton: [1785]), vol. 1, pp. 184, 186.
21 Charlotte Smith, *Emmeline, the Orphan of the Castle*, edited by Judith Stanton, vol. 2 of *The Works of Charlotte Smith*, 5 vols, general editor Stuart Curran (London: Pickering and Chatto, 2005), pp. 36, 35.

character and customs. In doing so, such sentimental novels use romantic narratives to raise questions about 'the exact point in the scale of civil society, to which the people of [Britain] have arrived', in Alexander's formulation.[22]

Gothic Histories

This sense of the connection between familial and national politics is perhaps most fully exploited in the 1787 novel *Alan Fitz-Osborne*, written by the Irish novelist Anne Fuller. Set in the reign of Henry III, this work has received very little critical attention, but is most often briefly mentioned for its ghost, the mother of the eponymous hero, who at one point hovers over the bed of her brother-in-law, dripping blood from the dagger that killed her onto her horrified murderer.[23] Jarlath Killeen, for example, describes Fuller as combining Thomas 'Leland's historical sensibility with Horace Walpole's supernatural excesses'.[24] The ghost's tale is a narrative of gendered persecution followed by political usurpation, and the text is insistent that the mechanisms of the two are connected. The villainous Walter Fitz-Osborne accuses his brother's wife Matilda of adultery, inflaming his brother's jealousy to the point where the elder Fitz-Osborne, absent on a crusade, commissions his wife's murder and loses himself to despair. This opens the way for Walter to take over the title and estate, and puts the disinherited Alan at his uncle's mercy. A strikingly similar dynamic is then found in a sub-plot, wherein a hermit (revealed to be a friend of the elder Fitz-Osborne) was similarly induced to suspect his wife, killed her, and dedicated his life to repentance and atonement. These tragedies are paralleled with national dynamics, where royal favourites 'regarded each other with jealousy and distrust' and 'sought to ruin [each other] in the opinion of the King'.[25] Like the novel's husbands, King Henry is 'fickle' and 'easily swayed to opposite opinions'; he is even persuaded to resent and suspect his son on 'no better ground than his favourite's malice'.[26] Walter uses the same tactics with his king as with his brother, and in both cases 'deceitful suggestions and present doubts swayed him more than the remembrance of past events'.[27] Marital injustice,

---

22 Alexander, *The History of Women*, vol. 1, p 103.
23 Anne Fuller, *Alan Fitz-Osborne: A Historical Tale*, 2 vols (Dublin, 1787), vol. 1, pp. 98–9.
24 Jarlath Killeen, *The Emergence of Irish Gothic Fiction: History, Origins, Theories* (Edinburgh: Edinburgh University Press, 2014), p. 171.
25 Fuller, *Alan Fitz-Osborne*, vol. 1, p. 110.
26 Fuller, *Alan Fitz-Osborne*, vol. 1, p. 143, vol. 2, p. 155.
27 Fuller, *Alan Fitz-Osborne*, vol. 2, p. 169.

disrupted inheritance and national instability are linked, as the 'public' and 'private' elements of the plot comment on each other.

In this context, the ghost's repeated appearances offer an important assurance that 'natural' justice and order will be reasserted in national as well as personal terms. The implicit presence of a higher authority is particularly important since the novel does not shy away from political turbulence. Within a plot detailing the aftermath of Magna Carta (the Provisions of Oxford and the Second Barons' War), Fuller offers sustained commentary on kingship and resistance:

> Providence has endued royalty with power, for the sole purpose of increasing the happiness and security of mankind. When a monarch, forgetful of this indispensible duty, would divest himself of the paternal character for that of a tyrant, the bands of obedience are loosed, and a nation, not habituated to slavery, will no longer regard him but as an idol of their own formation, which resistance can reduce to its primitive insignificance.[28]

In such passages, monarchy's potential for tyranny and corruption is made clear, but the novel also condemns rebellion as treason. It can do so largely because Prince Edward ('the Hope of England') provides a counterbalance to his father's negative example.[29] With Edward as his mentor, the hero Alan is not tempted by Simon de Montfort's arguments:

> Thou biddest me follow the general voice of an united nation. But what is this nation? All the truly noble, the generous, and the brave, cleave to the interests of their king and of their country; interests which, notwithstanding the arguments of sophistry, cannot be divided without the destruction of both. For the noisy and prostituted herd who find no happiness but in tumult, and no pleasure but in change ... Alan would indeed scorn to embrace their sentiments, or to imitate their conduct.[30]

The Gothic romance genre both enables and masks these political and historical reflections. The novel's Preface, for example, declares that truth is subordinate to fiction, but immediately goes on to say that 'this advantage is but apparent, and ... the laboured ornaments of [truth's] competitor serve but as foils to enhance the lustre of her own unvarnished and transcendant graces'.[31] Similarly, although the review in the *General Magazine* worried about the danger of 'confounding truth and falsehood' when 'mixing truth with fiction, and history with romance', it praises Fuller's 'great talents for

---

28 Fuller, *Alan Fitz-Osborne*, vol. 1, pp. 39–40.   29 Fuller, *Alan Fitz-Osborne*, vol. 1, p. 123.
30 Fuller, *Alan Fitz-Osborne*, vol. 1, pp. 174–5.   31 Fuller, *Alan Fitz-Osborne*, vol. 1, pp. ix–x.

historical composition'.³² Price, commenting on Fuller's final novel *The Son of Ethelwolf* (1789), suggests that 'Fuller's interest in history was coloured by ancient constitutionalism' and that her take on historical narrative emphasises the effects of lawgiving on the 'ordinary people'.³³ The choice of setting for *Alan Fitz-Osborne* clearly reflects this interest in ancient constitutional debates, though the focus on the effects of Henry's rule is tempered with a sense of his subjects' duties. There is also some scepticism here about the origins and authority of the law: legal changes are motivated by selfish political machinations rather than designed to bring about systemic improvements, and in any case national law does not always settle disputes, since the arbitration of external authorities (the Pope and the French king) is required at key points.

Fuller's reflections on sovereignty and on the causes and effects of domestic unrest thus contain both conservative impulses and those that are potentially politically disruptive. Even the passage cited above, in which Alan Fitz-Osborne rejects Simon de Montfort's temptations, is fraught with the language of division via the dual meaning of 'cleave'. These resonances are also, of course, heightened in the aftermath of the American Revolution; as Linda Colley points out, this 'was a *civil war*, not just in the sense that both sides had so much in common, but also in that each side was split within itself'.³⁴ It is perhaps unsurprising, then, that a notable feature of Gothic tales of the 1780s is their interest in exploring historical periods of civil war. This emphasis is particularly marked in Martha Harley's work. In *St Bernard's Priory* (1786; later extended and published as *The Priory of St Bernard* [1789]), buildings on the central estate have been 'rendered by civil war a desolate confusion' and the hero's backstory involves the upheaval caused by the fact that, 'At your birth this country was involved in all the horrors of a civil war.'³⁵ In her later novel *The Castle of Mowbray* (1788), the opening sentence tells us that the action takes place 'During the civil wars, which a few centuries ago disturbed the tranquillity of England', and we are soon reminded (in a somewhat mixed metaphor) that 'the sword of civil discord breathed around'.³⁶ There is also little sense that such conflict has an end date, since a moment of temporal shift provides the information that 'the civil

32 Anon., review of *Alan Fitz-Osborne*, *The General Magazine and Impartial Review* (December 1787): 367
33 Price, *Reinventing Liberty*, p. 40.
34 Linda Colley, *Britons: Forging the Nation, 1707–1837*, 2nd edition (New Haven and London: Yale University Press, 2005), p. 137.
35 Martha Harley, *St Bernard's Priory: An Old English Tale* (London, 1786), pp. 1, 15.
36 Martha Harley, *The Castle of Mowbray, an English Romance* (London, 1788), pp. 1, 19.

wars that desolated England [later] destroyed also the stately pile' containing a monument that is erected in the novel.[37]

This sense that the nation bears the scars of repeated domestic conflict adds nuance to the presence of Gothic ruins in narratives where the trope of ruination seems to outweigh historical verisimilitude. Despite its pre-Reformation temporal setting, for example, the climactic scene in Radcliffe's *The Castles of Athlin and Dunbayne* takes place in 'the ruins of an abbey, whose broken arches and lonely towers arose in gloomy grandeur through the obscurity of evening ... a monument of mortality and of ancient superstition'.[38] In *St Bernard's Priory*, Harley is similarly at pains to emphasise that the 'part [of the estate] where the old Priory had stood' is 'particularly ruinous'.[39] This depiction of religious buildings is reminiscent of Anna Laetitia Aikin's 'good Protestant' enjoyment of such ruins for the reminder of 'what we have escaped'; for Aikin, they serve to 'make posterity for ever thankful for this fairer age of liberty and light'.[40] Diane Long Hoeveler argues that such novels display 'bad conscience', in that the anachronism 'attempts to elide the very specific historical act carried out by Henry VIII and place the ruined Gothic abbey in the service of a trans-historical fantasy'.[41] Britain's Catholic heritage, and the traumas of its suppression, is downplayed by the pre-existing ruination of abbeys in these works.

However, the trope of ruination extends beyond religious buildings. In texts that emphasise civil war, the appearance of buildings that seem to be ruined before their time may also provoke reflection on the legacies of conflict. As James Kelly points out, this is a period in which 'ruins were recuperated not only aesthetically but politically, with the very idea of ruination allowing for meditation on historical conflicts both resolved and still open, and anticipation of the moment when current grandiloquent structures would fall to fragments'.[42] The affective power of ruins, in fact, seems to have enabled historico-political reflection in a way that undamaged

---

37 Harley, *The Castle of Mowbray*, p. 248.
38 Ann Radcliffe, *The Castles of Athlin and Dunbayne*, edited by Alison Milbank (Oxford: Oxford University Press, 1995), p. 102.
39 Harley, *St Bernard's Priory*, p. 1.
40 Anna Laetitia Barbauld, 'On Monastic Institutions', in *The Works of Anna Laetitia Barbauld*, edited by Lucy Aikin, 2 vols (London: Longman, Hurst, Rees, Orme, Browne, and Green, 1825), vol. II, pp. 195–213 (p. 196).
41 Diane Long Hoeveler, *The Gothic Ideology: Religious Hysteria and Anti-Catholicism in British Popular Fiction, 1780–1880* (Cardiff: University of Wales Press, 2014), p. 286, n.1.
42 James Kelly, 'The Politics of Ruin', in Michael Carter, Peter N. Lindfield and Dale Townshend (eds), *Writing Britain's Ruins* (London: The British Library, 2017), pp. 243–69 (p. 243).

structures did not. Thomas Whately argues in *Observations on Modern Gardening* (1770), for example, that 'an abbey, or a castle, if complete, can now be no more than a dwelling; the memory of the times, and of the manners, to which they were adapted, is preserved only in history, and in ruins', going on to remark that 'if the monument revive the memory of former times, we do not stop at the simple fact which it records, but recollect many more coæval circumstances'.[43] Even while omitting the specifics of religious conflict, then, the emphasis on ruination in historical Gothic narratives may encourage awareness of how the nation has been marked, and continues to be marked, by internal division.

This awareness is heightened when the destruction of Gothic buildings is depicted within the texts. In *The Castle of Mowbray*, the heroine Elwina is pursued by the lustful King Edward I and seeks refuge with Llewellyn of Wales, leading to the latter's downfall: 'Had Llewellyn ... sent Elwina out of his dominions, and submitted to Edward, the expiring embers of Cambrian liberty might have survived a little longer'.[44] This episode provokes the novel's most explicitly political reflections, centring on the contested cultural origins of British liberty. Here, that liberty is associated not with any version of Englishness, but with the doomed bardic nation, making Harley's work an example of how 'a residual immemorialist attachment to ancient British liberties persisted beyond mid-century, sanctioning ... literary recreations of free-spirited Celtic resistance to ... Plantagenet repression'.[45] The Welsh castle is destroyed in a conflagration that is framed as a defiant act: the warriors are exhorted to 'kindle the pile of liberty', and 'the bursting flames soon showed [the English conquerors] what a love of liberty was capable of executing'.[46] With 'the roofs ... falling in various places', the castle 'soon became a heap of flaming ruins'; later in the novel, the hero returns to 'the fatal ruin, and stood hours to contemplate it'.[47] The implication is that such ruins act as a memorial for what has been lost, as well as the compromises and complexities involved in building a modern British identity: 'Thus perished in one great noble end the remains of ancient liberty. Dispirited by their loss, rather than inspired by the same grand spirit of freedom, the

---

43 Thomas Whately, *Observations on Modern Gardening, Illustrated by Descriptions* (London, 1770), pp. 131, 155.
44 Harley, *The Castle of Mowbray*, p. 152.
45 Philip Connell, 'British identities and the politics of ancient poetry in later eighteenth-century England', *The Historical Journal* 49:1 (2006): 161–92 (p. 173).
46 Harley, *The Castle of Mowbray*, pp. 161, 162.
47 Harley, *The Castle of Mowbray*, pp. 163, 202.

people tamely submitted to the conqueror, and received from the afterwards noble descendants of Edward those privileges they continue to enjoy'.[48]

Gothic Pageantry

Stephen Conway has argued that 'the American conflict ... was a deeply intrusive event' in the lives of people living in Britain. In this light, the evocation of the histories and legacies of domestic conflict in Gothic writing of this period can be seen as part of the 'introspective reflection' that was prompted by defeat in America.[49] Reading Gothic narratives in this way, though, means acknowledging how the pageantry of the past can also provide a refuge from present conflicts. This dynamic is illustrated by the fact that, in May 1778, British officers responded to the recall of their beleaguered Commander-in-Chief, William Howe, by throwing him an elaborate farewell entertainment called the *Mischianza*, an event consisting chiefly of a medieval tournament.[50] This was, after all, the period in which 'the drive to refashion the self-image of Britain led to the "historical" category of Gothic being ... defined increasingly in terms of a proud military heritage', in Watt's account of the emergence of 'loyalist Gothic'.[51] First published a year after the Mischianza, Thomas Sedgwick Whalley's narrative poem *Edwy and Edilda*, for example, makes a clear link between national pride and chivalric spectacle. This ballad (which is so strongly influenced by Reeve's *The Old English Baron* that the 1783 Dublin edition claims her as its author)[52] opens with an encomium to 'the fame of [King] EGBERT's arms' and the 'tale of Britain's good',[53] and much of the second section is taken up with military games:

> A custom was in EGBERT's court.
> When bloody wars did cease,
> And doughty warriors [sic] arms were laid
> Upon the lap of peace;

---

48 Harley, *The Castle of Mowbray*, p. 164.
49 Stephen Conway, *The British Isles and the War of American Independence* (Oxford: Oxford University Press, 2000), p. 128.
50 For commentary on the Mischianza, see Linda Colley, *Britons*, pp. 147–8; Daniel O'Quinn, *Entertaining Crisis in the Atlantic Imperium, 1770–1790* (Baltimore: Johns Hopkins University Press, 2011), pp. 149–77.
51 Watt, *Contesting the Gothic*, p. 45.
52 [Thomas Sedgwick Whalley], *Edwy and Edilda: A Gothic Tale, in Five Parts. By the Author of the Old English Baron* (Dublin, 1783).
53 [Thomas Sedgwick Whalley], *Edwy and Edilda: A Tale, in Five Parts* (London, 1779), p. 2. All subsequent references are to this edition.

> Lest warlike arms and powers should rust,
> To mark the listed field
> Where Heroes, fam'd for val'rous deeds,
> The glittering lance might wield.[54]

In *The Old English Baron*, similar pageantry comes not in the form of a tournament but as a trial by single combat. This format makes it even more clear that might and right will ultimately be aligned: 'I trust in God and in the justice of my cause ... I have neither guilt, fear, nor doubt in me: I am so certain of success'.[55] Jonathan Dent has argued that Reeve emphasises 'religious revelation' so strongly in order to counter 'the increasingly secular nature of Enlightenment historiography', reading the novel as 'remind[ing] English readers of who they are and reassur[ing] them of their privileged place in God's providential scheme'.[56] Gothic ceremonies highlight the certainty of divine justice and provide comfort about the nation's status.

As well as celebrating martial prowess and dwelling on the aesthetic appreciation of 'Pageantry most rare', tournament scenes often redirect attention away from national upheaval, refocusing on gender dynamics and amatory relationships: 'Nor fame alone, nor love of arms, / Their beating bosoms fir'd, / A softer passion oft their hearts / More ardently inspir'd'.[57] In this way, rivalries can be framed as personal rather than political. Thus, in *The Castle of Mowbray*, a tournament involving Robert the Bruce is purely concerned with marital dynamics (his wife's accidental bigamy), despite the wider political upheavals explored elsewhere in the novel. In *Edwy and Edilda*, this tactic is more centrally embedded. When the villain Edbald murders Edwy, the question of Edwy's status has already been resolved, and Edbald attacks with the weapons he won by coming second in the tournament: a bow and arrows that were presented 'by thy own EDILDA's hand'.[58] Whalley's poem thus emphasises that the crime stems from individual pride and jealousy rather than anything systemic. Even while being used in the service of tragedy, the Gothic pageantry here retains its attractions and its associations with military pride.

Focusing on gender dynamics can, however, expose the desires that drive the national self-portraiture of such pageantry. One oddity of the Mischianza,

---

54 Whalley, *Edwy and Edilda*, p. 48.
55 Clara Reeve, *The Old English Baron*, edited by James Trainer, intro. by James Watt (Oxford: Oxford University Press, 2003), p. 87.
56 Jonathan Dent, *Sinister Histories: Gothic Novels and Representations of the Past, from Horace Walpole to Mary Wollstonecraft* (Manchester: Manchester University Press, 2016), p. 76.
57 Whalley, *Edwy and Edilda*, pp. 52, 48.   58 Whalley, *Edwy and Edilda*, p. 163.

for example, was the inclusion of Turkish costumes for the women involved in the tournament section. Daniel O'Quinn has analysed the way in which the 'deployment of colonial women in the chivalric/orientalist scene of the tournament carefully stabilises two mutually constitutive fantasies: one sexual and one imperial'. One involves the 'grateful approbation of martial performance' and the other emphasises 'that they have been liberated' and are returning 'to their rightful masters'.[59] Interestingly, domestic Gothic writing of the subsequent decade makes a similar link. Even setting aside the wholesale orientalism of William Beckford's *Vathek* (1786), orientalist scenes repeatedly become part of the spectacle that the Gothic offers. In *St Bernard's Priory*, for example, the tournament scene takes place in Palestine, and is part of a storyline in which a seemingly Muslim beauty is revealed to be Richard the Lionheart's 'long lost child; no longer Turkish Zoraide, but Christian Elmira!'[60] In Fuller's *Alan Fitz-Osborne*, similarly, a startlingly attractive Egyptian youth is revealed to be not only female but also a Christian, and the conflicts of the romance plot line combine with the broader historical clash of the crusades: the Sultan is 'inflamed at once with the hatred of Christianity, and the rage of disappointed love'.[61] This ensures that the emphasis is placed on the divide between Christian and Muslim, and any anxiety about Britain's Catholic past is displaced in favour of this greater alterity. Zulima is described as 'fair, beyond the utmost colouring of luxuriant fancy', and as a greater treasure than the 'inexhaustible wealth' of 'the most precious jewels of the East' that are intended for her dowry.[62] In gaining possession of her as his wife, then, Alan enacts an imperialist fantasy of appropriation.

Gothic Lineages

In Reeve's *The Old English Baron*, the 'peripheral, yet strangely emphasised' Arab/ Greek character Zadisky is Christianised and so 'restored to his true race', as Abby Coykendall puts it, in a manner that makes the actions of the British 'seem, at least in retrospect, altruistic and paternalistic interventions, rather than aggressive impositions from an outside force'.[63] In *Alan Fitz-Osborne*, Zulima's brother Mureddin is even more effectively subsumed

---

59 O'Quinn, *Entertaining Crisis*, p. 172.   60 Harley, *St Bernard's Priory*, p. 77.
61 Fuller, *Alan Fitz-Osborne*, vol. 2, p. 303.
62 Fuller, *Alan Fitz-Osborne*, vol. 2, pp. 299, 301.
63 Abby Coykendall, 'Gothic genealogies, the family romance, and Clara Reeve's *The Old English Baron*', *Eighteenth-Century Fiction* 17:3 (April 2005): 443–80 (pp. 472–3).

into the British narrative, becoming part of the domestic order as completely as his sister does: 'Edward presented Mureddin with the deeds of [the villainous uncle's] estates, and willed him to take the name of Fitz-Osborne. The son of the Soldan, now wholly English, restored the faded fame of the younger branch of that house to its pristine lustre.'[64] That Mureddin's 'newly acquired vassals ... blessed Heaven for having deprived them of their former masters', however, also complicates assumptions of racial superiority, raising questions about the inherent value of natively British bloodlines.[65]

The Gothic is, of course, centrally interested in disrupted and contaminated inheritances, in the reckoning that comes 'when father and villain are, or appear to be, one and the same'.[66] Walpole claimed that *Otranto* was 'grounded' on the 'moral ... that the sins of fathers are visited on their children to the third and fourth generation'.[67] Unsurprisingly, then, it is a trope that recurs in the texts that I have been discussing. The power of positive lineages is emphasised, as when *The Castle of Mowbray*'s heroine is protected from rape when a statue of her father seemingly comes to life: 'She shrieked, her voice was echoed through the rooms, nor did she call in vain ... a tremendous noise assailed their ears ... from its pedestal descended the statue of the earl Mowbray'.[68] At the same time, though, there is considerable anxiety about the legacies of shameful and immoral deeds. In *St Bernard's Priory*, the heroic characters struggle with their familial relationships with the villain Manston/De Courcy, thought to be Edmund's father: 'that wretch is father to Lord Edmund, and our uncle!'; 'Were Manston not the author of my being, this arm should chase the monster from the world.'[69] The consequent destabilisation of identity is emphasised by the unusual degree of slippage in the characters' names in this text. In Fuller's novel, Alan's status is damaged for much of the narrative not by uncertainty about the identity of his parents, but by a slander on their characters: the claim that their marriage was bigamous as a result of 'one deed of baseness' by his father. Alan laments that the 'stain' that 'contaminated his fame' is one that 'extends to me'.[70] These tensions are overcome in the eventual revelations of the truth in the plots' resolutions, but such storylines can be seen as working through an

---

64 Fuller, *Alan Fitz-Osborne*, vol. 2, p. 376.   65 Fuller, *Alan Fitz-Osborne*, vol. 2, p. 376.
66 Caroline Gonda, *Reading Daughters' Fictions 1709–1834: Novels and Society from Manley to Edgeworth* (Cambridge: Cambridge University Press, 1996), p. 141.
67 Horace Walpole, 'Preface to the First Edition' in *The Castle of Otranto*, edited by Nick Groom (Oxford: Oxford University Press, 2014), p. 6.
68 Harley, *The Castle of Mowbray*, p. 16.   69 Harley, *St Bernard's Priory*, pp. 21, 33.
70 Fuller, *Alan Fitz-Osborne*, vol. 1, p. 77; vol. 2, p. 270.

anxiety that Britain's forefathers may not have lived up to current moral standards. The family-romance resolutions thus connect to the idea that, as Reeve put it in the Preface to *The Old English Baron*, romance 'throws a veil' over the 'melancholy retrospect' offered by history's depiction of 'human nature'.[71]

Along the same lines, the 'noble peasant' motif (in which a seemingly low-born hero's true status is revealed) is rehearsed in both Reeve's *The Old English Baron* and Whalley's *Edwy and Edilda*, as well as in Radcliffe's *The Castles of Athlin and Dunbayne*. Interrogating the connection between merit and birth, these texts simultaneously reify class hierarchies and write middle-class perspectives into history. They lament 'that pride in noble minds / Should bear so large a part' and that 'outward circumstance ... Hath power to witch the eye',[72] but also emphasise that the hero is exceptional, that his qualities are incongruous with his supposed class position: 'I cannot help thinking you were born to a higher station than what you now hold.'[73] This is not quite the 'middle-class "merit in obscurity" creed' that Carol Margaret Davison sees as being incorporated into Reeve's work from the novel of sensibility,[74] but it does appropriate the hierarchies of the past to affirm middle-class values. Thus Edwy's behaviour and speech make 'amply' clear that his 'mind was with the grace / Of every virtue crown'd',[75] while, as Sue Chaplin points out, 'Reeve's "man of worth" is essentially an eighteenth-century man of sensibility committed to heroic action.'[76] Such values are thus written back into the past, gaining a lineage while also providing reassurance that the nation's heritage is morally sound.

The license with history that is enabled by the Gothic also allows the insertion of gendered perspectives into historical narratives. 'Feminised' approaches to the Gothic past in the period range from Reeve's morally improving didacticism (in which romance is directed 'to some useful, or at least innocent, end'),[77] to the imagination of female military heroism in Harley's *The Castle of Mowbray*, where the princess Isabel leads a successful charge to rescue her husband and dies to save him.[78] The Gothic also makes

---

71 Reeve, 'Preface to the Second Edition', *The Old English Baron*, p. 2.
72 Whalley, *Edwy and Edilda*, p. 146.   73 Reeve, *The Old English Baron*, p. 21.
74 Carol Margaret Davison, *Gothic Literature 1764–1824* (Cardiff: University of Wales Press, 2009), pp. 81–2.
75 Whalley, *Edwy and Edilda*, p. 146.
76 Sue Chaplin, 'Gothic Romance, 1760–1830', in Glennis Byron and Dale Townshend (eds), *The Gothic World* (London and New York: Routledge, 2014), pp. 199–209 (p. 204).
77 Reeve, 'Preface to the Second Edition', *The Old English Baron*, p. 3.
78 Harley, *The Castle of Mowbray*, pp. 20–3.

wider literary lineages available to appropriation by women writers, since 'masculine' genres can be accessed and explored via Gothic romance. For example, Reeve's influential literary history *The Progress of Romance* (1785) makes a strong case for a connection between romance and epic, arguing that romance is 'an *Heroic fable* ... Or ... an Epic in Prose', that romance and epic 'spring from the same root, – they describe the same actions and circumstances, – they produce the same effects', and that 'Epic Poetry is the parent of Romance.'[79] One review of *Edwy and Edilda* argued that the ballad is 'as perfectly *epic* as anything in ten-syllable verse' – though a correspondent with the journal vehemently disagreed.[80] It is Anne Fuller, though, who makes this connection explicit in her fiction, offering a Gothic epic that taps into nationalist sensibilities such as those expressed by William Hayley in 1782: 'Our generous Isle ... / Asks for her Chiefs the palm of Epic fame.' Hayley urged William Mason, author of the dramatic poems *Elfrida* [1752] and *Caractacus* [1759], to make epic's 'sacred fabric' of 'English form' and to 'gild Historic Truth with Fancy's beams!': 'To Patriot Chiefs unsung thy Lyre devote / And swell to Liberty the lofty note!'[81]

In focusing on the Plantagenet kings rather than the ancient British past, Fuller's exploration of liberty is not the uncomplicated celebration that Hayley might have envisaged. However, she does explicitly frame this Gothic 'Historical Tale' as a national epic. *Alan Fitz-Osborne* uses a quotation from Pope's *Iliad* as its epigraph, for example, and divides the action into 'Books' (as Fielding had done in his comic epic novels). Recognisably epic similes are used, particularly in relation to the heroic Prince Edward: 'As the mountain oak, when assailed by boisterous winds, bends its awful head to the tempest, yet remains unshaken in its roots, so the gallant Edward submitted to his fate, yet continued unbowed in spirit and in courage.'[82] The death of Simon de Montfort is even reminiscent of the death of Turnus at the end of Virgil's *Aeneid*: in Fuller, 'his furious soul fled indignant', while in Alexander Strahan's 1767 translation of Virgil's final book, 'Deep groaning, fled at once th'indignant soul.'[83] These intertextual echoes help to reinforce the sense that the novel is a

---

79 Clara Reeve, *The Progress of Romance, through Times, Countries, and Manners*, 2 vols (Colchester, 1785), vol. 1, pp. 13, 16, 25.
80 Anon., review of *Edwy and Edilda*, *The London Review of English and Foreign Literature* 9 (June 1779): 401–11 (p. 401); Anon., 'To the London reviewers', *The London Review* 10 (July 1779): 62–3 (p. 62).
81 William Hayley, *An Essay on Epic Poetry; in Five Epistles to the Revd. Mr. Mason, with Notes* (London, 1782), pp. 110, 112, 114.
82 Fuller, *Alan Fitz-Osborne*, vol. 1, p. 227.
83 Fuller, *Alan Fitz-Osborne*, vol. 2, p. 133; Alexander Strahan, *The Æneid of Virgil. Translated into Blank Verse*, 2 vols (London, 1767), vol. 2, p. 200 (Book XII, ll.1217–18).

national origin story. Just as the *Aeneid* explores a difficult past while pointing forward to the formation of Rome, so Fuller's narrative acknowledges and explores political ambiguities on the understanding that a glorious national future awaits, with its values personified by the future king, Edward.

In different ways, then, all of these domestic Gothic texts offer supplements to other forms of national history, using imaginative approaches to the past to explore Britain's Gothic inheritance. In Lee's *The Recess*, however, the ability to write female perspectives into historical narratives produces something more radical: not just 'a fictional alternative to Hume and Robertson', as Anne Stevens puts it, but a fundamental questioning of how 'history' is practised.[84] As Diana Wallace has claimed, this is a novel that reveals 'the subjective and constructed nature of historical representation'.[85] Recounting the tragic lives of the (fictional) twin daughters of Mary Queen of Scots, Lee focuses on stories that have been written out of national narratives – a more radical version of Hayley's 'Patriot Chiefs unsung', perhaps.

Appropriately, the Recess of the novel's title is a ruined monastic structure, described by Kelsey Kramer as 'a physical reminder of … a past that the Henrician Reformation aggressively sought to erase'.[86] Processes of erasure and destruction are not confined to one event, however; among other things, they are implicitly connected to eighteenth-century practices. As the novel progresses, the Recess's ruins are destroyed to improve the surrounding estate: 'the materials were wanted to erect a manufacture in the neighbourhood … while new plantations would … open the prospect'. Even Kenilworth, previously the scene of 'gay pageants', becomes a modern textile factory echoing with 'the noise of a hundred looms' – a 'desolation' that is described as its own kind of 'ruin'.[87] Depicting multiple possible sources of destruction and loss, then, Lee makes it clear that rupture with the past is inevitable, its lived experiences essentially irrecoverable.

In the face of this historical chasm, Lee's novel insists on the instability of any interpretation of the past. Indeed, the *Monthly Review* complained that the novel's mingling of romance and history 'brings a

---

84 Anne H. Stevens, *British Historical Fiction Before Scott* (Basingstoke: Palgrave Macmillan, 2010), p. 48.
85 Diana Wallace, *Female Gothic Histories: Gender, History and the Gothic* (Cardiff: University of Wales Press, 2013), p. 28.
86 Kaley A. Kramer, 'Haunting History: Women, Catholicism, and the Writing of National History in Sophia Lee's *The Recess*', in Julie A. Chappell and Kaley A. Kramer (eds), *Women During the English Reformations: Renegotiating Gender and Religious Identity* (Basingstoke: Palgrave Macmillan, 2014), pp. 129–44 (p. 129).
87 Sophia Lee, *The Recess; or, A Tale of Other Times*, edited by April Alliston (Lexington: The University Press of Kentucky, 2000), pp. 199, 274.

suspicion on truth itself'.[88] This becomes thematically central when the text offers competing, but equally compelling, responses to the same events in the narratives of the two sisters and their correspondents and interlocutors: 'how diametrically opposite were the impressions each took of his character!'; 'the sweet mistress of Essex had a very partial knowledge of his character, or information of his actions'; 'I ... found a thousand reasons for disputing a judgment which had hitherto been the rule of my own.'[89] Such repeated contradictions focus on the protagonists' assessments of their lovers, and are most often connected to accusations about the men's ambition. Cumulatively, this draws attention to the extent to which a desire for public recognition and power actuates *all* the novel's characters. The women express it through the heightened language of sentimental emotionality, but the '[h]igher, happier, and dearer prospects' that they aim for are born of '[d]reams of pride and grandeur'.[90] As each individual narrative is destabilised, the struggle for narrative control is explicitly politicised: 'popularity', as Essex points out, has 'dethroned monarchs'.[91]

Written records that might be taken to constitute historical 'proof' are also problematised. Wallace points out that the most obviously fictional element of the plot – the existence of the twin sisters – in fact comes from an unusually well-documented part of Mary's life: her miscarriage of Bothwell's twins in 1567.[92] Throughout the novel, textual evidence is contested. Thus, for example, papers 'from the first years of [Mary's] imprisonment' together 'with various other testimonials of [the sisters'] birth' are kept in 'a casket, which contained ... divers attestations'.[93] This description evokes historiographical debates about the 'Casket Letters', purportedly written by Mary Stuart to the Earl of Bothwell, which supposedly proved Mary's adultery and complicity in the death of her husband Lord Darnley.[94] As recently as 1782, Gilbert Stuart's *The History of Scotland* had defended Mary (against Hume, among others), by insisting that the 'letters were fabricated' and that the casket had in reality contained other papers.[95] *The Recess* imagines the fate of these alternative

---

88 B d k [Samuel Badcock], 'Art. 47. The Recess, or, A Tale of other Times', *Monthly Review; or, Literary Journal* (May 1783): pp. 455–6 (p. 455).
89 Lee, *The Recess*, pp. 155, 256, 316.   90 Lee, *The Recess*, pp. 149–50, 160.
91 Lee, *The Recess*, p. 215.   92 Wallace, *Female Gothic Histories*, pp. 40–1.
93 Lee, *The Recess*, pp. 35, 36.
94 For further discussion of how Lee responds to the debates about the 'Casket Letters', see Jane Elizabeth Lewis, *Mary Queen of Scots: Romance and Nation* (London: Routledge, 1998), pp. 137–46; Jonathan Dent, *Sinister Histories*, pp. 117–18.
95 Gilbert Stuart, *The History of Scotland: From the Establishment of the Reformation till the Death of Queen Mary*, 2 vols (London, 1782), vol. 1, p. 396.

papers, and both the power and the contingency of such evidence are made clear. When Matilda regains the 'casket ... contain[ing] all the testimonials of the Queen of Scots', she 'felt rich in these recovered rights'; her rights are created by the documentary record.[96] Concomitantly, those rights are obliterated when King James destroys the papers, gaining final control of the public narrative and writing the sisters out of history. Lee's Gothic tragedy thus exposes the power dynamics inherent in the relationship between text, historical memory and nation-building.

The decades between Walpole and Radcliffe, then, saw the publication of a rich and diverse range of Gothic-inflected texts. The political viewpoint of such writing varies – indeed, it is often internally ambiguous or inconsistent – but the dominant impulse of Gothic narrative in this period is its interest in national history. Domestic Gothic writing parallels the home and the nation, so that the stories of individuals reflect on national character. If the Gothic is 'a mode of history', in David Punter's famous formulation, these are the years that make it so.[97]

---

96 Lee, *The Recess*, p. 276.
97 David Punter, *The Literature of Terror: A History of Gothic Fictions from 1765 to the Present Day, Volume I: The Gothic Tradition* 2nd, revised edition (London and New York: Pearson Longman, 1996), p. 52.

I.II

Early British Gothic and the American Revolution

JAMES WATT

R. B. Heilman's study, *America in English Fiction 1760–1800: The Influences of the American Revolution*, includes Clara Reeve's *The Old English Baron: A Gothic Story* (1778) in an appendix of 'negative results' that lists the titles of novels 'in which [there are] no references to America'.[1] Reeve stated in her Preface that she wrote *The Old English Baron* 'upon the same plan' as *The Castle of Otranto* (1764), but she was also critical of Walpole for exceeding 'limits of credibility' and incorporating supernatural effects which 'instead of attention, excite laughter'.[2] Walpole in turn dismissed Reeve's imitation as a work 'reduced to reason and probability', calling it 'the most insipid dull thing you ever saw', and a conspicuously gendered reading has persisted of Reeve as a hesitant figure who awkwardly attempted to domesticate the boldness of Walpole's vision.[3] This essay will discuss how Reeve responded to Walpole not only by rejecting the attention-seeking extravagance of his work but also by choosing to situate her tale in fifteenth-century England. It will attempt to recover the political significance of this decision in the context of the early years of Britain's war in America, and it will consider the way in which – Heilman's point about its lack of 'reference' notwithstanding – the novel offers a highly allusive narrative of national reconciliation and repair. Even as Reeve claimed that her 'picture of Gothic times and manners' served the improving purposes of 'Romance', however, her work also acknowledges that its resort to the Gothic past is unable entirely to escape the 'melancholy retrospect' of 'History'.[4] With Reeve's prefatory distinction between history and romance

---

1 Robert Bechtold Heilman, *America in English Fiction: The Influences of the American Revolution* (Baton Rouge: Louisiana University Press, 1937), p. 437.
2 Clara Reeve, *The Old English Baron*, edited by James Trainer, intro. by James Watt (Oxford: Oxford University Press, 2003), pp. 2, 3.
3 Horace Walpole, letter to William Cole, 22 Aug 1778, in W. S. Lewis (ed.), *The Yale Edition of the Correspondence of Horace Walpole*, 48 vols (New Haven and London: Yale University Press, 1937–83), vol. 40, p. 379.
4 Reeve, *Old English Baron*, p. 2.

in mind, this essay will conclude by suggesting that through its mediation of *Otranto*, *The Old English Baron* helped to make the diverse resources of the Gothic past available to subsequent writers, and at the same time to ensure that its questioning of the nature of Britain's Gothic inheritance remained integral to the tradition of 'domestic Gothic' that it inaugurated.[5]

Gothic Virtue and Heroism

In the brief life of Reeve that he wrote to preface a later edition of *The Old English Baron*, Sir Walter Scott cited an undated letter from the author in which she described her early education:

> My father was an old Whig; from him I have learned all that I know; he was my oracle; he used to make me read the parliamentary debates while he smoked his pipe after supper. I gaped and yawned ... but, unawares to myself, they fixed my principles once and for ever. He made me read Rapin's History of England ... I read Cato's Letters ... I read the Greek and Roman Histories, and Plutarch's Lives; all these at an early age when few people of either sex can read their names.[6]

In an April 1791 letter to the Irish antiquary Joseph Cooper Walker, Reeve referred to the same course of reading, adding that she inherited from it 'A love of liberty, a hatred of Tyranny, an affection to the whole race of mankind, a wish to support their rights and properties'.[7] There is little biographical information about Reeve available, but in the light of her account of her Old Whig politics one might speculate that she would have been at the least sympathetic to the cause of American revolutionaries, who, in opposing government and taxation without their consent, often appealed to the tradition of 'Commonwealth' political thought with which Reeve was well acquainted. Although Reeve wrote her novel *Sir Roger de Clarendon* (1793) against the French Revolution, its Preface employs this same language of civic participation, presenting (after Plutarch's example) closer acquaintance with the 'great men' of the past as an antidote to the 'vile indolence, effeminacy, and extravagance of modern life and manners': 'When we read of our

---

5 I present Reeve's work as an 'inaugurating' text, rather than *Thomas Leland's Longsword, Earl of Salisbury* (1762), because of the influence of its mediation of *Otranto*.
6 Walter Scott, *Lives of the Novelists* (London: Oxford University Press, n.d.), p. 197.
7 Quoted in Gary Kelly, 'Clara Reeve', *Oxford Dictionary of National Biography* <www .oxforddnb.com / view / 10.1093 / ref:odnb / 9780198614128.001.0001 / odnb-9780198614128-e -23292?rskey=i1ZuY8&result=1> (last accessed 6 June 2018).

glorious ancestors, their actions ought to stimulate us to equal them, to support and maintain the honour of our country.'[8]

Reeve's best-known work was first published in 1777 as *The Champion of Virtue: A Gothic Story*, and her initial hailing of a 'virtue' in need of championing might be read as a statement of her Old Whig political affiliations. This location of virtue in a period of 'Gothic ... manners' suggestively alludes to the idea of Britain's 'ancient constitution' as well as perhaps to the theory of the Norman Yoke, according to which a pristine native liberty – variously Gothic, Saxon, or Old English – had been suppressed by the Conquest of 1066 and had to be recovered in the present. The theory of the Norman Yoke 'saw an extraordinary revival from about 1770', Gerald Newman has argued, and while American revolutionaries appealed to the historic rights of Englishmen against the tyranny of the British state, reformers in Britain campaigned for a return to practices such as annual elections which they associated with the distant past.[9] Ideas of historical virtue also had a broader resonance at this time, however, and were often cited in the context of less overtly politicised attempts to delineate the nation's cultural inheritance. Kathleen Wilson has argued that the Seven Years' War generated 'a re-thinking of Britain's own pasts', as commentators sought to conceive of a native freedom that remained uncompromised by empire and territorial expansion, and in the 1760s literary scholars such as Richard Hurd and Thomas Percy identified as a specifically 'Gothic' legacy the mutually beneficial social intercourse between the sexes that apparently characterised modern Britain.[10] Rather than invoke a lost birth-right in need of recovery, in other words, writers such as Hurd and Percy traced a continuity between the Gothic past, the Middle Ages and the present in the form of the 'refined gallantry' that originated in 'the antient manners of the German nations'.[11]

It is also important to emphasise that the association of 'Gothic times and manners' with the culture of 'chivalry and romance' discussed by Hurd made the Gothic past potentially congenial to British elites as well as to critics of the status quo. In her influential study of British national identity, Linda Colley describes the *Mischianza*, a mock-medieval tournament held on the banks of

---

8   Clara Reeve, *Memoirs of Sir Roger de Clarendon, The Natural Son of Edward Prince of Wales, Commonly Called the Black Prince; with Anecdotes of Many Other Eminent Persons of the Fourteenth Century*, 3 vols (London, 1793), vol. 1, pp. xxi, xii.
9   Gerald Newman, *The Rise of English Nationalism: A Cultural History, 1740–1830*, revised edition (New York: St. Martin's Press, 1997), p. 190.
10 Kathleen Wilson, *The Island Race: Englishness, Empire and Gender in the Eighteenth Century* (London: Routledge, 2003), p. 5.
11 Richard Hurd, *Letters on Chivalry and Romance* (London, 1762), p. 19.

the Delaware River near Philadelphia in May 1778 to mark the departure from America of the Commander-in-Chief of the British army General William Howe: 'in the face of doubt, disappointment, and vague premonitions of defeat', she states, pointing to Burgoyne's October 1777 surrender at Saratoga and other recent examples of military failure, 'the cream of the British officer corps sought a brief escape in an ordered and glamorous past'.[12] Daniel O'Quinn has since complicated Colley's account by focusing in detail on the oddness of this spectacle, which he presents as a self-consciously frivolous diversion – staged with a distant metropolitan audience partly in mind – rather than an idealising and corrective re-enactment of ongoing conflict.[13] For the purposes of this essay it is nonetheless useful to think about the way in which the Mischianza's chief orchestrator, Captain John André, appealed to a particular heritage of English military victory in his address to Howe, by calling up an era 'When great in arms our brave forefathers rose, / And loos'd the British Lion on his foes; / When the fall'n Gauls, then perjur'd too and base, / The faithless fathers of a faithless race, / First to attack, tho' still the first to yield, / Shrunk from their rage on Poictiers' laurel'd field'.[14] While the 1356 Battle of Poitiers offered an especially attractive reference point at this time (since English victory there, in O'Quinn's words, 'emerged from apparent defeat'), other military successes of the Hundred Years' War would go on to be invoked during Britain's war with revolutionary France, including by Reeve herself: the full title of *Sir Roger De Clarendon* presents him as 'the Natural Son of Edward Prince of Wales, Commonly Called the Black Prince', and it promises readers 'Anecdotes of Many Other Eminent Persons of the Fourteenth Century'.[15]

However, by early 1778 – when news of the defeat at Saratoga reached Britain – if not before, the progress of the war in America suggested to some that the nation had relinquished its reputation for martial prowess. Writing in June 1778, not long after France had entered the conflict on the revolutionary side, a contributor to the *London Evening Post* complained, for example, that 'Our men of rank and fortune have exchanged sexes with the soft and fair. They are fribbles and maccaronies, and not soldiers and heroes. A year or two of encampments and rigid discipline may restore them to virility and heroic hardiness; but alas! The constitution and power of England ... may in the

---

12 Linda Colley, *Britons: Forging the Nation 1707–1837* (New Haven: Yale University Press, 1992), p. 148.
13 Daniel O'Quinn, *Entertaining Crisis in the Atlantic Imperium, 1770–1790* (Baltimore: Johns Hopkins University Press, 2011), pp. 148–77.
14 Quoted in O'Quinn, *Entertaining Crisis*, p. 164.   15 O'Quinn, *Entertaining Crisis*, p. 165.

meantime be extinct'.[16] The idea of a national 'constitution' is literalised here and associated with – depleted – physical strength rather than the principles underpinning a system of government. Although Reeve's *The Champion of Virtue* predated the criticism of Britain's armed forces (in particular its senior ranks) that would gather pace after Saratoga, her story of 'Gothic times and manners' may have been understood by contemporaries in the context of the *London Evening Post*'s language of military vigour as much as of any Old Whig idea of pristine political virtue. Its opening paragraph indeed solicits the former reading, since it alludes both to the 1415 Battle of Agincourt (often cited alongside Poitiers and Crécy in 'Edwards and Henries' discourse) and to the history of the Crusades and of subsequent European conflict with an expansionist Ottoman empire:

> In the minority of Henry the Sixth, King of England, when the renowned John Duke of Bedford was Regent of France, and Humphrey the good Duke of Gloucester was Protector of England, a worthy Knight, called Sir Philip Harclay, returned from his travels to England, his native country. He had served under the glorious King Henry the Fifth with distinguished valour, had acquired an honourable fame, and was no less esteemed for Christian virtues than for decades of chivalry. After the death of his Prince, he entered into the service of the Greek Emperor, and distinguished his courage against the encroachments of the Saracens.[17]

The opening of Reeve's work sets up an essential antagonism between an English hero and familiar historical enemies while also, by referring to Turkish 'encroachment' in Europe, suggestively if obliquely acknowledging a distant contest over territory and sovereignty. If at the outset the novel appears to establish the political stability of Sir Philip's English home, however, as it develops its homecoming narrative it goes on to describe how home has become strange for the returning knight. First of all, Sir Philip has to prove his identity in order to regain possession of his family estate in Yorkshire after the death of his mother and sister during his time overseas. Then, when he subsequently goes to visit Lovel Castle, in the West of England, Sir Philip finds that Lord Lovel has died and that the castle is now in the hands of Lord Baron Fitz-Owen (the Baron of the title), to whom it had been sold by Sir Walter Lovel, his friend's younger brother, now living in Northumberland. While lodging in the nearby cottage of the peasant John

---

16 *London Evening Post* (9–11 June 1778), quoted in Robert W. Jones, *Literature, Gender and Politics in Britain during the War for America* (Cambridge: Cambridge University Press, 2011), p. 35.
17 Reeve, *Old English Baron*, p. 5.

Wyatt and his family, Sir Philip has 'strange and incoherent dreams' that anticipate the ensuing events of the work, and he encounters the virtuous Edmund Twyford ('as fine a youth as ever the sun shone upon', we are told), whom he seeks to adopt.[18] At an early stage, then, Reeve's work clearly signals that its plot will revolve around the uncovering of an act of usurpation and the restoration of a legitimate heir, with Edmund occupying a position akin to that of the 'noble, handsome and commanding' Theodore in Walpole's *Otranto*.[19] Edmund wants to remain a member of Fitz-Owen's household rather than enter Sir Philip's service, but while he is favoured by the Baron's younger son William and daughter Lady Emma, his presence is unwelcome to others, notably Wenlock and Markham, Fitz-Owen's nephews, who resent Edmund's qualities and help to prejudice the Baron's older son against him.

While it begins by defining the 'worthy Knight' Sir Philip against external enemies, therefore, Reeve's work is organised around a scenario of domestic strife that, as it is later revealed, has its roots in an act of fratricide – Sir Philip's friend Lord Lovel was murdered by his brother Sir Walter. The fact that Lovel Castle has changed hands not once but twice by the time that Sir Philip arrives there serves to complicate any straightforwardly allegorical reading of dispossession and restoration in the text. Moreover, the novel presents characters whose motivation appears to be narrowly personal: while Wenlock and Markham begrudge the attention that Lady Emma gives Edmund, the usurper Sir Walter Lovel still more overtly displays his sexual jealousy, finally confessing that his 'bad actions' derived from the envy he felt towards his brother, who gained the hand of the woman with whom he himself was in love.[20] At the same time, though, in view of the date of its composition, it is hard not to think about the larger political freighting of Reeve's work. Jay Fliegelman has persuasively argued for the symbolic significance of any representation of domestic relations in this period, and given that the war in America was seen by so many contemporaries as a familial struggle that involved the spilling of 'brothers' blood', it goes without saying that Sir Walter Lovel's murder of his kinsman is particularly resonant.[21] While Sir Philip and Edmund do not appear directly to represent a

---

18 Reeve, *Old English Baron*, p. 12.
19 Horace Walpole, *The Castle of Otranto*, edited by W. S. Lewis and E. J. Clery (Oxford: Oxford University Press, 1998), p. 54.
20 Reeve, *Old English Baron*, p. 91.
21 Jay Fliegelman, *Prodigals and Pilgrims: The American Revolution against Patriarchal Authority* (Cambridge: Cambridge University Press, 1982).

'side' or correspond to any historical actors in the ongoing conflict, Reeve's depiction of them and their endeavours similarly possesses a topical charge.

Dror Wahrman has argued that the American war generated a 'problem of identity' in Britain because 'internal strife destabilized the most basic distinctions between "us" and "them", good guys and bad guys, friends and foes'; one index of this confounding of distinctions, as already mentioned, is that American revolutionaries used a language of political opposition that had long been familiar to Britons.[22] *The Old English Baron* can be seen as indirectly addressing the problem of identity discussed by Wahrman, since Sir Philip's homecoming ultimately has a clarificatory impact, triggering a sequence of events that finally reveals Edmund to be the son and heir of the deceased Lord Lovel. Edmund's true status is heavily trailed, and his superior 'qualities' are further established by an early episode when the Baron sends the young men of Lovel Castle to France 'to learn the art of war, and signalize their courage and abilities'.[23] Reeve's work briefly refers here to Richard Duke of York's replacement of 'the great Duke of Bedford' as Regent of France (which took place in 1436) and how 'cities were lost and won' during this phase of the Hundred Years' War, but it makes no attempt to specify the details of this conflict, and, as in its opening paragraph, it presents France as a kind of eternal national foe.[24] Wenlock and Markham again appear as antagonists of Edmund during this French interlude, the function of which is to demonstrate his imperviousness to their plotting against him as well as his courage as a soldier. When, for example, they and others attempt to 'leave him to the enemy' by withdrawing at the last moment from a planned ambush on a French military convoy, Edmund's bravery ensures English victory anyway, as Reeve's sparse prose makes plain: 'Edmund advanced the foremost of the party; he drew out the leader on the French side; he slew him.'[25] Edmund is then presented to the Duke of York as 'the man to whom the victory was chiefly owing', although since he still thinks that he is a 'peasant' at this time he is unable to accept the knighthood that the Duke wishes to confer upon him.[26]

Frances Chiu points out that Wenlock describes Edmund as an 'upstart' just before his attempt to entrap him, and, emphasising that Edmund is an object of disdain to his enemies, she presents him as a 'portrait of the modern disenfranchised middle and lower-class

22 Dror Wahrman, *The Making of the Modern Self: Identity and Culture in Eighteenth-Century England* (New Haven: Yale University Press, 2004), p. 224.
23 Reeve, *Old English Baron*, p. 20.   24 Reeve, *Old English Baron*, p. 22.
25 Reeve, *Old English Baron*, pp. 24, 25.   26 Reeve, *Old English Baron*, p. 25.

Briton'.[27] If Reeve's depiction of the belittling of Edmund by haughty social superiors superficially rehearses the terms of Norman Yoke discourse, however, it remains the case that he is of aristocratic birth, and that the revelation of his true identity circumvents any tension between neglected merit and inherited privilege. As noted above, it is further significant that Edmund's virtue has a specifically military dimension, as is evident from Sir Philip's first encounter with him when he has just won an archery competition: 'I must ... take a view of this Edmund', Sir Philip declares.[28] Even as Reeve's account of Edmund's heroic deeds in France eschews direct engagement with debates about the legitimacy of the war in America, or the manner of its conduct, it can nonetheless be seen to constitute a 'performance of patriotism' of a kind that strives, in the words of Daniel O'Quinn, 'to figure forth a post-America British imperium'.[29]

Focusing primarily on stage plays performed between 1777 and 1784, O'Quinn suggests that the anticipation of defeat in America was a particular problem for Whigs, who saw in an American independence – with which they would instinctively have sympathised – the prospect of 'Liberty ... thriving elsewhere'.[30] This sense of liberty flourishing across the Atlantic while being compromised in Britain, O'Quinn argues, necessitated a search for 'new subjectivities and new social contracts suitable for the time to come', and together with Wahrman's analysis of a metropolitan 'problem of identity', O'Quinn's account of a Whig crisis of liberty helps to illuminate how Reeve may have responded to the American war even as she made no direct mention of it.[31] Her change of title from *The Champion of Virtue* to *The Old English Baron* arguably captures the way in which she sought to accommodate her 'fixed' Old Whig principles to the political circumstances of the present and future, since the later title not only gives the idea of public virtue an explicitly 'English' (rather than Classical republican) content but also signals its historical ballast and potentially enduring strength. By describing Edmund's exploits in fifteenth-century France, Reeve is able both to sidestep the rights and wrongs of the current conflict taking place in America and to invoke a conspicuously active virtue – witness the

27 Frances A. Chiu, '"Dark and dangerous designs": tales of oppression, dispossession, and repression, 1770–1800', *Romanticism on the Net* 28 (Nov 2002) <www.erudit.org/en/journals/ron/2002-n28-ron560/007205ar/> (last accessed 6 June 2018) (para. 11).
28 Reeve, *Old English Baron*, p. 13. 29 O'Quinn, *Entertaining Crisis*, p. 35.
30 O'Quinn, *Entertaining Crisis*, p. 34. 31 O'Quinn, *Entertaining Crisis*, p. 35.

association of military activity and 'exercise' – as an antidote to the effeminacy diagnosed in the *London Evening Post* and elsewhere.

At least in its French episode, then, Reeve's work enacts an (Old) 'Englishing' of public virtue in the terms of a history of martial prowess rather than a libertarian birth-right. While it is beyond the scope of this essay to consider the late eighteenth-century trajectory of 'radical patriotism', it is notable that Reeve here detaches a normative anti-Gallicanism from the reformist language of English liberties with which it was bound up in the rhetoric of a figure such as John Wilkes a decade or so earlier.[32] After Edmund's return from France, another suggestive episode shows Reeve again using her tale of 'Gothic times and manners' indirectly to reflect on and negotiate the crisis of the present. During a walk with his 'preceptor', Father Oswald, Edmund questions his companion about the 'preparations for building' that he observes at Lovel Castle, to which Oswald replies by telling him about Fitz-Owen's plans to construct a new apartment.[33] Edmund then asks why the Baron should take the trouble to do this when there is a vacant apartment on the other side of the castle, and Oswald in turn narrates a story about the mysterious death of its one-time occupant the former Lord Lovel on a military expedition in Wales, the suspicion of Lady Lovel that this was the result of foul play, and the subsequent conduct of Sir Walter Lovel, who, on the pretext of protecting his brother's grief-stricken widow, confined her in the now-empty chambers, where she died. Fitz-Owen accuses Edmund of speaking out of turn about the 'absurdity' of unnecessary building work, and, under pressure from his son Sir Robert and Wenlock, he orders Edmund to spend three nights in the old apartment to test Oswald's claims about its being haunted by its last residents.[34] Following his trial by combat in France, this second trial of Edmund's courage corroborates Oswald's story, because after dreaming of 'a Warrior, leading a Lady by the hand' and of being identified by the Lady as the 'sweet hope of a house that is thought past hope!', he hears a suit of armour crash to the floor and comes across portraits – turned to face the wall – of Lord and Lady Lovel, the former identified by Oswald as a striking resemblance to Edmund.[35] Reeve's work here signifies Edmund's legitimacy by using some of the same Gothic effects as *Otranto*, and like *Otranto* it describes contrasting reactions to apparently supernatural phenomena so that while Edmund searches for meaning,

---

32 Kathleen Wilson, *The Sense of the People: Politics, Culture and Imperialism in England, 1715–1785* (Cambridge: Cambridge University Press, 1995), pp. 206–36.
33 Reeve, Old English Baron, p. 27.   34 Reeve, Old English Baron, p. 33.
35 Reeve, Old English Baron, p. 38.

Wenlock and Markham (in their own later encounter with 'a man in compleat armour' in the apartment) succumb to terror: 'Wenlock sunk down in a swoon, and Markham had just strength enough to knock at the door'.[36]

Gothic Repair?

The story of the haunted apartment is politically resonant rather than simply derivative, since – beginning with Edmund's contrast between a costly new apartment and a functional old one – it clearly alludes to legal theorist Sir William Blackstone's *Commentaries on the Laws of England* (1765–9), which uses an architectural metaphor to describe the provenance and authority of English common law. Blackstone famously stated that 'We inhabit an old Gothic castle, erected in the days of chivalry, but fitted up for a modern habitant. The moated ramparts, the embattled towers, and the trophied halls, are magnificent and venerable, but useless. The inferior apartments, now converted into rooms of convenience, are cheerful and commodious, though their approaches are winding and difficult'.[37] Reeve's allusion to Blackstone in this episode offers another potentially remedial perspective on a Britain in crisis by calling up his *Commentaries*' highly detailed account of the long and slowly evolving history of English liberty. It is broadly fair to say that Blackstone's history of the laws of England contains the disruptive impact of the Norman Conquest, and implicit in Reeve's appeal to the Gothic castle as a symbol of continuity is the idea that a probably impending moment of ostensibly comparable magnitude – the break from Britain of its American colonies – would likewise leave the essential character of the nation and its freedoms unaffected.[38] It is notable in this respect that whereas its precursor text concludes with the collapse of the castle of Otranto, *The Old English Baron* not only keeps Lovel Castle intact but also presents it as finally welcoming home its rightful occupant. While 'A clap of thunder' shakes Otranto to its foundations, 'a sudden gust of wind' causes the gates of Lovel Castle to fly open, after which other internal doors, as the servant Joseph observes, 'open of their own accord to receive their master!'[39]

---

36 Reeve, *Old English Baron*, p. 68.
37 Sir William Blackstone, *Commentaries on the Laws of England*, 4 vols (Oxford, 1765–69), vol. 3, p. 268.
38 On Blackstone and the Conquest, see, for example, R. J. Smith, *The Gothic Bequest: Medieval Institutions in British Thought, 1688–1863* (Cambridge: Cambridge University Press, 1987), pp. 91–94.
39 Walpole, *Otranto*, p. 112; Reeve, *Old English Baron*, p. 115.

Household members such as Joseph and Oswald are shown to be especially ready to ascribe providential meaning to the scenes that they witness, and at the same time they are depicted as custodians of memory whose testimony helps to establish a clear narrative of what happened to Lord and Lady Lovel and their child; the peasants John Wyatt and Margery Twyford – Edmund's foster-parents, whose story, Oswald says, 'may be the means of making Edmund's fortune' – are also central in the latter process.[40] This reference to 'fortune' anticipates the way in which the novel goes on to shift between the romance mode through which it brings the past to light and various characters' more mundane concerns with (as the early nineteenth-century critic John Colin Dunlop put it) 'settlements, [the] stocking of farms, and household furniture'.[41] After Edmund's 'champion' Sir Philip defeats the usurping Sir Walter Lovel in formal combat, the work indeed adopts a strikingly legalistic idiom, as when it addresses some of the wider ramifications of Edmund's newly revealed status as the rightful heir of Lovel: Sir Robert expects his father to be compensated for the loss of the property that he had purchased in good faith, whereas Sir Philip thinks that Edmund deserves the arrears of his estate's income in addition to his restored inheritance. Reeve's primary solution to this problem of rival claims over the castle and its land again demonstrates the topicality of her work, however, and carries a symbolic freighting that appears to solicit allegorical interpretation. Sir Philip proposes that Edmund marry Fitz-Owen's daughter Lady Emma in order to unite the two families, and when he declares that the Baron 'will by this means, ingraft into [his] family, the name, title, and estate of Lovel', he at once invokes the language of fusion that is integral to Blackstone's account of historical process and draws attention to Reeve's recuperation of the idea of kinship alliance.[42] That the marriage of Edmund and Lady Emma is said to offer a model of 'conjugal affection and happiness' further demonstrates that Edmund is possessed of a modern, eighteenth-century sensibility, even as he is also presented as a member of an aristo-military caste.[43]

In view of O'Quinn's argument about contemporary intimations of a 'post-America' future, it is therefore tempting to read *The Old English Baron*'s tale of the restoration of Edmund Lovel and his connection by marriage to the Fitz-Owen family as a forward-looking fable of national

---

40 Reeve, *Old English Baron*, p. 49.
41 John Colin Dunlop, *The History of Fiction: Being a Critical Account of the Most Celebrated Prose Works of Fiction, from the Earliest Greek Romances to the Novels of the Present Age*, 3 vols (London, 1814), vol. 3, p. 184.
42 Reeve, *Old English Baron*, p. 110. 43 Reeve, *Old English Baron*, p. 134.

reconciliation and repair, built upon the foundations of Gothic virtue. As it ties up its loose ends the novel also describes another alliance that is similarly both personal and political. Sir Philip's friend Lord Clifford of Cumberland, the arbiter of his formal combat with the usurping Sir Walter Lovel, proposes that their encounter take place under the jurisdiction of Lord Graham, 'warden of the Scottish marches', and the later marriage of Lord Clifford's 'second daughter' and Lord Graham's 'eldest nephew' might be read as allegorising the future emergence of a new and inclusive Britishness.[44] (Lord Clifford marries his other daughter to Fitz-Owen's son Sir Robert, thereby including one of those previously hostile to Edmund in the work's final settlement too.) Toni Wein considers additional ways in which Reeve's work 'compose[s] an isolated region of England into a federation incorporating essential elements of what would become Great Britain', noting, for example, the significance of the 'expedition into Wales' from which Edmund's father failed to return.[45] While the matter-of-fact statement that the then monarch, Henry IV, 'chastised the Rebels' appears rather tantalisingly to allude to contemporary colonial rebellion (and if we read it as doing so, seems to cast it as illegitimate), the novel integrates Wales as well as Scotland into a larger union, for example by stating that after giving up his claim to Lovel Castle, Fitz-Owen resolved to 'repair [his] old castle in Wales, and reside there'.[46] Welsh cultural reference points are familiar not only to Lady Emma, who invokes 'Saint Winifred' on realising that Edmund is 'no peasant', but also to the more straightforwardly 'English' Edmund, whose preferred horse has the over-determined name of 'Caradoc'.[47]

Wein suggestively claims that Reeve further uses the category of 'internal foes' in order to help define this proleptic sense of Britishness.[48] If Reeve's work ultimately frustrates any attempt to read it as allegorising the American war itself, as I have argued, it comes closest to an allegorical mode in its representation of agents of discord who instigate familial conflict: Wein notes, for example, that while Wenlock and Markham attempt to frame Edmund as a figure plotting against his surrogate father, in particular when he disappears from the castle after his trial in the haunted apartment, 'Reeve

---

44 Reeve, *Old English Baron*, pp. 81, 123.
45 Toni Wein, *British Identities, Heroic Nationalisms, and the Gothic Novel, 1764–1824* (Basingstoke: Palgrave Macmillan, 2002), p. 72; Reeve, *Old English Baron*, p. 28.
46 Reeve, *Old English Baron*, pp. 28, 122.
47 Reeve, *Old English Baron*, pp. 72, 41; the name 'Caradoc' could refer to an ancestor of the Kings of Gwent but also to Caractacus, the leader of the Britons' resistance to Roman invasion.
48 Wein, *British Identities*, p. 75.

exonerates Edmund and turns the accusation back upon his accusers'.[49] It is significant too, however, that the novel presents its malefactors as potentially redeemable. Fitz-Owen tells Wenlock that by banishing him he wants to give him 'an opportunity of recovering his credit', and he assures Markham – after the latter has testified against his associate – that going abroad 'on ... business' on the Baron's behalf will similarly improve his standing in the eyes of others.[50] The usurper Sir Walter Lovel is also given the chance to lead a new and better life in exile, and following his banishment (which, like that of Wenlock, is permanent), he decides to eschew a penitential 'life of solitude and retirement' for 'the service of the Greek emperor, John Paleologus'.[51] He thus takes part in the conflict against Ottoman Turks from which Sir Philip, who proposes the terms of this exile, is depicted as returning in the novel's opening scene.

The 'internal foe' Sir Walter Lovel therefore ends the novel by enrolling himself in the European struggle to protect the territorial integrity of another imaginary bloc, Christendom. Even as Reeve's work thus invokes both earlier military heroes (such as the crusading King Richard I) and a longer history of conflict with 'Saracens', however, the specificity of its historical reference serves to undercut the rhetorical function of external adversaries in the text, as a foil against which a renewed sense of national character or reputation might be defined. Although the novel presents Sir Walter Lovel as having rediscovered the discipline of military activity and 'accepted a post in the emperor's army', in its closing moments it additionally states that Sir Philip's Greek servant Zadisky (the companion of the exiled knight on his 'pilgrimage to the Holy Land') 'foresaw, and lamented the downfall' of the Byzantine empire, 'and withdrew from the storm he saw approaching'; Zadisky – shrewdly, it is suggested – therefore opts for the life of retirement that Sir Walter Lovel rejects.[52] Whether or not Edward Gibbon was among the historians that Reeve read, the conclusion to her novel may allude to his extended narrative of imperial 'decline and fall' (the first volume of which was published in 1776), and it reminds readers that the enterprise of attempting to defend Europe against 'the encroachments of the Saracens', for all that it afforded honour to its participants, was ultimately a failure.[53]

The novel's engagement with the history of the reign of Henry VI still more clearly compromises its function as a fable of national

---

49 Wein, *British Identities*, p. 76.   50 Reeve, *Old English Baron*, p. 85.
51 Reeve, *Old English Baron*, p. 135.   52 Reeve, *Old English Baron*, pp. 119, 135.
53 Although Gibbon did not describe the fall of the Byzantine empire until the final volume of his work, published in 1788

reconciliation. While Edmund proves his courage in France against an even more familiar enemy, many of Reeve's first readers would have been aware that in 1453, shortly after the period in which the work is set (also the date of the fall of Constantinople), the end of the Hundred Years' War reduced the English presence in France to a foothold in Calais; when Reeve refers to Richard, Duke of York taking over as Regent of France, she briefly notes how in recent years a 'great part' of France had already 'revolted to Charles the Dauphin', the Valois claimant to the French throne.[54] The young Henry VI was crowned as King of France in 1431 and aspired to the sovereignty of both kingdoms, and the novel's acknowledgement of the impending demise of this ambition of dual monarchy might be read as consistent with its figuring of a 'post-America' future in which Britain would be relieved of a troublesome colonial encumbrance. Most readers would have seen the shortcomings of any such analogy between past and present, however, since after the final English defeat in Gascony in 1453, Henry VI suffered a mental breakdown that precipitated the dynastic conflict that would result in the Wars of the Roses (1455–85): Henry's cousin, Richard, Duke of York, claimed the Crown in 1460 before being killed by Lancastrian forces affiliated to Henry's wife, Margaret of Anjou, at the Battle of Wakefield at the end of the year. In other ways, too, readers may have been aware of the extent to which Reeve's work offers a highly idealised account of national union – the problem of national security that Wales posed was still unresolved at this time, and the loyalty to the Crown of the Lords of Wales, Baron Fitz-Owen's historical contemporaries, would not have been assured. If *The Old English Baron* is a narrative of homecoming that ostensibly tells an appealing story of 'home' eventually restored, therefore, this settlement is rendered unstable by what would probably have been recognised as the proximity of yet more domestic upheaval. When we situate the action of the novel in a longer fifteenth-century context, in other words, its festive conclusion, centred on Lovel Castle as 'a house of joy' open to all, looks like a deceptive lull before the eruption of a bloody civil war between rival houses.[55]

The Old English Baron is generally regarded as an unaccomplished work, and it contains a number of episodes that, as Reeve said of *Otranto*, unwittingly 'excite laughter'. This is the case, for example, when during Sir Philip's decisive combat with Lord Lovel, the latter falls and exclaims that he has

54 Reeve, *Old English Baron*, p. 22.   55 Reeve, *Old English Baron*, p. 132.

been slain, to which Sir Philip replies: 'I hope not ... for I have a great deal of business for you to do before you die.'[56] It is still difficult to escape Walpole's very quotable verdict on Reeve's attempt to follow him, and partly owing to his framing of *The Old English Baron* as a gauche imitation of *Otranto*, the significance of its historical setting has rarely been taken seriously.[57] Set against the reigns of other, much more celebrated monarchs in the pantheon of 'Edwards and Henries', notably Edward I, Edward III and Henry V, that of Henry VI seems an unlikely and rather unpromising historical focal point and subsequent works set during this time, such as Ann Radcliffe's narrative poem *St Alban's Abbey* (probably written in 1808–9), often appear to be similarly enigmatic.[58] In view of what Reeve said about the extent of her reading (for example of the Frenchman Paul de Rapin-Thoyras's *History of England*), however, it seems reasonable to suggest that her choice of the reign of Henry VI as a setting would have been deliberate and informed.[59] We might go further and speculate that by undercutting her own fable of national repair – by, albeit indirectly, responding to a moment of intra-familial crisis with reference to a period less than two decades before *another* civil war – Reeve's work offers a reflexive commentary on the function of the past in historical fiction, and on the forms of consolation and/or inspiration that it can and cannot provide. Reeve's Preface distinguishes between the 'melancholy' and 'amiable' perspectives respectively afforded by history and romance, as indicated above, and the main text of her work maps this contrast onto Henry VI and Edmund, and their experiences of 'minority' and maturity.[60]

When we situate *The Old English Baron* in the context of the late 1770s, then, its historical setting can be seen to call into question the contemporary applicability and rhetorical value of the cultural resources provided by the distant past. Even as this setting may have invited readers to interrogate the function of the past in the present, Reeve's depiction of the military prowess of Edmund, and to a lesser degree Sir Philip, nonetheless offers an un-ironic and idealising portrayal of Gothic heroism too. Not only does the novel juxtapose the unhappy historical figure of Henry VI with a romance hero

---

56 Reeve, *Old English Baron*, p. 88.
57 Although see Jonathan Dent, *Sinister Histories: Gothic Novels and Representations of the Past, from Horace Walpole to Mary Wollstonecraft* (Manchester: Manchester University Press, 2016), pp. 67–112, and Fiona Price, *Reinventing Liberty: Nation, Commerce and the British Historical Novel from Walpole to Scott* (Edinburgh: Edinburgh University Press, 2016), pp. 35–9.
58 St. Albans was the site of the conflict that signalled the start of the Wars of the Roses.
59 Dent, *Sinister Histories*, pp. 82–8 and 91–5.   60 Reeve, *Old English Baron*, p. 2.

whose coming of age is, in the end, triumphantly successful, but it also acknowledges the currency of seemingly more 'amiable' constructions of the past and the means by which they might be circulated. When Edmund's foster-mother Margery Twyford recalls how an 'old pilgrim' and former soldier named Edwin 'came ... into our parts ... and taught Edmund to read', for example, she states that 'he told him histories of wars, and Knights, and Lords, and great men; and Edmund took such delight in hearing him, that he would not take to any thing else'.[61] Just as Reeve herself – 'unawares' – had her principles 'fixed' by what her father read to her, Edmund is presented here as having been inspired (or indoctrinated) in his youth by the story-telling pilgrim. The 'great men' to whom Edmund is drawn seem to be rather different from the great men of Plutarch (to whom Reeve was introduced), and by referring in this way to Edmund's enthusiastic response to 'histories of wars', Reeve's work arguably anticipates how it might itself be read – albeit somewhat selectively – as a tale that celebrates a conspicuously martial Gothic virtue. When we consider the popularity of *The Old English Baron*, and the fact that it was still widely read when most Britons had long since forgotten about the crisis to which it obliquely responds, we can begin to appreciate the longer-term significance of its focus on 'Gothic times and manners' – and indeed to recognise how the nature of its resort to the heroic Gothic past may have helped to submerge memories of the American war.[62]

Clara Reeve's Legacy

To conclude this essay, I want to say a little more about the still under-discussed significance of Reeve's novel, and of the era of the American war more broadly, in the history of the Gothic. *The Old English Baron* can be seen as a 'procreative' text, to adopt Ann Rigney's term, precisely because of the way in which (as I have argued) its account of the Gothic past shifts between idealisation and exposure and thus invites subsequent re-writing.[63] Reeve aligned her work with the improving agency of romance, and in doing so she sought to redefine the meaning of native liberty by synonymising the Gothic and the 'Old English', and by associating the distant national past with

---

61 Reeve, *Old English Baron*, p. 53.
62 On the idea of the American Revolution's lack of lasting impact on Britain, see, for example, Eliga H. Gould, *The Persistence of Empire: British Political Culture in the Age of the American Revolution* (Chapel Hill: University of North Carolina Press, 2000), pp. 179–80.
63 Ann Rigney, *The Afterlives of Walter Scott: Memory on the Move* (Oxford: Oxford University Press, 2012), p. 92.

military – rather than political – virtue. 'History' nonetheless still casts a 'melancholy' shadow in the novel which in its sometimes idiosyncratic domestication of the Gothic, as evident especially in its focus on the reign of Henry VI, also opens up the nation's past for further scrutiny. Reeve's work was indeed to offer a model for other fictional investigations of the past, and, as Deborah Russell's essay in this volume demonstrates, a number of 'domestic Gothic' fictions, some of them clearly derivative of Reeve's – Martha Harley's *St Bernard's Priory* (1786), Anne Fuller's *Alan Fitz-Osborne* (1787), and the anonymous *The Castle of Mowbray* (1788), to name but a few – focused specifically on the Plantagenet era from Henry II (who came to the throne in 1154) through to Richard III (killed in battle in 1485).[64] Ann Radcliffe's first work, *The Castles of Athlin and Dunbayne* (1789), though set in an unspecified period in feudal Scotland, follows Reeve's example in its depiction of a noble peasant restored to his title, while her last novel, *Gaston de Blondeville* (published in 1826 but written around 1802–3), returns 'home' from continental Europe, the scene of her most celebrated fictions, to thirteenth-century England. *Gaston* nicely stages the different possibilities of the Plantagenet era for any enquiry into the history of the nation and its liberties, because while it invokes the Gothic virtue of Edward I ('the mighty ruler, who, by his wisdom and perseverance, bound up the wounds of his country, strengthened its sinews, and pruned away its exuberant vices'), its main focus on social tensions during the strife-ridden reign of his father Henry III frames the period as a moment in the making of modern Britain, offering parallels with the present in neither exemplary nor 'melancholy' terms.[65]

Sir Walter Scott, like Ann Radcliffe, clearly engaged with *The Old English Baron* and although he dismissed Reeve's work as 'sometimes tame and tedious', he paid silent tribute to its intellectual ambition in *Ivanhoe* (1819), which similarly takes a homecoming scene as the point of departure for an exploration of the dynamics of national unification.[66] Reeve's tale of dispossession and restoration, and in particular the episode of the haunted apartment that it features, may also have offered contemporaries an example to react against, however. Jeremy Bentham

---

64 Deborah Russell, 'Domestic Gothic Writing after Horace Walpole and before Ann Radcliffe' in this volume, pp. 222–42.
65 Ann Radcliffe, *Gaston De Blondeville; or, The Court of Henry III. Keeping Festival in Ardenne, a Romance. St Alban's Abbey, a Metrical Tale; With Some Poetical Pieces*, 4 vols (London, 1826), vol. 2, p. 137.
66 Scott, *Lives of the Novelists*, pp. 203–4.

wrote in *A Fragment on Government* (1776) that Blackstone 'should have considered, that it is not easier to *him* to turn the Law into a Castle, than it is to the imaginations of impoverished suitors to people it with Harpies', and this identification of the figurative potency of the castle anticipates how later writers would sometimes domesticate the Gothic in very different ways from Reeve.[67] Whereas Reeve's work offers a Blackstone-inflected representation of Lovel Castle as a locus of continuity and tradition, Sophia Lee's *The Recess* (1783–5), for example, uses Gothic architecture to help articulate a hitherto unknown history recovering the lives of the fictional daughters of Mary Queen of Scots, secretly raised beneath the ruins of St Vincent's Abbey: Lee's work presents a counter-history that also questions the processes of inclusion and exclusion by which accounts of the past are produced. Radcliffe followed *The Castles of Athlin and Dunbayne* with *A Sicilian Romance* (1790) – a work indebted to *The Recess* rather than *The Old English Baron* – in which the twin heroines struggle with their despotic father and finally discover that he has kept their mother prisoner in the family seat, the Castle of Mazzini.

One further index of the 'procreativity' of *The Old English Baron*, however, is that its haunted apartment episode can itself be seen to offer the germ of such heroine-centred 'female Gothic' plots. When Joseph recalls the mysterious death of Lord Lovel and how Sir Walter Lovel 'had the cruelty to offer love' to Lady Lovel and 'urged her to marry him', for example, he also states that 'one of her women heard her say that she would rather die than give her hand to the man who caused the death of her lord'.[68] Although this mention of Lady Lovel's act of resistance is both brief and second-hand, it indicates that there is a story to tell about her experience too. I have argued in this essay that Reeve's tale of 'Gothic times and manners' responded to the crisis of the American war by presenting what for the most part appears to be a forward-looking narrative of national reconciliation that imagines a 'post-America' future. If Reeve's main concern is with the 'championing' of Edmund's Gothic virtue, her acknowledgement of the untold story of Lady Lovel, like her situating of Edmund's restoration in a period

---

67 Jeremy Bentham, *A Fragment on Government*, edited by J. H. Burns and H. L. A. Hart (Cambridge: Cambridge University Press, 1988), p. 20; Wolfram Schmidgen, *Eighteenth-Century Fiction and the Law of Property* (Cambridge: Cambridge University Press, 2002), p. 171.

68 Reeve, *Old English Baron*, p. 44.

leading up to a civil war, nonetheless serves to qualify her narrative of his – and by extension the nation's – emergence with less 'amiable' (and indeed 'melancholy') perspectives on the past. Even as she appealed to the Gothic in order to negotiate a moment of crisis, therefore, Reeve's work also made it possible for her literary successors to treat the nation's Gothic inheritance as enduringly problematic as well as exceptional.

I.12

Gothic and the French Revolution, 1789–1804

FANNY LACÔTE

The period of the French Revolution, from 1789 to 1804, marked a distinct change in the type of fiction available on the French literary marketplace. Under the *Directoire*, from 1795 to 1799, novels of adventure and mystery competed with sentimental novels, pastoral novels and novels of manners, genres which had hitherto dominated the French literary scene; in addition to this, 76 per cent of novels published between 1796 and 1800 demonstrated either a serious or melancholic tone and subject-matter.[1] As this suggests, the fictions on offer to French readers during the revolutionary period were mostly 'dark', with a plot based on adventure and mystery, two characteristics of the Gothic mode that, across the Channel, was variously referred to as 'genre noir'[2], 'genre sombre'[3], 'romans noirs'[4] or, more intriguingly, 'romans diaboliques de l'Angleterre'.[5]

The graph (Fig.12.1) compares the number of English Gothic novels in French translation with the number of French 'romans noirs' published per year, republications of extant titles excepted.

After a decline during the Terror (1793–94), publications increased considerably from 1796 until 1798, the year that marked the *apogée* of the Gothic novel in France. This period also corresponds to that of the Directorial Terror – itself interposed between two waves of White Terror, in 1795 and 1799 respectively – and a regime in which individual freedom was suspended and censorship was re-established in ways that were perhaps more exacting

---

1 Angus Martin, Vivienne Mylne and Robert Frautschi, *Bibliographie du genre romanesque français, 1751–1800* (London: Mansell; Paris: France expansion, 1977), p. l.
2 Louis-Antoine Marquand, *Le Proscrit*, 4 vols (Paris: Le Normant, an XI–1803), vol. 1, p. xxiij.
3 Marquand, *Le Proscrit*, vol. 1, p. xxviij.
4 Nicolas-Alexandre Pigoreau, 'Tableau des romans noirs', in *Petite Bibliographie biographico-romancière ou dictionnaire des romanciers* (Paris: Pigoreau, 1821), pp. 353–4.
5 *Décade philosophique, littéraire et politique* (19 April 1799), p. 548.

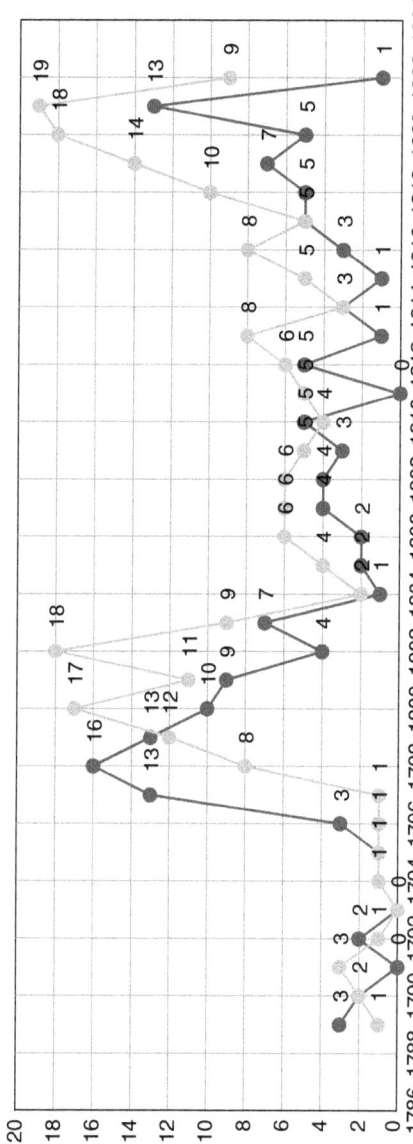

Fig.12.1: Graph of the number of French translations of the English Gothic novel and the number of French *romans noirs* published per year (1789–1822).

than during the *Ancien Régime*.[6] These historical facts challenge the critical claim that the vogue for Gothic fiction in France was concomitant with periods of political respite, assumptions which also make of the Gothic novel in France of the 1790s somewhat comforting, apolitical and escapist fantasies.[7]

The increase of translations from the English seems surprising, even paradoxical, given that the 1790s was not only the decade of revolutionary events but also the period during which England and France were at war with one another. Indeed, from 1792 to 1797, England joined the First Coalition against revolutionary France and in 1798 the two armies fought during the French campaign in Egypt. In addition, from 1789 onwards, republican propaganda maintained a climate of Anglophobia that lasted throughout the First French Empire (May 1804–April 1814; March 1815–July 1815).[8] This tense political relationship between the two nations seemed hardly favourable to the importation of a literary genre that originated from enemy shores. Contemporary critics and translators alike noticed the paradox. Among them was André Morellet, a prolific translator of Gothic novels, who noted in the Preface to his 1797 translation of Regina Maria Roche's *The Children of the Abbey* (1796) that:

> Malgré la guerre, qui depuis plus de quatre années, au grand dommage des deux nations, interrompt presque toute communication entre nous et le pays le plus riche en productions littéraires, un grand nombre de compositions anglaises du genre de celle que nous offrons ici au public, ont passé dans notre langue, et on en traduit sans cesse de nouvelles . . .[9]
>
> [Despite the war, which for more than four years, and to the great damage of the two nations, interrupts almost all communication between us and the richest country in literary productions, a large number of English publications in the genre of that which we offer here to the public have been translated in our language, and we are constantly translating new ones] . . .

---

6 Howard G. Brown, 'Mythes et massacres: reconsidérer la "terreur directoriale"', *Annales historiques de la Révolution française* 325 (July–September 2001): 23–52.

7 See Raymond Virolle, 'Vie et survie du roman noir', in P. Barbéris and C. Duchet (eds), *Manuel d'Histoire littéraire de la France* (Paris: Editions Sociales, 1972), pp. 138–47 (p. 146) and Daniel Hall, *French and German Gothic Fiction in the Late Eighteenth Century* (Bern: Peter Lang, 2005), p. 78.

8 Joëlle Prungnaud, 'La traduction du roman gothique en France au tournant du XVIIIe siècle', *TTR: traduction, terminologie, rédaction* 7:1 (1994): 11–46 (pp. 17–18).

9 All English translations in this chapter, unless otherwise stated, are my own. André Morellet, *Les Enfans de l'abbaye* 6 vols (Paris: Maradan, 1797), vol. I, p. 5.

Some French critics drew upon metaphorical notions of 'flooding'[10] to refer to the 'invasion' of English Gothic novels into the French literary marketplace, while others drew a parallel between the reign of Terror (1793–94) during the French Revolution and the 'terrors' contained within the novels themselves – 'terrible' fictions, it was held, that were utterly devoid of literary taste and value. In 1798, echoing English parodic critiques such as 'The Terrorist System of Novel Writing' (1797) by 'a Jacobin novelist' and the anonymous 'Terrorist Novel Writing' (1798), a journalist for the conservative *émigré* journal *Spectateur du Nord* noted that 'On diroit que les romanciers d'aujourd'hui, d'accord avec les révolutionnaires veulent nous accoutumer aux poignards, au poison, au sang, aux cadavres, à la terreur en un mot et au crime' [It could be said that, as if in agreement with revolutionaries, contemporary novelists seek to accustom us to daggers, poison, blood, corpses, in a word, to terror and to crime].[11] A few months later, the same newspaper observed with regard to the French translation of Matthew Gregory Lewis's *The Monk* (1796) that the novelist was paradoxically aiming to help 'faire oublier la terreur par la terreur' [forget terror with terror].[12]

Angela Wright has drawn attention to the extent to which often-unacknowledged acts of translation from French sources into English fuelled the genesis and production of Gothic fictions in Britain in the late eighteenth and early nineteenth centuries.[13] This chapter considers the question of France, England and the Gothic from a related yet different perspective: the translation of the English Gothic into French, and, with this, an account of how the Gothic mode in France became intricately inscribed in the political debates of the Revolution. I am less interested here in the 'terrorist' literary production itself than in those forsaken literary figures of late eighteenth-century France who mediated English Gothic fiction in the First French Republic between 1789 and 1804. These industrious translators, often working in haste and rarely signing their work, played a significant role, I argue, in the intercultural exchanges between France and England, despite the broader political tensions that played themselves out between the two nations.[14] While their

---

10 Philippe Werner Loos (ed.), *Journal général de la littérature de France* (Paris: Treuttel; Strasbourg: Würtz, 1800), p. 273.
11 *Spectateur du Nord, journal politique, littéraire et moral* (Hambourg: Fauche, January 1798), pp. 324–8 (p. 336).
12 *Spectateur du Nord* (Hambourg: Fauche, April 1798), p. 245.
13 Angela Wright, *Britain, France and the Gothic, 1764–1820: The Import of Terror* (Cambridge: Cambridge University Press, 2013).
14 It was not uncommon for two different translations of the same novel to be published at the same time.

works and the production and diffusion of such texts have received academic attention in the last few decades, French translators of the English Gothic novel officiating during the revolutionary events and under the First Republic have been mostly forgotten and overlooked. However, a study of the translators' backgrounds and an analysis of the stakes of translation is necessary in to order foster a fuller appreciation of the translators' role in the political dynamics of the French Revolution, a complex cultural and historical moment in which Gothic fiction came to play a crucial role.[15] This chapter links the translation of the English Gothic novel with various forms of political action in French society at the turn of the nineteenth century. First, it will address the translators' gender and social status, along with their political involvement during the revolutionary events. It will then focus on possible motives with regard to the choice of translation presented to French readerships. This particular study raises the notion of 'threshold'; that is, the type of literary works that were 'authorised' to cross the Channel and to enter revolutionary and republican territory. In the process, the argument will highlight the ways in which the English Gothic novel in French translation was received by contemporary critics and readers.

The French Translation of English Gothic Novels: A Woman's Business?

In France, the English Gothic novel reached its peak in 1798 following the success of Ann Radcliffe's fictions, which were quickly translated into French and which sparked a multitude of imitations. The literary and political writer Marie-Joseph de Chénier observed that, 'En général, il est à remarquer qu'en Angleterre, comme en France, ce sont des femmes qui figurent avec le plus de distinction parmi les romanciers modernes' [Broadly speaking, it should be noted that in England as in France, women figure with the greatest distinction among modern novelists].[16] At the turn of the century, the novel in France, as in England, was thus essentially considered women's business. Indeed, for Gothic fiction, statistics for the first wave of the genre in England (1764–1821) indicate a ratio of nine female novelists to one male,[17] as well as a

---

15 Jean-Luc Chappey, 'La traduction comme pratique politique chez Antoine-Gilbert Griffet de Labaume (1756–1805)', in Gilles Bertrand and Pierre Serna (eds), *La République en voyage 1770–1830* (Rennes: P.U.R., 2013), pp. 225–35 (p. 225).
16 Marie-Joseph de Chénier, *Tableau historique de l'état et des progrès de la littérature française depuis 1789* (Paris: Maradan, [1816], 1818), pp. 244–5.
17 Maurice Lévy, *Le Roman 'gothique' anglais, 1764–1824*, 2nd edition (Paris: Albin Michel, 1995), p. 150.

significant number of female translators.[18] Moreover, prevailing critical opinion held that the practice of translation, like other aspects of literary production, was a mercantile, even mercenary business, one akin, in its way, to prostitution and thus a sphere of cultural activity that was presided over by the weaker sex.[19]

However, the assumption that the Gothic novel as a fundamentally feminised mode is only accurate in Britain, for the preponderance of female over male writers and translators did not pertain in France. An analysis of 113 translations over the 32-year period from 1789 to 1821 indicates fifty-three male translators and twenty-two female translators, that is to say twice as many men as women, with thirty-eight remaining anonymous. This tendency becomes even more prevalent during the shorter, 15-year revolutionary and republican period between 1789 and 1804, during which a total of sixty translators includes thirty-five men, eight women and seventeen anonymous translators, for whom it is often impossible to identify the gender. Finally, when the time span is further reduced to the heyday of Gothic fiction in France (1797–1800), analysis reveals that, out of a total of forty translators (six of whom were anonymous), twenty-eight were men and only six were women. If the Gothic novel in Britain was a woman's business, Gothic fiction in France was an activity dominated by the male sex. Nonetheless, an account of some of the available biographical information pertaining to these women translators of British Gothic into French yields a number of important insights.

French Women Translators of British Gothic

Female translators of Gothic novels included a certain number of aristocrats: out of a total of twenty-five female translators for the period 1789–1821, eleven were aristocrats, that is to say almost half, while, in the revolutionary period between 1789 and 1804, six out of eight female translators were from aristocratic backgrounds. Louise-Marie-Victoire de Chastenay (1771–1855), known as Victorine de Chastenay, the translator of Ann Radcliffe's *Mysteries of Udolpho* (1794),[20] was a member of minor

---

18 Maurice Lévy, 'Du roman gothique au roman noir', in Catriona Seth (ed.), *Imaginaires gothiques: aux sources du roman noir français* (Paris: Desjonquères, L'Esprit des lettres, 2010), pp. 49–67 (pp. 54–5).
19 Elizabeth Durot-Boucé, 'Traducteurs et traductrices d'Ann Radcliffe, ou la fidélité est-elle une question de sexe ?', *Palimpsestes* 22 (2009): 101–28 (pp.101–2).
20 *Les Mystères d'Udolphe*, 4 vols (Paris: Maradan) 1797.

but ancient nobility.[21] Elisabeth-Charlotte-Pauline de Meulan (1773–1827), translator of Mary Hays' *Memoirs of Emma Courtney* (1796),[22] came from a noble and rich family of the *Ancien Régime*.[23] Marie-Françoise Gay Allart (1765–1821), who signed herself 'Mary Gay' in her translation of Radcliffe's *The Italian; or, the Confessional of the Black Penitents* (1796–7),[24] was descended from a bourgeois family that had been ennobled.[25] Cornélie-Pétronille-Bénédicte Wouters, translator of Mary Darby Robinson's *Walsingham; or, the Pupil of Nature* (1797),[26] was Baroness de Wasse, and Alexandrine-Louise Boutinon de Courcelles (1758–1826), translator of Elizabeth Jarvis's *Agatha; or, a Narrative of Recent Events* (1796),[27] was herself Countess de Guibert. Louise Rivarol, born Mather Flint (17?–1821) of British origins,[28] was married to the royalist pamphleteer Antoine Rivarol, who signed some of his works 'Comte Antoine de Rivarol'. If the noble origins of Rivarol are contested, his wife used the particle herself when she signed her translation.

The translation of the Gothic novel during the revolutionary events thus became a means of subsistence for those aristocrats of the *Ancien Régime* who had lost their privileged status. The families de Meulan[29] and de Wasse, for instance,[30] were financially ruined during the Revolution. Others, like de Chastenay, were forced to flee the capital during the Terror. Thereafter, the family of the translator of *Udolpho* found refuge in an old ruined abbey in Saint-Ouen,[31] a pile described in her memoirs as worthy of featuring in the most famous of Gothic novels.[32] This was quite a contrast for Victorine, who had once enjoyed life in Versailles with her parents.[33]

---

21 Raymond Trousson, *Une mémorialiste oubliée: Victorine de Chastenay* (Bruxelles: Académie royale de langue et de littérature françaises de Belgique, 2007), p. 1.
22 *La Chapelle d'Ayton, ou Emma Courtney*, 5 vols (Paris: Maradan, 1799).
23 Alexis-François Artaud de Montor (ed.), *Encyclopédie des gens du monde, répertoire universel des sciences, des lettres et des arts* 22 vols (Paris: Treuttel et Würtz, 1840), vol. 13, pp. 319–21.
24 *Éléonore de Rosalba, ou le Confessionnal des pénitens noirs*, 3 vols (Paris: Denné jeune, 1797).
25 Léon Séché, *Hortense Allart de Méritens dans ses rapports avec Chateaubriand, Béranger Lamenannais, Sainte-Beuve, G. Sand, Mme d'Angoult* (Paris: Société du Mercure de France, 1908), p. 33.
26 *D'Harcourt, ou l'Héritier supposé* 3 vols (Paris: Lepetit, 1798).
27 *Agatha, ou la Religieuse anglaise*, 4 vols (Paris: Maradan, 1797).
28 John Goldworth Alger, *Napoleon's British Visitors and Captives, 1801–1815* (London: Archibald Constable and Company, 1904), p. 149.
29 de Montor (ed.), *Encyclopédie des gens du monde*, vol. 13, pp. 319–21.
30 Fortunée Briquet, *Dictionnaire historique, littéraire et bibliographique des françaises et des étrangères naturalisées en France* (Paris: Treuttel et Würtz, 1804), p. 342.
31 Trousson, *Une mémorialiste oubliée*, p. 4.
32 Louise-Marie-Victorine de Chastenay, *Mémoires de Madame de Chastenay*, 2 vols (Paris: Plon, 1896), vol. 1, p. 185.
33 Chastenay, *Mémoires*, vol. 1, p. 116.

Barred from direct engagement in public life, women at the turn of the eighteenth century could only participate indirectly in political affairs. Their literary undertakings, in addition to providing for their needs, testified to their involvement in the socio-political context of 1790s French society and particularly in the great ferment of ideas provoked by the Revolution. Curiously, however, and despite their aristocratic backgrounds, most female translators appeared to have been supportive of revolutionary and republican ideals. The Baroness de Wasse, for example, was the author of a *Mémoire à l'Assemblée nationale, pour démontrer aux François les raisons qui doivent déterminer à admettre les Juifs indistinctement aux droits de Citoyens* (1790), a narrative that was based on the principles of equality and fraternity that were embraced by the Republic. During the Terror, she also published *La Famille émigrée, ou le Procédé généreux* (1793), a comedy dealing with the sensitive subject of exile and emigration during the Revolution. For her part, Mary Gay delivered a speech for a society called *Les Amis de la Liberté et de l'Égalité* in Chambery, performed on 18 March 1793 for the 'volunteers' of the Mont Blanc, who were recruited to defend borders when revolutionary France was threatened by the kingdoms of Bohemia and Hungary.[34]

The two translations by Mary Gary and Adélaïde-Gillette Billet Dufrénoy (1765–1825), respectively *The Italian* and Joseph Fox Junior's *Santa-Maria; or, the Mysterious Pregnancy* (1797), both give expression to anti-Catholic sentiments that were consistent with the anti-Clerical turn of the Revolution. *Agatha, ou la Religieuse anglaise* (1797), a translation of Elizabeth Jervis's *Agatha; or, a Narrative of Recent Events, a Novel* (1796), by the Countess de Guibert, is also related to contemporary events. The plot, praised in contemporary reviews, focuses on a heroine who is forced into a religious life against the backdrop of French revolutionary events.[35]

Other French translators of British Gothic fiction had been associated with influential political personalities of the time. Shortly after the revolutionary events, and at the time of her translation of *Udolpho*, Victorine de Chastenay was acquainted with individuals whose political views ranged from radicalism to conservatism, including Marie-Joseph de Chénier, Félicité de Genlis, François-René de Chateaubriand, Germaine de Staël and Thérésa Tallien. The diversity of the political views of Chastenay's acquaintances seems fitting given the fact that she was herself descended from a background that

34 Carla Hesse, *The Other Enlightenment: How French Women Became Modern*, Appendix A, 'Bibliography of French Women, 1789–1800' (Princeton, NJ: Princeton University Press, 2003), p. 157.
35 *Spectateur du Nord* (Hambourg: Fauche, January 1799), p. 18.

harboured ambivalent political opinions, including a conservative mother and a father who supported the French Revolution. Personal necessity required that she seek out the acquaintance of men in government themselves.[36] Among those was Pierre-François Réal, the Jacobin who had maintained a reputation as a terrorist until the Empire and who was responsible for the defence of the Count de Chastenay de Lanty when the latter was imprisoned for being suspected as an enemy of the Revolution.[37] During social events, Victorine also associated with Paul Barras, one of the directors of the *Directoire* from 1795 to 1799; Joseph Fouché, the historical Duke of Otranto and a fierce revolutionary terrorist; and Charles-Maurice de Talleyrand-Périgord, a defrocked priest, Minister of Foreign Affairs, member of the Third Estate and author of an article for the Constitution. Finally, Victorine met Napoléon Bonaparte on several occasions and sent him her works, including her translation of *Udolpho*, which the emperor placed in the library of the empress.[38]

Male Translators of Gothic fiction

Male translators of English Gothic, a group comprising a total of thirty-five men for the revolutionary and republican period (1789–1804), includes twelve aristocrats, two abbots and a defrocked priest. These numbers are the more significant when compared with that of the longer period of the first wave of the Gothic novel (1789–1821), which increases to seventeen members of the nobility and clergy out of fifty-three translators. Thus, the same observation can be made for the male as for the female translators of Gothic: the period of the French Revolution and the First Republic testified to the forced conversion of quite a few *ci-devants* and clergymen to literature in general and to translation in particular so as to earn a living. With men of letters, journalists, professors or civil servants momentarily turning to the translation of English Gothic novels, the translators, almost without exception, had a foot in the revolutionary upheaval, either directly through their actions or indirectly through their writings.

Among translators with harboured royalist political views or who stood as opponents of the Revolution stands Pierre-François Henry-Ragot (1759–1833), the historian from Nancy who trained to be a lawyer. Employed at the Ministry of Foreign Affairs in 1792, his career was

---

36 Chastenay, *Mémoires*, vol. I, p. iii.   37 Trousson, *Une mémorialiste oubliée*, pp. 5–6.
38 Trousson, *Une mémorialiste oubliée*, p. 11.

interrupted by the revolutionary events, to which he was so averse that he gave up his position.[39] His disgust for the Revolution and especially the politics of the *Directoire* notably features in his *Histoire du Directoire exécutif de la république française* (1801).[40] Henry had translated a certain Mr Singer's *Mystic Castle; or, Orphan Heir* (1796), a relatively successful novel whose title brings to mind the revolutionary events, notably the seizing or destruction of castles and the exile or execution of so many aristocrats. The plot takes place in the seventeenth century under the *Ancien Régime* and is centred on a ruined Gothic castle, the once-sublime interior of which is now decrepit and stained with blood, a testimony to the abuses and crimes committed within its walls. As the title of the novel suggests, Mowbray Castle, an architectural structure that alludes to the castle in Charlotte Smith's *Emmeline, the Orphan of the Castle* (1788), is a place of mystery, but also a place of revelation in which the orphan protagonist discovers that he is really of noble lineage. The light shed on the crimes perpetrated within the castle makes it uninhabitable in the eyes of the new heir and the building is therefore deserted before being demolished, an act of architectural demolition that encodes the will to make a clean break with the past and the obsolete Gothic architecture that embodies and represents it. Arguing, like Mary Wollstonecraft, John Thelwall, Catharine Macaulay and other 1790s radicals in Britain for the eradication of the material and immaterial legacies of the ancient past, the radicalism of the novel's ending conflicts with the conservative political orientation of its translator. Published concomitantly with Radcliffe's novels, the novel has been celebrated for its moral purpose and for its employment of the technique of the explained supernatural, a narrative turn that is fully integrated here with republican ideology.[41]

Two men, in particular, appear to have been more politically engaged than their compatriots, namely Louis-François Bertin de Vaux, known as Bertin l'Aîné (1766–1841) and Jean-Baptiste-Denis Desprès (1752–1832). The Revolution interrupted the religious career of the former.[42] Since Louis-

---

39 Alphonse Rabbe, Claude-Augustin Vieilh de Boisjolin and Charles-Augustin Sainte Beuve, *Biographie universelle et portative des contemporains*, 4 vols (Paris: Levrault, 1834), vol. 2, p. 2061.
40 Louis-Gabriel Michaud, *Biographie universelle ancienne et moderne*, 52 vols (Paris: C. Desplaces, Michaud, [1811–28] 1857), vol. 19, pp. 228–9.
41 See *Journal typographique et bibliographique* (Paris: P. Roux, 22 September 1797–21 September 1798), pp. 124–25.
42 Alphonse de Beauchamp, *Biographie moderne, ou Dictionnaire biographique, de tous les hommes morts et vivans* (Leipzig: Besson, 1806), pp. 411–12.

François's father had been the Duc de Choiseul's secretary, the political orientation of the Bertin family was well known.[43] It thus seems natural that Bertin l'Aîné turned to royalist journalism. During the Terror, he helped to draft several monarchist newspapers, including that of the *Éclair*.[44] Six years later, he founded with his brother the *Journal des Débats*, regarded by some as the most influential organ of literary criticism and monarchical opinion.[45] Simultaneously, he translated several English Gothic novels that all appear at the apex of the genre, including A. Kendall's *The Castle on the Rock; or, Memoirs of the Elderland Family* (1798); Francis Lathom's *The Midnight Bell, a German Story* (1798), in which Bertin directly comes out in favour of Catholicism and the *Ancien Régime*; the anonymous *Cavern of Death, a Moral Tale* (1794); and *Church of St Siffrid* (1797). In 1800, suspected by Napoléon of a royalist conspiracy, Louis-François was arrested and detained in the Temple prison for nine months. He was then banished at the same time as Alexandre Duval, author of a theatrical adaptation of *The Mysteries of Udolpho*,[46] and the conservative Chateaubriand, a close friend with whom he edited for a time the royalist journal *Mercure de France*.[47]

From 1783 to 1789, Jean-Baptiste-Denis Després, one of the translators of Lewis's *The Monk*, worked as a secretary for the Interior Ministry of the kingdom. At the start of the Revolution in 1789 and until 1792, he collaborated on a propagandistic periodical that criticised the Jacobins,[48] and for which he was imprisoned with Joseph-Alexandre-Pierre, Viscount de Ségur, in 1793.[49] Though Lewis's novel seems to conflict with the royalist sympathies of two of its translators, it constituted a choice of translation that perfectly fitted the ideology of the time, with its pro-revolutionary and anti-clerical dimension and its denunciation of the corruption of the *Ancien Régime*.[50] The novel was celebrated by republican critics for successfully portraying 'the monastic

---

43 William Duckett, *Dictionnaire de la conversation et de la lecture*, 16 vols (Paris: Firmin Didot, [1833] 1860), vol. 3, p. 90.
44 Beauchamp, *Biographie moderne*, p. 225.
45 de Montor (ed.), *Encyclopédie des gens du monde*, vol. 3, pp. 411–12.
46 Alexandre Duval, *Montoni, ou le Château d'Udolphe, drame en 5 actes et en prose, imité du roman Les mystères d'Udolphe* (Paris: Bureau dramatique, 1797).
47 de Beauchamp, *Biographie moderne*, pp. 411–12.
48 This might be the *Actes des Apôtres*, a periodical pamphlet created on 2 November 1789 by Jean-Gabriel Peltier.
49 Louis-Gabriel Michaud, *Biographie des hommes vivants* (Paris, Michaud, October 1816–February 1817), vol. 2, p. 387.
50 Pierre-Vincent Benoist, secretary of the Paris Commune in 1789, was a counter-revolutionary agent responsible for developing corruption in republican institutions. See Gustave Bord, *La Fin de deux légendes. L'affaire Léonard. Le baron de Batz* (Paris: Henri Daragon, 1909), pp. 91–2.

race',[51] and it has been compared in this regard to *La Religieuse*, Denis Diderot's anti-clerical novel that was written in 1780 and published in 1796, and which enjoyed considerable success and popularity at the time of the revolutionary events.[52]

A certain number of French translators of the British Gothic novel were either royalists or openly opposed to the Revolution, an observation that is both predictable and surprising. On the one hand, this is in keeping with the fact that, following the abolition of the monarchy and the privileges that they enjoyed, many aristocrats and a few members of the clergy were forced to turn to the pen as a means of subsistence. But on the other hand, the English Gothic novel that crossed the Channel during the First Republic was not a conservative but a liberal, even radical literary discourse, one that, as several critics have argued, reverberated strongly with republican ideology.[53] It therefore seems paradoxical that translators chose novels with an underlying political content that contradicted their own opinions. This is explained, however, by the strong presence of censorship at a time when the authorities were charged with the task of building a new national identity and tightly regulating its cultural productions. As the case of Desprès shows, translators of the Gothic thus participated, through the choice of works they offered to their readership, in the construction and diffusion of republican identity and ideology, sometimes despite their personal political views.[54]

---

51 *Décade philosophique, littéraire et politique* (April, May, June 1797), pp. 290–7.
52 *Spectateur du Nord* (Hambourg, Fauche, 29 January 1799), p. 17.
53 On the impact of the Revolution on the reception of the 1790s Gothic novel and Gothic's engagement with the revolutionary events in modern criticism, see, for example, Ronald Paulson, 'Gothic fiction and the French Revolution', *ELH* 48:3 (Autumn, 1981): 532–54 and *Representations of Revolution, 1789–1820* (New Haven and London: Yale University Press, 1983); Béatrice Didier, *Écrire la Révolution, 1789–1799* (Paris: P.U.F., 1989), pp. 217–27; Maggie Kilgour, *The Rise of the Gothic Novel* (London: Routledge, 1995); Daniel Hall, 'Rewriting the Revolution: Direct and Indirect Responses in the French Gothic Novel and Dramas', in Ben McCann and Daniel Hall (eds), *Rewriting the Political* (Exeter: Elm Bank Publications, 2000), pp. 9–18 and *French and German Gothic Fiction in the Late Eighteenth Century* (Bern: Peter Lang, 2005), pp. 113–48; Robert Miles, 'The 1790s: The Effulgence of Gothic', in Jerrold E. Hogle (ed.), *The Cambridge Companion to Gothic Fiction* (Cambridge: Cambridge University Press, 2002), pp. 41–62; Angela Wright, *Gothic Fiction: A Reader's Guide* (Basingstoke: Palgrave Macmillan, 2007), pp. 57–73; Katherine Astbury, 'Du gothique anglais au gothique français : le roman noir et la Révolution française', in Seth (ed.) *Imaginaires gothiques*, pp. 131–45; and Joseph Crawford, *Gothic Fiction and the Invention of Terrorism: The Politics and Aesthetics of Fear in the Age of the Reign of Terror* (London: Bloomsbury, 2013).
54 Other examples include Pierre-François Henry-Ragot (1759–1833), translator of Mr Singer's *Mystic Castle, or Orphan Heir* (1796); Jean-François André (1744–18?), who translated Felix Ellia's *Norman Banditti; or, the Fortress of Coutance* (1799) and the prolific Louis-François Bertin de Vaux, known as Bertin l'Aîné (1766–1841), translator of A.

A few translators occupied the more moderate end of the spectrum of political opinion during the revolutionary period. André Morellet (1721–1819), also known as 'l'abbé Morellet', was a translator of Gothic fiction who could be described as a 'man of the Enlightenment'. This clergyman, academician, pensioner of Louis XVI, friend of the philosophers and collaborator of the *Encyclopédie* (1751–1772) published essays on the situation, such as *Le Cri des familles* (1794), which generated interest[55] and probably influenced the implementation of the Decree of 6 June 1795, a ruling that stipulated the restitution of the family's properties to the heirs of those condemned to death by the revolutionary tribunals.[56] Following the loss of his privileges, as a direct result of the Revolution, Morellet was forced to live by his pen at the age of 70. He reluctantly turned to translations from the English, a language that he had acquired during journeys in England in 1772 and in 1784.[57] For a committed man of letters such as Morellet, the position of translator was clearly not an enviable one, subject, as it was, to considerable market fluctuations. He particularly deplored the 'malheureuse nécessité qui [l]'a forcé de perdre ainsi un temps précieux' ['unfortunate necessity that forced him to waste precious time'], a resource that he would rather have put to use in the composition of his own original literary works.[58] Nonetheless, his translations include successful English Gothic novels that were praised by French critics, such as Radcliffe's *Italian* (1796–7), Regina Maria Roche's *Children of the Abbey* (1796) and *Clermont* (1798), as well as Mary Charlton's *Phedora; or, the Forest of Minski* (1798), all of which feature the punishment of corrupted representatives of the *Ancien Régime* and the rewarding of virtuous protagonists, to whom title, fortune and property are returned at the end.

Charles Lucas's (17?–1854) *The Castle of Saint Donats; or, the History of Jack Smith* (1798), which became, under the pen of L. Billaut, *Le Château de Saint-Donats, ou Histoire du fils d'un émigré échappé aux massacres en France* (1802), was not an anodyne and politically inconsequential choice of translation since the alteration in the title clearly alluded to the French Revolution, in particular to the massacres during the Terror. Originally written by a clergyman, the novel was presented from the

---

Kendall's *The Castle on the Rock; or, Memoirs of the Elderland Family* (1798), Francis Lathom's *The Midnight Bell, a German Story* (1798), the anonymous *Cavern of Death, a Moral Tale* (1794), and *Church of St Siffrid* (1797).
55 André Morellet, *Mémoires de l'abbé Morellet, de l'Académie française, sur le dix-huitième siècle et sur la Révolution*, 2 vols (Paris: Ladvocat, 1821), vol. 2, p. 133.
56 Morellet, *Mémoires*, vol. 2, p. 133.
57 Durot-Boucé, 'Traducteurs et traductrices d'Ann Radcliffe', p. 104.
58 Morellet, *Mémoires*, vol. 2, p. 175.

outset as ideologically ambivalent in import.[59] In the Preface, the text is celebrated for morals that are said to be 'courageusement opposée à la contagion des principes destructifs de tout ordre social' [courageously opposed to the contagion of the destructive principles of all social order], that is to say as a seemingly counter-revolutionary and conservative work, a fiction opposed to the radical changes that were taking effect in French society at the turn of the century.[60] The translator Billaut further pointed out that the novel that he had chosen to translate was not the work of a republican and contained no outlandish opinions.[61] Pointing to the gap between the original publication date and that of the French translation, he explained that French political events did not allow the novel to be published in France immediately after its publication in England. However, although beginning as an initially conservative novel, the same Preface then provided the opportunity for the translator to highlight the benefits of the new political order in France[62] and to praise the new government.[63] Through the paratext, the translator thus justified a politically 'inadequate' publication that nonetheless provided the opportunity to address a still-sensitive issue.

Furthermore, the content of *The Castle of Saint Donats* resonates with political ambiguity. By depicting a ghost that turns out to be a Duke who has narrowly escaped the guillotine and who returns to his rightful position once order is restored, the narrative expresses a seemingly conservative dimension. Yet, this ending was also fully compatible with republican ideology. The coming of a new order at the end of the novel could serve as a metaphor for a new redeeming government, one which triumphs over obscurantism and the weight of the past once light has been shed on the crimes and mysteries hidden in the castle of Saint Donats, a structure of the *Ancien Régime* that has been built in the Gothic style. The Duke renouncing his title, a new heir inherits the castle and decides to renovate it. As in the fictions of the English novelist Charlotte Smith, the modernisation of the ancient Gothic structure, once restored to the rightful heir, might be read as a metaphor for the building up of a new society based on the ruins of the older one. It might also be read as the survivors' duty of remembrance towards the

---

59 Charles Lucas was curate of Avebury (see Charles Lucas, *The Infernal Quixote*, edited by M. O. Grenby (Peterborough, Ont.: Broadview, 2004), p. 9.
60 L. Billaut, *Le Château de Saint-Donats, ou Histoire du fils d'un émigré échappé aux massacres en France* (Tours: Brillault jeune; Paris: Onfroy, Fuchs, Debray, 1802), p. vij: 'courageusement opposée à la contagion des principes destructifs de tout ordre social'.
61 Billaut, *Le Château de Saint-Donats*, p. ix.   62 Billaut, *Le Château de Saint-Donats*, p. vi.
63 Billaut, *Le Château de Saint-Donats*, pp. x–xi.

symbols of a past and a powerful expression and embodiment of the heirs' awareness of the advent of a new era. As the example of the *Château de Saint Donats* indicates, if a few conservative Gothic novels crossed the Channel, they were offered to the French readership on two conditions: first, that they contain a certain apology to the new government under which they were published and, second, that they were the object of republican appropriation, thus illustrating the political and ideological malleability of the Gothic mode.

However, these novels were not the most successful in France during the revolutionary period. If many English and Irish Gothic novelists were conservative writers, their works were rarely translated in France.[64] In that regard, *The Castle of Saint Donats* was the exception that confirmed the rule. Conservative Gothic novels such as Horace Walpole's *The Castle of Otranto* (1764) and Clara Reeve's *The Champion of Virtue* (1777),[65] although reissued during the revolutionary period following the vogue of Radcliffe's novels in France, went almost unnoticed, while, with the exception of *Ethelwina* (1799), those of the prolific and ultra-conservative Thomas Isaac Horsley Curties were not translated into French.[66]

The most successful novels in France were those by liberal authors.[67] It seems curious that the category of translators with moderate political views features translators of Ann Radcliffe, Charlotte Smith and Regina Maria Roche, the last two of whom, at least in England, were hailed by the anti-Jacobin press as dangerous radicals. The political dimension of their novels, which either contradicted or did not exactly match the translator's political orientation, is explained by both commercial and ideological factors. On the one hand, French translators cashed in on the literary reputation and popularity of these three British novelists. On the other hand, they also made the careful choice to translate texts that contributed to the dissemination of new ideals, narratives which participated in the construction, transmission and reinforcement of the new republican identity.

Translations of *The Italian*, *The Children of the Abbey* and *The Castle of Saint Donats* were among the most successful during the French First Republic. This category included novels with plots seemingly celebrating the supernatural but in fact criticising Catholic superstition and opposing it to reason

---

64 Astbury, 'Du gothique anglais au gothique français, p. 136.
65 Reeve's novel was later published under the title of *The Old English Baron: A Gothic Story* (1778). French translations are based on both *The Champion of Virtue* and *The Old English Baron*.
66 Octave Henri Gabriel comte de Ségur, *Ethelwina*, 2 vols (Paris: F. Buisson, 1802).
67 Astbury, 'Du gothique anglais au gothique français', p. 136.

and modernity, notably through the use of the Radcliffean technique of the explained supernatural. It also comprised novels that turned away from Baroque aesthetics in order to embrace Classical precepts founded upon the principles of decorum, verisimilitude and moral purpose. The novel of terror published in France at the turn of the century is therefore a mode that demands such oxymoronic epithets as 'rational Gothic', 'classical Gothic' or 'Enlightenment Gothic'. This form of Gothic fiction challenges the long-held assumption that the mode arises primarily as a reaction to the forces of Enlightenment, logic and reason.[68]

Critics of *The Italian* in French translation celebrated its anti-clerical dimension and highlighted its portrayal of 'obscurantist' non-revolutionised countries, including the one in which the plot takes place. A journalist from the *Mercure français* congratulated Radcliffe for 'avoir retracé avec des couleurs si vives et si frappantes une partie des crimes de ce règne de prêtres' [having traced with such vivid and striking colours a part of the crimes of this reign of priests].[69] It seems, therefore, rather curious that André Morellet, despairing of being reduced by the Revolution to earning his own living, chose to translate *The Italian*, a novel that criticised the religious state that he himself embraced. Like *The Castle of Saint Donats, The Children of the Abbey*, also translated by Morellet, was celebrated by critics for its deeply moral dimensions. According to Auguste-Jean-Baptiste Defauconpret, for instance, the novel constituted safe and legitimate reading.[70] The journalist did not refer so much to the seemingly 'apolitical' nature of Roche's novel as to its anti-terrorist content. Like *The Italian* and many others novels published in France at the same time, *The Children of the Abbey* called for the restoration of social order after the fall of a violent and corrupted tyrannical regime while celebrating the advent of a new society created by the main protagonists, whose mission was to preserve it.

The most successful Gothic novels in France at the time of the revolutionary events retrospectively belong to what twentieth-century Anglo-American critics have described as the 'female Gothic'. If it has been re-examined over the years by critics of the Gothic novel and is now considered a fully-fledged sub-genre, this designation by Ellen Moers originally defined 'the work that

---

68 Such views, for example, are expressed in Andrew Smith and William Hughes (eds), *Empire and the Gothic: The Politics of Genre* (Basingstoke: Palgrave Macmillan, 2003).
69 *Mercure de France* (28 July 1797), p. 14, quoted in Alice M. Killen, *Le Roman terrifiant ou roman noir: de Walpole à Anne Radcliffe, et son influence sur la littérature française jusqu'en 1840* (Paris: Librairie ancienne Edouard Champion, 1924), p. 84.
70 *Magasin encyclopédique* (Paris: Fuchs, 1798), vol. 6, pp. 226–62.

women writers have done in the literary mode that, since the eighteenth century, we have called "the Gothic"'.[71] Female Gothic novels are 'terrifying' fictions mainly featuring the adventures of a heroine written by a female writer and aimed at a largely female readership; Moers's definition thus emphasised the gendered dimension of the sub-genre. French novels of this genre play the safe, somewhat naive and apolitical card, often from the outset, with a title usually including the first name of the heroine, be it Emma, Agatha or Éléonore. The latter, *Éléonore de Rosalba, ou le Confessionnal des pénitens noirs*, constitutes a particularly blatant case in the sense that the title of this French translation of *The Italian*, by a woman, emphasises the 'female Gothic' dimension of the novel by changing the focus from the male protagonist, Schedoni, to the female one, Éléonore de Rosalba. Upon closer consideration, though, the female Gothic plot allows for, among other things, the covert but no less pressing treatment of the themes of inheritance, family relations,[72] the importance of female emancipation and education.[73] As Katherine Astbury has observed, during the First Republic 'on voit une prolifération de romans qui utilisent leur représentation de la femme victime d'oppression comme commentaire sur les inégalités d'une société qui distribue de façon inéquitable le pouvoir, l'héritage et l'argent' [we see a proliferation of novels that use their portrayal of the woman victim of oppression as a commentary on the inequalities of a society that unequally distributes power, inheritance and money].[74] Under the cover of seemingly sentimental fictions aimed at women, female Gothic novels published in France during the revolutionary period thus served as a pretext for addressing more politically urgent topics. As observed by contemporary critics, these novels reverberated fully with the values disseminated by republican society and were therefore regarded as 'les héritiers de la pensée révolutionnaire' [the heirs of revolutionary thought].[75]

A survey of French translators of the British Gothic novel would be incomplete without an account of figures whose political opinions were favourable to revolutionary and republican ideals. The first was Basile-Joseph Ducos (1767–1836), translator of George Moore's *Grasville Abbey*

---

71 Ellen Moers, *Literary Women: The Great Writers* (London: The Women's Press, 1978), p. 90.
72 Hall, *French and German Gothic Fiction*, p. 20.
73 See Diane Long Hoeveler, *Gothic Feminism: The Professionalization of Gender from Charlotte Smith to the Brontës* (University Park: Pennsylvania State University Press, 1998).
74 Astbury, 'Du gothique anglais au gothique français', p. 136. Also see Hall, *French and German Gothic Fiction*, p. 20.
75 Astbury, 'Du gothique anglais au gothique français', p. 135.

(1797) and Mary Wollstonecraft's 'The Wrongs of Woman; or, Maria, a Fragment' (1798). Ducos came from a family whose revolutionary sympathies were undeniable. Indeed, François Ducos, Basile-Joseph's father, was administrator of the *Journal de la Montagne*, written by the 'Société des amis de la Constitution' and of which Basile-Joseph was a member, in parallel with his activity as editor for the *Lotographe*, which published minutes of the National Assembly meetings. Ducos was also the author of several travel accounts, all of which contain strongly anti-clerical elements.[76] Wollstonecraft's 'The Wrongs of Woman' is known for being a radical work supportive of French revolutionary ideals, while *Grasville Abbey*, as Diane Long Hoeveler has shown, is itself a highly anti-Catholic work.[77] Although the novel is set in Italy, critics did not fail to make the link with French events and refer to revolutionary France as a potential reservoir of terrifying fiction and welcoming ground for the 'noir' and the Gothic:

> Un pays qui a été si long-temps en proie aux guerres civiles, est sans doute plus convenable que tout autre pour y placer des événemens hors de l'ordre ordinaire des choses. Les brigandages, les meurtres, la dépopulation qui en est la suite, tous ces fruits des révolutions semblent préparer l'imagination à recevoir les impressions les plus sinistres.[78]

> [A country which has been for so long in the grip of civil wars is no doubt more suitable than any other for placing events outside the ordinary order of things. Banditry, murders, the consequent depopulation, all these fruits of the revolution seem to prepare the imagination to receive the most sinister impressions].

Ducos's political commitment thus helps us understand his two choices of translation, both published the same year, while Gothic fiction was at its peak in France.

An equally fascinating figure in the history of English–French Gothic translation was Jean-Baptiste Varney (1750–1831). Formerly a priest in Arras who gave up the religious habit after taking an oath to the French Constitution, Varney married and became a teacher in Pontoise before becoming director of a boarding school.[79] He had translated several Gothic

---

76 Isabelle Bour (ed.), *Maria, ou le Malheur d'être femme* (Saint-Etienne: Publications de l'Université de Saint-Etienne, 2005), p. 13.
77 Diane Long Hoeveler, *The Gothic Ideology: Religious Hysteria and Anti-Catholicism in British Popular Fiction 1780–1880* (Cardiff: University of Wales, 2014), notably pp. 232–9.
78 *Spectateur du Nord* (Hambourg: Fauche, April 1798), pp. 247–8.
79 Boris Noguès, 'Répertoire des professeurs et principaux de la faculté des arts de Paris aux XVIIe et XVIIIe siècles', November 2008 <http://rhe.ish-lyon.cnrs.fr/?q=pfap-record/6094> (last accessed 10 April 2016).

novels, including Ann Fuller's anti-Catholic novel *The Convent; or, the History of Sophia Nelson* (1786). The latter fiction, it is clear, constituted a particularly relevant choice of translation with regards to contemporary revolutionary events. Although published in English before the Revolution, it had been translated by a clergyman freed from his religious commitment by the revolutionary events and made available to the French readership the same year as Jacques-Marie Boutet de Monvel's anti-clerical play *Les Victimes cloîtrées*, that is to say, during the vogue of the *théâtre monacal* (so-called 'monkish plays'). The genre itself contains an obvious political purpose for it is born from the pen of partisans of the Revolution.[80] As a choice of translation fitting the ideological context, *The Convent* was far from being an isolated case, as we have seen with *The Italian* and *Santa-Maria*. These novels indicate that the anti-Catholicism of the British Gothic was appropriated and repurposed in the French revolutionary context, thus constituting examples of translation that directly inscribed the Gothic mode in France in contemporary revolutionary debates.

Some of the translators of English Gothic were doubly involved in the process of the diffusion of republican ideas, combining the role of translator with that of the printer-librarian-publisher or civil servant. One such figure is Théodore-Pierre Bertin (1751–1819), who travelled to England, where he studied English and Samuel Taylor's stenographic system, which he adapted to French.[81] Upon his return to France at the start of the Revolution, and thanks to his stenographic method, he transcribed the meetings of the *Assemblée Constituante*, the *Assemblée Législative* and the *Convention Nationale* for the newspapers; simultaneously and until 1812, he worked as a bookseller. In 1795, he became a pensioner of the *Convention Nationale*[82] during the reorganisation of the intellectual space by the Thermidorians – a political group whose members were involved in the *coup d'état* against Robespierre.[83] This status of pensioner of the government was shared with one of his fellow translators, François Soulès (1748–1809), translator of Radcliffe's *The Castles of Athlin and Dunbayne* (1789) and *The Romance of the Forest* (1791), and of Thomas Paine's radical *Rights of Man, being an answer to Mr. Burke's attack on the French Revolution* (1790). Thanks to his knowledge of the English language, Bertin published several translations of Gothic novels,

---

80 Astbury, 'Du gothique anglais au gothique français', p. 135.
81 To my knowledge, T.-P. Bertin is unrelated to the L.-F. Bertin previously mentioned.
82 François-Xavier de Feller, *Biographie universelle, ou Dictionnaire historique des hommes qui se sont fait un nom par leur génie* 12 vols (Paris: Gauthier frères, 1833), vol. 2, p. 269 and <http://data.bnf.fr/12903774/theodore-pierre_bertin/> (last accessed 28 May 2017).
83 Chappey, 'La traduction', p. 229.

including fictions by Maria Edgeworth, but also *Edgar, ou le Pouvoir du remords* (1800), translated from Richard Sickelmore junior's *Edgar; or, the Phantom of the Castle* (1798). His work as a translator, bookseller and stenographer under the different regimes, as well as his status as a pensioner of the government, suggest that Bertin was an active actor in the construction and diffusion of French republican ideas and identity.

Finally, Griffet de Labaume (1756–1805), a member of the lesser nobility, was perhaps more politically involved than any of his contemporaries discussed above. Before the Revolution, he collaborated on various periodicals such as the *Journal encyclopédique*, the *Mercure de France* and the *Censeur universel anglais*, the latter being one of the essential vectors of the exchanges between England and France.[84] In parallel with his journalistic activity, his work as a translator illustrates Labaume's role as a 'transmitter' of English culture in France, and this despite the tensions that existed between the two nations. During and after the revolutionary events, Labaume contributed to the *Magasin encyclopédique* and to the *Décade philosophique*, two periodicals ideologically in favour of the freedom and progress of civilisation and which clearly reveal Labaume's liberal political orientation.[85] In this regard, he probably shared similar political views to his fellow translator François Soulès. Labaume had translated Ottobah Cugano's *Thoughts and Sentiments on the Evil and Wicked Traffic of the Slavery and Commerce of the Human Species* (1787)[86] shortly before the Revolution and, like Soulès, he translated works of Paine, namely *Common Sense* (1776) and *Rights of Man*.[87] In 1795, Labaume obtained a position in the Interior Ministry, the division of Civic Instruction, a few years before he published his translations of English Gothic novels, such as Regina Maria Roche's *Children of the Abbey* (1796), critically acclaimed by the French press and the subject of a second translation by another exponent of the Enlightenment, André Morellet. Alongside his work for the government and his journalistic activity, his translations undoubtedly enabled him to play a significant role in the defence and diffusion of republican ideals.[88] Jean-Luc Chappey refers to a 'politicisation'[89] of Labaume's literary productions during the Revolution.[90] Indeed, according to a journalist for the

---

84 Patrice Bret and Jean-Luc Chappey, 'Pratiques et enjeux scientifiques, intellectuels et politiques de la traduction (vers 1660–vers 1840), vol. 1, Les enjeux politiques des traductions entre Lumières et Empire', *La Révolution française* 12 (2017):1–11 (p. 4).
85 See Chappey, 'La traduction', p. 232.
86 *Réflexions sur l'abolition de la traite et de l'esclavage des nègres* (1788).
87 *Sens commun* (1790) and *Théorie et pratique des droits de l'homme* (1792).
88 Chappey, 'La traduction', p. 231.   89 Chappey, 'La traduction', p. 228.
90 Chappey, 'La traduction', p. 228.

Décade, the political undertones of the works were what drove and informed Labaume's choices of translation: 'il choisit ceux qui pouvaient le mieux prouver son amour pour les hommes, son esprit philosophique et son patriotisme' [he continued to translate works, but he chose those who could best prove his love for men, his philosophical spirit and his patriotism].[91] As a reward for his commitment to the new institutions, and like his fellow translators Soulès and Bertin, Labaume became a pensioner of the *Convention Nationale* under the status of 'translator of several English works' for which he received an annual pension of 1,500 *livres*.[92]

Conclusion

The French translation of English Gothic, then, was predominantly a male concern. Biographical analysis also indicates that translators of the Gothic novel into French were both men and, to a lesser extent, women of a certain notoriety and, above all, personally involved in the political contexts of their time. As Jean-Luc Chappey wrote in 2013, 'L'attention actuelle portée aux traducteurs ne doit ... pas uniquement enrichir la sociologie du monde des Lettres, mais doit contribuer au renouvellement de l'histoire politique des périodes révolutionnaire et impériale' [The current attention paid to translators must not only enrich the sociology of the literary world, but must also contribute to the renewal of the political history of the revolutionary and imperial periods.][93] Given the political commitment of the translators, the hypothesis that the choice to translate Gothic novels is either purely commercial or randomly made can be interrogated. If the financial stake is not to be ignored, it would be more accurate to claim that the appeal of these fictions lay specifically in their commercial success and this is why they were considered by translators and publishers as potential vehicles for the diffusion of revolutionary and republican ideals. And yet, the revolutionary and republican context added an ideological dimension to the activity of the translator and filtered the type of production that entered France at a time during which the French Republic was creating and consolidating its new national identity, often in opposition to the enemy nation just across the Channel. At the very least, the analysis of the French translation of British Gothic fiction calls into question the claims of Annie Cointre and Annie Rivara, for whom international politics prior to the Consulate and the

---

91 *Décade philosophique* (Paris: Bureau de la Revue Philosophique, 1805), p. 183.
92 Chappey, 'La traduction', pp. 229–30.   93 Chappey, 'La traduction', p. 235.

Restoration had little impact on the translating activity and the choice of novels in France.[94] On the contrary, and as this chapter has shown, the vast majority of English Gothic novels translated into French during the period of the French Revolution are deeply implicated in contemporary political events and cannot always be reduced to a simple and uncomplicated statement of conservative politics. While, in keeping with the impulses of the Revolution, they tend to denounce the abuse of power and any form of tyranny, they refuse ultimately to come out in support of the Terror.[95] Moreover, if they call for the restoration of order after the chaos, it is the advent of a new order, of a new society, one free from guilt and the weight of the past, that they habitually celebrate. At the turn of the century, the publication of these terrifying, yet anti-Terror novels thus participated in the diffusion of republican values and coincided with the sociological emergence of a new and ever-growing 'democratic' French readership.[96] The question of English–French Gothic translation also brings to light the plight of those victims of the revolutionary events, including a certain number of aristocrats who turned to the translation of English Gothic novels as a means of ensuring their livelihood. Although curious, the contingency between the two partly explains the success of these fictions among a readership that had experienced revolutionary events first-hand. As Daniel Hall has argued, the Gothic novel of the turn of the nineteenth century is born of 'an obsession with an uncertain future, with the past affecting the present, with a search for stability and resolve in an age where the hero or heroine is never entirely sure of him/herself and is continually in the grip of real or imagined persecutors'.[97] If this type of fiction that depicts the terrifying adventures of individuals struggling with adversity was so successful in France, it is perhaps because several of their translators and readers had personally endured difficulties during or following the Revolution and had been, or still were, confronted with uncertainty regarding their own futures.

---

94 Annie Cointre and Annie Rivara (eds), *Recueil de préfaces de traducteurs de romans anglais, 1721–1828* (Saint-Étienne: Publications de l'Université de Saint-Étienne, 2006), p. 16.
95 Astbury, 'Du gothique anglais au gothique français', p. 142.
96 Paola Galli Mastrodonato, 'Romans gothiques anglais et traductions françaises: L'année 1797 et la migration de récits', *Neohelicon* 13:1 (1986): 287–320 (p. 291).
97 Hall, *French and German Gothic Fiction*, p. 140.

I.13

The Aesthetics of Terror and Horror: A Genealogy

ERIC PARISOT

If, as Aristotle claimed, tragedy rouses a compound emotion of pity (*éleos*) and fear (*phóbos*), then the two most significant literary movements of the eighteenth century – the sentimental and the Gothic – appear to represent a splitting of this feeling into distinct, primary modes of response. Fear, *phóbos*, is isolated above all as the driving passion of the Gothic. But as David Simpson observes, the eighteenth-century tendency was not to translate *phóbos* as fear, but instead as *terror*. 'Pity and terror' is the common Aristotelian phrase that can be found in many a translation or treatise across the century, from John Dryden, to Lord Kames, and Henry James Pye. 'This matters,' for Simpson, 'because it pushes terror into the realm of what is aesthetically productive or even desirable.'[1] This manifests in criticism, where terror is explored independently of the tragic as an important aesthetic and emotional experience, especially in relation to the Gothic and the sublime. Accordingly, this chapter traces the key developments in the aesthetics of terror and the coterminous experience of horror, from early-century formulations that conjoined the two to their gradual differentiation, highlighting the implications of these within the Gothic mode and beyond.

Terror/Horror: Common Ground

This genealogical survey begins with John Dennis's *The Grounds of Criticism in Poetry* (1704), in which terror is privileged as an 'Enthusiastick [sic] Passion' unrivalled in its capacity to give 'a great Spirit to Poetry'.[2] Much of Dennis's discussion of terror rehearses Longinus's conception of the sublime, namely that terror is often produced by the apprehension of power, whether

---

[1] David Simpson, 'Toward a theory of terror', *boundary 2* 41:3 (2014): 1–25 (p. 21).
[2] John Dennis, *The Critical Works of John Dennis*, 2 vols, edited by Edward Niles Hooker (Baltimore: John Hopkins University Press, 1967), vol. 1, p. 355.

common or grand; the degree to which terror is mingled with feelings of astonishment and admiration correlates with the strength of perceived power; and, accordingly, the most profound enthusiastic terror derives from religious ideas. '[N]othing is so terrible as the Wrath of infinite Power', he argues, as 'There is no flying or lying hid from the great universal Monarch.'[3] This has long-standing implications for the Gothic, a mode that is rarely far removed from the numinous and the holy. But more significant is Dennis's manoeuvre to carve out an independent critical space for terror by explicitly differentiating it from fear. Fear or terror 'is a disturbance of mind proceeding from an apprehension of an approaching evil, threatening destruction or very great trouble either to us or ours', Dennis unremarkably opines, but 'when the disturbance comes suddenly with surprise, let us call it terror; when gradually, fear'.[4] The importance of this distinction is threefold: first, it reinforces terror as a discrete emotional and aesthetic experience separable from other varieties of fear; second, it gestures towards an ensuing discussion of exactly how the sensation of terror operates, and, thus, how it can be manufactured artistically; and third, it refines our understanding of terror by introducing a temporal dimension, a critical technique applied frequently, if not consistently, in various eighteenth-century conceptions of terror and horror.

If terror for Dennis is a swift, startling passion, then it is also a transitory one that can subsequently produce pleasure: 'no Passion is attended with greater Joy than Enthusiastick [sic] Terror, which proceeds from our reflecting that we are out of danger at the very time that we see it before us'.[5] Dennis's notion of reflection here is not a conscious process but an innate, almost instantaneous response driven by our evolutionary impulse for self-preservation, as is the resultant sense of joy (or what some might call 'relief'). Nevertheless, Dennis's articulation of this process pre-empts comparable attempts to account for the pleasures of terror. Dennis's contemporary Joseph Addison, for instance, similarly claims that 'When we look on such hideous Objects, we are not a little pleased to think we are in no Danger of them ... so that the more frightful Appearance they make, the greater is the Pleasure we receive from the Sense of our own Safety', while Edmund Burke's concept of 'delight' (which will be discussed below) likewise depends upon terror's gradual dissipation.[6] If fear is a driving passion of the Gothic,

---

3 Dennis, *Critical Works*, vol. 1, p. 362.   4 Dennis, *Critical Works*, vol. 1, p. 356.
5 Dennis, *Critical Works*, vol. 1, p. 361.
6 Joseph Addison, 'Essay no. 418 (30 June 1712)', in Donald F. Bond (ed.), *The Spectator*, 5 vols (Oxford: Clarendon Press, 1965), vol. 3, p. 568; Edmund Burke, *A Philosophical*

then so is the thrill of terror-inducing objects that continues to draw us back. This 'paradox of the heart', as Anna Laetitia Aikin (later Barbauld) memorably calls it, remains a central theme in eighteenth-century discussions of terror and horror.[7]

Most crucially for the Gothic, the emotion of terror for Dennis 'signifies nothing at all to the purpose whether the danger is real or imaginary'. Irrespective of the source, terror is an emotion driven by the imagination, and when penetrated by those impressions of sight and sound – the two 'noble' senses which have a 'strict Affinity' with the imagination – and 'fir'd by that Agitation ... the very Objects themselves are set as it were before us, and consequently we are sensible of the same Passion that we should feel from the things themselves'.[8] This is obviously of critical importance to a fictional mode that aims to terrorise its readers by artificial means, but it also underscores the centrality of the imagination to Gothic aesthetics, paving the way to an endless variety of schemes designed to disturb a reader's imagination. As a transitory emotion fuelled by the imagination and often attended with instinctual pleasure, Dennis's conception of terror establishes a number of key considerations that are developed and explored in later formulations of terror and horror across the eighteenth century.

It is with Addison that horror comes into view. He offers little, however, to distinguish it explicitly from terror, primarily using 'horror' to describe the emotion attendant upon the sublime where Dennis before him, and Burke after him, use 'terror'. In his second essay on the pleasures of the imagination published in the *Spectator* (essay no. 412, 1712), Addison considers the delight with which we view natural scenes of greatness, the uncommon or the beautiful, despite the traces of incongruent horror that often accompany such pleasures. An instructive example can be found in his own description of his visit to Lake Geneva and the Alps:

> There are *Vista's* in it of a great Length, that terminate upon the Lake. At one Side of the Walks you have a near Prospect of the *Alps*, which are broken into so many Steps and Precipices, that they fill the Mind with an agreeable kind of Horror, and form one of the most irregular mis-shapen Scenes in the World.[9]

Enquiry into the Sublime and Beautiful, edited by James T. Boulton (London and New York: Routledge, 2008), p. 36.

7 Anna Laetitia Aikin, 'On the Pleasure Derived from Objects of Terror', in E. J. Clery and Robert Miles (eds), *Gothic Documents, A Sourcebook: 1700–1820* (Manchester and New York: Manchester University Press, 2000), pp. 127–9 (p. 128).

8 Dennis, *Critical Works*, vol. I, pp. 362–3.

9 Joseph Addison, *Remarks on Several Parts of Italy, &c. in the Years 1701, 1702, 1703* (London: 1726), p. 261.

The scene – expansive, stunning and strange as it is – meets all of Addison's criteria, and elicits a consuming sense of awe, what he describes as an 'agreeable ... Horror.' This same dynamic is described again in essay no. 412 in specific relation to novelty, which 'bestows Charms on a Monster, and makes even the Imperfections of Nature please us'.[10]

It is with this analogy that Addison unwittingly draws a crucial parallel between the enchantments of natural sublimity and those of supernatural tales. What Addison, following John Dryden, called this *'Fairie way of Writing'*, with its 'Fairies, Witches, Magicians, Demons, and departed Spirits ... raise a pleasing kind of Horrour [sic] in the Mind of the Reader, and amuse his Imagination with the Strangeness and Novelty of the Persons who are represented in them'.[11] Such paradoxical pleasures, to which Addison suggests we are all – but especially the English – naturally inclined, exert a powerful influence on impressionable minds, as witnessed in his observing 'several young Girls of the Neighbourhood sitting about the Fire with my Land-Lady's Daughters, and telling Stories of Sprits and Apparitions'. These young ladies – and one little boy 'who was so attentive of every Story, that I am mistaken if he ventures to go to bed by himself this Twelvemonth' – devotedly 'astonish and terrify one another' with 'these little Horrours [sic] of the Imagination', but while Addison initially revels in the description of the scene, he also issues a 'patriarchal' warning in at least two senses of that term.[12] On the one hand, imagining himself as a father, he advises care to protect children from overindulging in such imaginary pleasures, condoning 'a sound Imagination as the greatest Blessing of Life' provided it is yoked with 'clear Judgment'; without counterbalancing reason, a vigorous imagination becomes a 'Weakness'.[13] This is further exemplified by his rational demystification of local superstitions when describing his nocturnal stroll 'among the Ruins of an old Abby' elsewhere in the *Spectator* (essay no. 110, 1711). On the other hand, Addison's caution is heavily gendered, chiefly aimed, as it is, at the so-called weaker sex. These tales of supernatural horror and 'many other old Womens [sic] Fables of the like Nature' are primarily being enjoyed by young women – they are constructed by Addison, quite literally, as old wives' tales, fallacious stories passed from one generation of women to the next. Addison reconciles the two senses with the following counsel: 'since there are very few whose Minds are not more or less subject to these dreadful

---

10 Addison, 'Essay no. 412 (23 June 1712)' in Bond (ed.), *The Spectator*, vol. 3, p. 541.
11 Addison, 'Essay no. 419 (1 July 1712)', in Bond (ed.), *The Spectator*, vol. 3, pp. 570–1.
12 Addison, 'Essay no. 12 (14 March 1711)', in Bond (ed.), *The Spectator*, vol. 1, p. 53.
13 Addison, 'Essay no. 12 (14 March 1711)', in Bond (ed.), *The Spectator*, vol. 1, p. 54.

Thoughts and Apprehensions, we ought to arm our selves against them by the Dictates of Reason and Religion, *to pull the old Woman out of our Hearts ... and extinguish those impertinent Notions*' of fanciful youth.[14] In short, Addison fashions our predilection to delight in imaginary horrors as a feminine one, an enjoyment that must be exorcised by mature, masculine reason. These gendered associations prove to be powerful, enduring throughout the remainder of the century and beyond, as manifested in the late-century construction of Gothic readers as impressionable, largely foolish, young girls and, later, the twentieth-century critical construction of imaginary terrors as a hallmark of the 'female Gothic' (as opposed to the explicit, sensory, masculine horrors of Mathew Gregory Lewis and the German *Schauerroman*).[15]

Although Addison's use of the term 'horror', along with its gendered associations, is largely indistinguishable from what is later more commonly called 'terror', he does, however fleetingly, gesture towards a kind of horror that points to later conceptual divergences. In discussing the agreeable nature of sublime horror in essay no. 412, Addison inserts an important caveat: 'There may, indeed, be something so terrible or offensive, that the Horrour or Loathsomeness of an Object may over-bear the Pleasure which results from its *Greatness, Novelty, or Beauty*', but nevertheless, there is 'a Mixture of Delight in the very Disgust it gives us.'[16] Here, Addison admits to a *disagreeable*, repulsive kind of horror, of one that produces an overwhelming aversion that, at least in the first instance, excludes the possibility of pleasure. Elsewhere, during the account of his amble among the ruins of the abbey in essay no. 110, Addison admits to the way in which solemn darkness embellishes the 'supernumerary Horrours' of the scene.[17] As Dale Townshend suggests, the term 'supernumerary', which denotes that which 'is beyond or in excess of a usual, regular, stated, or prescribed number or amount', is used by Addison here to describe the psychological impact of sensory overstimulation.[18] This is instructively exemplified by Robert Blair's *The Grave* (1743), a graveyard poem that appropriately reprises Addison's phrase

---

14 Addison, 'Essay no. 12 (14 March 1711)', in Bond (ed.), *The Spectator*, vol. 1, p. 54.
15 For critical discussions of the female Gothic, see Juliann E. Fleenor (ed.), *The Female Gothic* (Montreal: Eden Press, 1983) and Diana Wallace and Andrew Smith (eds), *The Female Gothic: New Directions* (Basingstoke: Palgrave Macmillan, 2009).
16 Addison, 'Essay no. 412 (23 June 1712)', in Bond (ed.), *The Spectator*, vol. 3, p. 540.
17 Addison, 'Essay no. 110 (6 July 1711)', in Bond (ed.), *The Spectator*, vol. 1, p. 454.
18 *OED*, 1a; Dale Townshend, 'Gothic and the Cultural Sources of Horror, 1740–1820', in Xavier Aldana Reyes (ed.), *Horror: A Literary History* (London: The British Library, 2016), pp. 19–51 (p. 27).

to signal its macabre revelry in the sensory horrors of dying and death.[19] A new kind of horror emerges here; confounding, repugnant, and oppressive in its abundance, it is markedly removed from the genial pleasures of the sublime and the titillations of an active imagination, and one that is critically elucidated and creatively exploited later in the century.

While Edmund Burke's authoritative *A Philosophical Enquiry into the Origin of Our Ideas of the Sublime and Beautiful* (1757) follows Dennis by not explicitly distinguishing terror from horror, it does insistently posit terror as the central emotion of the sublime experience, critically expanding Dennis's conception of the term as it does so. Burke isolates the terror excited by the apprehension of pain and danger and fuelled by our instinct for self-preservation as 'the most powerful of all passions', and as such, 'the ruling principle of the sublime'; 'No passion so effectively robs the mind of all its powers of acting and reasoning', he claims, which goes some way to universalising what Addison saw as a largely feminine flaw.[20] Burke also clarifies the temporal relation between pleasure and terror by distinguishing 'pleasure' – as a positive experience linked with the beautiful rather than the sublime – from 'delight', a term specifically reserved for the pleasant 'sensations which accompanies the removal of pain or danger'.[21] In the hands of Dennis and Burke, terror takes shape as a sudden, surprising emotion that pivots upon the prospect of immediate danger, but one that paradoxically proves gratifying as it dissipates. But as Burke clarifies, 'When danger or pain press too nearly, they are incapable of giving any delight, and are simply terrible',[22] an important caveat that helps to differentiate the pleasurable terrors mediated by literature from actual, unremitting danger.

Burke's detailed exploration of the properties of sublime terror – such as power, vastness, obscurity and sensory privation – are adequately covered elsewhere, but these aesthetic qualities, both collectively and in isolation, yield significant literary results.[23] Burke highlights John Milton's description of Death in *Paradise Lost* (1667) as an example of 'judicious obscurity', which rouses the affective imagination by withholding full description, and, hence, complete knowledge of danger or its source; likewise, he points to William Collins's hazy personifications in his 'Ode to Fear' (1746), with Fear as 'shadowy' and insubstantial as

---

19 Jack G. Voller (ed.), *The Graveyard School: An Anthology* (Richmond, VA: Valancourt, 2016), p. 46.
20 Burke, *Philosophical Enquiry*, pp. 57–8.   21 Burke, *Philosophical Enquiry*, pp. 35–6.
22 Burke, *Philosophical Enquiry*, p. 40; cf. p. 46.
23 See Philip Shaw, *The Sublime* (London and New York: Routledge, 2006), pp. 48–71.

the emotion itself, eluding the mind's eye.[24] Where descriptive clarity restricts the imagination to the empirical senses, ambiguity leaves greater scope for imaginary, affective play. Obscurity is also aided by 'All *general* privations' such as '*Vacuity, Darkness, Solitude* and *Silence*', an aesthetic strategy usefully deployed in graveyard poetry.[25] Edward Young's *Night Thoughts* (1742–5), in particular, invests thoroughly in the sublimity of sensory privation and its potential to serve as a clean slate for the enthusiastic imagination: 'Nor Eye, nor list'ning Ear an object finds' in '*Silence*, and *Darkness*! Solemn Sisters! Twins / From antient *Night*, who nurse the tender Thought / To *Reason*'.[26] While Young aspires to 'anti-Gothic' reason in these cloistered conditions, he occasionally succumbs to their frightening capacities.[27] However, it is Radcliffe's Gothic landscapes that best exemplify the combined potential of these aesthetic qualities. When Emily St Aubert first lays sight on the eponymous castle in Ann Radcliffe's *The Mysteries of Udolpho* (1794), for instance, much of the structure is increasingly shrouded in failing light: as 'the light died away on its walls' and 'the rays soon faded ... its features became more awful in obscurity'. Most significant, though, is Emily's affective response, which by the pathetic fallacy bestows a solemn power upon Udolpho as 'the sovereign of the scene ... frown[ing] defiance on all', awakening 'terrific images in her mind' and increasing the 'fearful emotions' that had assailed her; Emily's 'imagination, ever awake to circumstance, suggested even more terrors, than her reason could justify'.[28] While terror may be subordinated to the sublime in Burke's treatise, in much Gothic literature the inverse equally applies.

Terror and Horror: Divergences

The differentiation of terror and horror, as two distinct species of fear with distinguishing aesthetic schemes, arguably begins after Horace Walpole's inaugurating Gothic novel, *The Castle of Otranto* (1764). Anna Laetitia

---

24 Burke, *Philosophical Enquiry*, p. 59; Roger Lonsdale (ed.), *The Poems of Thomas Gray, William Collins and Oliver Goldsmith* (London and New York: Longman, 1969), p. 418.
25 Burke, *Philosophical Enquiry*, p. 70.
26 Edward Young, *Night Thoughts*, edited by Stephen Cornford (Cambridge: Cambridge University Press, 1989), p. 37.
27 Andrew Smith, *Gothic Death 1740–1914: A Literary History* (Manchester: Manchester University Press, 2016), p. 21.
28 Ann Radcliffe, *The Mysteries of Udolpho*, edited by Bonamy Dobrée with notes and intro. by Terry Castle (Oxford: Oxford University Press, 2008), pp. 227–8.

Aikin's 'On the Pleasure Derived from Objects of Terror', an essay published in her and her brother John Aikin's collaborative *Miscellaneous Pieces, in Prose* (1773) as a theoretical reflection on the Gothic tale 'Sir Bertrand, a Fragment', is the next in a line of critical arguments about the mechanics of terror, and is one of the first critically to engage with Walpole's 'new species of romance'.[29] The scope of Aikin's essay is delineated clearly in the opening paragraph as she attempts to account for the delight with which we subject ourselves to 'pure terror', what Aikin calls a 'paradox of the heart'.[30] The pleasure of terror, Aikin suggests, is apparent in the way that supernatural tales and reports of natural and human disasters 'are devoured by every ear'.[31] It also manifests in our fascination with the extravagance of 'old Gothic romance' and 'Eastern tale[s]', in stories such as Walpole's *Otranto* and *The Arabian Nights' Entertainments* where 'the terrible is joined with the marvellous' to produce a 'mixed terror'.[32] Here, Aikin argues, our enthrallment is not necessarily proof of pleasure *per se*, but is mingled with 'the irresistible desire of satisfying curiosity', as we would sooner choose 'the smart pang of a violent emotion than the uneasy craving of an unsatisfied desire'.[33] But this does not account for the pleasures derived from 'well-wrought scenes of artificial terror', which in Aikin's scheme retain their connection to the 'sublime and [the] vigorous imagination'.[34] Where 'the excitement of surprise' or a 'strange and unexpected event awakens the mind', the 'agency of invisible beings' sparks the imagination, which 'explores with rapture the new world which is laid open to its view, and rejoices in the expansion of its powers. Passion and fancy co-operating elevate the soul to its highest pitch; and the pain of terror is lost in amazement.'[35]

In its focus on the experience of literary terror, Aikin's essay seemingly offers little to clarify its relation to horror, but a closer look at the first paragraph reveals otherwise:

> That the exercise of our benevolent feelings, as called forth by the view of human affections, should be a source of pleasure, cannot appear wonderful to one who considers that relation between the moral and natural system of

---

29 Horace Walpole, *The Castle of Otranto and The Mysterious Mother*, edited by Frederick S. Frank (Peterborough, Ont.: Broadview, 2003), p. 70.
30 Aikin, 'On the Pleasure Derived from Objects of Terror', pp. 127–8.
31 Aikin, 'On the Pleasure Derived from Objects of Terror', p. 128.
32 Aikin, 'On the Pleasure Derived from Objects of Terror', p. 128.
33 Aikin, 'On the Pleasure Derived from Objects of Terror', p. 129.
34 Aikin, 'On the Pleasure Derived from Objects of Terror', p. 129.
35 Aikin, 'On the Pleasure Derived from Objects of Terror', p. 129.

man, which connected a degree of satisfaction with every action or emotion productive of the general welfare. The painful sensation immediately arising from a scene of misery, is so much softened and alleviated by the reflex sense of self-approbation attending virtuous sympathy, that we find, on the whole, a very exquisite and refined pleasure remaining, which makes us desirous of again being witnesses to such scenes, instead of flying from them with disgust and horror ... But the apparent delight with which we dwell upon objects of pure terror, where our moral feelings are not in the least concerned, and no passion seems to be excited but the depressing one of fear, is a paradox of the heart, much more difficult of solution.[36]

While it is possible to suggest that the scope of the essay is broadly defined by its focus on the Gothic pleasures of fear to the exclusion of the sentimental pleasures of sympathetic pity, Aikin also implies a distinction between emotional processes that produce 'pure terror' on the one hand – the essay's primary focus – and the potential for 'disgust and horror' on the other. This differentiation pivots on the engagement of 'moral feelings'. What Aikin appears to propose is that the pleasurable 'exercise of our benevolent feelings' occurs if our moral sensibility is pricked by a painful scene, from which point two possibilities emerge. In the scenario being framed as the primary counterpart to the pleasures of terror, pain is mitigated by our 'virtuous sympathy', which encourages a sociable benevolence that not only gratifies our sense of self-worth but also rewards and perpetuates altruism; in short, we receive pleasure from doing good for others, which encourages us to continue to do so. Aikin does, however, allude to another possibility, where the painful impression may prove too great, overwhelming our moral and sympathetic imagination to the point of revulsion. This can prove especially so, as Aikin later argues, when scenes of horror approach recognisably common experience, which can produce 'an over-balance of pain'; where Addison suggests the spatially proximal might produce overbearing pain and danger, Aikin instead argues for the experientially proximal.[37] Like Dennis and Burke before her, Aikin details the sequential rise and fall of pain to describe experiences of fear, but, here, she constructs the purely aesthetic experience of terror as separate from emotional processes that implicate our moral sensibility, one of which is the repulsive experience of horror.

This is illustrated by Aikin's concluding example from Tobias Smollett's *Ferdinand Count Fathom* (1753). Admittedly, her distinction is clouded by her occasional slippage between 'terror' and 'horror', leading some to conclude

---

36 Aikin, 'On the Pleasure Derived from Objects of Terror', pp. 127–8.
37 Aikin, 'On the Pleasure Derived from Objects of Terror', p. 129.

that, like Burke's *Philosophical Enquiry*, the essay 'makes no attempt to differentiate' between the two.[38] And just as Aikin presents *Otranto* and *Arabian Nights'* in the concluding section to substantiate the kind of pleasure one might receive from the extravagant and marvellous, one might also argue that a 'strongly worked-up scene of natural horror' from Smollett's novel is invoked to exemplify her other category of terror, those 'well-wrought scenes' of literary artifice.[39] But reading 'natural horror' and 'artificial terror' synonymously seems too imprecise to bear scrutiny. Instead, the introduction of Smollett might be read as an unexpected manoeuvre to exemplify a third category of fear – horror – and its capacity to overwhelm because of its semblance with 'common nature'. The example, 'where the hero, entertained in a lone house in a forest, finds a corpse just slaughtered in the room where he is sent to sleep, and the door of which is locked upon him', seems to epitomise the type of painful scene that produces 'disgust and horror', the type of experience Aikin claims to exclude from this essay.[40] Upon 'the mortification' of finding a warm corpse in his cell, the eponymous hero Fathom finds the scene much too close – spatially, temporally and experientially – for comfort, filled 'with unspeakable horror' at the conclusion 'that he himself would undergo the same fate before morning'. His moral sensibility is disturbed by both the odious crime and the subsequent necessity to abandon 'scruple or remorse' when switching places with the cadaver to effect his escape.[41] Aikin appears to interpret natural as probable, enabling her to use a literary episode to exemplify 'natural horror', and while it adequately demonstrates how a reader can be thrilled by skilful artifice, it also simultaneously typifies what Aikin professes to dismiss in her Introduction: the overwhelming experience of morally repulsive horror. Aikin's essay, despite its ambiguities, points to the emergence of horror as a distinctive subjective state, a disorientating rather than elevating experience bound up with feelings of physical and/or moral abhorrence at the depraved, the inexpressible and the forbidden. And as later commentators discovered, such abhorrence is not always bound within the limits of the page.

In 'An Enquiry into those Kinds of Distress which excite Agreeable Sensations', another important essay published in *Miscellaneous Pieces, in*

---

38 Townshend, 'Gothic and the Cultural Sources of Horror', p. 34.
39 Aikin, 'On the Pleasure Derived from Objects of Terror', p. 129.
40 Aikin, 'On the Pleasure Derived from Objects of Terror', p. 129.
41 Tobias Smollett, *The Adventures of Ferdinand Count Fathom*, edited by Damian Grant (Oxford: Oxford University Press, 1978), pp. 85–6.

Prose, the Aikins' theorisations of horror would be further refined. Yet it was in James Beattie's 'Illustrations on Sublimity', an essay published in his *Dissertations Moral and Critical* (1783), that the corporeal shock of the unspeakable as an aspect of horror was further developed. Beattie primarily attempts here to differentiate the sources of the sublime from those of horror based on their actuality; the image of raging fire, he suggests, might produce feelings of astonishment and admiration in description but 'horror and sorrow' in reality.[42] 'In a word', Beattie clarifies, 'the Sublime, in order to give pleasing astonishment, must be either imaginary, or not immediately pernicious'.[43] From this premise Beattie endeavours to establish a different 'kind of horror', one activated by the natural *or* the imaginary, which 'though it make the blood seem to run cold, and produce a momentary fear, is not unpleasing, but may even be agreeable'.[44] Yet, the brand of horror that Beattie describes from this point seems rather familiar, as a 'pleasingly terrible' sensation stemming from natural scenes such as 'vast caverns, deep and dark woods, overhanging precipices', or from lively descriptions of the supernatural – in short, hardly a new conceptualisation.[45] He is, however, pointed in highlighting the corporeal effects of horror;[46] where Smollett describes Fathom's 'mortification' as a moment of extreme discomfort, Beattie speaks of a physical mortification, the congealing of life's essence as a momentary impression of death. To illustrate the point, Beattie draws upon Shakespeare's *Macbeth*, specifically when the witches are asked by Macbeth 'What is't you do?', to which they respond, 'A deed without a name' (IV.i.64–5). According to Beattie, this poetic encounter with the inexpressible, of something beyond natural experience and at the limits of language, induces a blood-curdling horror and an all-encompassing sense of astonishment in the reader.[47] Although Beattie labels this as an example of 'the true sublime', which further points to his struggle to distinguish a new form of horror from previous models of the sublime and terror, his emphasis upon somatic response advances a broad, emergent distinction between the sensory, visceral nature of horror and the psychological and imaginative mechanics of terror.[48]

It was not until the height of Gothic fiction's popularity in the 1790s, with Radcliffe at the peak of her powers and Matthew Gregory Lewis scandalising

---

42 James Beattie, *Dissertations Moral and Critical* (London and Edinburgh, 1783), pp. 614–15.
43 Beattie, *Dissertations*, p. 615.   44 Beattie, *Dissertations*, p. 615.
45 Beattie, *Dissertations*, p. 615. For a differing opinion, see Townshend, 'Gothic and the Cultural Sources of Horror', p. 34.
46 Townshend, 'Gothic and the Cultural Sources of Horror', p. 35.
47 Beattie, *Dissertations*, pp. 623–4.   48 Beattie, *Dissertations*, p. 624.

the reading public with *The Monk* (1796), that the aesthetics of terror and horror became fully differentiated in both fiction and critical discourse. While, as I have suggested, both Aikin and Beattie helped to define the aesthetic elements that would become the hallmarks of horror as distinct from more established notions of terror, it is Nathan Drake who is the first explicitly to contrast the two as separate species of Gothic fear. Given that his key contributions were published after Radcliffe's seminal *Udolpho* and *The Italian* (1796–7) and Lewis's *The Monk*, however, it is plausible to suggest that Radcliffe and Lewis, among others, were able to articulate the distinction creatively before critical definition.

Drake's 'On Gothic Superstition' and 'On Objects of Terror', both published in his collection *Literary Hours* (1798), are respectively concerned with supernatural and natural origins of terror. The theme of horror emerges in Drake's latter essay, where the defining difference centres not upon the objects themselves but upon artful moderation and degrees of revelation. Terror 'requires no small degree of skill and arrangement to prevent its operating more pain than pleasure', without which 'that thrilling sensation of mingled astonishment, apprehension and delight so irresistibly captivating to their generality of mankind' is more likely to cede to 'horror and disgust'.[49] Unadorned by literary artistry – such as the picturesque, the sublime, pathos, narrative deferral and the stimulation of suspense and curiosity – objects of terror 'would shock and appal every feeling heart'.[50] For Drake, the thrill of terror operates at 'the brink of horror', and the capacity to walk this fine line is a measure of literary genius.[51] This is no less true for supernatural objects of terror. The spirit world, according to Drake, delights the reader best when only occasionally visible, or by allusion rather than full disclosure. While Shakespeare is extolled as the paragon of such literary artifice, of Drake's contemporaries it is Radcliffe, 'the Shakspeare [sic] of Romance Writers', who can soften 'truly terrific' scenes with 'beautiful description, or pathetic incident' so that 'the impression of the whole never becomes too strong, never degenerates into horror'.[52]

This chief distinction invests in the *perception* of a fearful object, rather than the object itself, as that which defines affective response. An individual's perspective may well be singular, but it can also be mediated, and manipulated, by artistic means. Drake's emphasis on the way in which an object of

---

49 Nathan Drake, 'On Objects of Terror', in Clery and Miles (eds), *Gothic Documents*, pp. 160–3 (p. 160).
50 Drake, 'On Objects of Terror', p. 160.   51 Drake, 'On Objects of Terror', p. 161.
52 Drake, 'On Objects of Terror', p. 162.

terror is presented, and the literary skill required to effect it, helps to expose what hitherto, in various fragmented ideas, had been an underlying theme in this body of criticism. It additionally brings into focus the ways in which terror encourages one to dwell on one's own psychological state – the effect – while the overtness of horror demands concentration upon the cause of fear itself.[53]

Drake's division of terror and horror is also a patently hierarchical one, based on aesthetic as well as moral values. Where the conjuring of terror is celebrated as fine artistry, the painter or poet who indulges in the blatant shock of the horrific or cruel is 'surely unacquainted with the purport of his art'.[54] While terror is sanctioned as aesthetically desirable, horror is discarded to the realm of the non-aesthetic. Drake illustrates this hierarchical ordering with three examples: the scene of a grave-robber shuddering at the sight of a decayed corpse in an opened coffin, fleeing and unable to fully execute his crime; a Scottish ballad that relates a son's bloody execution of his father at the behest of his own mother; and, Walpole's closet-drama *The Mysterious Mother* (1768), which hinges upon the 'monstrous event' of 'a mother's premeditated incest with her own son, a catastrophe productive only of horror and aversion', a play, by Walpole's own admission, that was unfit for public staging.[55] In this context, Walpole's play is further illustration that extreme horror lies beyond the normative limits of experience, language and representation.[56] Moreover, all three examples portray crimes that defy basic morality, or even taboo; although not made explicit by Drake, it is apparent that they are aesthetically unpalatable in part because they are morally abhorrent.

Aesthetic and moral horror intersect most visibly in Lewis's *The Monk*, a novel that depicts, among other things, Ambrosio's carnal submission to Matilda's diabolic seductions; his doping, rape and murder of Antonia, later revealed to be his sister; his killing of Elvira, later revealed to be his mother; the deliberate incarceration of the pregnant Agnes, who is discovered emaciated while clutching her baby's corpse to her breast; and a rioting mob that executes the Prioress, beating her lifeless body into an unrecognisable 'mass

---

53 Rictor Norton, 'Aesthetic gothic horror', *Yearbook of Comparative and General Literature* 2 (1972): 31–40 (p. 36).
54 Drake, 'On Objects of Terror', p. 160.
55 Drake, 'On Objects of Terror', p. 161; Walpole, *The Castle of Otranto and The Mysterious Mother*, pp. 272, 275.
56 Townshend, 'Gothic and the Cultural Sources of Horror', p. 26.

of flesh, unsightly, shapeless, and disgusting'.[57] Samuel Taylor Coleridge took great exception to the novel in the *Critical Review* (February 1797), and his objections to its ghastly scenes share the same moral underpinnings as Drake's conception of horror. Pleasure, he claims, is the greatest ambition that a romance can claim, but Lewis's wanton lingering over such 'abominations' offers no such enjoyment; instead, the fiction is 'so frightful and intolerable, that we break with abruptness from the delusion'.[58] Like Drake, Coleridge also constructs a boundary 'beyond which terror and sympathy are deserted by the pleasurable emotions', a limit which the literary genius aspires 'to reach ... yet never pass'.[59] But what pushes the novel into the non-aesthetic realm of horror and disgust is not the '*physical* wonders' of Ambrosio's deeds, but the '*moral* miracle' of his unlikely transformation. Coleridge's censure, as Robert Miles interprets it, is founded on a conception of horror based not on '*physical* but *moral* violence', an aesthetic criterion that Miles credits to Coleridge but which can also be traced back to Drake and Aikin.[60]

The demarcation of terror from horror, however, is most completely realised in Radcliffe's novels and her exegetical dialogue 'On the Supernatural in Poetry', an excerpted essay that was written in 1802 but published posthumously in 1826. Radcliffe's construction of terror here is indebted to Burke's theories of sublime affect, especially his emphasis on the aesthetic potential of obscurity. In contrasting the ghosts of Banquo and King Hamlet in Shakespeare's *Macbeth* and *Hamlet* respectively, Radcliffe claims that Banquo's appearance provokes a horror 'sudden and strong' but 'transient', a cheap thrill of 'an inferior kind' when compared with 'the deep solemn feelings excited' in *Hamlet*, a 'gloomy and sublime kind of terror' that lingers 'long upon the mind'.[61] Radcliffe refines Dennis's and Burke's temporal definition of terror as a swift emotion; its onset may well be swift, but its diminishing is often not. 'Terror and horror are so far opposite', Radcliffe asserts in a key distillation of their contrariety, 'that the first expands the soul, and awakens the faculties to a high degree of life; the other contracts,

---

57 Matthew Gregory Lewis, *The Monk*, edited by Emma McEvoy (Oxford: Oxford University Press, 2008), p. 356.
58 *Critical Review* 2:19 (February 1797), in Clery and Miles (eds), *Gothic Documents*, 186.
59 *Critical Review* (February 1797), p. 187.
60 *Critical Review* (February 1797), p. 187; Robert Miles, *Ann Radcliffe: The Great Enchantress* (Manchester: Manchester University Press, 1995), p. 55.
61 Ann Radcliffe, 'On the Supernatural in Poetry', in Clery and Miles (eds), *Gothic Documents*, pp. 163–72 (p. 168).

freezes, and nearly annihilates them.'[62] Following Dennis and Burke, Radcliffe imbues terror with a quasi-religious hue, figuring it as an experience that momentarily transcends the empirical world to apprehend the existence of unfathomable power or another intangible world, and leaving a deep, haunting impression. But unlike her predecessors, Radcliffe juxtaposes the quasi-divinity of terror with the baseness of horror, an experience that forcibly grounds one in the mundane, sensory world, and never beyond. It is for this reason that Radcliffe redoubles Burke's investment in the affective and imaginative potential of obscurity as the primary aesthetic feature that distinguishes terror from horror. Reprising Burke's assertions that an object cannot 'strike the mind with its greatness' while we see it distinctly and 'perceive its bounds', and a 'clear idea is therefore another name for a little idea', Radcliffe suggests that the ghost of King Hamlet stimulates imaginary notions of grandeur where Banquo's ghost does not because the former is shrouded in 'uncertainty and obscurity'. Indeed, 'They must be men of very cold imaginations ... with whom certainty is more terrible than surmise.'[63] Radcliffe's brand of terror is fuelled by a vigorous imagination, but this is not new; what is novel, perhaps, is Radcliffe's concomitant claim that horror tyrannically obstructs our imagination in the same way that it usurps our bodies.

Radcliffe's terror is implied, the mere 'ghost of a ghost', never extending beyond the realms of probability.[64] This enables her sources of terror to be rationally explained – a distinguishing feature of her fiction. Just as Addison endorses reason and judgement to offset a vivid imagination, Radcliffe never leaves the Gothic imagination unfettered, ultimately reining in its visionary terrors with the natural and rational. As a review of *Udolpho* commonly attributed to Coleridge explains, 'mysterious terrors are continually exciting in the mind the idea of a supernatural appearance', keeping us 'upon the very edge and confines of the world of spirits and yet are ingeniously explained by familiar causes'.[65] But the explanation that pulls us back from the precipice of irrational horror is much delayed, allowing ample room for terror to take effect. The result, as another anonymous reviewer suggested, is that 'the

---

62 Radcliffe, 'On the Supernatural in Poetry', p. 168.
63 Burke, *Philosophical Enquiry*, p. 63; Radcliffe, 'On the Supernatural in Poetry', p. 168.
64 Andrew Smith, 'Hauntings', in Catherine Spooner and Emma McEvoy (eds), *The Routledge Companion to Gothic* (Abingdon: Routledge, 2007), pp. 147–54 (p. 147).
65 *Critical Review* 2:11 (August 1794), in Cheryl L. Nixon (ed.), *Novel Definitions: An Anthology of Commentary on the Novel, 1688–1815* (Peterborough, Ont.: Broadview, 2009), p. 291.

reader experiences in perfection the strange luxury of artificial terror, without being obliged for a moment to hoodwink his reason, or to yield to the weakness' – as Addison also called it – 'of superstitious credulity'.[66]

The power of suggestive terror and delayed explanation is most famously exemplified by Emily's lifting of the black veil in *Udolpho*. Upon unveiling what at first appears to be a concealed picture, Emily's curiosity and fascination turns to confounding horror; she instantly, and without utterance, faints, and upon gaining her senses, 'Horror occupied her mind, and excluded, for a time, all sense of past, and dread of future misfortune.'[67] The reader is led to believe that the horrid discovery is related to the suspicious disappearance of Signora Laurentini; indeed, Jane Austen's gullible Gothic reader Catherine Morland was certain that it was her skeleton.[68] Instead, hundreds of pages later, we discover that Emily had actually discovered a waxen figure of a decaying corpse that had once been used as a penitential prop. Natural and rational order is restored, but not after terror and suspense are embellished by imaginative speculation.

This example is often cited to underscore Radcliffe's specific affinity with terror, but a frequently overlooked feature of her method here is the depiction of horror to conjure terror. While the object that frightens Emily witless is artificial, it is perceived to be real at the precise moment of its discovery. Her state of horror, albeit unfounded, provokes our imaginary terror, until we are all eventually corrected by reason. Radcliffe speaks to the narrative relation between the two when discussing Milton's Satan, on whose 'brow sat horror plumed'; in a similar dynamic, Satan's image and 'the feeling of horror' is observed by Radcliffe to impart terror rather than horror in turn, for it 'is seen in glimpses through obscuring shades ... which excite the imagination to complete the rest'.[69] Set in different terms, one might say that Radcliffe draws a distinction between horror as a momentary failure of language, and terror as the communication of this failure along with the search for meaning through the very medium of language itself. Despite their divergence, in Radcliffe, terror and horror produce an unlikely harmony.[70]

---

66 *Monthly Review* 2:15 (November 1794), in Nixon (ed.), *Novel Definitions*, p. 294.
67 Radcliffe, *Mysteries of Udolpho*, p. 249.
68 Jane Austen, *Northanger Abbey*, edited by Susan Fraiman (New York and London: W. W. Norton and Co., 2004), p. 24.
69 Radcliffe, 'On the Supernatural in Poetry', pp. 168–9.
70 Jane Hodson, 'Gothic and the Language of Terror', in Angela Wright and Dale Townshend (eds), *Romantic Gothic: An Edinburgh Companion* (Edinburgh: Edinburgh University Press, 2016), pp. 289–305 (p. 304).

Revolutionary Terror and Horror

Towards the end of the eighteenth century, aesthetic terror and horror were politicised as their relation and value to the real world was questioned. Take, for instance, the critical controversy surrounding *The Monk*. For every Coleridge pained by its pernicious horror, there was an apologist to vouch for its forceful didactic potential. As defenders of the novel argued, the wicked transformation of characters, their libidinous deeds and shocking effects, and the triumph of vice in Lewis's narrative ought to be considered as sources of abhorrence rather than models for imitation, as negative moral lessons inculcated vividly in the cause of virtue.[71] Perhaps the most striking image of horror from the novel is the one of a starving, disoriented Agnes clasping her dead baby; not only is it visually disturbing to imagine, but it is also a moment in which pure innocence is sacrificed to the cruel tyranny of the Prioress. The murder of the innocent is something frequently threatened in eighteenth-century Gothic, but rarely fully realised. Yet the image is also painted in Robert Southey's ode 'To Horror' (composed 1791, published 1797), a poem that tritely lulls the reader into a false sense of familiarity with conventional tropes before unmasking the contemporary horrors of slavery and war, inviting the reader to 'pause' at the image of a sleeping mother in the snow embracing her son, already 'chill'd to an eternal rest'.[72] Where Aikin implies that moral engagement can result in either social benevolence or 'disgust and horror', Southey merges the two possibilities; Southey's horror has its own benignant potential, as a compelling force to rouse humanitarian concern. As Robert Miles posits, if 'one of the tenets of sensibility [is] that human beings are providentially disposed to react with horror and disgust to representations of malevolence', then this emotional energy can be appropriated to spur a reader's 'benevolent instincts' and 'sharpen their censorious ones'.[73] The aversive energy of horror, so often perceived as grounded in selfish concern, could evidently be channelled for the purposes of moral, social and political reform.

Commentators, however, were far more explicit in drawing a connection between terror, horror and the French Revolution. In satirical vignettes such

---

71 'An Apology for *The Monk*', *Monthly Mirror* 3 (April 1797), in Clery and Miles, *Gothic Documents*, pp. 191–6; and 'Vindication of *The Monk*', in Rictor Norton (ed.), *Gothic Readings: The First Wave, 1764–1840* (London: Leicester University Press, 2000), pp. 305–8.
72 Robert Southey, 'To Horror', in Voller (ed.), *The Graveyard School*, p. 218. For abolitionist literature as a literature of horror, see Joseph Crawford, *Gothic Fiction and the Invention of Terrorism* (London: Bloomsbury, 2013), p. 45.
73 Miles, *Ann Radcliffe*, p. 52.

as 'The Terrorist System of Novel Writing' (1797), signed by 'A Jacobin Novelist', and the anonymous 'Terrorist Novel Writing' (1798), fashionable Gothic fiction, in particular Radcliffe's novels, was ridiculed as a facile, formulaic derivative of Maximilian Robespierre's 'Reign of Terror' (1793–4). The former essay maintains that while it has 'been the fashion to advert to the horrid massacres which disgraced France' with 'abhorrence and indignation' – in keeping with the moralistic dynamics of horror outlined above – 'alas! ... just at the time when we were threatened with a stagnation of fancy, arose Maximilian Robespierre, with his system of terror, and taught our novelists that *fear* is the only passion they ought to cultivate, that to frighten and instruct were one and the same thing'.[74] The literary implications of the horrifying scenes in revolutionary France were, incidentally, not lost on the likes of Charlotte Smith, the Marquis de Sade and Germaine de Staël, all of whom commented on the necessary intensification of fictional terror and horror in the wake of this grim reality: in her Preface to the second volume of *The Banished Man* (1794), for instance, Smith suggests that an author 'can be at no loss for *real* horrors, if a novel must abound in horrors', and that the 'imagination, however fertile, can suggest nothing of individual calamity' that has not been 'exceeded' by the horrors of the Revolution.[75] But in 'The Terrorist System of Novel Writing', the conjunction of political and literary terror remains hazy at best. For Robespierre, terror was the strong arm of virtue and justice; 'If the driving force of popular government in peacetime is virtue', he declared to the National Convention on 5 February 1794, 'that of popular government during a revolution is both *virtue and terror* ... Terror is only justice that is prompt, severe, and inflexible; it is thus an emanation of virtue'.[76] This, of course, is something quite different from Radcliffe's fanciful terrors. Nevertheless, as Simpson observes, while 'The conjunction is not closely analysed', these systems of terror 'are not completely distinct', which 'leaves us with an open question' about their connection.[77]

Radcliffe's terror is never deadly, neither for us as readers nor for her trembling heroines, but it does perhaps offer a useful narrative model for the dissemination of political terror. In the episode of the black veil in

---

74 'The terrorist system of novel writing', *Monthly Magazine* 4, 21 (August 1797), in Norton (ed.), *Gothic Readings*, pp. 299–300.
75 Norton (ed.), *Gothic Readings*, p. 287. For de Sade and de Staël, see Peter Sabor, 'Medieval Revival and the Gothic', in H. S. Nisbet and Claude Rawson (eds), *The Cambridge History of Literary Criticism, Vol. IV: The Eighteenth Century* (Cambridge: Cambridge University Press, 1997), pp. 485, 488.
76 Crawford, *Gothic Fiction and the Invention of Terrorism*, p. 48.
77 Simpson, 'Toward a theory of terror', pp. 6–7.

Udolpho, we might recall that Emily's state of horror – unutterable and corporeally possessive – was very real. Emily is reacting less to what she sees, than its possible implications – that Montoni, her surrogate patriarch, is a scheming murderer. Radcliffe's narrative, in communicating this state and its continuing reverberations in Emily's life, is in turn intended to provoke terror in the reader, removed by degrees from the originating sight (and site) of horror linguistically and, as we continue to read, temporally. But as terror diminishes, so Radcliffe periodically and craftily prods the reader to remind us of the grave danger posed to the vulnerable Emily, and, in sympathising with her cause, we are only released from fear and anxiety when she is delivered from tyranny. We learn, like Emily, that the cause of her horror was artificial, but nonetheless, it still produces a chain effect of *real* emotion and behaviour. This is a compelling model for the propagation of political terror, whether set in eighteenth-century France or twenty-first century globalism: a horrific representation of power (whether actual or not, by Radcliffe's model, is seemingly irrelevant); the communication of its physical and emotional effect at the site of representation; and, occasional intimations of danger to revive the potency of the originating moment of horror and combat against its diminishing influence. What is more, both the literary model of terror and its political simulacrum demonstratively generate mania. Coleridge's disparaging portrayal of 'the devotees of the circulating libraries' as a multitude of barren brains entranced by the hackneyed 'delirium' of one author's imagination – a criticism that no doubt implicates the contemporary Gothic reader – might just as effectively describe the tyranny of fear over a (scared) witless populace.[78] Radcliffe, of course, ultimately releases the reader from her thrall: every novel must come to an end, and her rational explanations help to confine the spell of fear to its pages. Nonetheless, her 'system of terror' is one that efficiently capitalises upon the combined affective force of horror and terror, within or without the imaginary sphere, and whether for pleasurable or political ends – the creative culmination of a century of critical discourse.

The terror/horror nexus may be ever-changing in its complexities, but it has remained a cornerstone of Gothic aesthetics from the mode's eighteenth-century beginnings, and conceivably even earlier. Significantly, a host of crucial tensions have emerged from this nexus, giving impetus to critical

---

78 Samuel Taylor Coleridge, *Biographia Literaria*, 2 vols, edited by James Engell and W. Jackson Bate, in Kathleen Coburn (gen. ed.), *The Collected Works of Samuel Taylor Coleridge*, 16 vols (London: Routledge & Kegan Paul, 1971–2001), vol. 1, p. 48.

elucidation and creative practice. What, for instance, are the differences between real and artificial sources of fear? Are objects of fear best concealed or revealed? How does the supernatural bear relation to the natural? Should probability serve as a necessary limit or a point of departure? What role does chronological time play in the onset of fear – sudden or slow? Do men and women differ in their Gothic sensibilities, whether that be as readers or storytellers? Does the depiction of depraved deeds need to be bound by our moral code? How does one best express the inexpressible? The answers to these questions help to determine the boundaries between terror and horror as we now know it, while their endless variety of combinations give creative license to map and explore the interstices in between. But most crucially, they point to the primacy of aesthetics – to the different ways in which we portray and perceive a dreadful object as opposed to the intrinsic qualities of the object itself – in governing our emotional response.

1.14
Ann Radcliffe and Matthew Lewis

ANGELA WRIGHT

>   Thou not'st, like Radcliffe, with a painter's eye,
>   The pine-clad mountain and the stormy sky;
>   And, at thy bidding, to my wond'ring view
>   Rise the bold scenes Salvator's pencil drew:
>   On desert cliffs, I hear the raven's scream,
>   And mark the wat'ry moon's uncertain gleam:
>   'Tis thine to strike, with no inglorious hand,
>   The chords, that whilom echoed through the land,
>   When erst, at feudal grandeur's princely call,
>   The minstrel's song was heard in Gothic hall,
>   What time, around his hospitable board,
>   The hardy vassals hail'd their bounteous lord.
>   (Anon. [Henry Soame], *Epistle in Rhyme, to M.G. Lewis, Esq.*
>   *M.P. author of The Monk, The Castle Spectre, etc* [1798])[1]

The year 1798 witnessed the beginning of the consolidation of the very different authorial reputations of two of the decade's most famous Gothic authors, Ann Ward Radcliffe and Matthew Gregory Lewis. Whereas we now tend to separate these two writers according to their apparently differing approaches to the Gothic mode, with Radcliffe embracing the 'feminine' aesthetics of terror and Lewis the opposing 'masculine' practice of horror, in the late 1790s these two writers were frequently united in the minds of the reading public. 1798 was the watershed year in which, following the publication of Lewis's *The Monk* (1796) and Radcliffe's *The Italian* (1796–7), those distinctions between horror and terror that had respectively marked their practices began to be eroded by those who read them avidly. For some readerships, mentioning the works of Ann Radcliffe and Matthew Lewis in

---

1 Henry Francis Robert Soame, *Epistle in Rhyme, to M. G. Lewis, Esq. M.P. Author of The Monk, Castle Spectre, &c. With Other Verses. By the Same Hand* (London, 1798), p. 4.

the same breath seemed an acceptable, even an obvious, comparison to make. This chapter, then, offers less of an account of the differing aesthetic practices of Radcliffe and Lewis – the subject of several critical studies – than an historical contemplation of the symbiotic nature and interdependencies of their later works and consequent reputations.[2] Here, I seek to discover and account for a range of readers that chose to read, compare and mention simultaneously the works of both writers; that is, readers and critics who reflected on their similarities without pausing to articulate any major differences between them. Why, when we now consider Gothic authors of the 1790s, do we land first and foremost upon Radcliffe and Lewis? This, as I will proceed to argue, was in part due to the loud and sustained public calumniation of Matthew Lewis, MP, and the consequent literary defences of him. However much a source of chagrin this may have been to Ann Radcliffe, the close relationship between the two authors in the minds of their contemporary readers persisted throughout the Romantic period.

Ann Radcliffe and the 'Magic Spell of Genius'

Following her authorship of some of the decade's most enthusiastically consumed and widely reviewed titles, including *The Castles of Athlin and Dunbayne* (1789), *A Sicilian Romance* (1790), *The Romance of the Forest* (1791), *The Mysteries of Udolpho* (1794) and *The Italian* (1796–7), Ann Radcliffe had become one of the late eighteenth century's most critically acclaimed and financially successful authors. According to her first biographer Thomas Noon Talfourd, she earned the 'considerable' sums of £500 for *The Mysteries of Udolpho* and £800 for *The Italian*.[3] Talfourd went on to diminish the enormity of those successes by ascribing these amounts to the 'fashion of the times', though this says more about the transformations of literary tastes and practices in 1826 than it does about Radcliffe's reputation in the 1790s: in a

---

2 For an influential account of the Lewis/Radcliffe relationship, particularly in relation to Radcliffe's responses in *The Italian* to Lewis's *The Monk*, see Syndy M. Conger, 'Sensibility Restored: Radcliffe's Answer to Lewis's *The Monk*', in Kenneth W. Graham (ed.), *Gothic Fictions: Prohibition/Transgression* (New York: AMS Press, 1989), pp. 113–49.
3 This was the view of her official biographer Thomas Noon Talfourd, who was commissioned by Ann Radcliffe's husband William to compose the 'Memoir of the Life and Writings of Mrs Radcliffe' (1826), and which was presented as prefatory material to her posthumously published final novel and poems *Gaston de Blondeville; or, The Court of Henry III Keeping Festival in Ardenne, A Romance and St Alban's Abbey: A Metrical Tale; With Some Poetical Pieces*, 4 vols (London: Henry Colburn, 1826), vol.1, pp. 1–130 (p. 12).

publishing context in which the average amount payable for copyright was £10, Ann Radcliffe's earnings were, indeed, considerable.

With the focus upon independent, orphaned heroines who, over the course of three or four volumes, become the legal heirs to properties that have been unfairly taken from them, Ann Radcliffe pioneered a unique fusion of romance, travelogue and terror. Although most, if not all, of her narratives were set in the sixteenth century, her novels offered terrifying and all too credible glimpses into the fragility of women's rights during the late eighteenth century. Threats of physical violence pervade each tale, with heroines escaping the clutches of libertine villains such as the Duke de Luovo in *A Sicilian Romance*, the Marquis de Montalt in *The Romance of the Forest*, Montoni and his band of dissolute friends in *The Mysteries of Udolpho* and the monk, Father Schedoni, in *The Italian*. Those intimidations, however, never succeed in crushing Radcliffe's young heroines. Their successful evasions are, nonetheless, always framed by, and conditioned within, a cautionary tale concerning an older woman's suffering at the hands of others. In *A Sicilian Romance*, for example, the mother of the two heroines, having been imprisoned by her husband years ago, is recovered at the end of the novel by her daughter Julia. The *Critical Review* playfully questioned the credulity of the tale, noting that 'If our author again engages in this task, we would advise her not to introduce so many caverns with such peculiar concealments, or so many spring-locks which open only on one side.'[4] Radcliffe's subsequent novels seemingly absorbed this jocular advice. Here, the cautionary tales of older female characters remained embedded within the narrative frames until the conclusion of the story but emerged from the physical recesses of underground dungeons and caverns. In *The Mysteries of Udolpho*, Emily would finally uncover the sad fate of her deceased aunt who was forced into a marriage against her will; in *The Italian*, Elena discovers her mother taking refuge in a convent, subsequent to the sexual assault and forced marriage imposed upon her by the murderer of her husband. Echoes of the plot of Shakespeare's *Hamlet* stalked *The Italian*, but it always remained the choice of the older, wiser female to articulate the tales of sexual assault, betrayal and displacement. As E. J. Clery has observed, 'The story of a young woman, unprotected by family or fortune and submitted to a variety of dangers' was not

---

4 Review of Ann Radcliffe's *A Sicilian Romance*, *Critical Review; or, Annals of Literature* 1:350 (March 1791): 350.

unique to Radcliffe, but was instead surprisingly ubiquitous among both male and female authors of the eighteenth century.[5] Radcliffe's achievement, however, was more immediate and particular insofar as she mediated those plotlines through the frames of more cautionary stories from an older generation of women, almost as if the characters from the earlier prototypes of the heroine-centred romance were returning to warn their younger, more independent offspring.

The assessments of fellow authors, critics and amateurs alike confirmed Ann Radcliffe's ascendancy in the burgeoning tradition of Gothic romance, and firmly linked her craft with its signature evocation of terror. Towards the end of an ambiguous review of *The Mysteries of Udolpho* in the *Critical Review* in 1794, the reviewer, often identified as Samuel Taylor Coleridge, became one of the first critics to connect Radcliffe explicitly with Shakespeare. Borrowing a line from Thomas Gray's 'The Progress of Poesy' (1757), Coleridge allowed that the 'horror and thrilling fears' that so characterised the gifts of Shakespeare were also abundantly present in the writings of Ann Radcliffe.[6] His pronouncement paved the way for Nathan Drake's later, better-known assessment of Radcliffe as 'the Shak[e]spear of Romance writers' in his influential work of criticism *Literary Hours; or, Sketches Critical and Narrative* (1798).[7]

Radcliffe's association with Shakespeare was widely celebrated during the 1790s. Mary Wollstonecraft's *Maria; or, The Wrongs of Woman* (incomplete, but first published posthumously in 1798), for example, took pains to observe the distinctions between the Gothic romances of Radcliffe and the author's own more realistically grounded exploration of the fates of woman in present-day England by focusing upon the Shakespearean qualities of Radcliffe's *oeuvre*:

> Abodes of horror have frequently been described, and castles, filled with spectres and chimeras, conjured up by the magic spell of genius to harrow the soul, and absorb the wondering mind. But, formed of such stuff as dreams are made of, what were they to the mansion of despair,

---

5 E. J. Clery, 'Ann Radcliffe and D. A. F. de Sade: thoughts on heroinism', *Women's Writing* 1.2 (1994): 203–14 (p. 203).
6 Quoted in Dale Townshend and Angela Wright, 'Gothic and Romantic Engagements: The Critical Reception of Ann Radcliffe, 1789–1850', in Dale Townshend and Angela Wright (eds), *Ann Radcliffe, Romanticism and the Gothic* (Cambridge: Cambridge University Press, 2014), pp. 3–32 (p. 8).
7 Nathan Drake, *Literary Hours; or, Sketches Critical and Narrative* (Sudbury, 1798), p. 249.

in one corner of which Maria sat, endeavouring to recall her scattered thoughts![8]

Through these references to 'abodes of horror' and 'mansion of despair', the first connoting the eponymous castle in The Mysteries of Udolpho and the second a direct citation from The Romance of the Forest, Wollstonecraft subtly raised in the minds of her readership the example of Ann Radcliffe. As in her subtle invocations of the haunted battlements of Elsinore in this opening paragraph, it seems, at first, as if her allusion to harrowing 'the soul' echoes Act I, scene v of Hamlet, where the ghost of Hamlet's murdered father appears and warns his son as follows:

> I could a tale unfold whose lightest word
> Would harrow up thy soul, freeze thy young blood,
> Make thy two eyes like stars start from their spheres,
> Thy knotty and combinèd locks to part,
> And each particular hair to stand on end
> Like quills upon the fretful porcupine.
> But this eternal blazon must not be
> To ears of flesh and blood.[9]

Wollstonecraft's palimpsestic allusion to this most seductively terrifying of speeches from Hamlet in the opening to her highly political Gothic fiction is confidently reflexive, for it is channelled through Radcliffe's earlier reworkings of the same speech. In A Sicilian Romance, for example, Radcliffe had used 'I could a tale unfold' as an epigraph on the anonymous title page of the novel, and later, in 1794, she again used the speech as epigraph for Chapter Two of Volume I of The Mysteries of Udolpho. Evidently, this was a passage that resonated strongly with Radcliffe: in her 'Essay on the Supernatural in Poetry' (1826), an important reflection on the differences between horror and terror that, though separately published, was excerpted from the Introduction to her posthumously published romance Gaston De Blondeville (1826), Radcliffe commented upon 'the strange mixture of horror, pity, and indignation' that

---

8 Mary Wollstonecraft, Maria; or, the Wrongs of Woman, edited by Gary Kelly (Oxford: Oxford University Press, 1976), p. 75.
9 These lines from Hamlet (Act I, scene v, ll. 14–22) are cited from William Shakespeare, 'The Tragedy of Hamlet, Prince of Denmark', in The Norton Shakespeare, Based on the Oxford Edition, 2nd edition, edited by Stephen Greenblatt, Walter Cohen, Jean E. Howard, and Katharine Eisaman Maus, with an essay by Andrew Gurr (New York and London: W. W. Norton & Co., 2005), pp. 1683–784 (p. 1712).

the unfolding of the ghost's tale in *Hamlet* evokes.[10] Radcliffe's repeated return to this moment in her earlier fictions indicates its centrality to her aesthetic: the ghost's promise to unfold 'a tale' is a symbolic marker of both the potency of the past and the future's ability to uncover the secrets and injustices of that past. Wollstonecraft brilliantly bonded this Shakespearean allusion to 'the magic spell of genius', echoing and anticipating the ways in which others by the late 1790s had begun to speak of Radcliffe's 'enchanted' and 'enchanting' craft. Though framed as an attempt to differentiate her novel from the more anodyne enchantments of Radcliffe, Wollstonecraft's invocation of Radcliffe nonetheless paid homage her counterpart's superlative powers of literary wizardry.

The miscellany *The Weekly Entertainer* carried in 1796 a poetic clue as to precisely what readers prized and valued in Radcliffe's fiction. The extended epistle 'Verses written after reading Mrs Radcliffe's Romance of "The Forest"' touched upon the author's magisterial, celestial mastery of terror, commencing with these reverential lines:

> The pen of Radcliffe glows with hallow'd fires,
> Whose touch celestial brighten fancy's eye,
> That sees new worlds arise; and other objects views
> Of unknown wondrous form. Like lightning's glance
> With her we dart along the boundless air,
> To visit scenes impervious to the day,
> The drear recesses of some wilderness,
> Of forest wrapt in everlasting gloom.
> Where glimmering rays admitted thro' the trees
> Disclose the ruins of the antique tower;
> Or abbey rear'd by superstitious dread,
> Where, by the dying taper's light, the maid
> Tremblingly walks the spiral staircase steps
> Leading to spacious halls with ivy curtains hung;
> Thro' long-drawn aisles, with hoary moss o'ergrown,
> To lowly cells, dripping with dewy damps,
> Which stop the breath, and chill the vital blood.
>
> There terror makes his most frequented haunt,
> Arm'd with the shades of stratagems and plots;
> Fed by the night with skeletons and bones;

---

10 Ann Radcliffe, 'On the supernatural in poetry: by the late Mrs. Radcliffe', *The New Monthly Magazine and Literary Journal* 16:61 (January 1826): 145–52 (p. 148).

> Lull'd by the rustlings of the raven's wings,
> Which, with the hollow murmurings of the wind,
> Conspire to render terror still more dire.[11]

Like Shakespeare's own, Radcliffe's pen was thought to be tipped with divinity; in the view of this anonymous poet, it became a celestial gift that was capable of transporting the reader to 'new worlds', bringing to their view objects of 'unknown wondrous form'. Notably, this lengthy panegyric skirted around anything overtly political in Radcliffe's work: the closest that we get to any specific historical commentary is in the reference to the 'abbey rear'd by superstitious dread', a note that is in keeping with much anti-Catholic discourse in the period. Glossed over, too, are the specific crimes and terrors that beset the heroine Adeline, with the writer instead choosing to foreground the organic panoramas that are acoustically enhanced by 'the raven's wings' and the 'hollow murmurings of the wind'. Moreover, the Marquis de Montalt's villainous libertinism is alluded to yet also greatly attenuated in the poem's later admonition, 'But pleasure cloys, and every splendour fades; / Here giant pride exults, and jealousy torments'. Radcliffe's fictional talent resided for this poet in the revelation of new natural and imaginary worlds, in neutralising evil by showing its shortcomings amidst such natural splendour, but never in focusing in upon the young, forlorn and unprotected heroine and the terrors that assail her.

The 'Verses after reading Mrs Radcliffe's Romance of "The Forest' are thus more revealing in what they do not explore in Radcliffe's novel than in what they address. The reputation of Radcliffe's pen as cheering 'fancy's eye' was, by 1796, already culturally prominent. Through such a focus upon the 'pen of Radcliffe' instead of 'Mrs Ann Radcliffe', her novels became more palatable, her talents rendered more acceptable to a broad and politically diverse readership. In a third new edition of his satirical poem *The Pursuits of Literature* in 1797, for example, even the most conservative of critics, the Reverend Thomas James Mathias, had hailed Radcliffe as 'the mighty magician of THE MYSTERIES OF UDOLPHO', absolving her from the more politically seditious charges that he levelled against her female peers Charlotte Smith, Elizabeth Inchbald and Mary Robinson.[12] Questionably, for Mathias,

---

11 Anon., 'Verses written after reading Mrs. Radcliffe's romance of "The Forest"', *The Weekly Entertainer; or, Agreeable and Instructive Repository* 27:680 (Feb 22, 1796): 159–60 (p. 159).

12 Thomas J. Mathias, *The Pursuits of Literature: A Satirical Poem in Four Dialogues. With Notes* (London, 1797), p. 14. The first book of this poem first appeared in 1794, with further sections continuing to appear until 1797, but the reference to Radcliffe as the 'mighty magician' appeared only in a later revised edition of 1797.

Radcliffe's abilities to conjure were devoid of all political resonance.[13] Perhaps it was this very tendency – variously hinted at by authors as diverse as Wollstonecraft, Mathias and the anonymous poet of the 'Verses' – that secured Radcliffe's reputation as a novelist of alternative worlds and vistas and the magical enabler of her readers' imaginations. Her ascendancy in the realm of Gothic romance certainly persisted well into the nineteenth century. Walter Scott, for one, would famously anoint her as the 'first poetess of romantic fiction', while John Colin Dunlop would single out the 'very powerful interest' provoked by her works in contrast to the 'servility' of her numerous imitators.[14]

Although it is less easy to discern the critical insights of those who read Ann Radcliffe purely for pleasure, the demand for her novels at subscription libraries around the country confirms her popularity. We have the vivid snapshot, for example, of a young Sheffield apprentice, Joseph Hunter, who returned frequently to Sheffield's subscription Surrey Street Library in order to try to borrow the second volume of Radcliffe's three-volume masterpiece *The Italian*. When he eventually got to read this volume of the novel, Hunter noted in the journal where he recorded his reading and impressions of works, 'Finished the 2nd volume of Mrs. Radcliffe's The Italian. She is the best writer in her way of any body I ever heard of.'[15] For diarist Thomas Green, as for many eighteenth-century readers, Radcliffe excelled first and foremost because of her attention to natural scenery. In 1797, completing his reading of *The Italian*, Green records that 'In the vivid exhibition of the picturesque of nature, in the delineation of strong and dark character, in the excitation of horror by physical and moral agency, I know not that Mrs. R. has any equal.'[16] At first glance, Radcliffe's reputation as the 'best writer in her way', as 'the first poetess of romantic fiction' who soared far above those

13 For further discussion of Ann Radcliffe and politics, see Angela Wright, *Britain, France and the Gothic, 1764–1820: The Import of Terror* (Cambridge: Cambridge University Press, 2013), pp. 88–119 and James Watt's chapter 'Ann Radcliffe and Politics', in Townshend and Wright (eds), *Ann Radcliffe*, pp. 67–82.
14 Walter Scott, 'Prefatory Memoir to Mrs Ann Radcliffe', in *The Novels of Mrs Ann Radcliffe … To Which Is Prefixed, a Memoir of the Life of the Author*, Novelist's Library, Vol. X. (London: Hurst, Robinson and Co, 1824), pp. i–xxxix (p. iv); John Colin Dunlop, *The History of Fiction: Being a Critical Account of the Most Celebrated Works of Fiction, From the Earliest Greek Romances to the Novels of the Present Age*, 2nd edition, 3 vols (Edinburgh: James Ballantyne and Co, for Longman, Hurst, Rees, Orme and Brown, 1816), vol. 3, pp. 468–9.
15 'The Journal of Joseph Hunter', British Library Add MSS 24,879, fol. 17v, 02/06/1798.
16 Thomas Green, *Extracts from the Diary of a Lover of Literature* (Ipswich: John Rawe, 1810), quoted in Rictor Norton (ed.), *Gothic Readings: The First Wave* (London: Leicester University Press, 2000), p. 347.

who produced comparatively pale copies of her style and plots, seemed to be unimpeachable.

'Wonder-working Lewis, Monk or Bard'[17]

With the burgeoning admiration for Radcliffe's authorial craft, however, there inevitably came the desire to emulate. The young Matthew Gregory Lewis, Member of Parliament, ambassador, translator, editor, poet and playwright, had begun his literary excursions through writing plays for the theatre, composing in 1791 a drama called *The Epistolary Intrigue* that was first rejected by the theatres at Covent Garden and Drury Lane. Posted abroad to revolutionary Europe, he admired Radcliffe's work to such an extent that he acknowledged to his mother in correspondence that he was inspired by Radcliffe's *The Mysteries of Udolpho* to complete the three-volume Gothic romance *The Monk*.[18] As early as 1969, Lewis's nod to Radcliffe in correspondence with his mother prompted the critic Robert D. Hume to cast Lewis's novelistic production *The Monk* in the guise of Gothic usurper. In his essay 'Gothic versus Romantic: A Revaluation of the Gothic Novel', Hume accused Lewis of setting out, 'quite deliberately, to overgo Mrs Radcliffe', thus casting Radcliffe herself in the role of the heroine and Lewis in the role of the Gothic villain.[19] Hume's view was emphatically judgemental, echoing those of many down the ages who had claimed that *The Monk* was decidedly inferior to the romances of Radcliffe, and that the author himself was lacking in both modesty and self-restraint in his bid to usurp the position of one whom Thomas De Quincey would later dub the 'great enchantress of that generation'.[20] In his very attempt to compare the two authors, however, Hume's argument unwittingly followed the impulses of some of the more benign readers and critics of both authors from the 1790s, several of whom had begun to regard Ann Radcliffe and Matthew Lewis as undisputed equals.

In their footnote to Byron's assessment of Matthew Lewis as 'Wonder-working Lewis, Monk or Bard' in his satire *English Bards and Scots Reviewers*

---

17 My subheading here is taken from Lord Byron's assessment of his friend Matthew Lewis in his poem *English Bards and Scots Reviewers* (London: James Cawthorn, 1809).
18 See Margaret Baron-Wilson, *Life and Correspondence of M. G. Lewis, Author of 'The Monk,' 'Castle Spectre,' &c. With Many Pieces in Prose and Verse, Never Before Published*, 2 vols (London: Henry Colburn, 1839), vol. 1, p. 123.
19 Robert D. Hume, 'Gothic versus romantic: a revaluation of the gothic novel', *PMLA* 84:2 (March 1969): 282–90(p. 285).
20 Thomas De Quincey, *The Works of Thomas De Quincey, Vol. II: Confessions of an English Opium-Eater, 1821–1856*, edited by Grevel Lindop (London: Pickering & Chatto, 2000), p. 147.

(1809), a line that celebrated Lewis's role as the influential collector and compiler of short Gothic tales and ballads in his collection *Tales of Wonder* (1801), Byron's nineteenth-century editors offered a dispassionate, cursory assessment of Lewis that established some of the major paradoxes of the writer's career:

> Matthew Gregory Lewis, M.P. for Hindon, never distinguished himself in Parliament, but mainly, in consequence of the clever use he made of his knowledge of the German language, then a rare accomplishment, attracted much notice in the literary world, at a very early period of his life. His Tales of Terror; the drama of the Castle Spectre; and the romance called the Bravo of Venice … but above all, the libidinous and impious novel of The Monk, invested the name of Lewis with an extraordinary degree of celebrity, during the poor period which intervened between the obscuration of Cowper, and the full display of Sir Walter Scott's talents in the 'Lay of the Last Minstrel'.[21]

Lewis's authorial reputation was extensive, but not only did *The Monk*, his Gothic romance described above as 'libidinous and impious', risk eclipsing his other achievements in the public eye, it also threatened to overshadow the more well-established Gothic romances of his erstwhile inspiration, Ann Radcliffe. Published in 1796, the novel had a longer percolation than some critics allow, being commenced while Lewis was in Paris much earlier in 1791. It reflects, as André Parreaux and Ronald Paulson have suggested, an earnest engagement with the mob terror of the French Revolution, but also a deep familiarity with French literary sources, including Denis Diderot's anti-clerical novel *La Religieuse* (completed c. 1780; published posthumously in 1796) and the novels of the Marquis de Sade. Indeed, Matthew Gregory Lewis's linguistic abilities extended far beyond his translation of Goethe's *Faust* for the group assembled at the Villa Diodati during the Summer of 1816, a detail that is explored in Volume II of *The Cambridge History of the Gothic*. During his time in revolutionary Paris, Lewis also attended the theatre frequently, and read more than he allowed to his mother. Later, back in England, he would continue to translate a number of German and French romances, novels and plays, including *The Minister. A Tragedy* (unperformed; published 1797); *Rolla; or, The Peruvian Hero* (unperformed; published 1799); *The Harper's Daughter; or, Love and Ambition* (performed 1803; published 1813); *Rugantino: or, The Bravo of Venice* (performed 1805; published 1806); *Venoni; or, The Novice of St Mark's*

---

21 *The Works of Lord Byron, Complete in One Volume. With notes by Thomas Moore, Lord Jeffrey, Sir Walter Scott, Bishop Heber, Samuel Rogers, Professor Wilson, J. G. Lockhart, George Ellis, Thomas Campbell, Rev. H. H. Milman, etc.* (London: John Murray, 1842), p. 425.

(1809); *The Bravo of Venice, A Romance* (1805); and *Feudal Tyrants; or, The Counts of Carlsheim and Sargans* (1806). If Gothic fiction was frequently derided as a foreign 'German' import, this was due in no small part to Lewis's skills as a translator.

Lewis's first published novel, *The Monk*, is a heady combination of the author's acknowledged and unacknowledged reading. In the 'Advertisement' to the text, Lewis rather haphazardly selected some sources by which he had been inspired, listing the story of Santon Barsisa as related in *The Guardian*, the tradition of the Bleeding Nun in Germany, and other Danish and Spanish sources. But nowhere did he list his inspirations from Diderot and Sade, for he was astute enough to appreciate that these revolutionary, anti-clerical works would be frowned upon by the anxious literary establishment of 1790s Britain. Nor did Lewis focus upon what he drew from his female contemporaries. For instance, one can deduce from the physical descriptions of Antonia's figure in Chapter One as 'light and airy as that of an Hamadryad' that he took inspiration from other tales on the Hamadryad – a nymph who lives in a tree and dies when the tree dies – that appeared in *The Guardian*, as well as from Elizabeth Carter's poem 'To —, on his Design of Cutting down a Shady Walk' (1745), which focused in upon a weeping Hamadryad in its very first stanza: 'In plaintive Notes, that tun'd to Woe / The sadly sighing Breeze / A weeping Hamadryad mourn'd / Her Fate-devoted Trees.'[22] Lewis drew upon literary representations of the mythical figure of the Hamadryad to offer dramatic irony in his initial depiction of Antonia, for we know from the very first chapter of the novel that, despite what the subtitle promises, this is quite explicitly not a romance. From Radcliffe's *Udolpho*, Lewis also drew upon the tale of Signora di Laurentini, the tragic figure who, tempted, seduced and abandoned, haunts the margins of the text. The focus in *The Monk* upon four females with varying amounts of agency – Antonia the passive victim; Matilda the demon sorceress who seduces Ambrosio; Agnes the unwilling convert who is imprisoned upon the discovery of her pregnancy; and the embedded tale of the Bleeding Nun – offers us a compassionate if relentlessly bleak view of female autonomy and fate. This was a theme that Lewis pursued throughout his career, from his spectacular supernatural tragedy *The Castle Spectre* (performed 1797; published

---

22 Elizabeth Carter, 'To a Gentleman, on his Design of Cutting down a Shady Walk', in *Poems on Several Occasions* (London, 1762), p. 39.

1798) through to his short Gothic drama entitled *The Captive* (performed 1803), a theatrical adaptation of Wollstonecraft's *Maria* that told the story of a wife imprisoned by her husband.

'Libidinous' and 'impious', the editorial terms used to describe *The Monk* in the footnote to Byron's poem, did not do justice to Lewis's deeply intertextual meditation on the limited choices imposed upon women, a meditation that was inspired as much by his female counterparts as by any of the sources that he listed in the 'Advertisement' to *The Monk*. Although, as Michael Gamer has observed, initial responses to *The Monk* were relatively benign, it was when Lewis, buoyed up by the initial reception, began to sign himself from the second edition onwards as 'M.G. Lewis, Esq. M.P.' that the fury of the critical establishment was unleashed.[23] Writing for the *Critical Review*, Coleridge objected to the '*blending*, with an irreverent negligence, [of] all that is most awfully true in religion with all that is most ridiculously absurd in superstition', further deploring the novel's highly visual, even pornographic, qualities as '*libidinous minuteness*'.[24] It may well have been Coleridge's phrasing here that prompted a swiftly revised second edition of *The Italian* in 1797, revisions which consistently frustrate and curtail the eroticism of the visual field. Coleridge's attention to the text's 'libidinous' nature was certainly in the minds of Byron's nineteenth-century editors as they summarised Lewis's career so dismissively in their footnote. Lewis's major transgression, however, came from his fateful combination of parliamentary business with novel-writing. This blending was nothing new, as such figures as Horace Walpole, William Beckford and, later, Byron himself, demonstrated, but it was the insouciant acknowledgement of his legislative status on the title page of his blasphemous and highly sexualised novel that particularly incensed his critics. At the end of his review for the *Critical Review*, Coleridge observed, 'Yes! The author of the Monk signs himself a *Legislator!* We stare and tremble.'[25] Mathias, who had elsewhere in *The Pursuits of Literature* singled out Ann Radcliffe for praise, went further in his condemnation, also drawing attention to the 'name, style, and title' that were prefixed to *The Monk*:

> Who does *not know*, that he is a member of Parliament? ... we can feel that it is an object of moral and of national reprehension, when a Senator openly

---

23 Michael Gamer, 'Genres for the prosecution: pornography and the gothic', *PMLA* 114:5 (October 1999): 1043–54 (p. 1047).
24 Samuel Taylor Coleridge, review of *The Monk*, *Critical Review* 2:19 (February 1797): 194–200 (p. 197).
25 Coleridge, review of *The Monk*, p. 198.

and daringly violates his first duty to his country. There are wounds, and obstructions, and diseases in the political, as well as in the natural, body, for which the removal of the part affected is alone efficacious.[26]

Mathias accused Lewis firmly and hysterically of 'state parricide' and suggested in his inflamed rhetoric that Lewis should be surgically removed from the 'body politic' and summarily placed on trial for obscenity. Although there is doubt and speculation as to whether Mathias's encouragement of the Attorney General Sir John Scott actually succeeded, with Lewis's first biographer Margaret Baron-Wilson claiming that Scott was 'actually instructed', the effects upon Lewis's familial relationships and burgeoning literary career were decisive.[27] Lewis set about altering subsequent editions of the novel and began to focus his talents thereafter more firmly upon the stage, producing his Gothic tragedy *The Castle Spectre* at Drury Lane Theatre in December 1797, and then a suite of other dramas, including, among a host of other non-original dramatic works, *Village Virtues: A Dramatic Satire. In Two Parts* (1796); *Adelmorn, the Outlaw: A Romantic Drama, in Three Acts* (performed and published 1801); *Alfonso, King of Castile: A Tragedy in Five Acts* (published 1801; performed 1802); *Adelgitha; or, The Fruits of a Single Error. A Tragedy in Five Acts* (published 1806; performed 1807); *The Wood Daemon; or, 'The Clock Has Struck', A Grand Romantic Melo Drama, in Three Acts* (performed 1807); *Timour the Tartar. A Grand Romantic Melo-Drama, in Two Acts* (1811); and *One O'Clock! Or, The Knight and the Wood Daemon. A Grand Musical Romance, in Three Acts* (1811).

'Like Radcliffe'

Seemingly retreating from the dangers of sole authorship into the 'safer', more collaborative practices of the drama, it is possible that Lewis found himself somewhat intimidated by Coleridge, Mathias and others, for contrary to the expectations that their loaded invective suggest, *The Monk* continued to be consumed and celebrated by the reading public.[28] While the opening and plotline of Radcliffe's *The Italian* have been widely read as providing a salutary corrective to Lewis's *The Monk*, we have no clear evidence as to

---

26 Thomas James Mathias, Preface to vol. IV of *The Pursuits of Literature: A Satirical Poem in Four Dialogues. With Notes.* July 1797, 8th revised edition (London, 1798), p. 242.
27 Baron-Wilson, *Life and Correspondence of M. G. Lewis*, vol. 1, pp. 153–4.
28 For an account of Lewis's retreat from authorship into the more collaborative practices of the drama, see Michael Gamer, 'Authors in effect: Lewis, Scott, and the gothic drama', *ELH* 66 (1999): 831–61.

how Radcliffe viewed the 'libidinous minuteness' of Lewis's text.[29] Furthermore, despite Lewis's reticence in his 'Advertisement' to *The Monk* in declaring his inspiration from his fellow Gothic romancer, other authors, by 1798, began to make that associative leap, assuring the continued presence of both Radcliffe and Lewis in the select pantheon of Gothic writers deemed worthy of mention. Henry Soame's anonymous 'Epistle in Rhyme to M.G. Lewis, Esq. M.P.' impressively ran to twelve pages in its panegyric to Lewis's authorial craft. Central to Soame's tribute was the explicit comparison between both authors that I have used as the epigraph to this chapter. Soame's eulogy perhaps over-reached itself when it claimed that Lewis had noted 'like Radcliffe, with a painter's eye / The pine-clad mountain and the stormy sky', going on to compare Lewis's craft with that of the painter Salvator Rosa. The comparison acknowledged Radcliffe but sought to place Lewis's engagement with the aesthetics of the seventeenth-century Italian Baroque painter on a par with that of Ann Radcliffe. Radcliffe, who awkwardly and anachronistically had her narrator in *The Mysteries of Udolpho* observe that 'This was such a scene as Salvator would have chosen, had he then existed, for his canvas', imagined her characters inhabiting the painted landscapes of Salvator Rosa and Claude Lorrain in a self-conscious homage to the artists.[30] Accordingly, she became justifiably, although narrowly, celebrated for her use of imaginative landscapes. By contrast, there is no measure by which one could argue that Lewis's claustrophobic romance, *The Monk*, places anywhere near as much emphasis upon such wild and torrid landscapes until the conclusion of his narrative, when Ambrosio's body is dashed on the cliffs in punishment for his sins. Soame's extended epistle nonetheless chose to frame the shared achievements of both authors through the frame of the 'painter's eye', perhaps skirting around some of the more controversially perceived deficiencies in Lewis's craft as he did so. In the extended title of Soame's epistle, Lewis was referred to as the author of both *The Monk* and *The Castle Spectre*. In contrast to this astute attempt to draw attention to Lewis's considerable talents as a playwright, the many dramatisations and theatrical adaptations of Radcliffe's works were, by contrast, critically excoriated, with a footnote observing that 'This operation is by the perpetrators and

---

29 For a recent account of the connections and departures between Radcliffe and Lewis in *The Italian*, see Jerrold E. Hogle's chapter 'Recovering the Walpolean Gothic: *The Italian; or, The Confessional of the Black Penitents* (1796–97)', in Townshend and Wright (eds), *Ann Radcliffe*, pp. 151–67 (especially pp. 151–2).
30 Ann Radcliffe, *The Mysteries of Udolpho*, edited by Bonamy Dobrée with notes and intro. by Terry Castle (Oxford: Oxford University Press, 1998), p. 30.

newspaper writers termed *dramatizing*.'³¹ A particular invective was weighed against James Boaden's adaptation of Radcliffe's *The Romance of the Forest* as *Fontainville Forest* (1794), with Soame dismissively referring to Boaden as a 'scribbler'. What emerged from this somewhat digressive footnote is significant: Soame was unimpressed with dramatic adaptations of Radcliffe, but he revalorised the original dramaturgy of the main subject of his poem, Matthew Lewis, and so extended his fame. Albeit partly in the different formal and generic realms of drama and romance, Lewis and Radcliffe were placed on the same plane in terms of genius and talent, with Soame going even further by comparing Lewis with Dante. The inference here was that Lewis possessed a genius superior to that of Radcliffe through his own manifold excursions into the world of Gothic theatre.

Soame did not hesitate in adding Lewis's legislative role of MP to the title of his defence of Lewis. Mathias's and Coleridge's invective against Lewis's straddling of the seemingly conflicting roles of MP and author was taken up by a range of different authors for a range of different purposes. In some respects, the opprobrium of Mathias and Coleridge backfired spectacularly, as it kept *The Monk* very much at the forefront of readers' imaginations and memories. A far less well-known satire of Lewis, 'The Old Hag in a Red Cloak. A Romance', which appeared in *The Spirit of Anti-Jacobinism for 1802*, capitalised upon an infantilised, feminised version of the notorious author, figuring 'little Mat', 'an M.P.', as perilously inscribed within a more sinister version of the Little Red Riding Hood fairy tale. Over the course of twenty-seven quatrains, Lewis is cursed and hounded by a series of fairy-tale characters. This bizarre flight of satirical invective, however, imagined a 'sisterly' Ann Radcliffe joining Lewis's mother in an attempt to save his life:

> As Blue-beard for blood loudly howl'd o'er his wife,
> And Sister Ann pleaded so well for his life;
> Mat's favourite spectre he saw dance in air,
> And he gave up his spirit a prey to despair.³²

---

31 Henry Francis Robert Soame, *Epistle in Rhyme*, p. 8. Here, as in the footnote discussed above, a particular invective was weighed against James Boaden's adaptation of Radcliffe's 1791 romance *The Romance of the Forest*, with Boaden being referred to as a 'scribbler'.

32 Anon., 'The Old Hag in a Red Cloak. A Romance', in *The Spirit of Anti-Jacobinism for 1802: Being a Collection of Essays, Dissertations, and Other Pieces, in Prose and Verse, on Subjects Religious, Moral, Political, and Literary*. (London, 1802), pp. 324–7 (p. 327). This poem was attributed to one Mr Jekyll in the editorial notes accompanying Byron's 'English Bards and Scotch Reviewers' in *The Works of Lord Byron, Complete in One Volume*, p. 425.

The poem further poked fun at Lewis's 'epilogues, sonnets, and lady-like rhyme', bonding his work firmly to a feminised form of fiction and warning him, at the conclusion, to 'write common sense'. Lewis's excursions into the realms of imagination and fancy were thus connected for contemporary readers to Radcliffe's imaginative excursions. Here, though, the passing allusion to Radcliffe's practice did not exempt her, but instead made her an abettor to Lewis's extravagant and seemingly 'feminine' literary pursuits.

In the wake of the publication of *The Monk* and *The Italian*, Radcliffe and Lewis from 1798 onwards were often placed together, be that in a symbiotic, comparative or even competitive literary environment. The Marquis de Sade's critical work *Idées sur les romans* (1800), for example, placed Radcliffe and Lewis in competition with each other as it attempted to theorize 'these new novels' in relation to the revolutionary tremors of Europe. For Sade, however, the 'bizarre flights of Mrs. Radcliffe's imagination' fell considerably short of the superiority of *The Monk*.[33] Nonetheless, his views on the superior merits of Lewis to Radcliffe were fairly exceptional, not simply for his ranking of the one above the other, but for his throwing them into competition with one another at all.

Robert Miles has also observed that 'Ann Radcliffe and Matthew Lewis were the two most significant Gothic novelists of the 1790s, an estimate of their importance shared by their contemporaries.'[34] Beyond the examples that I have offered already, the impression of them as jointly significant and equal in their imaginative abilities is confirmed by several authors. The reading journal maintained by Mary Godwin and Percy Bysshe Shelley shows both young authors reading *The Monk* and *The Mysteries of Udolpho* together in 1815. In *Northanger Abbey* – the novel that Jane Austen began writing in 1797 under the title *Susan* but which, though dated 1818, was published posthumously in late 1817 – the author also offers us a glimpse of how symbiotically connected the two authors were. Chapter Seven portrays the odious character John Thorpe confusing the authorship and novels of Radcliffe and Lewis. When Catherine Morland questions Isabella Thorpe's brother, '"Have you ever read Udolpho, Mr Thorpe?"', he first responds by mentioning *The Monk*. Of course, this is not necessarily an indication that he believes *The Monk* to have been written by Radcliffe, but instead is a marker

---

33 D. A. F, Marquis de Sade, *Idées sur le roman* (1800), translated as 'Ideas on the Novel' trans. Leonard de Saint-Yves, quoted in Angela Wright, *Gothic Fiction: A Reader's Guide to Essential Criticism* (Basingstoke: Palgrave Macmillan, 2007), p. 64.
34 Robert Miles, 'Ann Radcliffe and Matthew Lewis', in David Punter (ed.) *A New Companion to the Gothic* (Oxford: Wiley-Blackwell, 2012), pp. 93–109 (p. 93).

of how closely associated in the minds of contemporary readers the work of both authors was. The conversation between Catherine and John Thorpe slowly unspools to reveal that the latter's opinions concerning the merits of Radcliffe and Lewis are merely an insipid and confused regurgitation of the opinions of others:

> 'Novels are all so full of nonsense and stuff; there has not been a tolerably decent one come out since Tom Jones, except the Monk; I read that t'other day; but as for all the others, they are the stupidest things in creation.'
> 'I think you must like Udolpho, if you were to read it; it is so very interesting.'
> 'Not I, faith! No, if I read any it shall be Mrs Radcliffe's; her novels are amusing enough; they are worth reading; some fun and nature in *them*.'
> 'Udolpho was written by Mrs. Radcliffe', said Catherine, with some hesitation, from the fear of mortifying him.[35]

Thorpe's opinion that Radcliffe is 'worth reading' while other authors are not is certainly not formed from his own careful perusal and comparison of Radcliffe's romances with those of other writers from the decade. With the phrase 'worth reading', Austen draws attention instead to the way in which Thorpe's opinions of literary value are formed from the journals of his age, such as the *Monthly Magazine*, the *Analytical* and the *Monthly Review*. Crucially, however, *The Monk* is presented as the other exception to Thorpe's unfounded excoriation of novels: 'there has not been a tolerably decent one come out since Tom Jones, except the Monk', he observes. If Austen is using Thorpe as a passive eavesdropper on, and mouthpiece for, a tranche of readers and critics, then *The Monk* too rises as an exception. Neither compared nor, indeed, confused explicitly with the works of Radcliffe, *The Monk* and the novels of Ann Radcliffe stand out here as 'decent' and 'worth reading'. We know, of course, that Thorpe's opinion is by no means representative of that of Austen herself, who takes pains in *Northanger Abbey* to draw her readers' attention to the richness of Gothic writing in the 1790s, introducing to them through the reading list of the fictional Miss Andrews a far broader selection of contemporary Gothic titles. Nevertheless, it is the titles of Radcliffe and Lewis that are drawn into conversations beyond their generic boundaries, with *The Monk* being compared to *Tom Jones* (1749) by Henry Fielding – perhaps for a shared irreverence of tone, libertine sentiment or focus upon an abandoned infant – and *Udolpho* being compared with Fanny Burney's 1796 novel *Camilla*.

---

35 Jane Austen, *Northanger Abbey*, edited by Marilyn Butler (Harmondsworth: Penguin, 2005), p. 45.

John Thorpe, however, attempts to compensate for not knowing that *Udolpho* was composed by Ann Radcliffe by observing:

> 'No sure; was it? Aye, I remember, so it was; I was thinking of that other stupid book, written by that woman they make such a fuss about, she who married the French emigrant.'
> 'I suppose you mean *Camilla*?'
> 'Yes, that's the book; such unnatural stuff! however much the female side of the partnership wished otherwise.'[36]

As if to disguise and excuse his inadequate knowledge of Radcliffe, Thorpe draws her fiction into comparison with the work of Burney, but only as 'that other stupid book', suggesting that 'the French emigrant' whom Burney married had a part to play in the 'unnatural stuff' of the novel. Burney's marriage to the French emigré Alexandre-Jean-Baptiste d'Arblay had taken place in 1793, prior to the publication of *Camilla*, and Thorpe's opinions here ventriloquise those of some who disapproved of the writer's conjoining with a Frenchman. But of interest here, most specifically, are the ways in which this exchange illustrates the depth of Catherine's reading. Not only do we see her luxuriating in *The Mysteries of Udolpho*, but she is also conversant with the works of Samuel Richardson (elsewhere she discusses her judgement of *Sir Charles Grandison* [1753]) and Frances Burney.

John Thorpe's dismissive view of Burney's *Camilla* was certainly not one shared by Jane Austen, nor, indeed, by Ann Radcliffe. Burney's own endorsement of a cautious sensibility in her heroines clearly informed the characterisations and cautions against the over-indulgent sensibility that Radcliffe portrayed across her fiction. But Radcliffe was less celebrated for this connection with Burney than she was for her inspirational use of landscapes. In 1819, for example, we encounter a similar judgemental comparison between Radcliffe and Burney by William Hazlitt:

> I must say I like Mrs Radcliffe's romances better, and think of them oftener [than those of Fanny Burney]: and even when I do not, part of the impression with which I survey the full-orbed moon shining in the blue expanse of heaven, or hear the wind sighing through autumnal leaves, or walk under the echoing archways of a Gothic ruin, is owing to repeated perusal of the Romance of the Forest and the Mysteries of Udolpho.[37]

---

36 Austen, *Northanger Abbey*, p. 45.
37 William Hazlitt, *Lectures on the English Comic Writers* (London, 1819), p. 250.

Hazlitt, like the anonymous author who praised *The Romance of the Forest* in *The Weekly Entertainer* in 1796, delighted as much in the acoustics of Radcliffe's fiction, her attention to a sighing wind or echoing archways, as he did in the 'full-orbed moon' invoked in several of her descriptions. And yet, in the precise language that he used here, there resounds an echo of an echo, a memory of a memory. For these provide not so much the comparison between Radcliffe and Burney that he articulates, but rather retrace the convoluted path of connections between Ann Radcliffe and Matthew Lewis that I have explored in this chapter. For references to the 'full-orbed moon' return an attuned reader to *The Monk* rather than to Radcliffe's romances, and to the descriptions of the demonic temptress Matilda's feigned attempt to stab herself in the breast as the 'Moonbeams' dart 'upon the beauteous Orb'.[38] Whether Radcliffe liked it or not, for Romantic-era readers the fate of her works became firmly linked to Lewis's scandalous Gothic romance.

38 Matthew Lewis, *The Monk: A Romance*, edited by Nick Groom (Oxford: Oxford University Press, 2016), pp. 51–2.

1.15

The Gothic Novel Beyond Radcliffe and Lewis

YAEL SHAPIRA

'Imitation' is a key term in critical reactions to Romantic-era British Gothic fiction in its day, and one used over and over by reviewers and periodical writers to describe the many Gothic works published between 1790 and 1820. Key features of the Gothic novel – a haunted medieval castle, a relentless villain, a persecuted maiden, a dynastic mystery, violent deaths and more – were already in place in Horace Walpole's *The Castle of Otranto* (1764) and appeared again in a handful of later works, such as Clara Reeve's *The Old English Baron* (1778); but then, in the 1790s and early 1800s, novels containing these distinctive elements became somewhat of a cultural deluge. For observers of the outpour the reason seemed obvious: it lay in the phenomenal success of two Gothic authors, Ann Radcliffe (1764–1823) and Matthew Gregory Lewis (1775–1818).

Having made a modest start with *The Castles of Athlin and Dunbayne* (1789), Radcliffe went on to publish a series of increasingly well-received Gothic romances – *A Sicilian Romance* (1790), *The Romance of the Forest* (1791), *The Mysteries of Udolpho* (1794) and *The Italian* (1796–97) – before disappearing from the literary scene (a sixth work, *Gaston De Blondeville* and its accompanying texts, appeared posthumously in 1826). Lewis's *The Monk* (1796) offered a darker, explicitly erotic twist on Radcliffe's materials; the scandal that surrounded it only whetted the public appetite for more tales of horror. Faced with a steady flow of new Gothic fictions, many of them by obscure or anonymous authors, Romantic-era reviewers frequently framed their brief evaluations as a scornful comparison between 'originals' and 'imitations': Radcliffe and Lewis, they claimed, created the model – and everyone else followed, with varying degrees of success and 'genius' or talent (the latter usually dismissed as minimal).

Thus, for example, the *Critical Review* describes Isabella Kelly's *The Abbey of St. Asaph* (1795) as having been written in 'humble imitation of the well-known novels of Mrs. Radcliffe' and therefore 'duly equipped with all the appurtenances of ruined towers, falling battlements, moats, draw-bridges, Gothic porches, tombs, vaults, and apparitions'.[1] Sir Walter Scott sums up the prevalent view of Radcliffe's relation to her contemporaries when he blames the end of her publishing career on those 'servile imitators' who 'prophaned' her work.[2] Though more scandalous and thus less commonly held up as a worthy exemplar, Lewis is also invoked as both the original on which other novels are based, and the yardstick by which they are found wanting. Reading George Moore's *Theodosius de Zulvin, The Monk of Madrid* (1802), a reviewer for the *Monthly Register* has no doubt about source of the novelist's plot and central ideas: 'To the youthful production of Lewis's ardent genius, the author is evidently indebted for the general outline of his story, as well as for many of its subordinate features.' Declining to enumerate the 'various imitations of *the Monk* which Mr. Moore has introduced into his pages', the writer archly comments that he might have used Lewis's 'model ... to greater advantage'.[3]

From the perspective now offered by book historians, the Romantic period does indeed appear to have provided strong incentives for writers to follow successful literary models – but also, significantly, for publishers to emphasise the similarities between different titles, signalling that they belonged to the same 'type' of fiction. In what ways and to what degree such books were indeed the same is, as we will see, another matter. The abolition of perpetual copyright by the courts in 1788 injected new vigour and competition into the publishing industry, causing a leap in the production of novels. What drove the demand for new fiction was the growing dominance of the circulating libraries, some of them owned by publishers – most famously, William Lane of the Minerva Press – who commissioned and printed their own inventory. Seeking a steady flow of fresh and appealing titles, Lane and similarly-minded publishers provided an unprecedented opportunity for inexperienced authors, many of them women, who were willing to work quickly and for low pay; they wrote book after book, all the while keeping a close eye on what was proving popular in the novel market.[4] As Anthony Mandal, Edward

---

1 Anon., review of *The Abbey of St. Asaph*, *The Critical Review* 14 (July 1795): 349.
2 Walter Scott, 'Prefatory Memoir to Mrs. Ann Radcliffe', in *The Novels of Mrs. Ann Radcliffe [...] to Which is Prefixed, a Memoir of the Life of the Author* (London: Hurst, Robinson & Co., 1824), pp. i–xxxix (p. xiv).
3 Anon., review of *Theodosius de Zulvin, The Monk of Madrid*, *The Monthly Register and Encyclopedian Magazine* (February 1803): 326.
4 See Anthony Mandal, 'Gothic and the Publishing World, 1780–1820', in Glennis Byron and Dale Townshend (eds), *The Gothic World* (London and New York: Routledge, 2014),

Jacobs, Franz J. Potter and others have shown, these factors combined with the favourable reception of Lewis and Radcliffe to create the 'flood' of Gothic novels in the 1790s and early 1800s.[5] In what we would today describe as a concentrated 'branding' effort, many titles featured what Robert Miles calls Gothic 'marketing cues' – monks, nuns, mysteries, ghosts, castles, abbeys – indicating that they belonged to the same category of fiction.[6] Library catalogues further reinforced the sense of kinship by grouping novels together and alphabetising them by title; works whose titles began with the word 'castle', for example, would thus normally be listed one after the other, and may well have been placed together on the library shelf.[7]

But were the novels thus grouped together really nothing more than 'imitations' of Lewis and Radcliffe, if we take this term to mean, as the reviewers seem to suggest, the simple, mechanical and therefore not very interesting replication of prominent features? One reason why we do not yet have a well-founded answer to this question is that the modern study of Romantic-era Gothic has until recently remained circumscribed by the same conviction that Romantic reviewers themselves expressed – namely, that if we venture beyond the handful of now-canonical Gothic 'originals', we will find only more of the same, but done far less well. If twentieth-century Gothic scholarship sought to reclaim a literature that had long been regarded as the 'skeleton in the closet' of respectable eighteenth-century writing, in Anne Williams's words, it ironically did so by disavowing its own set of embarrassing relics.[8] As a result, whereas the works of Radcliffe, Lewis, Horace Walpole, Mary Shelley and a few others have been subject to every kind of analysis in the last decades, the many Gothic novels penned by the era's most prolific and successful authors – Eliza Parsons, Isabella Kelly, Francis Lathom, Elizabeth Meeke, T. J. Horsley Curties and others – have

---

pp. 159–71 and James Raven, 'Production', in Peter Garside and Karen O'Brien (eds), *The Oxford History of the Novel in English, Vol. II: English and British Fiction 1750–1820* (Oxford: Oxford University Press, 2015), pp. 3–28.

5 Mandal, 'Gothic and the Publishing World', in Byron and Townshend (eds), *The Gothic World*; Franz J. Potter, *The History of Gothic Publishing, 1800–1835: Exhuming the Trade* (Basingstoke: Palgrave Macmillan, 2005); Edward H. Jacobs, *Accidental Migrations: An Archeology of Gothic Discourse* (Lewisburg: Bucknell University Press, 2000), chapter 5 and 'Ann Radcliffe and Romantic Print Culture', in Dale Townshend and Angela Wright (eds), *Ann Radcliffe, Romanticism and the Gothic* (Cambridge: Cambridge University Press, 2014), pp. 49–66.

6 Robert Miles, 'The 1790s: The Effulgence of Gothic', in Jerrold E. Hogle (ed.), *The Cambridge Companion to Gothic Fiction* (Cambridge: Cambridge University Press, 2002), pp. 41–62 (p. 41).

7 Jacobs, *Accidental Migrations*, pp. 177–84.

8 Anne Williams, *Art of Darkness: A Poetics of Gothic* (Chicago: Chicago University Press, 1995), p. 1.

received only nominal attention. Their neglect is part of a broader critical disinterest and even scorn towards 'trade Gothic', a term that encompasses not only circulating-library novels but Gothic bluebooks, chapbooks and magazine tales too.[9]

Joining a recent surge of interest in this neglected corpus, the present chapter aims, as its title suggests, to offer an overview of Romantic-era Gothic fiction that extends beyond the usual focus on Radcliffe and Lewis. In venturing outside the traditional bounds of Gothic literary history, however, I will keep those bounds firmly in sight, since an essential first step on the way to a broader narrative of the Gothic's evolution is to challenge the all-too-simple label of 'imitation', a concept the precise historical meaning of which in this period and context has been fruitfully reopened to debate by Elizabeth Neiman and Hannah Hudson's recent work on the Minerva Press.[10] That trade-Gothic authors were influenced by the most prominent Gothic novels of their times is undeniable: they set their plotlines in crumbling abbeys and castles, depicted heroines on the run from scheming villains and gave hints of supernatural activity that either did or did not turn out to have a rational explanation. Yet if we do not immediately dismiss such resemblances as 'imitations', and, instead, look at them more closely, we will find a great deal of suggestive difference too, indicating that we need a broader vocabulary to describe the relations between trade Gothic and canonical Gothic – not just imitation, but adaptation, appropriation, critique or subversion.

In exploring what happens in Gothic novels beyond Radcliffe and Lewis, therefore, I will focus especially on those moments in trade-Gothic fiction that *do* resemble the more famous works of the time: that resemblance is precisely where the inadequacy of the term 'imitation' becomes most apparent. As Hudson has noted, 'While many studies of the gothic focus on Radcliffe's novels alone or compare them to an undifferentiated mass of "Minerva gothics," there is much to gain from reading these novels alongside each other and on relatively equal terms.'[11] Reading both Radcliffe and Lewis

---

9 See Potter, *History of Gothic Publishing*.
10 Elizabeth A. Neiman, 'A new perspective on the Minerva Press's "derivative" novels: authorizing borrowed material', *European Romantic Review* 26:5 (2015): 633–58; Hannah Doherty Hudson, 'The Myth of Minerva: Publishing, Popular Fiction, and the Rise of the Novel', unpublished PhD thesis (Stanford University, 2013).
11 Hannah Doherty Hudson, 'Sentiment and the Gothic: Failures of Emotion in the Novels of Mrs Radcliffe and the Minerva Press', in Albert J. Rivero (ed.), *The Sentimental Novel in the Eighteenth Century* (Cambridge: Cambridge University Press, 2019), pp. 155–72 (p. 156).

on 'equal terms' with their forgotten contemporaries, I will show, places in doubt long-held assumptions about the 'servile' attitude of trade-Gothic authors towards their celebrated peers. In the sections that follow, I therefore offer two complementary discussions of trade-Gothic novels and their complex, ambivalent relation to Radcliffe and Lewis.

I begin with Eliza Parsons's *The Castle of Wolfenbach* (1793), an author and a novel whose histories exemplify the material circumstances shaping most Romantic-era Gothic fiction. Though Parsons, like many other trade-Gothic authors, was working quickly while registering market trends, especially the recent success of Radcliffe's Gothic romances, her novel is not in any simple sense an imitation of Radcliffe, since both writers, I argue, offer parallel yet significantly *dis*similar adaptations of the same already-popular plotline. Parsons's sharp divergence from Radcliffe in key aspects of her Gothic, moreover, suggests that *The Castle of Wolfenbach* and other novels of its kind may have catalysed Radcliffe's subsequent authorial choices, exerting an influence on her (albeit of the negative kind) that scholarship has yet to explore. The second section of the essay seeks to further challenge the idea of uncomplicated 'imitation' by looking at the variations that two other Minerva novelists, Isabella Kelly and Francis Lathom, offer on a celebrated piece of Gothic narrative: Lewis's episode of the Bleeding Nun, that well-known inset tale from *The Monk*. Precisely because of the Nun's considerable fame, I argue, its re-emergence in Kelly's *Eva* (1799) and more implicit presence in Lathom's *The Midnight Bell* (1798) enrich rather than impoverish their respective fictions. Not only do Kelly and Lathom refashion and reposition the tale that they borrow from Lewis, but the memory of its 'original' incarnation in *The Monk* – as Lewis admitted, he was himself adapting a German legend – hovers over Kelly's and Lathom's revisions of it, adding poignancy and ideological significance to their retellings.

Experimentation and Innovation: Parsons's *The Castle of Wolfenbach*

Having been 'accustomed to affluence, and for many years blessed with prosperity', Eliza Parsons lost her merchant husband at the age of 50; an impoverished mother of eight, she now depended for her livelihood on the favour of others and her own resourcefulness as a writer.[12] It was thus that

---

12 Eliza Parsons, *The History of Miss Meredith; A Novel*, 2 vols (London, 1790), vol. 1, p. v. On Parsons's biography, see Karen Morton, *A Life Marketed as Fiction: An Analysis of the Works of Eliza Parsons* (Kansas City: Valancourt Books, 2011), chapter 2.

she began, at the age of 50, the 17-year writing career during which she would publish 19 novels and one play. Despite her success as a novelist, she continued to battle poverty for the rest of her life and lived under constant threat of arrest, as she vividly described in her appeals for the financial support of the Royal Literary Fund.[13]

Parsons's economic circumstances are typical of the conditions under which many, if not most, Gothic novels of the period were produced. The ambitious literary experiments conducted by Radcliffe and Lewis – the middle-class wife of a newspaper editor and the son of a well-connected upper-class family, respectively – were the exception rather than the rule in a marketplace where financial need drove most literary production. There is no question that the sums that Radcliffe received for the copyrights of *The Mysteries of Udolpho* (£500) and *The Italian* (£800) were extreme outliers; most novelists sold the copyright to their novels for around £10.[14] Therefore, while novel-writing may have been an acceptable pursuit for a distressed gentlewoman such as Parsons, it was hardly a lucrative one. To bring in even a modest income, a writer of fiction had to be quick, inventive and responsive to market trends.

Given the centrality of Gothic to the output of the Minerva Press, J. F. Hughes and other publishing houses that specialised in the high-paced, low-pay production of new titles, it seems safe to assume that most Gothic (or at least Gothic-sounding) novels of the period were written swiftly, and that they were often written by authors who also worked in other popular genres, including historical fiction, sentimental fiction and the novel of manners. In many cases, writers tried out the effect of combining Gothic materials with the conventions of these other fictional forms. What seems like a deluge of Gothic fiction in the period 1790–1820 may therefore contain fewer distinctly 'Gothic' novels than the count of keywords in titles alone suggests, an issue that scholars have begun to tackle as they look more closely at the texts themselves.[15] As Mandal has recently shown, for example, despite the prolific Mrs Meeke's fondness for naming abbeys, castles and priories in her titles, her many novels are at heart 'sentimental melodrama[s]' rather than Gothic

---

13 Jennie Batchelor, 'The claims of literature: women applicants to the Royal Literary Fund, 1790–1810', *Women's Writing* 12 (2005): 505–21.
14 Rictor Norton, *Mistress of Udolpho: The Life of Ann Radcliffe* (London: Leicester University Press, 1999), pp. 94, 125; Mandal, 'Gothic and the Publishing World', p. 163.
15 See especially Deborah Anne McLeod, 'The Minerva Press', unpublished PhD thesis (University of Alberta, 1997), chapter 3.

romances.[16] In her years as a Minerva novelist, Kelly likewise experimented with different blends of Gothic and sentimental conventions: Gothic settings and plotlines thoroughly dominate some of her works (for example, *The Ruins of Avondale Priory* [1796]), while elsewhere appearing only in isolated incidents within sentimental tales and/or fictions criticising the foibles of fashionable society (for example, *Madeline, or, the Castle of Montgomery* [1794] and *Joscelina* [1797]).

It was on such a path of quick experimentation with generic possibilities that Parsons, too, embarked in 1791: encouraged by the positive reception of her privately published first novel, *The History of Miss Meredith* (1790), she began working with William Lane. Possibly solicited by Lane following the success of her debut work, her first Minerva publication was another novel of manners, *The Errors of Education* (1791).[17] The Minerva Press published 10 of her novels over a period of six years, three of them appearing in the same year, 1793. Parsons was working unusually fast, having fallen deeper into debt when an injury left her bedridden for months; continuing to write in a genre that had already served her well, she thus produced two additional novels of manners, *Woman as She Should Be* and *Ellen and Julia*, in 1793.[18] She was also, however, willing to try new things. In *The Castle of Wolfenbach*, her third novel that year, she turned to the tale of terror, probably inspired by Radcliffe's recent success.

The Castle of Wolfenbach begins at the eponymous castle, where the path of one beleaguered heroine intersects with that of another. Matilda Weimar, a beautiful orphan of unclear origins, is fleeing the sexual advances of her guardian when she arrives at the castle, where she unexpectedly discovers Victoria, Countess of Wolfenbach, imprisoned there by her husband for many years. Parsons's convoluted narrative follows the gradual working-out of both women's predicaments: Matilda grapples with her guardian's efforts to force her into marriage, and she must also confront the mystery of her origins if she is to become a suitable bride for her would-be suitor, the Count de Bouville. Victoria, meanwhile, needs not only to escape her captivity (as she does soon after the novel's beginning) but to free herself of her husband's coercion and rejoin her family, including the son taken from her in infancy. Both plotlines eventually reach their happy ending: Victoria's dying husband confesses his crimes, leaving her free to remarry, while

---

16 Anthony Mandal, 'Mrs. Meeke and Minerva: the mystery of the marketplace', *Eighteenth-Century Life* 42:2 (2018): 131–51 (p. 140).
17 Morton, *A Life Marketed as Fiction*, p. 48.   18 Morton, *A Life Marketed as Fiction*, p. 48.

Matilda discovers her illustrious family heritage, finds the mother she believed dead and finally marries her beloved Bouville.

Various critics have pointed to the similarities of plot between *The Castle of Wolfenbach* and Radcliffe's *A Sicilian Romance* and *The Romance of the Forest*.[19] But if Parsons repeats Radcliffean structures and themes, she does so with enough suggestive divergence to indicate that she is not simply replicating Radcliffe's Gothic, but appropriating Gothic materials to suit her own intentions. We can see this complexity by probing deeper into the most obvious link between *The Castle of Wolfenbach* and Radcliffe's fiction: the tale of a husband who secretly imprisons his wife. Such a story provided the resolution to the central mystery of *A Sicilian Romance*, whose heroine, Julia, ultimately discovers that her 'dead' mother, the Marchioness of Mazzini, has been locked up in a dungeon for 15 years by her husband, Julia's father. Given the positive reception of Radcliffe's novels, and if we adhere to the prevalent assumption that they were mechanically imitated by lesser writers, it may seem only logical that Victoria's story in *The Castle of Wolfenbach* is a retelling of the Marchioness's.

There is, however, another possibility, one that becomes compelling when we look closely at the best-selling fictional work which in all likelihood influenced Radcliffe herself: 'The History of the Duchess of C.*** – written by Herself', an inset narrative within Stéphanie Félicité de Genlis's best-selling novel *Adèle et Théodore* (1782), anonymously translated into English as *Adelaide and Theodore, or letters on Education* in 1783. Based on what the author insisted was a true story, *The History of the Duchess* told of an Italian noblewoman's 9-year incarceration by her husband, who announced her death to the world and even built an ornate tomb in her memory while secretly keeping her prisoner. As Gillian Dow has shown, the novel was an immediate hit among British readers, with four editions appearing by 1796 and two magazines running rival translations; the tale of the Duchess gained a popularity of its own, appearing in a 1787 anthology, *The Beauties of Genlis*, and subsequently published as a separate novella well into the nineteenth century.[20] As implied by the naming of her characters in *The Romance of the Forest*, Radcliffe was an

---

19 For example, Morton, *A Life Marketed as Fiction*, chapter 7; Angela Wright, 'Disturbing the Female Gothic: An Excavation of the Northanger Novels', in Diana Wallace and Andrew Smith (eds), *The Female Gothic: New Directions* (Basingstoke: Palgrave Macmillan, 2009), pp.60–75 (p. 67); and Diane Long Hoeveler's introduction to Eliza Parsons, *The Castle of Wolfenbach*, edited by Diane Long Hoeveler (Kansas City: Valancourt Books, 2007), pp. vii–xiv (pp. x–xi).
20 Gillian Dow, '*Northanger Abbey*, French fiction, and the affecting history of the Duchess of C***', *Persuasions* 32 (2010): 28–45 (pp. 35–6).

admirer of Genlis's work – but so, apparently, was Parsons: her version of the incarcerated wife tale suggests that rather than simply follow in Radcliffe's footsteps, she also read the *History of the Duchess*, formed her own opinion of it, and responded to it independently in her fiction. Victoria's account of how 'My blood chilled when I entered the gates' of the Castle of Wolfenbach echoes the reaction of Genlis's young heroine, whose shudder as she rides over the drawbridge into her own husband's castle prompts him to respond with cold mirth: '"What is the matter with you, said he? The ancient appearance of this castle seems to surprise you. What! do you think you are entering a prison!"'[21] No parallel detail appears in *A Sicilian Romance*, where Radcliffe's Marchioness de Mazzini simply awakens one day in the 'hideous abode' that her husband has prepared for her beneath the castle.[22] Intriguingly, it was only a year *after* Parsons's novel that Radcliffe, too, echoed the same moment in Genlis by having Emily feel a pang of foreboding as 'the carriage-wheels rolled heavily under the portcullis' of the Castle of Udolpho, filling her with the uneasy sense that 'she was going into her prison'.[23] Influence, then, does not flow here from Radcliffe to Parsons in the simple, self-evident way that traditional views of Radcliffe and her 'imitators' might lead us to expect; at the very least, the two authors are offering independent adaptations of a common intertext. Moreover, one may even begin to wonder about the effect that Radcliffe's lesser-known contemporaries had on her writing (a possibility to which I will return below): might it have been a rival retelling of the Duchess' tale – maybe even *Castle of Wolfenbach* – that prompted Radcliffe to revisit Genlis's precedent in *Udolpho*, this time echoing a resonant detail that she had previously left out?

Parsons's tale resembles Genlis's more than Radcliffe's in other ways as well. Like the Duchess's husband, the Count of Wolfenbach creates an elaborate counterfeit funeral, complete with a coffin that holds a 'figure or bundle, wrapt in a sheet' (Genlis specifies that a wax effigy of the Duchess is buried in her stead).[24] Moreover, where Radcliffe insists on the flawless conduct of her Marchioness, Parson's Victoria, like Genlis's Duchess, commits what both she and her society consider to be an offence against wifely virtue. Though neither is actively adulterous, both women stray from their

---

21 Parsons, *Castle of Wolfenbach*, p. 95; Stéphanie Félicité de Genlis, *Adelaide and Theodore; or Letters on Education*, 3 vols (London, [1783]), vol. 2, p. 206.
22 Ann Radcliffe, *A Sicilian Romance*, edited by Alison Milbank (Oxford: Oxford University Press, 1998), p. 176.
23 Ann Radcliffe, *The Mysteries of Udolpho*, edited by Bonamy Dobrée (Oxford: Oxford World Classics, 1998), p. 227.
24 Parsons, *Castle of Wolfenbach*, p. 99.

culture's uncompromising codes of female fidelity in marriage: the Duchess writes to a friend confessing her aversion to her husband and her lingering feelings for another man, while Victoria secretly corresponds with her concerned former suitor. The inclusion of this indiscretion allows Parsons, like Genlis, to interrogate the absolute ideal of wifely fidelity touted by conduct-book literature, contrasting the slim margin of error allowed to women with the unfettered power granted to husbands over them. Though both works are deeply concerned with female self-examination, neither treats the imprisoned wife's transgression as deserving of such severe consequences.

Parsons, in fact, goes farther than Genlis in pointing out the discrepancy between crime and punishment, as she provides an especially candid description of the Count's aggression. Having caught her in the act of receiving a missive from the Chevalier De Montreville, her former suitor, the Count delivers a 'dreadful blow' to his pregnant wife's head before dragging in the Chevalier himself, 'with his mouth bound, his hands tied, and every mark of cruel treatment'. He then proceeds to murder Victoria's suspected lover before her eyes, stabbing him with a dagger 'through several parts of his body' until 'his blood flowed in torrents, and with groans he fell on his face and expired'. Locked into a closet for the night with the dead man, Victoria loses consciousness and when she finally awakens, her 'clothes covered with blood', the sight of 'the unhappy murdered Chevalier' causes her to go into labour, delivering the son whom her husband will soon take away.[25] As Angela Wright notes, 'Parsons deviates from the Radcliffean model ... in the far more explicitly violent depiction of marital conflict', turning *The Castle of Wolfenbach* into 'a novel about marital violence' that exposes, far more effectively than does Radcliffe's fiction, 'the bloody consequences of a forced, loveless marriage'.[26]

The unflinching portrayal of the violence inside the Castle of Wolfenbach is significant, moreover, as the positively 'un-Radcliffean' aspect of Parsons's novel, which, in another sharp departure from Radcliffe, also features a young heroine who proves quite able to handle such gruesome sights. Shortly after the beginning of the story, Matilda enters Victoria's apartment in the Castle of Wolfenbach with the servant, Joseph: 'What a scene presented itself! a woman on the bed weltering in blood! Both uttered a cry of horror, and ran to the bed; it was the elderly attendant of the lady dead, by a

---

25 Parsons, *Castle of Wolfenbach*, pp. 97–8.
26 Wright, 'Disturbing the Female Gothic', pp. 67, 68.

wound in her throat.'²⁷ Though her first response is, appropriately enough, to faint, Matilda then rouses herself sufficiently to investigate further, and eventually even concerns herself with the fate of Victoria's murdered attendant. 'I cannot be easy under the idea, that the poor woman above should lie there to decay', she says to Joseph, '"is there no way to place her in a decent manner?' When Joseph proposes that the body be put inside a trunk, Matilda proceeds to suggest what no Radcliffe heroine would ever even consider: '"Now, Joseph", (said she) "I will assist you to bring the body down." "You, my lady!" (cried he, staring at her.) "Yes", (rejoined she;) "let us go up."'²⁸ Though Joseph manages in the end to lift the body himself, its disposal is still described as an act in which Matilda, too, participates: 'They deposited the unfortunate woman in the chest, which was fastened down, and without speaking a single word returned to the parlour.'²⁹

If such a scene seems unlikely to modern-day readers, it is because we have formed our notions of how both women writers and Gothic heroines relate to bodily horror on the basis of Radcliffe's *The Mysteries of Udolpho*. The avoidance of gruesome imagery is now considered an essential component of Radcliffean Gothic: as she explained in a posthumously published essay, Radcliffe aimed to evoke in her reader the delicate reaction of terror, which 'expands the soul, and awakens the faculties to a high degree of life', and not the blunter response of horror, which 'contracts, freezes, and nearly annihilates them'.³⁰ *The Mysteries of Udolpho* was her masterful display of aesthetic theory put to practice, most famously in the black-veil scene. The figure behind the veil at the Castle of Udolpho causes Emily to lose consciousness, but what she sees is not described to the reader for several hundred pages. When, towards the novel's end, the narrator finally discloses what Emily saw, it turns out to have been not, as Emily thought, a worm-riddled corpse but a wax effigy. The key element in Radcliffe's strategy is not only the narrator's ultimate revelation that the dead body is a fake – a move that parallels her more famous method for controlling sensationalist materials, the so-called 'explained supernatural' – but the care that Radcliffe takes to defuse the scene's horrific potential by separating Emily's experiences from those of the reader. Emily sees and, as though to prove the need for her creator's artistic manoeuvres, promptly faints; the reader, meanwhile, is protected by Radcliffe's delay in narration from the same deflating (because

---

27 Parsons, *Castle of Wolfenbach*, p. 26.   28 Parsons, *Castle of Wolfenbach*, pp. 28–9
29 Parsons, *Castle of Wolfenbach*, p. 30.
30 Ann Radcliffe, 'On the supernatural in poetry. By the late Mrs. Radcliffe', *New Monthly Magazine* 16: 61 (1826): 145–52 (pp. 149, 150).

overwhelming) aesthetic reaction of horror and, left to imagine what was there behind the veil, is allowed to experience the more delicate and sublime response of terror.[31]

Strikingly, however, Radcliffe did not handle the encounter with the dead body with anything like this level of sophistication in her earlier novels, where sightings of ghastly human remains were brief but straightforward – the 'receptacle for the murdered bodies of the unfortunate people who had fallen into the hands of the banditti' that Julia and Hippolitus stumble upon in *A Sicilian Romance*, for example, or the skeleton that Pierre La Motte finds inside a trunk deep within the deserted abbey in *The Romance of the Forest*.[32] The latter instance may have been influenced by the similar discovery of a corpse in Tobias Smollett's *The Adventures of Ferdinand, Count Fathom* (1753), which had been praised by John and Anna Laetitia Aikin in 1773 as the 'best conceived, and most strongly worked-up scene of mere natural horror' that they could remember.[33] But something happened between the appearance of *The Romance of the Forest* in 1791 and the publication of *The Mysteries of Udolpho* in 1794: what had seemed to Radcliffe (and the Aikins before her) an unexceptionable, even necessary moment for a tale of terror apparently struck her as requiring more thoughtful handling, and in *Udolpho*, rather suddenly, she turned the encounter with human remains into an extremely self-aware, carefully managed scene. What, we might ask, prompted this shift?

Though all we can do is speculate, *The Castle of Wolfenbach* raises some interesting possibilities about the extent to which Radcliffe was not only shaping the Gothic fiction of her day but responding to it as it developed. When we ask ourselves what Ann Radcliffe read, the answers spring to mind readily enough: Shakespeare, Milton, Spenser, Tasso, Gray, Collins and a host of other pre-Romantic poets – those writers, in other words, from whom she quotes generously in her novels. But unlike other authors of her time, most famously Jane Austen in *Northanger Abbey* (written 1798–99; published late 1817; dated 1818), Radcliffe does not openly acknowledge or cite other novelists. Her romances do suggest a familiarity with prominent fictions of her time: she must have read not only *The Monk*, to whose excesses she responded in *The Italian*, but earlier works offering precedents of Gothic

---

31 For a fuller discussion of this strategy see Yael Shapira, *Inventing the Gothic Corpse: The Thrill of Human Remains in the Eighteenth-Century Novel* (Basingstoke: Palgrave Macmillan, 2018), chapter 4.
32 Radcliffe, *A Sicilian Romance*, 166; Ann Radcliffe, *The Romance of the Forest*, edited by Chloe Chard (Oxford: Oxford University Press, 1986), p. 54.
33 J. and A. L. Aikin, *Miscellaneous Pieces, in Prose* (London, 1773), p. 126.

terror, such as Smollett's *Ferdinand, Count Fathom*, already mentioned, Walpole's *The Castle of Otranto* and Reeve's *The Old English Baron* (to which Radcliffe's first novel, according to Rictor Norton, gives a 'gracious salute').[34] These fictions, however, are present in Radcliffe's novels only as echoes, not as explicit allusions; it was through the foregrounded and systematic association of her writing with a tradition of poetry, not prose, that she pursued what critics have characterised as a determined course of self-elevation.[35] The lack of explicit reference to fiction is, I would argue, part of the same strategy: however well she might have known them, Radcliffe never openly concedes familiarity with 'Cecilia, or Camilla, or Belinda', the novelistic heroines so cheerfully championed by Austen's narrator; and she certainly never signals so much as a vague awareness of those Gothic fictions with which her more obscure contemporaries were filling the library shelves.[36]

If, however, we consider the timing of the publication of *The Castle of Wolfenbach* – in 1793, during the three years, an unusually long gap for early Radcliffe, between *The Romance of the Forest* and *The Mysteries of Udolpho* – and factor in the gruesome imagery that Parsons includes without apology, we might begin to ask ourselves whether Radcliffe might have been more aware of what was going on in contemporary fiction than we have had reason to believe. Might she have actually read Parsons's novel, or others like it? If more and more novels in the Gothic vein were appearing (and 1793, as Miles notes, witnessed a particular upsurge in the production of Gothic-sounding titles), and if such novels were coming to be associated with shocking description and grisly sights, might that have prompted Radcliffe to create the elaborate frame that surrounds *Udolpho*'s most startling spectacle?[37] Was it the pressure exerted by association with Minerva novelists like Parsons that caused her to begin handling her own corpses so carefully, tying her fiction to the aesthetically privileged discourse of the sublime to distinguish herself from the commercial Gothic mêlée around her?

Even if novels like Parsons's had only a negative impact on Radcliffe, prompting her to careful manoeuvres of self-differentiation, acknowledging that impact already complicates our understanding of the Gothic novel's evolution, traditionally described as a dichotomous struggle between

---

34 Norton, *Mistress of Udolpho*, p. 58.
35 E. J. Clery, *Women's Gothic: From Clara Reeve to Mary Shelley* (Tavistock: Northcote House, 2000), pp. 54–9. Norton's tally of literary citations in Radcliffe's work confirms her avoidance of explicit references to fiction; see *Mistress of Udolpho*, pp. 49–50.
36 Jane Austen, *Northanger Abbey, Lady Susan, The Watsons, Sanditon*, edited by James Kinsley and John Davie (Oxford: Oxford World's Classics, 2003), p. 24.
37 Miles, 'The 1790s', p. 42.

Radcliffe and Lewis only. Recognising that trade Gothic might have influenced Radcliffe, and not only the other way around, is also a necessary corrective to some unexamined assumptions that have shaped the modern study of Radcliffe's romances. In failing to even consider such a possibility, critical practice has too-unquestioningly aligned itself with hyperbolic Romantic depictions of Radcliffe as a solitary genius existing apart from the commercial fray, the 'mighty magician ... bred and nourished by the Florentine Muses in their sacred solitary caverns', or the 'poetess' so 'disgusted' with the numerous lowly fictions inspired by her work that she ceased publishing altogether.[38] Compounded by Radcliffe's own strategic avoidance of overt references to other novels, such idealised portraits of her authorship have kept us from fully exploring her relations to the bustling fiction marketplace in which she operated. And if reading Radcliffe and Parsons together raises new questions about Radcliffe, it certainly provides grounds for revising what we assume about the writers of trade Gothic: though it shares plot elements and themes with Radcliffe's novel, *The Castle of Wolfenbach* is not in any simple way 'Radcliffean'. As we will see, while other trade-Gothic novelists also found inspiration in the work of leading Gothic authors, they, like Parsons, were not nearly as 'servile' and 'slavish' or even as 'humble' as the reviews would have us believe.

Trade Gothic's Bleeding Nuns: Isabella Kelly and Francis Lathom

The work of Isabella Kelly (c. 1759–1857) and Francis Lathom (1774–1832) offers another compelling vantage point onto the tangle of admiration, creative license and even defiance with which trade-Gothic writers invoked the more celebrated Gothic works and writers of the day. Kelly's circumstances are strikingly similar to Parsons's: forced by her husband's debts and eventual death to seek a way of supporting her young children, she published seven novels with Lane between 1794 and 1801, and four subsequent novels with other publishers, as well as a volume of poetry and several non-fiction works. A second marriage left her quickly widowed again, and she, like Parsons, continued to battle poverty for the rest of her life.[39] Lathom was no less

---

38 [Thomas James Mathias,] *The Pursuits of Literature, a Satirical Poem, in Four Dialogues. With Notes*, 8th edition (Dublin: P. Byrne, 1798), p. 51; Scott, 'Prefatory Memoir', pp. iv, xiv.

39 See 'Kelly, Isabella', in Susan Brown, Patricia Clements, and Isobel Grundy (eds), *Orlando: Women's Writing in the British Isles from the Beginnings to the Present*

prolific, though in his case the role of financial necessity is less clear-cut: the son of a wealthy merchant family from Norwich, he was also a dramatist and actor for the local theatre company, and in the course of his career he wrote seven plays, 10 Gothic novels and 11 contemporary domestic novels. A crisis of an uncertain nature (some have speculated about a homosexual relationship) caused him to leave Norwich in 1810; a separation from his wife ensued, as did a rift with his father that affected Lathom's inheritance.[40] Though it is not likely that he was ever as close to destitution as Parsons and Kelly, he did describe himself as an author who worked for money, claiming in the Preface to an 1807 novel that it is 'a sufficient sanction for an author whose remuneration is to arise from gratifying the public taste, to apply his pen to such subjects as interest the feeling of the majority'.[41]

Like Parsons, both Kelly and Lathom clearly followed market trends: having included only a modicum of Gothic content in her first novel, *Madeline; or, The Castle of Montgomery* (1794), Kelly followed up with a series of novels in which, as noted above, she experimented with increasing levels of Gothic materials. Lathom's debut novel, *The Castle of Ollada* (1795), is strongly indebted to Walpole's *Castle of Otranto*, a connection made clear and even flaunted by the use of such names as Hippolita and Theodore; the titles of some of Lathom's subsequent novels, including *Mystery, A Novel* (1800), *Astonishment!!! A Romance of a Century Ago* (1802) and *The Impenetrable Secret, Find it Out!* (1805), indicate his continued willingness to play the generic typing game. Yet if Kelly and Lathom were influenced by the Gothic successes of their day, they retained a compelling measure of independence before them, not just emulating, but adapting and reinventing. This becomes evident if we look at how both novelists appropriated one of the most famous Gothic figures of their day: Lewis's Bleeding Nun.

Appearing in the tale of star-crossed lovers Raymond and Agnes in *The Monk*, the Bleeding Nun is a spectre who haunts Lindenberg Castle, dressed in a bloodstained habit and veil and bearing a lamp and a dagger. When Raymond, believing that she is Agnes in disguise, inadvertently pledges his love to the ghost, the Nun begins to appear nightly by his bedside: an animated 'Corse' with the 'paleness of death ... spread over her features',

---

(Cambridge: Cambridge University Press Online, 2006) <http://orlando.cambridge.org> (last accessed 12 April 2018).
40 Potter, *History of Gothic Publishing*, pp. 131–34.
41 Preface to *The Fatal Vow; or, St. Michael's Monastery* (1807), quoted in Montague Summers, *The Gothic Quest: A History of the Gothic Novel* (New York: Russell & Russell, 1938; reissued 1964), p. 175.

she fixes Raymond with the glare of her 'lustreless and hollow' eyes and kisses him on the mouth with her 'cold lips'.[42] Raymond wastes away under the Nun's power until he is saved by the fortuitous intervention of the Wandering Jew, who reveals to him her true story: she is Beatrice de la Cisternas, Raymond's ancestor, a nun who broke her holy vows to live with her baron lover, murdered him at the instigation of his brother, and was stabbed to death by the brother in turn. Arranging for her proper burial, Raymond finally lays Beatrice to rest, releases himself from her control, and ends the haunting of Lindenberg Castle.

A much-praised element of Lewis's novel, the story of the Bleeding Nun went on to become a popular success in its own right, featured in plays, chapbooks and magic-lantern shows.[43] But the Nun obviously also appealed to trade-Gothic novelists – not only Kelly and Lathom, whom I will discuss below, but T. J. Horsley Curties, who included his own tale of the ghostly 'Bleeding Nun of St. Catherine' in *Ancient Records; or, The Abbey of St. Oswythe* (1801) and apparently also wrote a separate, shorter version published the same year, 'The Ruins of the Abbey of St. Martin'.[44] Their adaptations of this memorable figure have not been critically examined, probably because they would seem the epitome of uninteresting 'imitation'. Yet the insistent memory of *The Monk* is precisely what makes the Bleeding Nun figures in novels after Lewis so intriguing; the resulting stories, with their blend of the familiar and the divergent, are surprisingly thought-provoking, as the two following examples will show.

Kelly's *Eva* is a multi-generational tale of female suffering focused on three women, all named Eva and all subject to the violent manipulations of ambitious men. The first Eva, Countess of Bellegarvine, marries one such man but lives to regret it when his cruel mistreatment of their son leads to the latter's suicide. She dies and leaves her daughter, also named Eva, at the mercy of her father, who forces her to marry a man whom she despises, Sir Reginald Glen Bolton. At the time of their marriage, Eva discovers that Sir Reginald has disinherited his infant niece, whom she adopts, names Eva as well, and raises as her own. The youngest Eva, too, finds herself persecuted by a domineering man, her adopted brother; his relentless pursuit causes Eva

---

42 Matthew Lewis, *The Monk*, edited by Howard Anderson (Oxford: Oxford University Press, 1995), pp. 160–1.
43 Diane Long Hoeveler, 'Gothic Adaptation, 1764–1830', in Byron and Townshend (eds), *The Gothic World*, pp. 185–98 (p. 186).
44 Dale Townshend, 'T. I. Horsley Curties, romance, and the gift of death', *European Romantic Review* 24:1 (2013): 23–42 (pp. 27–8).

and her mother much suffering until the final untangling of the plot leads to the conventional happy ending.

As noted above, Kelly, like Parsons, wove Gothic materials into sentimental fictions and tales of contemporary manners; *Eva* is a blend of all three, with the Gothic components concentrated almost entirely in the novel's first volume, in the episode that surrounds the second Eva's forced marriage. Furious at her refusal to marry Sir Reginald, Eva's father whisks her away to the Nunnery of Wanleymere, 'a low, heavy and irregular building, erected in a gloomy style of Gothic architecture'.[45] With the Gothic setting in place, the rumour of supernatural activity is quick to follow: as Eva soon learns from her maid, the nunnery is supposedly haunted by the ghost of a certain Lady Agatha. When her candle accidentally goes out at night, Eva finds herself faced with a terrifying sight: 'a pale, glimmering light in a remote corner of the room', which 'quivered as if moved by a short breath' and was soon 'raised from the pedestal by a power as yet to her invisible'.[46] Advancing towards her, she sees a 'female figure, bearing the lamp ... The form was tall, and not inelegant; the attitude that of dejection; it was habited in black, but a white transparent veil floated around it, through which could be discovered a countenance pale, and expressive of despair, yet touchingly delicate, and affectingly composed'.[47]

To Eva's astonishment, the spectral figure speaks: 'Fear not' she says to Eva; 'Destined bride of savage Reginald Glen Bolton, fear not me, but promise to poor, murdered Agatha protection for her child!' Laying down a packet, she adds: 'Receive these testimonies – no other evidence is wanted; demand the child, and Agatha can rest!' Having delivered her message, the figure receives the stunned Eva's silent assent: gazing at 'the spectre's face with speechless, yet expressive meaning', Eva raises her prayer book to her lips and kisses it, sealing 'the unuttered, yet most awful, vow, by fervently pressing her lips to the sanctified page'.[48] The figure then glides away into the darkness.

Few devoted readers of Gothic fiction in 1799 could have failed to recognise the provenance of Kelly's spectral nun, but they would also have noted the significant changes Kelly introduces into her borrowed plotline. Those changes are evident even before the mystery of the moment is unravelled, in the very nature of the encounter between the heroine and the mysterious figure. The Nun herself is markedly unlike Beatrice, whose repulsive

---

45 Isabella Kelly, *Eva. A Novel*, 3 vols (London, 1799), vol. 1, p. 146.
46 Kelly, *Eva*, vol. 1, p. 159.   47 Kelly, *Eva*, vol. 1, p. 160.
48 Kelly, *Eva*, vol. 1, pp. 161, 162.

physicality was Lewis's particular embellishment of a German folk legend: as Syndy M. Conger notes, 'the blood stains, the wound, the dagger, the "rotting fingers," and the icy kiss of death on the lips' were all his invention.[49] Elsewhere in her fiction, Kelly proves entirely willing to indulge in Lewis-style gruesome description.[50] Here, however, she seems determined to reverse the effect of Lewis's graphic realism, stressing the 'touchingly delicate' features visible behind the Nun's veil.

No less significant is Kelly's revision of the nature of the encounter between the Nun and the living witness whom she haunts. For Raymond, the Nun's visits are a source of 'horror too great to be described', causing his voice to fail and his 'nerves' to be 'bound up in impotence'.[51] Between the Nun's ghastly appearance and Raymond's revulsion and fear, it is little wonder that modern critics see the Nun as an expression of *The Monk* 's pervasive strain of misogyny – in various readings, 'a projection of the castrating woman who is also a bringer of death', a 'living corpse' whose touch 'introduces decay and impotence into Raymond's body', or a 'figure of ... materiality and mortality' that 'demarcate[s] the limitations of masculine freedom'.[52] It is therefore all the more striking that Kelly turns her echo of Lewis's famous scene into an encounter between two women, the 'affectively composed' nun and the young, harassed bride-to-be who, despite her deep fears for herself, recognises that she is being called upon to perform a sacred task – a task, moreover, entrusted to her on behalf of a third woman, the 'poor, murdered Agatha'.

Although the power of the moment as an incursion of the supernatural is later dispelled by Kelly's choice of a rational explanation – the nun, it turns out, is not really a ghost, but rather a disguised friend of Agatha, Sir Reginald's dead sister – its force and implications are not diminished, especially since the encounter proves empowering to Eva in an entirely practical way. Brought to the altar for her own forced nuptials, she hears the priest ask 'If any man can shew just cause why these two may not be lawfully joined', and shocks Sir Reginald by stopping the wedding herself: I'am not a man', she

---

49 Syndy M. Conger, *Matthew G. Lewis, Charles Robert Maturin and the Germans: An Interpretative Study of the Influence of German literature on Two Gothic Novels* (Salzburg: Institut für Englische Sprache und Literatur, Universität Salzburg, 1976), p. 103.
50 Shapira, *Inventing the Gothic Corpse*, pp. 158–64.   51 Lewis, *The Monk*, p. 160.
52 See, respectively, Marie Mulvey-Roberts, 'From Bluebeard's Bloody Chamber to Demonic Stigmatic', in Wallace and Smith (eds), *The Female Gothic*, pp. 98–114 (p. 106); Adriana Craciun, *Fatal Women of Romanticism* (Cambridge: Cambridge University Press, 2003), p. 119; and Alison Milbank, 'Bleeding Nuns: A Genealogy of the Female Gothic Grotesque', in Wallace and Smith (eds) *The Female Gothic*, pp. 76–97 (pp. 81, 82).

declares, 'yet... Knowest thou no impediment, Sir Reginald... no act of justice to be performed, no restitution to be made, no wrath appeased, no rights asserted?'[53] Armed with the packet of documents that the 'ghost' left in her possession, Eva is able to exact justice for Agatha, whose story we now learn: opposed to her runaway marriage, Sir Reginald murdered Agatha's husband and then, after Agatha died in childbirth, stole the inheritance due to his infant niece, who becomes the novel's third Eva. It is the intervention of the adapted 'Bleeding Nun', a figure of feared emasculation that here becomes an agent of female solidarity, that Kelly allows her matrilineage of Evas to assert some measure of power and control over their fates, in a work that otherwise richly documents their persistent abuse by powerful men.

A more muted yet compelling echo of the Bleeding Nun appears at a key moment in Francis Lathom's *The Midnight Bell* (1798). The convoluted plot of Lathom's second Gothic composition begins and ends with the mystery of Cohenburg Castle, whose young heir, Alphonsus, is rudely expelled from his home and family existence. After his father is murdered, Alphonsus's mother, having at first accused his uncle of fratricide, then contradicts her own earlier plea for revenge, asserts the uncle's innocence and frantically demands that he leave: 'observe thy mother's words, nor ask their explanation:—instantly fly this castle, nor approach it more, as you value life!—as you value heaven!'[54] Alphonsus's elaborate adventures in *The Midnight Bell* lead him to the woman he soon marries, Lauretta; her own mysterious family history, eventual reunion with her long-lost father and numerous other extrapolated narratives make up the lengthy bulk of the novel.

Eventually, however, Alphonsus returns to his ancestral castle, now said to be haunted and with a ghostly bell ringing out every night: the locals believe that the ghost of the murdered Count 'tolls the bell to call somebody in, that it may reveal the murder of its body to them, and frighten them into promising to revenge its death'.[55] Naturally, Alphonsus cannot rest until he makes his way at night inside the castle; when he returns the next day, 'a frantic wildness was depicted on his countenance, and his stretched eyes were fixed on vacancy'. Pressed by the anxious Lauretta and her father to reveal what happened, he finally unfolds a barely coherent tale about encountering his dead mother in the castle:

---

53 Kelly, *Eva*, vol. 1, p. 203.
54 Francis Lathom, *The Midnight Bell, A German Story, Founded on Incidents in Real Life*, 3 vols (London, 1798), vol. 1, p. 25.
55 Lathom, *Midnight Bell*, vol. 3, p. 118.

> It was in the dead of the night that I saw her; *did I not tell you that she had a burning lamp in her hand? . . . But she was dead: her cheeks were pale and sunk;* my disobedience called her from the grave: I would fain see her once more, and kneel for her forgiveness: and would she then but calm her angry looks, I should die happy.[56]

Once again, we meet a spectral female bearing a lamp, and this time, unlike in Kelly, we again encounter a Lewisian emphasis on the deadness of the face with its pale, sunken cheeks. Yet once again, however, what makes the moment fascinating is the combined effect of familiarity and strangeness. Like Raymond, Alphonsus is distraught, but for different reasons: rather than the ghastly alter ego of his lover, he encounters a macabre version of his mother, Anna, an apparition who he believes is angry with him for disobeying her orders and returning home. Enfeebled, like Raymond, by the female ghost he believes he saw, he too seeks release through the intercession of another man – in his case, a local friar that he begs to go to the castle on his behalf and 'pray for me forgiveness for my disobedience, of my mother's shade'.[57]

What follows continues the narrative parallel to the Bleeding Nun tale: the friar, like the Wandering Jew, tells the story that will set Alphonsus free and lay the ghostly female to rest. But the similarity, once again, opens up into difference that adds depth and poignancy to Lathom's story. Alphonsus now finally learns the terrible secret that destroyed his family: his father, irrationally suspicious of his wife, convinced his brother to test Anna's virtue by making sexual advances towards her. Fearful that her brother-in-law would attack her, she saw an intruder in her room one night and stabbed him, only to discover that she had killed her own husband. Though clearly indebted to *Hamlet* (like so many other Gothic fictions of its day), *The Midnight Bell* also invites the reader to compare Anna's story to that of that famous lamp-bearing dead woman from *The Monk*. Both Anna and Beatrice are caught in deadly sexual triangles, but whereas Beatrice's murder might be seen as her just deserts for her many sins, Anna is the guiltless victim of senseless male jealousy and manipulation. There is a sad irony to the fact that, despite their dissimilar circumstances, both women end up in the same place, as ghosts forced to haunt the place of their undoing; in Anna's case, moreover, the ghostly status is self-inflicted, the expression of a guilt that can

---

56 Lathom, *Midnight Bell*, vol. 3, p. 168; italics added.
57 Lathom, *Midnight Bell*, vol. 3, p. 197.

never be assuaged. Near mad with grief and remorse, she has the friar 'circulate an immediate report of her death'. While her tormented brother-in-law withdraws to a monastery of his own, she becomes the spectre haunting her own former home in an endless ritual of penance: it is she who tolls the bell each night for the 'double purpose', as the friar explains, 'of keeping idle visitors from the castle, under the idea of its being haunted', and summoning the monks to hold nightly prayers over her dead husband's coffin.[58]

The reader familiar with Lewis can thus ponder the implications of the analogy between Beatrice and Anna's restless 'walking', as well as between their respective 'exorcisms'. The Bleeding Nun is finally subdued by the two men – the Wandering Jew and her descendent, Raymond – and her disruptive power is dispelled when she is buried in the ancestral plot. But since she is imprisoned by her own guilt, Anna remains locked in her 'spectral' role, refusing to rejoin the living by seeing her son or even bless him, since (as she tells the friar) 'her blessing would fall a curse' upon him.[59] Instead she confirms her own status as nun, recluse and quasi-ghost by withdrawing to a convent, where she soon dies. To her son alone is left some semblance of comfort, since he is 'little doubtful of her forgiveness in a happier state, for the commission of an involuntary crime'.[60]

The celebrity and success of Radcliffe and Lewis in the 1790s and beyond were impressive, even daunting, and affiliation with them could be a form of self-promotion for lesser-known Gothic writers. But even as they made various gestures of deference and indebtedness towards the predominant Gothic authors of their time and echoed their work liberally, trade-Gothic authors, as I have shown, were engaged in something more complicated and interesting than simply replicating pieces of *Udolpho* or *The Monk*. What emerges when we approach their work with curiosity rather than inherited disdain is not the trickle-down model of literary impact asserted in most histories of the Gothic, but a vibrant scene of experimentation with the narrative and tonal possibilities of Gothic materials. These experiments were conducted simultaneously by multiple authors, Radcliffe and Lewis among them, who were reading each other's work and responding to it by trying out different styles, generic blends and ideological emphases. As scholarship

---

58 Lathom, *Midnight Bell*, vol. 3, pp. 223, 226.   59 Lathom, *Midnight Bell*, vol. 3, p. 233.
60 Lathom, *Midnight Bell*, vol. 3, pp. 243–4.

begins to pay attention to the multiple stories these forgotten authors told – as it begins, that is, to retrieve the embarrassing skeleton of trade Gothic from the proverbial closet – the story of how the Gothic itself developed is likewise becoming a more nuanced, comprehensive and compelling one.[61]

[61] The research presented in this chapter was supported by the Israel Science Foundation (grant no. 128/15).

1.16

Oriental Gothic: Imperial-Commercial Nightmares from the Eighteenth Century to the Romantic Period

DIEGO SAGLIA

The eighteenth century was a turning-point in the relations between Britain and the East, as the former's domination of, and investment in, increasingly substantial portions of Asia resulted in political, economic and cultural forms of 'maniacal hyperproductivity'.[1] This process drew upon age-old visions of the East as a site of excess – a place that was immeasurably ancient and vast, and characterised by omnipotent rulers, a hypertrophic luxuriance, overabundant wealth, overwhelmingly physical and sensual bodies, and uncontainably irregular and profuse imagination and arts. Marilyn Butler aptly described the Orient in eighteenth-century culture as an idealised world of 'visions of wealth and luxury', a 'land of magic, ingenious contrivances, treasure, love-intrigue and powerful arbitrary caliphs'.[2] More broadly, Eastern excess lay also in its exorbitance, its being outside Western norms and principles. Oscillating between fact and fiction, order and disorder, this construct belongs to what Georges Bataille defined as the other side of rational (capitalist) production and its attendant cultural-political regime – an 'accursed share' that sees 'no growth but only a luxurious squandering of energy in every form' through irrational expenditure and destruction.[3] Both time- and culture-specific, the fateful encounter of Gothic and Orientalist aesthetics and discourses in the eighteenth century unleashed a wave of unsettling fantasies that tapped into the fears and desires of a British culture in thrall to a demonised but irresistibly captivating 'other'.

Though originating from the global aspirations of Enlightenment cultural geography, Oriental Gothic paradoxically presents anti-Enlightenment and

---

1 Srinivas Aravamudan, *Enlightenment Orientalism: Resisting the Rise of the Novel* (Chicago and London: University of Chicago Press, 2012), p. 2.
2 Marilyn Butler, 'Orientalism', in David B. Pirie (ed.), *The Penguin History of Literature: The Romantic Period* (London: Penguin, 1994), pp. 395–447 (pp. 395–6).
3 Georges Bataille, *The Accursed Share: An Essay on General Economy, Vol. I: Consumption*, trans. by Robert Hurley (New York: Zone Books, 1991), p. 33.

anti-modern tendencies that throw into relief the unsayable and the repressed in opposition to rationalist notions of self and polity, identity and culture.[4] Yet Oriental Gothic was also inextricable from eighteenth- and early nineteenth-century processes of transformation and modernisation based on territorial expansion and commercial imperialism; in particular, pertaining both to archaic, unchangeable Asia and developing, thrusting Europe, trade constitutes an unsettling connection between their would-be opposed temporalities. In turn, in this transitional phase, Oriental Gothic is an imaginative site of real and metaphorical exchanges, yoking together the transcendental and the material to bring to the surface Britain's imperial-commercial fears and anxieties.

To explore this variegated context, this chapter traces three intersecting storylines centred on textual sources and modes of writing, commerce and empire, and the use of bodies respectively. These three narratives are interconnected by the governing trope of conflicted exchange (the prefix *meta*, as in *metaphor* and *metonymy*, aptly signalling 'movement across'), on the one hand, and material and immaterial circulation of individuals, cultures and economic systems, on the other. Addressing Edward Said's undifferentiated 'pre-romantic and romantic representations of the Orient as an exotic locale',[5] this chapter explains how the timelessness of the East – its eternal, immutable barbarism and uncontainable excess – was reshaped and put to use within Gothic in relation to specific historical conditions, producing powerful fictional translations of an increasingly globalised experience of the world.

Textual Exchanges – East to West

The East came to the European eighteenth century as an imaginative archive through such repositories as Antoine Galland's *Les Mille et une nuits* (1704–17) or Barthélemy d'Herbelot's *Bibliothèque orientale* (1697, which Galland completed and published after d'Herbelot's death), and as a densely material dimension, a space of trade and empire. It became part of a narrative of imperial acquisition and control informed both by the material sublime of

---

4 As Smith and Hughes note, 'The Enlightenment ... produces its own doubles' since it tries 'to account for what it by definition cannot know and in the process draws attention to its own failings.' See Andrew Smith and William Hughes, 'Introduction: The Enlightenment Gothic and Postcolonialism', in Andrew Smith and William Hughes (eds), *Empire and the Gothic: The Politics of Genre* (Basingstoke and New York: Palgrave Macmillan, 2010), pp. 1–12 (pp. 2–3).
5 Edward W. Said, *Orientalism: Western Conceptions of the Orient* (London: Penguin, 1991), p. 118.

unlimited luxury and wealth and by the intangible sublimity of power, the numinous and the supernatural. In the British cultural domain, it was Galland's highly creative 'translation' of the *Arabian Nights' Entertainments*, in French first and in English soon thereafter, that introduced seductively disquieting ways of imagining the East that variously anticipated Oriental Gothic.

The English translation of the *Nights* went into its eighteenth 'edition' by 1793, a figure that practically doubled in the subsequent 40 years thanks to reprints and new translations.[6] As they continued to be read, the tales also continued to fascinate and, indeed, unsettle the imagination of generations; for the *Nights* and Oriental tales more generally could also be sources of fear, as in the exemplary cases of Samuel Taylor Coleridge and Thomas De Quincey, who, as children, had been terrified by the stories of 'Zayn al-Asnam' and Aladdin respectively.[7] Anna Laetitia Aikin acknowledged the frightening potential of Oriental tales in 'On the Pleasure Derived from Objects of Terror' (1773), where she observes that 'The old Gothic romance and the Eastern tale, with their genii, giants, enchantments, and transformations ... will ever retain a most powerful influence on the mind' thanks to their 'wildnesses of the imagination'.[8] For Aikin, Oriental tales are crucial instances of the oxymoronic pleasure issuing from 'objects of terror', as she notes that 'The more wild, fanciful, and extraordinary are the circumstances of a scene of horror, the more pleasure we receive from it' and proceeds to illustrate this process through the effect on readers of the many 'examples of the terrible joined with the marvellous' in the *Nights*.[9]

It is, of course, difficult to determine with any degree of certainty whether the narrative complexities of the story-within-story format of the *Nights* actually bore on the Gothic technique of embedding visible in William Beckford's *Vathek* (written in 1782; translated into English by Samuel Henley without Beckford's consent as *An Arabian Tale* in 1786); Mary Shelley's *Frankenstein* (1818; 1831) or Charles Robert Maturin's *Melmoth the Wanderer* (1820). Yet the plots, motifs and general irregularity of the stories in the *Nights*, as well as those of other popular Oriental tales, exerted a pervasive

---

6 Peter L. Caracciolo, 'Introduction: "Such a store house of ingenious fiction and of splendid imagery"', in Peter L. Caracciolo (ed.), *The Arabian Nights in English Literature: Studies in the Reception of The Thousand and One Nights into British Culture* (Basingstoke and London: Macmillan, 1988), pp. 1–80 (p. 6).
7 Robert Irwin, *The Arabian Nights: A Companion* (London and New York: I. B. Tauris, 2005), pp. 266–7.
8 J. and A. L. Aikin, *Miscellaneous Pieces, in Prose* (London, 1773), p. 122.
9 Aikin and Aikin, *Miscellaneous Pieces*, p. 126.

and lasting influence on Gothic authors and texts. Horace Walpole, an enthusiast of the *Nights* who saw in them 'a wildness ... that captivates', produced a collection of *Hieroglyphic Tales* (1785) in imitation of Anthony Hamilton's popular parodies of the *Nights* written in French and circulating in manuscript in the early part of the century.[10] William Beckford, a distant relative of Hamilton on the maternal side, admired his narratives and was deeply familiar with the *Nights* and other sources of Orientalist lore from an early age. Matthew Gregory Lewis admired *Vathek*, translated Hamilton's tales into English and, in the advertisement to *The Monk* (1796), acknowledged that the 'first idea' for the novel was suggested to him by 'the story of *Santon Barsisa*', a tale of a saintly monk tempted into rape and murder by the devil, published in *The Guardian* in 1713 and taken from Pétis de la Croix's *Turkish Tales* (1707–8).[11] Robert Southey's turn to the East was influenced by Beckford's *Vathek* and Walter Savage Landor's epic *Gebir* (1798), and he specifically found inspiration for *Thalaba, the Destroyer* (1801) in the description of the Dom Daniel cavern, inhabited by the evil magician Maugraby and his fellow sorcerers, in one of Robert Heron's *Arabian Tales; or, A Continuation of the Arabian Nights Entertainments* (1792). As for the later Gothic output, it may suffice to mention that both Mary Shelley and Charles Robert Maturin inserted revealing references to the *Nights* in *Frankenstein* and *Melmoth*, which therefore feature significant and sometimes overlooked connections with the fictional-ideological universe of Oriental Gothic.

Between the eighteenth century and the Romantic period, intersections of the East and the Gothic produced such intricate webs of texts, geo-political relations and economic exchanges that a critical approach focusing on lines of influence and source-hunting would merely deliver further confirmation of ceaseless interactions. In contrast, this chapter examines how this encounter was grounded on intertextual exchanges that simultaneously crystallised textual transcriptions of commercial exchanges and imperial transactions – a perspective combining both the idea of the East as an imaginative and textual archive and its status as 'an integral part of European *material* civilization and culture'.[12]

---

10 Quoted in Robert L. Mack, 'Introduction', in Robert L. Mack (ed.), *Oriental Tales* (Oxford: Oxford University Press, 1992), pp. vii–xlix (p. xix). On Anthony Hamilton, see Ros Ballaster, *Fabulous Orients: Fictions of the East in England 1662–1785* (Oxford: Oxford University Press, 2005), pp. 2–4, 98–100.
11 Mathew Gregory Lewis, *The Monk*, edited by Howard Anderson (Oxford: Oxford University Press, 1973), p. 6.
12 Said, *Orientalism*, p. 2.

Nightmares of Trade and Empire

Through their representation of economies converging on despotic figures, as well as on unchecked exchange and circulation, Oriental tales contributed to making Oriental Gothic a crucible of the anxieties raised by Britain's expanding geo-political and economic horizons. Once more, the *Nights* are exemplary in this respect, being peopled with arbitrary rulers, merchants, shopkeepers and slave traders, and portraying the markets, auctions, caravanserais and bazaars of Baghdad and Cairo; these features duly reappeared in such derivatives as James Ridley's *Tales of the Genii* (1764), *The Tales of Inatulla* translated by Alexander Dow (1768) and Heron's *Arabian Tales*. On the basis of this long-standing association of the East and commerce, Oriental Gothic re-envisioned familiar Gothic themes and motifs from a global perspective, one in which the potentially nightmarish outcomes of commercial imperialism chimed with concerns raised by proto-globalisation. In other words, through its Oriental inflections Gothic was the product of, and a primary site of imaginative engagement with, what C. A. Bayly has termed the 'first age of truly global imperialism, 1760–1830', which saw the emergence of 'global networks of people, monetary transactions, and ideas'.[13]

In contrast to earlier panegyrics to the civilising force of *le doux commerce*, in the second half of the eighteenth century, trade came under attack by embattled detractors such as Guillaume Thomas François Raynal and Adam Ferguson. In their examinations of the 'predicaments of empire, militarism, and political despotism' between the Seven Years War and the end of the American Revolution, both emphasised how the beneficial aspects of commerce had been increasingly contaminated by expansionism, protectionism, rivalry and power struggles.[14] For Ferguson and the Scottish conjectural historians more generally, commerce 'had undermined Gothic institutions and had destroyed the feudal nobilities that dominated Europe after the fall of Rome'.[15] It was a transformative, modernising energy that had *de-Gothicised* the West. And yet, as the central plank in a developing global economic order, they also condemned it as an instrument of exploitation that contributed to *re-Gothicising* the West by fostering a 'regular and constant system of oppression', a 'global system of competitive commerce' that simultaneously raised 'the stakes in the ancient quest for territorial empire'.[16]

---

13 C. A. Bayly, *The Birth of the Modern World, 1780–1914: Global Connections and Comparisons* (Oxford and Malden, MA: Basil Blackwell, 2004), pp. 45, 42.
14 Iain McDaniel, *Adam Ferguson in the Scottish Enlightenment: The Roman Past and Europe's Future* (Cambridge, MA and London: Harvard University Press, 2013), p. 107.
15 McDaniel, *Adam Ferguson*, p. 107.   16 McDaniel, *Adam Ferguson*, pp. 110, 117.

These questions gained prominence in Gothic fiction thanks to Sophia Lee's popular *The Recess; or, a Tale of Other Times*, a novel about the (imaginary) twin daughters of Mary, Queen of Scots, first published in 1783–5 and one of the most enduringly influential early Gothic texts. Though most of its narrative centres on Renaissance England and Ireland, a short central section recounts the travails and torments of one of the princesses, Matilda, in the West Indies. Abducted to Jamaica, she experiences the dehumanising effects of commercial and territorial empire, is caught up in a slave rebellion and subsequently imprisoned, while her health is progressively undermined by suffering, privation and the tropical climate. This section, which speaks directly to eighteenth-century geo-political and socio-economic concerns, connects the Gothic imagination with mid- to late-century denunciations of an increasingly globalised capitalist imperialism. In Janina Nordius's words, Lee's novel 'instigates a tradition within gothic literature that locates the source of fear and horror to, on the one hand, enlightened humanist values and, on the other, the cultural and racial oppression that has come to form an integral part of the eurocentric political and economic agenda'.[17] Oriental Gothic displaced these questions to Asia, employing figurations of remoteness and otherworldliness to convey anxieties over uncontrolled circulation, unmonitored borders and unstoppable processes of production and exchange, invasion, contamination and metamorphosis – all related to the acceleration of interconnections and transformations activated by commercial relations.

A crucial work in this vein is *Vathek*, its titular Caliph hailed from the outset as the 'Sovereign of the world', an Oriental-style hyperbole that suggests the universal scope of Beckford's tale. Vathek is immediately introduced as the pinnacle of a political and economic structure centred on his capital as the hub of a whole system of control and consumption.[18] The city of Samarah and the Palace of Alkoremi, from where his mandates spread outwards over the entire kingdom, are the points of convergence of its economic output. This is visible in the accumulation of objects and products not only in the palace but also, more symbolically, in his magical tower, which concentrates the country's wealth ('Immense treasures had been lavished upon it') and is a site of irrational expenditure and destruction of resources – an architectural

---

17 Janina Nordius, 'A tale of other places: Sophia Lee's *The Recess* and colonial gothic', *Studies in the Novel* 34:2 (2002): 162–76 (pp. 164–5).
18 William Beckford, *Vathek*, edited by Roger Lonsdale (Oxford: Oxford University Press, 1970), p. 11.

realisation of Bataille's 'accursed share'.[19] As the place where Vathek and his mother Carathis engage in the dark arts, the tower signifies the terrifying side of economic production and consumption, here transfigured in the representation of the Caliph's political and supernatural power over his unimaginably vast domains.

The unexpected arrival at court of the grotesquely deformed *giaour* sets the action in train within the context of a fatal exchange. A traveller from 'a region of India, which is wholly unknown', this mysterious figure is laden with 'extraordinary ... merchandize' and 'beautiful commodities'.[20] Though Vathek is initially repulsed by the monstrous aspect of this 'rude merchant', 'joy succeeded to this emotion of terror, when the stranger displayed to his view such rarities as he had never before seen'.[21] These slippers, knives and sabres are 'not less admirable for their workmanship than for their splendour' and 'enriched with gems, that were hitherto unknown'.[22] It is these objects, purchased with 'all the coined gold ... from his treasury', that inspire him to set out on his imperial progress and a doomed quest for the treasures of the pre-Adamite sultans and, with truly global aspirations, the 'talismans that control the world'.[23]

Reworking the motif of merchants and traders in Oriental tales, this scene conveys the destructive potential of commercial transactions by combining the age-old fascination of Eastern luxury and *mirabilia* with contemporary conceptions of the East as a space of imperial-economic activity and acquisition. Since the nightmares in *Vathek* originate within an international trading network, they also foreshadow the increasingly global reach of British commercial and colonial power: if the *giaour* is a 'monstrous embodiment of the slave economy on which Beckford's vast fortune depended', by the same token he figures 'the potentially destructive allure of Britain's own rapidly growing Eastern empire'.[24] Relatedly, Vathek's hellward expedition reads as a fictional analogue of the countless diplomatic, military and exploratory forays into the East undertaken by England and Britain since the early modern era.

By collapsing political and economic issues into the autobiographically resonant bizarrerie of *Vathek*, Beckford – whose family wealth came from

---

19 Beckford, *Vathek*, p. 38.   20 Beckford, *Vathek*, pp. 14, 5, 6.
21 Beckford, *Vathek*, pp. 7, 5.   22 Beckford, *Vathek*, p. 5.
23 Beckford, *Vathek*, pp. 6, 22.
24 James Watt, 'Orientalism and Empire', in Richard Maxwell and Katie Trumpener (eds), *The Cambridge Companion to Fiction in the Romantic Period* (Cambridge: Cambridge University Press, 2008), pp. 129–42 (p. 130).

Jamaican sugar plantations, merchant interests and financial investments on the London stock exchange – narratively translated the intricate system of 'chains of causation' and 'modes of connection' that, at the turn of the century, were laying the ground for later developments of globalisation.[25] In his solidly documented visionary extravaganza, the fabled wealth and timeless terrors of the Orient are fitted into a narrative of commercial exchange and imperial exploration and conquest. Thus *Vathek* depicts the East as terrifying not merely because of its otherness, but also because it features processes of commercial circulation that make it not only 'out there', relegated to a safe distance, but also potentially bring it 'over here'. This thematic and ideological pattern is recurrent in much Romantic-period Oriental Gothic, more or less conspicuously pervading its textual canon.

A coded inscription of these concerns is offered by Charlotte Dacre's *Zofloya; or, The Moor* (1806), whose title-character hints at contemporary debates on slavery,[26] while being also connected with two major centres of the history of imperialism and commercial capitalism in the Renaissance – Venice and Granada. A year later, Matthew Gregory Lewis, whose *The Monk* was one of Dacre's models in *Zofloya*, published 'The Anaconda' (*Romantic Tales*, 1808), where he offered an explicit treatment of the threats of commercial-imperial exchanges in an Eastern setting. Set within a humorous frame, this tale retrospectively narrates the encounter of Western colonists in Ceylon with the terrifying snake. 'The Anaconda' stands out for its unsettling atmosphere of commercial-imperial terror and horror based on an effective use of claustrophobia, suspense, multiple dangers and *coups de théâtre*; also, its colonial setting resonates strongly with Lewis's status as a plantation owner and the author of *Journal of a West India Proprietor*, which, though published in 1834, covered earlier visits to his Jamaican estates. In the external frame of the tale, the busybodies of a provincial English town are suspicious of the returning colonial entrepreneur Everard and accuse him of coming by his wealth by murdering a certain Anne O'Condor (a transparent, tellingly Irish, garbling of the exotic name of the snake). To clear his reputation, he reveals how he obtained his fortune in a narrative that weaves him and the snake into an intricate series of metaphorical and real exchanges.

---

25 David Armitage and Sanjay Subrahmanyam, 'Introduction: The Age of Revolutions, c. 1760–1840 – Global Causation, Connection, and Comparison', in David Armitage and Sanjay Subrahmanyam (eds), *The Age of Revolutions in Global Context, c. 1760–1840* (Basingstoke and New York: Palgrave Macmillan, 2010), pp. xii–xxxii (p. xiv).

26 Kim Ian Michasiw, 'Charlotte Dacre's Postcolonial Moor', in Andrew Smith and William Hughes (eds), *Empire and the Gothic*, pp. 35–55 (p. 52).

Everard begins by confirming that his 'fortune was made in the island of Ceylon' and that Seafield, his aptly named employer, had left England 'in pursuit of fortune to the East', where the 'capricious goddess ... showered her favours upon his head with the most unwearied profusion'.[27] This context of acquisition, production and superabundance is a reprise of the myth of the Orient as a *cornucopia* that symbolically generates the snake that appears on Seafield's estate and traps him in a pavilion from which Everard and some native servants try to rescue him. Excess is written all over the slithery body of the gigantic (feminised) reptile, with her repulsively fascinating 'enormous thickness', 'the singular richness and beauty of her tints' and the unearthly speed and strength with which she 'dart[s] herself from tree to tree with tremendous leaps'.[28] Straddling the natural and the supernatural, Lewis's anaconda is an extremely physical creature, his description insisting on its bulk, movements, skin, jaw, eyes and the 'black tongue' it uses to separate the flesh from the bones of its victims.[29] Indeed, it is an almost too potent token of the terrors of Eastern otherness, thanks, too, to the material-symbolic nexus of abjection present in the references to rotting and decay associated with 'the pestilential vapours, constantly exhaling' from its jaws, which prove fatal for the trapped plantation owner.[30]

By interlinking Seafield, his employee and later heir Everard, and the deadly snake, Lewis conjures up a network of exchanges that throws into relief a desirable yet uncontrollable Eastern profusion and Western commercial and territorial acquisitiveness. In the process, the anaconda is more than a terrifying cypher for the East dealing out retribution to the exploitative Western characters: it stands also for the West and its global expansionism, as intimated by its infectious vapours and its description as 'the most voracious animal in nature'.[31] Such economically induced contagion is fittingly Janus-faced. Exchange is figured as a destabilising force that both enriches the West and undermines it (witness the emaciated form of the rescued but dying Seafield). However, if the snake's victim is a colonist, its 'beneficiary' is yet another colonial entrepreneur, the now wealthy Everard. As it concludes with his inheriting his master's fortune, the tale announces the unstoppable self-renewal of a system of imperial, colonial and

---

27 Matthew Gregory Lewis, 'The Anaconda', in Peter Haining (ed.), *Great British Tales of Terror: Gothic Stories of Horror and Romance 1765–1840* (Harmondsworth: Penguin, 1973), pp. 82–132 (p. 94).
28 Lewis, 'The Anaconda', pp. 104, 103, 113.   29 Lewis, 'The Anaconda', p. 106.
30 Lewis, 'The Anaconda', p. 120.   31 Lewis, 'The Anaconda', p. 121.

commercial control and exploitation that, as suggested above, could also be read as an allusion to the closer colonial domain of Ireland.[32]

In addition to being the most enduring Romantic-period inscription of monstrosity, Mary Shelley's *Frankenstein* (1818) also presents significant links to commercial and Oriental themes. Though critics have amply explored the novel's engagements with Orientalist discourse and the Creature's racial and imperial implications, this focus can be expanded further by recovering its reworking of themes related to the East and (fatal) commercial exchanges within a plot that, as its internal calendar suggests, is set in the last decade of the eighteenth century.[33] Pervading its different narrative levels, this knot of issues informs its evocation of a nightmare of potentially global proportions, including yet also exceeding the Creature's direct threat to Victor Frankenstein, his relatives and friends.

Victor's narrative, and particularly the visionary glimpse which sets off his project, are rooted in the *Nights*, since he confesses to Captain Robert Walton: 'I was like the Arabian who had been buried with the dead, and found a passage to life aided only by one glimmering … light.'[34] With this reference to Sindbad's fourth voyage, Victor seeks to explain himself to himself and to Walton through one of the most popular characters in the *Nights*, one whose tales mix the real and the fantastic, the supernatural and the material, and who is both a sailor and 'a merchant from the city of Baghdad', his first adventure involving other merchants and business deals with them.[35] Sindbad's restless travelling signifies the unstoppable nature of commercial circulation and depicts the Orient as a network of lines of exchange; but, in addition, Sindbad himself becomes a traded item when, on his seventh and last voyage, he is captured and sold to a merchant who employs him to hunt for ivory, which, in the tale's happy conclusion, the merchant partly gifts to him.

Victor's binding of his 'great and overwhelming' discovery to an East crossed by trading routes and commercial interests unveils a widespread presence of references to commerce and the Orient in the novel. Walton

---

32 See Julia Wright, 'Lewis's "Anaconda": gothic homonyms and sympathetic distinction', *Gothic Studies* 3:3 (2001): 262–78.
33 For a summary of these interpretations by, among others, H. L. Malchow, Joseph W. Lew, D. S. Neff and Anne K. Mellor, see Elizabeth A. Bohls, *Romantic Literature and Postcolonial Studies* (Edinburgh: Edinburgh University Press, 2013), pp. 167–74.
34 Mary Shelley, *Frankenstein: The 1818 Text*, edited by Marilyn Butler (Oxford: Oxford University Press, 1993), p. 35.
35 Robert L. Mack (ed.), *Arabian Nights' Entertainments* (Oxford: Oxford University Press, 1995), pp. 142–3.

mentions the merchants in the Russian port of Archangel a mere few paragraphs before his reference to Coleridge's 'The Rime of the Ancient Mariner', thus entwining symbolic-metaphysical wandering and practical, commercially motivated travelling.[36] Within Victor's narrative, this link re-emerges in Henry Clerval's story, where trade is explicitly associated with the Orient. The son of a Geneva merchant who expects him to follow in his professional footsteps, Clerval aspires to be both a merchant and a man of culture and, on joining Victor at Ingolstadt, gives free rein to his Orientalist passion by studying Asian languages and poetry and writing stories in the style of the *Nights* – both pursuits converging into his plan to become a colonial administrator in the 1831 edition.[37]

The Creature's inset narrative connects this thematic-ideological nexus with historic cycles of imperial conquest and global expansion in the tale of the 'sweet Arabian' Safie. Her father a Turkish merchant (and a stereotypically untrustworthy Oriental, at that) and her mother an enslaved Christian Arab (thus essentially a traded commodity), Safie is at the centre of exchanges which, in objectifying her, bear importantly on her role as an analogue of the Creature, who shares her process of learning and development. In this light, the Orient lies at the heart of the novel not merely because Safie's tale is literally placed halfway through it, but also because of its central role in unleashing the Creature's destructive force. It is Safie's lover, Felix de Lacey, who instructs her about her own identity as an Oriental through Constantin de Volney's *Les Ruines: ou méditations sur les révolutions des empires* (1791; translated into English as *The Ruins; or, A Survey of the Revolutions of Empires* in 1792), where she reads about her own 'slothful' people.[38] Similarly, it is Felix who precipitates the final transformation of the Creature, teaching him to become evil by violently chasing him from the de Laceys' hut: 'thanks to the lessons of Felix, and the sanguinary laws of man, I have learned how to work mischief'.[39]

Featuring in the frame (Walton), Victor's narrative (Clerval and Victor's mother, Caroline Beaufort, the daughter of a failed merchant) and the Creature's narrative (Safie), trade and the East are directly pertinent to the novel's tragic events, though also to its less conspicuous but equally disturbing foreshadowings. And their association with the Creature is the most

---

36 Shelley, *Frankenstein*, pp. 9–10.
37 Shelley, *Frankenstein*, pp. 21–8, 49–50, 51, 216, 225. See Joseph W. Lew, 'The deceptive other: Mary Shelley's critique of orientalism in *Frankenstein*', *Studies in Romanticism* 30:2 (1991): 255–83 (pp. 262–4).
38 Shelley, *Frankenstein*, p. 95.   39 Shelley, *Frankenstein*, p. 118.

significant locus of the three, since the starting point of his destructive agency lies in an Orientalised context. Moreover, commerce and the East bear on the global threat posed by the Creature's potential spreading of violence, since his reproduction is envisaged as a contagion that is ultimately a form of circulation akin to that of mercantile and imperial expansion.[40] Victor conceives of the possible effects of his experiment in global terms, for, when he laments 'I had turned loose into the world a depraved wretch', one who 'might desolate the world', he conjectures the end of the human race.[41] Concurrently, the Creature's imagined contagion depends on the interconnectedness of a commercially intertwined globe where it moves around freely and rapidly – crossing the seas just like Victor or Walton (for instance, he boards 'a vessel bound for the Black Sea') and, at the end, appearing suddenly in front of Walton on board the ship 'returning to England', so that for an instant the Creature seems to be bound for the readers' own country and imperial metropole.[42] These concerns continued to stimulate Mary Shelley's reflections on the catastrophes generated by commerce, and she reprised them in her dystopian novel *The Last Man* (1826), where Constantinople returns as the capital of a failing empire, a commercial *entrepôt* between East and West and the original place of the lethal epidemic that destroys humankind.[43]

The encounter between the Orient and Western commercial imperialism takes on nightmarish proportions in Maturin's *Melmoth*, too, where the claustrophobic atmospheres of the Inquisition in 'Tale of the Spaniard' contrast with the transoceanic vistas and anxieties of 'Tale of the Indians'. The latter issues a vigorous denunciation of commercial imperialism and colonialism, re-echoing late eighteenth-century critiques and resonating with the author's own troubled sense of Irishness.[44] Sharing the Iberian theme of 'Tale of the Spaniard', 'Tale of the Indians' stands out from the novel's other narratives for its central position and because it features Melmoth as most actively torturing his designated victim, Immalee. A daughter of nature, she

---

40 See Miranda Burgess, 'Transporting *Frankenstein*: Mary Shelley's mobile figures', *European Romantic Review* 25:3 (2014): 247–65.
41 Shelley, *Frankenstein*, pp. 57, 119.   42 Shelley, *Frankenstein*, pp. 172, 184.
43 See Joseph W. Lew, 'The Plague of Imperial Desire: Montesquieu, Gibbon, Brougham, and Mary Shelley's *The Last Man*', in Tim Fulford and Peter J. Kitson (eds), *Romanticism and Colonialism: Writing and Empire, 1780–1830* (Cambridge: Cambridge University Press, 1998), pp. 261–78 and Alan Bewell, *Romanticism and Colonial Disease* (Baltimore and London: Johns Hopkins University Press, 1999), pp. 296–314.
44 See Massimiliano Demata, 'Discovering Eastern Horrors: Beckford, Maturin, and the Discourse of Travel Literature', in Smith and Hughes (eds), *Empire and the Gothic*, pp. 13–34 (pp. 24–31).

is a Spanish castaway left as a child on an uninhabited island in the Indian Ocean. Her life is bound up with global trade from the outset, since, as the young Isidora, she is taken to the East Indies to join her father, a merchant who had moved there to restore him 'to opulence, and to the hope of vast and future accumulation'.[45] The bulk of the tale concerns her survival and transformation into a goddess of nature and love by the superstitious locals, until Melmoth starts to tempt her to take on his curse while educating her by showing her the mainland, its people and customs.

As Immalee's island is not far from the routes of 'the gallant and well-manned vessels of Europe', her tale is regularly punctuated by references to commerce and contacts between different lands and cultures.[46] These ships are tokens of Europe's greater technological advancement over the East in comparison with 'the clumsy, and ill-managed vessels of the Rajahs, that floated like huge and gilded fish tumbling in uncouth and shapeless mirth on the wave'.[47] They are also instruments of evil, which the narrator presents in political and economic terms through the eyes of Melmoth, who gazes at 'the European vessels full of the passions and crimes of another world, – of its sateless cupidity, remorseless cruelty, its intelligence, all awake and ministrant in the cause of its evil passions, and its very refinement operating as a stimulant to more inventive indulgence, and more systematized vice'.[48] He observes them as they 'approach to traffic for "gold, and silver, and the souls of men;" – to grasp, with breathless rapacity, the gems and precious produce of those luxuriant climates ... to discharge the load of their crimes, their lust and their avarice, and after ravaging the land, and plundering the natives, depart, leaving behind them famine, despair, and execration'.[49] Though these ships belong to different European powers, Maturin implicitly links them to English commercial interests since Immalee's island is located 'not many leagues from the mouth of the Hoogly', the river on the banks of which Calcutta would be built (the Nawab of Bengal granted the area to the East India Company in 1690; the tale is set between 1680 and 1684).[50]

Immalee's is a story of innocence perverted doubling as a tale about the perversion of global relations through the demonically expansionistic and exploitative geo-economic system developed and exported worldwide by European imperial powers since the Renaissance. As such, 'Tale of the

---

45 Charles Maturin, *Melmoth the Wanderer*, edited by Douglas Grant, intro. by Chris Baldick (Oxford: Oxford University Press, 1989), p. 502.
46 Maturin, *Melmoth*, p. 298. 47 Maturin, *Melmoth*, p. 298.
48 Maturin, *Melmoth*, p. 300. 49 Maturin, *Melmoth*, p. 300.
50 Maturin, *Melmoth*, p. 272.

Indians' endows the novel's other narratives of imprisonment and subjection with broader implications by attaching them to a panorama of exploitation functioning through interconnection and circulation. In this tale, the 'chains of causation' and 'modes of connection' of early globalism become vectors of unmitigated evil. A reimagining of the Wandering Jew and thus closely associated with temporal and spatial transit, Melmoth is inextricable from a global matrix that is once again rooted in the East and which ultimately constitutes a much more effective locus of terror in the novel than the protagonist himself, who, all considered, is relatively ineffectual since he targets very few victims and manages to drive to perdition only two of them, one being Immalee/Isidora.

In Oriental Gothic works, what was usually construed as the immutable and static Orient becomes a space of contact, movement and exchange, which attracts the West and binds it to itself, this enticement turning into a double-edged threat with apocalyptically global implications. Even as it represents other cultures and economic systems, Oriental Gothic more or less overtly addresses Western forms of territorial and economic control and expansion, as well as their destructive potential on a global scale. Thus, the power of Oriental Gothic texts lies also in their making visible *here*, an *out there* that is unimaginably vast in its geographical extension and astonishingly intricate in its geo-political and economic mechanisms and effects.

Gothic Bodies in the East

The imperial-commercial theme permeating, and thus somehow homogenising, the corpus of Oriental Gothic bears crucially on its representations of male and female bodies. In *Vathek*, Beckford displays the Caliph's violent use of human bodies, starting from the innocent children sacrificed to ingratiate the *giaour* in the opening pages; Dacre's *Zofloya* throws into bold relief the Moor's bartered and exchanged body, which then casts an irresistibly physical spell on the novel's villainess Victoria; in *Frankenstein*, Shelley presents the exotic body of Safie as an object of negotiation caught between Felix de Lacey's desire and her father's using her to secure his help to escape from prison. The implications of the fatal exchange and circulation gather momentum with early nineteenth-century Oriental Gothic, as appears from such representative texts as Southey's *The Curse of Kehama* (1810), Byron's and Shelley's Orientalist verse from the 1810s, Thomas Moore's *Lalla Rookh* (1817), Richard Lalor Sheil's tragedy *Bellamira* (1818), Thomas De Quincey's *Confessions of an English Opium-Eater* (1822), Walter Scott's 'The Surgeon's

Daughter' (1827) and the anonymous *The Lustful Turk* (1828). In these works, commercial traffic within a context of Eastern trade and imperial economics characterises the treatment and fate of human bodies.

In particular, Oriental Gothic customarily places bodies under the figurative and symbolic jurisdiction of the Eastern despot, which since the eighteenth century had concentrated Western concerns with absolute political power (the despot's body as the ultimate normative nucleus), a centralised economy (all production and consumption converges on him) and the control of bodies (the tyrant as the pivot of the court and harem). As Alain Grosrichard remarks, this conception of Oriental absolutism, intended as a negative counterpart to Western political practices, was based on a figure who 'is and has everything' within a 'concentric and centralized' system dominated by a 'despotic economy' which Gothic turns into a terrifying physical economy.[51]

George Colman the Younger's phenomenally successful *Blue-Beard; or, Female Curiosity!* (Drury Lane, 16 January 1798) offered eager theatregoers a revision of the tale of the wife-murdering monster in a Turkish setting centred on Abomelique, a tyrannical 'Bashaw, with Three Tails', and his 'magnificent Castle' containing the notorious 'blue chamber'.[52] The beautiful and innocent, though fatally curious, Fatima is given by her father to Abomelique in exchange for favours and wealth (the bashaw has 'wealth and power' and is versed in 'mystick spells, and hellish incantations').[53] The prey of his appetites, Fatima is taken away to the castle, where, contravening Abomelique's prohibition, she enters the blue chamber, an 'inner apartment' offering a concentration of Gothic horrors – a visually arresting crowd of 'flying Phantoms, sheeted Spectres, skipping Skeletons' – and the place where her transgression will bring about the tyrant's destruction.[54]

A denunciation of despotism and oppression fitting both revolutionary and counter-revolutionary discourse, the play is yet another inscription of the economic-commercial features of Oriental Gothic. Enshrining a 'luxury of wealth', the castle is the hub of Abomelique's hoarding economy, which Colman explicitly links to trade.[55] Indeed, with an incongruous turn that can only be explained in light of the economic implications of Oriental Gothic,

---

51 Alain Grosrichard, *The Sultan's Court: European Fantasies of the East*, trans. by Liz Heron (London and New York: Verso, 1998), pp. 64, 67, 71.
52 George Colman the Younger, 'Blue-Beard; or, Female Curiosity!', in Jeffrey N. Cox and Michael Gamer (eds), *The Broadview Anthology of Romantic Drama* (Peterborough, Ont.: Broadview, 2003), pp. 75–96 (p. 79).
53 Colman, 'Blue-Beard', p. 79.   54 Colman, 'Blue-Beard', p. 84.
55 Colman, 'Blue-Beard', p. 89.

the text suddenly veers to commercial language when, near the end, the villain explains his absence from the castle owing to his having 'accounts to settle, – with traders, – Merchants from Gallipoli', refers to his involvement with 'worldly business' and 'negotiation', and mentions his familiarity with the 'Day-book' of 'Commerce'.[56] The spectacular finale in which, Don Giovanni-like, Abomelique sinks 'beneath the earth' while a 'volume of Flame' arises seals the destruction of the lethal connection of commerce, hoarding and the enslavement and subsequent immolation of female bodies centred on the bashaw's despotic figure.[57]

This nexus of bodies, politics and economics continued to metamorphose and ripple across Oriental Gothic works well into the 1810s and 1820s. Published in 1810, Southey's *Kehama* tellingly opens with a striking depiction of the imperial economy of the Gothic East during the night-time rituals held in the capital of the evil eponymous rajah. The epicentre of his political and economic power, as in *Vathek*, the city is where the 'accursed share' takes over through an expenditure of natural resources and human bodies. In Book I, Southey traces a scene of *sati* enriched by a superabundance of luxurious trappings and placed under the all-controlling eye of the rajah hailed as the 'King of the world' and 'master of mankind' – a scene that confirms the poem's thematisation of a destructive centripetal economy.[58] This initial expenditure returns in Book VIII, where Kehama massacres a crowd guilty of foiling a rite to endow him with god-like powers, and in Book XIV with the self-immolation of the worshippers of Juggernaut under the wheels of its giant chariot. The heroine Kailyal gives a name and a face to these countless anonymous bodies as the low-caste woman who challenges Kehama's power with the help of her father Ladurlad. She appears in the opening procession scene, where she is to be killed in order to revenge the death of Kehama's son, murdered by Ladurlad to protect her from his threatened rape, and then she reappears in the procession of Juggernaut as the idol's destined bride. Yet, as in *Blue-Beard*, these iterated attempts at sacrificing her as a sexualised object to Kehama's centripetal economy merely reinforce the events leading to his final defeat.

Though he notoriously counted *Kehama* among Southey's 'unsaleables' in a letter to Thomas Moore, in the 1810s, Byron, together with Moore and Shelley, repeatedly drew inspiration from it and from Southey's earlier

---

56 Colman, 'Blue-Beard', p. 93. 57 Colman, 'Blue-Beard', p. 96.
58 I. 77, 81. Robert Southey, *The Curse of Kehama*, edited by Daniel Sanjiv Roberts, in *Robert Southey: Poetical Works 1793–1810*, general editor Lynda Pratt, 5 vols (London: Pickering and Chatto, 2004), vol. 4, pp. 1–191 (p. 11).

Thalaba, reworking their Gothicised depictions of despotism, imperial expansionism and sexual politics.[59] Byron determinedly mined Oriental materials with Gothic inflections in his metrical tales set in an Ottoman-dominated Levant, which he also imagined as a space of transit and exchange. Oriental despots preside over these narratives – Hassan in *The Giaour* and Seyd in *The Corsair*, for instance – their association with the harem ensuring that the possession and arbitrary use of (female) bodies plays a central role in their lawless, violent universe. Though Gothic in different ways (*The Giaour* more obviously so, with its references to death by drowning in a sack and vampirism), both poems cast this physical economy within narratives of attempted rebellion against an oppressively centripetal regime, as the nameless *giaour* and Conrad the pirate infiltrate the centre of tyrannical power and connect with the body of the woman in the harem (Leila and Gulnare) with dire consequences. In the 1820s, Byron reprised this situation in the Constantinople cantos of *Don Juan* (Cantos V–VI), where the protagonist is captured by Levantine pirates, sold on the slave market, purchased by the sultana Gulbeyaz and smuggled into the imperial harem in female disguise for her own pleasure. In this parodic inversion of a familiar Orientalist and Oriental Gothic topos, the subversive figure is Gulbeyaz herself; by contrast, the Western man does not break into the *seraglio* but is introduced into it through cross-dressing and ultimately ends up sleeping, or perhaps not, surrounded by countless Oriental female bodies. An apparently humorous depiction of an Eastern economy of superabundance, luxury and joyous expenditure, this episode, much like the *Arabian Nights*, is nonetheless under the constant threat of death by beheading, impaling or, as in *The Giaour*, drowning in a sack.

In 1817, Shelley published *Laon and Cythna*, immediately revised and retitled *The Revolt of Islam*, a visionary political epic set between Greece ('Argolis') and Constantinople ('The Golden City'). This highly symbolic, intricate work borrows freely from the Oriental Gothic theme of a centripetal economic and political system sustained by a physical economy centred in the despot – here, the sultan in his palace surrounded by his eunuchs and harem women. In the same year, Thomas Moore reinterpreted this formula in *Lalla Rookh*, his hugely popular collection of framed metrical tales set in the East. His adherence to the Oriental Gothic imaginary is especially visible in the longer narratives of 'The Veiled Prophet of Khorassan' and 'The Fire-

---

59 To Thomas Moore, 28 August 1813, in Leslie A. Marchand (ed.), *Byron's Letters and Journals*, 13 vols (London: John Murray, 1973–4), vol. 3, p. 101.

Worshippers', which focus on different manifestations of the desire for global domination and imperial conquest. Both poems cast female bodies – the Bokharan harem slave Zelica in 'The Veiled Prophet' and the Arab Hinda in 'The Fire-Worshippers' – as the meeting-points of historical and political tensions which, once again, read as coded allusions to global expansionism.

This representation of bodies at the mercy of global forces continued to resurface well into the 1820s, producing a variety of textual outcomes. In De Quincey's 'The Pains of Opium' from the *Confessions*, the body subjected by the fatal Oriental exchange is that of the English opium-eater himself, rendered passive and enslaved by an exotic substance that feminises and turns him into a point of contact and exchange between East and West, concentrating in himself both Oriental trade and the centralising sway of an Eastern potentate (opium is, after all, 'the legitimate centre' of the Eater's narrative).[60] A more literal figuration is offered by the anonymous pornographic novel *The Lustful Turk* (1828), an epistolary exchange between a sexually enslaved Englishwoman, her friend in England and the Dey of Algiers, among others. Explaining in great detail the usual round of sexual acrobatics, the novel harnesses the terror of the woman imprisoned in the harem to intensify the (male) reader's pleasure.[61] At the same time, this graphic rendition of multiple sexual expenditures is significantly set in one of the infamous Barbary states, notorious for their piratical activities and human trafficking, and the epicentre of a Mediterranean network – peopled with Turks, Greeks, Italians and French – centred on the trade of European female bodies. Scott's contemporaneous 'The Surgeon's Daughter' (1827) comparably, though much more demurely, focused on the transformation of a Scottish woman into a pawn of imperial games involving an Indian prince and Western adventurers gone native, and thus into a sexual object traded for favour and preferment. If the skills of the Dey of Algiers finally endear him to his English sex slave, Scott's villain, a renegade European, is killed by being stamped upon by the elephant he believed 'awaited his occupancy' in the tale's gruesome climax.[62]

---

60 Thomas De Quincey, *Confessions of an English Opium-Eater and Other Writings*, edited by Grevel Lindop (Oxford: Oxford University Press, 1985), p. 78.
61 See Steven Marcus, *The Other Victorians: A Study of Sexuality and Pornography in Mid-Nineteenth-Century England* (New Brunswick and London: Transaction, 2009), pp. 197–216.
62 Walter Scott, *Chronicles of the Canongate*, edited by Claire Lamont (London: Penguin, 2003), p. 284. See also Tara Ghoshal Wallace, 'The elephant's foot and the British mouth: Walter Scott on imperial rhetoric', *European Romantic Review* 13:3 (2002): 311–24.

Eighteenth-century and Romantic-era Gothic has an undeniably international thematic scope – from the crusades mentioned in *The Castle of Otranto* in the 1760s, to the African slaves in Lewis's *The Castle Spectre* in the 1790s and the voyages round the Cape of Good Hope in the late 1820s plays on the Flying Dutchman. The East occupies a special place in this global map, as the traditional competing other and 'cultural contestant' of the West, as well as the object of repeated Western economic, diplomatic and territorial forays.[63] Encapsulating the intricate web of an unfolding global order and its threats, Oriental Gothic is an expression of what Saree Makdisi terms 'worldly Romanticism'.[64] By the same token, its terrifying scenarios are inflections of 'the inevitability of human contact, over distances and at speeds and intensities hitherto unknown' conjured up by the 'experience of globalization' and, specifically, the worldly imaginary Evan Gottlieb defines as 'Romantic globalism'.[65]

This chapter has traced a narrative in which late eighteenth-century literature appeared to respond to these challenges by elaborating forms of Oriental Gothic which were then bequeathed to the Romantic era, where they took on increasingly detailed features and came to constitute a set of – admittedly uneven and often more allusive than referential – imaginative reactions to the emergence of capitalist modernity and its effects. This exotic brand of Gothic explores the disorienting and terrifyingly global effects of commercial and imperial developments by compressing them into cultural artefacts that make them disturbingly present and *over here*, replacing sanitised distance with frightening proximity and even intimacy. As a particularly effective '*language* of panic', Oriental Gothic specialised in conveying the unthinkably vast expanse of the global and its intersecting mechanisms of travel, importation, traffic and transit, border crossings, invasions and contaminations.[66] From the eighteenth century to the late Romantic era, it continuously conjured up perturbing vistas linking the familiar and the exotic, inspiring both fascination and revulsion, and tapping into the anxieties generated by a system of globalised synchronicities and interconnections that have shaped the world and unsettled the imagination to this day.

---

63 Said, *Orientalism*, p. 1.
64 Saree Makdisi, 'Introduction: worldly romanticism', *Nineteenth-Century Literature* 65:4 (2011): 429–32.
65 Evan Gottlieb, *Romantic Globalism: British Literature and Modern World Order, 1750–1830* (Columbus: Ohio State University Press, 2014), p. 2.
66 H. L. Malchow, *Gothic Images of Race in Nineteenth-Century Britain* (Stanford: Stanford University Press, 1996), p. 4.

1.17

The German 'School' of Horrors: A Pharmacology of the Gothic

BARRY MURNANE

In his 1827 survey of over 50 years of the reception of German literature in Britain, Thomas Carlyle highlighted a significant stereotyping of German writing as being loaded with 'vulgar horrors, and all sorts of showy exaggeration'.[1] As a prominent translator and mediator of German writing in Britain Carlyle knew what he was talking about, even if his retrospective account suggests that the influence of the German 'School' of 'vulgar horrors' had long since waned since its post-revolutionary pinnacle in the 1790s. This was when the *Analytical Review* in 1796 could accuse German writers like Veit Weber of 'giving unbounded licence to ... imagination' and of being 'extravagant' and prone to 'luxuriousness'.[2] In this discursive construction of a stereotype of the German Gothic, one of the most powerful *dispositifs* was that of toxicology and pharmacology. While Hester Lynch Piozzi speaks negatively of the 'contagious phrenzy' that seized Britain in the 1790s aided by 'German plays and novels of a new sort, filled with ... phantasmagorie' freely available from promoters of 'cheap repository',[3] William Hazlitt speaks more positively of German Gothic as causing a 'fine hallucination' and 'noble madness' when it hits 'the temper of men's minds'.[4] In literary criticism around 1800, German Gothic is conceived as impacting on the reader's mental and moral health, sometimes positively, but usually in a toxic, poisonous manner. On a thematic level, meanwhile, pharmaceuticals and

---

1 Thomas Carlyle, 'The state of German literature', *The Edinburgh Review* 46 (1827): 304–51 (p. 313).
2 Anon., 'Art. IX. The Black Valley; a Tale from the German by Veit Weber', *The Analytical Review* 23 (Jan.–June 1796): 507–10 (p. 507). Veit Weber is the *nom de plume* of Leonhard Wächter.
3 Hester Lynch Piozzi, *Retrospective; or, A Review of the Most Striking and Important Events, Characters, Situations, and Their Consequences, Which the Last Eighteen Hundred Years Have Presented to the View of Mankind*, 2 vols (London, 1801), vol. 1, pp. 511–12.
4 William Hazlitt, *Lectures Chiefly on the Dramatic Literature of the Age of Elizabeth. Delivered at the Surrey Institution* (London, 1820), pp. 346–7.

poisons have a powerful presence in many plots, as for example in E. T. A. Hoffmann's Gothic anti-*Bildungsroman*, *Die Elixiere des Teufels* (1815) [The Devil's Elixirs]. Using this guiding pharmacological rhetoric of horror, this chapter will provide an introduction to the German 'School' of horrors in its late-Enlightenment and Romantic contexts, outlining the productive interactions between Germany and Britain that generated long-lasting effects in subsequent Gothic discourse.

Gothic's Toxic Poetics

For early British critics, German Gothic fiction was synonymous with an image of Germany as a depraved site of necromancy, secret societies and wanton violence, the 'mailed knights, secret tribunals, monks, spectres, and banditti' of which Carlyle speaks.[5] Bemoaning 'the close and more artificial veil of German literature' in which European radicals were supposedly dispersing their revolutionary politics, Hannah More, for example, in 1799 writes:

> Poetry as well as prose, romance as well as history … have thus been employed to instil the principles of Illuminatism, while incredible pains have been taken to obtain able translations of every book which was supposed likely to be of use in corrupting the heart or misleading the understanding. In many of these translations, certain stronger passages, which, though well received in Germany, would have excited disgust in England, are wholly omitted in order that the mind may be more certainly, though more slowly, prepared for the full effect of the same poison to be administered in a stronger degree in another period.[6]

German Gothic and its burgeoning translation industry in Britain were linked both thematically and socially with depravity, and, almost from the outset, were discussed in the material terms of consumerism and consumption. Where Carlyle speaks of 'extravagance', the reviewer in the *Analytical Review* speaks of 'showy exaggeration' and 'luxuriousness', all of which More sees here as spreading corruption throughout society. She identifies as toxic a brand of literature emerging from Germany, one that is driven by suspense and sensation, or *frisson*. This is best captured in the German term for the Gothic novel, *Schauerroman*, meaning literally a novel that causes one

---

5 Carlyle, 'The state', p. 313.
6 Hannah More, *Strictures on the Modern System of Female Education*, 2 vols (London, 1799), vol. 1, pp. 42–3.

to shudder or shiver. *Frisson* is also central to later accounts of German Gothic: Hansjörg Garte speaks of 'Spannung' [suspense] in the context of the Gothic novel and locates this in terms of the bodily affective poetics of German theories of tragedy, while Jörg Schönert speaks of a 'Sensationsgier' [craving for sensationalism] at the heart of these novels around 1800.[7]

What is even more remarkable about More's critical account is that this toxic poetics thrives even in the redacted and censored forms in which these German novels were published in Britain; indeed the dangers are paradoxically intensified by the abridgments that had been introduced to save the British audience from the worst excesses of the German texts. It seems as though Germany's horrors are despicable dangers in even their most sanitised of forms. As a supposed letter to the editor of the *Anti-Jacobin* in 1798 put it, 'The industrious importers of German dramatic *poison* have been obligated to mangle and pare their commodities, in order to make them vendible; – the grand champion of sedition, and chief of *whitewashers*, has been induced to advise his drunken adherents, to obey the laws.'[8] These visions of the literary scene in Germany anchor a stereotype of the 'German School' in pharmacological terms, a trope that is perhaps more familiar to modern readers from Henry Tilney's corrective warning about the excesses of Gothic fiction in Jane Austen's *Northanger Abbey* (written 1798–9; published late 1817; dated 1818). According to Tilney, Catherine Morland must learn that the horrid stories of intrigue, conspiracy and murder that she has encountered in such novels are not transferable or applicable to British culture. Catherine is told that the 'dreadful nature of the suspicions' she has are the product of a 'riot in [her] own brain' brought on by her unhealthy reading habits.[9] Austen's novel not only refers to translations of actual German works (K. F. Kahlert's *The Necromancer* [1792; trans. 1794] and Carl Grosse's *Horrid Mysteries* [1796])[10] in

---

7 Hansjörg Garte, *Kunstform Schauerroman* (Leipzig: Carl Garte, 1935), pp. 9–10; Jörg Schönert, 'Schauriges Behagen und distanzierter Schrecken: Zur Situation von Schauerroman und Schauererzählung im literarischen Leben der Biedermeierzeit', in Alberto Martino (ed.), *Literatur in der sozialen Bewegung* (Tübingen: Niemeyer, 1977), pp. 27–92. (p. 28). See also Michael Hadley, *The Undiscovered Genre: A Search for the German Gothic Novel* (Berne: Peter Lang, 1978); and Patrick Bridgwater, *The German Gothic Novel in Anglo-German Perspective* (Amsterdam and New York: Rodopi, 2013).
8 Anon, 'Letter to the editor', *The Anti-Jacobin Review* 1 (December 1798): 700–1.
9 Jane Austen, *The Novels of Jane Austen, Vol. 5: Northanger Abbey and Persuasion*, edited by R. W. Chapman (Oxford: Oxford University Press 2015), pp. 197, 113.
10 [K. F. Kahlert], *Der Geisterbanner. Eine Wundergeschichte aus mündlichen und schriftlichen Traditionen* (Vienna, 1792); Kahlert, *The Necromancer; or, The Tale of the Black Forest* (London: Skoob books, 1989); Carl Grosse, *Der Genius* (Halle/Saale, 1790–4); Grosse, *The Genius; or, The Mysterious Adventures of Don Carlos de Grandez*, trans. by Joseph

the list of 'horrid novels' consumed by Catherine, but also includes English works that were obviously hoping to profit from the German influx: Francis Lathom's supposed 'German story Founded on Incidents of Real Life', *The Midnight Bell* (1798); Eliza Parson's 'German Story', *The Castle of Wolfenbach* (1793); and her 'German Tale,' *The Mysterious Warning* (1796).[11]

Such polemical accounts of the German 'School' of horrors obscure the real sources and production conditions of the texts that Catherine Morland and her real-life fellow readers consumed around 1800. It is evident in the context of Austen's novel that 'German' is a term also used to describe home-grown British fiction in the Gothic mode; indeed, as becomes clear in the memoires of writers like Hester Lynch Piozzi and More, the 'German School' is also used as a synonym for all that is negative about home-grown British culture in its entirety. In a review of Ann Radcliffe's *The Italian* (1796–97), the *Anti-Jacobin* writes: 'In the meantime, the wildness, the mysterious horror of many situations and events in Mrs Radcliffe are rather German than English: they partake of Leonora's spirit: they freeze, they "curdle up the blood." They are always incredible: they are, apparently, supernatural.'[12] The notorious link between Germany and the Gothic continued well into the nineteenth century, as Edgar Allan Poe's famous dictum that his terror came from the soul rather than from Germany suggests.[13]

In some respects, these British conceptions of German literature were as much the product of British translators and publishers as they were based on actual German texts. Many novels underwent significant semantic changes in the course of translation, and many translators were either linguistically poorly trained or were German speakers living in Britain but with little literary training. Both groups tended to produce stylistically questionable texts.[14] In Peter Teuthold's translation for the Minerva Press in 1794, for example, the exorcist of Kahlert's *Der Geisterbanner* becomes the more mysterious 'necromancer'. Such changes are visible not so much on the level of

---

   Trapp (London, 1796); Grosse, *Horrid Mysteries: A Story*, trans. by Peter Will (London, 1796).
11 Austen, *Novels*, p. 40.
12 Anon., 'Art. V. *The Italian*', *The Anti-Jacobin Review* 7 (September 1800): 27–30 (p. 28).
13 Edgar Allan Poe, 'Preface for Tales of the Grotesque and Arabesque', in *Collected Works of Edgar Allan Poe, Vol. 2: Tales and Sketches, 1831–1842*, edited by Thomas Ollive Mabbott (Cambridge, MS: Belknap Press of Harvard University Press, 1978), p. 473.
14 Barry Murnane, 'Importing home-grown horrors? The English reception of the Schauerroman and Schiller's *Der Geisterseher*', *Angermion* 1 (2008): 51–83; Silke Arnold-de Simine, '"Lost in Translation"? Die englische Übersetzung von Benedikte Nauberts *Herrmann von Unna*', in Barry Murnane and Andrew Cusack (eds), *Populäre Erscheinungen. Der deutsche Schauerroman um 1800* (Munich: Fink, 2011), pp. 121–33.

content; instead, amendments on a micro-level radicalise the horror in the text. If in Kahlert's text one reads 'Furchtbar schwebte der Geist meiner Mutter einher; – meine Sinne verließen mich' [The ghost of my mother floated terrifyingly into the room; – my senses forsook me], Teuthold writes 'The ghost of my mother hovered before my eyes with a grim, ghastly look; a chilly sweat bedewed my face and my senses forsook me';[15] 'Himmel, wie ward mir' [Heavens, what are these sensations] becomes 'Merciful heaven! How I was chilled with horror.'[16] When a bolt of lightning strikes down Volkert during his final confession, the psychological narrative has been completely abandoned by Teuthold in order to revel in a horrific aesthetic of violence and the sublime: 'anticipating the pleasure it would afford me to strike my enemies with terror by my sudden appearance and to feast my eyes on the pangs of the devoted victims of my vengeance'.[17] The English text is littered with such revisions, and it is clear that Teuthold considers this to be in the interests of British taste and expectations, rather than the other way around.[18]

Similar recontextualisations also influenced the reception of Benedikte Naubert's *Ritterroman* [novel of chivalry] *Herrmann von Unna* (1788).[19] Celebrated in her day, Benedikte Naubert was largely forgotten other than as a writer of fairy tales, and indeed the traditional accounts of the German Gothic novel that focused on Goethe, Schiller, Grosse and others often neglected her role as a formative figure in developing the Gothic both in Germany and across Europe as a whole.[20] *Herrmann von Unna*, a sentimental *Ritterroman*, was by far her most successful work in Britain and tells the story of Ida, the illegitimate daughter of a nobleman raised in a middle-class family in Nürnberg, who appears at the court of King Wenceslas and instantly becomes the Empress's favourite.[21] She falls in love with Herrmann von Unna, before becoming tied up in a series of conspiracies, which employ secret tribunals to separate her from Herrmann and imprison her falsely in

---

15 Kahlert, *Geisterbanner*, p. 34; Kahlert, *Necromancer*, p. 15. All translations from the German in this chapter are my own, unless otherwise indicated.
16 Kahlert, *Geisterbanner*, p. 20; Kahlert, *Necromancer*, p. 16.
17 Kahlert, *Necromancer*, p. 138.
18 Daniel Hall, *French and German Gothic Fiction in the Late Eighteenth Century* (Bern: Peter Lang. 2005), pp. 22–4; see also Alan Menhennet, 'Schiller and the Germanico-terrific romance', *Publications of the English Goethe Society*, 51 (1980–1): 22–57.
19 Barry Murnane, 'Radical Translations. Dubious Anglo-German Cultural Transfer in the 1790s', in Maike Oergel (ed.), *(Re)-Writing the Radical* (Berlin: De Gruyter, 2012), pp. 44–60.
20 See Hilary Brown, *Benedikte Naubert (1756–1819) and Her Relations to English Culture* (Leeds: Maney, 2005).
21 [Benedikte Naubert], *Herrmann von Unna. Eine Geschichte aus den Zeiten der Vehmgerichte* (Leipzig, 1788).

The German 'School' of Horrors: A Pharmacology of the Gothic

various dungeons and convents. Ida is accused of witchcraft, murder and high treason and in order to assist her, her adoptive father becomes a member of the so-called *Vehmgericht*, or Secret Tribunal. When the young couple, Herrmann and Ida, are united at last, their happy ending is undermined somewhat by Herrmann being elected as a member of the tribunal's opaque power structures. Naubert's original remained essentially a sentimental romance, very much along the lines of Sophia Lee's *The Recess* (1783–5) or Ann Radcliffe's *The Romance of the Forest* (1791). An anonymous English translation of Naubert's novel appeared in 1794, which seems to have been translated from the French of Baron de Bock.[22] There are numerous amendments in the English text that seem to have their origin in Bock's historical studies, all of which heighten the importance of the secret tribunals in the novel. Whereas the episodes involving the *Vehmgericht* were merely one element of the two-volume German work, the English translation includes Bock's 'Essay on the Secret Tribunal' as an extended Foreword. Prefacing the novel with Bock's polemical study obviously emphasised the *Vehmgericht* and the conspiratorial elements of the plot for an English readership.[23] Naubert's novel was even adapted for the stage by James Boaden and performed in Covent Garden in 1795 as *The Secret Tribunal*.[24] There were also competing stage adaptations around 1800, including a previous dramatic adaptation in German, Johann Nepomuk Komarek's *Ida oder Das Vehmgericht* (performed and printed in Vienna in 1792), a French version of which seems to have been the main source of Boaden's adaptation.[25] Given that these were versions of a pre-Revolutionary text set in a climate of political paranoia in 1794, significant contextual difference began to colour its reception.

Naubert's example suggests that the paths of cultural transfer themselves were no less important in generating the image of a horrific German School of writing. Rather than adhering to any meaningful systematisation that would allow solid differentiation between German and English works, the international nature of these literary relations can be highly confusing. For example, Johann Heinrich Zschokke's bandit-novel *Aballino der große Bandit*

---

22 [Benedikte Naubert], *Hermann of Unna. A Series of Adventures of the Fifteenth Century, in which the Proceedings of the Secret Tribunal under the Emperors Winceslaus and Sigismond are Delineated. In Three Volumes. Written in German by Professor Kramer* (London, 1794) and *Herman d'Unna, ou Aventures arrivées au commencement du quinzieme siècle [Texte imprimé], dans le temps où le tribunal secret avoit sa plus grande influence*, trans. by Baron de Bock (Paris, 1791).
23 See Arnold-de Simine, '"Lost in Translation"', pp. 130–1.
24 James Boaden, *The Secret Tribunal* (London, 1795).
25 Johann Nepomuk Komarek, *Ida oder Das Vehmgericht* (Pilsen und Leipzig, 1792).

(1794) was translated for British readers by Matthew Gregory Lewis as *The Bravo of Venice*, followed by his stage adaptation *Rugantino* (in the Covent Garden Theatre) in 1805. Besides this obvious link, a ballet or pantomime going by the title *Abelino; or, The Robber's Bride*, claiming to be a dramatic version of Lewis's translation, was performed at the Coburg Theatre in April 1805 and Robert Elliston performed and published a play going by the title of *The Venetian Outlaw* (1805) that claimed to be an original work, but which was in fact an adaptation of Pixérécourt's French stage-version of Zschokke's novel.[26] It is most likely these paths of translation and transmission led to the popular association of German writing with Gothic drama in particular. Between Germany, France and Britain – as well as in the interchange between translation, adaptation and original work – it becomes difficult to distinguish any one single point of origin for that which has come to be known in the English-speaking world as 'the Gothic', never mind ascertain a clear sense of what is 'German' about the German School of horror.

For all the talk of the Gothic novel in *Northanger Abbey*, German Gothic was first and foremost associated with such dramatic adaptations rather than with the *Ritter-, Räuber-, und Schauerromane* themselves in Britain.[27] Samuel Taylor Coleridge's critique of the German Gothic in his 1816 review of Charles Maturin's *Bertram* of the same year (again, another home-grown title rather than a German work in the proper sense) is a critique of 'modern jacobinical *drama*',[28] and it is to the 'German stage' in particular that the *Anti-Jacobin* objects with its polemical campaign against the radical 'SYSTEM comprehending not Politics only, and Religion, but Morals and Manners,

---

26 [Johann Heinrich Daniel Zschokke], *Abaellino der große Bandit* (Frankfurt und Leipzig, 1794), no pag.; J. H. D. Zschokke, *Aballino der große Bandit. Ein Trauerspiel in fünf Aufzügen, nach der Geschichte dieses Namens von demselben Autor* (Leipzig, Frankfurt a. d. Oder, 1795); Matthew Gregory Lewis, *The Bravo of Venice. A Romance* (London, 1805); Lewis, *Rugantino; or, The Bravo of Venice* (London, 1806); Robert Elliston, *The Venetian Outlaw* (London, 1805); René Charles Guilbert de Pixérécourt, *L'homme a trois visages* (Paris, 1801), no pag.; see also Karl S. Guthke, *Englische Vorromantik und deutscher Sturm und Drang: M.G. Lewis' Stellung in der Geschichte der deutsch-englischen Literaturbeziehungen* (Göttingen: Mayer und Müller, 1958), pp. 201–3.

27 See in this regard Jeffrey N. Cox, *In the Shadows of Romance* (Athens, OH: Ohio University Press, 1987); Paul Ranger, *Gothic Drama in the London Patent Theatres* (London: Society for Theatre Research, 1991); Michael Gamer, *Romanticism and the Gothic: Genre, Reception, and Canon Formation* (Cambridge: Cambridge University Press, 2000); Diego Saglia, 'Gothic Theatre', in Glennis Byron and Dale Townshend (eds), *The Gothic World* (London and New York: Routledge, 2014), pp. 354–65; and Francesca Saggini, *The Gothic Novel and the Stage* (London: Pickering & Chatto, 2015).

28 Samuel Taylor Coleridge, *The Collected Works of Samuel Taylor Coleridge, Vol. 7, Biographia Literaria*, edited by James Engell and W. Jackson Bate (Princeton, NJ: Princeton University Press, 1984), p. 221

and generally whatever goes to the composition or holding together of Human Society' in German literature.[29] Even respectable literary journals like the *British Critic* or the *Monthly Review* joined in this chorus of fearful criticism: 'In the present state of the drama, when pasteboard pageantries and German spectres have almost driven Shakespeare and Congreve from the stage, we cannot but applaud any attempt to "hold the mirror up to Nature."'[30] The apparent popularity and infamy of drama is an important indication that it is unhelpful to limit the role of German literature within the emergent field of Gothic literature around 1800 to prose fiction alone. Indeed Wordsworth refers in the 1800 Preface to the *Lyrical Ballads* to 'frantic novels, sickly and stupid German tragedies'.[31] As we have begun to see, German novels were also available as stage adaptations, in redacted versions as prologues, harlequinades or epilogues, adapted into popular illustrated prose formats based on these stage versions in widely available chapbooks and bluebooks, and ultimately also into popular visual culture in the form of pantomimes, tableaux and phantasmagoria shows.

The British afterlife of J. K. A. Musäus's 'Die Entführung' (1787), one of his *Volksmärchen der Deutschen*, illustrates this generic multiplicity paradigmatically and leads us to arguably the most prominent 'German' writer of the era, Matthew Gregory Lewis. 'Die Entführung' gained notoriety in an abridged and recontextualised form as a central episode in Lewis's *The Monk* (1796), since when it has been better known as 'The Bleeding Nun'. This inset tale of supernatural horror in which Don Raymond tells Don Lorenzo about his attempted elopement with the latter's sister, Agnes, is essentially a retelling of German poet Gottfried August Bürger's spectral ballad 'Lenore' (1773) through the narrative frame of Musäus's text.[32] This realistic framework is the first major piece of recontextualisation from the German original, as it locates a narrative that was marked as a fairy tale (or *Volksmärchen*) in Musäus's original text firmly in the actual reality of Madrid, thereby generating the *frisson* required by Lewis's fantastic narrative. Musäus's tale, on the other hand, is a convoluted 'anecdote' (to use the sub-title that he himself

---

29 Anon., 'Poetry', *The Anti-Jacobin, or Weekly Examiner. In Two Volumes* (London, 1799), vol. 2, pp. 415–16.
30 Anon., review of Joanna Baillie's *Plays on the Passions*, *Monthly Review* 27 (1798): 66–9 (p. 66).
31 William Wordsworth, 'Preface to *Lyrical Ballads* (1800)', in *The Prose Works of William Wordsworth*, Vol. 1, edited by W. J. B. Owen and Jane W. Smyser (Oxford: Clarendon, 1974), p. 128.
32 On the relationship between Musäus and Lewis, see Guthke, *Englische Vorromantik*, pp. 176–83; I return to the role of Bürger in Lewis's novel below.

provided) about Lauenstein Castle that stretches over several hundred years, starting with the pre-history of the castle as a convent, how the dispossessed and disinterred nuns are said to have haunted the castle until an exorcist banished all but one of them, and finally finishing with a tale of love and intrigue between Emilia and a soldier named Fritz in the Thirty Years War who plan to use the nun's appearance to elope. This prefigures Lewis's love story between Raymond and Agnes, with Fritz mistaking the ghost of the last remaining nun for Emilia and pledging his love for her so that her ghostly skeleton haunts him nightly. Musäus only mentions the visitation of the ghost in passing and it is here that the differences to Lewis's more horrific version become clear:

> Wie die Glocke zwölfe schlug, öffnete sich die Türe, die verlorne Reisegefährtin trat herein; doch nicht in Gestalt der reizenden Emilie, sondern der gespenstischen Nonne, als ein scheußliches Geripp. Der schöne Fritz wurde mit Entsetzen gewahr, daß er sich schlimm vergriffen hatte, schwitzte Todesschweiß, hob an sich zu kreuzen und zu segnen, und alle Stoßgebetlein zu intonieren, die ihm in der Angst einfielen.[33]

> [As the clock struck twelve the door opened and his missing companion entered, only in the guise of the ghostly nun, a horrific skeleton rather than his attractive Emilie. Fair Fritz suddenly realised with revulsion that he had made an awful mistake, started sweating profusely, began making the sign of the cross, blessing himself, and reciting all the prayers he could think of in his state of horror.]

The ghost of The Bleeding Nun in *The Monk*, on the other hand, is elaborately developed and highly visual, the first-person perspective focusing in depth on the affect produced by what is clearly a violent ghostly presence rather than a light-hearted spectral apparition:

> A figure entered, and drew near my Bed with solemn measured steps. With trembling apprehension I examined this midnight Visitor. God Almighty! It was the Bleeding Nun! It was my lost Companion! Her face was still veiled, but She no longer held her Lamp and dagger. She lifted up her veil slowly. What a sight presented itself to my startled eyes! I beheld before me an animated Corse. Her countenance was long and haggard; Her cheeks and lips were bloodless; The paleness of death was spread over her features, and her eyeballs fixed steadfastly upon me were lustreless and hollow.[34]

33 Johann Karl August Musäus, *Volksmärchen der Deutschen*, 5 vols (Gotha, 1787), vol. 5, p. 271.
34 Matthew Gregory Lewis, *The Monk*, edited by Emma McEvoy (Oxford: Oxford University Press, 1995), p. 124.

The explicit visuality of this horrific figure owes much to Lewis's reception of another German text, Gottfried August Bürger's 'Lenore', which was translated from German into English six times in total in 1796, most notably by Norwich-based William Taylor, one of the foremost mediators of German literature around 1800.[35] Although Bürger's ballad does indeed provide an important pretext for Lewis's 'Germanic' poems 'Alonzo the Brave and Fair Imogine' and 'The Water-King', both originally published in *The Monk* and subsequently anthologized in Lewis's collection *Tales of Wonder* (1801), it is notable that both The Bleeding Nun and 'Die Entführung' feature female spectres rather than the male spectre in Bürger's poem.[36] The pattern of heightening the horrific visuality in this manner is reproduced at various junctures, not least in a comparison of the respective exorcisms. Musäus's text is certainly not devoid of the supernatural, featuring as it does an exorcist who banishes the ghost, but again this is narrated almost in passing while the use of 'Unfug' [nonsense] reduces the horror to a matter of ludicrousness.[37] Lewis, by contrast, develops an episode of radical, visual horror: 'Curiosity would not suffer me to keep my eyes off his face: I raised them, and beheld a burning Cross impressed upon his brow. For the horror with which this object inspired me I cannot account, but I never felt its equal!'[38]

This first stage of intertextual appropriation by Lewis was followed by multiple less official and legitimate instances, including plays, ballets, pantomimes and chapbooks such as *The Bleeding Nun of the Castle of Lindendorff; or, The History of Raymond and Agnes* (1799). Such popular visualisations drew on Lewis's appropriation and recontextualisation of 'Die Entführung' rather than on Musäus's story itself. It was presumably the visuality of Lewis's version that made the transition of the Gothic tale onto the stage relatively simple, starting with the 1797 production of his play *The Castle Spectre*, where the ghost of Evelina that appears in Conway Castle was modelled on the description of 'The Bleeding Nun' ('a tall female figure, her white and flowing garments spotted with blood').[39] The Bleeding Nun enjoyed a stage afterlife of different proportions in less mainstream or legitimate theatrical contexts thereafter, featuring as a 'ballet pantomime', *Airs, Glees, and Choruses in a New Grand Ballet Pantomime of Action, Called Raymond and Agnes; or the Castle of Lindenbergh*, performed in the Covent Garden theatre in 1797 and organised

---

35 Taylor's translation 'Lenora' was published in *The Monthly Magazine* 2 (1796), pp. 135–8.
36 See Douglass H. Thomson, 'Introduction', in Matthew Lewis, *Tales of Wonder*, edited by Douglass H. Thomson (Toronto: Broadview Press, 2009), pp. 15–17.
37 Musäus, *Volksmärchen*, vol. 5, p. 272.   38 Lewis, *The Monk*, p. 133.
39 Matthew Gregory Lewis, *The Castle Spectre* (London, 1798), p. 79.

by Charles Farley. A melodramatic version of 'The Bleeding Nun' in two acts entitled *Raymond and Agnes, the Travellers Benighted* (published in 1804, performed in 1809) was attributed to Lewis himself, although Montague Summers seems to think it more likely that Henry William Grosette was the author; it also appeared with the alternative subtitle *The Bleeding Nun of Lindenberg*.[40] This success seems to have encouraged James Boaden (already well known for his adaptations of Ann Radcliffe's novels, most notably *Fountainville Forest* – a version of Radcliffe's *Romance of the Forest*) to produce a dramatic adaptation of his own, *Aurelio and Miranda* (1798); oddly enough, however, he opted to remove the Nun herself from his dramatic adaptation, as the advertisement to the play outlines:

> THIS play is avowedly founded on the Romance of the MONK. The Author enters not into the discussion which that work has produced. His attempt has been to dramatise the leading incident of the Romance, without recourse to supernatural agency.[41]

Boaden mainly reproduces the structure, sequence and content of Lewis's plot, but rather than privileging the supernatural episodes in Germany, the play focuses on the brutal events in Madrid, albeit without the novel's gratuitous sex and violence.[42]

As this example shows, German and Gothic drama offered a dramatic mode that was multi-generic, heavily intertextual and loaded with spectacular effects: texts move across generic borders just as easily as they move across national and cultural borders. Hester Piozzi captures these contradictory moments well: 'taste, no longer classical, cried out for German plays and novels of a new sort, filled with what the Parisians call ... phantasmagoria'.[43] Though most closely associated with magic lantern shows and popular visual entertainment, the phantasmagoria became an affect-driven performative poetics energised by suspense and fear rather than text-based drama, and was familiar from popular, vernacular traditions such as the burlesque, vaudeville and non-patent theatres. The permeability of German Gothic texts across genres seems to have been a crucial means of achieving popularity and maximum cultural reach in Britain, with German, Gothic and drama becoming almost synonymous with one another around

---

40 Montague Summers, *The Gothic Quest* (London: The Fortune Press, 1938), p. 228.
41 James Boaden, *Aurelio and Miranda* (London, 1799), unpaginated Preface.
42 See David Christopher, 'Matthew Lewis's *The Monk* and James Boaden's *Aurelio and Miranda* – from text to stage', *Theatre Notebook* 65 (2011): 152–70.
43 Piozzi, *Retrospective*, vol. 2, pp. 511–12.

1800. On the evidence of the texts and plays discussed here, Germany's claim to 'ownership' of these horrors is open to debate. Nevertheless, by focusing on the deviation from classical taste that stretches generic conventions to breaking point, Piozzi does help us to understand what was meant by 'German' around 1800, and helps us to understand what confused and discomforted critics in equal measures.

Notwithstanding the problems of origins discussed here, British critics sought to differentiate – however insecurely – between English and German tastes. When T. J. Mathias declared 'No Congress props our Drama's falling state, / The modern ultimatum is, 'Translate.' / Then sprout the morals of the German school; / The Christian sinks, the Jacobin bears rule',[44] German literature served him as a cultural shorthand for all that was bad about modernity. Such diagnoses are of interest in establishing an understanding of what the adjective 'German' meant in Britain around 1800. On the one hand, 'German' refers to a morally and aesthetically problematic form of literature originating – or at least purporting to originate – in Germany; but equally – and indeed no less disturbingly – so, it seems to function as a master metaphor for a modern, home-grown British depravity of taste: 'But we are decidedly of the opinion, that neither the taste of a British public will be improved, nor their morals meliorated, by the importation of any productions of the German stage, in the present state of German literature.'[45] German Gothic is a noxious brew that aids the self-destruction of Britain's national character.

Gothic Pharmacology

These metaphors are well chosen, given that noxious, toxic brews and drafts are central motifs and plot devices in many of these works, both in their genuine German and their titular British incarnations. In Zschokke's romance *Abaellino; der große Bandit*, we are presented with the story of the Graf Obizzo of Naples who, having been betrayed by his family, escapes to Venice where he assumes the dual identity of a Florentine nobleman named Flodoard and a penniless beggar who, because of being mistreated by the Venetian aristocrat he helped to save from the robbers, himself becomes a feared robber and murderer known as Abaellino. He engages with the thieves whose weapons of choice are poison and daggers, and although he ultimately

---

44 T. J. Mathias, *The Shade of Alexander Pope on the Bank of the Thames. A Satirical Poem* (London, 1799), pp. 56–60.
45 Anon., 'Art. The theatre', *The Anti-Jacobin Review* 1 (October 1798): 479–81 (p. 481).

aims to serve the state and turn the robbers over to the authorities, poisonous daggers are central to the adventure narrative.[46] This remains the case both in Zschokke's own dramatic adaptation *Abällino*[47] and in the various translations and adaptations, including Matthew Gregory Lewis's *The Bravo of Venice*.[48] Likewise in Grosse's *Der Dolch* (1796–7) [The Dagger], poisonous drafts play a central role. The novel tells the story of the dysfunctional court of a German prince, with an open conflict both between the prince and his courtiers and between the Baron von St. and his wife, Albertina von F., and various plots of sexual and romantic intrigue. At the end of the first part of the novel, a dramatic interview between the Baron (who has been cheating on Albertina) and his wife features a goblet of lemonade concealing poison that she only barely manages to avoid drinking.[49] In Lewis's *The Monk*, Ambrosio is able to gain access to Antonia's room in volume three by engaging Matilda to procure a sleep-inducing branch of myrtle. Meanwhile, in the inset narrative of the Bleeding Nun, Don Raymond only barely avoids being murdered through poisoning at the hands of the band of robbers in the forest outside Strasbourg – where he has taken refuge for the night – because the lady of the house takes pity on him and warns him. Similar scenes of poisoning feature in Radcliffe's *The Mysteries of Udolpho* (1794) and Charlotte Dacre's *Zofloya* (1806). The motif of the dangerous draft is also at the heart of a later Gothic novel that is heavily influenced by Lewis's *The Monk*: E. T. A. Hoffmann's *Elixiere des Teufels* (1815). Inspired by *The Monk*, this novel tells the story of a young monk and talented orator, Medardus, who succumbs initially to the temptations of craving adoration from his audience, and then to the eponymous elixir, a secretive draft entrusted to him which fuels his imagination and oratory skills, but also his desire for physical pleasure. He is sent on a mission to Rome to remove him from these temptations, but with his sensual desires thus awoken, the journey becomes a disaster, with Medardus succumbing to deception, incest and murder. At the end of the novel it even seems as though Medardus is merely living through a punishment for an original act of sin by one of his ancestors (a painter who, likewise, succumbed to earthly rather than spiritual aesthetic pleasures, having drunk from a similar intoxicating draft in pursuit of an ideal work of art many generations ago).

When More, Mathias and the Anti-Jacobins accused writers, translators, publishers and booksellers of engaging in similar acts of poisoning, the

---

46 See, for example, Zschokke, *Abaellino*, p. 41.
47 See, for example, Zschokke, *Abällino*, pp. 60–5.
48 See, for example, Lewis, *Bravo*, pp. 34–5 and 140–2.
49 Carl Grosse, *Der Dolch* (Berlin, 1794), pp. 77–80.

aspersion involved an uncanny doubling of such plot devices. They also, however, implicitly transferred thematic elements from individual works onto a different level of discourse. Thus More writes of people who recommend German works to young females that '[b]y allowing their minds to come into contact with such contagious matter, they are irrevocably tainting them' and warns that 'the heart once infected with this newly medicated venom, subtil [sic] though sluggish in its operation, resembles what travellers relate of that blasted spot the dead-sea, where those devoted cities once stood which for their pollutions were burnt with fire from heaven ... All is death'.[50] Similarly, the *Anti-Jacobin Review* criticised Britain's 'depravity of taste, as displayed in the extreme eagerness for foreign productions', going as far as to suppose that there was 'a systematic design to extend such depravity by a regular importation of exotic poison from ... the new German School'.[51]

In his Prologue to *The Secret Tribunal* (1795), James Boaden makes a similar argument, albeit one that comes out in support of the affect-centred performances of his Gothic melodrama. He starts by lamenting the lack of formal coherence in other plays of the period, knowing full well that his play is no different: 'LONG hath the tragic muse, in secret mourn'd / Her pow'r abused, her empire overturn'd, / Her sacred laws in mixt confusion tost; / Her rights insulted, and her virtues lost.' This is not to suggest that Boaden intended to remedy this confusion, for he goes on to claim that his inclination is 'To waken Feeling, and to touch – The heart'.[52] His aim with the play is thus to reach his viewers through a limited plot focus and the tight, tension-inducing structure. In this regard, Boaden lays the groundwork for the judgement of a rather unlikely successor, William Hazlitt. In his lecture 'On the German Drama' (1816) Hazlitt, despite having little or no knowledge of German, reflected positively on Goethe's *Werther* (1774) and on Schiller's *Die Räuber* (1781) [The Robbers], both of which he held to be central to the 'canon' of the German School around 1800. Hazlitt finds that 'a German tragedy is a good thing. It is a fine hallucination: it is a noble madness and as there is a pleasure in madness ... there is a pleasure in reading a German play to be found in no other'.[53] Hazlitt is heavily influenced by August Wilhelm Schlegel here, whose *Vorlesungen über dramatische Kunst und Literatur* he had reviewed in John Black's English translation of 1805 [*Lectures on Dramatic Literature*]. Although he rejected Schlegel's philosophical bent, Hazlitt did

---

50 More, *Strictures*, pp. 45 and 51.
51 Anon., 'Preface', *The Anti-Jacobin Review* 4 (August to December 1799): vi–xvi (pp. vi–vii).
52 Boaden, *Tribunal*, no pag.   53 Hazlitt, *Lectures*, p. 346.

share the German's Romantic allegiance to the primacy of the imagination in the creation and reception of art. For him, the plays act pharmacologically, 'hitting the temper of men's minds': 'It embodies ... in the glare of the senses ... the extreme opinions which are floating in our time.'[54] Hazlitt praises the radical politics rejected by conservative critics that are purportedly expressed in these plays; as a result, the *pharmakon* of the 'German School' proves healing rather than toxic in his account. The affect-based poetics of Friedrich Schiller's *Die Räuber* is the epitome for him of the way in which literature can 'throw off that load of bloated prejudice, of maddening pride and superannuated folly' that makes up the 'factitious drapery of society'.[55] Boaden and Hazlitt, although very different writers, engage in precisely the kind of affective melodramatic poetics that seemed so dangerous to critics like Coleridge, More and the Anti-Jacobins; what is 'poison' and 'venom' for the one group is the curative principle for the others.

By deploying the theme of poisoning on a different discursive level, the fantastic content matter of the German texts and plays is no longer the sole issue for British critics. Rather, this trope takes on a different status, functioning as a means of modelling and problematising the productive powers of the imagination and their dangers as aesthetic categories in the processes of writing, reading and spectatorship more generally. The production, translation and consumption of the *Schauerroman* is modelled as being pharmacological itself, and pharmacology is the poetological model according to which German Gothic texts are seen to be produced. This is an old argument, of course: in *The Phaedrus*, Plato had already declared literature to be a *pharmakon*, that dubious substance that can both cure and kill. The link between literature and pharmacy lies in the illusory/simulacral quality of representation – the alchemy of imagination. Readers are tricked into accepting the phantasmagoric shadows of the literary world as real, and in the worst-case scenario they could lose contact with reality altogether. These dangers of the imagination are precisely the issue that Austen's Henry Tilney raises in relation to Catherine Morland's reading in *Northanger Abbey*. He claims that she has begun to interpret the world as a Gothic novel, thus slipping off into a phantasmagoric delirium induced by the poisonous pills of her Gothic reading.

Interestingly, the term *Schauer* in the German word for the Gothic novel, *Schauerroman*, adds some weight to these British critiques, implying as it does an affective poetics that draws deliberately on discussions of the mind–body

---

54 Hazlitt, *Lectures*, p. 347.   55 Hazlitt, *Lectures*, p. 350.

dualism with the shudder being understood as a bodily/nervous manifestation of mental/emotional horror.[56] This becomes clear in the reaction of conservative critics, such as Johann Georg Heinzmann, to the effects of reading such novels on the moral, intellectual and physiological health of readers. For Heinzmann, the new reading pleasures of late-Enlightenment popular literature cause readers to experience 'Visionen, Delire, fleischliche[] Begierden' [visions, states of delirium, pleasures of the flesh], whereby the combination of the corporeal ('fleischlich') and mental ('visions') is deliberate. Accordingly, the effects of these reading practices are also figured as affecting the body, with reading producing a list of physical and psychological side effects:

> Kopfschmerzen, schwache Augen, Hitzblattern, Podagra, Gicht, Hämorrhoiden, Engbrüstigkeit, Schlagflüsse, Lungenknoten, geschwächte Verdauung, Verstopfung der Eingeweide, Nervenschwäche, Migräne, Epilepsie, Hypochondrie, Melankolie, die gewöhnlichsten Krankheiten; unsre Lebenssäfte stocken und faulen; häßliche Leidenschaften: Traurigkeit, Unwillen, Mißvergnügen, Eifersucht und Neid, Trotz und Eigendünkel ...[57]

> [Headaches, poor eyesight, boils, podagra, gout, haemorrhoids, constriction of the breast, strokes, constriction of the airways, weakened ability to digest food, constipation, weak nerves, migraines, epilepsy, hypochondria, melancholy, the usual illnesses; our vital forces stagnate and putrefy; horrid passions: sadness, indignation, displeasure, jealousy and enviousness, defiantness and conceit.]

The excitement of the powers of imagination thus impacts on the mind and body, on the intellectual and physiological capacities, in equal measure. Notably, Heinzmann discusses this mind–body dualism in pharmacological terms: authors of popular literature understand 'wie sie mit grosser Kunst und grosser Anstrengung ihre giftigen Pillen vergolden, damit sie desto leichter hinunter gehen' [how to coat their poisonous pills with great skill and effort in gold so that they may be swallowed all the easier].[58]

---

56 Barry Murnane, 'Haunting (Literary) History: An Introduction to German Gothic', in Andrew Cusack and Barry Murnane (eds), *Popular Revenants: German Gothic and Its International Reception, 1800–2000* (Rochester, NY: Camden House, 2012), pp. 10–43 (pp. 11–13).
57 Johann Georg Heinzmann, *Über die Pest der deutschen Literatur. Appel an meine Nation über Aufklärung und Aufklärer; über Gelehrsamkeit und Schriftsteller; über Büchermanufakturen, Rezensenten, Buchhändler; über moderne Philosophen und Menschenerzieher; auch über mancherley anderes, was Menschenfreyheit und Menschenrechte betrifft* (Bern, 1795), pp. 450–51.
58 Heinzmann, *Über die Pest*, p. 133.

At the heart of such claims – as indicated in the discussion of Hazlitt's lecture 'On the German Drama' above – is the changing conceptualisation of the role that the imagination plays in literary creativity and reception. In contrast to the Enlightenment, during which imagination was viewed as a property for translating sensual empirical data into ideas, a form of writing emerged in the final third of the eighteenth century which recognised imagination as a productive capacity in its own right. The imagination here is reconfigured as being capable of creating images out of ideas which then become indistinguishable from the outside world; this is the essence of what Immanuel Kant in the *Critique of Pure Reason* (1781) calls 'productive imagination'.[59] The aesthetic moment of *aisthesis* is replaced by *poiesis*, the constructive power of the writer's fantasy, and, hence, the source of a model of literature that is no longer content with *mimesis* of reality but seeks instead to create its own illusory or simulated realities. This development in late eighteenth-century aesthetics is by no means limited to Gothic works, but it was arguably the Gothic that profited most from the new-found importance of the imagination and its ability to generate imaginary worlds – as Terry Castle's famous account of the phantasmagoric spaces of the mind in the works of Ann Radcliffe has shown.[60] For both British and German critics around 1800, but also in modern accounts of the German Gothic, popular romance is envisaged as functioning in an analogous manner to psychoactive medicinals.

This account has sought to locate the aesthetic models of the Gothic within emergent anthropological paradigms of the imagination and affective patterns of literary reception developing in late-Enlightenment and Romantic philosophy and literature across Europe, using the transnational and transmedial cipher of the 'German School' to reconstruct this discursive transformation.[61] It has also argued that, around 1800, the 'German School' was a shifting descriptor in three central respects. First, 'German' functions as a catch-all term for both home-grown British and genuinely German works adhering to these new aesthetic patterns and best captured in the German term *Schauer*, thereby aiding British critics in their attempts to order and control the expanding popular literary market around 1800. Second, these

---

59 Immanuel Kant, *The Critique of Pure Reason*, trans. and edited by Paul Guyer and Allan W. Wood (Cambridge: Cambridge University Press, 2000), pp. 238–40.
60 Terry Castle, *The Female Thermometer: 18th-Century Culture and the Invention of the Uncanny* (Oxford: Oxford University Press, 1995).
61 Jürgen Barkhoff, '"The echo of the question, as if it had merely resounded in a tomb": The Dark Anthropology of the *Schauerroman* in Schiller's *Der Geisterseher*', in Cusack and Murnane (eds), *Popular Revenants*, pp. 44–59.

works look backward towards the Enlightenment and its corporeal aesthetics of reception (the bodily affectivity described by Boaden), and forward towards Romanticism's interrogation of subjectivity and its poetics based on the productive powers of the imagination (the noble madness described by Hazlitt). Third, Gothic and 'German' figure in both cases as synonyms for one another, and both are described in pharmacological terms: whereas conservative critics on both sides of the Channel viewed this imaginative and affective poetics with grave reservation and encoded it within a toxicological framework, Romantic writers and critics – such as Boaden, Lewis, Hoffmann and, later, Hazlitt – identify an aesthetically and even politically positive valence to the 'German School' as a means of 'curing' aesthetic taste and social disorder. Both sides could draw upon a thematic basis for these judgements, with pharmaceuticals and poisons playing a key role in the plots of many of the works discussed above. Whether as poison or cure, the 'German School of Horrors' was clearly a powerful *pharmakon* in the aesthetic repositories of the late eighteenth century.

1.18

Gothic and the History of Sexuality

JOLENE ZIGAROVICH

As George E. Haggerty asserts in *Queer Gothic*, 'Gothic fiction gave sexuality a history in the first place.'[1] Early Gothic novels such as Horace Walpole's *The Castle of Otranto* (1764) focus on usurped patrilineage and non-normative sexual relations that threaten domesticity. For the Gothic, sexual aberrance coincides with other non-normative economic, gender and racial characteristics.[2] With its monstrous villains, the Gothic thereby invents the 'human' as counter to these broad identity categories: white, male heterosexuals of privilege. It is no coincidence that the first, introductory volume of Michel Foucault's *The History of Sexuality* (1976; trans. 1978) investigates the normative impact of approaching sex in terms of 'sexuality' during the same period that sees rise of the Gothic novel. Foucault argues that the sexualities that gradually emerge in the eighteenth and nineteenth centuries were part of a new normative paradigm. With Foucault's theory, we can see the Gothic as part of the period's discursive 'machinery'. With its supernatural trappings and remote, medieval settings, the Gothic novel seemingly distances itself from contemporary subject formation as it explores and experiments with transgressive sexualities. Across a variety of discursive practices, this chapter will first examine how these anxieties about a post-Enlightenment sexuality generate regulation. Next, it will explore this effect on late eighteenth- and early nineteenth-century Gothic narrative, a form which consistently depicts and dramatises non-normative sexualities, acts and characters, producing pathology and perversion, yet ultimately condemning and punishing these potentials and possibilities in order to re-establish the dominant, heteronormative practice. The aim is to demonstrate that, from a Foucauldian

---

[1] George E. Haggerty, *Queer Gothic* (Urbana and Chicago: University of Illinois Press, 2006), p. 5.
[2] Eve Kosofsky Sedgwick's *The Coherence of Gothic Conventions* (New York: Arno Press, 1980) is an early study of the intersection of class and sexuality in the Gothic.

perspective, transgressive sexualities encountered in the Gothic embody both liberatory and restrictive potentials, and that non-heteronormative desires and acts are simultaneously the product and limit of biopower.

Foucault, Biopower and the Gothic

The influence on Gothic studies of the work of French philosopher, new-historian and sociologist Michel Foucault cannot be understated. A primary focus of Foucault's work resides in the theory that the institutionalisation of human knowledge, as discourse, shaped and constituted the human subject as such.[3] His highly influential theory of biopower rests on examining the socially marginalised, and illuminating constructs that determine the practices of inclusion and exclusion (*Madness and Civilization* [1961; trans. 1964]; *Discipline and Punish* [1975; trans. 1977]). According to Foucault, the taxonomic fields of medicine, law, anthropology, criminology, pedagogy and psychology were all agents of power insofar as they functioned to name, control and regulate the sexuality that they simultaneously helped to produce. These power mechanisms, he claims, 'functioned in such a way that discourse on sex ... became essential. Toward the beginning of the eighteenth century, there emerged a political, economic, and technical incitement to talk about sex'.[4] Sex was not something one simply judged, he explains, 'it was a thing one administered. It was in the nature of a public potential; it called for management procedures; it had to be taken charge of by analytical discourses. In the eighteenth century, sex became a "police" matter.'[5] In the interest of the state's power, there arose a necessity of regulating sex through public discourses. Eighteenth-century examples of biopower include the emergence of 'population' as an economic and political problem that governments must study and control; the policing of children's schools; and the monitoring of children's sex. Foucault recognises that as the Church lost its hold, so 'innumerable institutional devices and discursive strategies' were deployed in the eighteenth century to regulate adolescent sex.[6] Through pedagogy, medicine and economics, sex became both a secular concern and a matter of the state, eventually requiring the social body as a whole to place itself under regulation.

3 Robert Miles, *Gothic Writing, 1750–1820: A Genealogy* (Manchester: Manchester University Press, 2002), p. 95.
4 Michel Foucault, *The History of Sexuality, Volume I: An Introduction*, trans. by Robert Hurley (New York: Vintage, 1990), p. 23.
5 Foucault, *History of Sexuality*, p. 24.   6 Foucault, *History of Sexuality*, p. 30.

Foucault's attack upon the so-called 'repressive hypothesis' in *The History of Sexuality, Volume I* posits, against the claims of a psychoanalytic and Marxist study such as Steven Marcus's *The Other Victorians* (1966), that the nineteenth century was not an era in which sexuality was socially silenced; rather, it was a period characterised by 'the multiplication of discourses' pertaining to sex, even to the extent that it witnessed the discursive 'invention' of the notion of 'sexuality' itself. In particular, the introductory volume to *The History of Sexuality* discusses those deemed deviant by a new medicalisation of sexuality. Foucault argues that 'what came under scrutiny was the sexuality of children, mad men and women, and criminals; the sexuality of those who did not like the opposite sex; reveries, obsessions, petty manias, or great transports of rage'.[7] This taxonomy intersects with feminist, queer and, more recently, transgender theories, areas that have been sutured with Gothic studies and the Gothic novel from the outset. Foucauldian theory can thus help to explain the marginalised, sexually deviant and gender non-conforming subjects that we so often encounter in the Gothic, illuminating the spaces that the Gothic creates for these subjects, and then describing the powers that subsequently demonise (and often torture and expel) these same figures.

From the beginning, Foucault's work on sexuality was developing beyond an interest in the power relations attendant upon notions of sexuality: the multi-volume *The History of Sexuality* was indeed intended to be a genealogy of the formation of the human subject, from ancient Greco-Roman culture up to Foucault's twentieth-century present. In Volume I, he argues that modern power created new forms of sexuality by inventing discourses about it (using the emergence of the homosexual as a distinct category in the nineteenth century, for example). In his account, these distinct categories (defined by psychological, physiological and even genetic characteristics) were actively produced and manufactured by the power system of the modern discourse of sexuality (*scientia sexualis*). Foucault develops a history of sexuality and subjectivity that is often aligned with his history of the modern prison. As with the criminals discussed in *Discipline and Punish*, the sexually 'abnormal' were controlled by the powers of observation and normalising judgements. Both projects thus sought to provide a genealogy not just of criminality and sexuality, but of modern biopower too – a history of the subject as, invariably, 'subject to' modern forms of power. As both projects ultimately argue, we are not only controlled as objects of disciplines

---

7 Foucault, *History of Sexuality*, pp. 38–9.

that have expert knowledge of us but are also regulated as the self-scrutinising subjects of our own knowledge. Foucault thereby questions the ideal of a modern sexual liberation.[8] The irony of our endless preoccupation with sexuality, he claims, is that we somehow think it is coterminous with resistance.

Both Anne Williams and Robert Miles have argued that late eighteenth-century Gothic romance is an important cultural agent in the deployment of Foucault's conceptualisation of modern sexuality. In *Gothic Writing, 1750–1820: A Genealogy*, Miles asks, 'Given the permissiveness and increased care of the child around the end of the eighteenth century, and the stress on happiness in marriage, why were Gothic novels – reflective of the highly repressive patriarchal patterns of the seventeenth century rather than present reality – so popular?'[9] Referencing Foucault's argument in *The History of Sexuality* concerning the regulation of sexuality in the eighteenth century through marriage, Miles maintains that:

> As sexuality detached itself from the deployment of alliance, with its juridical and religious backing, a new discursive field is created and problematised. This problematising gave rise to the deployment of sexuality which overlapped, interpenetrated and contradicted its threatened predecessor, the deployment alliance. During this prolonged moment of uncertainty, tension and ambivalence, Gothic writing begins to take familiar shape, spun from the discourses the moment itself engendered ... At its simplest, the plot of Gothic romance is a threat to primogeniture, the arranged marriage gone wrong through the advent of a desire that proves literally unruly.[10]

Indeed, the Gothic novel emerges at a time when so-called 'classical' discourses on marriage, sexuality and procreation – Foucault's notion of 'ancient alliance' – were being critiqued and replaced by emergent, more modern, notions of 'sexuality'. 'Unnatural' or 'perverse' sexuality thereby emerges in a variety of discursive practices, both to resist and to reinscribe normative ideas of gender and sexuality.

The drawing together of Foucauldian concepts of the proliferation of discourses with the emergence of Gothic literature at the end of the eighteenth century is, indeed, revealing. Foucault speculates that up to the end of the period, three major codes governed sexual practices. While canonical law, civil law and 'the Christian pastoral' determined the division

---

8 Foucault, *History of Sexuality*, p. 159.
9 Miles, *Gothic Writing*, p. 25. See also Anne Williams, *Art of Darkness: A Poetics of Gothic* (Chicago: University of Chicago Press, 1995).
10 Miles, *Gothic Writing*, p. 25.

between licit (legal, marital, reproductive) and illicit (non-reproductive) acts in order to 'constitute a sexuality that is economically useful and politically conservative',[11] the Gothic novel reinforced heteronormative sexuality and dramatised acts of sexual surveillance. Yet it simultaneously participated in a narrative form of sexology; the Gothic can fruitfully be read as a discursive practice that delineates sexual irregularities and deviations. While legal sanctions multiplied in this era, and while psychological taxonomies annexed 'sexual irregularities' to mental illness, heteronormativities were being defined and upheld by numerous discourses (philosophical and literary), including the Gothic. In fact, we might easily align Foucault's list of abnormalities with several well-known Gothic plots. As he writes, 'What came under scrutiny was the sexuality of children' (William Beckford's *Vathek* [1786)] and the later, posthumously published, *The Episodes of Vathek*), 'mad men and women, and criminals' (Horace Walpole's *The Castle of Otranto*; Ann Radcliffe's *The Mysteries of Udolpho* [1794]; Matthew Lewis's *The Monk* [1796]); 'the sexuality of those who do not like the opposite sex' (*Vathek*, *The Episodes*; Radcliffe's *The Romance of the Forest* [1791]); and 'reveries, obsessions, petty manias, or great transports of rage' (most Gothic novels, including *Otranto*, *The Monk*, *Udolpho*, Thomas De Quincey's *Confessions of an English Opium-Eater* [1821] and James Hogg's *The Private Memoirs and Confessions of a Justified Sinner* [1824] (my emendations)).[12] In order to reinforce norms, these 'peripheral sexualities' were explored (but also condemned) by Gothic authors and deemed 'unnatural.' The Gothic novel thus attests to Foucault's abandoning of a repressive hypothesis; rather, it is one of many markers of the 'visible explosion of unorthodox sexualities' and 'multiplication of disparate sexualities' by which the discursive installation of modern sexuality was characterised.[13] Later, during the nineteenth century, this would become known as the 'implantation of the perverse', that discursive means through which *scientia sexualis* extended its reach over a range of aberrant pleasures and sexual practices. The Gothic is thus a device of 'excitation and incitement', as well as a discursive practice that 'stirred up people's fears'.[14] As Haggerty has aptly put it, 'The connections between the history of sexuality (and the growth of sexology) and the gothic are not necessarily coincidental. They haunt each other with similarities.'[15] Steven Bruhm concurs, maintaining that 'Sexuality, as it comes to us through a history of Freudian, post-Freudian and queer thought, is nothing short of

11 Foucault, *History of Sexuality*, p. 37.
13 Foucault, *History of Sexuality*, p. 49.
15 Haggerty, *Queer Gothic*, p. 51.
12 Foucault, *History of Sexuality*, pp. 38–9.
14 Foucault, *History of Sexuality*, pp. 48, 53.

Gothic in its ability to rupture, fragment, and destroy both the coherence of the individual subject and of the culture in which that subject appears.'[16]

As several scholars have shown, binary gendered models fail to account for the diversity of gender and sexual expressions that we encounter in late eighteenth-century culture, an era in which gender and sexuality were being realigned along the binary essentialist model that Thomas Laqueur has influentially called the 'two-sex' model of sex: the conflation of female bodies with femininity, male bodies with masculinity, and non-normative bodies with perversity.[17] As gender and sexuality were being renegotiated, so the danger from the dominant perspective is found to be embodied in the Gothic threat. Extreme, perverse, violent, excessive and masochistic desires find their home in Gothic writing, and violently oppose and undermine the sexual status quo even as they are ultimately rendered functional of it. In the late eighteenth and early nineteenth centuries, we see authors invoking radical sex far more often than other forms of desiring so as to dramatise the blatant transgression of desire and challenge social boundaries and regulations, not only in the Gothic novel, but in popular pornography, prostitute and libertine literature, and even canonical literature of the age too. Charlotte Dacre's *Zofloya; or, The Moor* (1806), for example, can be seen as a consequence of pornographic fiction such as John Cleland's *Memoirs of a Woman of Pleasure* (1748), Diderot's *Les Bijoux Indiscrets* (1748) and Sade's *Die Philosophie im Boudoir* (1795); whore biographies such as Defoe's *Moll Flanders* (1722), *Memoirs of the Celebrated Miss Fanny M* (anon. 1758) and *The Life and Actions of that Notorious Bawd Susan Wells* (anon. 1753); and French libertine literature such as Sade's *L'Histoire de Juliette* (1801) and Laclos's *Les Liaisons dangereuses* (1782).[18] This exploration of tabooed desire is employed by writers in part to reaffirm the power of the normative, but also to carve out spaces for potential non-normative resistance to power. Because of this, the pederast, homosexual, molly, incest perpetrator, hermaphrodite and the gender non-conforming subject (such as Mary Frith, Charlotte Charke, Chevalier d'Eon and others), all incite regulation, prohibition and further discourse. Frith, or 'Moll Cutpurse', was a notorious cross-dressing pickpocket whose adventures were sensationalised in several biographies. Charke, the cross-dressing

---

16 Steven Bruhm, 'Gothic Sexualities', in Anna Powell and Andrew Smith (eds), *Teaching the Gothic* (Basingstoke: Palgrave Macmillan, 2006), pp. 93–106 (p. 93).
17 See Thomas Laqueur's argument in *Making Sex: Body and Gender from the Greeks to Freud* (Cambridge, MA and London: Harvard University Press, 1990).
18 Samuel Richardson's *Clarissa* (1748) can also be seen as an English libertine influence. Dacre contributed to the tradition with her novel, *The Libertine*, in 1807.

and gender fluid actress, was daughter of the playwright Colley Cibber. The Chevalier d'Eon, a proto-transgender figure, was not only a male French spy, but openly cross-dressed and identified as female for decades. Well-known figures such as these openly defied traditional gender boundaries and saw their 'eccentricities' and images circulated in print throughout the eighteenth century.

With the eighteenth-century emergence of the modern British state, and the gradual shift from a domestic to a market economy, the imperatives of social reproduction changed the way in which familial and gender relations were understood. Thus, sexuality became a market tool, not only for regulation, as Foucault claims, but also for the redefinition of familial and gender norms. Paul-Gabriel Boucé identifies what he calls a 'constant problem' of the Enlightenment: 'how individuals could indulge their own sexual passions without danger to the social world'.[19] By producing a horrifying sexual reality, Matthew Lewis, William Beckford, Charlotte Dacre and others expose the process of control that Foucault came later to describe as a pathologisation of pleasure. This force – the cultural system that commodifies desire and renders it lurid and pathological – is embodied in Gothic anxiety. It is the Foucauldian 'deployment of sexuality' that the Gothic prefigures, in that sexuality defies social containment and threatens power even if it is ultimately the product of it.

Policing Genders and Sexualities

Gothic sexuality, a sexuality intersected with transgressions and taboos, is both demanded and forbidden; necrophilia, incest and other forms of 'perverse' Gothic sex represent cultural deviation, yet, at the same time, their discursive practices mobilise the possibilities of a resistance to power. As conceptualised by Lee Edelman, George Haggerty, Ian McCormick, George Rousseau and Kristina Straub, the queer, hermaphrodite, pederast and perpetrator of incest can also be viewed as figures of non-identity that require urgent gestures of social control, management and punishment.[20] The early modern belief that sexual persecution was necessary for social order was rooted in both religious and patriarchal belief systems. As Laqueur, Faramerz Dabhoiwala and other historians of sexuality have noted, in sixteenth-century

19 Paul-Gabriel Boucé, *Sexuality in Eighteenth-Century Britain* (Manchester: Manchester University Press, 1998), p. 20.
20 Jolene Zigarovich, 'Introduction', in Jolene Zigarovich (ed.), *Sex and Death in Eighteenth-Century Literature* (New York: Routledge, 2013), pp. 1–28 (p. 10).

England harsh laws were passed that policed sexuality. Dabhoiwala estimates that up to 90 per cent of the litigation handled by ecclesiastical courts involved extramarital sex, adultery, prostitution and sodomy (a capital offence starting in 1534).[21] In 1552, a revision of canon law meant that adulterers could face life in prison or exile. Sexual transgressors were often publicly humiliated (whipped, branded) throughout the period. As Rictor Norton, Ian McCormick, Dale Townshend and others have detailed, the Vere Street Coterie is one such notorious Romantic-era example. In 1810, twenty-seven men were arrested in a London molly-house, the eighteenth-century term for a social or sexual meeting-place for what we would today term homosexual males. Six of the convicted who had been found guilty of sodomy were pilloried in the Haymarket; a 46-year-old man and 16-year-old boy were hanged at Newgate.[22] Homoerotic activity in the period, of course, lacked a specific definition and sense of legal and administrative identity particular to itself, and fell 'together with other sexual aberrations such as incest, bestiality and necrophilia, under the general category of "sodomy"'.[23] Ian McCormick traces several trials for such sexual acts, including *The Trial of Thomas Andrews, for Sodomy* (1761) and *The Trial of Richard Branson, for an Attempt to commit Sodomy, on the Body of James Fassett* (1760).[24] The prosecutors in these trials often described the perpetrators as 'monsters', their sexual acts as 'poisons', 'infections' and 'diseases' that were capable of being spread to other men. The sodomite also challenged eighteenth-century notions of masculinity. Pamphlet literature and trial records from the period reinforced the sense of a satirised subculture of mollies and effeminate men. As McCormick notes, 'Attitudes to sodomy hardened in terms of an offence to manners and morals; but increasingly its regulation was as much social ostracism as prosecution.'[25] The spectacle of court cases thus gave the impression of regulation, while an eighteenth-century homosexual subculture persisted and even flourished.

As recent scholars have argued, by the mid-eighteenth-century, sexual mores in England and Europe had undergone somewhat of a revolution.

---

21 Faramerz Dabhoiwala, *The Origins of Sex: A History of the First Sexual Revolution* (Oxford: Oxford University Press, 2012), p. 13.
22 See Rictor Norton, *Mother Clap's Molly House: The Gay Subculture in England, 1700–1830* (London: Chalford Press, 2006) and Ian McCormick's multi-volume *Sexual Outcasts, 1750–1850*, 4 vols (London: Routledge, 2000).
23 Dale Townshend, '"Love in a convent": or, Gothic and the Perverse Father of Queer Enjoyment', in William Hughes and Andrew Smith (eds), *Queering the Gothic* (Manchester: Manchester University Press, 2011), pp. 11–35 (p. 23).
24 See McCormick's *Sexual Outcasts, 1750–1850*, vol. 2.
25 McCormick, *Sexual Outcasts, 1750–1850*, vol. 2, p. 11.

Dabhoiwala, for example, has identified a backlash against extreme Puritanism, especially among the upper classes and those in the sexually liberal court of Charles II. In their study of eighteenth-century gender contestation and fluidity, Julia Epstein and Kristina Straub have observed that the boundary between biological sex, gender identity and erotic practices was 'unsettlingly fluid', a state of affairs that persisted across the long eighteenth century.[26] Thomas King has argued for a radical discontinuity between the 'pederastic subjection' characteristic of earlier sexual–social relations and modern gendered 'liberal subjectivities'.[27] Recognising this more liberal understanding of gender, Susan S. Lanser remarks that the vast majority of eighteenth-century people 'lived outside heterosexual dyads ... wittingly or unwittingly transgressed heteronormative rubrics, and disturbed the culture of "his-and-hers" through a wide range of material and representational practices'.[28] And yet, despite this seemingly liberal and fluid sense of gender and sexuality, a growing codification of gender binaries was emerging. The regulation of homosexuality, hermaphroditism, gender inversion and other forms of 'social monstrosity' figured prominently in the development of 'regimes of normalisation', modern-day equivalents of which remain decidedly in place today.[29] Marriage was seen as a customary reinforcer and protector of heteronormativity; with the 1753 Marriage Act, for instance, the British Parliament set the conditions for consensual heterosexual marriages. By the late eighteenth century, the growing prospect that enduring love could be found inside marriage was subject to increasing idealisation. Yet the medical and juridical apparatuses of surveillance often proved difficult to deploy. As urban populations grew, and as the mass media of print culture circulated ideas about alternative sexualities and a well-travelled, global population emerged, so sexual surveillance in England and Europe became increasingly difficult to enforce. In fact, though sexuality continued to be policed in a variety of important ways

---

26 Julia Epstein and Kristina Straub, *Body Guards: The Cultural Politics of Gender Ambiguity* (New York: Routledge, 1991), p. 2.
27 Thomas King, *The Gendering of Men, 1600–1750: The English Phallus* (Madison: University of Wisconsin Press, 2004), p. 12.
28 Susan S. Lanser, 'Of Closed Doors and Open Hatches: Heteronormative Plots in Eighteenth-Century (Women's) Studies', in Ana de Freitas Boe and Abby Coykendall (eds), *Heteronormativity in Eighteenth-Century Literature and Culture* (New York: Routledge, 2015), pp. 23–40 (p. 25).
29 See Michel Foucault, *Abnormal: Lectures at the Collège de France, 1974–1975*, trans. by Graham Burchell (New York: Picador, 2003), pp. 1–29.

during the nineteenth century, the machinery of public punishment had been largely abandoned.³⁰

However, any too overt and extravagant an expression of sexual profligacy, at least among the genteel, still stood at odds with the strictures of self-restraint, moral conformity and decency: the gentleman risked becoming a libertine and if his expressions of masculinity were seemed to be lacking, he was in danger of being taken for a fop. Discursive practices thus still attempted to police non-reproductive, non-heteronormative forms of sexuality. A persistent eighteenth-century example is *Onania*, a text about the vices of masturbation that Foucault himself discusses. In the 1776 edition of *Onania or, the Heinous sin of, Self Pollution and all its frightful consequents (in both sexes)*, the anonymous author states in the Preface that:

> This practice is so frequent, and so crying an offence, especial among the male youth of this nation, that I have reason to imagine, a great many offenders would never be guilty of it, if they had been thoroughly acquainted with the heinousness of the crime, and the sad consequences to the body as well as the soul, which may, and often do, ensue upon it.³¹

Self-pollution, here, is identified as a 'national' disease, one that pertains as much to France as to Britain. The campaign against masturbation in which *Onania* participates was driven by explicit political, ideological and economic motives, including middle-class concerns about self-control, marriage and population growth; medical concerns about venereal disease; and religious notions of 'uncleanness'. Though the treatise claims that it wishes to 'cure' the cultural body of onanism through detailing its numerous harms, the tract actually instructs and details the pleasures of masturbation, thereby inspiring or, in Foucauldian terms, 'inciting', pleasure in its readers. This policing yet simultaneously titillating discursive structure is directly relevant to the Gothic, a genre that, from its origins, was charged with similar possibilities.

Gothic Fiction, Sexual Transgression and Regulation

As Dale Townshend has argued, 'With the rise of the discourse of *scientia sexualis*, a new, decidedly modern discursive arrangement was implemented,

---

30 Foucault, *Abnormal*, p. 358. Foucault argues that self-policing replaces the public machinery of sexual surveillance and punishment.
31 M. D. T. Bienville, *Nymphomania; or, A Dissertation Concerning the Furor Uterinus*, trans. by Edward Sloane Wilmot (London, 1775), p. 4.

ordering and constituting its subjects according to a range of new criteria and demanding that they fulfill a number of discursive requirements.'[32] The deployment of sexuality thereby produces a continual extension of areas for the maximisation of power and control. 'Unnatural' sexuality, from Manfred's near-incestuous desire for his future daughter-in-law Isabella in *The Castle of Otranto* to Victoria's miscegenetic desire for the Moor in *Zofloya*, came to characterise desires and acts that resisted eighteenth-century institutionalised discourses of heterosexual marriage and procreation. With its exotic locales and medieval settings, the Gothic novel marginalises and distances itself as it simultaneously critiques contemporary discourses of marriage and sexuality. While novels such as *Vathek*, *The Mysteries of Udolpho*, *The Monk* and *Zofloya* discipline and punish their sexual perpetrators, they concurrently register defiance and resistance to these same institutional norms.

Lewis's *The Monk* is perhaps one of the most blatant examples of this disciplining and defiance: it explores homoeroticism and criminal sexualities such as necrophilia and incest, but then relegates its perpetrators to prisons and hell. Most of these transgressive sexual acts are centred on Ambrosio, the monk whose moral descent involves disturbing sexual and violent crimes. Lewis introduces Ambrosio as a young monk who has fascinated the inhabitants of Madrid: 'The adoration paid him by young and old, by man and woman, is unexampled. The grandees load him with presents; their wives refuse to have any other confessor; and he is known through all the city by the name of The Man of Holiness.'[33] He appeals to both men and women, and this attractiveness is itself grounded in his masochistic denial of pleasure: 'He is reported to be so strict an observer of chastity, that he knows not in what consists the difference of man and woman. The common people therefore esteem him to be a saint.'[34] Yet, Ambrosio's lack of knowledge also leads him into what initially reads as a same-sex affair when the young novitiate Rosario joins the monastery:

> A sort of mystery enveloped this youth, which rendered him at once an object of interest and curiosity ... He seemed fearful of being recognised, and no one had ever seen his face. His head was continually muffled up in his cowl; yet such of his features as accident discovered, appeared the most

---

32 Dale Townshend, *The Orders of Gothic: Foucault, Lacan, and the Subject of Gothic Writing, 1764–1820* (New York: AMS Press, 2007), p. 55.
33 Matthew Gregory Lewis, *The Monk: A Romance*, edited by Christopher MacLachlan (London: Penguin, 1998), pp. 18–19.
34 Lewis, *The Monk*, p. 19.

beautiful and noble ... The youth had carefully avoided the company of the monks: he answered their civilities with sweetness, but reserve, and evidently showed that his inclination led him to solitude. To this general rule the superior was the only exception. To him he looked up with a respect approaching idolatry: he sought his company with the most attentive assiduity, and eagerly seized every means to ingratiate himself in his favour.[35]

Sensing Rosario's attraction to him, Ambrosio returns the attention:

Ambrosio on his side did not feel less attracted towards the youth; with him alone did he lay aside his habitual severity. When he spoke to him, he insensibly assumed a tone milder than was usual to him; and no voice sounded so sweet to him as did Rosario's ... Ambrosio was every day more charmed with the vivacity of his genius, the simplicity of his manners, and the rectitude of his heart: in short, he loved him with all the affection of a father. He could not help sometimes indulging a desire secretly to see the face of his pupil; but his rule of self-denial extended even to curiosity, and prevented him from communicating his wishes to the youth.[36]

Ambrosio finds himself attracted to Rosario 'with all the affection of a father', but this attraction uses the same language that had traditionally been used to express heteronormative desire in eighteenth-century novels: 'vivacity', 'simplicity of manner', 'rectitude of heart' and an objectification of the youthful face. Notably, Lewis will later deploy the gender-fluid body to redirect this homoerotic potential.

One of the most notorious of Ambrosio's sexual crimes involves the chaste Antonia, the object of the monk's insatiable desires. Not yet aware that Antonia is his sister, Ambrosio utilises supernatural means to overpower and rape her. He is aided by Matilda (the cross-dressing Rosario and gender-fluid demon) who instructs Ambrosio as follows:

There is a juice extracted from certain herbs known but to a few, which brings on the person who drinks it the exact image of death. Let this be administered to Antonia: you may easily find means to pour a few drops into her medicine. The effect will be throwing her into strong convulsions for an hour: after which her blood will gradually cease to flow, and heart to beat: a mortal paleness will spread itself over her features, and she will appear a corse to every eye.[37]

Matilda further suggests that once she is 'dead' Antonia be buried in the church vaults: '[T]heir solitude and easy access render these caverns favourable to your designs. Give Antonia the soporific draught this evening: eight-

---

35 Lewis, *The Monk*, pp. 40–1.   36 Lewis, *The Monk*, p. 41.   37 Lewis, *The Monk*, p. 284.

and-forty hours after she has drank it, life will revive in her bosom. She will then be absolutely in your power: she will find all resistance unavailing, and necessity will compel her to receive you in her arms.'[38] Tainting Antonia's medicine with drops from 'the fatal phial' that has been procured at the convent's pharmacy, Ambrosio later returns to the house to witness her painful 'death'. He is satisfied that 'Antonia had drunk the opiate, was buried in the vaults of St Clare, and absolutely at his disposal'.[39] Surrounded by putrid half-corrupted bodies, the comatose Antonia arouses Ambrosio, 'strengthen[ing] his resolution to destroy Antonia's honour'.[40] When she begins to awaken, Ambrosio 'clasp[s] her to his bosom almost lifeless with terror, and faint with struggling', and gradually makes himself 'master of her person' while refusing to desist from his 'prey' till he 'had accomplished his crime and dishonour of Antonia'.[41] It is then that the reader learns that Ambrosio has in fact raped an unconscious victim. Horrified by his actions, Ambrosio stabs Antonia, simultaneously consummating and destroying his necrophilic, Sadean desires.

As this scene suggests, novels like *The Monk*, in fact, deploy a discourse of libertinism that reflects the hypocrisy of the seemingly demure sexual agenda of Radcliffe's *The Mysteries of Udolpho* and other Gothic fictions of feminine modesty and sensibility. Markman Ellis, for instance, uses Lewis's Ambrosio as a case study of Enlightenment sexuality.[42] In Lewis's narrative, Ambrosio's progress towards sin is driven by his desire to be free from the restraints of his monastic institutionalisation. When he finds his liberty, he indulges all of his desires and lusts, rather than the moral capacities (chastity, virtue, faith) that he thought he represented. Ambrosio's pursuit of the erotic can be taken to epitomise revisionist Enlightenment constructions of sexuality. 'Manly' libertinism associated a construction of masculinity with a particular philosophical and political platform. The libertine, like the rake, was characterised by dissolute licentiousness, simultaneously offering a mode of philosophical enquiry and a form of political engagement. In *The Monk*, Lewis appropriates the discourse of libertinism to his contestation of orthodox manners and morals: in this sense, libertinism is a critique of the sentimental

---

38 Lewis, *The Monk*, p. 284.
39 Lewis, *The Monk*, p. 323. Lewis's mingling of sex and death takes the drugged rape scene to disturbing levels (in fact, it is a rewriting of the notorious 'rape while surrounded by rotting corpses' scene from the Marquis de Sade's *Justine; or The Misfortunes of Virtue* [1791]).
40 Lewis, *The Monk*, pp. 324–5.   41 Lewis, *The Monk*, p. 328.
42 Markman Ellis, *The History of Gothic Fiction* (Edinburgh: Edinburgh University Press, 2003).

transformation of the patriarchal model of female domesticity. Contradicting Christian orthodoxy, new libertine discourse posited that the pursuit of sexual pleasure was good and natural.[43] In his *Treatise of Human Nature* (1739–40), the Scottish moral philosopher David Hume posited erotic attraction or the 'natural appetite betwixt the sexes' as the 'first and original principle of human society'.[44] Roy Porter concludes that, 'These naturalistic and hedonistic assumptions—that Nature had made men to follow pleasure, that sex was pleasurable, and that it was natural to follow one's sexual urges—underpinned much Enlightenment thought about sexuality.'[45] Sexual pursuit and pleasure had now found their alignment with the discourse of liberty.

This liberty 'unnaturally' extends to female characters such as Dacre's Victoria di Loredani, a figure who transgresses the limits of desire but, more importantly, also offers new potentials for gender spectrums and identities. In particular, Dacre aligns Victoria with Lewis's characterisations in *The Monk*. Echoing the scene of Antonia's drugged rape and stabbing is Victoria's rape of Henriquez in Dacre's *Zofloya*. Frustrated that her brother-in-law rejects her romantic advances and only finds the fair and delicate Lilla attractive, Victoria seeks a remedy from Zofloya, a figure who, like Lewis's Matilda, is really Satan in disguise. Only with the assistance of Zofloya's potions does Victoria's body morph into Lilla's so that Henriquez is tricked into having sex with her. When Henriquez awakes after having slept with Victoria while drugged, he is horrified at her transformed appearance: 'Those black fringed eyelids, reposing upon a cheek of dark and animated hue—those raven tresses hanging unconfined—oh, sad! oh, damning proofs!—Where was the fair enamelled cheek—the flaxen ringlets of the delicate Lilla?'[46] Devastated with the knowledge that he has been deceived by Victoria, Henriquez stabs himself to death. With Victoria, Dacre gender-reverses the typical libertine plot and simultaneously rejects and reinforces stereotypes and fears about passionate and sexualised women.

Sexual liberation – its pleasures *and* dangers – is, of course, a persistent theme in early Gothic romance. As Adriana Craciun, Ellis and others have observed, Dacre's Victoria and Lewis's Ambrosio are both spectacularly

---

43 Roy Porter, 'Mixed Feelings: The Enlightenment and Sexuality in Eighteenth-Century Britain', in Paul-Gabriel Boucé (ed.), *Sexuality in Eighteenth-Century Britain* (Manchester, Manchester University Press, 1982), pp. 1–27 (pp. 4–5).
44 David Hume, *A Treatise of Human Nature*, 3 vols (London, 1739–40), vol. 3, p. 53.
45 Porter, 'Mixed Feelings', p. 4.
46 Charlotte Dacre, *Zofloya; or, The Moor*, edited by Kim Ian Michasiw (Oxford: Oxford University Press, 1997), p. 221.

unable to control their passions. Craciun and Ellis situate this within the contemporary debate regarding the nymphomaniac, a woman who displays insatiable sexual desires and appetites. A popular treatise by the French physician M. D. T. Bienville, translated as *Nymphomania; or, A Dissertation Concerning the Furor Uterinus* (1775), describes the 'symptoms' of one particular case study: 'At the mere sight of a handsome man or beautiful woman, my body became restless, an expression of pleasurable possession spread over my face; I could scarcely conceal the violence of my desires.'[47] Craciun aligns this description with Victoria's insatiable desire for Henriquez: 'The frantic woman, incapable of restraining her emotion, cast herself at his feet, and seizing his hand – 'Henriquez! she cried, 'Henriquez, my soul adores you!— behold me at your feet,—I offer you all,—all that I possess—my hand in marriage—grant me but your love!'[48] In *The Monk*, the narrator describes Ambrosio's reaction to Antonia's drugged and naked body in terms similar to those employed in Bienville's case study: 'desires were raised to that frantic height, by which Brutes are agitated'.[49] For Ellis, the rhetoric and symptoms reveal Ambrosio as a type of nymphomaniac, a victim rather than the master of the desires that provoke within him responses akin to rage or madness.[50]

Victoria's fearless appetite for sexual knowledge and pleasure was in fact the focus of much moral disapproval in contemporary reviews of Dacre's text. In the same way that Ambrosio's sexual and moral liberation is inspired and directed by the infernal influence of Lewis's Matilda, so the sexual and moral liberation of Dacre's Victoria is influenced by Satan in the form of the seductive Moor. Dacre also deliberately describes Victoria's eventual submission to Zofloya's will as a marriage, and his attempts to convince her to depend on him are expressed in the language of romantic courtship. As Craciun puts it, 'Here Dacre highlights the subjecting (not liberatory) function of heterosexuality and its central institution, marriage.'[51] Notable is the fact that Bienville's *Nymphomania* embodies the contradictory claims regarding sexual difference and women's propensity for sexual desire and pleasure. He argues that women's sexuality is natural and that its suppression is 'capable of ... causing a revolution, and disorder in the physical system of their nature', while simultaneously emphasising 'the fragility of [women's] nature' and their greater vulnerability to their distinctly sexualised bodies, which

---

47 Quoted in Ellis, *The History of Gothic Fiction*, p. 92.   48 Dacre, *Zofloya*, p. 195.
49 Lewis, *The Monk*, p. 260.   50 See Ellis, *The History of Gothic Fiction*, pp. 90–3.
51 Adriana Craciun, 'Introduction', in *Zofloya; or, The Moor*, by Charlotte Dacre, edited by Adriana Craciun (Peterborough, Ont.: Broadview, 2003), pp. 9–32 (pp. 15–16).

therefore demand regulation.[52] Like Foucault later, Bienville argues that the ultimate danger in nymphomania is social disorder through corporeal disorder.[53] Thrown into the abyss by Satan, the mutilated bodies of Ambrosio and Victoria can thus be read as representative of the fragmented subject, the instabilities within the self that emerge in the face of uncontrolled and uncontrollable desire. Throughout the later eighteenth century, the body becomes an agent of sexual response in its very emotional organisation. The medicalisation of desire can clearly be traced back to the medical and scientific literature of the age. Thus, while the Gothic offers new options for sexuality, it exposes at the same time a threateningly repressed and repressive system of control. The tensions between the ideological imperatives of the age and bodily, sexual and gender expression are rich places for further critical exploration.

In its resistance to the gender binary, the companionate marriage and the growing codification of heterosexuality, late eighteenth-century Gothic fiction famously depicts several graphic examples of sexual and gender play. Alongside Lewis's Rosario/ Matilda, Beckford's *Vathek* is a particularly compelling case. As Kenneth W. Graham has observed, 'Homosexuality, libertinism, necrophilia, and incest' are all present in *Vathek*.[54] The eponymous character rebels against a benign yet restrictive Islam in order to embrace sensuality and forbidden knowledge. The luscious descriptions of Gulchenrouz, Vathek's courtship of Nouronihar, the incident of Carathis and the ghouls, and the Nouronihar–Gulchenrouz relationship all point to non-heteronormative sexuality (such as pederasty) in the orientalised realm of the supernatural, the exotic and the foreign. In one especially remarkable scene, the *giaour* commands the blood of fifty of 'the most beautiful sons of thy vizirs and great men', and as Vathek's mother Carathis remarks, 'There is nothing so delicious, in his estimation, as the heart of a delicate boy palpitating with the first tumults of love.'[55] Such indulgences, however, are seldom left unpunished. In Beckford's companion-piece, *The Episodes of Vathek*, blatant pederasty and homoeroticism are punished, the 'perpetrators' relegated to eternal torture in hell. Through Beckford's revisions of 'The History

---

52 Bienville, *Nymphomania*, pp. 160, vii.   53 See Bienville, *Nymphomania*, p. 70.
54 Kenneth W. Graham, 'Introduction', in *Vathek with The Episodes of Vathek*, by William Beckford, edited by Kenneth W. Graham (Peterborough, Ont.: Broadview, 2001), pp. 17–40 (p. 25).
55 William Beckford, *Vathek with the Episodes of Vathek*, edited by Kenneth W. Graham (Peterborough, Ont.: Broadview, 2001), pp. 65, 126.

of the Two Princes and Friends, Alasi and Firouz', Firouz's sex shifts. In this first version of the tale, Prince Alasi, whose heart 'throbbed with tenderness and breathed only for sensual delights', offers protection to Firouz, 'a young boy more beautiful than the morning star', who uses his beauty to corrupt Alasi, destroy his marriage and his kingdom, and eventually cause his descent into hell.[56] In the revised version of the tale, Beckford transitions the male Firouz into the female Firouzkah and creates the pattern that Lewis would later follow with Rosario in *The Monk*. An 'episode' that he initially wrote to depict same-sex desire was eventually defused for the reading public through strategic appropriation of a cross-dressing (and potentially transgender) body. Defying biological norms, these bodies are concurrently fetishised and disciplined. In *Vathek*, hell-dwellers are punished with marked bodies, and such renderings offer a more common depiction of hell: Vathek and other transgressors must 'wander in an eternity of unabating anguish'.[57] Receiving their ultimate punishment within Eblis, the offenders assume a burning heart: 'their hearts immediately took fire, and they, at once, lost the most precious gift of heaven: HOPE'.[58] Those in Eblis are certainly monstrous and 'unnatural' criminals, their flaming hearts not only a punishment but a marker of sexual transgression brandished and shared by the community of hell.[59]

In the vaults of *The Monk*, similarly, Ambrosio commits his act of incest: inscribed as a dark and hidden psychogeographical locus, the labyrinth and the act of incestuous gratification signal the horrifying dissolution of familial bonds, a cautionary, paternal lesson on the dangers of excessive passion.[60] The absence of symbolic and legal restraints in these subterranean zones that exist beyond the bounds of a paternalistic order confers absolute freedom and complete sovereignty, a return, perhaps, to the power of feudal lordship. Hidden from the eye of observation, Gothic labyrinths, abbeys and castles are, like Foucault's reading of Bentham's designs for the Panopticon in *Discipline and Punish*, an effect of the Enlightenment's 'fear of darkened spaces' and a cultural

---

56 Beckford, *Vathek*, pp. 151, 153.   57 Beckford, *Vathek*, p. 148.
58 Beckford, *Vathek*, p. 147.
59 Additionally, Beckford's flaming heart may allude to the punishment often inflicted upon those condemned to burning at the stake, a common early modern punishment for those who engaged in sodomitical practices. For a helpful discussion of Eblis and its inhabitants, see Jeremy Chow, 'Go to Hell: William Beckford's Skewed Heaven and Hell', in Jolene Zigarovich (ed.), *TransGothic in Literature and Culture* (New York: Routledge, 2018), pp. 53–76.
60 Fred Botting, 'The Gothic Production of the Unconscious', in Glennis Byron and David Punter (eds), *Spectral Readings: Towards a Gothic Geography* (Basingstoke: Macmillan, 1999), pp. 11–36 (p. 29).

attempt to render them visible and legible.⁶¹ Similar to the fate of the transgressors in Beckford's *Episodes*, Ambrosio's criminal acts (murder, rape, incest) and 'unnatural' sexuality (his nymphomania, necrophilic and homoerotic desires) are relegated in the end to hell.

In Dacre's revisioning and regendering of Lewis's transgressive Monk, Victoria, too, must necessarily experience a similar punishment. In fact, she is a unique and powerful example of 'unnatural' gender characterisation and sexuality. *Zofloya* expresses sexual freedom and the desire for knowledge to be gained from sex, yet the narrative ultimately condemns and executes its female transgressor for having sought it. This exploration of transgressive female sexuality can be understood in Foulcauldian terms: 'rather than a massive censorship, beginning with the verbal proprieties imposed by the Age of Reason', Foucault writes, 'what was involved was a regulated and polymorphous incitement to discourse'.⁶² Kim Ian Michasiw observes that, in *Zofloya*, Dacre 'entertains the possibility of a woman's desire—usually a transgressive one—being achieved, only to sweep that possibility away irrevocably'.⁶³ Yet the entire novel that participates in discursive 'incitement' provocatively displays and indulges Victoria's passions. As with Lewis's *The Monk*, we are voyeurs until the novel's final pages, having been witnesses throughout to the possibility of spectacular gender variance. Notoriously, Victoria is unrepentant and unapologetic, attitudes best exemplified in her sexual fantasies involving the servant-Moor, Zofloya, who is Satan in disguise. Overtly threatening sexuality, a staple of masculine Gothic forms in writers such as Lewis, is fundamentally rewritten here. Transforming Lewis's Faustian monk Ambrosio, who gives in to desire and falls at the hands of Satan, Dacre uniquely dramatises the fall of woman in the figure of Victoria, who sacrifices herself for her sexual indulgences. Victoria is also a fully realised version of Radcliffe's Laurentini di Udolpho, whose transgressions in *The Mysteries of Udolpho* simply provide a moral lesson concerning the dangers of excessive passion. In this way, Dacre's Victoria can be seen as somewhat of a Victor/Victoria figure, one who is aligned with male sexual aggressiveness and limitlessness, and who embodies, as Dacre puts it, a 'furor of conflicting passions'.⁶⁴ In fact, Dacre permits her to indulge all of these

---

61 Michel Foucault, *Power/Knowledge: Selected Interviews and Other Writings, 1972–1977*, edited by Colin Gordon, trans. by Colin Gordon, Leo Marshall, John Mepham and Kate Sopher (New York: Pantheon Books, 1980), p. 53.
62 Foucault, *History of Sexuality*, p. 34.
63 Kim Ian Michasiw, 'Introduction', in *Zofloya; or, The Moor*, by Charlotte Dacre, edited by Kim Ian Michasiw (Oxford: Oxford University Press, 1997), vii–xxxvii (p. viii).
64 Dacre, *Zofloya*, p. 134.

passions and illicit sexual liaisons. In depicting an anti-heroine with an insatiable sexual appetite, Dacre dramatises the monstrous results of post-Enlightenment female desire.[65]

Waging war against nineteenth-century bourgeois values, the aristocratic and sexually threatening Victoria receives her just punishment in falling into the devil's arms and being consigned to hell. And, as Craciun has so effectively argued, 'nymphomaniacal degeneration' leads to social disorder; in a post-Sadean world, Dacre's novels show how portraits of destructive women leave neither vice nor virtue intact, but demonstrate how both categories, not just the 'unnatural' one, are socially constructed and similarly destroyed.[66] More recently, Haggerty has argued that through the passions of its heroine, *Zofloya* 'makes a mockery of the heteronormative power of marriage and family'.[67] In his reading, Victoria exists 'to demonstrate how thrilling it can be' to give in to weaknesses and passions.[68] Though such interpretations of Victoria are insightful, we might also read Victoria as a gender-fluid and, as such, fundamentally unintelligible character who is ultimately rejected and destroyed by her culture. *Zofloya* also opposes distinct gender binaries in a blatant manner, most directly through Zofloya and Victoria. The resulting gender continuum is not ultimately forbidden; rather, it is indulged and then necessarily relegated to destruction in the abyss at the novel's end.

Beyond this, Dacre's novel distinctly fits within a contemporary trans-paradigm of gender and sexuality in several important ways. As Foucault and others have shown, 'binary gendered models fail to account for the diversity of gender and sexual expressions in the era', one in which gender and sexuality were being realigned along the binaric, essentialist lines.[69] Foucault explains in his Introduction to the memoirs of Herculine Barbin, a nineteenth-century French hermaphrodite or intersex person, that the objective of social institutions was to restrict 'the free choice of indeterminate individuals'.[70] Although the liberalism of his interpretations has subsequently

---

65 Diane Long Hoeveler, 'Charlotte Dacre's *Zofloya*: a case study in miscegenation as sexual and racial nausea', *European Romantic Review* 8:2 (1997): 185–99.
66 Craciun, 'Introduction', p. 23.
67 George E. Haggerty, 'The Failure of Heteronormativity in the Gothic Novel', in Boe and Coykendall (eds), *Heteronormativity*, pp. 131–49 (pp. 139–40).
68 Haggerty, 'The Failure of Heteronormativity', p. 142.
69 Ranita Chatterjee, 'Charlotte Dacre's Nymphomaniacs and Demon-Lovers: Teaching Female Masculinities', in Ben Knights (ed.), *Masculinities in Text and Teaching* (New York: Palgrave Macmillan, 2008), pp. 75–89 (p. 81).
70 Michel Foucault, *Herculine Barbin: Being the Recently Discovered Memoirs of a Nineteenth-Century French Hermaphrodite*, trans. by Richard McDougall (New York: Pantheon Books, 1980), p. 8.

been disputed, Foucault observes that during the Middle Ages hermaphroditism was widely accepted; when people demonstrated the physical or mental traits of the opposite sex they could openly choose their gender identifications, opening gender itself up to a sense of performance and play. Yet in the eighteenth and nineteenth centuries, this openness was generally restricted. As Foucault argues, medical, legal, social and cultural discourses increasingly required that bodies conform to gender norms, with medical experts seeking to locate and define one true sex in every person. There are, indeed, numerous eighteenth-century medical treatises dedicated to the hermaphrodite, a figure that is associated with Gothic rhetoric throughout: 'mongrell', 'promiscuous', 'monster', 'deformed', 'unnatural' are some of the terms that abound.[71] In Giles Jacob's *Tractatus de Hermaphroditis* (1718), we find various speculations about the causes of an ambiguous body or 'double anatomy' (humours, divine punishment, the health of the womb, excess of seed, and so on). One text that partly supports Foucault's claims is George Arnaud de Ronsil's influential *A Dissertation on Hermaphrodites* (1750), which offers medical interventions to fix genital 'deformities':

> There are others ... which call for all the attention of the surgeon, and in which his understanding and dexterity become of extraordinary use; who leaving to the bare speculative physician, the painful but honourable province of finding out the mysterious causes, his principal concern is to lend a helping-hand to those who are thus disfigured by nature.[72]

The surgeon, here, is seen as someone who will restore that 'perfect harmony, which forms the object of our admiration'. Hermaphroditism was considered to be a deviation or departure from the law of nature and, in order to restore nature's intention, 'monstrous' bodies had to be normalised and intersexed persons were forced into choosing a binary sex in order to curtail the threat that their indeterminacy posed to social and civil order.

---

71 For instance, Giles Jacob's *Tractatus de Hermaphroditis* (1718) includes a chapter on 'hermaphrodites, unnatural births, generation of monsters', and uses the terms 'deformed' and 'deformity' throughout. James Parsons's *A Mechanical and Critical Enquiry Into the Nature of Hermaphrodites* (1741) traces the historical association of the hermaphrodite with promiscuity and describes the hermaphrodite as a 'monster in Nature'. Joshua Poole's *The English Parnassus* (1657) defines the hermaphrodite as 'ambiguous, promiscuous, mixed, sex-confused, mongrel, neuter, effeminate'.

72 George Arnaud, *A Dissertation on Hermaphrodites* (London, 1750), pp. 433–5. See McCormick's *Sexual Outcasts, 1750–1850, Volume I: Sexual Anatomies*, which anthologises numerous treatises on hermaphroditism and other genital differences. Ruth Gilbert's *Early Modern Hermaphrodites: Sex and Other Stories* (New York: Palgrave Macmillan, 2002) provides an excellent eighteenth-century historiography and challenges Foucault's notion that there was ever 'free choice'.

Dacre's characterisation of the feminised demon Zofloya and the hypersexualised and increasingly masculine Victoria can be seen to represent this restriction and violent reaction against unintelligibility. As Ranita Chatterjee demonstrates, Dacre's novel does not fit easily into a binary model of gender and sexuality; rather, it defies categorisation as 'Female' or 'Male' Gothic and thus can be described as 'queer', as can the novel's 'female masculine' heroine herself.[73] More than 'queer', however, Victoria's character is also proto-trans: as an example of what we might term 'transgothic', Dacre's novel – and its masculinised heroine/villain Victoria – best illustrates the unfettered and violent passion that intersects genders and sexualities in the early Gothic novel.[74]

Dacre leaves her readers with the enduring and ever-shifting portrait of a powerful and destructive figure – one that shocked and appalled her contemporary readers, dissolving, as it does, boundaries between male and female, demonic paternal order and degenerative female desire. Earlier in the novel, the narrator underscores this mobile, shifting identity by declaring: 'The mind of Victoria was supremely elastic.'[75] In fact, her transition is a new source of Gothic fear: her 'elasticity' and mutability empower her not only to transgress social and gender boundaries, but to create a new space for exploration and development too. This proto-trans identification might be broached through Jack Halberstam's conception of transgender. Expanding the common understanding of transgender as migration, as a moving back and forth between the gender binary, Halberstam argues for a politics of transgender mobility.[76] Transgender proliferates gender binaries and opens up a *mobile* space beyond and between simple male–female categorisations; in *Zofloya*, Dacre conceived an early literary form of this perpetual movement, strangeness and shifting. Though necessarily destroyed so that the social order might be reconstituted and reaffirmed, Victoria resonates as a destabilising figure, and Dacre's radical vision of gender continuums seems singular and distinctive in early female Gothic writing.[77]

---

73 Chatterjee, 'Nymphomaniacs and Demon Lovers', pp. 80–81.
74 For a fuller discussion of transgothic theory, see Jolene Zigarovich's introduction, 'Transing the Gothic', in Zigarovich (ed.), *TransGothic in Literature and Culture*, pp. 1–22.
75 Dacre, *Zofloya*, p. 65.
76 Jack Halberstam, *Female Masculinity* (Durham, NC: Duke University Press, 1998), p. 164.
77 In Dacre's subsequent novel, *The Libertine* (1807). she includes a cross-dressing minor character. Gabrielle appears as 'Eugene' through a good portion of the novel, demonstrating Dacre's sustained interest in the dramatic power of gender fluidity.

While *Zofloya* constructs a distinctive Gothic subjectivity in its representation of culturally outlawed sexual desire, it also carves out a new space for a range of sexual and gender options. The bodies of Victoria and Zofloya literally represent this widening space. As a revised version of Lewis's Matilda and Beckford's sorceress Carathis from *Vathek*, Victoria develops and increases in power as the novel progresses. Notably, Victoria's body shifts, transforms and transitions. Lilla is the pale foil to Victoria, whose body grows larger and darker over the course of the narrative: 'Her figure, though above the middle height, was symmetry itself; she was the tall and graceful antelope.'[78] Simultaneously, Victoria's physical transformation reveals late eighteenth-century anxieties that the sexual binary was neither fixed nor natural. In fact, the Gothic novel can be seen as a discursive mode for challenging eighteenth-century categorisations and definitions of individuals based upon their biology. Flexible and dynamic, the Gothic allows for this ever-shifting identification. In a well-known example from Lewis's *The Monk*, the young novitiate Rosario befriends Ambrosio in the monastery and later exposes his breast to Ambrosio, revealing his biological gender as female:

> She had torn open her habit, and her bosom was half exposed. The weapon's point rested upon her left breast: and, oh! that was such a breast! The moon beams darting full upon it enabled the monk to observe its dazzling whiteness: his eye dwelt with insatiable avidity upon the beauteous orb: a tension till then unknown filled his heart with a mixture of anxiety and delight; a raging fire shot through every limb; the blood boiled in his veins, and a thousand wild wishes bewildered his imagination.[79]

She admits that her name is actually Matilda, and that she has cross-dressed to access Ambrosio in the monastery. As a rigorously chaste monk, Ambrosio seems to be experiencing his first sexual arousal, but that desire cannot be reduced to heterosexual attraction; it depends, rather, on the combination of male and female traits that Rosario/Matilda presents, and that forbidden combination is precisely what excites the Monk. Homoerotic desire here is buried beneath a tableau of heterosexual libidinal excess, the monastery or convent being what Clara Tuite terms a 'pornotopic setting'.[80] At the end of

---

78 Dacre, *Zofloya*, p. 76. Earlier described as a 'hyena', Victoria is now an 'antelope', the hyena's natural prey, suggesting a shift in violence.
79 Lewis, *The Monk*, pp. 84–5.
80 Clara Tuite, 'Cloistered closets: enlightenment pornography, the confessional state, homosexual persecution and *The Monk*', *Romanticism on the Net* 8 (1997) <www.erudit.org/en/journals/ron/1997-n8-ron420/005766ar/> (last accessed 5 January 2019). Quotation from paragraph 17.

the novel, it is appropriate that Matilda reveals herself as a demon working in the service of Satan so as to construct the Monk's fall from grace: his attraction to the gender-fluid Rosario/Matilda must be seen as demonic. And while Lewis's cross-dressing Matilda does not overthrow prevailing social hierarchies, and although her repudiation of established value systems and her sensual indulgences do not ultimately rewrite patriarchal policy, her critiques and transgressions of established, prescribed gender roles are nonetheless notable, as is her shifting spectrum of genders and sexes.[81] Matilda's gender fluidity aligns her with Dacre's Zofloya, but also, most powerfully, with Victoria. In fact, Victoria usurps male power, destroying both the masculine and traditional modes of femininity, and through this she expands the potential for new gender identities and modes.[82] Lewis's demon Rosario/Matilda and Dacre's Victor/Victoria are compelling examples of the subversive capabilities of Gothic literature, graphically figuring the period's questioning of stable, 'natural', normative bodies and genders. The dismantling of Female and Male Gothic categories and the extension and expansion of queer Gothic opens up the space for redefinitions and continued destabilisations.

Yet, we must at least acknowledge that, as Foucault has argued, the promise of 'liberated' sexual desire is power's most attractive ruse.[83] In those notoriously utopian closing moments of *The History of Sexuality: An Introduction*, we encounter the promise of a world of light, of 'bodies and pleasures unfettered by the weight of the social denominations that define them all the way down'.[84] In this regard, perhaps we might envision Dacre's novel as a step towards the violent separation of the subject from the social deemed necessary, but not wholly possible, in Foucault's reverse-Whiggish vision of history. Gothic endings must necessarily reinforce paternal order and heteronormativity. Like so many other Gothic plots, the ending of *Udolpho* does precisely this: a divine Father is invoked to preside over Emily's companionate heterosexual marriage to Valancourt and to emphasise the law that rewards virtue and punishes vice. Though brimming with transgression and 'immoral' desire, early Gothic fictions remain preoccupied by the laws regulating society and domesticity, and reinforce the necessity of

---

81 Nowell Marshall reads Rosario as trans male. See his chapter 'Beyond Queer Gothic: Charting the Gothic History of the Trans Subject in Beckford, Lewis, Byron', in Zigarovich (ed.) *TransGothic in Literature and Culture*, pp. 25–52.
82 Beatriz González Moreno, 'Gothic excess and aesthetic ambiguity in Charlotte Dacre's *Zofloya*', *Women's Writing* 14:3 (2007): 419–34 (p. 428).
83 Foucault, *History of Sexuality*, p. 16.   84 Foucault, *History of Sexuality*, p. 159.

a moral resolution. As Fred Botting has put it, 'Power and desire, law and transgression, produce, and repress, complex webs of relations rather than forge absolute and inviolable limits.'[85] The concern with non-normative genders and sexualities in the Gothic mode is situated in a network of relations and policing. Necessarily, Gothic fiction dramatises the monstrosity of lawlessness and sexual liberation. In this manner we can perceive Gothic fiction as being a part of the 'discursive explosion' of sexuality over the three centuries that Foucault's revisionist history of sexuality traces. As Foucault observes, 'Where there is desire, the power relation is already present.'[86] We know that Gothic fiction exploits illicit desires and indulges non-heteronormative sexuality, yet, as Foucault reminds us, these discursive practices simultaneously serve the interests of biopower. Surveillance, discipline and punishment are thereby reinvigorated and reinforced. As Angela Wright has argued, more recent theories of gender and sexuality perhaps offer better accounts of the complexity of gender and sexuality representations within Gothic fiction.[87] This is one of the many reasons why Gothic has remained so fertile a place for critical and theoretical exploration. And in our current political climate, it is even more relevant to look back to the Gothic romances of the Romantic era in order to explore the fears provoked by the French Revolution, the issues of nationhood and foreignness, and the growing awareness of gender identities and sexualities. Gothic writers were early exemplars of discursive critique, dramatising unconscious fears and political repression. Though Foucault's legacy has not gone unchallenged, his theories are sutured with the Gothic throughout. Imprisoned by discursive practices that police and discipline, the eighteenth-century subject found the incitement and escalating discourse of sex reinforced in Gothic fiction, yet within its pages we also find glimpses of the possibility of resistance to the power-wielding discourse of modern sexuality itself.

---

85 Botting, 'The Gothic Production of the Unconscious', p. 28.
86 Foucault, *History of Sexuality*, p. 81.
87 Angela Wright, *Gothic Fiction: A Reader's Guide* (Basingstoke: Palgrave Macmillan, 2007), p. 143.

1.19

Gothic Art and Gothic Culture in the Romantic Era

MARTIN MYRONE

There is no art history of the Gothic. Nor, perhaps, should there be. Notwithstanding occasional attempts to valiantly assert a genre of 'Gothic Art' with a clear identity, the concept, or at least the phrase, has not achieved general currency.[1] The researcher seeking out that precise term in search engines and library databases will still more than likely be led to historical works relating to medieval art and architecture than to anything linked directly to what we might describe as a 'Gothic' imagination at work in the visual culture of the Romantic era. While these may provide certain rewards in their evocative illustrations, they are unlikely to answer very directly the researcher's needs. The same researcher who persists will probably find their way to the substantial body of literature around the Gothic Revival in architecture and design in the long eighteenth century. The relationship between the Gothic Revival and the Gothic as a literary genre is, however, not clearly defined, and is neither directly causal nor wholly incidental. The literary Gothic may have a medieval setting, but it may not; artists and writers promoting the 'Gothic Revival' may address questions of imagination and the fantastic associated with the literary genre, but they may not. Horace Walpole's Strawberry Hill and William Beckford's Fonthill Abbey are equally landmarks in the context of literary histories of the Gothic and art-historical accounts of the Gothic Revival. Those iconic architectural productions have an undoubted relationship to the literature of terror and fantasy that we have come to designate as 'Gothic'. But whether the same can be said of ornamental design that makes use of the pointed arches and slim columns of medieval architecture in the period is a moot point. Is a Wedgwood jug with

---

[1] Graham Ovenden, 'Gothic Art', in Marie Mulvey-Roberts (ed.), *The Handbook of the Gothic* (Basingstoke: Palgrave Macmillan, 2009), pp. 127–8; David Punter and Glennis Byron, *The Gothic* (Oxford: Blackwell, 2004), pp. 36–7.

Gothic tracery part of a larger cultural phenomenon that we might designate as the Gothic? Is it 'Gothic Art'?

This is not to say, though, that there has not been a great deal of thinking about the visual in relation to the Gothic in the Romantic era. On the contrary, a leading feature of the study of the Gothic as a cultural phenomenon over the last 20 years has been an intensifying interest in the mode's visual dimensions. Where once restricted to a fairly well-established canon of literary texts, the field of Gothic studies now embraces theatrical presentation, popular print, landscape views, gardening and interior design, optical technologies and side-shows, quite aside from a determined emphasis on the imagistic character of Gothic literary texts themselves. Besides those specifically topical or generic interests, scholarship has also, increasingly, embraced a sense of the visuality of Gothic cultural productions; 'Gothic', David Punter asserts, 'provides an image language for bodies and their terrors'.[2] Hence a recent study of a specific Gothic motif, that of the corpse, defines its subject as 'an *image* of a dead body *rendered with deliberate graphic bluntness* in order to excite and entertain' (emphasis added), even while addressing a range of literary materials in the form of eighteenth-century novels.[3]

If the Gothic scholarship that has flourished over the last two or three decades has vigorously explored forms of Gothic sensation, visual culture, spectacle or visuality, it has not generally had as its primary point of focus those materials that have traditionally been the object of the art history of the Romantic era: oil paintings, watercolours and drawings, and the more aesthetically ambitious, autonomous forms of printmaking (larger, single-sheet prints in line engraving or mezzotint), the relatively high status of which, compared to crafts and decorative arts, was being actively affirmed at this historical moment by the operation of art institutions (art theory, criticism, academies and art exhibitions). Book illustrations, caricature prints, graphic ephemera and advertising material, usually anonymous or attributed to obscure figures, have featured more often than reproductions of oil paintings by the famous artists associated with Romanticism. There may be strictly economic and practical factors in play here: reproducing pictures from major art collections has been expensive and accessing those images often difficult. Illustrated art books cost that much more to produce, and, since art history is a smaller field of study, the uptake is relatively smaller. There may

---

2 David Punter, *Gothic Pathologies: The Text, The Body and The Law* (Basingstoke: Macmillan, 1998), p. 14.
3 Yael Shapira, *Inventing the Gothic Corpse: The Thrill of Human Remains in the Eighteenth-Century Novel* (Basingstoke: Palgrave Macmillan, 2018), p. 1.

also be some issue with the resilience of disciplinary boundaries that divide art history from cultural history and literary studies, and the value systems that hierarchise texts and textual matters above the pictorial. But fundamentally, and rather more historically interesting, is the fact that there are simply relatively fewer works in 'fine art' media that could convincingly be classed as 'Gothic', and which could plausibly sustain interrogation as manifestations specifically of 'Gothic' culture. We are, in seeking out a Gothic art in Romantic-era media and in contexts outside of book illustration and popular culture, repeatedly pushed towards what can appear to be the penumbra of the Gothic as a phenomenon, towards literary authors and genres that may overlap with or be adjacent to the Gothic, but which do not seem wholeheartedly, full-bloodedly so: Shakespeare, John Milton, folklore, bardic poetry, the Bible, Orientalism, the picturesque, literary tourism and the likes.

This chapter is dedicated to thinking about those works of art and the possibility of that meaningful relationship with the Gothic in the late eighteenth and early nineteenth centuries, while attending to a circumscribed notion of art and the artist as these conceptual categories were achieving definition over the same timeframe. It also recognises that as the field of Gothic studies has further mutated and expanded, the possibilities for understanding such relationships have increased considerably. It is now possible to reassess such major figures in the history of art, narrowly defined, as Giovanni Battista Piranesi, Henry Fuseli, William Blake and even the Spanish painter Francisco Goya as also implicated in the Gothic in a number of fundamental ways. If this has been the product of formal scholarship by literary and cultural historians, it has also been manifested in the several exhibitions dedicated to Gothic topics in the visual arts.[4]

In what follows, I suggest that the intersection of the Gothic and art, narrowly defined, may also have some special heuristic value. The value of taking the visual arts into account as art in addressing the Gothic may be primarily in its unsettling and disruptive effects, which may help to expose the dynamism of cultural forms taking shape in irregular and even volatile ways between media, between high and low, the commercial and the esoteric, the rarefied and the popular. At the same time, it may set a certain limit or outer horizon for what threatens to be an endlessly proliferating concept. As much as we may welcome the dissolution of such boundaries within a field of research that might better be termed 'visual culture studies'

---

4 Martin Myrone (ed.), *Gothic Nightmares: Fuseli, Blake and the Romantic Imagination* (London: Tate Publishing, 2006); Felix Krämer (ed.), *Dark Romanticism: From Goya to Max Ernst* (London: Gestalten UK Ltd, 2012).

or something similar, the instrumental force accorded to the idea of *art* as such from the late eighteenth century is critically important. The historical boundary around 'art', contingent, artificial, vested as it is, became a definite and increasingly purposeful force within cultural activity in precisely the Romantic period. It is more than coincidental that the chronology of the original phase of Gothic literary and cultural production (roughly, 1760–1830) matches that of the development of aesthetics as philosophical discourse, and the 'invention of art' as a relatively autonomous field of activity.[5] This occurred with the institution from the mid-eighteenth to the early nineteenth century of regular public art exhibitions, of art criticism as a genre, museum display and national heritage, and the crystallisation of the figure of 'the artist' as a special kind of social actor.[6] Thinking about the Gothic in the comparatively rarefied context as that of the institutionalised field of art as it was taking shape in the Romantic period may have a certain clarifying and disruptive force.

In Search of Gothic Art

If one of the obstacles to apprehending a 'Gothic Art' has been the unclear relationship between the Gothic Revival and Gothic literary phenomena, this relationship, in recent years, has been actively reassessed. Michael Charlesworth, for instance, has noted that 'Despite their historical coherence and inter-relatedness, the areas of architecture and the Gothic novel are now very rarely discussed as parts of a whole cultural movement.'[7] The modern analysis of the literature and visual culture of the Gothic Revival by Charlesworth and others has done much to suggest some greater common ground with the literature of terror, in deeply entrenched anxieties about religion and gender, and in profound nostalgia for a lost medieval past which might be explored in deconstructive and psychoanalytic terms. Looking to the key examples of Strawberry Hill and Beckford's architectural extravagances, Peter N. Lindfield and Dale Townshend observe that 'Gothic Revivalist architecture was to a large extent motivated by the desire to exceed paternal

---

5 Larry Shiner, *The Invention of Art: A Cultural History* (Chicago: University of Chicago Press, 2001).
6 See Geraldine Pelles, 'The image of the artist', *The Journal of Aesthetics and Art Criticism* 21:2 (Winter 1962): 119–37.
7 Michael Charlesworth (ed.), *The Gothic Revival 1720–1870: Literary Sources & Documents*, 3 vols (Mountfield, East Sussex: Helm Information, 2002), vol. 1, p. 5.

architectural example', engaging therein a psychodrama central to Gothic literary terror.[8]

These are shifts that have opened the way to thinking about a large body of images of ruins, historical landscapes, sites and topographical views that might ostensibly have been undertaken for antiquarian, touristic or documentary purposes, but which gained a special charge and value from their resonance with Gothic themes. The British landscape being rediscovered and represented in the heyday of Romantic tourism was, as a recent collection has asserted, a 'Gothic Britain'.[9] Thus is provided a context in which at least some images by such iconic Romantic artists as J. M. W. Turner and John Constable might be reassessed as drawing their visual potency from Gothic sources. The wounded-looking hollow of Hadleigh Castle in Constable's famous image might then be seen not only registering, as the art-historical literature has variously asserted, the depth of his emotional despair in the wake of his wife's death, nor only a generic picturesque interest in ruins, or even a professional gambit in laying claim to the sublime tragedy that might be given form through the native landscape, but also a specifically Gothic sense of the uncanny violence of the medieval ruin. Given the bone-like chalkiness of Constable's palette, the shattered edges of the castle's walls and the solid but spongy protuberances on the shore, we might even begin to indulge the idea that there was a corpse-like quality to these historic structures, all rendered with the 'graphic bluntness' of the Gothic aesthetic (Fig. 19.1).

The overlap and interaction between the literature and artistic productions of antiquarianism, national tourism and Gothic Revival, and the Gothic of terror and the supernatural is a developing field of enquiry.[10] Take the Gothic as, more reductively, a canon of literary texts occupied with supernatural, terrible or horrific themes in historical or alien settings, and the relationship with art as one of illustration, and the field of enquiry shrinks considerably. Gothic novels did carry illustrations, of course. We still lack a corpus of Romantic book illustration to be able to gauge the situation more precisely,

---

8 Peter N. Lindfield and Dale Townshend, 'Reading Vathek and Fonthill Abbey: William Beckford's Architectural Imagination', in Caroline Dakers (ed.), *Fonthill Recovered: A Cultural History* (London: UCL Press, 2018), pp. 284–301 (p. 296).
9 William Hughes and Ruth Heholt (eds), *Gothic Britain: Dark Places in the Provinces and Margins of the British Isles* (Cardiff: University of Wales Press, 2018). See also Michael Carter, Peter N. Lindfield and Dale Townshend (eds), *Writing Britain's Ruins* (London: British Library Publishing, 2017).
10 See Dale Townshend, *Gothic Antiquity: History, Romance, and the Architectural Imagination, 1760–1840* (Oxford: Oxford University Press, 2019).

Fig.19.1: John Constable, *Hadleigh Castle, The Mouth of the Thames – Morning after a Stormy Night* (1829). Yale Center for British Art, Paul Mellon Collection.

but this kind of work was generally considered to be limited in its ambitions.[11] The engravings that were a feature of select Gothic novels and collections were rather modest in character. Designing for illustration would lead to the creation of drawings or watercolours, perhaps small cabinet paintings in oils. These might be included in art exhibitions, but did not generally garner critical attention. The makers of these images were often anonymous, and it is hard to distinguish named individuals within this field who could be identified specifically with Gothic illustrations.

There are, nonetheless, instances of the task of artists and publishers investing considerably more into illustrations relating to texts with Gothic associations. Most notably in several regards there were William Blake's illustrations for Robert Blair's *The Grave* (1743), a prime manifestation of what we can now acknowledge as 'Blake's Gothic aesthetic' (Fig. 19.2).[12] Blake's controversial but famed designs made great play of spirit forms,

---

11 See Ian Haywood, Susan Matthews and Mary L. Shannon (eds), *Romanticism and Illustration* (Cambridge: Cambridge University Press 2019).
12 Sibylle Erle, '"On the Very Verge of legitimate Invention": Charles Bonnet and William Blake's Illustrations to Robert Blair's *The Grave* (1808)', in Carol Margaret Davison (ed.), *The Gothic and Death* (Manchester: Manchester University Press 2017), pp. 34–47.

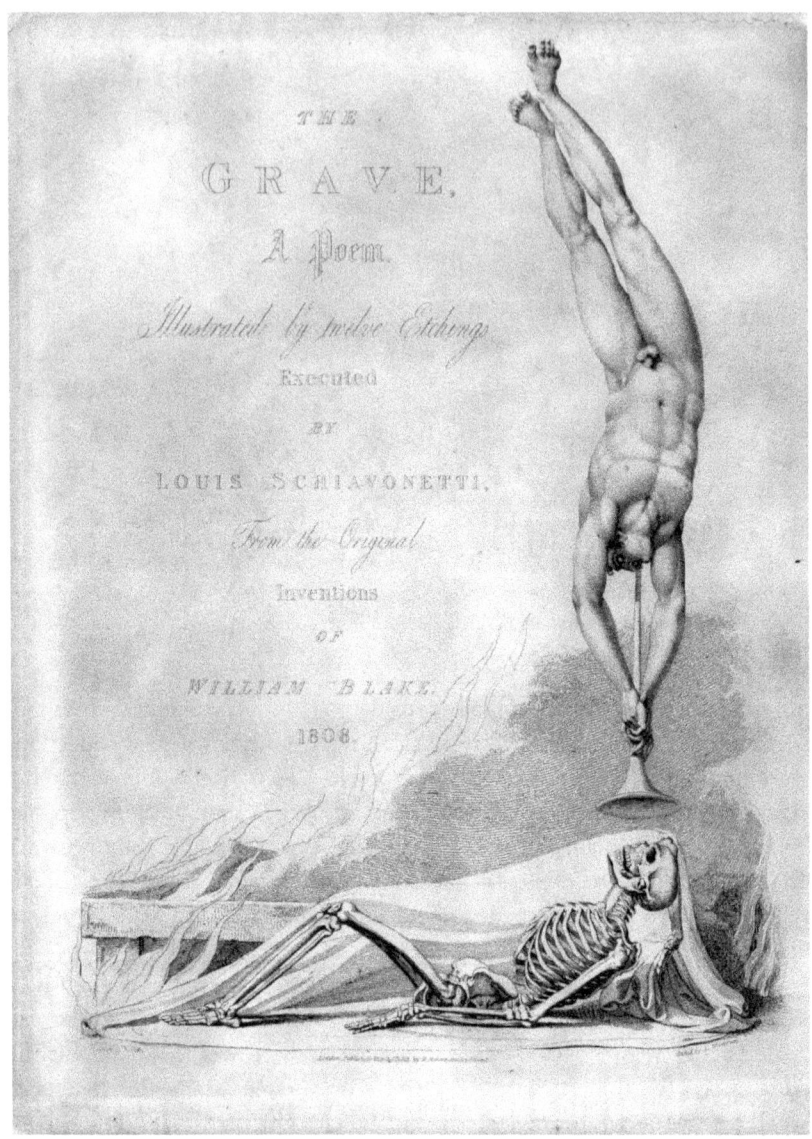

Fig.19.2: Print made by Luigi Schiavonnetti after William Blake. Title page to Robert Blair's *The Grave, a Poem* (1808, published 1813). Yale Center for British Art, Paul Mellon Collection.

visionary antics and medieval Gothic forms, and if, as Chris Bundock and Elizabeth Effinger have recently observed, Blake remains somewhat of a

Fig.19.3: Theodor von Holst, Frontispiece to Mary Shelley's *Frankenstein* (1818), revised edition published by Colburn and Bentley, London 1831. Steel engraving in book 93 x 71 mm. Wikimedia Commons.

'spectral, marginal figure' in the 'robust and expanding field of Gothic studies', this was largely because of the distinction imposed within Blake studies between Gothic Revival and Gothic horror.[13] Theodor von Holst's design for Richard Bentley and Henry Colburn's 1831 edition of Mary Shelley's *Frankenstein* (1818) is a further rare exception of a direct illustration to a Gothic novel that obtains additional art-historical interest. Von Holst was well known for his supernatural and romantic imagery, but was basically a jobbing artist who was never professionally settled.[14] His frontispiece to the 1831 edition of Shelley's novel presents a full-blooded Gothic scene, featuring an arched window with Gothic tracery, moonlight, a skeleton, and the look of terror and alarm on the figure of Frankenstein, who seems to be wearing distinctly medieval-looking costume, escaping through the door (Fig.19.3). Holst, well versed in German literature and a self-consciously romantic figure, admired Henry Fuseli and knowingly adopted his pictorial mannerisms, including long-legged heroes and limp maidens, as well as a predilection for figures wearing skin-tight leggings.

The production of such designs required from the originating artist a watercolour or drawing, or at most a small-scale oil painting. There were fewer substantial paintings directly taking up Gothic literary themes. One notable exception, Nathaniel Grogan's *Lady Blanche Crosses the Ravine Guided*

---

13 Chris Bundock and Elizabeth Effinger (eds), *William Blake's Gothic Imagination: Bodies of Horror* (Manchester: Manchester University Press 2018), p. 1.
14 Max Browne, *The Romantic Art of Theodor von Holst, 1810–1844* (London: Lund Humphries 1994).

by the Count and St Foix: A Scene from 'The Mysteries of Udolpho' (1790s; National Gallery of Ireland, Dublin), takes its theme from Ann Radcliffe's best-known romance but bears no intimations of horror and terror beyond the Burkean sublimity invoked by the rushing cataract over which the painting's subjects cautiously pick their way. Catherine Blake's startling little painting *Agnes* (c. 1800; Fitzwilliam Museum, Cambridge) is notable, then, as a direct illustration of one of the most shocking scenes in Matthew Gregory Lewis's *The Monk* (1796), for Agnes is a nun nursing her dead baby in a filthy dungeon. If such graphic bluntness was commonplace in the more shocking kind of Gothic literature that Lewis's novel epitomised, it was, ironically, scarce in the context of graphic art. Henry Fuseli's *The Fire King* (1811; V&A Museum, London) lifts its subject from Walter Scott and from his contribution to the iconic collection edited by Lewis, *Tales of Wonder* (1801). We might count John Martin's *Sadak* (1812; St Louis Art Museum) an exercise in rendering vaulting volcanic scenery in shocking reds and oranges, taking as its source a fantastic story in James Ridley's *Tales of the Genii* (1764) and calculated to cause a sensation when it was exhibited at the Royal Academy in 1812. But that calculation was based not only on the expectation of maximum optical impact, in the context of an art display dominated by the more muted colours of fashionable portraiture and naturalistic landscape painting, but also on the surprise factor of such fantastical subject matter. Gothic literary texts were very rarely referenced by artists seeking to make a name for themselves in the mainstream contexts of exhibition and publication.

When, in 1783, Horace Walpole observed that 'Of late, Barry, Romney, Fuseli, Mrs Cosway & others, have attempted to paint Deities, Visions, Witchcraft &c, but have only been bombast & extravagant, without true dignity', he was noting how a number of high-profile artists had taken to exhibiting pictures with shocking and unusual subject matter of a sort which we would now readily identify with the Gothic aesthetic.[15] But it is worth noting that the artists he namechecked – the Irish history painter James Barry, the fashionable portraitist and frustrated painter of the sublime George Romney, the Swiss-born painter of the fantastic and horrible Henry Fuseli, and the Classical subject painter Maria Cosway – were not looking to Gothic literature for their sources. The paintings that Walpole had seen at the art exhibitions of the previous decade or so were instead drawn from Greek tragedy, from Shakespeare, Edmund

---

15 From Walpole's annotations to the Royal Academy exhibition catalogue from 1783, Lewis Walpole Library, Yale University.

Spenser and Milton, occasionally from modern poetry, and sometimes, though rarely, from folkloric sources. They were pictures that, in claiming association with generally canonical – and deeply familiar – literary materials, were also laying claim to a certain kind of intellectual and cultural authority for their authors. Whatever the 'bombast' of the resulting works, and however calculated they may have been in addressing a contemporary audience for art tending to a taste for direct spectacle and sensational visual effects rather than profundity and subtlety, the artists wanted also to claim a degree of cultural prestige. This balanced combination of visual extravagance, literary populism and cultural canonicity was a key gambit in late eighteenth-century art, apparent in the multitude of often quite ambitious pictures on literary themes by a range of exhibiting artists, and especially in the phenomenon of the literary galleries organised in the 1780s and 1790s. These were initiated by commercial publishers and involved commissioning pictures, sometimes rather large pictures, by leading artists on set literary themes, with the aim of exhibiting these and promoting interest in the engraved reproductions that would follow. These projects – run most notably in London by Thomas Macklin, John Boydell, Robert Bowyer and, in Dublin, by James Woodmason – led to artists producing images with supernatural and terrible content that were overtly Gothic in character. The Shakespearean imagery commissioned by Boydell and Woodmason, in particular, featured ghosts, witches and fairies in some abundance. Given how recent scholarship has deepened our understanding of Shakespeare's Gothicism in the eighteenth century, we are not out of place in viewing an image such as Fuseli's rendering of Hamlet for Boydell's Shakespeare Gallery as a committedly Gothic image (Fig.19.4).[16] In the absence of extensive state or church patronage for modern art, these were pictures that were simultaneously commercially orientated to the same market for sensation as that exploited by the Minerva Press, while also aspiring to high cultural prestige and nationalist sentiment through embodying works by the most acclaimed figures in English literary culture.[17]

---

16 John Drakakis and Dale Townshend (eds), *Gothic Shakespeares* (Abingdon: Routledge, 2008); Christy Desmet and Anne Williams (eds), *Shakespearean Gothic* (Cardiff: University of Wales Press, 2009); Elisabeth Bronfen and Beate Neumeier (eds), *Gothic Renaissance: A Reassessment* (Manchester: Manchester University Press, 2014).

17 See Luisa Calè, 'Blake and the Literary Galleries', in Sarah Haggarty and Jon Mee (eds), *Blake and Conflict* (Basingstoke: Palgrave Macmillan, 2008), pp. 185–209.

Fig.19.4: Robert Thew after Henry Fuseli, *Hamlet, Prince of Denmark: Act I, Scene iv, Platform before the Palace of Elsineur [sic] – Hamlet, Horatio, Marcellus and the Ghost* (1803). Yale Center for British Art, Yale Art Gallery Collection, Gift of John Gerli, B.A. 1932.

The Gothic Autonomy of Art

As Jon Klancher has argued, the failure of the print market during the long years of the French Wars, and the collapse of the literary galleries, with the Shakespeare Gallery being famously dispersed by lottery in 1804, was a pivotal moment for artists.[18] Having seen in such commercial enterprises an opportunity to forge an art that was both financially rewarding and critically credible, and a means by which modern British artists could attach themselves to the swelling nationalism of the era, these failures pushed them instead to claim a higher degree of creative autonomy. Artists, as Klancher contends, were more inclined to set out their claims through literary production of their own, eschewing middlemen to claim authorial rights. The developments that Klancher observes can be fruitfully cast as constituting

---

18 Jon Klancher, *Transfiguring the Arts and Sciences: Knowledge and Cultural Institutions in the Romantic Age* (Cambridge and New York: Cambridge University Press, 2013).

an episode in the 'autonomisation' of art, the larger historical process unfolding from the later eighteenth century by which art was endowed with a new self-sufficiency. There were paradoxes in this emerging situation. As Geraldine Pelles has observed in a long-neglected essay on the image of the artist around 1800, 'around the same time it had at least become established, the new conceptual system of the fine arts began to disintegrate. For along with the greater distinction accorded painting and the painter in a relatively autonomous realm, art also came to be regarded as a generalized creative activity, and the artist as the archetype of a diffuse creative quality'.[19]

There are certain aspects to this autonomisation that could be evoked as Gothic. The archetype of the inspired artist, working feverishly in cloistered surroundings or, better still, in rags in a lonely attic, has its own Gothic resonances. Meanwhile, if art arose from the labours of isolated creative work (rather than in collective efforts in the workshop, or at the behest of a master or patron); if its effects were that much more mysterious; and if the sources of inspiration enigmatic, the artist could appear consequently as a supernatural actor. As William Vaughan has observed, the period under discussion here sees particular importance attached to the idea of the artist as a 'magician', as part of the wholesale secularisation of magic and the supernatural through the eighteenth century and an effort to secure the value of art in the context of the fluid uncertainties of modernity.[20]

The figure who exemplifies this perhaps unexpected common ground between the autonomisation of art and the Gothic aesthetic is Henry Fuseli. While the direct illustration of Gothic sources in formats and media conforming to the definition of art as such were scarce, the works of art that appear most wholeheartedly Gothic are those by Fuseli that, paradoxically, lack a clear literary source. The iconic work in this regard is Fuseli's *The Nightmare*, the sole exhibit included by the artist in the Royal Academy exhibition of 1782 (artists would generally hedge their bets and demonstrate their productivity and virtuosity by showing several works at a time).[21]

---

19 Geraldine Pelles, 'The image of the artist', p. 126.
20 William Vaughan, 'Magic in the Studio', in Ann Bermingham (ed.), *Sensation & Sensibility: Viewing Gainsborough's Cottage Door* (New Haven and London: Yale University Press, 2005), pp. 165–79.
21 See Nicolas Powell, *Fuseli – 'The Nightmare'* (London: Allen Lane, 1973); Myrone, *Gothic Nightmares*; Andrei Pop, 'Sympathetic spectators: Henry Fuseli's nightmare and Emma Hamilton's *Attitudes*', *Art History* 34 (2011): 934–57; Martin Postle, '1782: Sir Joshua Buys a Gainsborough', *The Royal Academy of Arts Summer Exhibition: A Chronicle, 1769–2018*, edited by Mark Hallett, Sarah Victoria Turner and Jessica Feather (London: Paul Mellon Centre for Studies in British Art, 2018) <https://chronicle250.com/> (last accessed 2 July 2019).

Nestling on the walls of the Academy in the company of a multitude of fashionable portraits, the occasional theatrical and Classical scenes, and pictures of more mundane subjects such the immediately adjacent canvases *Portraits of horses and dogs belonging to the Hon. Mr Pitt* and *Cattle*, this canvas had an immense impact. 'The Night Mare by Mr. Fuiseli [*sic*]', wrote a critic, 'like all his productions, has strong marks of genius about it; but hag-riding is too unpleasant a thought to be agreeable to any one, and is unfit for furniture or reflection.'[22] Horace Walpole dismissed it as 'Shocking', and it was clearly this painting, among others, that he had in mind when he railed against the 'bombast[ic] & extravagant' strain within contemporary British art.[23] It was being lampooned by caricaturists as early as 1784, and has never left the public imagination since. It was caricatured, emulated, copied throughout the nineteenth century, and has resurfaced in the art, satire and cinema of the twentieth, circulating not only in the Anglophone world but far beyond. It was a point of reference for the Danish artist Nicolai Abildgaard, for Goya in Spain, for comic artists in Germany, the Netherlands and Honoré Daumier in France, among others. The image was resurrected for the publicity for Ken Russell's film *Gothic* (1984), and re-staged within the film itself. It remains a favourite format for satirists down to the present day.

The painting was engraved officially in 1783 and several times without permission (Fig.19.5). At least two early oil versions by Fuseli are documented; the Frankfurt version of 1790–1 (Goethe-Museum, Frankfurt) adjusts the composition and renders the female figure a more ghostly, if more contorted, presence. It was this version that was engraved for an edition of Erasmus Darwin's *Botanic Garden* in 1806. This picture is almost as frequently reproduced in modern times as the first version, apparently hanging in reproduction in Sigmund Freud's apartment, cited by Carl Gustav Jung and Ernest Jones and featuring memorably as the cover of Penguin Books' widely read *Three Gothic Novels* (1964). Fuseli was still painting a further version towards the end of his life in the 1820s, and this was engraved as well.

For an image that seems most obviously to have encapsulated an idea of the Gothic, it is important to observe that, though Mary Shelley alludes to it in her description of the death of Elizabeth in *Frankenstein*, it has no prior and specific anchorage in Gothic literature, and originally no self-evident literary reference at all. It was exhibited under the unusually enigmatic title of *The night-mare*: enigmatic because pictures with literary, historical or even specific

22 *The Morning Chronicle and Public Advertiser*, 9 May 1782.
23 See W. T. Whitley, *Artists and Their Friends in England, 1700–1799*, 2 vols (London: Medici Society, 1928), vol. 2, p. 37; Myrone, *Gothic Nightmares*, p. 35.

Fig.19.5: Engraving after Henry Fuseli's *The Nightmare*. Wellcome Collection. CC BY.

cultural content would routinely be catalogued with the source authority named, and often accompanied by lines from the original source text. Fuseli himself did this on several occasions. Whatever literary or cultural reference there may have been in the painting, what is certain is that such was not revealed, not even in the catalogue entry when it was exhibited at the Royal Academy in 1782, nor subsequently when it was engraved with lines from Erasmus Darwin's yet-unpublished natural history poem, *The Loves of the Plants* (1789), attached to it.

Still, there remains a possibility that Fuseli had in mind a specific literary source for what has become his best-known painting. Thomas Middleton's Jacobean tragedy, *The Witch*, written between 1613 and 1617 but only published from a manuscript in 1778, includes a reference to the foul, incestuous imp 'Firestone' heading out with his Nightmare 'to overlay a fat parson's daughter'. The folkloric allusions of the image are manifold, too, in the figure of the 'nightmare'; in the presence of an incubus (further lifted from Classical sources); and in its allusions to the fairy-tale tradition, the evil imps and dwarves of which all feasibly provide the model for Fuseli's evil figure. Then there is the possibility of scientific allusions, either in reference to contemporary understanding of sleep paralysis, or the effects of narcotics, stimulants and diet. We are left to speculate as to whether the horse and imp are meant to be supernatural figures, manifestations of the woman's fantasies or allegorical representations. The sickly glitter of the painting itself suggests a perverse or ironic re-working of the playfully erotic images to be found in French, and sometimes English, painting and illustration, with the dishevelled boudoir interior characteristically to be found in such compositions transformed into a gloomy and claustrophobic setting.

Whatever its origins, Fuseli left the source material for *The Nightmare* tantalisingly undisclosed. The following year, he mischievously drew attention to this aspect of his artistic practice when he showed *Percival Delivering Belisane from the Enchantment of Urma* in 1783, claiming in the catalogue that the subject was drawn from the 'Provencal Tales of Kyot', an authentic-sounding source for what was, in fact, a fabrication. 'Kyot' had been identified by the medieval German knight-poet Wolfram von Eschenbach as the source matter for the romance *Parzival*, written in the early thirteenth century and first published in 1477. But there is no documented Kyot, and no known literary work had been attributed to him. Von Eschenbach had claimed that Kyot's text was itself a translation from an Arabic manuscript discovered in the Spanish city of Toledo, the centre for manuscript studies in the medieval period and a vital contact zone between European and Arab cultures. Thus, in claiming that the source of his 'Urma' pictures was to be found in 'Kyot', Fuseli proposes that his picture shows a subject taken from a

Fig.19.6: John Raphael Smith after Henry Fuseli, *Belisane and Parcival under the Enchantment of Urma* (1782). Paul Mellon Fund. Courtesy of the National Gallery of Art, Washington.

non-extant text, which was in turn meant to be a translation of another text that, itself, never existed. In so doing, Fuseli was laying claim to exemplary Gothic origins, the Arab and European sources for romance literature having been subject to extensive scholarly enquiry in the work of Richard Hurd, Thomas Percy and Thomas Warton in previous decades. Fuseli went on to publish a mezzotint that appeared to show a further episode in the story, the narrative of which, of course, never actually existed beyond these images (Fig.19.6). Similarly, his numerous drawings and pictures on the theme of 'Ezzelin and Meduna' featured a haggardly witch, a beautiful maiden as victim and a long-limbed hero of the Crusades in situations redolent of a variety of Gothic literary sources but not definitely linked with any existing textual materials.

Fuseli himself admitted that he had invented the names and situations for several of his key pictures in a letter to his patron William Roscoe in 1791:

> Your Approbation of my proposal for painting Small pictures to make the Large ones go on, gives me much pleasure; there is hardly an interesting

Subject, I may well say, from Homer to Shakespeare – or in the records of History – that at one time or other I have not bestowed, at least a Cursory thought on, so that my Stock will not be easily exhausted: but Situations as I have Combined Such as _Ezelin, Belisane_ &c; Philosophical Ideas made intuitive, or Sentiment personified, suit, in my opinion, Small Canvases eminently – Want You any thing You will let me know.[24]

Such license may reflect what Fuseli was develop into an element of his artistic theory, as explored by Christopher Heppner in connection with William Blake's visual practice: the idea that, by pursuing the representation of elemental or essential qualities, proper names are almost irrelevant. Heppner notes that while 'Fuseli writes strongly about the superfluousness of proper names', he was also deeply anxious that, in practice, such an art, freed from the convention of names, might become unintelligible, and that in his own painting he made use of established monikers for his characters 'with extremely few exceptions'.[25] While this is clearly true, it does not diminish the significance of what was basically a short-lived experiment at the turn of the 1780s. Much like Horace Walpole's gestures in The Castle of Otranto (1764), Fuseli's inventions of the early 1780s were constituted through a distinctly 'Gothic' manoeuvre, the dizzying play of false appearances and fraudulent claims, forgery and fakery, captured in Jerrold E. Hogle's rightly celebrated phrase, 'ghost of the counterfeit'.[26]

The titles and proper names Fuseli provided for his fantasy pictures of the early 1780s provided no greater orientation beyond establishing the broad generic terms of the picture. They point to art functioning in new ways, circulating in the context of new visual technologies and within new contexts for cultural consumption, sometimes coincident with or even occasionally dependent upon literary sources of the Gothic, but more generally demonstrating the conditions of Gothic production itself: sensationalism, consumerism and the disruption of the hierarchies of genre, taste and value. Of Fuseli it was noted that 'with such incomprehensible sublimity are his subjects sometimes handled' that a work was once mistakenly hung upside down by the workmen at the Academy.[27] Another critic noted:

---

24 David H. Weinglass (ed.), *The Collected English Letters of Henry Fuseli* (Millwood: Kraus International NY, 1982), p. 74.
25 Christopher Heppner, *Reading Blake's Designs* (Cambridge: Cambridge University Press, 1995), p. 81.
26 See Jerrold E. Hogle, 'The Ghost of the Counterfeit in the Genesis of the Gothic', in Allan Lloyd Smith and Victor Sage (eds), *Gothick Origins and Innovations* (Amsterdam: Rodopi, 1994), pp. 23–33.
27 Anon., *Letters from an Irish Student in England to his Father in Ireland*, 2 vols (London: C. Cradock & W. Joy, 1809), vol. 2, p. 140.

> It is a difficult task to estimate the merits of this artist's work, by any rule or criterion by which we judge of others. Pictures are, or ought to be, a representation of natural objects, delineated with taste and precision. Mr *Fuseli* gives us the human figure, from the recollection of its form, and not from the form itself; he seems to be painting every thing from fancy, which renders his work almost incomprehensible, and leaves no criterion to judge of them by, but the imagination.[28]

What may define the literary Gothic is its ambiguous, indefinite narrative content – the uncertain lineaments of story or of pictorial or architectural space. But what defines Gothic art is that it retained certain public, moral functions even if its relationship with public culture was parasitic. There is enough of Michelangelo in Fuseli, for instance, and the pictures are sufficiently ambitious in their medium and format, to qualify for a place on the walls of the Royal Academy. Indeed, Fuseli himself secured a place within the artistic establishment when he became a Royal Academician and, subsequently, Professor of Painting and Keeper at the Academy. It was this very prominence, however, that fired up his fiercest critics. For Fuseli was not to be so readily dismissed as sensationalist and commercial 'trash' of the same ilk as the magic lanternists and Grub Street illustrators of the day. When the Reverend Bromley sought to belittle Fuseli in his *A Philosophical and Critical History of the Fine Arts* of 1793, it was by pitching him against the history painter Benjamin West's vision of the heroic, a mode anchored in 'heroic fact' and politically sound to boot. Where West sought out subjects from 'real history', and depicted them with close attention to historical details, Fuseli was a mere fantasist and in this respect not unlike the purveyors of cheap literary romance:

> The *night-mare, little red riding hood, the shepherd's dream,* or any dream that is not marked in authentic history as combined with the important dispensations of Providence, and many other pieces of a visionary and fanciful nature, are speculations of as exalted a stretch in the contemplation of such a mind as the finest lessons that ever were drawn from religion, or morals, or useful history. And yet the painter, who should employ his time on such subjects, would certainly amuse the intelligent no more than the man who should make those subjects the topics of a serious discourse. But what good has the world, or what honour has the art, at any time derived from such light and fantastic speculations?[29]

---

28 *Public Advertiser*, 22 May 1786.
29 Robert Anthony Bromley, *A Philosophical and Critical History of the Fine Arts*, 2 vols (London: Printed for the Author, 1793–5), vol. 1, pp. 36–7.

Fuseli, by this time an Academician, stood accused of a lightness and a tendency towards fantasising that was seen to constitute a departure from art's moral and social purpose. He thus helps to mark out, involuntarily, the new-found autonomy of the artist. The precise conjunction of the Gothic with this aesthetic independence has been described by E. J. Clery in her account of the shift of the supernatural from the realm of superstitious belief to that of spectacle, the movement, as she phrases it, into 'an autonomous realm of the aesthetic, the awakening of a sensibility detached from truth'.[30] At this point, Fuseli's Gothic art is revealing not only of the kinds of professional gambits encouraged by the commercialisation of art, nor only of the autonomy being newly claimed by artists, nor of the uncertain legibility and cultural status of artworks, but of a still larger transformation. A connection can then be drawn with the forbidding architectural fantasies of Piranesi, or with Goya, now acknowledged as 'Spain's foremost Gothic painter'.[31] The famed etchings and the sequence of 'black paintings' of the latter evoke dark horrors from folklore, historical experience and the imagination.

These artists equally seem to be 'attempting to represent in visual terms this unstable, haunted space which today might rightly assume the name Gothic'.[32] But we might want to push the case further, moving away from any sense of dependency upon literary precedent, and provide a sharper definition of the relationship between Gothic art, as art, and the larger Gothic culture. The historical rise in the Romantic period of the autonomy of the artist and of the artwork is a hallmark of modernity, a modernity that was not propelled merely by disinterested philosophical reflection nor even by the internal psychic struggles of the individual artist, but also by commercial instincts and interests insofar as these could be reconciled with the shifting ideas of cultural prestige. Fuseli seems precisely to be a forerunner of the contemporary artist in the radical uncertainty that was expressed about the value of his art: he was variously considered a genius, a cynic or a madman. The sensational Gothicism of his art only drew spectacular attention to these uncertainties. A painter of a landscape, portrait or legitimate Classical theme

---

30 E. J. Clery, 'Laying the Ground for Gothic: The Passage of the Supernatural from Truth to Spectacle', in Valeria Tinkler-Villani and Peter Davidson (eds), *Exhibited by Candlelight: Sources and Developments in the Gothic Tradition* (Amsterdam: Rodopi, 1995), pp. 65–74.

31 See Xavier Aldana Reyes, *Spanish Gothic: National Identity, Collaboration and Cultural Adaptation* (Basingstoke: Palgrave Macmillan, 2017).

32 Gilda Williams, 'Defining a Gothic Aesthetic in Modern and Contemporary Visual Art', in Glennis Byron and Dale Townshend (eds), *The Gothic World* (London and New York: Routledge 2014), pp. 412–25 (p. 421).

might be considered a good artist or a bad artist, but is scarcely likely to be accounted as shocking, abysmal or exploitative as a painter of nightmares and fairies drawn from imagination. The same equivocation accompanies much contemporary art that has been classed as having Gothic qualities, in the cinematic productions which seem curiously to connect high and low, exploitation and aesthetic aspiration, or the visual art of Damien Hirst and the Chapman Brothers that are products of a global gallery system but which confrontationally offer low-cultural debasement.[33] The motifs of the Gothic in the context of the visual arts served to register the terror and unease of the new cultural situation at the end of the eighteenth century: the ambiguous, contested, interminable character of art in the modern era. That a full-blooded Gothic art resurfaces only intermittently in the history of 'high art' exposes not only the volatility and inconstancy of Gothic culture, nor the irreconcilability of the Gothic and art, but also the general ambivalence towards the indeterminacies of art in the modern era.

33 Christoph Grunenberg (ed.), *Gothic: Transmutations of Horror in Late Twentieth Century Art* (Boston: Institute of Contemporary Art, 1997); Gilda Williams (ed.), *The Gothic* (London: Whitechapel, 2007); Williams, 'Defining a Gothic Aesthetic'.

I.20

Time in the Gothic

ROBERT MILES

Gothic Time

In order to understand time in the Gothic, one must first understand the historical moment out of which the first Gothic novels emerged. Literary history provides us with a rich archive of theoretical accounts, beginning with Friedrich's Schiller's, in *On Naïve and Sentimental Poetry* (1795–6), written during the very midst of the Gothic's rise. The late eighteenth century distinguishes itself as a moment of 'radical reflexivity'[1] that forever creates a chasm between the naïve and the sentimental, the direct and the 'reflective',[2] the magical and the disenchanted. This was the period that witnessed, as T.S. Eliot might have put it, the final 'dissociation of sensibility';[3] or, to use a different idiom, the final fragmenting of pre-modern lifeworlds as the process of secularisation completed itself.[4] And this was the period in which the supernatural, as revealed religion, was recuperated as the divine in nature, as natural supernaturalism.[5]

The most recent exploration of this moment, by the philosopher Charles Taylor, is also its richest and most extensive. Drawing explicitly on Schiller's naïve/sentimental distinction,[6] Taylor reads the late eighteenth century as

---

1 Colin Jager, 'This Detail, This History: Charles Taylor's Romanticism', in Michael Warner, Jonathan VanAntwerpen and Craig Calhoun (eds), *Varieties of Secularism in a Secular Age* (Cambridge, MA: Harvard University Press, 2013), pp. 166–92 (p. 169).
2 Friedrich Schiller, *On the Naïve and Sentimental in Literature*, trans. Helen Watanabe-O'Kelly (Manchester: Carcanet Press, 1981), p. 14.
3 T. S. Eliot, 'The Metaphysical Poets', in Vincent B. Leitch (ed.), *The Norton Anthology of Theory and Criticism*, 3rd edition (New York: W. W. Norton & Co., 2018), pp. 891–8 (p. 896).
4 Vincent P. Pecora, *Secularization and Cultural Criticism: Religion, Nation, and Modernity* (Chicago: University of Chicago Press, 2006), p. 7.
5 M. H. Abrams, *Natural Supernaturalism: Tradition and Revolution in Romantic Literature* (New York: W.W. Norton & Co., 1971), p. 13.
6 Colin Jager, 'Language Within Language: Reform and Literature in *A Secular Age*', in Florian Zemmin, Colin Jager and Guido Vanheeswijk (eds), *Working with A Secular Age: Interdisciplinary Perspectives on Charles Taylor's Master Narrative* (Berlin & Boston: Walter de Gruyter, 2016), pp. 207–28 (p. 207).

the point in Western History in which secularisation had completed itself at the level of 'background', so that it was now a part of an array of norms firmly embedded in our 'modern social imaginary'.[7] Background and social imaginary are key terms for Taylor, as they indicate the nature of his project, which is, in a way, pre-philosophical. That is, he aims to delineate – to provide a fine-grained analysis of – the attitudes that constitute a common mentality, but which are so deeply embedded in culture as to become, in effect, invisible. Drawing on the work of John Searle and Hubert Dreyfus, who in turn draw upon Ludvig Wittgenstein, Martin Heidegger and Michael Polanyi,[8] Taylor describes background as follows:

> It is in fact that largely unstructured and inarticulate understanding of our whole situation, within which particular features of our world show up for us in the sense they have. It can never be adequately expressed in the form of explicit doctrines, because of its very unlimited and indefinite nature. That is another reason for speaking here of an 'imaginary' and not a theory.[9]

A background is not a set of theories and arguments that may be philosophically tested and explored; rather, it is a set of attitudes, assumptions and norms – constituted by innumerable cultural practices – that colour, and indeed shape, our understanding of the world. Taylor's *A Secular Age* (2007) is an extensive exploration of just one such assumption that has become naturalised within the Western modern social imaginary: the assumption that whether and where an individual might or might not locate a sense of fullness in life (Taylor's expansive term for religious belief) is a matter for the individual. It is a lifestyle choice, as we might now put it. Taylor advances the acceptance of this belief as a non-controversial given, at the level of mass culture, as a more reliable working hypothesis for understanding secularisation, as opposed to the two most common ways of viewing it: the separation of church and state, or the withering away of established religion.[10]

Taylor's self-confessed grand narrative bridges a before and an after: before the Axial age, and some (admittedly protracted) time after. Before was a time in which the self was embedded within nature, was part of a seamless lifeworld, but, in being so, suffered porous boundaries between inside and out, between a self and supernatural powers controllable, if at all, through good and bad magic. In the enchanted pre-modern world, animism is rife,

---

7 Charles Taylor, *A Secular Age* (Cambridge, Mass.: Belknap Press of Harvard University Press, 2007), pp. 172–3.
8 Taylor, *A Secular Age*, p. 794, n. 12.   9 Taylor, *A Secular Age*, p. 173.
10 Taylor, *A Secular Age*, pp. 1–22.

spirits of ancestors stalk the land, some intent on ill, some on good. Time, for its part, is double. Or rather, time is simply a function of earthly existence, of duration. Time is something we enter, on birth, and leave again, on death. In the supernatural world there is no time, only a timeless present. Earthly time, then, is a matter of marking time, until time ends, a marking that runs in circles, like the seasons, a period of iteration and repetition, rather than linear progression. The modern self, by contrast, is 'disembedded'[11] from nature, is alienated from it. It is 'buffered'[12] and 'punctual',[13] meaning atomised as an autonomous individual girded by 'rights'.[14] Time is no longer perceived as circular, but linear.

In Taylor's reading, the cusp between late Enlightenment and Romanticism is the period in which our modern notions of subjectivity and secularity have completed the process of having become embedded as *background* – have become invisible norms. It is the sense of finality, of irreversible modernity, that brings about the first, florid imagining of the one-way bridge we have crossed, one lamented, famously, by Richard Hurd as the loss of a 'world of fine fabling', the price paid for the 'revolution' of modernity.[15] The Gothic is a mash-up of the before and the after, a superimposition of a version of the lost enchanted world on disenchanted modernity; a version, because the Gothic subsists within Romantic irony, within a sentimental consciousness where the 'naïve' can never be recaptured, only imitated. In his letters, Samuel Taylor Coleridge expresses his admiration for the 'simplicity and naturalness' of Matthew Lewis's language in his Gothic play, *The Castle Spectre* (1797): 'This, I think, a rare merit: at least, I find, I cannot attain this innocent nakedness, except by *assumption*. I resemble the Duchess of Kingston, who masqueraded in the character of "Eve before the Fall", in flesh-coloured Silk.'[16] In imitating the 'world of fine fabling' that we have lost through modernity, the Romantic poet discovers himself wearing the linguistic equivalent of pink silk. Or, to adopt a different idiom, the Gothic is irreversibly 'camp':[17] it is aware that the 'naïve' that it adopts is always already the 'sentimental' in disguise.

11 Taylor, *A Secular Age*, p. 156.   12 Taylor, *A Secular Age*, pp. 37–42.
13 Charles Taylor, *Sources of the Self: The Making of the Modern Identity* (Cambridge, MA: Harvard University Press, 1989), p. 159.
14 Charles Taylor, *Modern Social Imaginaries* (Durham, NC: Duke University Press, 2004), p. 4.
15 E. J. Clery and Robert Miles (eds), *Gothic Documents, A Sourcebook: 1750–1820* (Manchester and New York: Manchester University Press, 2000), p. 77.
16 Ernest Hartley Coleridge (ed.), *Letters of Samuel Taylor Coleridge*, 2 vols (London: William Heinemann, 1895), vol. 1, p. 238.
17 Susan Sontag, 'Notes on Camp', in *A Susan Sontag Reader* (New York: Farrar/Giroux, 1982), pp. 105–20.

Time in Ann Radcliffe

The novels of Ann Radcliffe have come to the fore in Gothic studies in recent years, in part because she is the author who dramatises, most eloquently, the cultural poetics of this newly embedded secular subjectivity. Radcliffe's texts are extraordinary for the ways in which they stage, and dramatise, what, in Taylor's terms, we might call the faltering of the buffered self. In one respect this is no more than what we might expect from a reading of Sigmund Freud's essay on the uncanny: after all, the failure of the buffered self is also a failure to 'surmount' the 'primitive' beliefs that were common to the infancy of the race, such as telepathy, doubling and animism – all common features of the pre-modern, enchanted, porous self.[18] As the buffered self falters, so the porous self emerges once more, along with a universe – enchanted and uncanny – of spirits, shape-shifters and boundary-crossers. Radcliffe's romances are extraordinary, then, in the degree and thoroughness with which they imagine the collapse of the 'buffered self', which is always held before us on the verge of dissolution. As a result, Radcliffe's heroine, typically, finds herself constantly on the verge of being pitched back out of modern linear time, into the repetitions and circularities of 'dream' time.

Charles Taylor once again helps us understand what is at stake. 'The move to a horizontal, direct-access world, interwoven with an embedding in secular time', he writes, 'had to bring with it a different sense of our situation in time and space. In particular it brings different understandings of history and modes of narration.'[19] This brings out a paradox: secular time is also continuous with the modern notion of 'deep time' that emerged around the end of the eighteenth century beginning with the work of the Scottish geologist James Hutton (1726–97). Deep time is when linearity extends to the vanishing point, which is to say, the point of sublimity: it is thus cognate with Immanuel Kant's mathematical sublime, but also with Kant's sublime more generally, where the mind falls back in astonishment at its inability to cope with the task at hand. The imagination takes a stab at envisioning mathematical infinity, but, as it does so, reason informs us of the inability of our imaginations to match the conceptions of reason. It is then that the mind buckles, where this buckling is the experience of the sublime.

---

18 Sigmund Freud, 'The "Uncanny"', in James Strachey (ed. and trans.), *The Standard Edition of the Complete Psychological Works of Sigmund Freud, Vol. XVII: An Infantile Neurosis and Other Works* (London: The Hogarth Press, 1955), pp. 219–52 (pp. 240, 247).
19 Taylor, *A Secular Age*, p. 714.

If the sublime is one bookend of the modern experience of time, the other, as Taylor notes, is narrative, and along with it, growth and maturation: 'We can no longer describe' the rightness of the present order 'as the emergence of a self-realizing order lodged in higher time', as was the case in the old, enchanted order; 'The category that is at home in secular time is rather that of growth, maturation, drawn from the organic realm. A potential within nature matures.'[20] Alastair MacIntyre has influentially argued that this sense of self as the subject of story – where our lives are the stuff of narrative, a 'potential that matures' – has deep Aristotelian/Christian roots. In particular, the pre-Enlightenment sense of there being unproblematically known ends to life, a telos derived from the great chain of being, where each link has a telos fitted to its station, was instrumental to this narrativising habit. Virtue, for Aristotle, was defined by our telos, the ends proper to our station, king or peasant. To die in a state of virtue was also to die happy, in both the older, stoic, Greek sense, and in its Christian guise.[21] As MacIntryre reasons,

> If a human life is understood as a progress through harms and dangers, moral and physical, which someone may encounter and overcome in better and worse ways and with a greater or lesser measure of success, the virtues will find their place as those qualities the possession and exercise of which generally tend to success in this enterprise and the vices as qualities which likewise tend to failure. Each human life will then embody a story whose shape and form will depend upon what is counted as a harm and danger and upon how success and failure, progress and its opposite, are understood and evaluated.[22]

By the late Enlightenment the notion of nature- or God-given ends had evaporated under the philosophical heat applied by Baruch Spinoza, David Hume, Kant and others.[23] The narrativising habit remained, however, as an aspect of the modern social imaginary.

It is the sense of story, of each self being on a journey with a starting place and a meaningful end, that imparts our sense of time in the novel, of meaningful duration, with episodes, chapters and incremental change. It is Jane Austen who, more than any other novelist of the period, realises this sense of self, story and time. It is especially evident in *Pride and Prejudice* (1813), where Elizabeth Bennet marks a moment of partial self-knowledge by exclaiming:

---

20 Taylor, *Modern Social Imaginaries*, p. 175.
21 Darrin M. McMahon, *Happiness: A History* (New York: Grove Press, 2006), p. 7.
22 Alasdair MacIntyre, *After Virtue*, 3rd edition (Notre Dame: University of Notre Dame Press, 2007), p. 144.
23 Alasdair MacIntyre, *After Virtue*, p. 54.

'How despicably I have acted!' she cried; 'I, who have prided myself on my discernment! I, who have valued myself on my abilities! who have often disdained the generous candour of my sister, and gratified my vanity in useless or blameable mistrust! How humiliating is this discovery! Yet, how just a humiliation! Had I been in love, I could not have been more wretchedly blind! But vanity, not love, has been my folly ... Till this moment I never knew myself.'[24]

Lack of candour, abundant vanity and a surfeit of both pride and prejudice – Elizabeth Bennet envisions herself in the midst of her life story where she steers by the virtues, even as she is drawn into the back eddies of personal vice. Elizabeth may feel that she has finally arrived in the safe harbour of self-knowledge, but the attentive reader soon perceives that she is still mid-way on her journey. It is the sense of narrative, of journeying from one state to another with a meaningful goal in mind, that imparts a sense of time, of growth and change to *Pride and Prejudice*: otherwise life would be no more than a random succession of moments.

And that is how recent critics working on Radcliffe and time describe her romances: as a succession of moments, days and scenes,[25] as a 'phantasmagoria' in which the ligaments that bind experience into a shape made meaningful by duration, goals and virtues to steer by have all snapped, so that, as Terry Castle argues, the phantasmal and the real blend into each other as undifferentiated sense data.[26] To use the terminology of Radcliffe's time, this is the point at which the line separating real from 'ideal' presence is forever blurring.[27] Another way of putting this difference between Austen and Radcliffe is that the former perfects the *Bildungsroman* by heightening its social realism, whereas the latter writes a kind of 'anti-*Bildungsroman*'. Rather than pictures in a life segmenting it into a meaningful history, with significant periods and an arc tracing an intelligible silhouette, Radcliffe writes a form of fiction in which the autonomous self is forever on the point of inward collapse. In the final analysis, the Radcliffean heroine triumphs not by learning, by acknowledging, knowing and performing acts of virtue that help her realise her true ends in life, thus getting from here to there, but rather by

---

24 Jane Austen, *Pride and Prejudice*, edited by Robert P. Irvine (Peterborough, Ont.: Broadview 2002), p. 22.
25 Michael Paulson, 'Out of time: temporal conflict in Ann Radcliffe's *The Mysteries of Udolpho*, *European Romantic Review* 30:5 (2019): 595–614.
26 Terry Castle, 'The Spectralization of the Other in *The Mysteries of Udolpho*', in Laura Brown and Felicity A. Nussbaum (eds), *The New Eighteenth Century: Theory, Politics, English Literature* (London and New York: Routledge, 1991), pp. 231–53.
27 Henry Home, Lord Kames, *Elements of Criticism*, 3rd edition, 2 vols (Edinburgh, 1765), vol. 1, p. 82.

simple endurance, by resisting the forces that would have her collapse back in on herself:

> When they returned to the chateau, Lady Blanche conducted Emily to her favourite turret, and from thence they rambled through the ancient chambers, which Blanche had visited before ...
>
> While Emily looked from one of the casements, she perceived, with surprise, some objects, that were familiar to her memory;—the fields and woods, with the gleaming brook, which she had passed with La Voisin, one evening, soon after the death of Monsieur St. Aubert, in her way from the monastery to her cottage; and she now knew this to be the chateau, which he had then avoided, and concerning which he had dropped some remarkable hints.
>
> Shocked by this discovery, yet scarcely knowing why, she mused for some time in silence ... The music, too, which she had formerly heard, and, respecting which La Voisin had given such an odd account, occurred to her, and, desirous of knowing more concerning it, she asked Dorothée whether it returned at midnight, as usual, and whether the musician had yet been discovered.
>
> 'Yes, ma'amselle', replied Dorothée, 'that music is still heard, but the musician has never been found out, nor ever will, I believe; though there are some people, who can guess.'
>
> 'Indeed!' said Emily, 'then why do they not pursue the enquiry?'
>
> 'Ah, young lady! enquiry enough has been made—but who can pursue a spirit?'
>
> Emily smiled, and, remembering how lately she had suffered herself to be led away by superstition, determined now to resist its contagion; yet, in spite of her efforts, she felt awe mingle with her curiosity, on this subject ...[28]

This scene from *The Mysteries of Udolpho* (1794) is especially rich for understanding Radcliffe's way with time. It is a deeply layered moment. It occurs mid-way through the romance; it looks back at what has already happened, while anticipating what is yet to come. At its core is resistance to the 'contagion of superstition' that threatens to infect, and dissolve, Emily's sense of her own personhood.

The personhood of Radcliffe's heroines is held in suspension between two alternative versions of the sublime. Both are inflected by what Taylor calls 'kairotic knots'.[29] 'Kairos' means a right, critical or opportune moment. In 'homogenous, empty time' (Taylor is quoting Walter Benjamin's description

---

28 Ann Radcliffe, *The Mysteries of Udolpho*, edited by Bonamy Dobrée with notes and intro. by Terry Castle (Oxford: Oxford University Press, 2008), pp. 489–90.
29 Taylor, *A Secular Age*, p. 54.

of modern secular time) kairotic knots occur 'in the stories we tell about ourselves'. These are moments 'whose nature and placing calls for reversal, followed by others demanding rededication'. The secular example that Taylor gives, at the level of nationalist historiography, is revolution, where the national purpose is made clear, and acts of rededication made. But in 'the pre-modern era, the organizing field for ordinary time came from ... higher times'.[30] The revolution in Elizabeth Bennet's understanding, where she rededicates herself to the principle of self-knowledge, would be just such a personal, secular, kairotic knot. A 'pre-modern' example, on the other hand, would be the result of some kind of supernatural intervention, one providing a glimpse into 'higher times'. The sublime in Radcliffe pivots around moments that act, simultaneously, as sacred and profane kairotic knots.

The lengthy passage quoted above is a perfect example. In order to appreciate the ways in which this is so, we have to identify its numerous layers. The mixture of 'curiosity' and 'awe' offers us our deepest clue. It glances back at two significant moments in the romance, either of which could be the previous occasion where Emily had 'suffered herself to be led away by superstition'. The nearest in time is the moment that Emily lifts the veil, dropping unconscious on the spot, her mind overcome, filled with 'horror' to the exclusion of all else. The narrator explains the source of Emily's shock by tracking her train of association as she wandered the chambers of Udolpho, enjoying the 'view of ancient grandeur' – that is, from 'the strange history of the former possessor of the edifice' (Signora Laurentini), to

> the conversation of Annette, together with the circumstance of the veil, throwing a mystery over the subject, that excited a faint degree of terror. But a terror of this nature, as it occupies and expands the mind, and elevates it to high expectation, is purely sublime, and leads us, by a kind of fascination, to seek even the object, from which we appear to shrink.[31]

Awe, terror, curiosity, plus a safe vantage point, equals the 'pure' sublime, as the reader knows from Edmund Burke.[32] Expecting simple terror (an affair of the imagination), Emily is confronted by complex horror (the decaying body of Laurentini, as she has been to led to believe from Annette's garbled

---

30 Taylor, *A Secular Age*, p. 54. 31 Radcliffe, *Mysteries of Udolpho*, p. 248.
32 Edmund Burke, *A Philosophical Enquiry into the Origins of Our Ideas of the Sublime and Beautiful* (London, 1757), pp. 13–14.

account).³³ In the tension between 'buffered' and 'porous', the latter – a self whose boundaries are defensible only through magic or superstition – appears to be triggered by the threat of violence, by the imago of the violated female body. But this, as we shall see, is only a single layer.

Sensational though it is, Laurentini's history (as related by Annette) is not strictly supernatural, and Emily may be thinking of the previous time that she smiled at the threat of superstition before her mind succumbed to its 'contagion'. It occurs during her first visit to the Chateau-le-Blanc with her ailing father. Here they meet La Voisin, a peasant whose own life's story weirdly doubles that of St Aubert.³⁴ A haunting strain of music floats through the air. La Voisin comments:

> 'They say it often comes to warn people of their death, but I have heard it these many years, and outlived the warning.'
> Emily, though she smiled at the mention of this ridiculous superstition, could not, in the present tone of her spirits, wholly resist its contagion.
> 'Well, but, my good friend', said St. Aubert, 'has nobody had courage to follow the sounds? If they had, they would probably have discovered who is the musician.'³⁵

This passage brings two more layers into focus. The first is the superstition that hearing spectral music is a harbinger of death, a pre-modern kairotic knot. The second is that the death that matters is the death of the father. Although St Aubert plays the role of Enlightenment sceptic in discounting music as a fatal harbinger, it is certainly true for him, as he dies shortly after this episode. The association of superstition, contagion (the porous self) and the 'pure' sublime (the mixture of awe and curiosity) is later re-emphasised in the scene in which Emily attempts to burn her father's papers, and as she does so, finds herself being viewed by the ghost of her father as she approaches her task with a blend of 'curiosity and terror'.³⁶

The sublime in Radcliffe, then, pivots in two directions, one towards modernity and the secular, buffered self, the other back towards an enchanted world of porous subjectivity. The former is associated with the paternal imago, and terror, the latter with the maternal, and horror. The one tends towards the profane, the other to the supernatural. In either case,

---

33 For the terror/horror distinction in the Gothic, see Robert Miles, 'Ann Radcliffe and Matthew Lewis', in David Punter (ed.), *A New Companion to the Gothic* (Oxford: Wiley-Blackwell, 2012), pp. 94–109 (p. 94).
34 Robert Miles, 'The surprising Mrs Radcliffe: *Udolpho*'s artful mysteries', *Women's Writing* 22:3 (2015): 300–16 (p. 302).
35 Radcliffe, *Mysteries of Udolpho*, p. 68.   36 Radcliffe, *Mysteries of Udolpho*, p. 103.

symbolically, these experiences – where the heroine's personhood comes under threat – are generally signalled by the presence of a turret, a room with a window, or a threshold of some kind. Here Emily gazes from a window in the paternal home of La Vallée after the death of her father:

> The deep repose of the scene, the rich scents, that floated on the breeze, the grandeur of the wide horizon and of the clear blue arch, soothed and gradually elevated her mind to that sublime complacency, which renders the vexations of this world so insignificant . . . Emily forgot Madame Cheron and all the circumstances of her conduct, while her thoughts ascended to the contemplation of those unnumbered worlds, that lie scattered in the depths of aether, thousands of them hid from human eyes, and almost beyond the flight of human fancy. As her imagination soared through the regions of space, and aspired to that Great First Cause, which pervades and governs all being, the idea of her father scarcely ever left her; but it was a pleasing idea, since she resigned him to God in the full confidence of a pure and holy faith.[37]

Here the sublime stretches (in clear homage to Anna Laetitia Barbauld's 'A Summer Evening's Meditation' [1773]) to the intergalactic and the imaginative stupefaction of deep time where linearity stretches to its vanishing point. It is a secular kairotic knot presided over by the father's imago, the 'idea' that 'scarcely ever left her'.

The father's association with the buffered self is underlined by the first appearance of the word 'contagion' in the narrative. It is initially used by St Aubert in his Polonius-like advice to his daughter:

> 'A well-informed mind,' he would say, 'is the best security against the contagion of folly and of vice. The vacant mind is ever on the watch for relief, and ready to plunge into error, to escape from the languor of idleness. Store it with ideas, teach it the pleasure of thinking; and the temptations of the world without, will be counteracted by the gratifications derived from the world within. Thought, and cultivation, are necessary equally to the happiness of a country and a city life; in the first they prevent the uneasy sensations of indolence, and afford a sublime pleasure in the taste they create for the beautiful, and the grand; in the latter, they make dissipation less an object of necessity, and consequently of interest.'[38]

The passage is part insight, part misdirection. Insight, because it sketches the dynamics of the buffered self: from the redoubt of a well-stocked and cultivated 'world within' – an image of the autonomous self – so that the contagion of 'vice' may be resisted. Misdirection, because vice is not the

37 Radcliffe, *Mysteries of Udolpho*, pp. 113–14.   38 Radcliffe, *Mysteries of Udolpho*, p. 6.

quarter from which the danger will come – rather, it is from those incorrigible mental experiences that immediately fill the 'vacant' mind, whether the unveiled image of the violated female body or the 'superstitious', abject sublime.

We now have all the pieces we need to appreciate the extended passage quoted above, and how it represents the Gothic sense of time. The scene is witnessed across a threshold (a 'casement'), an image of the autonomous, 'punctual' self.[39] Emily's gaze aestheticises nature, in the manner of the well-stocked mind urged by her father: 'the fields and woods, with the gleaming brook, which she had passed with La Voisin'. The phrasing appears to be building towards the kind of landscape description that pervades the novel: one where 'thought and cultivation . . . afford a sublime pleasure in the taste they create for the beautiful, and the grand'. The momentum towards the paternal, secular, 'buffered' sublime is interrupted, however, by the familiarity of the scene. A memory surfaces of a previous encounter with this landscape, where Emily's father hinted at mysteries connected to the family, and to the chateau that she now recollects from her earlier visit. 'Shocked by this discovery', she attends to the music that now floats through the forest, which she had also previously heard. Time threatens to collapse, in the manner of Marcel Proust's 'madeleine' moment. In the period since her first visit to the environs of Chateau-le-Blanc, much has happened to Emily. Her father has died; she is taken to the Apennines by her aunt; she endures imprisonment at Udolpho, before escaping through extraordinary feats of endurance and resistance. Through it all, she has developed her character by cleaving to her father's advice, his tutelage and education. It is not the music itself that precipitates the temporary collapse of Emily's carefully cultivated, buffered self; instead, it is Annette's hint that the music is the work of a spirit, a creature of the enchanted world. The sublime overcomes Emily, which is to say that she is undone by the mixture of 'awe and curiosity' that is its defining mark. The reader has to wait before she can appreciate fully the nature of this moment of the superstitious sublime. We must follow the leads, from the music, to the nun Sister Agnes who plays it, to the revelation that the nun is in fact Laurentini, to Emily's aunt, the Marchioness, murdered by Laurentini, and finally to Emily's buried fear that the Marchioness is in fact her biological mother. As we do, we experience the pivot in Radcliffe's representation of the sublime, from the 'pure', paternal version, an instrument of the buffered self (a sublime of terror), to the maternal, which the

---

39 Charles Taylor, *Sources of the Self*, p. 159.

heroine experiences as the failure to surmount the beliefs of the enchanted world (an anti-sublime of horror). The apparent *Bildungsroman* tracing Emily's education and development collapses back into past time. Rather than the linearity of modernity, Emily's experience of the kairotic moment, where music and memory overlap with each other, leads to a reversal and the fear of rededication to ambiguous 'higher times'. Rather than an upward narrative drive towards a character formed on paternal principles, Emily's experience of the haunting music throws her back into circularity, repetition and the ghost of the violated maternal body (traceable through the pattern of association that has become visible by the novel's end: that is, from Laurentini, as both repentant nun and mouldering body, to the Marchioness she poisoned, to the Marchioness as Emily's imagined, murdered mother).

The Tale of Terror

In her seminal essay, 'On the Pleasure Derived from Objects of Terror' (1773), Anna Laetitia Aikin had earlier expanded upon the modern paradox of 'the apparent delight with which we dwell upon the objects of pure terror', including, as examples, 'tales of ghosts and goblins', as well 'murders, earthquakes, fires, murders'.[40] Anna Laetitia Aikin, together with her brother John in the accompanying Gothic tale 'Sir Bertrand, a Fragment' (1773), both anticipate, and fuel, the fad for the uncanny that overwhelmed the Romantic reading public. Taylor finds this moment significant:

> Perhaps the clearest sign of the transformation of our world is that today many people look back to the world of the porous self with nostalgia. As though the creation of a thick emotional boundary between us and the cosmos were now lived as a loss. The aim is to try to recover some measure of this lost feeling. So people go to the movies about the uncanny in order to experience a frisson. Our peasant ancestors would have thought us insane. You can't get a frisson from what is really in fact terrifying you.[41]

Taylor's comments effectively bring together the Burkean and Radcliffean sublimes. As with Burke, the sublime frisson that comes from an exposure to the cosmos in all its terrifying mystery is only enjoyed by a self that is safe and 'buffered'; but as with Radcliffe, the deepest frisson comes not from the

---

40 Anna Laetitia Aikin, 'On the Pleasure Derived from Objects of Terror', in E. J. Clery and Robert Miles (eds), *Gothic Documents, A Sourcebook: 1750–1820* (Manchester and New York: Manchester University Press, 2000), pp. 127–9 (p. 128).
41 Taylor, *A Secular Age*, p. 38.

imaginative exposure to the immensities of deep time, nor from the unfathomable hand of the creator obscured by the veil of nature, but from a reimagining of the porous self.

It is a curious fact of the rise of the Gothic that the fear underlying the porous self – the fear of once more finding oneself vulnerable to the contagion of superstition that re-enchants and re-animates the world – is resolutely gendered as feminine, not just in its putative audience, but in the subject suffering the 'contagion', a word that nicely catches the abjection at work in the Enlightenment construction of 'superstition'. And so it is with the tale of terror, the poetic version of the Gothic that, for a few years in the early 1800s, swept all before it, beginning with Matthew Gregory Lewis's edited collection, *Tales of Wonder* (1801) and its anonymous 'companion' volume, *Tales of Terror* (1801).[42] Featuring such luminaries as Walter Scott, Robert Southey and Lewis himself, these collections set the fashion for the tale of terror, typically, a faux-Medieval ballad featuring romantic love, the supernatural and death. The fashion had a very particular origin: Edinburgh in the late summer of 1794. It was there that Anna Laetitia Barbauld 'electrified' an audience by reading aloud Gottfried August Bürger's 'Lenore' (1773), translated by her ex-student William Taylor of Norwich (with the title changed to 'Lenora').[43] Although he missed the reading, Walter Scott heard about and requested a copy of Taylor's translation, an event that Scott later credited for instilling in him the desire to become a poet.[44]

'Lenora' is set in the Middle Ages, during the reign of the English king, Richard I. Lenora anxiously waits for the return of her beloved from the Crusades. It is a poem of two halves. The first half tells the story of Lenora's despair; of how her betrothed William's 'fellow-soldiers come back' from the Holy Land, but without her beloved; and how her mother is unable to allay Lenora's distress in the midst of others rejoicing. Becoming ever more frantic, Lenora declares:

---

42 Douglass H. Thomson (ed.), 'Introduction', *Tales of Wonder*, by Matthew Gregory Lewis (Peterborough, Ont.: Broadview, 2010), pp. 13–36 (p. 34).

43 The precise year in which Barbauld recited Bürger's poem in Edinburgh has been the source of considerable disagreement among critics. While some cite the year as 1793, I follow here the dates of September–October 1794, as cited in the chronology included in William McCarthy and Elizabeth Kraft's definitive edition of Barbauld's works, *Anna Letitia Barbauld: Selected Poetry and Prose* (Peterborough, Ont.: Broadview, 2002), p. 35. For an alternative dating, see the editorial Introduction to Walter Scott, *An Apology for Tales of Terror* <www.walterscott.lib.ed.ac.uk/works/poetry/apology/introduction.html> (last accessed 10 February 2019).

44 Anon., 'The worthies of Norwich', *Littell's Living Age* no. 1836 (August 23, 1879): 451–70 (p. 462).

> 'O mother, mother! gone is gone:
> My hope is all forlorn;
> The grave mie onlye safeguarde is—
> O, had I ne'er been borne!'[45]

The second half tells the story of a single, protracted moment. Lenora commits the unpardonable sin of despair; or rather, despair happens to her:

> And so despaire did rave and rage
> Athwarte her boiling veins;
> Against the Providence of God
> She hurlde her impious strains.   (ll. 85–9)

Her damnation is immediate. This is the next stanza but one:

> When harke! abroade she hearde the trampe
> Of nimble-hoofed steed;
> She hearde a knighte with clank alighte,
> And climb the staire in speede.   (ll. 93–6)

As the reader soon deduces, it is Death that comes to call. Ballads naturally tell a story, but, from this moment on, there really is no story to tell. Lenora is already dead and in the grave. Narrative, on the other hand, is about duration and time. Taylor squares the circle through repetition. In the elongated moment of Lenora's damnation and death, where she is escorted to the grave by a ghostly simulacrum of her beloved William, the following stanza is repeated three times after intervals of nine and six stanzas:

> Tramp, tramp, across the land they speede;
> Splash, splash, across the see:
> 'hurrah! the dead can ride apace;
> Dost feare to ride with mee?'   (ll. 157–60)

Taylor's translation describes a warp in time: a moment has become an eternity, in which Lenora rides with her beloved until 'an yren-grated grate / Soon biggens to their viewe' (ll. 229–30). Taylor slyly refers to the formal principle that he uses to create a sense of extended, or warped time. Death declares:

> Look up, look up, and airy crewe
> In roundel daunces reele:
> The moone is bryghte, and blue the nyghte,
> Mayst dimlie see them wheele.   (ll. 197–200)

---

45 William Taylor, 'Lenora', in Thomson (ed.), *Tales of Wonder*, pp. 222–31 (p. 225, ll. 61–4). All subsequent quotations are cited parenthetically in the text.

While not a strict roundel, the second half of the ballad proceeds through the roundel's typical structure of a repeated refrain. Within this repeating structure (an endless 'wheele') there is the apparent linear movement of time. Death declares:

> I weene the cock prepares to crowe;
> The sand will soone be runne:
> I snuffe the earlye morning aire;
> Downe, downe! our worke is done. (ll. 221–4)

In the warp of time the night has stretched to accommodate a ride of a 'thousand miles' (l. 123); on the other hand, despite the hourglass and its running sand, it is a mere instant. For as the poem also makes clear, Death here is a figure for a kind of black magic. The point is made through a locked-door mystery:

> And soon she herde a tinkling hande,
> That twirled at the pin;
> And thro' her door, that open'd not,
> These words were breathed in.
>
> 'What ho! what ho! thy dore undoe;
> Art watching or asleepe?
> My love, dost yet remember mee,
> And dost thou laugh or weep?' (ll. 97–104)

Lenora is undone, as it were, from the inside: 'All in her sarke, as there she lay, / Upon his horse she sprung' (ll. 145–6). In one respect this is a version of the Gothic's familiar master-trope of live burial, where unwanted barriers remain firm and wanted ones leak like sieves. Death declares:

> All as thou ly'st upon thy couch,
> Aryse, no longer stop;
> The wedding guests thy coming waite,
> The chamber dore is ope. (ll. 121–4)

The chamber door here is the grave; in a few stanzas we have segued – through an extended chiasmus – from Lenore's locked bedroom door, which, though locked, is open, to the burial chamber, whose door, though open, is forever closed to those who would leave.

There is, of course, a respectable theological veneer insulating the poem's Gothicism. Lenora despairs of God's mercy, and like Dr Faustus, who commits the same sin, she is punished with eternal damnation. The Gothic nature of the poem emerges once we ask at what point is Lenora damned? The answer appears to be this stanza:

> Go out, go out, my lampe of life;
>   In grislie darkness die:
> There is no mercye, sure, above!
>   For ever let me lie.   (ll. 65–8)

Lenora's mother, horrified, exclaims:

> Almighty God! O do not judge
>   My poor unhappy childe;
> She knows not what her lips pronounce,
>   Her anguish makes her wilde.   (ll. 69–72)

It is, evidently, already too late. Lenora is dammed the moment that she utters the declarative 'Go out, go out, my lampe of life'! As if to underline the point, Taylor repeats the line two stanzas later. Lenora is either already outside of a temporal world, where things change, or she crosses her Rubicon with the second declaration. Either way, we are beyond conventional theological territory, where even the determined Faustus is given several chances to repent. Lenore has none: the magic of words undoes her. In 'Lenora', a curse has become a sure-fire performative.

Worse, it leads to her immediate death. No sooner has she damned herself through her incautious words, than – as we have seen – death comes to call. This is Gothic in the familiar sense that it describes a universe from which God the benevolent father may be absent, but God as a jealous and malevolent force outside any moral logic remains. To put it another way, the supernatural realm has collapsed back into a primitive world of good and bad magic, one as irrational as the other, where the uncanny's terrifying power is undimmed – in Lenora's case, the uncanny power of words to turn utterance into performance.[46]

'Christabel'

Taylor's translation of Bürger's 'Lenore' reprises many of the same elements that we later encounter in Radcliffe's *Udolpho*. Both texts feature the figuration of what Charles Taylor would call the porous self, which is to say, a self vulnerable to invasive, malevolent magic; this magic is in turn represented as

---

[46] In his essay on the uncanny, Freud refers to the supernatural tendency of words to become deeds as the 'omnipotence of thoughts'.

uncanny; the porous self is gendered female; there is a contrast between linear time associated with narrative and subject development (if negatively so in the first half of 'Lenora'), and a circular time of repetition, of repeating 'wheels', that is outside or beyond ordinary secular time; and, finally, both texts feature 'kairotic knots', or temporal warps. When Lenora commands her lamp of light to go out she initiates a reversal in her life fortunes, immediately provoking a warp in time, just as time collapses and reverses for Emily when the contagion of superstition overcomes her.

It is the nature of genres rapidly to turn 'meta'; once a genre's first practitioners have developed that genre's narrative vocabulary and syntax, the way is clear for subsequent writers to develop a reflexive practice in which the animating principles of the genre are not just reproduced, but commented upon. Such is the case with Samuel Taylor Coleridge's 'Christabel' (1816), which takes the elements we have so far seen in Radcliffe and Burger/Taylor, and fashions them into a fascinating commentary on the Gothic's relation to modernity. In his 1816 Preface to 'Christabel', Coleridge protests against the charge of plagiarism that he expects to receive for echoing the method of Walter Scott's *The Lay of the Last Minstrel*, published to great acclaim in 1805, on the grounds that Coleridge had completed the fragment we now have before 1800.[47] Like many of Coleridge's public pronouncements, the claim is more smokescreen than disculpation, for the work that his method flatters is obviously not Scott's, but Taylor's *Lenora*, first published to great acclaim in 1796, two years before 'Christabel' was even started. 'Christabel' (like many other Tales of Terror) is not only a reworking of what Henry James would call Taylor's donnée, 'his subject, his idea',[48] but his poetic method of 'medievalising' the ballad. While Taylor's stylistic influence is more pronounced in *The Rime of the Ancient Mariner* (1798) at the level of the stanza, it is also present in Coleridge's main stylistic innovation in 'Christabel', which is to capture the driving rhythm of Taylor's translation by subordinating syllables to accents, or stresses. In his Preface to the poem, Coleridge tells us that though the number of syllables per line 'may vary from seven to twelve, yet in each line the accents will be found to be only four'. Coleridge claims that the number of syllables varies in relation to 'some transition in the nature of the imagery or passion',[49] but the

---

47 Samuel Taylor Coleridge, 'Preface to "Christabel"', in Duncan Wu (ed.), *Romanticism: An Anthology*, 4th edition (Oxford: Wiley-Blackwell, 2012), pp. 659–60 (p. 659).
48 Henry James, *The Art of Fiction* <https://public.wsu.edu/~campbelld/amlit/artfiction.html> (last accessed 10 February 2019).
49 Coleridge, 'Preface to "Christabel"', in Wu (ed.) *Romanticism: An Anthology*, p. 659.

overall effect of retaining four strong stresses per line (which is what a stress-timed metre allows one to do) is to create a marked sense of time: not quite a metronome, but a pronounced pulsation, nonetheless.

This stylistic innovation is important, because it underlines the main division in the poem, which is between the world depicted and the means of depicting it. The world depicted is an enchanted world of magic, transference, porous boundaries between this world and a supernatural one, of an interconnected lower and higher time. We are, however, buffered from this world through the means of its depiction. The narrative that tells us about the goings-on in the world of the poem is itself the product of a 'modern', post-enchantment subjectivity, in the manner of, for example, Horace Walpole's *The Castle of Otranto* (1764), which describes in the first Preface to the novel a pre-Reformational world through the self-conscious style of a post-Reformational polemicist. Coleridge had a deep, intuitive, agonised relationship to Romantic irony. He was painfully self-conscious of his own distance from the kind of naïve openness to the world that marked genuine products of original genius. Coleridge dramatises this self-consciousness through his narrator, who manifestly is incapable of understanding the world of enchantment unfolding before him. He can pedantically parse what he sees, or sentimentally gloss the goings on that he describes; but directly access the naïve worldview of his subjects he cannot do. Like any other modern, self-conscious poet, he can simulate, rather than share in, the kind of bygone culture that produced worlds of 'fine fabling'. In Taylor's terms, the buffering of the narrator's subjectivity insulates him from the terrors of the enchanted world. One of the marks of this buffering is the linear sense of time that is subliminally communicated to the reader through the clock-like regularity of the rhythm. The narration is marked by regular, linear time, whereas the world depicted is frequently warped and cyclical.

Taylor's *donnée* is divulged in the first stanza of 'Lenora':

> At break of day, with frightful dreams
> Lenora struggled sore:
> My William, art thou slaine, say'd she,
> Or dost thou love no more?   (ll. 1–4)

Are Lenora's dreams so frightful because her erotic desires overpower religious prudence (for which she is punished), or are they frightful because Death already has his sights on Lenora, as a vulnerable soul, and so primes her mind with equivocal dreams (in the manner of much subsequent Gothic writing, from Radcliffe's *The Romance of the Forest* [1791], through to Matthew

Gregory Lewis's *The Monk* [1796] and Charlotte Dacre's *Zofloya* [1806])? Coleridge borrows Taylor's idea, unpacking it in the process:

> The lovely lady, Christabel,
> Whom her father loves so well,
> What makes her in the wood so late,
> A furlong from the castle gate?
> She had dreams all yesternight
> Of her own betrothèd knight;
> Dreams that made her moan and leap
> As on her bed she lay in sleep;
> And she in the midnight wood will pray
> For the weal of her lover that's far away.   (ll. 23–32)

Coleridge takes the same subject matter (a young girl pining for her absent betrothed) but adds elements that thicken the plot. In Radcliffean terms, it is as if the narrator were an agent of the father who, rather than instilling into the heroine the buffering virtues of sensibility, reads them into her behaviour, so that he interprets her as a feminine subject disciplined by patriarchal virtues. Once cued into the unreliability of the narrator, the reader begins to spy a consistent gap between the world that Christabel inhabits and the one projected onto that world by the narrator. Taylor tells us outright that Lenora's dreams were 'frightful', whereas the reader of 'Christabel' is left to intuit as much, once they begin to read past the narrator's speculative glosses:

> She stole along, she nothing spoke,
> The sighs she heaved were soft and low,
> And naught was green upon the oak
> But moss and rarest misletoe:
> She kneels beneath the huge oak tree,
> And in silence prayeth she.   (ll. 33–8)

The narrator reads Christabel as a figure of innocence: she goes to the woods to pray for her betrothed's well-being. But why the sighs 'soft and low'? Why does she steal, as if she were a guilty thing? If her father loves her so well, why does she need to put distance between herself and the castle in order to 'pray' for her lover, if, indeed, praying is what she is doing? Finally, why does the narrator pass over the detail of the mistletoe, which was used in the period of the poem as protection against witches and demons? Read in the light of 'Lenora', we come to understand that the narrator is suppressing the central question: is Christabel tormented by transgressive desire? Is she already haunted by demons, despite the mistletoe? Are these, in fact, one and the same question? Freud, of course, supplies a ready answer, but in order to understand how Coleridge represents time we need to suspend our Freudian disbelief for a moment.

After she kneels to 'pray', the following happens:

> The lady sprang up suddenly,
> The lovely lady Christabel!
> It moaned as near, as near can be,
> But what it is she cannot tell.— (ll. 39–42)

Has Christabel silently transgressed, in the manner of Lenora? The question arises because the world misunderstood by the buffered narrator is one of magic, of good and bad spirits, animism, and a strange and intense form of telepathy where words and looks have occult powers (a form Freud termed the 'omnipotence of thoughts', borrowing the phrase from one of his patients).[50] What connection is there between Christabel's dreams that make her 'moan and leap', and the 'moan' that she now hears?

> The night is chill; the forest bare;
> Is it the wind that moaneth bleak?
> There is not wind enough in the air
> To move away the ringlet curl
> From the lovely lady's cheek;
> There is not wind enough to twirl
> The one red leaf, the last of its clan,
> That dances as often as dance it can,
> Hanging so light, and hanging so high,
> On the topmost twig that looks up at the sky. (ll. 45–54)

The moaning, we shortly discover, comes from Geraldine, who appears to be some kind of evil spirit in the guise of an abused Gothic heroine. Although baffled by her sudden appearance, the narrator's question-and-answer routine (which he reverts to whenever the supernatural intrudes) is nevertheless revealing. Given that it is a windless night, speculation that it is the wind that moans is obviously pointless, but it prompts an illuminating illustration, the 'one red leaf . . . That dances as often dance it can'. John Ruskin used this as a prime example of the 'pathetic fallacy', which involves, in the act of 'morbid' personification, the poetic ascription of agency to nature: in other words, animism.[51] In Charles Taylor's terms, the locution 'pathetic fallacy' performs

---

50 Freud, 'The "Uncanny"', in Strachey (ed. and trans.), p. 240.
51 John Ruskin, *Modern Painters* <www.ourcivilisation.com/smartboard/shop/ruskinj/> (last accessed 10 February 2019).

the cultural work of identifying and demystifying 'animism', thus disembedding the human subject from nature, buffering it in the process. But in the world that Geraldine inhabits, animism is very much alive.

We can see this by following the permutations of the word 'moan'. It next appears in association with the old mastiff bitch that guards the castle:

> The mastiff old did not awake,
> Yet she an angry moan did make!
> And what can ail the mastiff bitch?
> Never till now she uttered yell
> Beneath the eye of Christabel.
> Perhaps it is the owlet's scritch:
> For what can ail the mastiff bitch?   (ll. 142–8)

The buffered narrator is once again all at sea. Despite his cluelessness, the reader deduces that the dog moans, angrily, because she senses the approach of an evil spirit. This equation is made explicit later on, when, after her night of ambiguous seduction, Geraldine wipes Christabel's memory through a kind of curse, so that reporting 'Thou heard'st a low moaning,/ And found'st a bright lady, surpassingly fair' is alone 'in her power to declare' (ll. 261–64). But in bard Bracy's prophetic dream, matters are turned upside down:

> For in my sleep I saw that dove,
> That gentle bird, whom thou dost love,
> And call'st by thy own daughter's name—
> Sir Leoline! I saw the same
> Fluttering, and uttering fearful moan,
> Among the green herbs in the forest alone.   (ll. 519–24)

Regardless of the accuracy of bard Bracy's dream, an equation is now drawn between Christabel and Geraldine, where both are apparently discovered in the woods moaning in distress. A Freudian reading would interpret Geraldine as an externalisation of Christabel's repressed desire, and, therefore, as her double. But in a Tayloresque reading, the important point to note is that the world of the poem is one in which boundaries are porous, or easily crossed, and where the boundary is alternatively protected, or surrendered, by white or black sorcery, by the white, protective magic of the 'wandering mother' (l. 199), and her surrogate, the mastiff bitch, or the invasive black magic of Geraldine. In an animistic world, spirits are constantly moving across thresholds, from one body to the next. Thus Christabel, invaded by Geraldine:

> A snake's small eye blinks dull and shy;
> And the lady's eyes they shrunk in her head,
> Each shrunk up to a serpent's eye
> And with somewhat of malice, and more of dread,
> At Christabel she looked askance!
> One moment and the sight was fled!
> But Christabel, in dizzy trance
> Stumbling on the unsteady ground
> Shuddered aloud, with a hissing sound;
> And Geraldine again turned round,
> And like a thing, that sought relief,
> Full of wonder and full of grief,
> She rolled her large bright eyes divine
> Wildly on Sir Leoline.   (ll. 571–84)

If bard Bracy's dream is true, the moaning dove is Christabel and the snake strangely throttling / embracing her is Geraldine. But now, through 'forced unconscious sympathy' (l. 598), Christabel takes on Geraldine's serpentine characteristics ('hissing'). The telepathy between them is so profound that, syntactically at least, we do not know who rolls her eyes wildly on Sir Leoline: Christabel or Geraldine. The next stanza expatiates further on this strange interchange of personalities:

> So deeply she had drunken in
> That look, those shrunken serpent eyes,
> That all her features were resigned
> To this sole image in her mind:
> And passively did imitate
> That look of dull and treacherous hate!   (ll. 589–94)

The two girls are now effectively one.

Or rather, that is how the narrator construes it. In his telling, the aggressive and perverse Geraldine stamps her image on the soft wax of Christabel's impressionable innocence, on 'the maid, devoid of guile and sin'. The alternative interpretation – and it is a view that we can surmise that the narrator is striving to keep at bay – is that there is indeed an alarming mobility between the souls of the girls, with the spirit of the one occupying the other, and vice versa. Within the poem, animism – the ability of spirits to wander and cross boundaries, physical or magic – is gendered female, from the ghost of Christabel's mother, punningly dubbed 'wandering mother' (that is, hysteria, the rising womb), to Geraldine, who breaches the castle's defenses by crossing its threshold with Christabel's help.

Opposed to animism is the male world of the Castle, a figure for the buffered self. Each of the poem's two parts begin by dwelling on time:

> 'Tis the middle of night by the castle clock,
> And the owls have awakened the crowing cock;
> Tu—whit! Tu—whoo!
> And hark, again! the crowing cock,
> How drowsily it crew.
> Sir Leoline, the Baron rich,
> Hath a toothless mastiff bitch;
> From her kennel beneath the rock
> She makes answer to the clock,
> Four for the quarters, and twelve for the hour;
> Ever and aye, moonshine and shower,
> Sixteen short howls, not overloud;
> Some say, she sees my lady's shroud. .   (ll. 8–13)

The castle clock beats out the rhythms of secular time in opposition to a ghost – 'my lady's shroud'. The mastiff bitch appears to occupy a mediating position between the supernatural and disenchanted worlds: on the one hand she echoes, and reproduces, the demarcations of chronological time with bizarre precision; on the other, she is in touch with the spirit world. This structure (empty, linear time marked by a chronometer; a world out of time; and a mediating figure) is reproduced at the start of Part II.

> 'Each matin bell', the Baron saith,
> 'Knells us back to a world of death'.
> These words Sir Leoline first said,
> When he rose and found his lady dead:
> These words Sir Leoline will say
> Many a morn to his dying day!   (ll. 320–6)

The matin bell marks the middle of the night – the witching hour. The matin bell knells us back to a world of death because it acts as a reminder of modern, empty, homogenous time, time parcelled by the ticking of a clock, where the dead stay dead: hence the need to memorialise them. For the Baron, time has become an essential element of the ritual he uses to buffer himself against death.

> And hence the custom and law began
> That still at dawn the sacristan,
> Who duly pulls the heavy bell,
> Five and forty beads must tell

> Between each stroke—a warning knell,
> Which not a soul can choose but hear
> From Bratha Head to Wyndermere.   (ll. 326–32)

The Baron imposes his chronometric 'time' on others, the souls who cannot chose not to hear it, as a stay against time. Here bard Bracy occupies the mediating place as he comments on how the knell bounces round the valley: 'Three sinful sextons' ghosts are pent, / Who all give back, one after t'other, / The death-note to their living brother' (ll. 341–3). Through his privileged position as bard, Bracy is in touch with both worlds: the buffered world of the castle locked fast within secular time, and the animistic world of nature, of ambulatory spirits, and timeless repetitions and cycles. In this respect the narrator is the antithesis of bard Bracy. The narrator is a poet of fancy, of limited understanding, of 'sentiment', as Schiller would say, meaning 'speculative' and detached, whereas Bracy retains his prophetic character, directly in touch with animistic principles that enlivened past worlds of fine fabling. The narrator is thus locked within the temporal understanding of modernity, of a linear secular time; insofar as he represents bard Bracy, he gives voice to an understanding, and experience of time (warped, cyclical, without obvious demarcations) he otherwise cannot comprehend, an especially vicious form of Romantic irony.

Ultimately time in the Gothic turns on the presence of the Gothic cusp, the tendency of Gothic writing to choose a setting that illustrates Hurd's 'revolution', where the animistic world of fine fabling – of ancient ballads and feudal beliefs – overlaps with the modern world that has supplanted it. For Charles Taylor, imagining the Gothic cusp and toying with the uncanny becomes possible, and, indeed, desirable precisely because the modern, punctual, buffered self has become the unquestioned norm. Early practitioners of the Gothic seemed intuitively to have understood this. Like someone enjoying the Burkean sublime, they imagine the terrors of the supernatural world from the safe vantage point of the buffered self, and as they do so they inscribe the basic temporal contrast of the Gothic, which is between the premodern world of ghosts (timeless, circular, repetitious, with porous boundaries between self and other, this world and the next), and the empty, chronometric, homogenous time of modernity.

Select Bibliography

All quoted sources are referenced in full in the footnotes to the chapters in this volume. Rather than repeat that information here, this Select Bibliography lists only longer works, and for the most part excludes duplicate editions of the same text, as well as shorter historical reviews and articles.

Abrams, M. H., *Natural Supernaturalism: Tradition and Revolution in Romantic Literature* (New York: W.W. Norton & Co., 1971).

Addison, Joseph, *Remarks on Several Parts of Italy, &c. in the Years 1701, 1702, 1703* (London, 1726).

Adelman, Janet, *Suffocating Mothers: Fantasies of Maternal Origin in Shakespeare's Plays, Hamlet to the Tempest* (New York and London: Routledge, 1992).

Aikin, J. and A. L. Aikin, *Miscellaneous Pieces, in Prose* (London, 1773).

Akenside, Mark, *The Pleasures of Imagination. A Poem in Three Books* (London, 1744).

Aldana Reyes, Xavier, *Spanish Gothic: National Identity, Collaboration and Cultural Adaptation* (Basingstoke: Palgrave Macmillan, 2017).

Alger, John Goldworth, *Napoleon's British Visitors and Captives, 1801–1815* (Westminster: Archibald Constable and Co., 1904).

Allan, Juliet, 'New light on William Kent at Hampton Court Palace', *Architectural History* 27 (1984): 50–8.

Al-Rawi, Ahmed K., 'The Arabic ghoul and its Western transformation', *Folklore* 120:3 (2009): 291–306.

Amory, Patrick, *People and Identity in Ostrogothic Italy, 489–554* (Cambridge: Cambridge University Press, 1997).

Anderson, Benedict, *Imagined Communities: Reflections on the Origin and Spread of Nationalism* (London: Verso, 1983).

Anderson, W. B., *Sidonius Apollinaris: Poems and Letters*, trans. by W. B. Anderson, 2 vols (Cambridge, MA and London: Harvard University Press, 1936).

Anon., *Powis Castle; or, Anecdotes of an Ancient Family*, 2 vols (London, 1788).

Aravamudan, Srinivas, *Enlightenment Orientalism: Resisting the Rise of the Novel* (Chicago and London: University of Chicago Press, 2012).

Armitage, David, *The Ideological Origins of the British Empire* (Cambridge: Cambridge University Press, 2000).

Armitage, David and Sanjay Subrahmanyam, 'Introduction: The Age of Revolutions, c. 1760–1840 – Global Causation, Connection, and Comparison', in David Armitage and Sanjay Subrahmanyam (eds), *The Age of Revolutions in Global* Context, *c. 1760–1840* (Basingstoke and New York: Palgrave Macmillan, 2010), pp. xii–xxxii.

Arnaud, George, *A Dissertation on Hermaphrodites* (London, 1750).

Arnold, Jonathan J., M. Shane Bjornlie and Kristina Sessa (eds), *A Companion to Ostrogothic Italy* (Leiden: Brill, 2016).

Arnold-de Simine, Silke, '"Lost in Translation"? Die englische Übersetzung von Benedikte Nauberts *Herrmann von Una*', in Barry Murnane and Andrew Cusack (eds), *Populäre Erscheinungen. Der deutsche Schauerroman um 1800* (Munich: Fink, 2011), pp. 121–33.

Astbury, Katherine, 'Du gothique anglais au gothique français: le roman noir et la Révolution française', in Catriona Seth (ed.), *Imaginaires gothiques: aux sources du roman noir français* (Paris: Desjonquères, 2010), pp. 131–45.

Austen, Jane, *Pride and Prejudice*, edited by Robert P. Irvine (Peterborough, Ont.: Broadview 2002).

Austen, Jane. *Northanger Abbey*, edited by Susan Fraiman (New York and London: W. W. Norton and Co., 2004).

Ayres, Philip, *Classical Culture and the Idea of Rome in Eighteenth-Century England* (Cambridge: Cambridge University Press, 1997).

Backscheider, Paula, *Spectacular Politics: Theatrical Power and Mass Culture in Early Modern England* (Baltimore: Johns Hopkins University Press, 1993).

Baines, Paul and Edward Burns (eds), *Five Romantic Plays, 1768–1821* (Oxford: Oxford University Press, 2000).

Baldwin, Edward [William Godwin], *The Pantheon, or, Ancient History of the Gods of Greece and Rome*, 2nd edition (London, 1809).

Ballaster, Ros, *Fabulous Orients: Fictions of the East in England 1662–1785* (Oxford: Oxford University Press, 2005).

Banks, Joseph, *The Endeavour Journal of Joseph Banks, 1768–1771*, edited by J. C. Beaglehole, 2 vols (Sydney: Public Library of New South Wales, 1962).

Barbauld, Anna Laetitia, *The Works of Anna Laetitia Barbauld*, edited by Lucy Aikin, 2 vols (London, Longman, Hurst, Rees, Orme, Browne, and Green, 1825).

Barkhoff, Jürgen, '"The echo of the question, as if it had merely resounded in a tomb": The Dark Anthropology of the *Schauerroman* in Schiller's *Der Geisterseher*', in Andrew Cusack and Barry Murnane (eds), *Popular Revenants: The German Gothic and Its International Reception, 1800–2000* (Rochester, NY: Camden House, 2012), pp. 44–59.

Baron-Wilson, Margaret, *Life and Correspondence of M. G. Lewis, Author of 'The Monk,' 'Castle Spectre', &c. With Many Pieces in Prose and Verse, Never Before Published*, 2 vols (London: Henry Colburn, 1839).

Barney, Stephen A., W. J. Lewis, J. A. Beach and Oliver Berghof (eds), *The Etymologies of Isidore of Seville*, trans. by Stephen A. Barney, W. J. Lewis, J. A. Beach and Oliver Berghof (Cambridge: Cambridge University Press, 2006).

Barnish, S. J. B., *Cassiodorus: Selected Variae* (Liverpool: Liverpool University Press, 1992).

Bataille, Georges, *The Accursed Share: An Essay on General Economy, Vol. I: Consumption*, trans. by Robert Hurley (New York: Zone Books, 1991).

Batchelor, Jennie, 'The claims of literature: women applicants to the Royal Literary Fund, 1790–1810', *Women's Writing* 12 (2005): 505–21.

Bate, Jonathan, 'Shakespeare and the Rival Muses: Siddons versus Jordan', in Robyn Asleson (ed.), *Notorious Muse: The Actress in British Art and Culture, 1776–1812* (New Haven: Yale University Press, 2003), pp. 81–103.
Bayly, C. A., *The Birth of the Modern World, 1780–1914: Global Connections and Comparisons* (Oxford and Malden, MA: Basil Blackwell, 2004).
Beattie, James, *Dissertations Moral and Critical* (London and Edinburgh, 1783).
Beauchamp, Alphonse de, *Biographie moderne, ou Dictionnaire biographique, de tous les hommes morts et vivans* (Leipzig: Besson, 1806)
Beckert, Sven, *Empire of Cotton: A Global History* (New York: Vintage, 2014).
Beckford, William, *An Arabian Tale, from an Unpublished Manuscript: With Notes Critical and Explanatory*, edited and translated by Samuel Henley (London, 1786).
Beckford, William, *Vathek with the Episodes of Vathek*, edited by Kenneth W. Graham (Peterborough, Ont.: Broadview, 2001).
Bentham, Jeremy, *A Fragment on Government*, edited by J. H. Burns and H. L. A. Hart (Cambridge: Cambridge University Press, 1988).
Bentley, Richard (ed.), *Q. Horatius Flaccus, ex recensione & cum notis atque emendationibus Richardi Bentleii* (Cambridge, 1711).
Berndt, Guido M. and Roland Steinacher (eds), *Arianism: Roman Heresy and Barbarian Creed* (Farnham: Ashgate, 2014).
Bettenson, Henry, *St Augustine: City of God*, intro. by John O'Meara (London: Penguin Books, 1984).
Bewell, Alan, *Romanticism and Colonial Disease* (Baltimore and London: Johns Hopkins University Press, 1999).
Bienville, M. D. T., *Nymphomania; or, A Dissertation Concerning the Furor Uterinus*, trans. by Edward Sloane Wilmot (London, 1775).
Billaut, L., *Le Château de Saint-Donats, ou Histoire du fils d'un émigré échappé aux massacres en France* (Tours: Brillault jeune; Paris: Onfroy, Fuchs, Debray, 1802).
Blackmore, Sir Richard, *Alfred. An Epick Poem* (London, 1723).
Blackstone, William, *Commentaries on the Laws of England*, 4 vols (Oxford, 1765–69).
Blair, Hugh, *A Critical Dissertation on the Poems of Ossian, the Son of Fingal* (London, 1763).
Blair, Hugh, *Lectures on Rhetoric and Belles Lettres*, 2 vols (London, 1783).
Blair, Robert, *The Grave. A Poem*, 2nd edition (London, 1743).
Blockley, R. C., *The Fragmentary Classicising Historians of the Later Roman Empire*, 2 vols (Liverpool: Francis Cairns, 1981–3).
Blood, Harold Christian, *Some Versions of Menippea*, unpublished PhD dissertation, University of California, Santa Cruz, 2011.
Boaden, James, *The Secret Tribunal* (London, 1795).
Boaden, James, *Aurelio and Miranda* (London, 1799).
Boaden, James, *Memoirs of Mrs. Siddons*, 2 vols (London, 1827).
Boaden, James, 'Fontainville Forest, A Play', in Steven Cohan (ed.), *The Plays of James Boaden* (New York: Garland, 1980), pp. 1–70.
Boaden, 'The Italian Monk', in Steven Cohan (ed.), *The Plays of James Boaden* (New York: Garland, 1980), pp. 1–78.
Boucé, Paul-Gabriel, *Sexuality in Eighteenth-Century Britain* (Manchester: Manchester University Press, 1998).

Select Bibliography

Bohls, Elizabeth A., *Romantic Literature and Postcolonial Studies* (Edinburgh: Edinburgh University Press, 2013).
Bond, Donald F. (ed.), *The Spectator*, 3 vols (Oxford: Clarendon Press, 1965).
Bond, Donald F. (ed.), *Critical Essays by Joseph Addison, with Four Essays by Richard Steele* (Oxford: Clarendon Press, 1970).
Bord, Gustave, *La Fin de deux légendes. L'affaire Léonard. Le baron de Batz* (Paris: Henri Daragon, 1909).
Botting, Fred, 'The Gothic Production of the Unconscious', in Glennis Byron and David Punter (eds), *Spectral Readings: Towards a Gothic Geography* (Basingstoke: Macmillan, 1999), pp. 11–36.
Botting, Fred, *Gothic*, 2nd edition (Abingdon and New York: Routledge, 2014).
Bour, Isabelle (ed.), *Maria, ou le Malheur d'être femme* (Saint-Etienne: Publications de l'Université de Saint-Etienne, 2005).
Bret, Patrice and Jean-Luc Chappey, 'Pratiques et enjeux scientifiques, intellectuels et politiques de la traduction (vers 1660–vers 1840) – vol. 1 – Les enjeux politiques des traductions entre Lumières et Empire', *La Révolution française* 12 (2017): 1–11.
Bridgwater, Patrick, *The German Gothic Novel in Anglo-German Perspective* (Amsterdam and New York: Rodopi, 2013).
Briquet, Fortunée, *Dictionnaire historique, littéraire et bibliographique des françaises et des étrangères naturalisées en France* (Paris: Treuttel et Würtz, 1804).
Bromley, Robert Anthony, *A Philosophical and Critical History of the Fine Arts*, 2 vols (London: Printed for the Author, 1793–95).
Bronfen, Elisabeth and Beate Neumeier (eds), *Gothic Renaissance: A Reassessment* (Manchester: Manchester University Press, 2014).
Brown, Hilary, *Benedikte Naubert (1756–1819) and Her Relations to English Culture* (Leeds: Maney, 2005).
Brown, Howard G., 'Mythes et massacres: reconsidérer la "terreur directoriale"', *Annales historiques de la Révolution française*, 325 (July–September 2001): 23–52.
Browne, Max, *The Romantic Art of Theodor von Holst, 1810–1844* (London: Lund Humphries 1994).
Bruhm, Steven, 'Gothic Sexualities', in Anna Powell and Andrew Smith (eds), *Teaching the Gothic* (Basingstoke: Palgrave Macmillan, 2006), pp. 93–106.
Bryant, Julius, 'From "Gusto" to "Kentissime": Kent's Designs for Country Houses, Villas, and Lodges', in Susan Weber (ed.), *William Kent: Designing Georgian Britain* (New Haven and London: Yale University Press, 2013), pp. 183–241.
Bugg, John, 'The other interesting narrative: Olaudah Equiano's public book tour', *PMLA* 121:5 (2006): 1424–42.
Bundock, Chris and Elizabeth Effinger (eds), *William Blake's Gothic Imagination: Bodies of Horror* (Manchester: Manchester University Press 2018).
Burgess, Miranda, 'Transporting *Frankenstein*: Mary Shelley's mobile figures', *European Romantic Review* 25:3 (2014): 247–65.
Burnet, Gilbert, *A Collection of Several Tracts and Discourses Written in the Years 1677, to 1704*, 3 vols (London, 1704).
Burnet, Gilbert, *Some Letters, containing An Account of What Seem'd Most Remarkable in Travelling Through Switzerland, Italy, Some Parts of Germany, &c.*, 3rd edition ([London?] 1708).

Burke, Edmund, *A Philosophical Enquiry into the Origin of Our Ideas of the Sublime and Beautiful*, edited by Adam Phillips (Oxford: Oxford University Press, 1990).

Burke, Edmund, *The Writings and Speeches of William Burke, Vol. V*, edited by P. J. Marshall and William B. Todd (Oxford: Oxford University Press, 1991).

Burke, Edmund, 'Speech on Opening of Impeachment', 15 February 1788, in *The Writings and Speeches of Edmund Burke, Vol. VI*, edited by P. J. Marshall and William B. Todd (Oxford: Oxford University Press, 1991), pp. 269–312.

Butler, Marilyn, 'Orientalism', in David B. Pirie (ed.), *The Penguin History of Literature: The Romantic Period* (London: Penguin, 1994), pp. 395–447.

Byron, Glennis and Dale Townshend (eds), *The Gothic World* (London and New York: Routledge, 2014).

Calè, Luisa, 'Blake and the Literary Galleries', in Sarah Haggarty and Jon Mee (eds), *Blake and Conflict* (Basingstoke: Palgrave Macmillan, 2008), pp. 185–209.

Camden, William, *Britannia: or A Chorographical Description of Great Britain and Ireland, together with the Adjacent Islands*, 2 vols (London, 1722).

Cameron, Alan, *Claudian: Poetry and Propaganda at the Court of Honorius* (Oxford: Oxford University Press, 1970).

Cameron, Ed, *The Psychopathology of the Gothic Romance: Perversion, Neuroses and Psychosis in Early Works of the Genre* (Jefferson: McFarland, 2000).

Campbell, Jill, '"I am no giant": Horace Walpole, heterosexual incest, and love among men', *Eighteenth Century* 39:3 (1998): 238–60.

Caracciolo, Peter L., 'Introduction: "Such a store house of ingenious fiction and of splendid imagery"', in Peter L. Caracciolo (ed.), *The Arabian Nights in English Literature: Studies in the Reception of The Thousand and One Nights into British Culture* (Basingstoke and London: Macmillan, 1988), pp. 1–80.

Carey, Brycchan, *British Abolitionism and the Rhetoric of Slavery: Writing, Sentiment, and Slavery, 1760–1807* (Basingstoke: Palgrave Macmillan, 2005).

Carlyle, Thomas, 'The state of German literature', *The Edinburgh Review* 46 (1827): 304–51.

Carretta, Vincent, *George III and the Satirists* (Athens, GA: University of Georgia Press, 1990).

Carter, Michael, Peter N. Lindfield and Dale Townshend (eds), *Writing Britain's Ruins* (London: The British Library, 2017).

Castle, Terry, *Masquerade and Civilization: The Carnivalesque in Eighteenth-Century Culture and Fiction* (Stanford, CA: Stanford University Press, 1989).

Castle, Terry, 'The Spectralization of the Other in *The Mysteries of Udolpho*', in Laura Brown and Felicity A. Nussbaum (eds), *The New Eighteenth Century: Theory, Politics, English Literature* (London and New York: Routledge, 1991), pp. 231–53.

Castle, Terry, *The Female Thermometer: 18th-Century Culture and the Invention of the Uncanny* (Oxford: Oxford University Press, 1995).

Caulfield, James, *Memoirs of the Celebrated Persons Composing the Kit-Cat Club: With a Prefatory Account of the Origin of the Association* (London, 1821).

Cawelti, John G., *Adventure, Mystery, and Romance: Formula Stories as Art and Popular Culture* (Chicago: University of Chicago Press, 1976).

Chaplin, Sue, 'Gothic Romance, 1760–1830', in Glennis Byron and Dale Townshend (eds), *The Gothic World* (London and New York: Routledge, 2014), pp. 199–209.

Chappell, Julie A. and Kaley A. Kramer (eds), *Women During the English Reformations: Renegotiating Gender and Religious Identity* (Basingstoke: Palgrave Macmillan, 2014).

Chappey, Jean-Luc, 'La traduction comme pratique politique chez Antoine-Gilbert Griffet de Labaume (1756–1805)', in Gilles Bertrand and Pierre Serna (eds), *La République en voyage 1770–1830* (Rennes: P.U.R., 2013), pp. 225–35.

Charlesworth, Michael (ed.), *The Gothic Revival 1720–1870: Literary Sources & Documents*, 3 vols (Mountfield, East Sussex: Helm Information, 2002).

Chastenay, Louise-Marie-Victorine de, *Mémoires de Madame de Chastenay*, 2 vols (Paris: Plon, 1896).

Chatterjee, Ranita, 'Charlotte Dacre's Nymphomaniacs and Demon-Lovers: Teaching Female Masculinities', in Ben Knights (ed.), *Masculinities in Text and Teaching* (New York: Palgrave Macmillan, 2008), pp. 75–89.

Chatterton, Thomas, *Complete Works*, edited by Donald S. Taylor and Benjamin B. Hoover, 2 vols (Oxford: Clarendon Press, 1971).

Chénier, Marie-Joseph de, *Tableau historique de l'état et des progrès de la littérature française depuis 1789* (Paris: Maradan, [1816], 1818).

Chiu, Frances A., '"Dark and dangerous designs": tales of oppression, dispossession, and repression, 1770–1800', *Romanticism on the Net* 28 (Nov 2002) <www.erudit.org/en/journals/ron/2002-n28-ron560/007205ar/> (last accessed 6 June 2018).

Chippendale, Thomas, *The Gentleman and Cabinet-Maker's Director: Being a Large Collection of the Most Elegant and Useful Designs of Household Furniture, in the most Fashionable Taste*, 3rd edition (London, 1762).

Chow, Jeremy, 'Go to Hell: William Beckford's Skewed Heaven and Hell', in Jolene Zigarovich (ed.), *TransGothic in Literature and Culture* (New York: Routledge, 2018), pp. 53–76.

Christopher, David, 'Matthew Lewis's *The Monk* and James Boaden's *Aurelio and Miranda* – from text to stage', *Theatre Notebook* 65 (2011): 152–70.

Clark, Kenneth, *The Gothic Revival: An Essay in the History of Taste*, 2nd edition (Harmondsworth: Penguin Books, 1962).

Clarke, Stephen, 'Horace Walpole's Architectural Taste', in Peter Sabor (ed.), *Horace Walpole: Beyond the Castle of Otranto*, special feature in *1650–1850 Ideas, Æsthetics, and Inquiries in the Early Modern Era* 16 (2009): 223–44.

Clarke, Stephen, '"Lord God! Jesus! What a house!": describing and visiting Strawberry Hill', *Journal for Eighteenth-Century Studies* 33:3 (September 2010): 357–80.

Clarke, Stephen, *The Strawberry Hill Press & Its Printing House: An Account and an Iconography* (New Haven and London: Yale University Press, 2011).

Clarke, Stephen (ed.), *Horace Walpole: Selected Letters* (New York, London and Toronto: Everyman's Library, 2017).

Clarkson, Thomas, *The History of the Rise, Progress, and Accomplishment of the Abolition of the African Slave-Trade by the British Parliament*, 2 vols (London, 1808).

Clery, E. J., 'Ann Radcliffe and D. A. F. de Sade: thoughts on heroinism', *Women's Writing* 1:2 (1994): 203–14.

Clery, E. J., 'Laying the Ground for Gothic: The Passage of the Supernatural from Truth to Spectacle', in Valeria Tinkler-Villani and Peter Davidson (eds), *Exhibited by Candlelight: Sources and Developments in the Gothic Tradition* (Amsterdam: Rodopi, 1995), pp. 65–74.

Clery, E. J., *The Rise of Supernatural Fiction, 1762–1800* (Cambridge: Cambridge University Press, 1995).

Clery, E. J., *Women's Gothic: From Clara Reeve to Mary Shelley* (Tavistock: Northcote House, 2000).

Clery, E. J. and Robert Miles (eds), *Gothic Documents, A Sourcebook: 1700–1820* (Manchester and New York: Manchester University Press, 2000).

Clive, Robert, *Lord Clive's Speech in the House of Commons, 30th March 1772* (London,1772).

Cobb, James *The Haunted Tower* (London, 1796).

Cockburn, John, *The History and Examination of Duels* (London, 1720).

Cointre, Annie and Annie Rivara (eds), *Recueil de préfaces de traducteurs de romans anglais, 1721–1828* (Saint-Étienne: Publications de l'Université de Saint-Étienne, 2006).

Coleridge, Ernest Hartley (ed.), *Letters of Samuel Taylor Coleridge*, 2 vols (London: William Heinemann, 1895).

Coleridge, Samuel Taylor, *Biographia Literaria*, 2 vols, edited by James Engell and W. Jackson Bate, in Kathleen Coburn (Gen. ed.), *The Collected Works of Samuel Taylor Coleridge*, 16 vols (London: Routledge & Kegan Paul, 1971–2001).

Coleridge, Samuel Taylor, 'Preface to *Christabel*', in Duncan Wu (ed.), *Romanticism: An Anthology*, 4th edition (Oxford: Wiley-Blackwell, 2012), pp. 659–60.

Colley, Linda, *Britons: Forging the Nation, 1707–1837*, 2nd edition (New Haven and London: Yale University Press, 2005).

Collins, Roger, *Visigothic Spain 409–711* (Oxford: Blackwell Publishing, 2004).

Colman, George the Younger, 'Blue-Beard; or, Female Curiosity!', in Jeffrey N. Cox and Michael Gamer (eds), *The Broadview Anthology of Romantic Drama* (Peterborough, Ont.: Broadview, 2003), pp. 75–96.

Colvin, H. M., 'Gothic survival and gothick revival', *The Architectural Review* 103 (1948): 91–8.

Colvin, Howard, *A Biographical Dictionary of British Architects 1600–1840*, 4th edition (New Haven and London: Yale University Press, 2008).

Colvin, Howard, 'Henry Flitcroft, William Kent and Shobdon Church, Herefordshire', in David Jones and Sam McKinstry (eds), *Essays in Scots and English Architectural History: A Festschrift in Honour of John Frew* (Donington: Shaun Tyas, 2009), pp. 1–8.

Conger, Syndy M., *Matthew G. Lewis, Charles Robert Maturin and the Germans: An Interpretative Study of the Influence of German literature on Two Gothic Novels* (Salzburg: Institut für Englische Sprache und Literatur, Universität Salzburg, 1976).

Conger, Syndy M., 'Sensibility Restored: Radcliffe's Answer to Lewis's *The Monk*', in Kenneth W. Graham (ed.), *Gothic Fictions: Prohibition/Transgression* (New York: AMS Press, 1989), pp. 113–49.

Connell, Philip, 'British identities and the politics of ancient poetry in later eighteenth-century England', *The Historical Journal* 49:1 (2006): 161–92.

Conway, Stephen, *The British Isles and the War of American Independence* (Oxford: Oxford University Press, 2000).

Cooper, Anthony Ashely, Earl of Shaftesbury, *Characteristicks of Men, Manners, Opinions, Times*, 3 vols (London, 1711).

Copeland, Nancy E., '"Simple art and simple nature": Sarah Siddons *versus* Ann Crawford', *RECTR* 2nd series 2:1 (1987): 54–61.

Cowper, William, *The Poems of William Cowper*, edited by John D. Baird and Charles Ryskamp (Oxford: Oxford University Press, 1995).

Cox, Jeffrey N., *In the Shadows of Romance* (Athens, OH: Ohio University Press, 1987).

Cox, Jeffrey N. (ed.), *Seven Gothic Dramas, 1789–1825* (Athens, OH: Ohio University Press, 1992).

Cox, Jeffrey N., 'Gothic Drama', in Marie Mulvey-Roberts (ed.), *The Handbook of the Gothic* (New York: New York University Press, 2009), pp. 131–5.

Coykendall, Abby, 'Gothic genealogies, the family romance, and Clara Reeve's *The Old English Baron*', *Eighteenth-Century Fiction* 17:3 (April 2005): 443–80.

Craciun, Adriana, *Fatal Women of Romanticism* (Cambridge: Cambridge University Press, 2003).

Craciun, Adriana, 'Introduction', in *Zofloya; or, The Moor*, by Charlotte Dacre, edited by Adriana Craciun (Peterborough, Ont.: Broadview, 2003), pp. 9–32.

Crawford, Joseph, *Gothic Fiction and the Invention of Terrorism: The Politics and Aesthetics of Fear in the Age of the Reign of Terror* (London: Bloomsbury, 2013).

Cugoano, Ottabah, *Thoughts and Sentiments on the Evil of Slavery* (London, 1787).

Cumberland, Richard, 'The Carmelite: A Tragedy', in Roberta F. S. Borkat (ed.), *The Plays of Richard Cumberland*, 6 vols (New York: Garland, 1982), vol. 3, pp. 1–72.

Dabhoiwala, Faramerz, *The Origins of Sex: A History of the First Sexual Revolution* (Oxford: Oxford University Press, 2012).

Dacre, Charlotte, *Zofloya; or, The Moor*, edited by Kim Ian Michasiw (Oxford: Oxford University Press, 1997).

Dalrymple, William, 'The East India Company: The original corporate raiders', *The Guardian* (4 March 2015). <www.theguardian.com/world/2015/mar/04/east-india-co mpany-original-corporate-raiders> (last accessed 27 March 2019).

Davenant, Charles, *Essays upon I. The Balance of Power. II. The Right of Making War, Peace, and Alliances. III. Universal Monarchy* (London, 1701).

Davison, Carol Margaret, *Gothic Literature 1764–1824* (Cardiff: University of Wales Press, 2009).

Davoli, Sylvia, *Lost Treasures of Strawberry Hill: Masterpieces from Horace Walpole's Collection* (London: Scala, 2018).

Day, Thomas and John Bicknell, *The Dying Negro, A Poetical Epistle, Supposed to Be Written by a Black (Who lately shot himself on board a vessel in the river Thames;) to His Intended Wife* (London, 1773).

De Beer, E. S., 'Gothic: origin and diffusion of the term; the idea of style in architecture', *Journal of the Warburg and Courtauld Institutes* 11 (1948): 143–62.

De Bruyn, Frans, 'Edmund Burke's gothic romance: the portrayal of Warren Hastings in Burke's writings and speeches on India', *Criticism* 29:4 (1987): 415–87.

Defoe, Daniel, *Jure Divino: A Satyr. In Twelve Books* (London, 1706).

Defoe, Daniel, *Robinson Crusoe*, edited by Thomas Keymer (Oxford: Oxford University Press, 2007).

Demata, Massimiliano, 'Discovering Eastern Horrors: Beckford, Maturin, and the Discourse of Travel Literature', in Andrew Smith and William Hughes (eds), *Empire and the Gothic: The Politics of Genre* (Basingstoke and New York: Palgrave Macmillan, 2010), pp. 13–34.

Denham, John, *Coopers-Hill. A Poem* (London, 1709).

Dennis, John, *The Advancement and Reformation of Modern Poetry. A Critical Discourse, in Two Parts* (London, 1701).
Dennis, John, *Britannia Triumphans; or, The Empire Sav'd, and Europe Deliver'd. By the Success of her Majesty's Forces under the Wise and Heroick Conduct of his Grace the Duke of Marlborough. A Poem* (London, 1704).
Dennis, John, *The Critical Works of John Dennis*, 2 vols, edited by Edward Niles Hooker (Baltimore: John Hopkins University Press, 1967).
Dent, Jonathan, *Sinister Histories: Gothic Novels and Representations of the Past, from Horace Walpole to Mary Wollstonecraft* (Manchester: Manchester University Press, 2016).
De Quincey, Thomas, *Confessions of an English Opium-Eater and Other Writings*, edited by Grevel Lindop (Oxford: Oxford University Press, 1985).
Desmet, Christy and Anne Williams (eds), *Shakespearean Gothic* (Cardiff: University of Wales Press, 2009).
Dewing. H. B. (ed.), *Procopius: History of the Wars*, 5 vols (Cambridge, MA and London: Harvard University Press, 1914–28).
Didier, Béatrice, *Écrire la Révolution, 1789–1799* (Paris: P.U.F., 1989).
Dirks, Nicholas B., *The Scandal of Empire: India and the Creation of Imperial Britain* (Cambridge, MA: Harvard University Press, 2006).
Dobrée, Bonamy and Geoffrey Webb (eds), *The Complete Works of Sir John Vanbrugh, Vol. 4* (London: Nonesuch Press, 1928).
Dobson, Michael, *The Making of the National Poet: Shakespeare, Adaptation, and Authorship, 1660–1769* (Oxford: Clarendon Press, 1992).
Dow, Gillian, '*Northanger Abbey*, French fiction, and the affecting history of the Duchess of C***', *Persuasions* 32 (2010): 28–45.
Downes, Kerry, *Hawksmoor* (London: A. Zwemmer, 1959).
Downes, Kerry, *Sir Christopher Wren: The Design of St Paul's Cathedral* (London: Trefoil in association with Guildhall Library, 1988).
Doyle, Laura, *Freedom's Empire: Race and the Rise of the Novel in Atlantic Modernity, 1640–1940* (Durham, NC: Duke University Press, 2008).
Drakakis, John and Dale Townshend (eds), *Gothic Shakespeares* (Abingdon and New York: Routledge, 2008).
Drake, Nathan, *Literary Hours; or, Sketches Critical and Narrative* (London, 1798).
Drinkwater, John and Hugh Elton (eds), *Fifth-Century Gaul: A Crisis of Identity?* (Cambridge: Cambridge University Press, 1992).
Dryden, John, *King Arthur; or, The British Worthy* (London, 1691).
Dryden, John (trans.), *The Works of Virgil: Containing His Pastorals, Georgics and Æneis*, 3 vols, 3rd edition (London, 1709).
Duckett, William, *Dictionnaire de la conversation et de la lecture*, 16 vols (Paris: Firmin Didot, [1833] 1860).
Duff, William, *An Essay on Original Genius; and Its Various Modes of Exertion in Philosophy and the Fine Arts, particularly in Poetry* (London, 1767).
Duncombe, John, *The Feminiad, a Poem*, edited by Jocelyn Harris (Los Angeles: Williams Andrew Clark Memorial Library, 1981).
Dunlop, John Colin, *The History of Fiction: Being a Critical Account of the Most Celebrated Prose Works of Fiction, from the Earliest Greek Romances to the Novels of the Present Age*, 3 vols (London, 1814).

Durot-Boucé, Elizabeth, 'Traducteurs et traductrices d'Ann Radcliffe, ou la fidélité est-elle une question de sexe?', *Palimpsestes* 22 (2009): 101–28.

Eastlake, Charles Locke, *A History of the Gothic Revival* (London: Longmans, Green and Co., 1872).

Eliot, T. S., 'The Metaphysical Poets', in Vincent B. Leitch (ed.), *The Norton Anthology of Theory and Criticism*, 3rd edition (New York: W. W. Norton & Co., 2018), pp. 891–8.

Ellis, Markman, *The History of Gothic Fiction* (Edinburgh: Edinburgh University Press, 2003).

Elliston, Robert, *The Venetian Outlaw* (London, 1805).

Epstein, Julia and Kristina Straub, *Body Guards: The Cultural Politics of Gender Ambiguity* (New York: Routledge, 1991).

Equiano, Olaudah, *The Interesting Narrative and Other Writings*, edited by Vincent Carretta (London: Penguin, 2003).

Erle, Sibylle, '"On the very Verge of legitimate Invention": Charles Bonnet and William Blake's Illustrations to Robert Blair's *The Grave* (1808)', in Carol Margaret Davison (ed.), *The Gothic and Death* (Manchester: Manchester University Press 2017), pp. 34–47.

Evelyn, John, *An Account of Architects and Architecture, Together, with an Historical, Etymological Explanation of Certain Terms, Particularly Affected by Architects* (London, 1706).

Favret, Mary A., *War at a Distance: Romanticism and the Making of Modern Wartime* (Princeton, NJ: Princeton University Press, 2010).

Fear, Andrew T., *Orosius: Seven Books of History against the Pagans*, trans. by Andrew T. Fear (Liverpool: Liverpool University Press, 2010).

Feller, François-Xavier de, *Biographie universelle, ou Dictionnaire historique des hommes qui se sont fait un nom par leur génie*, 12 vols (Paris: Gauthier frères, 1833).

Felton, D., *Haunted Greece and Rome: Ghost Stories from Classical Antiquity* (Austin: University of Texas Press, 1999).

Fielding, Henry, *The History of Tom Jones, A Foundling*, 6 vols (London, 1749).

Fingesten, Peter, 'Topographical and anatomical aspects of the gothic cathedral', *The Journal of Aesthetics and Art Criticism* 20:1 (Autumn, 1961): 3–23.

Fleenor, Juliann E. (ed.), *The Female Gothic* (Montreal: Eden Press, 1983).

Fliegelman, Jay, *Prodigals and Pilgrims: The American Revolution against Patriarchal Authority* (Cambridge: Cambridge University Press, 1982).

Foote, Samuel, *The Nabob; A Comedy* (London, 1778).

Foucault, Michel, *Herculine Barbin: Being the Recently Discovered Memoirs of a Nineteenth-Century French Hermaphrodite*, trans. by Richard McDougall (New York: Pantheon Books, 1980).

Foucault, Michel, *Power/Knowledge: Selected Interviews and Other Writings, 1972–1977*, edited by Colin Gordon, trans. by Colin Gordon, Leo Marshall, John Mepham and Kate Soper (New York: Pantheon Books, 1980).

Foucault, Michel, *The History of Sexuality, Volume I: An Introduction*, trans. by Robert Hurley (New York: Vintage, 1990).

Foucault, Michel, *Abnormal: Lectures at the Collège de France, 1974–1975*, trans. by Graham Burchell (New York: Picador, 2003).

Frank, Frederick S., *The First Gothics: A Critical Guide to the English Gothic Novel* (New York and London: Garland Publishing, 1987).

Franklin, Michael, J., 'Accessing India: Orientalism, Anti-"Indianism" and the Rhetoric of Jones and Burke', in Tim Fulford and Peter J. Kitson (eds), *Romanticism and Colonialism: Writing and Empire, 1780–1830* (Cambridge: Cambridge University Press, 1998), pp. 48–66.

Freeman, Lisa A., *Antitheatricality and the Body Public* (Philadelphia: University of Pennsylvania Press, 2017).

Freud, Sigmund, 'A Special Type of Object Choice Made by Men', in *The Standard Edition of the Complete Psychological Works of Sigmund Freud, Vol. XI: Five Lectures on Psycho-Analysis, Leonardo da Vinci and Other Works* (London: The Hogarth Press, 1910), pp. 163–76.

Freud, Sigmund, 'The "Uncanny"', in James Strachey (ed. and trans.), *The Standard Edition of the Complete Psychological Works of Sigmund Freud, Vol. XVII: An Infantile Neurosis and Other Works* (London: The Hogarth Press, 1955), pp. 219–52.

Friedman, Terry, 'The transformation of York Minster, 1726–42', *Architectural History* 38 (1995): 69–90.

Fry, Paul H., 'Classical Standards in the Period', in Marshall Brown (ed.), *The Cambridge History of Literary Criticism, Vol. 5: Romanticism* (Cambridge: Cambridge University Press, 2000), pp. 7–28.

Fuller, Anne, *Alan Fitz-Osborne: A Historical Tale*, 2 vols (Dublin, 1787).

Galli Mastrodonato, Paola, 'Romans gothiques anglais et traductions françaises: L'année 1797 et la migration de récits', *Neohelicon* 13:1 (1986): 287–320.

Gamer, Michael, 'Authors in effect: Lewis, Scott, and the gothic drama', *ELH* 66 (1999): 831–61.

Gamer, Michael, 'Genres for the prosecution: pornography and the gothic', *PMLA* 114:5 (October 1999): 1043–54.

Gamer, Michael, *Romanticism and the Gothic: Genre, Reception, and Canon Formation* (Cambridge: Cambridge University Press, 2000).

Genlis, Stéphanie Félicité de, *Adelaide and Theodore; or Letters on Education*, 3 vols (London, [1783]).

Garte, Hansjörg, *Kunstform Schauerroman* (Leipzig: Carl Garte, 1935).

Geraghty, Anthony, *The Architectural Drawings of Sir Christopher Wren at All Souls College, Oxford: A Complete Catalogue* (Aldershot: Ashgate, 2007).

Gerrard, Christine, *The Patriot Opposition to Walpole: Politics, Poetry, and National Myth, 1725–1742* (Oxford: Clarendon Press, 1994).

Gifford, William, *The Satires of Decimus Junius Juvenalis* (London, 1802).

Gilbert, Ruth, *Early Modern Hermaphrodites: Sex and Other Stories* (New York: Palgrave Macmillan, 2002).

Gillespie, Stuart, *English Translation and Classical Reception: Towards a New Literary History* (Malden: Wiley-Blackwell, 2011).

Goddu, Teresa A., 'The African American Slave Narrative and the Gothic', in Charles L. Crow (ed.), *A Companion to American Gothic* (Malden: John Wiley, 2014), pp. 71–83.

Godwin, William, 'Of History and Romance' <www.english.upenn.edu/~mgamer/Etexts/godwin.history.html> (last accessed 17 June 2019).

Goffart, Walter, *The Narrators of Barbarian History (A.D. 550–800): Jordanes, Gregory of Tours, Bede, and Paul the Deacon* (Princeton, NJ: Princeton University Press, 1988).

Goffart, Walter, *Barbarian Tides: The Migration Age and the Later Roman Empire* (Philadelphia: University of Pennsylvania Press, 2006).

Goldsmith, Oliver, 'The Monthly Review (May 1757)', in Arthur Friedman (ed.), *The Collected Works of Oliver Goldsmith*, 5 vols (Oxford: Clarendon, 1966), vol. 1, pp. 12–13.

Gonda, Caroline, *Reading Daughters' Fictions 1709–1834: Novels and Society from Manley to Edgeworth* (Cambridge: Cambridge University Press, 1996).

Gottlieb, Evan, *Romantic Globalism: British Literature and Modern World Order, 1750–1830* (Columbus, OH: Ohio State University Press, 2014).

Gould, Eliga H., *The Persistence of Empire: British Political Culture in the Age of the American Revolution* (Chapel Hill: University of North Carolina Press, 2000).

Greenblatt, Stephen, *Will in the World: How Shakespeare Became Shakespeare* (New York: W. W. Norton, 2004).

Greene, Jack P., *Evaluating Empire and Confronting Colonialism in Eighteenth-Century Britain* (Cambridge: Cambridge University Press, 2013).

Gregory the Great, <www.tertullian.org/fathers/index.htm#Gregory_Dialogues> (last accessed 8 August 2019).

Griffin, Robert J., *Wordsworth's Pope: A Study in Literary Historiography* (Cambridge: Cambridge University Press, 2005).

Groom, Nick, *The Gothic: A Very Short Introduction* (Oxford: Oxford University Press, 2012).

Groom, Nick, 'Eighteenth-Century Gothic before *The Castle of Otranto*', in Joanne Parker (ed.), *The Harp and the Constitution: Myths of Celtic and Gothic Origin in Modern Europe* (Leiden and Boston: Brill, 2016), pp. 26–46.

Groom, Nick, 'Romanticism before 1789', in David Duff (ed.), *The Oxford Handbook of British Romanticism* (Oxford: Oxford University Press, 2018), pp. 13–29.

Grosrichard, Alain, *The Sultan's Court: European Fantasies of the East*, trans. by Liz Heron (London and New York: Verso, 1998).

Grosse, Carl, *Der Genius* (Halle/Saale, 1790–4).

Grosse, Carl, *Der Dolch* (Berlin, 1794).

Grosse, Carl, *The Genius; or, The Mysterious Adventures of Don Carlos de Grandez*, trans. by Joseph Trapp (London, 1796).

Grosse, Carl, *Horrid Mysteries: A Story*, trans. by Peter Will (London, 1796).

Grunenberg, Christoph (ed.), *Gothic: Transmutations of Horror in Late Twentieth Century Art* (Boston: Institute of Contemporary Art, 1997).

Guillery, Peter and Michael Snodin, 'Strawberry Hill: building and site', *Architectural History* 38 (1995): 102–28.

Guthke, Karl S., *Englische Vorromantik und deutscher Sturm und Drang: M.G. Lewis' Stellung in der Geschichte der deutsch-englischen Literaturbeziehungen* (Göttingen: Mayer und Müller, 1958).

Gwynn, David M., *The Goths: Lost Civilizations* (London: Reaktion Books, 2017).

Haan, Estelle, *Thomas Gray's Latin Poetry* (Brussels: Latomus, 2000).

Hadley, Michael, *The Undiscovered Genre: A Search for the German Gothic Novel* (Berne: Peter Lang, 1978).

Haggerty, George E., *Unnatural Affections: Women and Fiction in the Later 18th Century* (Bloomington: Indiana University Press, 1998).

Haggerty, George E., *Men in Love: Masculinity and Sexuality in the Eighteenth Century* (New York: Columbia University Press, 1999).

Haggerty, George E., 'Walpoliana', *Eighteenth-Century Studies* 34:2 (Winter 2001): 227–49.

Haggerty, George E., *Queer Gothic* (Urbana and Chicago: University of Illinois Press, 2006).

Haggerty, George E., 'Queering Horace Walpole', *Studies in English Literature 1500–1900* 46:3 (2006): 543–61.

Haggerty, George E., 'The Failure of Heteronormativity in the Gothic Novel', in Ana de Freitas Boe and Abby Coykendall (eds), *Heteronormativity in Eighteenth-Century Literature and Culture* (New York: Ashgate, 2014), pp. 131–49.

Halberstam, Jack, *Female Masculinity* (Durham, NC: Duke University Press, 1998).

Hall, Daniel, 'Rewriting the Revolution: Direct and Indirect Responses in the French Gothic Novel and Dramas', in Benn McCann and Daniel Hall (eds), *Rewriting the Political* (Exeter: Elm Bank publications, 2000).

Hall, Daniel, *French and German Gothic Fiction in the Late Eighteenth Century* (Bern: Peter Lang, 2005).

Halsall, Guy, *Barbarian Migrations and the Roman West, 376–568* (Cambridge: Cambridge University Press, 2007).

Hamilton, Walter, *Ammianus Marcellinus: The Later Roman Empire (A.D. 354–378)*, trans. by Walter Hamilton, intro. and notes by Andrew Wallace-Hadrill (London: Penguin Books, 1986).

Hamm, Jr, Robert B., '*Hamlet* and Walpole's *The Castle of Otranto*', *Studies in English Literature 1500–1900* 49:3 (Summer, 2009): 667–92.

Harley, Martha, *St Bernard's Priory: An Old English Tale* (London, 1786).

Harley, Martha, *The Castle of Mowbray, an English Romance* (London, 1788).

Harney, Marion, *Place-Making for the Imagination: Horace Walpole and Strawberry Hill* (Farnham: Ashgate, 2013).

Harries, Jill, *Sidonius Apollinaris and the Fall of Rome, A.D. 407–485* (Oxford: Oxford University Press, 1994).

Harris, Eileen, 'Batty Langley: a tutor to freemasons (1696–1751)', *Burlington Magazine* 119: 890 (1977): 327–35.

Harris, John, 'A William Kent discovery: designs for Esher Place, Surrey', *Country Life* (14 May 1959): 1076–8.

Harris, John, 'Esher Place, Surrey', *Country Life* (2 April 1987): 94–7.

Hart, Vaughan, *Nicholas Hawksmoor: Rebuilding Ancient Wonders* (New Haven and London: Yale University Press, 2002).

Hart, Vaughan, *Sir John Vanbrugh: Storyteller in Stone* (New Haven and London: Yale University Press, 2008).

Hayley, William, *An Essay on Epic Poetry; in Five Epistles to the Revd. Mr. Mason, with Notes* (London, 1782).

Haywood, Ian, Susan Matthews and Mary L. Shannon (eds), *Romanticism and Illustration* (Cambridge: Cambridge University Press 2019).

Hazen, Allen T., *A Bibliography of the Strawberry Hill Press* (New Haven: Yale University Press, 1942).

Hazlitt, William, *Lectures on the English Comic Writers* (London, 1819).

Hazlitt, William, *Lectures Chiefly on the Dramatic Literature of the Age of Elizabeth. Delivered at the Surrey Institution* (London, 1820).

Headley, Gwyn, *Follies, Grottoes & Garden Buildings* (London: Aurum, 1999).

Heather, Peter, *Goths and Romans, AD 332–489* (Oxford: Clarendon Press, 1991).

Heather, Peter, *The Goths* (Oxford: Blackwell Publishing, 1996).

Heather, Peter (ed.), *The Visigoths from the Migration Period to the Seventh Century: An Ethnographic Perspective* (Woodbridge: The Boydell Press, 1999).
Heather, Peter, *The Fall of the Roman Empire: A New History* (London: Macmillan, 2005).
Heather, Peter, *Empires and Barbarians: Migration, Development and the Birth of Europe* (London: Macmillan, 2009).
Heather, Peter and John Matthews, *The Goths in the Fourth Century* (Liverpool: Liverpool University Press, 1991).
Heiland, Donna, *Gothic and Gender: An Introduction* (Oxford: Blackwell, 2004).
Heilman, Robert Bechtold, *America in English Fiction: The Influences of the American Revolution* (Baton Rouge: Louisiana University Press, 1937).
Heinzmann, Johann Georg, *Über die Pest der deutschen Literatur. Appel an meine Nation über Aufklärung und Aufklärer; über Gelehrsamkeit und Schriftsteller; über Büchermanufakturen, Rezensenten, Buchhändler; über moderne Philosophen und Menschenerzieher; auch über mancherley anderes, was Menschenfreyheit und Menschenrechte betrifft* (Bern, 1795).
Henry, Robert, *The History of Great Britain, from the First Invasion of It by the Romans under Julius Cæsar*, 6 vols (London, 1771–93).
Hepburn, Robert, *A Discourse concerning Fews and Superiorities, Shewing That the Rigid Observance of Them Is Inconsistent with the Nature of the British Constitution* (Edinburgh, 1716).
Heppner, Christopher, *Reading Blake's Designs* (Cambridge: Cambridge University Press, 1995).
Hermanson, Anne, *The Horror Plays of the English Restoration* (Farnham: Ashgate Publishing, 2014).
Hesse, Carla, *The Other Enlightenment: How French Women Became Modern*, Appendix A, 'Bibliography of French Women, 1789–1800' (Princeton, NJ: Princeton University Press, 2003).
Highfill, Philip, A., Kalman A. Burmin and Edward A. Langhans (eds), *A Biographical Dictionary of Actors, Actresses, Musicians, Dancers, Managers and Other Stage Personnel in London, 1660–1800* (Carbondale: Southern Illinois University Press, 1973–93).
Hillgarth, J. N., *The Visigoths in History and Legend* (Toronto: Pontifical Institute of Mediaeval Studies, 2009).
Hodson, Jane, 'Gothic and the Language of Terror', in Angela Wright and Dale Townshend (eds), *Romantic Gothic: An Edinburgh Companion* (Edinburgh: Edinburgh University Press, 2016), pp. 289–305.
Hoeveler, Diane Long, 'Charlotte Dacre's *Zofloya*: a case study in miscegenation as sexual and racial nausea', *European Romantic Review* 8:2 (1997): 185–99.
Hoeveler, Diane Long, *Gothic Feminism: The Professionalization of Gender from Charlotte Smith to the Brontës* (University Park: The Pennsylvania State University Press, 1998).
Hoeveler, Diane Long, 'Introduction', *The Castle of Wolfenbach* by Eliza Parsons, edited by Diane Long Hoeveler (Kansas City: Valancourt Books, 2007), pp. vii–xiv.
Hoeveler, Diane Long, *Gothic Riffs: Secularizing the Uncanny in the European Imaginary, 1780–1820* (Columbus, OH: Ohio State University Press, 2010).
Hoeveler, Diane Long, 'Gothic Adaptation, 1764–1830', in Glennis Byron and Dale Townshend (eds), *The Gothic World* (London and New York: Routledge, 2014), pp. 185–98.

Hoeveler, Diane Long, *The Gothic Ideology: Religious Hysteria and Anti-Catholicism in British Popular Fiction, 1780–1880* (Cardiff: University of Wales Press, 2014).

Hogan, Charles B., *The London Stage: Part 5, 1776–1800: A Critical Introduction* (Carbondale: Southern Illinois University Press, 1968).

Hogle, Jerrold E., 'The Ghost of the Counterfeit in the Genesis of the Gothic', in Allan Lloyd Smith and Victor Sage (eds), *Gothick Origins and Innovations* (Amsterdam: Rodopi, 1994), pp. 23–33.

Hogle, Jerrold E., 'Recovering the Walpolean Gothic: *The Italian; or, The Confessional of the Black Penitents* (1796–97)', in Dale Townshend and Angela Wright (eds), *Ann Radcliffe, Romanticism and the Gothic* (Cambridge: Cambridge University Press, 2014), pp. 151–67.

Home, Henry Lord Kames, *Elements of Criticism*, 3rd edition, 2 vols (Edinburgh, 1765).

Home, John, 'Douglas: A Tragedy', in James S. Malek (ed.), in *The Plays of John Home* (New York: Garland, 1980), pp. 7–75.

Hudson, Hannah Doherty, 'The Myth of Minerva: Publishing, Popular Fiction, and the Rise of the Novel', unpublished PhD thesis, Stanford University, 2013.

Hudson, Hannah Doherty, 'Sentiment and the Gothic: Failures of Emotion in the Novels of Mrs. Radcliffe and the Minerva Press', in Albert J. Rivero (ed.), *The Sentimental Novel in the Eighteenth Century* (Cambridge: Cambridge University Press, 2019), pp. 155–72.

Hughes, Ian, *Stilicho: The Vandal Who Saved Rome* (Barnsley: Pen & Sword Military, 2010).

Hughes, William and Andrew Smith (eds), *Queering the Gothic* (Manchester: Manchester University Press, 2009).

Hughes, William and Ruth Heholt (eds), *Gothic Britain: Dark Places in the Provinces and Margins of the British Isles* (Cardiff: University of Wales Press, 2018).

Hurd, Richard, *Letters on Chivalry and Romance* (London, 1762).

Hurd, Richard, *The Works of Richard Hurd*, 8 vols (London, 1811).

Hume, David, 'Letter XLII', in *Letters of David Hume to William Strahan*, edited by G. Birkbeck Hill (Oxford: Clarendon Press, 1888), pp. 155–7.

Hume, David, *A Treatise of Human Nature*, edited by L. A. Selby-Bigge (Oxford: Clarendon Press, 1888).

Hume, Robert D., 'Gothic versus romantic: a revaluation of the gothic novel', *PMLA* 84:2 (March 1969): 282–90.

Innes, Thomas, *A Critical Essay on the Ancient Inhabitants of the Northern Parts of Britain, or Scotland*, 2 vols (London, 1729).

Irwin, Robert, *The Arabian Nights: A Companion* (London and New York: I. B. Tauris, 2005).

Jacobs, Edward H., *Accidental Migrations: An Archaeology of Gothic Discourse* (Lewisburg: Bucknell University Press, 2000).

Jacobs, Edward H., 'Ann Radcliffe and Romantic Print Culture', in Dale Townshend and Angela Wright (eds), *Ann Radcliffe, Romanticism and the Gothic* (Cambridge: Cambridge University Press, 2014), pp. 49–66.

Jager, Colin, 'This Detail, This History: Charles Taylor's Romanticism', in Michael Warner, Jonathan VanAntwerpen and Craig Calhoun (eds), *Varieties of Secularism in a Secular Age* (Cambridge, MA: Harvard University Press, 2013), pp. 166–92.

Jager, Colin, 'Language Within Language: Reform and Literature in *A Secular Age*', in Florian Zemmin, Colin Jager and Guido Vanheeswijk (eds), *Working with A Secular Age: Interdisciplinary Perspectives on Charles Taylor's Master Narrative* (Berlin & Boston: Walter de Gruyter, 2017), pp. 207–28.

James, Henry, *The Art of Fiction* <https://public.wsu.edu/~campbelld/amlit/artfiction.html> (last accessed 10 February 2019).

Jauss, Hans Robert, 'Modernity and literary tradition', trans. by Christian Thorne, *Critical Inquiry* 31 (2005): 329–64.

Jenkins, Bethan M., *Between Wales and England: Anglophone Welsh Writing of the Eighteenth Century* (Cardiff: University of Wales Press, 2017).

Jephson, Robert, 'The Count of Narbonne', in Temple James Maynard (ed.), *The Plays of Robert Jephson* (New York: Garland, 1980), pp. 1–61.

Jestin, Loftus, *The Answer to the Lyre: Richard Bentley's Illustrations for Thomas Gray's Poems* (Philadelphia: University of Pennsylvania Press, 1990).

Johannesson, Kurt, *The Renaissance of the Goths in Sixteenth-Century Sweden*, trans. by James Larson (Berkeley and Los Angeles: University of California Press, 1991).

Johnson, Paul, *The Birth of the Modern: World Society, 1815–1830* (London: Phoenix Giant, 1996).

Johnson, Samuel, *A Dictionary of the English Language*, 2 vols (London, 1755–6).

Johnson, Samuel, *Mr Johnson's Preface to His Edition of Shakespear's [sic] Plays* (London, 1765).

Johnson, Samuel, *Dr Johnson: Poetry and Prose*, edited by Mona Wilson (Cambridge, MA: Harvard University Press, 1967).

Johnson, Samuel, 'Life of Dryden', in John H. Middendorf (ed.), *Lives of the Poets*, The Yale Edition of the Works of Samuel Johnson, vols 21–3 (New Haven: Yale University Press, 2010).

[Kahlert. K. F.], *Der Geisterbanner. Eine Wundergeschichte aus mündlichen und schriftlichen Traditionen* (Vienna, 1792).

Kahlert, K. F., *The Necromancer; or, The Tale of the Black Forest* (London: Skoob books, 1989).

Kalter, Barrett, 'DIY gothic: Thomas Gray and the medieval revival', *ELH* 70:4 (2003): 989–1019.

Kant, Immanuel, *The Critique of Pure Reason*, trans. and edited by Paul Guyer and Allan W. Wood (Cambridge: Cambridge University Press, 2000).

Kelly, Christopher, *Attila the Hun: Barbarian Terror and the Fall of the Roman Empire* (London: Vintage Books, 2008).

Kelly, Gary, 'Clara Reeve', *Oxford Dictionary of National Biography* <https://doi-org.ezproxy.mmu.ac.uk/10.1093/ref:odnb/23292> (last accessed 6 June 2018).

Kelly, Gary, 'Clara Reeve, Provincial Bluestocking: From the Old Whigs to the Modern Liberal State', in Nicole Pohl and Betty A. Schellenberg (eds), *Reconsidering the Bluestockings* (San Merino: Huntington Library, 2002), pp. 105–25.

Kelly, Isabella, *Eva. A Novel*, 3 vols (London, 1799).

'Kelly, Isabella', in Susan Brown, Patricia Clements, and Isobel Grundy (eds), *Orlando: Women's Writing in the British Isles from the Beginnings to the Present* (Cambridge: Cambridge University Press Online, 2006) <http://orlando.cambridge.org> (last accessed 12 April 2018).

Kelly, James, 'The Politics of Ruin', in Michael Carter, Peter N. Lindfield and Dale Townshend (eds), *Writing Britain's Ruins* (London: The British Library, 2017), pp. 243–69.

Ketton-Cremer, R. W., *Horace Walpole: A Biography*, 3rd edition (London: Methuen & Co., 1964).

Kilgour, Maggie, *The Rise of the Gothic Novel* (London: Routledge, 1995).

Killeen, Jarlath, *The Emergence of Irish Gothic Fiction: History, Origins, Theories* (Edinburgh: Edinburgh University Press, 2014).

Killen, Alice M., *Le Roman terrifiant ou roman noir: de Walpole à Anne Radcliffe, et son influence sur la littérature française jusqu'en 1840* (Paris: Librairie ancienne Edouard Champion, 1924).

King, Thomas, *The Gendering of Men, 1600–1750: The English Phallus* (Madison: University of Wisconsin Press, 2004).

King, William, 'Animadversions on the Pretended Account of Danmark', in *Miscellanies in Prose and Verse* (London, [1709]), pp. 51–2.

Klancher, Jon, *Transfiguring the Arts and Sciences: Knowledge and Cultural Institutions in the Romantic Age* (Cambridge and New York: Cambridge University Press, 2013).

Kliger, Samuel, 'Whig aesthetics: a phase of eighteenth-century taste', *ELH* 16:2 (June 1949): 135–50.

Kliger, Samuel, *The Goths in England: A Study in Seventeenth- and Eighteenth-Century Thought* (Cambridge, MA: Harvard University Press, 1952).

Komarek, Johann Nepomuk, *Ida oder Das Vehmgericht* (Pilsen und Leipzig, 1792).

Krämer, Felix (ed.), *Dark Romanticism: From Goya to Max Ernst* (London: Gestalten UK Ltd, 2012).

Kramer, Kaley A. 'Haunting History: Women, Catholicism, and the Writing of National History in Sophia Lee's *The Recess*', in Julie A. Chappell and Kaley A. Kramer (eds), *Women During the English Reformations: Renegotiating Gender and Religious Identity* (Basingstoke: Palgrave Macmillan, 2014), pp. 129–44.

Kramnick, Jonathan Brody, *Making the English Canon: Print-Capitalism and the Cultural Past, 1700–1770* (Cambridge: Cambridge University Press, 1999).

Kulikowski, Michael, *Rome's Gothic Wars: From the Third Century to Alaric* (Cambridge: Cambridge University Press, 2007).

Langhorne, John and William Langhorne, *Plutarch's Lives, translated from the original Greek*, 3rd edition, 6 vols (London, 1778).

Langley, Batty and T. Langley, *Ancient Architecture: Restored, and Improved, by a Great Variety of Grand and Useful Designs, Entirely New in the Gothick Mode for the Ornamenting of Buildings and Gardens Exceeding Every Thing That's Extant* (London, 1741–2).

Langley, Philippa and Michael Jones, *The King's Grave: The Search for Richard III* (New York: St. Martin's Press, 2013).

Lanser, Susan S., 'Of Closed Doors and Open Hatches: Heteronormative Plots in Eighteenth-Century (Women's) Studies', in Ana de Freitas Boe and Abby Coykendall (eds), *Heteronormativity in Eighteenth-Century Literature and* Culture (New York: Routledge, 2015), pp. 23–40.

Laqueur, Thomas, *Making Sex: Body and Gender from the Greeks to Freud* (Cambridge, MA and London: Harvard University Press, 1990).

Lathom, Francis, *The Midnight Bell, A German Story, Founded on Incidents in Real Life*, 3 vols (London, 1798).

Lee, Sophia, *The Recess; or, A Tale of Other Times*, edited by April Alliston (Lexington: The University Press of Kentucky, 2000).

Lenski, Noel, *Failure of Empire: Valens and the Roman State* (Berkeley and London: University of California Press, 2002).

Leslie, Charles, *Masonry: A Poem* (Edinburgh, 1739).

Lévy, Maurice, *Le Roman 'gothique' anglais, 1764–1824*, 2nd edition (Paris: Albin Michel, 1995).
Lévy, Maurice, 'Du roman gothique au roman noir', in Catriona Seth (ed.), *Imaginaires gothiques: aux sources du roman noir français* (Paris: Desjonquères, L'Esprit des lettres, 2010).
Lew, Joseph W., 'The deceptive other: Mary Shelley's critique of orientalism in *Frankenstein*', *Studies in Romanticism* 30 (1991): 255–83.
Lew, Joseph W., 'The Plague of Imperial Desire: Montesquieu, Gibbon, Brougham, and Mary Shelley's *The Last Man*', in Tim Fulford and Peter J. Kitson (eds), *Romanticism and Colonialism: Writing and Empire, 1780–1830* (Cambridge: Cambridge University Press, 1998), pp. 261–78.
Lewis, Isabella, *Terrific Tales* (Chicago: Valancourt Books, 2006).
Lewis, Jane Elizabeth, *Mary Queen of Scots: Romance and Nation* (London: Routledge, 1998).
Lewis, Matthew Gregory, *The Castle Spectre*, 2nd edition (London, 1798).
Lewis, Matthew Gregory, *The Love of Gain* (London, 1799).
Lewis, Matthew Gregory, *The Bravo of Venice. A Romance* (London, 1805).
Lewis, Matthew Gregory, *Rugantino; or, The Bravo of Venice* (London, 1806).
Lewis, Matthew Gregory, 'The Anaconda', in Peter Haining (ed.), *Great British Tales of Terror: Gothic Stories of Horror and Romance 1765–1840* (Harmondsworth, Penguin, 1973), pp. 82–132.
Lewis, Matthew Gregory, *The Monk*, edited by D. L. Macdonald and Kathleen Scherf (Peterborough, Ont.: Broadview, 2004).
Lewis, Wilmarth Sheldon, *Collector's Progress* (New York: Knopf, 1951).
Lewis, W. S., 'The genesis of Strawberry Hill', *Metropolitan Museum Studies* 5:1 (June 1934): 57–92.
Lewis, W. S. (ed.), *The Yale Edition of Horace Walpole's Correspondence*, 48 vols (New Haven and London: Yale University Press, 1937–83).
Lewis, W. S., 'Horace Walpole, Antiquary', in Richard Pares and A. J. P. Taylor (eds), *Essays Presented to Sir Lewis Namier* (London: Macmillan & Co., 1956), pp. 178–203.
Lewis, W. S. (ed.), *Notes by Horace Walpole on Several Characters of Shakespeare* (Farmington: privately printed, 1940).
Lindfield, Peter N., 'The Countess of Pomfret's gothic revival furniture', *The Georgian Group Journal* xxii (2014): 77–94.
Lindfield, Peter N., '"Serious gothic" and "doing the ancient buildings": Batty Langley's *Ancient Architecture* and *Principal Geometric Elevations*', *Architectural History* 57 (2014): 141–73.
Lindfield, Peter N., *Georgian Gothic: Medievalist Architecture, Furniture and Interiors, 1730–1840* (Woodbridge: Boydell and Brewer, 2016).
Lindfield, Peter N., 'Heraldry and the architectural imagination: John Carter's visualisation of *The Castle of Otranto*', *The Antiquaries Journal* 96 (2016): 291–313.
Lindfield, Peter N., '"Hung Round with the Helmets, Breast-Plates, and Swords of Our Ancestors": Allusions to Chivalry in Eighteenth-Century Gothicism?', in Barbara Gribling and Katie Stevenson (eds), *Chivalry and the Vision of the Medieval Past* (Woodbridge: Boydell and Brewer, 2016), pp. 61–98.
Lindfield, Peter N. and Dale Townshend, 'Reading Vathek and Fonthill Abbey: William Beckford's Architectural Imagination', in Caroline Dakers (ed.), *Fonthill Recovered: A Cultural History* (London: UCL Press, 2018), pp. 284–301.

Link, Frederick, 'Introduction', in Frederick M. Link (ed.), *The Plays of John O'Keeffe*, 4 vols (New York: Garland, 1981), vol. 1, pp. vii–lxxii.

Little, David M., and George M. Kahrl (eds), *The Letters of David Garrick*, 3 vols (Cambridge, MA: Harvard University Press, 1963).

Lloyd Smith, Allan, *American Gothic Fiction: An Introduction* (New York and London: Continuum 2004).

Lonsdale, Roger (ed.), *The Poems of Thomas Gray, William Collins and Oliver Goldsmith* (London and New York: Longman, 1969).

Lonsdale, Roger (ed.), *The New Oxford Book of Eighteenth-Century Verse* (Oxford: Oxford University Press, 1984).

Loos, Philippe Werner (ed.), *Journal général de la littérature de France* (Paris: Treuttel; Strasbourg: Würtz, 1800).

Lucas, Charles, *The Infernal Quixote*, edited by M. O. Grenby (Peterborough, Ont.: Broadview, 2004).

Maas, Michael (ed.), *The Cambridge Companion to the Age of Justinian* (Cambridge: Cambridge University Press, 2005).

Maas, Michael (ed.), *The Cambridge Companion to the Age of Attila* (Cambridge: Cambridge University Press, 2015).

MacIntyre, Alasdair, *After Virtue*, 3rd edition (Notre Dame: University of Notre Dame Press, 2007).

Mack, Robert L., 'Introduction', in Robert L. Mack (ed.), *Oriental Tales* (Oxford: Oxford University Press, 1992), pp. vii–xlix.

Mack, Robert L. (ed.), *Arabian Nights' Entertainments* (Oxford: Oxford University Press, 1995).

Maenchen-Helfen, Otto J., *The World of the Huns: Studies in Their History and Culture* (Berkeley and London: University of California Press, 1973).

Makdisi, Saree, 'Introduction: worldly romanticism', *Nineteenth-Century Literature* 65:4 (2011): 429–32.

Malchow, H. L., *Gothic Images of Race in Nineteenth-Century Britain* (Stanford: Stanford University Press, 1996).

Malek, James S., 'Introduction', in *The Plays of John Home*, edited by James S. Malek (New York: Garland, 1980), pp. vii–xliii.

Mandal, Anthony, 'Gothic and the Publishing World, 1780–1820', in Glennis Byron and Dale Townshend (eds), *The Gothic World* (London and New York: Routledge, 2014), pp. 159–71.

Mandal, Anthony, 'Mrs. Meeke and Minerva: the mystery of the marketplace', *Eighteenth-Century Life* 42:2 (2018): 131–51.

Marchand, Leslie A. (ed.), *Byron's Letters and Journals*, 13 vols (London: John Murray, 1973–94).

Marcus, Steven, *The Other Victorians: A Study of Sexuality and Pornography in Mid-Nineteenth-Century England* (New Brunswick and London: Transaction, 2009).

Marquand, Louis-Antoine, *Le Proscrit*, 4 vols (Paris: Le Normant, an XI–1803).

Marshall, Nowell, 'Beyond Queer Gothic: Charting the Gothic History of the Trans Subject in Beckford, Lewis, Byron', in Jolene Zigarovich (ed.), *TransGothic in Literature and Culture* (New York: Routledge, 2018), pp. 25–52.

Martin, Angus, Vivienne Mylne and Robert Frautschi, *Bibliographie du genre romanesque français, 1751–1800* (London: Mansell; Paris: France expansion, 1977).

Mascov, Johann Jakob, *The History of the Ancient Germans; Including that of the Cimbri, Celtæ, Teutones, Alemanni, Saxons, and Other Ancient Northern Nations*, 2 vols (London and Westminster, 1737 [1738]).

Mathias, T. J., *The Pursuits of Literature. A Satirical Poem in Four Dialogues. With Notes*, 7th edition (London, 1798).

Mathias, T. J., *The Shade of Alexander Pope on the Bank of the Thames. A Satirical Poem* (London, 1799).

Mathisen, Ralph W. and Danuta Shanzer (eds), *Society and Culture in Late Antique Gaul: Revisiting the Sources* (Aldershot: Ashgate, 2001).

Maturin, Charles Robert, *Melmoth the Wanderer*, edited by Douglas Grant, intro. by Chris Baldick (Oxford: Oxford University Press, 1989).

Maynard, Temple, 'Introduction', in *The Plays of Robert Jephson*, edited by Temple Maynard (New York: Garland, 1980), pp. vii–xxvii.

McCarthy, Michael, *The Origins of the Gothic Revival* (New Haven and London: Yale University Press, 1987).

McCarthy, William, *Anna Letitia Barbauld: Voice of the Enlightenment* (Baltimore: Johns Hopkins University Press, 2008).

McConnell Stott, Andrew, *What Blest Genius? The Jubilee that Made Shakespeare*, 2nd edition (New York: W. W. Norton, 2019).

McCormick, Ian, *Sexual Outcasts, 1750–1850*, 4 vols (London: Routledge, 2000).

McDaniel, Iain, *Adam Ferguson in the Scottish Enlightenment: The Roman Past and Europe's Future* (Cambridge, MA and London: Harvard University Press, 2013).

McDouall [MacDowall], Andrew, Lord Bankton, *An Essay upon Feudal Holdings, Superiorities, and Hereditary Jurisdictions, in Scotland* (London, 1747).

McGann, Jerome J., *The Beauty of Inflections: Literary Investigations in Historical Method and Theory* (Oxford: Oxford University Press, 1988).

McMahon, Darrin M., *Happiness: A History* (New York: Grove Press, 2006).

Menhennet, Alan, 'Schiller and the Germanico-terrific romance', *Publications of the English Goethe Society*, 51 (1980–81): 22–57.

Meziere, Harriet, *Moreton Abbey; or, The Fatal Mystery*, 2 vols (Southampton, [1785]).

Michasiw, Kim Ian, 'Introduction', in *Zofloya; or, The Moor*, by Charlotte Dacre, edited by Kim Ian Michasiw (Oxford: Oxford University Press, 1997), pp. vii–xxxvii.

Michasiw, Kim Ian, 'Charlotte Dacre's Postcolonial Moor', in Andrew Smith and William Hughes (eds), *Empire and the Gothic: The Politics of Genre* (Basingstoke and New York: Palgrave Macmillan, 2010), pp. 35–55.

Michaud, Louis-Gabriel, *Biographie des hommes vivants* (Paris: Michaud, October 1816–February 1817).

Michaud, Louis-Gabriel, *Biographie universelle ancienne et moderne*, 52 vols (Paris: C. Desplaces, Michaud, [1811–28] 1857).

Mierow, Charles C., *Jordanes: The Origin and Deeds of the Goths* (Cambridge: Speculum Historiale; New York: Barnes & Noble, 1960).

Milbank, Alison, 'Bleeding Nuns: A Genealogy of the Female Gothic Grotesque', in Diana Wallace and Andrew Smith (eds), *Female Gothic: New Directions* (Basingstoke: Palgrave Macmillan, 2009), pp. 76–97.

Milbank, Alison, *God and the Gothic: Religion, Romance, and Reality in the English Literary Tradition* (Oxford: Oxford University Press, 2018).

Miles, Robert, *Ann Radcliffe: The Great Enchantress* (Manchester: Manchester University Press, 1995).

Miles, Robert, *Gothic Writing, 1750–1820: A Genealogy* (Manchester: Manchester University Press, 2002).

Miles, Robert, 'The 1790s: The Effulgence of Gothic', in Jerrold E. Hogle (ed.), *The Cambridge Companion to Gothic Fiction* (Cambridge: Cambridge University Press, 2002), pp. 41–62.

Miles, Robert, 'Ann Radcliffe and Matthew Lewis', in David Punter (ed.), *A New Companion to the Gothic* (Oxford: Wiley-Blackwell, 2012), pp. 93–109.

Miles, Robert, 'The surprising Mrs Radcliffe: *Udolpho*'s artful mysteries', *Women's Writing* 22:3 (2015): 300–16.

Miles, Robert, 'History/Genealogy/Gothic: Godwin, Scott and Their Progeny', in Jerrold E. Hogle and Robert Miles (eds), *The Gothic and Theory: An Edinburgh Companion* (Edinburgh: Edinburgh University Press, 2019), pp. 33–52.

Minma, Shinobu, 'General Tilney and tyranny: *Northanger Abbey*', *Eighteenth-Century Fiction* 8:4 (July 1996): 503–18.

Miscellaneous Poems and Translations. By Several Hands, edited by Richard Savage (London, 1726).

Moers, Ellen, *Literary Women: The Great Writers* (London: The Women's Press, 1978).

Moore, John, *Zeluco*, edited by Pamela Ann Perkins (Kansas City: Valancourt Books, 2008).

Moorhead, John, *Theoderic in Italy* (Oxford: Oxford University Press, 1992).

Mordaunt Crook, J., *John Carter and the Mind of the Gothic Revival* (London: The Society of Antiquaries of London, 1995).

More, Hannah, *Strictures on the Modern System of Female Education*, 2 vols (London, 1799).

Morellet, André, *Les Enfans de l'abbaye*, 6 vols (Paris: Maradan, 1797).

Morellet, André, *Mémoires de l'abbé Morellet, de l'Académie française, sur le dix-huitième siècle et sur la Révolution*, 2 vols (Paris: Ladvocat, 1821).

Moreno, Beatriz González, 'Gothic excess and aesthetic ambiguity in Charlotte Dacre's *Zofloya*', *Women's Writing* 14:3 (2007): 419–34.

Morin, Christina, *The Gothic Novel in Ireland, c. 1760–1829* (Manchester: Manchester University Press, 2018).

Morton, Karen, *A Life Marketed as Fiction: An Analysis of the Works of Eliza Parsons* (Kansas City: Valancourt Books, 2011).

Mowl, Timothy, *Horace Walpole: The Great Outsider* (London: Faber & Faber, 2010).

Mowl, Timothy and Brian Earnshaw, *An Insular Rococo: Architecture, Politics and Society in Ireland and England, 1710–1770* (London: Reaktion, 1999).

Mulligan, Hugh, 'The Lovers, an African Eclogue', in *Poems Chiefly on Slavery and Oppression* (London, 1788), pp. 23–31.

Mulvey-Roberts, Marie, 'From Bluebeard's Bloody Chamber to Demonic Stigmatic', in Diana Wallace and Andrew Smith (eds), *The Female Gothic: New Directions* (Basingstoke: Palgrave Macmillan, 2009), pp. 98–114.

Murnane, Barry, 'Importing home-grown horrors? The English reception of the Schauerroman and Schiller's *Der Geisterseher*', *Angermion* 1 (2008): 51–83.

Murnane, Barry, 'Haunting (Literary) History: An Introduction to German Gothic', in Andrew Cusack and Barry Murnane (eds), *Popular Revenants: German Gothic and Its International Reception, 1800–2000* (Rochester, NY: Camden House, 2012), pp. 10–43.

Murnane, Barry, 'Radical Translations. Dubious Anglo-German Cultural Transfer in the 1790s', in Maike Oergel (ed.), *(Re)-Writing the Radical* (Berlin: De Gruyter, 2012), pp. 44–60.

Murphy, Arthur, *The Literary Magazine: or Universal Review*, April 1757 (March 15–April 15, 1757), 3 vols (London 1757).

Musäus, Johann Karl August, *Volksmärchen der Deutschen*, 5 vols (Gotha, 1787).

Mydla, Jacek, 'The gothic as a mimetic challenge in two post-*Otranto* narratives', *Image & Narrative* 18: 3 (2017): 80–93.

Myrone, Martin (ed.), *Gothic Nightmares: Fuseli, Blake and the Romantic Imagination* (London: Tate Publishing, 2006).

[Naubert, Benedikte], *Herrmann von Unna. Eine Geschichte aus den Zeiten der Vehmgerichte* (Leipzig, 1788).

[Naubert, Benedikte], *Herman d'Unna, ou Aventures arrivées au commencement du quinzieme siècle [Texte imprimé], dans le temps où le tribunal secret avoit sa plus grande influence*, trans. by Baron de Bock (Paris, 1791).

[Naubert, Benedikte], *Hermann of Unna. A Series of Adventures of the Fifteenth Century, in which the Proceedings of the Secret Tribunal under the Emperors Winceslaus and Sigismond are Delineated. In Three Volumes. Written in German by Professor Kramer* (London, 1794).

Nechtman, Tillman W., *Nabobs: Empire and Identity in Eighteenth-Century Britain* (Cambridge: Cambridge University Press, 2010).

Neiman, Elizabeth A., 'A new perspective on the Minerva Press's "derivative" novels: authorizing borrowed material', *European Romantic Review* 26:5 (2015): 633–58.

Newman, Gerald, *The Rise of English Nationalism: A Cultural History, 1740–1830*, revised edition (New York: St. Martin's Press, 1997).

Newman, John, 'The Architectural Setting', in Nicholas Tyacke (ed.), *The History of the University of Oxford, Vol. 4* (Oxford: Clarendon, 1997), pp. 135–78.

Nicholson, *The Solitary Castle: A Romance of the Eighteenth Century*, 2 vols (London, 1789).

Nisbet, Alexander, *An Essay on the Ancient and Modern Use of Armories* (London, 1718).

Nixon, Cheryl L. (ed.), *Novel Definitions: An Anthology of Commentary on the Novel, 1688–1815* (Peterborough, Ont.: Broadview, 2009).

Noguès, Boris, 'Répertoire des professeurs et principaux de la faculté des arts de Paris aux XVIIe et XVIIIe siècles', November 2008 <http://rhe.ish-lyon.cnrs.fr/?q=pfap-record/6094> (last accessed 10 April 2016).

Norman, Larry F., *The Shock of the Ancient: Literature and History in Early Modern France* (Chicago: University of Chicago Press, 2011).

Norton, Rictor, 'Aesthetic gothic horror', *Yearbook of Comparative and General Literature* 2 (1972): 31–40.

Norton, Rictor, *Mistress of Udolpho: The Life of Ann Radcliffe* (London: Leicester University Press, 1999).

Norton, Rictor (ed.), *Gothic Readings: The First Wave, 1764–1840* (London: Leicester University Press, 2000).

Norton, Rictor, *Mother Clap's Molly House: The Gay Subculture in England, 1700–1830* (London: Chalford Press, 2006).

O'Brien, Karen, *Narratives of Enlightenment: Cosmopolitan History from Voltaire to Gibbon* (Cambridge: Cambridge University Press, 1997).
O'Keeffe, John, *A Short Account of the New Pantomime called Omai; or, A Trip Round the World* (London, 1785).
O' Keeffe, John, 'The Castle of Andalusia', in Frederick M. Link (ed.), *The Plays of John O'Keeffe*, 4 vols (New York: Garland, 1981), vol. 1, pp. 1–82.
O'Quinn, Daniel, *Staging Governance: Theatrical Imperialism in London, 1770–1800* (Baltimore: The Johns Hopkins University Press, 2005).
O'Quinn, Daniel, *Entertaining Crisis in the Atlantic Imperium, 1770–1790* (Baltimore: Johns Hopkins University Press, 2011).
Ovenden, Graham, 'Gothic Art', in Marie Mulvey-Roberts (ed.), *The Handbook of the Gothic* (Basingstoke: Palgrave Macmillan, 2009), pp. 127–8.
Owen, Jeremy, *The Goodness and Severity of God, in his Dispensations, with respect unto the Ancient Britains* (London, 1717).
Parry, Graham, *Trophies of Time: English Antiquarians of the Seventeenth Century* (Oxford and New York: Oxford University Press, 1995).
Parsons, Eliza, *The History of Miss Meredith; A Novel*, 2 vols (London, 1790).
Paulson, Michael, 'Out of time: temporal conflict in Ann Radcliffe's *The Mysteries of Udolpho*', *European Romantic Review* 30:5 (2019), forthcoming.
Paulson, Ronald, 'Gothic fiction and the French Revolution', *ELH* 48:3 (Autumn, 1981): 532–54.
Paulson, Ronald, *Representations of Revolution, 1789–1820* (New Haven and London: Yale University Press, 1983).
Pearce, Edward, *The Great Man: Sir Robert Walpole: Scoundrel, Genius and Britain's First Prime Minister* (London: Jonathan Cape, 2007).
Pearson, Jacqueline, *Women's Reading in Britain 1750–1835: A Dangerous Recreation* (Cambridge: Cambridge University Press, 1999).
Pecora, Vincent P., *Secularization and Cultural Criticism: Religion, Nation, and Modernity* (Chicago: University of Chicago Press, 2006).
Pelles, Geraldine, 'The image of the artist', *The Journal of Aesthetics and Art Criticism* 21:2 (Winter 1962): 119–37.
Pennington, Montagu (ed.), *Letters from Mrs. Elizabeth Carter, to Mrs. Montagu, Between the Years 1755 and 1800*, 3 vols (London, 1817).
Percy, Thomas, *Reliques of Ancient English Poetry: Consisting of Old Heroic Ballads, Songs, and Other Pieces of Our Earlier Poets, (Chiefly of the Lyric Kind). Together with Some Few of Later Date*, 3 vols (London, 1765).
Peterson, Martin S., *Robert Jephson (1736–1803): A Study of His Life and Works* (Lincoln, NE: University of Nebraska Press, 1930).
Philips, Ambrose, *The Free-Thinker: or, Essays of Wit and Humour*, 3rd edition, 3 vols (London, 1739).
Phillips, Mark Salber, *Society and Sentiment: Genres of Historical Writing in Britain, 1740–1820* (Princeton, NJ: Princeton University Press, 2000).
Pigoreau, Nicolas-Alexandre, 'Tableau des romans noirs', in *Petite Bibliographie biographico-romancière ou dictionnaire des romanciers* (Paris: Pigoreau, 1821).
Pinkerton, John (ed.), *Walpoliana*, 2 vols (London, 1799).

Piozzi, Hester Lynch, *Retrospective; or, A Review of the Most Striking and Important Events, Characters, Situations, and Their Consequences, Which the Last Eighteen Hundred Years Have Presented to the View of Mankind*, 2 vols (London, 1801).

Pixérécourt, René Charles, *L'homme a trois visages* (Paris, 1801).

Poe, Edgar Allan, 'Preface for Tales of the Grotesque and Arabesque', in *Collected Works of Edgar Allan Poe, Vol. 2: Tales and Sketches, 1831–1842*, edited by Thomas Ollive Mabbott (Cambridge, MA: Belknap Press of Harvard University Press, 1978), p. 473.

Pointon, Marcia, 'Dealer in magic: James Cox's jewelry museum and the economics of luxurious spectacle in late-eighteenth-century London', *History of Political Economy* 31 (1999): 423–51.

Polidori, John, *The Vampyre and Ernestus Berchtold; or, the Modern Oedipus*, edited by D. L. Macdonald and Kathleen Scherf (Peterborough, Ont: Broadview, 2008).

Pop, Andrei, 'Sympathetic spectators: Henry Fuseli's *Nightmare* and Emma Hamilton's Attitudes', *Art History* 34 (2011): 934–57.

Pope, Alexander, *An Essay on Criticism* (London, 1713 [1712]).

Pope, Alexander (ed.), *The Works of Shakespear*, 6 vols (London, 1725).

Pope, Alexander, *Minor Poems*, edited by Norman Ault and John Butt (London: Methuen, 1964).

Porter, James I., 'What Is "Classical" about Classical Antiquity?', in James I. Porter (ed.), *Classical Pasts: The Classical Traditions of Greece and Rome* (Princeton, NJ: Princeton University Press, 2006), pp. 1–68.

Porter, Roy, 'Mixed Feelings: The Enlightenment and Sexuality in Eighteenth-Century Britain', in Paul-Gabriel Boucé (ed.), *Sexuality in Eighteenth-Century Britain* (Manchester: Manchester University Press, 1982), pp. 1–27.

Postle, Martin, '1782: Sir Joshua Buys a Gainsborough', *The Royal Academy of Arts Summer Exhibition: A Chronicle, 1769–2018*, edited by Mark Hallett, Sarah Victoria Turner and Jessica Feather (London: Paul Mellon Centre for Studies in British Art, 2018) <https://chronicle250.com/> (last accessed 2 July 2019).

Potter, Franz J., *The History of Gothic Publishing, 1800–1835: Exhuming the Trade* (Basingstoke: Palgrave Macmillan, 2005).

Powell, Nicolas, *Fuseli – 'The Nightmare'* (London: Allen Lane, 1973).

Pratt, Samuel Jackson, *Humanity; or, the Rights of Nature, A Poem* (London, 1788).

Price, Fiona, *Reinventing Liberty: Nation, Commerce, and the Historical Novel from Walpole to Scott* (Edinburgh: Edinburgh University Press, 2016).

Price, Joseph, *Five Letters, from a Free Merchant in Bengal, to Warren Hastings, Esq* (London, 1778).

Prior, James, *Memoir of the Life and Character of the Right Hon. Edmund Burke*, 2nd edition, 2 vols (London: Baldwin, Cradock and Joy, 1826).

Prior, James, *Life of Edmond Malone, Editor of Shakespeare*, 2 vols (London: Smith, Elder and Co., 1860).

Prungnaud, Joëlle, 'La traduction du roman gothique en France au tournant du XVIIIe siècle', *TTR: traduction, terminologie, redaction* 7:1 (1994): 11–46.

Punter, David, *The Literature of Terror: A History of Gothic Fictions from 1765 to the Present Day*, revised edition, 2 vols (London: Pearson Longman, 1996).

Punter, David, *Gothic Pathologies: The Text, The Body and The Law* (Basingstoke: Macmillan, 1998).

Punter, David (ed.), *A New Companion to the Gothic* (Chichester: Wiley-Blackwell, 2012).

Punter, David and Glennis Byron, *The Gothic* (Oxford: Blackwell, 2004).

Quinn, Vincent, 'Graveyard Writing and the Rise of the Gothic', in Angela Wright and Dale Townshend (eds), *Romantic Gothic: An Edinburgh Companion* (Edinburgh: Edinburgh University Press, 2016), pp. 37–54.

Rabbe, Alphonse, Claude-Augustin Vieilh de Boisjolin and Charles-Augustin Sainte Beuve, *Biographie universelle et portative des contemporains*, 4 vols (Paris: Levrault, 1834).

Radcliffe, Ann, *Gaston De Blondeville; or, The Court of Henry III. Keeping Festival in Ardenne, a Romance. St Alban's Abbey, a Metrical Tale; With Some Poetical Pieces*, 4 vols (London, 1826).

Radcliffe, Ann, 'On the supernatural in poetry. By the late Mrs. Radcliffe', *New Monthly Magazine and Literary Journal* 16:61 (1826): 145–52.

Radcliffe, Ann, *The Romance of the Forest*, edited by Chloe Chard (Oxford: Oxford University Press, 1986).

Radcliffe, Ann, *The Castles of Athlin and Dunbayne*, edited by Alison Milbank (Oxford: Oxford University Press, 1995).

Radcliffe, Ann, *The Mysteries of Udolpho*, edited by Bonamy Dobrée with notes and intro. by Terry Castle (Oxford: Oxford University Press, 1998).

Radcliffe, Ann, *A Sicilian Romance*, edited by Alison Milbank (Oxford: Oxford University Press, 1998).

Radcliffe, Ann, *The Italian*, edited by Robert Miles (London: Penguin Books, 2000).

Ranger, Paul, *Gothic Drama in the London Patent Theatres* (London: Society for Theatre Research, 1991).

Raven, James, 'Production', in Peter Garside and Karen O'Brien (eds), *The Oxford History of the Novel in English, Vol. II: English and British Fiction 1750–1820* (Oxford: Oxford University Press, 2015), pp. 3–28.

Reeve, Clara, *Original Poems on Several Occasions* (London, 1769).

Reeve, Clara, *The Progress of Romance, through Times, Countries, and Manners*, 2 vols (Colchester, 1785).

Reeve, Clara, *Plans of Education with Remarks on the System of Other Writers* (London, 1792).

Reeve, Clara, *Memoirs of Sir Roger de Clarendon, The Natural Son of Edward Prince of Wales, Commonly Called the Black Prince; with Anecdotes of Many Other Eminent Persons of the Fourteenth Century*, 3 vols (London, 1793).

Reeve, Clara, *The Old English Baron*, edited by James Trainer, intro. by James Watt (Oxford: Oxford University Press, 2003).

Reeve, Matthew M., 'Dickie Bateman and the gothicization of Old Windsor: architecture and sexuality in the circle of Horace Walpole', *Architectural History* 56 (2013): 97–131.

Reeve, Matthew M., 'Gothic architecture, sexuality and license at Horace Walpole's Strawberry Hill', *Art Bulletin* 95:3 (September 2013): 411–39.

Reeve, Matthew M., '"A Gothic Vatican of Greece and Rome": Horace Walpole, Strawberry Hill, and the Narratives of Gothic', in Matthew M. Reeve (ed.), *Tributes to Pierre du Prey: Architecture and the Classic Tradition from Pliny to Posterity* (London: Harvey Miller Publishers, 2014), pp. 185–209.

Richardson, Alan, 'Introduction', in *Slavery, Abolition, and Emancipation: Writings in the British Romantic Period*, edited by Debbie Lee and Peter J. Kitson, 8 vols (London: Pickering and Chatto, 1999), vol. 4, pp. ix–xxvi.

Richardson, Alan, 'Introduction', in *Three Oriental Tales: Complete Texts with Introduction, Historical Contexts, Critical Essays*, edited by Alan Richardson (Boston: Houghton Mifflin, 2002), pp. 1–14.

Rigney, Ann, *The Afterlives of Walter Scott: Memory on the Move* (Oxford: Oxford University Press, 2012).

Rix, Robert W., *The Barbarian North in Medieval Imagination: Ethnicity, Legend, and Literature* (New York and London: Routledge, 2015).

Robins, George and Dudley Costello, *A Catalogue of the Classic Contents of Strawberry Hill Collected by Horace Walpole* (London, 1842).

Robinson, Charles E. (ed.), *Mary Shelley: Collected Tales and Stories* (Baltimore: Johns Hopkins University Press, 1992).

Rogers, Brett M. and Benjamin Eldon Stevens (eds), *Classical Traditions in Modern Fantasy* (New York: Oxford University Press, 2017).

Rolfe, J. C., *Ammianus Marcellinus, Vol. III: Latter Part: The History of King Theoderic* (Cambridge, MA and London, Harvard University Press, 1939).

Roman, Cynthia, 'The Art of Lady Diana Beauclerk: Horace Walpole and Female Genius', in Michael Snodin, with Cynthia Roman (eds), *Horace Walpole's Strawberry Hill* (New Haven and London: Yale University Press, 2009), pp. 155–69.

Rosenfeld, Sybil, *Georgian Scene Painters and Scene Painting* (Cambridge: Cambridge University Press, 1981).

Rowan, Alistair John, 'Batty Langley's Gothic', in Giles Robertson and George Henderson (eds), *Studies in Memory of David Talbot Rice* (Edinburgh: Edinburgh University Press, 1975), pp. 197–215.

Rudé, George, *The Crowd in History: A Study of Popular Disturbances in France and England, 1730–1848* (New York: John Wiley, 1964).

Rushton, Edward, *West-Indian Eclogues* (London, 1787).

Ruskin, John, *Modern Painters* <www.ourcivilisation.com/smartboard/shop/ruskinj/> (last accessed 10 February 2019).

Sabor, Peter (ed.), *Horace Walpole: The Critical Heritage* (London and New York: Routledge & Kegan Paul, 1987).

Sabor, Peter, 'Medieval Revival and the Gothic', in H. S. Nisbet and Claude Rawson (eds), *The Cambridge History of Literary Criticism, Volume IV: The Eighteenth Century* (Cambridge: Cambridge University Press, 1997), pp. 470–88.

Sabor, Peter (ed.), *The Court Journals and Letters of Frances Burney, Volume I* (Oxford: Clarendon Press, 2011).

Sachs, Jonathan, *Romantic Antiquity: Rome in the British Imagination, 1789–1832* (Oxford: Oxford University Press, 2010).

Sage, Victor (ed.), *The Gothick Novel: A Casebook* (Basingstoke: Macmillan, 1990).

Saggini, Francesca, *The Gothic Novel and the Stage* (London: Pickering & Chatto, 2015).

Saglia, Diego, 'Gothic Theatre', in Glennis Byron and Dale Townshend (eds), *The Gothic World* (London and New York: Routledge, 2014), pp. 354–65.

Saglia, Diego, '"A portion of the name": Stage Adaptation of Radcliffe's Fiction, 1794–1806', in Dale Townshend and Angela Wright (eds), *Ann Radcliffe, Romanticism and the Gothic* (Cambridge: Cambridge University Press, 2014), pp. 219–36.

Saglia, Diego, 'Staging Gothic Flesh: Material and Spectral Bodies in Romantic-Period Theatre', in Lilla Maria Crisafulli and Fabio Liberto (eds), *The Romantic Stage: A Many-Sided Mirror* (Amsterdam: Rodopi, 2014), pp. 161–84.

Saglia, Diego, 'The Gothic Stage: Visions of Instability, Performances of Anxiety', in Angela Wright and Dale Townshend (eds), *Romantic Gothic: An Edinburgh Companion* (Edinburgh: Edinburgh University Press, 2016), pp. 73–94.

Said, Edward W., *Orientalism: Western Conceptions of the Orient* (London: Penguin, 1991).

Savage, Nicholas, 'Kent as Book Illustrator', in Susan Weber (ed.), *William Kent: Designing Georgian Britain* (New Haven and London: Yale University Press, 2013), pp. 412–47.

Scarborough, Dorothy, *The Supernatural in Modern English Fiction* (New York and London: G. P. Putnam's Sons, 1917).

Schaff, Philip (ed.), *The Principal Works of St. Jerome*, trans. by W. H. Freemantle (Grand Rapids: Wm. B. Eerdmans Publishing, 1892).

Schiller, Friedrich, *On the Naïve and Sentimental in Literature*, trans. Helen Watanabe-O'Kelly (Manchester: Carcanet Press, 1981).

Schmidgen, Wolfram, *Eighteenth-Century Fiction and the Law of Property* (Cambridge: Cambridge University Press, 2002).

Schönert, Jörg, 'Schauriges Behagen und distanzierter Schrecken: Zur Situation von Schauerroman und Schauererzählung im literarischen Leben der Biedermeierzeit', in Alberto Martino (ed.), *Literatur in der sozialen Bewegung* (Tübingen: Niemeyer, 1977), pp. 27–92.

Scott, Walter, 'Prefatory Memoir to Mrs. Ann Radcliffe', in *The Novels of Mrs. Ann Radcliffe . . . to Which Is Prefixed, a Memoir of the Life of the Author* (London: Hurst, Robinson & Co., 1824), pp. i–xxxix.

Scott, Walter, 'Clara Reeve', in Ioan Williams (ed.), *Sir Walter Scott on Novelists and Fiction* (London: Routledge & Kegan Paul, 1968), pp. 94–101.

Scott, Walter, *Chronicles of the Canongate*, edited by Claire Lamont (London: Penguin, 2003).

Scott, Walter, *An Apology for Tales of Terror* <www.walterscott.lib.ed.ac.uk/works/poetry/apology/introduction.html> (last accessed 10 February 2019).

Scott, Walter, *Lives of the Novelists* (London: Oxford University Press, n.d.).

Séché, Léon, *Hortense Allart de Méritens dans ses rapports avec Chateaubriand, Béranger Lamenannais, Sainte-Beuve, G. Sand, Mme d'Angoult* (Paris: Société du Mercure de France, 1908).

Sedgwick, Eve Kosofsky, *The Coherence of Gothic Conventions* (New York: Arno Press, 1980).

Selden, John, *The Duello, or, Single Combat: From Antiquity Derived into This Kingdom of England* (London [1711?]).

Shakespeare, William, *The Plays of William Shakespeare*, edited by Samuel Johnson, 8 vols (London, 1765).

Shakespeare, William, *1. Henry IV*, edited by A. R. Humphreys (London: Arden Shakespeare, 2000).

Shakespeare, William, *A Midsummer Night's Dream*, edited by Harold Brooks (London: Arden Shakespeare, 2004).

Shakespeare, William, *Hamlet: The Texts of 1603 and 1623*, The Arden Shakespeare, edited by Ann Thompson and Neil Taylor (London: Bloomsbury, 2006).

Shapira, Yael, *Inventing the Gothic Corpse: The Thrill of Human Remains in the Eighteenth-Century Novel* (Basingstoke: Palgrave Macmillan, 2018).
Shaw, Philip, *The Sublime* (London and New York: Routledge, 2006).
Shelley, Mary, 'Roger Dodsworth: The Reanimated Englishman', in Betty T. Bennett and Charles E. Robinson (eds), *The Mary Shelley Reader* (New York and Oxford: Oxford University Press, 1990), pp. 274–82.
Shelley, Mary, *Frankenstein: The 1818 Text*, edited by Marilyn Butler (Oxford: Oxford University Press, 1993).
Shelley, Mary, *The Last Man*, edited by Morton D. Paley (Oxford: Oxford University Press, 1994).
Shelley, Mary, *Valperga: or, The Life and Adventures of Castruccio, Prince of Lucca*, edited by Tilottama Rajan (Peterborough, Ont.: Broadview Press, 1998).
Shiner, Larry, *The Invention of Art: A Cultural History* (Chicago: University of Chicago Press, 2001).
Simpson, David. 'Toward a theory of terror', *boundary 2* 41:3 (2014): 1–25.
Sivan, Hagith, *Galla Placidia: The Last Roman Empress* (Oxford: Oxford University Press, 2011).
Smith, Andrew, 'Hauntings', in Catherine Spooner and Emma McEvoy (eds), *The Routledge Companion to Gothic* (Abingdon: Routledge, 2007), pp. 147–54.
Smith, Andrew, *Gothic Death 1740–1914: A Literary History* (Manchester, Manchester University Press, 2016).
Smith, Andrew and Hughes, William (eds), *Empire and the Gothic: The Politics of Genre* (Basingstoke: Palgrave Macmillan, 2003).
Smith, Andrew and William Hughes, 'Introduction: The Enlightenment Gothic and Postcolonialism', in Andrew Smith and William Hughes (eds), *Empire and the Gothic: The Politics of Genre* (Basingstoke and New York: Palgrave Macmillan, 2010), pp. 1–12.
Smith, Charlotte, *Emmeline, the Orphan of the Castle*, edited by Judith Stanton, vol. 2 of *The Works of Charlotte Smith*, 5 vols, general editor Stuart Curran (London: Pickering and Chatto, 2005).
Smith, R. J., *The Gothic Bequest: Medieval Institutions in British Thought, 1688–1863* (Cambridge: Cambridge University Press, 1987).
Smollett, Tobias. *The Adventures of Ferdinand Count Fathom*, edited by Damian Grant (Oxford: Oxford University Press, 1978).
Snodin, Michael, with Cynthia Roman (eds), *Horace Walpole's Strawberry Hill* (New Haven and London: Yale University Press, 2009).
Soame, Henry Francis Robert, *Epistle in Rhyme, to M. G. Lewis, Esq. M.P. Author of The Monk, Castle Spectre, &c. With Other Verses. By the Same Hand* (London, 1798).
Soane, John, *Plans, Elevations and Sections of Buildings* (London, 1788).
Sontag, Susan, 'Notes on Camp', in *A Susan Sontag Reader* (New York: Farrar/Giroux, 1982), pp. 105–20.
Southey, Robert, 'The Curse of Kehama, edited by Daniel Sanjiv Roberts', in *Robert Southey: Poetical Works 1793–1810*, general editor Lynda Pratt, 5 vols (London: Pickering and Chatto, 2004), vol. 4, pp. 1–191.
The Spectator, 8 vols (London, [1712–13] [1713]).
Spelman, Henry, *Reliquiæ Spelmannianæ*, 2 vols (London, 1723).
Spenser, Edmund, *Works*, edited by John Hughes, 6 vols (London, 1715).

Staves, Susan, 'Douglas's Mother', in John. H. Smith (ed.), *Brandeis Essays in Literature* (Waltham, MA: Brandeis University Press, 1983), pp. 51–67.

Steele, Richard, *The Lucubrations of Isaac Bickerstaff Esq; in Five Volumes*, 5 vols (London, 1720).

Stein, Mark, 'Who's Afraid of Cannibals? Some Uses of the Cannibal Trope in Olaudah Equiano's *Interesting Narrative*', in Brycchan Carey, Markman Ellis and Sara Salih (eds), *Discourses of Slavery and Abolition: Britain and its Colonies, 1760–1838* (Basingstoke: Palgrave Macmillan, 2004), pp. 96–107.

Stevens, Anne H., *British Historical Fiction Before Scott* (Basingstoke: Palgrave Macmillan, 2010).

Stevenson, Jane, *Women Latin Poets: Language, Gender, and Authority from Antiquity to the Eighteenth Century* (Oxford: Oxford University Press, 2005).

Stevenson, William, *Remarks on the Very Inferior Utility of Classical Learning* (Manchester, 1796).

Stocking, Rachel L., *Bishops, Councils, and Consensus in the Visigothic Kingdom, 589–633* (Ann Arbor: University of Michigan Press, 2000).

Strahan, Alexander, *The Æneid of Virgil. Translated into Blank Verse*, 2 vols (London, 1767).

Stramaglia, Antonio, *Res inauditae, incredulae: Storie di fantasmi nel mondo greco-latino* (Bari: Levante editori, 1999).

Straub, Kristina, Misty G. Anderson and Daniel O'Quinn (eds), *The Routledge Anthology of Restoration and Eighteenth-Century Drama* (New York and London: Routledge, 2017).

'Strawberry Hill.—by Lady Morgan', *New Monthly Magazine* 17 (August 1826): 121–8, and September 1826, pp. 256–67.

Stuart, Gilbert, *The History of Scotland: From the Establishment of the Reformation till the Death of Queen Mary*, 2 vols (London, 1782).

Summers, Montague (ed.), *The Castle of Otranto and The Mysterious Mother* (London: Constable, 1924).

Summers, Montague, *The Gothic Quest* (London: The Fortune Press, 1938).

Talfourd, Thomas Noon, 'Memoir of the Life and Writings of Mrs Radcliffe', in Ann Radcliffe, *Gaston de Blondeville, or, The Court of Henry III Keeping Festival in Ardenne, A Romance and St Alban's Abbey: A Metrical Tale; With Some Poetical Pieces*, 4 vols (London: Henry Colburn, 1826), vol.I, pp. 1–130.

Taylor, Charles, *Sources of the Self: The Making of the Modern Identity* (Cambridge, MA: Harvard University Press, 1989).

Taylor, Charles, *Modern Social Imaginaries* (Durham, NC: Duke University Press, 2004).

Taylor, Charles, *A Secular Age* (Cambridge, MA: Belknap Press of Harvard University Press, 2007).

Taylor, David Francis, *Theatres of Opposition: Empire, Revolution, and Richard Brinsley Sheridan* (Oxford: Oxford University Press, 2012).

Taylor, Gary, *Reinventing Shakespeare: A Cultural History from the Restoration to the Present* (Oxford: Oxford University Press, 1989).

Taylor, William, 'Lenora', in Douglass H. Thomson (ed.), *Tales of Wonder*, by Matthew Gregory Lewis (Peterborough, Ont.: Broadview, 2010), pp. 222–31.

Temple, William, *An Introduction to the History of England* (London, 1695).

Temple, William, *Miscellanea: The Second Part. In Four Essays*, 2nd edition (London, 1690).

Thomas, David (ed.), *Restoration and Georgian England 1660–1778* (Cambridge: Cambridge University Press, 1989).

Thomas, Helen, *Romanticism and Slave Narratives: Transatlantic Testimonies* (Cambridge: Cambridge University Press, 2004).

Thompson, E. A., revised by Peter Heather, *The Huns* (Oxford: Blackwell Publishing, 1996).

Thomson, Douglass H. (ed.), 'Introduction', *Tales of Wonder*, by Matthew Lewis (Peterborough, Ont.: Broadview, 2010), pp. 13–36.

Thomson, James, *Alfred: A Masque* (London, 1740).

Thorpe, Lewis, *Gregory of Tours: The History of the Franks* (Harmondsworth: Penguin Books, 1974).

Tompkins, J. M. S., *The Popular Novel in England: 1770–1800* (London: Methuen & Co., 1932).

Townshend, Dale, *The Orders of Gothic: Foucault, Lacan, and the Subject of Gothic Writing, 1764–1820* (New York: AMS Press, 2007).

Townshend, Dale, 'Gothic and the Ghost of Hamlet', in John Drakakis and Dale Townshend (eds), *Gothic Shakespeares* (Abingdon and New York: Routledge, 2008), pp. 60–97.

Townshend, Dale, '"Love in a convent": or, Gothic and the Perverse Father of Queer Enjoyment', in William Hughes and Andrew Smith (eds), *Queering the Gothic* (Manchester: Manchester University Press, 2011), pp. 11–35.

Townshend, Dale, 'T. I. Horsley Curties, romance, and the gift of death', *European Romantic Review* 24:1 (2013): 23–42.

Townshend, Dale, 'Gothic and the Cultural Sources of Horror, 1740–1820', in Xavier Aldana Reyes (ed.), *Horror: A Literary History* (London: The British Library, 2016), pp. 19–51.

Townshend, Dale, *Gothic Antiquity: History, Romance, and the Architectural Imagination, 1760–1840* (Oxford: Oxford University Press, 2019).

Townshend, Dale and Angela Wright (eds), *Ann Radcliffe, Romanticism and the Gothic* (Cambridge: Cambridge University Press, 2014).

Townshend, Dale and Angela Wright, 'Gothic and Romantic Engagements: The Critical Reception of Ann Radcliffe, 1789–1850', in Dale Townshend and Angela Wright (eds), *Ann Radcliffe, Romanticism and the Gothic* (Cambridge: Cambridge University Press, 2014), pp. 3–32.

Townshend, Dale and Angela Wright, 'Gothic and Romantic: An Historical Overview', in Angela Wright and Dale Townshend (eds), *Romantic Gothic: An Edinburgh Companion* (Edinburgh: Edinburgh University Press, 2016), pp. 1–34.

Toynbee, Paget and Leonard Whibley (eds), *Correspondence of Thomas Gray*, 3 vols (Oxford: Clarendon Press, 1935).

Toynbee, Paget Jackson, 'Horace Walpole's journals of visits to country seats &c.', *Walpole Society* 16 (1927–28): 8–80.

Toynbee, Paget Jackson, *Strawberry Hill Accounts: A Record of Expenditure in Building Furnishing, &c Kept by Mr Horace Walpole from 1747 to 1795* (Oxford: Clarendon Press, 1927).

Tracy, Ann B., *The Gothic Novel, 1790–1830: Plot Summaries and an Index to Motifs* (Lexington: University Press of Kentucky, 1981).

Troide, Lars E. (ed.), *Horace Walpole's Miscellany, 1786–1795* (New Haven: Yale University Press, 1978).

Trousson, Raymond, *Une mémorialiste oubliée: Victorine de Chastenay* (Bruxelles: Académie royale de langue et de littérature françaises de Belgique, 2007).

Trusler, John, *A Descriptive Account of the Islands Lately Discovered in the South-Seas* (London, 1778).

Tuite, Clara, 'Cloistered closets: enlightenment pornography, the confessional state, homosexual persecution and *The Monk*', *Romanticism on the Net* 8 (1997) <www.erudit.org/en/journals/ron/1997-n8-ron420/005766ar/> (last accessed 5 January 2019).

Turnbull, Paul, 'The Chief Mourner's Costume: Religion and Political Change in the Society Islands, 1768–73', in Michelle Hetherington and Paul Morley (eds), *Discovering Cook's Collections* (Canberra: National Museum of Australia, 2009), pp. 41–57.

Uden, James, 'Gothic Fiction, the Grand Tour, and the Seductions of Antiquity: John Polidori's *The Vampyre* (1819)', in Roberta Micallef (ed.), *Illusions and Disillusionment: Travel Writing in the Modern Age* (Boston: Ilex Foundation, 2018), pp. 58–77.

Uden, James, 'Horace Walpole, gothic classicism, and the aesthetics of collection', *Gothic Studies* 20:1 (2018): 44–58.

Uden, James, *Spectres of Antiquity: Classical Literature and the Gothic* (New York: Oxford University Press, forthcoming).

Upcott, William (ed.), *The Miscellaneous Writings of John Evelyn, Esq. F.R.S* (London, 1825).

Vardy, John, *Some Designs of Mr. Inigo Jones and Mr. Wm. Kent* (London, 1744).

Varma, Devendra P., *The Gothic Flame: Being a History of the Gothic Novel in England* (London: Arthur Baker Ltd, 1957).

Vaughan, William, 'Magic in the Studio', in Ann Bermingham (ed.), *Sensation & Sensibility: Viewing Gainsborough's Cottage Door* (New Haven and London: Yale University Press, 2005), pp. 165–79.

Verstegan, Richard, *A Restitution of Decayed Intelligence: In Antiquities Concerning the Most Noble and Renowned English Nation* (Antwerp, 1605).

Virolle, Raymond, 'Vie et survie du roman noir', in P. Barbéris and C. Duchet (eds), *Manuel d'Histoire littéraire de la France* (Paris: Editions Sociales, 1972), pp. 138–47.

Voller, Jack G. (ed.), *The Graveyard School: An Anthology* (Richmond, VA: Valancourt, 2016).

Voltaire [Arouet, François-Marie] *Letters Concerning the English Nation* (London, 1778).

Wahrman, Dror, *The Making of the Modern Self: Identity and Culture in Eighteenth-Century England* (New Haven: Yale University Press, 2004).

Wainwright, Clive, *The Romantic Interior: The British Collector at Home, 1750–1850* (New Haven and London: Yale University Press, 1989).

Wallace, Diana, *Female Gothic Histories: Gender, History and the Gothic* (Cardiff: University of Wales Press, 2013).

Wallace, Diana and Andrew Smith (eds), *The Female Gothic: New Directions* (Basingstoke: Palgrave Macmillan, 2009).

Wallace, Tara Ghoshal, 'The elephant's foot and the British mouth: Walter Scott on imperial rhetoric', *European Romantic Review* 13 (2002): 311–24.

Walpole, Horace, *Anecdotes of Painting in England; with Some Account of the Principal Artists; and Notes on Other Arts; Collected by G. Vertue, and Now Digested from His MSS*, 4 vols (Strawberry Hill: Printed by Thomas Farmer, 1762–71 [1780]).

Walpole, Horace, *Hieroglyphic Tales* (Twickenham, 1785).

Walpole, Horace, *The Works of Horatio Walpole, Earl of Orford*, 5 vols (London: Printed for G. G. and J. Robinson and J. Edwards, 1798).

Walpole, Horace, *The Yale Edition of Horace Walpole's Correspondence*, 48 vols, edited by W. S. Lewis (New Haven: Yale University Press, 1937–83).

Walpole, Horace, 'Notes by Horace Walpole on Several Characters of Shakespeare', in Wilmarth Sheldon Lewis (ed.), *Miscellaneous Antiquities* (Windham, CT: Hawthorne House, 1940), pp. 5–7.

Walpole, Horace, *Historic Doubts on the Life and Reign of Richard the Third*, edited by P. W. Hammond (Gloucester: Alain Sutton, 1987).

Ward-Perkins, Bryan, *The Fall of Rome and the End of Civilization* (Oxford: Oxford University Press, 2005).

Ward-Perkins, Bryan, 'Where Is the Archaeology and Iconography of Germanic Arianism?', in David M. Gwynn and Susanne Bangert (eds), *Late Antique Archaeology 6: Religious Diversity in Late Antiquity* (Leiden: Brill, 2010), pp. 265–89.

Walpole, Horace, *The Castle of Otranto*, edited by Nick Groom (Oxford: Oxford University Press, 2014).

Warton, Thomas, *Observations on The Fairy Queen of Spenser*, 2nd edition, 2 vols (London, 1762).

Watt, James, *Contesting the Gothic: Fiction, Genre and Cultural Conflict, 1764–1832* (Cambridge: Cambridge University Press, 1999).

Watt, James, 'Orientalism and Empire', in Richard Maxwell and Katie Trumpener (eds), *The Cambridge Companion to Fiction in the Romantic Period* (Cambridge: Cambridge University Press, 2008), pp. 129–42.

Watt, James, 'Ann Radcliffe and Politics', in Dale Townshend and Angela Wright (eds), *Ann Radcliffe, Romanticism and the Gothic* (Cambridge: Cambridge University Press, 2014), pp. 67–82.

Webb, John, *A Vindication of Stone-Heng Restored: in which the Orders and Rules of Architecture Observed by the Ancient Romans, are Discussed*, 2nd edition (London, 1725).

Webb, Timothy, 'Haunted City: The Shelleys, Byron, and Ancient Rome', in Timothy Saunders, Charles Martindale, Ralph Pite and Mathile Skoie (eds), *Romans and Romantics* (Oxford: Oxford University Press, 2012), pp. 203–24.

Weber, Susan (ed.), *William Kent: Designing Georgian Britain* (New Haven and London: Yale University Press, 2013).

Wein, Toni, *British Identities, Heroic Nationalisms, and the Gothic Novel, 1764–1824* (Basingstoke: Palgrave Macmillan, 2002).

Weiner, Jesse, Benjamin Eldon Stevens and Brett M. Rogers (eds), *Frankenstein and its Classics: The Modern Prometheus from Antiquity to Science Fiction* (London: Bloomsbury, 2018).

Weinglass, David H. (ed.), *The Collected English Letters of Henry Fuseli* (Millwood: Kraus International NY, 1982).

West, Shearer, 'Roles and Role Models: Montagu, Siddons, Lady Macbeth', in Elizabeth Eger (ed.), *Bluestockings Displayed: Portraiture, Performance and Patronage, 1730–1830* (Cambridge: Cambridge University Press), pp. 164–86.

[Whalley, Thomas Sedgwick], *Edwy and Edilda: A Tale, in Five Parts* (London, 1779).

[Whalley, Thomas Sedgwick], *Edwy and Edilda: A Gothic Tale, in Five Parts. By the Author of the Old English Baron* (Dublin, 1783).

Whately, Thomas, *Observations on Modern Gardening, Illustrated by Descriptions* (London, 1770).

White, James, *Earl Strongbow: The History of Richard de Clare and the Beautiful Geralda*, 2 vols (London, 1789).

White, Roger, 'The Influence of Batty Langley', in J. Mordaunt Crooke (ed.), *A Gothick Symposium at the Victoria and Albert Museum* (London: Victoria and Albert Museum, 1984), no. pag.

White, Roger, 'William Kent and the Gothic Revival', in Susan Weber (ed.), *William Kent: Designing Georgian Britain* (New Haven and London: Yale University Press, 2013), pp. 247–69.

Whitley, W. T., *Artists and Their Friends in England, 1700–1799*, 2 vols (London: Medici Society, 1928).

Wilberforce, William, *A Letter on the Abolition of the Slave Trade* (London, 1807).

Williams, Abigail, *Poetry and the Creation of a Whig Literary Culture, 1681–1714* (Oxford: Oxford University Press, 2005).

Williams, Anne, *Art of Darkness: A Poetics of Gothic* (Chicago: Chicago University Press, 1995).

Williams, Gilda (ed.), *The Gothic* (London: Whitechapel, 2007).

Williams, Gilda, 'Defining a Gothic Aesthetic in Modern and Contemporary Visual Art', in Glennis Byron and Dale Townshend (eds), *The Gothic World* (London and New York: Routledge 2014), pp. 412–25.

Williams, Helen Maria, *A Poem on the Bill Lately Passed for Regulating the Slave Trade* (London, 1788).

Wilson, Jon, *India Conquered: Britain's Raj and the Chaos of Empire* (London: Simon & Schuster, 2016).

Wilson, Kathleen, *The Sense of the People: Politics, Culture and Imperialism in England, 1715–1785* (Cambridge: Cambridge University Press, 1995).

Wilson, Kathleen, *The Island Race: Englishness, Empire and Gender in the Eighteenth Century* (London: Routledge, 2003).

Wilson, Penny, 'Classical Poetry and the Eighteenth-Century Reader', in Isobel Rivers (ed.), *Books and their Readers in Eighteenth-Century England* (New York: St. Martin's Press, 1982), pp. 69–96.

Wilt, Judith, *Ghosts of the Gothic: Austen, Eliot and Lawrence* (Princeton, NJ: Princeton University Press, 1980).

Wolf, Kenneth Baxter, *Conquerors and Chroniclers of Early Medieval Spain*, 2nd edition (Liverpool: Liverpool University Press, 1999).

Wollstonecraft, Mary, *Maria; or, the Wrongs of Woman*, edited by Gary Kelly (Oxford: Oxford University Press, 1976).

Womersley, David (ed.), *Augustan Critical Writing* (London: Penguin Books, 1997).

Wood, Jamie P., *The Politics of Identity in Visigothic Spain: Religion and Power in the Histories of Isidore of Seville* (Leiden: Brill, 2012).

Wood, Marcus, 'Introduction', in *The Poetry of Slavery: An Anglo-American Anthology 1764–1865*, edited by Marcus Wood (Oxford: Oxford University Press, 2003), pp. xi–xxxiv.

Worrall, David, *Theatric Revolution: Drama, Censorship and Romantic Period Subcultures 1773–1832* (Oxford: Oxford University Press, 2006).

Worrall, David, 'The Political Culture of Gothic Drama', in David Punter (ed.), *A New Companion to the Gothic* (Chichester: Wiley-Blackwell, 2012), pp. 148–60.
Worsley, Giles, 'The origins of the gothic revival: a reappraisal: the Alexander Prize essay', *Transactions of the Royal Historical Society* 3 (1993): 105–50.
Worsley, Giles, *Classical Architecture in Britain: The Heroic Age* (New Haven and London: Yale University Press, 1995).
Wren, Christopher, *Parentalia: Or, Memoirs of the Family of the Wrens: Viz., of Matthew, Bishop of Ely, Christopher, Dean of Windsor, Etc. But Chiefly of Sir Christopher Wren in Which Is Contained, Besides His Works, a Great Number of Original Papers and Records* (London, 1750).
Wren, Christopher, 'Tom Tower, Christ Church, Oxford (1681–2)', *The Wren Society* 5 (1928): 17–23.
Wright, Angela, *Gothic Fiction: A Reader's Guide* (Basingstoke: Palgrave Macmillan, 2007).
Wright, Angela, 'Disturbing the Female Gothic: An Excavation of the Northanger Novels', in Diana Wallace and Andrew Smith (eds), *The Female Gothic: New Directions* (Basingstoke: Palgrave Macmillan, 2009), pp. 60–75.
Wright, Angela, *Britain, France and the Gothic, 1764–1820: The Import of Terror* (Cambridge: Cambridge University Press, 2013).
Wright, Angela and Dale Townshend (eds), *Romantic Gothic: An Edinburgh Companion* (Edinburgh: Edinburgh University Press, 2016).
Wright, Julia, 'Lewis's "Anaconda": Gothic homonyms and sympathetic distinction', *Gothic Studies* 3:3 (2001): 262–78.
Young, Edward, *The Complaint* (London, 1743).
Young, Edward, *Conjectures on Original Composition* (London, 1759).
Zigarovich, Jolene, 'Introduction', in Jolene Zigarovich (ed.), *Sex and Death in Eighteenth-Century Literature* (New York: Routledge, 2013), pp. 1–28.
Zigarovich, Jolene, 'Transing the Gothic', in Jolene Zigarovich (ed.), *TransGothic in Literature and Culture* (New York: Routledge, 2018), pp. 1–22.
[Zschokke, Johann Heinrich Daniel], *Abaellino der große Bandit* (Frankfurt und Leipzig, 1794).
Zschokke, J. H. D., *Aböllino der große Bandit. Ein Trauerspiel in fünf Aufzügen, nach der Geschichte dieses Namens von demselben Autor* (Leipzig, Frankfurt a. d. Oder, 1795).

Index

The Abbey of St. Asaph (Kelly, I.), 323–4
Abildgaard, Nicolai, 418
abolitionist Gothic, 191–7
 supernatural terrors and, 197
Addison, Joseph, 56–7, 64, 81–2, 143, 163, 174
 on terror, 286–9
Adelman, Janet, 150
Adelmorn, the Outlaw (Lewis, M. G.), 212–13
The Advancement and Reformation of Modern
  Poetry (Dennis, J.), 76, 77
The Adventures of Ferdinand, Count Fathom
  (Smollett, T.), 334
aesthetic relativism, 88
aesthetics of association, 125–40
 Classical compared to Gothic architecture,
  129–30
Aikin, Anna Laetitia, 290–9, 334, 347, 437. See
 also Barbauld, Anna Laetitia
Aikin, John, 214, 334, 437
Akenside, Mark, 55, 81–2, 85
Alaric, 22, 24, 30–3
 as military leader, 31–3
 Sack of Rome by, 32–3, 45–6
Alexander, William, 228
Alfred (Blackmore, R.), 48
Alfred the Great, 48
Amalasuintha, 38–9
American Revolution, British Gothic and
 haunted apartment as metaphor for, 252–8
 heroism during, 244–52
 The Old English Baron and, 244–58
 virtue and, 244–52
Anderson, Benedict, 163–4
Andrews, Miles Peter, 199–200, 213
Anecdotes of Painting in England (Walpole,
  H.), 129
The Anonymous Valesianus, 24, 38
anti-Catholic sentiment, during French
  Revolution, 269, 279–80

anti-Enlightenment themes, in Oriental
  Gothic fiction, 345–6
Apollinarius, Sidonius, 24, 35
Aquitaine Kingdom, 33–6
 boundaries of, 34
 Codex Euricianus, 35
 Huns during, 34–5
Arabian Nights' Entertainments (Galland, A.),
  185, 347–8
 authors influenced by, 347
 Gothic fiction influenced by, 347–8
 objects of terror in, 347
 translations of, 347
Arabs, Visigothic Spain conquered by,
  24, 42–3
architecture, Gothic
 aesthetics of association for, 125–40
 Classical compared to Gothic
  architecture, 129–30
 imaginative response to, 127
 during long eighteenth century, 52–6
 medievalist literature and, 60
 religious influences on, 54–6
archive fever, in Gothic fiction, 9
Ariosto, Ludovico, 75
Aristotle, 73
Ars Poetica (Horace), 73, 165–6
Ascham, Roger, 74
Astbury, Katherine, 278
Athalaric, 38–9
Athaulf, 33–4
Attila (as Hun military leader), 34–5, 36
Augustine of Hippo, 32
Austen, Jane, 9, 366–7, 430–1
 time in, comparisons to Radcliffe's use,
  431–2

Bacon, Nathaniel, 43, 72
The Banditti (O'Keeffe, J.), 220–1

484

Banks, Joseph, 180–1
Barbauld, Anna Laetitia, 435, 438. *See also* Aikin, Anna Laetitia
Baron-Wilson, Margaret, 316
Barry, James, 414
Battle of Culloden, 56
Battle of Hexham (Colman, G. the Younger), 218
Bayly, C. A., 349
Beattie, James, 294
Beckford, William, 315
  Vathek, 184–90, 236, 347–8
  as Oriental Gothic fiction, 350–2
  sexual transgression in, 397–8
The Beggar's Opera (Gay, J.), 198
Bentham, Jeremy, 259–60
Bentley, Richard, 122, 413
Bicknell, John, 191–3
Bienville, M. D. T., 396–7
Bill of Rights (1689), 43
Blackmore, Sir Richard, 48
Blackstone, William, 223, 252, 412
Blair, Hugh, 5
Blair, Robert, 55, 70, 183
Blake, Catherine, 413–14
Blake, William, 408, 411–13, 422
blank verse, in Gothic poetry, 81–2
Bleeding Nun, in *The Monk*, 337–8
  adaptations of, 373–4
  in *Eva*, 339–40
  in *The Midnight Bell*, 342–3
Bluebeard; or, Female Curiosity! (Colman, G. the Younger), 359–60
Boaden, James, 198–9, 374, 377
bodies, representation of
  in German Gothic fiction, 380–1
  in Oriental Gothic fiction, 358–63
Boethius, 24, 38
Botting, Fred, 70
Boucé, Paul-Gabriel, 388
Bowyer, Robert, 415
Boydell, John, 415
Boyle, Richard, 110
Bram Stoker's Dracula (film), 16
Braulio of Zaragoza, 42
The Bravo of Venice (Lewis, M. G.), 376
Britain
  Goths in, during long eighteenth century, 48–9, 50–1
  Gothic visual arts in, 410
  mass immigration into, as global terror, 184
  national identity through resistance to foreign empires, 181–2
  public perceptions of global terrors, by British people, 180–4
  of Catholic despotism, 182
  of enslavement by Spanish, 182
  of mass immigration, 184
Britannia (Camden, W.), 46, 47
Browne, Thomas, 141
Bruhm, Steven, 386–7
Bundock, Chris, 411–13
Bunyan, John, 60–1
Bürger, Gottfried August, 373, 438–41
Burke, Edmund, 10, 52, 165, 189–90, 218
  on terror, 289–90, 433–4
Burney, Frances, 320–1
  Radcliffe compared to, 321–2
Burton, Tim, 17
Byron, George Gordon (Lord), 312–13, 361

Caesar, Julius, 45
Caleb Williams (Godwin, W.), 11
Camden, William, 46, 47
Cameron, Ed, 151
Camilla (Burney, F.), 320–1
The Canterbury Tales (Chaucer, G.), 88
Carey, Brycchan, 191–2
Carlyle, Thomas, 364, 365–6
The Carmelite (Cumberland, R.), 209–10
Carter, Elizabeth, 168–9, 314
Carter, John
  The Death of Matilda, 134, 136
  The Entry of Frederick [sic] into the Castle of Otranto, 133–4
Cassiodorus, 24
Castle, Terry, 145
The Castle of Andalusia (O'Keeffe, J.), 207–8
The Castle of Ollada (Lathom, F.), 337
The Castle of Otranto (Walpole, H.), 1, 5, 19, 130–40, 205. *See also* historical Gothic
  counter-Reformation in, 2
  fragmentation of the Classical, 162
  as Gothic novel, 45
  Hamlet and, comparisons to, 151–2
  hyper-fictionality of, 94
  preface of, 7
  Protestant Reformation in, 2
The Castle of Wolfenbach (Parsons, E.), 327–36
  at Minerva Press, 328–9
  publication of, timing of, 335
  similarities to previous works, 330
  The History of the Duchess of C*** written by Herself, 330–2
  violence in, 332–3

485

Index

The Castle Spectre (Lewis, M. G.), 198–9, 317–18, 428
The Castles of Athlin and Dunbayne (Radcliffe, A.), 222, 259
Catherine of Aragon, 1–2
  Legatine Court and, 1
Catholic despotism, 182
Catholicism
  in Garrick's Jubilee, Roman Catholic rituals as part of, 145–6
  Gothic architecture influenced by, 54–5
  in Visigothic Spain, 40–1
Cato (Addison, J.), 163
The Champion of Virtue (Reeve, C.), 5, 171, 245
Chaplin, Sue, 238
Chappey, Jean-Luc, 281–2
Characteristicks of Men, Manners, Opinions, Times (Cooper, A. A., third Earl of Shaftesbury), 78–80
Charlemagne, 35–6, 39–40
Charlesworth, Michael, 409–10
Charlton, Mary, 274
Chatterton, Thomas, 64–6, 131
Chaucer, Geoffrey, 88
Chénier, Marie-Joseph de, 266
The Children of the Abbey (Roche, R. M.), 264, 274
Chippendale, Thomas, 53
Chiu, Frances, 249–50
Christabel (Coleridge, S. T.)
  public response to, 442
  time in, 441–9
Churchill, Charles, 63
Chute, John, 122
City of God (Augustine of Hippo), 32
Clark, Kenneth, 69–70, 98
Clarkson, Thomas, 193
the Classical
  in *The Castle of Otranto*, fragmentation of, 162
  in *Frankenstein*, 177–8
  gender prejudice and, 167–73
  genre and, 167–73
  the Gothic and, 176–8
  languages, 164
  oppressive influence of, 162–7
  Romantic-era authors and, 178–9
Classical architecture, Gothic architecture compared to, 129–30
Classical learning, in Visigothic Spain, 41–2
Claudian, 24
Clery, E. J., 135–7, 222, 306–7, 424
Clovis (King), 35–6

Cobb, James, 199–200, 213
Codex Euricianus, 35
Colburn, Henry, 413
Coleridge, Samuel Taylor, 298–9, 307, 347, 370–1, 428
  Christabel, 441–9
  public response to, 442
Colley, Linda, 245–6
Colman the Younger, George, 199–200, 218, 359–60
Colvin, Howard, 98–9
Commentaries on the Laws of England (Blackstone, W.), 252
commerce and trade, as theme, in Oriental Gothic fiction, 349–58
Conjectures on Original Composition (Young, E.), 162–3
The Consolation of Philosophy (Boethius), 24, 38
Constable, John, 410, 411
The Convent; or, the History of Sophia Nelson (Fuller, A.), 279–80
Conway, Stephen, 234
Cooper, Anthony Ashley (third Earl of Shaftesbury), 61, 72, 78–80, 81–2
Coopers-Hill (Denham, J.), 54
Coppola, Francis Ford, 16
The Corsair (Byron), 361
Cosway, Maria, 414
The Count of Narbonne (Jephson, R.), 204–7
counter-Reformation, in *The Castle of Otranto*, 2
Cowper, William, 184
Cox, James, 188, 214
Crimson Peak (film), 17
Critique of Pure Reason (Kant, I.), 380
Cugoano, Ottobah, 191
Cumberland, Richard, 204–6, 208–9
  The Carmelite, 209–10
The Curse of Kehama (Southey, R.), 360
Curties, T. J. Horsley, 325–6, 338

Dabhoiwala, Faramerz, 388–9
Dacre, Charlotte, 352–4, 376, 395, 399–404
d'Alembert, Jean le Rond, 4
Darwin, Erasmus, 418–20
Davenant, Charles, 51
Davison, Carol Margaret, 199–200, 238
Day, Thomas, 191–3
The Death of Matilda (Carter, J.), 134, 136
Defoe, Daniel, 50, 60–1
De l'origine des loix, des arts, et des sciences et leurs progrès chez les anciens peuples (Goguet, A.-Y.), 4

486

Index

De origine actibusque Getarum (Getica)
  (Jordanes), 25
Denham, John, 54, 72
Dennis, John, 75–8, 81–2, 143
  The Grounds of Criticism in Poetry, 77–8,
    284–5
  on terror, 284–5
Dent, Jonathan, 9, 234–5
depravity, in German Gothic fiction, 365–75
De Quincey, Thomas, 347, 358–9, 362
Derrida, Jacques, 9
Diderot, Denis, 4, 272–3
discovered document, as literary convention,
  in Gothic fiction, 7, 9
Dobson, Michael, 142
Dodsworth, Roger, 14–15
domestic Gothic writing
  early literary foundations for, 222–3
  ghosts in, 229
  Gothic histories, 229–34
  lineage themes, 236–42
  pageantry, 234–6
  satirical Gothic, 223–7
  superstition, 225
  sentimental Gothic, 227–9
  ruination trope in, 232–3
  theoretical approach to, 222–3
Don Juan (Byron), 361
Douglas (Home, J.), 200–3
  longevity of, 201
  plot devices in, 202–3
  violent themes in, 202
Dow, Alexander, 349
Doyle, Laura, 181–2
Dracula (Stoker, Bram), 29–30
  Freudian influences in, 15
  historical elements in, 15–16
The Dracula Tape (Saberhagen, F.), 16
Dracula Untold (film), 16
Drake, Nathan, 307
Dryden, John, 61, 82–5, 143, 199, 284
Dryer, John, 69–70
Duff, William, 57–8
Duncombe, John, 168–9
Dunlop, John Colin, 310–11
Duval, Alexandre, 272
The Dying Negro (Bicknell, J. and Day, T.),
  191–3

Earl Strongbow (White, J.), 223–4
Eastlake, Charles Locke, 97–8
Edelman, Lee, 388
Edgeworth, Maria, 280–1

Effingher, Elizabeth, 411–13
Elegy Wrote in a Country Churchyard
  (Gray), 55–6
Eliot, T. S., 151–2, 426
Die Elixiere des Teufels (Hoffmann, E. T. A.),
  365, 376
Ellen and Julia (Parsons, E.), 329
Ellis, Markman, 5–6
Elliston, Robert, 369–70
Emmeline, the Orphan of the Castle (Smith, C.),
  228–9, 271
*Encyclopédie, ou dictionnaire raisonné des
  sciences, des arts et des métiers*
  (d'Alembert, J. le Rond and Diderot,
  D.), 4
Die Entführung' (Musäus, J. K. A.), 371–2
*The Entry of Frederick [sic] into the Castle of
  Otranto* (Carter, J.), 133–4
The Epistolary Intrigue (Lewis, M. G.), 312
Equiano, Olaudah, 194, 195–7
The Errors of Education (Parsons, E.), 329
An Essay on Romance (Scott, W.), 11
Etymologies (Isidore of Seville), 24, 41–2
Euric (King), 35
Eva (Kelly, I.), 338–41
  Bleeding Nun references in, 339–40
  ghosts in, 339–40
  supernatural in, 340–1
Exclusion Crisis, 72, 220

The Faerie Queene (Spenser, E.), 58, 88
  structure of, 88–9
Farley, Charles, 373–4
Favret, Mary, 214–15
fear. *See* horror; terror
female translators, of English Gothic fiction
  novels, 266–70
Ferguson, Adam, 3
feudalism, among Goths, during long
  eighteenth century, 50
fiction, Gothic. *See also specific genres*
  Arabian Nights' Entertainments as influence
    on, 347–8
  challenging genres in, 167–73
  Foucault on, 383–8
  gender prejudice in, 167–73
  during long eighteenth century, popular
    meaning of, 45
  terror in, 289–90
Fielding, Henry, 53, 154, 320–1
Fletcher, John, 141
Fontainville Forest (Boaden, J.), 198–9
Foote, Samuel, 187

Foucault, Michel, 3, 11
  on Gothic fiction, 383–8
  The History of Sexuality, 382–8, 404–5
  on sexuality, 382–8
Frank, Frederick S., 224
Frankenstein; or, the Modern Prometheus (Shelley, M. W.)
  Classical themes in, 177–8
  history in, 11–12
  literary influences on, 177–8
  as Oriental Gothic Fiction, 354–6
  Paradise Lost and, 12
Franks, Visigoths and
  military defeat of, 35–6
  in Spain, 40–1
Frederick of Hanover (Prince), 48
French Revolution
  anti-Catholic sentiment, 269, 279–80
  English Gothic fiction novels available during
    economic and social status of translators, 267–8, 269–70
    female translators of, 266–70
    male translators of, 270–82
    translations of, 266–83
  French Gothic novels available during, 262–6
    English translations of, 263
    liberal themes in, 276
    opposition to, 273
    support for, 278–9
    women barred from political engagement, 269
Freud, Sigmund. *See also* psychoanalysis
  Dracula influenced by, 15
Fry, Paul, 164
Fuller, Anne, 229, 230–2, 239, 279–80
Fuseli, Henry, 408, 413–14, 416, 421
  artistic references for, 420–3
  The Nightmare, 417–18, 419

Galla Placidia, 33–4
Galland, Antoine
  Arabian Nights' Entertainments, 185, 347–8
  authors influenced by, 347
  Gothic fiction influenced by, 347–8
  objects of terror in, 347
  translations of, 347
Galliano, John, 17
Gallic Wars, 45
Gamer, Michael, 315
Garrick, David, 201, 208–9, 221
Garrick's Jubilee, for Shakespeare, 143–6
  Roman Catholic rituals as part of, 145–6
Gaskell, Elizabeth, 164
Gaston De Blondeville (Radcliffe, A.), 259
Gay, John, 154, 198
Der Geisterbanner (Kahlert, K. F.), 367–8
gender. *See also* women
  the Classical and, 167–73
  policing of, in Gothic fiction, 388–91
Genlis, Stéphanie Félicité de, 330–2
Gepids, 36
German Gothic fiction. *See also* Lewis, Matthew Gregory; *The Monk*; *specific works*
  bodily representations in, 380–1
  critical review of, 370–1
  definition and scope of, 380
  depravity as theme in, 365–75
  horror elements of, 367
  pharmacology in, 375–81
  poisoning, 378
  stereotyping in, 364–5
  toxic poetics as element of, 365–75
Germania (Tacitus), 25
The Ghost (Churchill, C.), 63
'ghost of the counterfeit', 422
ghosts and ghostliness
  in domestic Gothic writing, 229
  in *Eva*, 339–40
  as Gothic element, 175–6
  in *The Midnight Bell*, 342–3
The Giaour (Byron), 361
Gibbon, Edward, 10
Gillespie, Stuart, 174–5
global terrors, perceptions by British people, 180–4
  Catholic despotism, 182
  enslavement by Spanish, 182
  of mass immigration, 184
Glorious Revolution of 1688, 43, 50, 72
Goddu, Teresa A, 196–7
Godwin, William, 9–10, 13–14, 199–200
  historical romancer in, 10–11
Goguet, Antoine-Yves, 4
Goldsmith, Oliver, 218, 223
Gothic, as concept. *See also specific topics*
  after Bill of Rights, 43
  the Classical and, 176–9
  definition of, 22, 25
  ghosts and ghostliness and, 175–6
  after Glorious Revolution of 1688, 43
  in long eighteenth century. *See* long eighteenth century
  Orientalist empires and, 184–90

Index

nabobs, 187
Romantic era, 178–9
Gothic architecture. *See* architecture
Gothic drama
  creation of, 204–10
  as genre, 200
  orchestration of, 214–19
  as political, 217–19
  production elements of, 211–14
Gothic histories, in domestic writing, 229–34
Gothic literature. *See* literature
The Gothic Novel in Ireland, c. 1760–1829 (Morin, C.), 69
The Gothic Quest (Summers, M.), 67–8
Gothic Revival (Clark, K.), 69–70
Gothic Revival, of 1760s, 86–93
  aesthetic relativism and, 88
  dating of, 99
  genesis of, 99–100
  'Gothic survival' as distinct from, 87
  literary antiquarianism, 91–2
  public endorsement of, 87
Gothic Revival architecture
  aesthetic schism in, among architects, 100
  dating of, 99
  definition and scope of, 99–100
  expertise gap in, 99–100
  genesis of, 99–100
  Hawksmoor and, 100, 104–7
    architectural style, 104–6
    use of medieval forms, 106–7
  Kent and, 100, 110–15
    architectural style, 110–14
  knowledge gaps in, 99–100
  Langley and, 53, 100, 115–19, 122
    architectural style, 115–17
  McCarthy and, 97–8
  Strawberry Hill villa, 96–7, 120–5
    design themes at, 124–5
    Gothic style of, 121–2
    restoration of, 96–7
    sexual narrative implicit in, 137–8
  Vanbrugh and, 100, 107–9
    architectural style, 107–9
  Wren and, 100, 101–4
    architectural style, 101–4
'Gothic survival', 87
Gothic theatre. *See* theatrical plays
Gothick Constitution, 51–2
Goths. *See also* Ostrogoths; Visigoths
  Alaric and, 22, 24, 30–3
    as military leader, 31–3
    Sack of Rome by, 32–3, 45–6
  archaeological evidence of, 27–8
  Sîntana de Mureș-Černjachov culture, 27–8, 29
  as barbarians, 47
  Camden on, 46
  in Classical civilisation, 47
  as foreign invaders, 44
  during Gallic Wars, 45
  Germanic tribes as, 25–6
  Greuthungi and, 30
    farming settlements for, 30–1
  Huns and, 26, 28–30
    archaeological evidence of, 29–30
  literary sources, 23–5
    Classical Greece, 23
    Classical Latin, 23
  during long eighteenth century, 45–52
    in Britain, 48–9, 50–1
    feudalism among, 50
    Gothick Constitution, 51–2
    political governance among, 48–52
    regional integration of, 48
  migration of, 25–6, 27, 29–30
    from Scandza Island, 27–8
  nomenclature for, 25–6
  relation to the Gothic, 22–3
  in Renaissance, depictions of, 22–3
  Roman Empire and, cultural influences on, 28–30
    Alaric as military leader and, 31–3
    through Christianity, introduction of, 29
    Sack of Rome, by Alaric, 32–3
    under Valens, 30
  social structures for, 27
  Tervingi and, 30
    farming settlements for, 30–1
  Theodosius I and, treaty with, 30–1
  values for, 62–3
Goya, Francisco, 408
Graham, Kenneth W., 397
Gray, Thomas, 55–6, 70, 124, 307
  Walpole and, quarrels with, 155–6
Greenblatt, Stephen, 143, 147
Gregory the Great (Pope), 39
Greuthungi, Goths and, 30
  farming settlements for, 30–1
Grogan, Nathaniel, 413–14
Groom, Nick, 68
Grosette, Henry William, 373–4
Grosrichard, Alain, 359
Grosse, Carl, 366–7
The Grounds of Criticism in Poetry (Dennis, J.), 77–8, 284–5

Hadleigh Castle, 410, 411
Haggerty, George, 134–5, 214–15, 382, 388
Hall, Daniel, 283
Hallett, William, 122
Hamilton, Anthony, 347–8
Hamlet (Shakespeare, W.), 149–51
  The Castle of Otranto and, comparisons to, 151–2
  female sexuality in, 150–1
Hamm, Robert B., Jr, 149
Harney, Marion, 126
Harris, Thomas, 214
Hart, Joseph, 143
Hastings, Warren, 189–90
haunted apartment metaphor, American Revolution and, 252–8
Hawksmoor, Nicholas, 100, 104–7
  architectural style, 104–6
  use of medieval forms, 106–7
Hazlitt, William, 321–2, 364, 377–8
Heidegger, Martin, 427
Heilman, R. B., 243
Heinzmann, Johann Georg, 379
Henry, Robert, 3
  The History of Great Britain, from the First Invasion of It by the Romans Under Julius Caesar, 3–5
    legitimacy of, 4–5
    literary influences on, 4
    Walpole's response to, 6–7
Henry VIII (King), 48, 54
  Legatine Court and, 1
Heppner, Christopher, 422
Heptameron, 158–9
Hermann von Unna (Naubert, B.), 368–70
  translations of, 369
hermaphroditism, 401–2
Heron, Robert, 348
Higson, Andrew, 17
The Historian (Kostova, E.), 16
Historic Doubts on the Life and Reign of Richard the Third (Walpole, H.), 153
historical Gothic, for Gothic literature
  Gothic Revival, 86–93
    aesthetic relativism and, 88
    'Gothic survival' as distinct from, 87
    literary antiquarianism, 91–2
    public endorsement of, 87
  Longsword, Earl of Salisbury, 67–9, 93–5
    reviews of, 94
    methodological approach, 69–71
    origins of, 68
    in early plays, 70

  in scholastic philosophy, 70
  poetry in, 71–86
    in blank verse, 81–2
    Gothick poetry, 74–5, 81–2
    rhyme in, 73–4, 81–2
  political context for, 71–86
    Exclusion Crisis and, 72
    Glorious Revolution and, 72
    Tories and, 82–85
    War of Spanish Succession, 72
    Whigs and, 72, 81–2. *See also* Cooper, Anthony Ashley
historical romancer, in Gothic fiction, 10–11
historical writing, Gothic fiction and, relationship between, 9
historicism, in Gothic fiction
  challenges to, 7–9
  distrust of history, 11–15
  trends in, 5–7
historiography, in Gothic fiction, 15–16
history
  in *Frankenstein*, 11–12
  in Gothic fiction, 5–7
  romance and, differences between, 6
The History of England (Hume, D.), 3
The History of English Poetry (Warton, T.), 92
The History of Great Britain, from the First Invasion of It by the Romans Under Julius Caesar (Henry, R.), 3–5
  legitimacy of, 4–5
  literary influences on, 4
  Walpole's response to, 6–7
The History of King Lear (Tate), 148
The History of Miss Meredith (Parsons, E.), 329
The History of Roger Dodsworth (Shelley, M. W.), 14–15
The History of Scotland During the Reigns of Queen Mary and James VI (Robertson, W.), 3, 8
The History of Sexuality (Foucault, M.), 382–8, 404–5
The History of the Duchess of C*** written by Herself (Genlis, F. de), 330–2
History of the Gothic Revival (Eastlake, C. L.), 97–8
History of the Kings of the Goths (Isidore of Seville), 24, 41
The History of Tom Jones (Fielding, H.), 53
Hoeveler, Diane Long, 232, 279
Hoffmann, E. T. A., 365, 376
Hogle, Jerrold E., 422
homosexuality, in Gothic fiction, 389
Horace, 73, 165–6

Horace Walpole: The Great Outsider (Mowl, T.), 149
horror
  in German Gothic fiction, 367
  moral, 296–7
  in *The Mysteries of Udolpho*, 301–2, 333–4
  revolutionary, 300–3
  terror and, distinction from, 290–9
Howe, William, 234
Hudson, Hannah, 326
Hughes, James Fletcher, 174
Hume, David, 3–5, 201, 395
Hume, Robert D., 312
Huns
  in Aquitaine Kingdom, 34–5
  Attila as military leader, 34–5, 36
  Gepids' defeat of, 36
  Goths and, 26, 28–30
    archaeological evidence of, 29–30
  Ostrogoths under rule of, 36
Hurd, Richard, 59–60, 63, 87–8, 94–5, 164, 421
Hutton, James, 429

ibn Ziyad, Tariq, 42
Iffland, August Wilhelm, 44
imperialisation, as literary theme, 349–58
incest themes, 131–3
Inchbald, Elizabeth, 310–11
Innes, Thomas, 54–5
An Institute of the Laws of Scotland (McDouall, A.), 51
The Institution of the Order of the Garter (West, G.), 60
Interesting Narrative (Equiano, O.), 194, 195–7
Isidore of Seville, 26, 41
  Etymologies, 24, 41–2
  Visigothic Spain and, 41–2
The Italian (Radcliffe, A.), 176, 274
Italy
  Ostrogoths in, 24, 26
    destruction of, 24
  Stilicho in, 31–2

Jacobs, Edward H., 324–5
Jacobs, Giles, 401
Jauss, Hans Robert, 161
Jephson, Robert, 199–200, 204–7
John (Pope), 39
Johnson, Samuel, 58, 91–2, 143, 199
Jommelli, Niccolò, 215
Jordanes, 24, 25
  on migration of Goths, 25–6, 27, 29–30
Jure Divino (Defoe, D.), 50

Justin (Emperor), 38
Juvenal, 175

Kahlert, K. F., 367–8
kairotic knots, 432–3
Kant, Immanuel, 380, 429
Kelly, Isabella, 323–4, 325–6, 336–44
  Bleeding Nun and, in works of, 337–8, 339–40
  Eva, 338–41
    Bleeding Nun references in, 339–40
    ghosts in, 339–40
    supernatural in, 340–1
  Madeline; or, The Castle of Montgomery, 337
Kelly, James, 232–3
Kelly, Michael, 213
Kent, William, 100, 110–15
  architectural style, 110–14
Ketton-Cremer, R. W., 150
Killeen, Jarlath, 69, 229
Klancher, Jon, 416–17
Kliger, Samuel, 71–2
Knox, John, 54–5
Kostova, Elizabeth, 16
Kramer, Kelsey, 240

Labaume, Griffet de, 281–2
Landor, Walter Savage, 348
Lane, William, 329
Langhorne, John, 94, 174
Langley, Batty, 53, 100, 115–19, 122
  architectural style, 115–17
Laon and Cythna (Shelley, P. B.), 361–2
Laqueur, Thomas, 387
The Last Man (Shelley, M. W.), 13–14, 176, 356
Lathom, Francis, 325–6, 336–44, 366–7
  Bleeding Nun and, 337–8
  The Castle of Ollada, 337
  The Midnight Bell, 341–3
    Bleeding Nun references in, 342–3
    ghosts in, 342–3
Lectures on Rhetoric (Blair, H.), 5
Lee, Sophia, *The Recess*, 5, 7–8, 11, 223, 240, 259–60
  as Oriental Gothic fiction, 350
Legatine Court, 1
Leland, Thomas, 229
  Longsword, Earl of Salisbury, 67–9, 93–5
  reviews of, 94
Lenore (Bürger, G. A.), 373, 438–41
Leovigild (King), in Visigothic Spain, 40–1
  resistance to, 41
Leslie, Charles, 53–4

491

Letters on Chivalry and Romance (Hurd, R.), 63, 87–8, 164
Lewis, Matthew Gregory, 312–22. *See also The Monk*
  Adelmorn, the Outlaw, 212–13
  authorial reputation of, 313–14
  The Bravo of Venice, 376
  Byron on, 312–13
  The Castle Spectre, 198–9, 317–18, 428
  The Epistolary Intrigue, 312
  Hume, R. D., on, 312
  literary influences of earlier works, 373–4
  Miles on, 319–20
  Radcliffe's work as influence on, 312, 316–22
  as theatrical producer, 316
  theoretical approach to, 304–5
Lewis, Wilmarth Sheldon, 96–7, 138
The Libertine (Dacre, C.), 402
Life of Aemilius Paulus (Plutarch), 172–3
Lindfield, Peter N., 134, 409–10
lineage themes, 236–42
literary antiquarianism, 91–2
literary terror, 291–2
literature, Gothic. *See also* historical Gothic; *specific authors*; *specific topics*; *specific works*
  archive fever in, 9
  contemporary historical writing and, 9
  definition of, 5–6
  discovered document as convention in, 7, 9
  historical romancer in, 10–11
  historicism in
    challenges to, 7–9
    distrust of history, 11–15
    trends in, 5–7
  historiography in, 15–16
  during long eighteenth century, 56–63
    imagination as theme in, 57–8
    Shakespeare and, 58
  Marxist influences in, 15
  politicisation of, 16
  postmodernist elements in, 15, 17
  in popular culture, 17
  post-structuralism in, 15
  psychoanalysis as influence in, 15
  scope of, 5–6
  Ulfila, as apostle to Goths, 29
Lives (Plutarch), 173, 174
Lives of the Fathers of Merida, 41
Lloyd, Hannibal Evans, 44
Locke, John, 75
long eighteenth century (c. 1680–1800), Gothic and
  cultural politics during, 52–6
    in architecture, 52–6
    fiction novel during, popular meaning of, 45
    Glorious Revolution during, 43, 50, 72
    Goths during, 45–52
      in Britain, 48–9, 50–1
      feudalism among, 50
      Gothick Constitution, 51–2
      political governance among, 48–52
      regional integration of, 48
    literature during, 56–63. *See also specific authors*; *specific works*
      imagination as theme in, 57–8
      Shakespeare and, 58
    as social concept, 43
Longsword, Earl of Salisbury (Leland, T.), 67–9, 93–5
  reviews of, 94
Loutherbourg, Philippe-Jacques de, 180
The Love Song of J. Alfred Prufrock (Eliot, T. S.), 151–2
Lowndes, Thomas, 130
Lucas, Charles, 274–6

Macaulay, Thomas Babington, 126, 223
Mackenzie, Henry, 227–8
Macklin, Thomas, 415
Macpherson, James, 63–4, 131
Madeline; or, The Castle of Montgomery (Kelly, I.), 337
Makdisi, Saree, 363
The Making of the National Poet: Shakespeare, Adaptation, and Authorship (Dobson, M.), 142
male translators, of English Gothic fiction novels, 270–82
Mallet, David, 69–70
Mandal, Anthony, 324–5
Mann, Horace, 122
Marcellinus, Ammianus, 23–4, 29
Marcus, Steven, 384
Maria; or, The Wrongs of Woman (Wollstonecraft, M.), 307–8
marriage, sexuality and, 390–1
Martel, Charles, 35–6
Martha Peake (McGrath, P.), 16
Martin, John, 414
Marxism, in Gothic fiction, 15
Mason, William, 131, 155, 239
Masona of Merida (Bishop), 41
Masquerade and Civilization (Castle, T.), 145

mass immigration, into Britain, 184
Mathias, T. J., 222, 310–11, 375
Maturin, Charles Robert, 347–8
  Melmoth the Wanderer, 9, 19, 356–8
McCarthy, Michael, 97–8
McCormick, Ian, 388, 389
McDouall, Andrew, 51
McGrath, Patrick, 16
Meeke, Elizabeth, 325–6
Melmoth the Wanderer (Maturin, C. R.), 9, 19, 356–8
Melville, Herman, 11
Metahistory (White, H.), 15
Meziere, Harriet, 228
Michasiw, Kim Ian, 399
Middleton, Thomas, 420
The Midnight Bell (Lathom, F.), 341–3
  Bleeding Nun references in, 342–3
  ghosts in, 342–3
A Midsummer Night's Dream (Shakespeare, W.), 58, 166–7
Miles, Robert, 11, 325, 385
  on Lewis, M. G., 319–20
  on Radcliffe, A., 319–20
Miller, Sanderson, 100
Milton, John, 12, 69–70
Minerva Press, 326, 328–9
The Minstrel of the North (Stagg, J.), 45
Moers, Ellen, 277–8
Moll Flanders (Defoe, D.), 60–1
The Monk (Lewis, M. G.), 312–22
  Bleeding Nun in, 337–8
  adaptations of, 373–4
  in *Eva*, 339–40
  in *The Midnight Bell*, 342–3
  sexuality in, 403–4
  regulation of, 392–5
  sexual transgression in, 398–9
  Tom Jones compared to, 320–1
Montagu, Elizabeth, 143
Moore, George, 324
Moore, Thomas, 358–9, 360–1
moral horror, 296–7
More, Hannah, 365
Morellet, André, 281–2
Moreton Abbey (Meziere, H.), 228
Morin, Christina, 69
Morland, Catherine, 9, 196, 319–20, 366–7
Mowl, Timothy, 149, 155
Mr. Johnson's Preface to His Edition of Shakespear's [sic] Plays (Johnson, S.), 91–2
Mulligans, Hugh, 193

Die Mündel (Iffland, A. W.), 44
Murphy, Arthur, 203
Musäus, J. K. A., 371–2
The Mysteries of Udolpho (Radcliffe, A.), 173–4, 176, 317, 319
  Coleridge review of, 298–9, 307
  horror in, 301–2, 333–4
  landscapes in, 290
  time in, 432–4, 435–7
  translations of, 267–8, 269
The Mysterious Mother (Walpole, H.), 121, 159–60
  incest themes in, 131–3
  setting for, 135–7

The Nabob (Foote, S.), 187
nabobs, 187
natural terror, 293
Naubert, Benedikte, 368–70
The Nephews (Lloyd, H. E.), 44
New Historicism, 11
New History (Zosimus), 24, 32
Newman, Gerald, 245
Das Nibelungenlied (The Song of the Nibelungs), 39–40
Nieman, Elizabeth, 326
Night Thoughts (Young, E.), 55, 57
The Nightmare (Fuseli, H.), 417–18, 419
Nordius, Janina, 350
Norman, Larry, 163
Northanger Abbey (Austen, J.), 9, 366–7
Norton, Rictor, 389
Nymphomania; or, A Dissertation Concerning the Furor Uterinus (Bienville, M. D. T.), 396–7

O'Brien, Karen, 5
Odovacer, 36
Of History and Romance (Godwin, W.), 9–10, 13–14
Of Poetry (Temple, W.), 56
O'Keefe, John, 180, 204, 207–8, 220–1
The Old English Baron (Reeve, C.), 5, 162, 171, 223. See also *The Champion of Virtue*
  American Revolution and, 244–58
  Radcliffe influenced by, 259
Olympiodorus of Thebes, 24
O'Quinn, Daniel, 236, 246
The Order of Things (Foucault, M.), 3
Oriental Gothic fiction
  anti-Enlightenment themes in, 345–6
  Arabian Nights' Entertainments, as seminal work, 185, 347–8

Oriental Gothic fiction (cont.)
  authors influenced by, 347
  Gothic fiction influenced by, 347–8
  objects of terror in, 347
  translations of, 347
  commerce and trade as themes in, 349–58
  Eastern excesses as element of, 345
  Frankenstein, 354–6
  imperialisation as theme in, 349–58
  literary development of, origins of, 346–8
  Melmoth the Wanderer, 356–8
  The Recess, 350
  representation of bodies in, 358–63
  terror elements in, 347
  Vathek, 350–2
  Zofloya, 352–4
Orientalist empires, 184–90
  nabobs, 187
Original Poems on Several Occasions (Reeve, C.), 168
The Origins of the Gothic Revival (McCarthy, M.), 97–8
Orosius, Christian, 24
Ossianics (Macpherson, J.), 63–4
Ostrogoths, 22, 36–40
  Athalaric and, 38–9
  decline of, 38–40
    through military warfare, 39–40
  divisions among, 38
  Gepids, 36
  under Hun rule, 36
  in Italy, 24, 26
    destruction of Ostrogoth state, 24
  languages used among, 37–8
  legal systems for, 37–8
  Odovacer and, 36
  religion of, 37–8
  under Theodoric the Amal, 36–8
    Amalasuintha, 38–9
    family rule after death of, 38–9
    marriage alliances under, 37
    unification of Ostrogoths under, 37
  under Totila, 39
  Visigoths and, division from, 25, 26
The Other Victorians (Marcus, S.), 384
Otway, Thomas, 198
Owenson, Sydney, Lady Morgan, 138–9

pageantry, in domestic Gothic writing, 234–6
Paine, Thomas, 280–1
Paradise Lost (Milton, J.), 12
Parnell, Thomas, 70
Parreaux, André, 313

Parsons, Eliza, 325–6, 366–7
  The Castle of Wolfenbach, 327–36
    at Minerva Press, 328–9
    publication of, timing of, 335
    similarities to previous works, 330–2
    violence in, 332–3
  Ellen and Julia, 329
  The Errors of Education, 329
  The History of Miss Meredith, 329
  Lane and, 329
  Woman as She Should Be, 329
Paulson, Ronald, 313
Pearce, Edward, 154
Pelles, Geraldine, 416–17
Penny Dreadful, 17
Percy, Thomas, 64, 421
Petrarch, 75
pharmacology, in German Gothic fiction, 375–81
  poisoning, 378
Phillips, Mark Salber, 5
A Philosophical Enquiry into the Origin of Our Ideas of the Sublime and Beautiful (Burke, E.), 52, 165
Pierre, Joseph-Alexandre, 272
Pierre; or, the Ambiguities (Melville, H.), 11
Piozzi, Hester Lynch, 364, 367, 374–5
Piranesi, Giovanni Battista, 408
Platzner, Robert L., 200
pleasure, pathologisation of, 388
Pleasures of Imagination (Akenside, M.), 55, 85
Plutarch, 172–3
Poe, Edgar Allan, 367
Poem on the Bill Lately Passed for Regulating the Slave Trade (Williams, H. M.), 193–4
Poetics (Aristotle), 73
poetry, Gothic
  in historical Gothic canon, 71–86
    in blank verse, 81–2
    Gothick poetry, 74–5, 81–2
    rhyme in, 73–4, 81–2
  toxic poetics, in German Gothic fiction, 365–75
The Poetry of Slavery (Wood, M.), 191–2
poisoning, 378
Polanyi, Michael, 427
Pope, Alexander, 52, 60, 69–70, 143
pornotopic settings, 403–4
postmodernism, in Gothic fiction, 15, 17
  in popular culture, 17
post-structuralism, in Gothic fiction, 15
Potter, Franz J., 324–5
Pratt, Samuel Jackson, 193

Prévost, Antoine François, 11
Price, Fiona, 224
Pride and Prejudice (Austen, J.), 430–1
Prince Arthur (Blackmore, R.), 48
Procopius, 24
The Progress of Poesy (Gray, T.), 307
The Progress of Romance (Reeve, C.), 169–72
Protestant Reformation, in *The Castle of Otranto*, 2
Protestantism, Gothic architecture and, 54–6
psychoanalysis, Gothic fiction influenced by, 15
The Psychopathology of the Gothic Romance (Cameron, E.), 151
Punter, David, 2, 70, 242, 407
Pye, Henry James, 284

Queer Gothic (Haggerty, G. E.), 382
Quinn, Vincent, 70

Radcliffe, Ann, 8, 176
  Burney compared to, 321–2
  The Castles of Athlin and Dunbayne, 222, 259
  critical success of, 305–12
    among literary peers, 310–11
  Gaston De Blondeville, 259
  influence of other novelists on, 334–5
  The Italian, 176, 274
  Miles on, 319–20
  The Mysteries of Udolpho, 173–4, 176, 317, 319
    Coleridge review of, 298–9, 307
    horror in, 301–2, 333–4
    landscapes in, 290
    time in, 432–4, 435–7
    translations of, 267–8, 269
  The Old English Baron as influence on, 259
  public response to, 309–10
  The Romance of the Forest, 8, 176
    adaptations of, 318
  Romantic-era Gothic fiction output, 323. *See also* specific works
  Shakespeare and, 307–8
  St Alban's Abbey, 257
  terror in works of, 297–9, 301–2
  theoretical approach to, 304–5
  Thorpe on, 320–1
  Wollstonecraft and, 307–9
Die Räuber (Schiller, F.), 377–8
Reccared, in Visigothic Spain, 41
The Recess (Lee, S.), 5, 7–8, 11, 223, 240, 259–60
  as Oriental Gothic fiction, 350
Reeve, Clara
  The Champion of Virtue, 5, 171, 245

literary legacy of, 258–61
The Old English Baron, 5, 162, 171, 223
  American Revolution and, 244–58
  Radcliffe influenced by, 259
Original Poems on Several Occasions, 168
The Progress of Romance, 169–72
Reeve, Matthew M., 139–40
Reliques of Ancient English Poetry (Percy, T.), 64, 91–2
Renaissance, Goths in, depictions of, 22–3
Res Gestae (Marcellinus), 23–4
A Restitution of Decayed Intelligence (Verstegan, R.), 47
revolutionary horror, 300–3
revolutionary terror, 300–3
rhyme
  in barbarian nations, 61–2
  in Gothic poetry, 73–4, 81–2
Richardson, Samuel, 321
Ridley, James, 349, 414
Robertson, William, 3, 8
Robinson, Mary, 310–11
Robinson Crusoe (Defoe, D.), 60–1
Roche, Regina Maria, 264, 274, 281–2
Roderic (King), 42
Roman Empire
  Gallic Wars, 45
  Goths and, cultural influences on, 28–30
    Alaric as military leader and, 31–3
    through Christianity, introduction of, 29
    Sack of Rome, by Alaric, 32–3, 45–6
    under Valens, 30
The Romance of the Forest (Radcliffe, A.), 8, 176
  adaptations of, 318
Romantic-era Gothic fiction. *See also* Lewis, Matthew Gregory; Radcliffe, Anne
  'branding' of, 325
  the Classical and, 178–9
  history and, differences between, 6
  imitation of previous works in, 323, 325–6
  publishing houses for, 326
  as trade Gothic fiction, 325–6. *See also* Kelly, Isabella; Lathom, Francis; Parsons, Eliza
    Minerva Press, 326, 328–9
  'worldly Romanticism', 363
Romney, George, 414
Ronsard, Pierre de, 75
Ronsil, George Arnaud de, 401
Roscoe, William, 421–2
Rousseau, George, 388
Rowe, Nicholas, 208–9
Rowley, Thomas, 65

Index

ruination trope, in sentimental Gothic, 232–3
Rushdie, Salman, 16
Rushton, Edward, 193

Saberhagen, Fred, 16
Sachs, Jonathan, 175–6
Sack of Rome, by Alaric, 32–3, 45–6
Said, Edward, 346
Samuel, Richard, 168–9
Satire (Juvenal), 175
satirical Gothic, 223–7
  superstition in, 225
Scandza Island, migration of Goths from, 27–8
Schiavonnetti, Luigi, 412
Schiller, Friedrich, 377–8, 426
Schlegel, August Wilhelm, 377–8
Schoenbaum, Samuel, 143
The Scholemaster (Ascham, R.), 74
Schönert, Jörg, 366
Scott, Walter, 11, 171, 310–11, 358–9
Scottish Enlightenment, historians of, 3
The Seasons (Thomson, J.), 50
The Secret Tribunal (Boaden, J.), 377
A Secular Age (Taylor, C.), 427–8
Sedgwick, Eve Kosofsky, 185
sentimental Gothic, 227–9
  ruination trope in, 232–3
A Sentimental Journey (Sterne, L.), 131
Seven Books of History against the Pagans (Orosius), 24
sexual narratives, Strawberry Hill villa and, 137–8
sexual transgression, in Gothic fiction, 391–405
  homosexuality, 389
  in *The Monk*, 398–9
  through taboo behaviours, 387–8
  in *Vathek*, 397–8
  in *Zofloya*, 395, 399–404
sexuality, in Gothic fiction
  binary gendered models in, 387–8
  in expanding market economy, 388
  hermaphroditism and, 401–2
  historical development of, 382
  in *The History of Sexuality*, 382–8, 404–5
  marriage and, 390–1
  in *The Monk*, 403–4
  regulation of sexuality, 392–5
  sexual transgression in, 398–9
  pathologisation of pleasure in, 388
  policing of gender in, 388–91
  pornotopic settings, 403–4
  regulation of, 391–405
    in *The Monk*, 392–5

social context for
  contemporary changes in, 389–91
  stigma as result of, 391
  types of, 388–91
Shakespeare, William, 58
  critics of, 143
  cultural presence of, 142–51
  Garrick's Jubilee for, 143–6
  Roman Catholic rituals as part of, 145–6
  Hamlet, 149–51
  The Castle of Otranto and, comparisons to, 151–2
  female sexuality in, 150–1
  A Midsummer Night's Dream, 58, 166–7
  Radcliffe and, 307–8
  after Restoration, 142–4
  audience response to, 146–7
  Walpole and, 156–60
Shame (Rushdie), 16
Sheil, Richard Lalor, 358–9
Shelley, Mary Wollstonecraft, 271, 319
  Frankenstein
    Classical themes in, 177–8
    history in, 11–12
    literary influences on, 177–8
    as Oriental Gothic Fiction, 354–6
  Paradise Lost and, 12
  history in works of, 11–15
  The History of Roger Dodsworth, 14–15
  The Last Man, 13–14, 176, 356
  Radcliffe and, 307–9
  Valperga, 12–13
Shelley, Percy Bysshe, 175–6, 361–2
Sheridan, Richard B., 214
Shields, William, 180
Shore, Gary, 16
Sickelmore, Richard, 280–1
Siddons, Sarah, 208–9
Simpson, David, 284
Sîntana de Mureș-Černjachov culture, 27–8, 29
Sleepy Hollow (film), 17
Smith, Allan Lloyd, 17
Smith, Charlotte, 228–9, 271, 275–6, 310–11
Smollett, Tobias, 292–3, 334
Snodin, Michael, 98
Solitary Castle, 224–5, 226
The Song of the Nibelungs (*Das Nibelungenlied*), 39–40
Southerne, Thomas, 208–9
Southey, Robert, 348, 358–9, 360
Spain. *See also* Visigothic Spain

enslavement of British people, as terror, 182
Spenser, Edmund, 58, 69–70, 88
St Alban's Abbey (Radcliffe, A.), 257
Stagg, John, 45
stereotyping, in German Gothic fiction, 364–5
Sterne, Laurence, 62, 63, 131
Stilicho, 31–2
Stoker, Bram, *Dracula*, 29–30
　Freudian influences in, 15
　historical elements in, 15–16
Strahan, William, 3
Straub, Kristina, 388
Strawberry Hill villa, 96–7, 120–5
　design themes at, 124–5
　Gothic style of, 121–2
　restoration of, 96–7
　sexual narrative implicit in, 137–8
Stuart, Charles Edward, 145–6
Stuart, Gilbert, 3, 241
suggestive terror, 299
Summers, Montague, 67–8
supernatural
　in *Eva*, 340–1
　terror and, 295
supernatural terror, 197, 295. *See also* global terrors
superstition, 225
　terror and, 295
Swift, Jonathan, 62, 154
Symmachus, 38

Tacitus, 25, 45
Talfourd, Thomas Noon, 305–6
Tasso, Torquato, 75
Tate, Nahum, 148
Taylor, Charles, 426–8, 429, 445–6
　kairotic knots, 432–3
Taylor, David Francis, 219
Taylor, Gary, 142–3
Temple, Sir William, 43, 46, 56, 61–2, 72
terror. *See also* global terrors, perceptions by British people
　Addison on, 286–9
　aesthetics of, 294–5, 296–7
　Aikin, A. L., on, 290–9
　in *Arabian Nights' Entertainments*, 347
　Burke on, 289–90, 433–4
　definition and scope of, 284–90
　Dennis on, 284–5
　distinction from horror, 290–9
　as driving passion of Gothic, 284
　in Gothic fiction, 289–90
　hierarchy of, 296
　horror and
　　distinction from terror, 290–9
　　moral, 296–7
　　in *The Mysteries of Udolpho*, 301–2
　　revolutionary, 300–3
　literary, 291–2
　natural, 293
　in Oriental Gothic fiction, 347
　in Radcliffe's works, 297–9, 301–2
　revolutionary, 300–3
　suggestive, 299
　supernatural forces and, 295
　superstition and, 295
Tervingi, Goths and, 30
　farming settlements for, 30–1
Teuthold, Peter, 367–8
theatrical plays, Gothic
　entertainment as purpose of, 206–7
　of Exclusion Crisis, 220
　Gothic drama
　　creation of, 204–10
　　as genre, 200
　　orchestration of, 214–19
　　as political, 217–19
　　production elements of, 211–14
　origins of, 198
　plays in, breadth of, 199–200. *See also specific works*
Theobald, Lewis, 143
Theodoric I (King), 34
Theodoric II (King), 35
Theodoric the Amal (King), 36–8
　Amalasuintha, 38–9
　family rule after death of, 38–9
　marriage alliances under, 37
　unification of Ostrogoths under, 37
Theodosius de Zulvin, the Monk of Madrid (Moore, G.), 324
Theodosius I (Emperor), 30–1
Thomas, Helen, 195
Thomson, James, 50, 182
Thorpe, John, 320–1
Thoughts and Sentiments on the Evil of Slavery (Cugoano, O.), 191
time, as concept
　in *Christabel*, 441–9
　historical context for, 426–8
　in *Lenore*, 438–41
　in Radcliffe's works, 429–37
　　comparisons to Austen's use of time, 431–2
　　The Mysteries of Udolpho, 432–4, 435–7

time, as concept (cont.)
  Taylor, C., on, 426–8
  terror and, 437–41
Tom Jones (Fielding, H.), 320–1
Tories, historical Gothic and, 82–85
Toro, Guillermo del, 17
Totila (King), 39
Townshend, Dale, 149, 389, 391–2
toxic poetics, in German Gothic fiction, 365–75
trade. *See* commerce and trade
translations, of Gothic fiction
  Arabian Nights' Entertainments, 347
  female translators, of English Gothic fiction novels, 266–70
  of French Gothic fiction novels, into English, 263
  during French Revolution, 266–83
  Hermann von Unna, 369
  male translators, 270–82
  The Mysteries of Udolpho, 267–8, 269
transmigrations
  definition of, 141
  natural, 141
  in Shakespeare's works, 141–2
Treatise of Human Nature (Hume, D.), 3–5, 395
Tristam Shandy (Sterne, L.), 62, 63
Trusler, John, 181
Tuite, Clara, 403–4
Turner, J. M. W., 410
Tyrrell, James, 72

United States (US). *See* American Revolution

Valens (Emperor), 30
Valperga; or, the Life and Adventures of Castruccio, Prince of Lucca (Shelley, M. W.), 12–13
Vanbrugh, John, 100, 107–9
  architectural style, 107–9
Varma, Devendra, 70
Varney, Jean-Baptiste, 279
Vathek (Beckford, W.), 184–90, 236, 347–8
  as Oriental Gothic fiction, 350–2
  sexual transgression in, 397–8
Venice Preserved (Otway, T.), 198
Verstegan, Richard, 47, 72
violence
  in *The Castle of Wolfenbach*, 332–3
  in *Douglas*, 202
virtue, American Revolution and, 244–52
Visigothic Spain, 24, 26, 40–3
  Arab conquest of, 24, 42–3

Catholicism in, 40–1
Christian learning in, 41–2
Classical learning in, 41–2
decline and fall of, 42, 43
Franks in, 40–1
Isidore of Seville and, 41–2
under Leovigild, 40–1
  resistance to, 41
political instability in, 42–3
under Reccared, 41
regional boundaries for, 40–1
Visigoths, 22
  Aquitaine Kingdom, 33–6
  boundaries of, 34
  Codex Euricianus, 35
  Huns during, 34–5
  Athaulf, 33–4
  decline of, 35–6
  Euric, 35
  Franks' defeat of, 35–6
  Galla Placidia, 33–4
  military strength of, 35
  Ostrogoths and, division from, 25, 26
  in Spain. *See* Visigothic Spain
  Theodoric I, 34
  Theodoric II, 35
visual arts, in Gothic culture. *See also specific artists*
  autonomy of, 416–25
  balance with commercial factors, 415
  in Britain, 410
  definition of, 423, 424–5
  in Gothic Revival movement, 409–10
  Hadleigh Castle, 410, 411
  heuristic value of, 408–9
  history of, 406–7
  scholarship on, 407–8
    modern analysis in, 409–15
  Walpole on, 414–15, 418
Volney, Constantin de, 355
von Holst, Theodor, 413

Wahrman, Dror, 249
Wallace, Diana, 240
Walpole, Horace, 2, 7, 14, 59–60, 315, 347–8. *See also The Castle of Otranto*
  aesthetics of association for, 125–40
    Classical compared to Gothic architecture, 129–30
    imaginative response to, 127
  Anecdotes of Painting in England, 129
  Gray and, quarrels with, 155–6

Historic Doubts on the Life and Reign of Richard the Third, 153
The History of Great Britain, from the First Invasion of It by the Romans Under Julius Caesar and, response to, 6–7
The Mysterious Mother, 121, 159–60
  incest themes in, 131–3
  setting for, 135–7
  Shakespearean conventions used by, 156–60
  Strawberry Hill villa, 96–7, 120–5
    design themes at, 124–5
    Gothic style of, 121–2
    restoration of, 96–7
    sexual narrative implicit in, 137–8
  on visual artists, 414–15, 418
War (Procopius), 24
War of Spanish Succession, 72
Warburton, William, 143
Warton, Thomas, 59, 92, 124, 129, 223, 421
Watt, James, 171, 224
West, Gilbert, 60
Whalley, Thomas Sedgwick, 234–5
Whately, Thomas, 232–3
Whigs, historical Gothic and, 72, 81–2. *See also* Cooper, Anthony Ashley
White, Hayden, 15
White, James, 223–4
Wilberforce, William, 191
Will in the World (Greenblatt, S.), 147
William of Orange, 56
Williams, Abigail, 72
Williams, Anne, 385

Williams, Helen Maria, 193–4
Wilson, Jon, 186
Wilson, Kathleen, 245
Wilt, Judith, 216
Wittgenstein, Ludvig, 427
Wittiza (King), 42
Wollstonecraft, Mary, 307–8
Woman as She Should Be (Parsons, E.), 329
women
  during French Revolution, barriers to political engagement, 269
  in *Hamlet*, female sexuality in, 150–1
  as translators, of English Gothic fiction novels, 266–70
Womersley, David, 72
Wood, Marcus, 191–2
Woodmason, James, 415
Wordsworth, William, 174–5
'worldly Romanticism', 363
Worrall, David, 218
Wrangham, Francis, 174–5
Wren, Christopher, 100, 101–4
  architectural style, 101–4
Wright, Angela, 91, 265, 405

Young, Edward, 55, 57, 70, 164

Zeno (Emperor), 36
Zofloya; or, The Moor (Dacre, C.), 352–4, 376, 395
  sexual transgression in, 395, 399–404
Zosimus, 24, 32
Zschokke, Johann Heinrich, 369–70

For EU product safety concerns, contact us at Calle de José Abascal, 56–1°, 28003 Madrid, Spain or eugpsr@cambridge.org.